Modes of Comparison

THE COMPARATIVE STUDIES IN SOCIETY AND HISTORY BOOK SERIES

Raymond Grew, Series Editor

Comparing Muslim Societies:
Knowledge and the State in a World Civilization
   Juan R. I. Cole, editor

Colonialism and Culture
   Nicholas B. Dirks, editor

Constructing Culture and Power in Latin America
   Daniel H. Levine, editor

Time: Histories and Ethnologies
   Diane Owen Hughes and Thomas R. Trautmann, editors

Cultures of Scholarship
   S. C. Humphreys, editor

Comparing Jewish Societies
   Todd M. Endelman, editor

The Construction of Minorities: Cases for Comparison
Across Time and Around the World
   André Burguière and Raymond Grew, editors

States of Violence
   Fernando Coronil and Julie Skurski, editors

Modes of Comparison: Theory and Practice
   Aram A. Yengoyan, editor

# Modes of Comparison

## Theory & Practice

Aram A. Yengoyan, Editor

THE UNIVERSITY OF MICHIGAN PRESS
*Ann Arbor*

Copyright © by the University of Michigan 2006
All rights reserved
Published in the United States of America by
The University of Michigan Press
Manufactured in the United States of America
⊛ Printed on acid-free paper
2009   2008   2007   2006      4   3   2   1

*A CIP catalog record for this book is available from the British Library.*

Library of Congress Cataloging-in-Publication Data

Modes of comparison : theory and practice / Aram A. Yengoyan, editor.
     p. cm. — (The comparative studies in society and history book
series)
   Includes bibliographical references.
   ISBN-13: 978-0-472-09918-4 (cloth : alk. paper)
   ISBN-10: 0-472-09918-3 (cloth : alk. paper)
   ISBN-13: 978-0-472-06918-7 (pbk. : alk. paper)
   ISBN-10: 0-472-06918-7 (pbk. : alk. paper)
   1. History— Philosophy.   2. Anthropology—Philosophy.
I. Yengoyan, Aram A.
II. Series.
D16.8.M697     2006
901—dc22                                          2005029463

*This volume is dedicated to*
RAYMOND GREW
*for his forty years of creative*
*inspiration and guidance with*
Comparative Studies in Society and History.

# Acknowledgments

Grateful acknowledgement is given to *Comparative Studies in Society and History* (*CSSH*) for permission to reproduce the following articles in revised form:

"Frazer, Leach, and Virgil: The Popularity (and Unpopularity) of *The Golden Bough*" by Mary Beard first appeared in *CSSH* 34: 203–24.

"Regulation Theory, Post-Marxism, and the New Social Movements" by George Steinmetz originally appeared in *CSSH* 36: 176–212.

"Cowries and Conquest: Toward a Subalternate Quality Theory of Money" by C. A. Gregory. Originally appeared in *CSSH* 38: 195–217.

"The Cities of Avignon and Worms as Expressions of European Community" by Beverly Heckart originally appeared in *CSSH* 31: 462–90.

"Flowers and Bones: Approaches to the Dead in Anglo-American and Italian Cemeteries" by Jack Goody and Cesare Poppi originally appeared in *CSSH* 36: 146–75.

"Race, Ethnicity, Species, and Breed: Totemism and Horse-Breed Classification in America" by John Borneman originally appeared in *CSSH* 30: 25–51.

"Global Violence and Nationalizing Wars in Eurasia and America: The Geopolitics of War in the Mid-Nineteenth Century" by Michael Geyer and Charles Bright originally appeared in *CSSH* 38: 619–57.

We also thank the American Historical Association for permission to republish "The Case for Comparing Histories" by Raymond Grew, which originally appeared in *American Historical Review* 85: 763–78.

# Contents

161 Pontiusus

# Illustrations

# Introduction

## On the Issue of Comparison

*Aram A. Yengoyan*

What is distinctive about modern anthropology is the comparison of
embedded concepts (representations) between societies differently
located in time or space. The important thing in this comparative
analysis is not their origin (Western or non-Western), but the forms
of life that articulate them, the powers they release or disable.
Secularism—like religion—is such a concept.

—Asad 2003: 17

The idea of comparative analysis and enquiry in the social sciences and the
humanities has had a long and varied trajectory over the past two centuries, but more so since 1900. Some of the early problems of what comparison meant and what were its aims are still with us; other problems such
as the role of comparison in theory construction, generalizations, and a
focus on the particular are still critical matters of debate.

Yet, the topic of comparison has embraced a wide range of issues and
themes which in many cases have added a new and critical insight for
understanding the complexities of what social scientists are attempting to
explicate. To a certain extent, the interest in comparison is an old phenomenon, one that goes back to the ancients, yet it is not limited to any
particular historical continuity. But, I think it would be acceptable to note
that the increasing interest in comparison and an interest in other places
and spaces converge with the rise of historical consciousness in a society,
culture, political entity, etc. As this form of consciousness was expressed in
and through old institutions, the creation of new institutions and social
forms, and gradual changes in the matrix of economic and political complexity, it became evident that there was another out there. In the writings

of Diderot, Voltaire, and others of their time, we find an increasing sense of what were other societies outside of France, which in turn, over time, sharpened the idea of what it meant to be French.

With the emergence of national histories both in the past and present and in the work of national scholars, historical work of this kind asked questions primarily of itself. To an extent, the growing interest in comparison by historians worked against national histories, but its lasting impact was to expand on them. A case in point is the ongoing interest by French writers in French feudalism, which turned the corner through the work of comparativists and historically minded anthropologists who saw the problem of feudalism with a different lens, some of them coming from China, Russia, and Japan. If comparison partly de-nationalized national histories, it also created a set of enquiries, which were disruptive of what was assumed as logical and natural. Within the social sciences some disciplines, such as history and anthropology, are more comparative than others, and within the humanities many aspects of the study of literature are now carried out within fields such as comparative literature, critical theory, and cultural studies.

This essay and the articles in the volume all address a variety of issues that have a bearing on what comparison entails and how it relates to constructs in the social sciences/humanities. Even a basic question, such as "what are we comparing," brings forth a range of concerns, some of which we can say something about, and yet it also creates a vigilance for identifying potential problems. Some of these general issues and concerns are addressed in the following discussion. We must always be concerned with the problem of time and space. What are the implications and problems of comparing entities and forms which are markedly different through time and space? Such differences cannot be glossed over by broad and vague categories that might minimize the nuances of particular features, which might or might not be understood. How does one define change both in terms of its micro- and macro-parameters, and what does change mean? In many cases historians and anthropologists see change differently. What are the reasons for this? And of course, one must ask if the idea of comparison can deal with change at all, especially if the form of comparison is based on categories which are not only static, but are intricately linked to a particular historical and cultural milieu. Thus comparisons that are primarily synchronic might stress the static quality of categories, but any type of diachronic comparison must understand the limiting quality of employing static categories over time.

The use of categories cross-culturally through time and across space presents special and possibly insurmountable problems. How valid are categories even within the context from which they are generated? One can critique categories which initially start as temporal but are ultimately conveyed as eternal. Marx's critique of Ricardo's labor theory of production, for example, was based on how categories from one historical time become eternal structures, thus minimizing the dynamics of change within the complexities of nineteenth-century capitalism. In some directions, Marx's critique of the imperative category in theoretical analysis resonates in the works of Nietzsche, Foucault, and some present-day post-modern writers. Thus, categories like labor, production, or profit, let alone religion, become binding to a particular period of time and yet over time assume a life of their own. For anthropologists this is of greater concern since we move our categories from one context to another with little forethought. In this kind of practice, the "facts" not only reify the categories; they also reaffirm the theoretical basis. Even within the context of comparing mortuary practices, bones, and flowers in Italy and England, the paper by Jack Goody and Cesare Poppi gives clear warning of how one might be misled unless one's categories are contextualized prior to comparing and theorizing. Here the problem must initially be comprehended as one of translation, and all translations to a certain extent are subjective (see essays by Goody and Poppi and by Yengoyan). Even at the level of translation, we must admit subjectivity into our enquiry. Yet saying this, we must also be careful not to relegate subjectivity only to translation, thus concluding that only the universal or semi-universal is objective. Both sides of this contrast are wrong.

Apart from various arguments on method, which will be discussed later, comparison and comparative history is initially based on hunches and speculations that can be invaluable. Some cases of comparison might be productive, others might not, but regardless of the results, comparison creates new and unique insights which might reflect on older issues, or they can direct us to different arenas of interpretation. Like all speculations, some work and some do not, but generally new vistas are set forth.

In general, these insights and interpretations usually start from our own intellectual heritage as the source of what we try to comprehend for other places and in other times. Sometimes the direction of the source can be reversed, although this does not occur very often. A good example of this reverse direction occurs in an analysis of the role of totemism in military divisions in World War I. Linton (1924) noted that totemic groupings, insignia, personal appellation, group solidarity and inter-group rivalries, and animal mascots were part of how the American Expeditionary Forces (A.E.F.) were organized as the Rainbow Division, composed of a series of exclusive and inclusive namesakes. Furthermore, each of these namesakes were group guardians that were based on omens, some of them cautionary, others prescriptive. In many ways, this was the structure of how totemic systems work, yet it was clear to Linton that the richness of content which might be found in societies such as Australian Aboriginals did not exist. Cases such as the A.E.F. might be rare, but it does provide a perspective from which one might compare and reflect upon one's own society.

Comparison and comparative enquiry is not a method per se, nor is it to be equated with theory construction. Theories might emerge from comparisons, such as a global history, but most comparative work is regional and smaller-scale. From each of these types of comparison (global, regional, small-scale), far-reaching theories might develop, but the development of theory is not the original aim of most comparative studies. If theory is to explain and predict events and facts, the most critical aims of comparison are to make discoveries through different ways of seeing things—by drawing forth new, unique, and possibly odd implications that bear on what is being compared—and to direct our attention to other contexts which on their surface might appear to have no connection.

Historically, comparison has been conducted in a variety of ways. For Durkheim, comparison was based on the initial analysis of a single case (like religion among the Arunta/Aranda of central Australia) from which a set of general propositions was established as the foundations of religious structure, action, and thought. For historical sociologists from Weber onward, comparison resulted from the semblance and contrast of different historical trajectories, with the aim of isolating forces, which would explain differences and similarities. Anthropology has had a long and varied understanding of what comparison embraces. The comparative method under Radcliffe-Brown was based on the creation of a taxonomy of social units, which were compared from one society to another with the goal of forging social laws, which ideally underlie all societies as principles of social structure. Within the American historical school, especially in the work of Benedict, comparison was a matter of writing cultural portraits of different societies which were contrasted as a means of setting forth the idea of difference. Although there have been major shifts from Benedict's position, the idea of cultural portraits remains critical in the writings of Geertz and others.

Culture, both the concept and as practice, poses a number of special and difficult problems in regards to comparison. Apart from how culture is defined, which is a moot issue, it is commonly understood as the last or least factor in developing comparative understandings. A number of assumptions have a direct or indirect bearing on this situation, many of them quite complex.

Historically, especially within American anthropology, culture has been associated with what is particular—a local and bounded unit. Anthropologists have finally moved away from the boundedness of culture, but the stress on particularism and localism is still common. In part this reflects that many societies see *themselves* as local, and stress differences between themselves and adjacent groups. Yet, the problem for social scientists dealing with comparative issues is that they normally conceive of culture as the source of difference in which comparisons either fail or are not fully realized. Thus, if all else in societies is predictable, and a comparison does not yield significant conclusions, the problem must be with culture. It is culture that does not follow the predicted trajectory. Or culture may simply be utilized to explain why local matters are different.

An example of this kind of thinking is found in how economy is projected against culture. If one cannot predict an outcome from economic models, which in theory are logical and rational, culture is employed to account for why the model did not work and what was not predictable. Culture, which is normally invoked at the last instance, is used to answer what economic structuration will not.

Thus, the conservative quality of culture is also an attribute of inertia to change. Institutions and political structures might change through economic transformations or revolutions, but the source of change is seldom if ever realized in culture. In Burguière's contribution to this volume, he states, "Braudel speaks of *mentalités* as 'jails' of the *longue durée,* which means that they play neither a creative nor even an active role in the historical process but can merely use the force of inertia to resist change. Only economic and social structures are active forces in the making of history."

This position is hardly unique to the stress on *mentalités* in the *Annales* school of French intellectual thought, since its foundational roots are in Durkheim and the whole of the *L'Année Sociologique.* But it is not only a French matter. The American anthropologist A. L. Kroeber wrote on the subject as early as 1917. For Kroeber, one of the characteristics of culture was what he called "ballast." In this sense, culture as ballast promoted stability over time, categories of thought and action which were meaningful for cultural participants, and a sense of repose.

Another issue regarding the ability to deal with culture in a comparative context is the matter of commensurability. As noted in Poppi's post-script to this volume, the analysis of culture starts from and concludes on the idea of difference(s). This poses a continuous problem for comparison, which must assume some measure of commensurability from the initial determination of why the comparison is being done. This is a critical problem and one that creates methodological concerns, because comparison invokes semi-universal categories which are invoked as mediating entities between local practice and a range of common practical problems which every society encounters.

Comparison, fraught as it is with a number of insurmountable method-ological and theoretical problems, is carried out in a variety of ways. Some of them work better in particular contexts, while some yield different results that can be tested or may be converted into middle-range theory. As a form of thought experiment, comparison opens up new possibilities for the analysis of new problems and/or a rethinking of older issues.

### Changes and Revisions in the Idea of Comparison

Anthropological interest in comparison goes back to late nineteenth-century cultural evolutionary schemes which by the 1910s had run their course. Yet, from the inception of anthropology the interest in comparison has held sway in theoretical development. Just as the evolutionists saw their enterprise as one of science, approaches since World War II have all used the purported scientific method as the dominant framework to anchor comparative findings. Murdock envisioned comparison as part of his universal and global scheme of seeing bounded units as the subjects of cross-cultural analysis through which particular hypotheses could be tested. Cultural propositions could be tested using cross-cultural files, which at that time were located at Yale University. The concern for writing cross-cultural laws about human behavior was another expression of the rise of behaviorism in the social sciences, beginning in the 1920s and continuing throughout the 1970s.

While such schemes were global, the comparative method under Rad-cliffe-Brown was more limited in scope. Working within a Durkheimian framework, he saw social science as the comparison of social typologies through which a variety of societies could be reduced to a limited number of types and sub-types, which could be further compared. By comparing types through ethnographic cases, Radcliffe-Brown argued that certain universal principles underlay all particular societies, and that these principles were finite. Critical here was the shift from culture to society as the focus of analysis. Not only was society the basis of British social anthropology, society and social action had jobs to accomplish. Society was not as variable, particular, and unique as was culture. Social laws were universal and could be inductively derived and tested, while culture was more open ended, and had no universal forms. Simply put, culture was too "messy." Both Murdock and Radcliffe-Brown insisted that the comparative method was anthropology's version of the scientific method. Both claimed that through their frameworks they were doing grand theory and, above all, that their methodologies were objective.

Grand theory has had a long and dominant role in anthropology. From the 1940s onward, the American anthropologist Julian Steward developed various evolutionary frameworks to account for the rise of early states. Though his approach was more limited in scope, it too was seen to be comparative, scientific, and objective. The most recent version of grand theory is Lévi-Straussian structuralism; global, comparative, and above all and like its predecessors, objective. The source or basis of comparison here is the unconscious, key features of which Lévi-Strauss postulates as universal, though not Freudian. Lévi-Strauss has never wavered from the assertion that his approach is scientific.

In general, historians have not insisted that science is the anchor of their comparisons. At various times, historians have dabbled in discussions of what a scientific approach might add to historical understanding, but most of these attempts have had little lasting impact. History remains divided and spread across the social sciences and the humanities, and this has helped spare the profession from endless debates as to what a science of history would be like, or what this would add to the totality of historical understanding.

The fundamental issue is that history was and is committed to the importance of contextualizing phenomena. Cultural meanings and their nuanced twists over time are critical in ascertaining the kinds of internal contradictions which historical events take and the forms of complexity which settle on contexts as layers of patina. Only in the past three decades has anthropology come to realize the importance of context. We have learned from Edmund Wilson's *To the Finland Station* that history is still in part the writing and also the acting of the past. Though historians may not do it as Wilson did, the creative insight of their efforts has spared them from endless debates over objectivity.

There are, however, conjunctions between anthropology and history, and they revolve around the idea of relativism. Both fields have their intellectual foundations in relativism, although what they attribute to relativism might differ. In anthropology, extreme relativism must deny any form of comparison. If one adheres to a position that all events are unique, particular, and contextualized, then comparison in any form is not an issue. Anthropologists differ on this matter, but few would accept that we must start and end as extreme relativists. Nonetheless, the even less extreme forms of relativism can cause strain, because anthropology first and foremost sees itself as a theoretical enterprise. As already noted, theory construction should not be equated with comparison, for they are fundamentally different enterprises. But if relativism is on one side of the equation and in its essence denies the viability of comparison and theory, the latter two must respond to the dilemma. And indeed, as anthropology has had an increasing impact on theory, relativism in its various expressions has receded. For many, this shift is still a problem that will always exist.

There are parallels in the way history has dealt with relativism. Historians might envision relativism as a way of promoting the uniqueness and the integrity of national histories, against converting them into regional, areal, or global concerns. The writing of national histories has been linked to a romanticism or, better yet, a relativistic romanticism or a romanticized relativism. From such a perspective, theory and comparison are non-issues and must be avoided.

## The Question of Method

At one time historians and anthropologists might have used terms like "the comparative method" as if it was a single all encompassing method. Linked to this approach was the conviction that comparison was connected to entities which were comparable, like systems in which the unit of analysis was semi-hermetic. Thus nations/states/cultures/global histories were a hermetic which could be projected through time and space. These days are now past, and we all realize that such entities are not bounded and linked to a particular space. Thus comparison is carried out in many ways and there is no single methodology which we label as "the comparative method." Debate continues, however, and closure on this matter has been elusive.

A range of subjects must be discussed as they impinge on what we do as part of the comparative enterprise. There are a number of ways in which comparative projects emerge, some based on hunches and speculations, others built from broader categories such as colonial policy, slavery, migration, or gender. But one typically works from a case study or site which might yield results that have broader implications for other cases. Even when case studies initially appear to be highly specific, sometimes critical implications can be drawn from them. An excellent example of moving from case studies to comparison is Kelly's (1984) analysis of how indigenous society was presented to West African colonies and Vietnam during French colonial rule. Through the analysis of grade school books, Kelly showed how certain cultural features were stressed and others marginalized as the books projected what it meant to be a West African or a Vietnamese, and how these differences could be embraced within the French colonial canopy.

Case studies must always be contextualized, and thus comparison is not simply a matter of putting forward a one-to-one semblance between features which are more evidently critical to the aims of the writer. Contextualization is a thorny issue and it is a concern which cannot be dismissed for the sake of theoretical clarity. One of the benefits of contextualization is that context does not only deal with the factual; it can also bring forth information which might not be evident from what is factually derived. By tacking back and forth from the factual to the counterfactual, one must ask under what conditions some event or structure did not occur or could not emerge. Counterfactual arguments have a long history in philosophical thought and one of their contributions, apart from illuminating what something is *not,* is to sharpen the kinds of enquiries one makes of what is factual. Ideally, any type of comparison must deal with the problem of counterfactuals since they yield analytical trajectories which would not be apparent through comparing one factual case study to another.

Another methodological issue is raised by questions of separateness and distance in time and space. Traditionally, comparisons have invoked the idea that if what is being compared shares some common time and space, the findings will be more powerful. Or one can make comparisons that are distant but that fall within a general category, such as Kelly's work on educational policy and practice within the French colonial system.

Another problem is posed by cases which on the surface might appear to be radically different, with little in common. The article by Geyer and Bright compares the emergence of Germany and the United States in the nineteenth century as they relate to global and colonial developments during that period. On the surface, it might look as if not much can be said, but as the authors note, the parallel emergence of these two future world powers occurred during a period of the nineteenth century which historians have usually interpreted as one of peace. Thus, the comparison of the role of the United States within the context of the Western hemisphere and Germany in the context of continental Europe may be understood as different versions of manifest destiny which resulted in hegemonic domination in contested but not overarching territories.

Methodological formalism is a concern that has dominated many aspects of comparative work. Formalism implies a sense of control over the number and kinds of variables which are employed in comparison. By defining fewer variables as critical to a problem, one may assume that one's findings will be more precise and more amenable to testing in other contexts. Some historical studies have employed this method, but it has been more common in the social sciences such as anthropology, sociology, and economics. The rigor of such methods and the questions they ask of the empirical evidence can result in interesting conclusions, but sometimes the findings are difficult to extend beyond the empirical universe and context under study. In many ways this type of work can appear overly mechanistic, but in some cases the results have been critical.

The current concern with presentism also raises methodological questions. Although presentism is a critical theoretical position in postmodernism and especially in the writings of Foucault, its foundations are best exemplified in Nietzsche's writings on history. The presentist position correctly argues that histories have different narratives, but is the narrative a projection of the present narrative on the past? If so, a clear understanding of various expressions of present narratives is a methodological imperative for understanding how the past is portrayed. By projecting backwards into time and space, the presentist position argues that we never really know the past, which is only employed to justify the present. As a philosophical concern, the presentist perspective has methodological relevance. Does doing history only maintain and verify the present? If presentism seeks the present in the past, to what extent are earlier historical narratives muted? If various historical epochs were once understood as the "thought of an age," can we ever understand these earlier periods as a set of narratives which must be captured in prior texts that no longer exist?

Methodologically, presentism in history generates a number of challenging questions which may have no closure. At best we must be cautious regarding what we are doing and the extent to which narratives are compounded into versions of the present. This is also an issue in comparative analysis, one which has similarities to the writing of cultural portraits in anthropology. Cultural portraits are pictures, a form of art in which the reader moves from one portrait to another. Comparatively, the reader makes judgments on what is pleasing or acceptable, and what is not. Such discriminations are partly subjective, yet in each case the portrait must resonate with one's prior text which is the basis of circumspection. At best, the historian and the anthropologist can identify those prior texts which are essential to unpacking questions of what is necessary to make sense of what is out there.

Comparisons are not scientific nor do they exhaust all possibilities. Durkheim envisioned sociology as a scientific field, but that can only be accomplished with a conviction that laws can be generalized from single, particular contexts. Few comparativists would fully adhere to the position set forth by Durkheim, but the methodology of generalization from cases remains critical to us nevertheless. In Adas' contribution to this volume, he generalizes on how European and Indian forms of scientific enquiry dealt with different issues, and yet there was exchange between the two forms of thought. This exchange resulted in a number of new developments on both sides, yet scientific enquiry in India remained Indian. Analysis of the two-way flow of ideas between colonizer and colonized must include a methodological concern with contingencies, with changing individual and collective agencies, and with the negotiation of competing and conflicting epistemologies.

The rise of comparative histories—of gender relations and colonialism, slavery, migration and immigration, and more recently transnationalism—all emerge from a single case or context from which issues are carried into other contexts. Through comparison, the initial assumptions from the original case can be questioned and rethought, and this forces us to ask why some features exist in some cases but not in others.

Comparison can deal with either questions of larger processes *or* particular patterns that can be elicited from limited historical processes, but neither ever exhausts what might be possible, nor can we ever account for the full spectrum of cases. It is here that, methodologically, one might turn to the possibilities of contrafactuals, for they force us to ask why particular possibilities do not exist empirically even though they could exist logically. In both kinds of enquiry (factual and counterfactual), the outcome will be the pursuit of questions as hunches and speculations.

## Old Issues, New Directions

Comparisons have been expressed in a variety of ways, and thus there is no single method which encompasses the range of work. Furthermore, the implications which comparison generates are not only based on comparing particular cases or by comparing cases which fall within particular categories of analysis. In many cases, the minute analysis of a particular case *per se* will generate issues and questions which primarily result from the case, and in most situations these findings cannot be predicted beforehand. Similarly, when the historian enters archival work and the anthropologist new and possibly radical contexts, the detailed and rich variation encountered may yield questions that can be set forth for possible comparison. Inferences of this type usually result from the intellectual curiosity of the researcher who asks why something exists and what it means. An excellent example of this kind of probing and analysis is Diane Hughes' (1986) detailed and provocative study of earrings, culture, and social conflict in the art of Florentine Italy.

Aesthetics is probably the most culture-bound phenomenon which comparative work encounters, and in many ways it is the most challenging. Categories for aesthetic analysis hardly exist, and those that do are usually not very interesting. Aesthetics convey ideas of beauty and truth which give cultures their sense of uniqueness as well as what was once called their *geist* or spirit. Art historians have dealt with this issue for decades. Aesthetic understandings of particular times and spaces are the most culture-bound entities which comparativists encounter. Though it is difficult to generalize beyond particular contexts, studies of aesthetics offer rewards not only in understanding of the arts themselves, but also in the light they can shed on societal tensions expressed and mediated within the aesthetic domain, as Hughes (1986) has demonstrated.

The vitality of comparison requires us to reflect on our different ways of knowing things. This kind of knowing requires detailed analysis and knowledge of the historical narratives which are entangled within any given context. At any one time, our categories replicate the different narratives which emerge as a variety and combination of tropes which change over time and within any presentistic context. Categories are hardly neutral, and thus the art historian and the historian must always be attentive to unpacking them. Normally we compare by contextualization, which we assume means exploring the milieu which works in and through the categories. Yet comparison can and does exist primarily by the comparing of contexts which might be more productive than the category itself. Stoler (2001), working within a colonial and post-colonial framework, has brilliantly analyzed and demonstrated how certain cultural features in American colonial history not only resonate within post-colonial frameworks, but also how empires and their legal codes created varying contexts which must be comprehended as competing narratives from empire in and through regional and local responses.

Modernity/modernities as categories of comparative analysis have come to the fore in how we understand the present. Ironically, the interest in modernity seems to have emerged after the rise of postmodernity, leaving one to ponder why and how this inversion was manifest. The roots of modernity go back to the nineteenth century, though the present currency of writings on the subject seem to indicate that it represents a new wave of analysis. While the rise of modernity occurred throughout societies and nations in Europe, it was understood as a remaking of the social fabric, partly as a result of European industrial development after 1870. Probably the best analyses of modernity from that time, and perhaps ever, are found in the writings of Georg Simmel (1858–1918), the German sociologist/cultural philosopher who saw the basic problem as one of commodification in its many forms. While Simmel notes how society, class, personal relations, and values were redrawn alongside the endless growth of objective culture, social bonds and group affiliations no longer existed vis-à-vis one another. Each new strand of interaction was reshaped and meditated through commodities, and new institutions assumed an almost unquestioned existence in the quotidian life of society. Thus categories like leisure, travel and vacation, adornment and style, space and privacy, and the public sphere all emerged as differing expressions of commodification and modernity. As Simmel notes, such drastic changes could not always be internalized by individuals as part of what he labels "subjective culture." The breakdown of older norms and the vacuity of new structures resulted in forms of alienation and distanciation between individuals and groups.

The issue of modernity as a category embraces a number of critical concerns which cannot be subsumed under a single category. One of these is the contrast commonly drawn between secularism and traditionalism. If secularism is cast as part of modernism along with increasing degrees of rationality and bureaucracy, the focus on traditionalism becomes even more a response to what many parts of the world interpret as another penetration of Western hegemony. However, cultural and religious responses must never be interpreted solely as only a reaction to external forces. A case in point is the current debates regarding Islamic thought and action as it is comprehended within contemporary Western perspectives on Orientalism. Islam as a cultural structure becomes more focused and vocal as the vehicle that embraces what can be labeled as Occidentalism, in which an external critique of the "West" takes on a high degree of visibility. Furthermore, modernities in the plural always rest upon cultural and political foundations. Thus, one can talk of "Asian Modernities" or "Southeast Asian Modernities" as a means of depicting the hybridization of modernity as a contextualized debate being carried out in many nation states.

Comparisons of global history in its various contexts raises the critical theoretical issue of just when the state reigns supreme over society and vice-versa. As Geyer and Bright point out, in the global imperialism of the nineteenth century the state was supreme over society. The question to ask, however, is how a re-action or re-balancing occurs whereby society regains supremacy. This is a vital problem of comparative analysis and one which must initially be examined on a case by case basis within the various contours of imperialism and post- imperialistic structural changes. There is no single pathway to understanding this, and in some cases one can argue that the state always in the end reigns or regains its supremacy.

Another implication of the state/society contrast is the emergence of what is now called the subaltern. What subaltern studies stress is that either the state or society creates the subaltern. The creation, which initially may have occurred through the employment of force based on social divisions within society is normalized and routinized through legislation, which stresses that these societal cleavages are natural. India and South Africa are the best cases of legislation reifying the inequities of society. For the comparativist, the analysis of such cases must include not only how the subaltern is created in various contexts, but also how the explicit and implicit facets of laws and legislation are manifest. Culturally, each of these contexts might take on a different veneer, but there are nonetheless structural similarities across the different cases. On the overt cultural level in particular cases, one must be cognizant of the language of legislation through which drastic forms of internal control are "softened" to make laws appear as natural, non-draconian, and semi-palatable. Any comparison of such cases requires an initial detailed analysis of particular contexts from which overt and covert implications can be elicited for further analysis.

The move from local to regional histories and global history should not be approached as a one-way process in which globalization brings forth an increasing homogeneity, which gradually works from the global to the local. Comparative historians are well aware that resonance at the local level may take many different expressions. It is valid to argue that broad similarities may emerge, but in most cases cultural differences are not only rendered but are enhanced. Local differences are not only internally generated based on traditions, they are normally magnified in terms of the oppositions which exist between adjacent societies. Propinquity creates and enhances differences which in most cases are historically based. One need not travel to central Australia to observe this pattern in Aboriginal Australian cultures, it is more pleasurable to go from England to France and back. Historians and anthropologists have stressed this form of inversion in their work and many ethnographic and historical works support this kind of analysis. Although the stress on national traditions may at one time have appeared excessive, the impact of globalization can create different patterns of response which defy prediction.

Many of this volume's papers deal with the issue of translation. As I have noted, aesthetics is a most difficult aspect of culture to translate across different contexts. Translations can be done through the application of comparable categories in two or more cases, but one must always be cautious if the comparison brings forth something new and unique, or if it reaffirms the categories and thus makes the case analysis a mere vehicle for broadening categories or enhancing theoretical clarity. To bridge differences in such cross-case analyses, one usually deals with a meta-language from which particular features of each case are contrasted.

Again we must be cautious in how far the meta-language is used, because particular cases, be they cultures or languages, may not resonate with the meta-language. On the other hand, apart from aesthetics, many features of what we would label as parts of society can be understood through meta-languages which expand on certain features in terms of their linkages with other aspects of society.

Translation, like any comparative agenda, emerges from the research problems which are being explored. Just as comparison is not a methodology, the idea of translation must not be combined with any form of methodology. For some scholars, translation is not only the beginning but also an end. Thus, for comparative work as well as translation, the rigor of one's attempt must be first and foremost the strength of one's research problem.

## The Organization of the Volume: Categories and Essays

In the organization of the various essays into relatively meaningful categories, it will be evident to the reader that a certain amount of overlap exists from essay to essay and from category to category. Discrete categories do not work since all of the essays move in a variety of ways which, in turn, illuminate certain features that were neither evident nor intended by the authors. The categories have been set up as a means of eliciting new insights or uniqueness, to try to illuminate old and new things.

Section I, *On Thinking Comparatively,* covers a range of past and present concerns with how comparative analysis is related to theoretical concerns within the social sciences and humanities. The range of the essays is broad, and the insights they provide on how comparison has been perceived in the past speak to many contemporary issues.

André Burguière provides an insightful review of philosophical and intellectual debates in the early creation of *Annales* from its inception in 1929 to the present, and analyzes transformations of the founding visions as set forth by Marc Bloch and Lucien Febvre.[1] Following Durkheim, Bloch and Febvre were committed to making history a form of positivism though taking it in many directions different from what Durkheim meant by positivism as a scientific endeavor of his time. Although Bloch and Febvre focused on the idea of *mentalités,* there were differences in what they meant by it. But the real issue was to move history and the social sciences forward as a generalizing science in which the role and dominance of the individual was dethroned. The analysis of *mentalités* was based on looking at cultural and social facts from the inside. This perspective was based not only on the facts of collective consciousness but also on how thoughts and actions of the individual emanated from collective structures and behaviors.

Both Bloch and Febvre had an aversion toward theories which were implanted on the phenomena, and thus in the long run destroyed or altered the very nature of the subject matter and empirical evidence which they were attempting to describe and interpret. This totalizing framework dealt with intellectual production as it connected with the social and material life that was under investigation. Thus Marxism and Freudianism in their many variants were suspect, although Febvre remained intrigued by the emotions.

Here Burguière refers to the study of *mentalités* as anthropological history. What is meant by this new concept is an ability to deal with the science of change (which was critical to Bloch) and to absorb an interest in subjectivities expressed in and through periods of rapid change such as early modernity in France. Here again we encounter the issue of culture versus economy, with culture seen as the inertia to change. Anthropological history also partially shifts the investigation from quantitative to qualitative features. The diversity and complexity of the historical process is enhanced through the determinations of comparisons in which differences are readily brought to light. Differences, however, are not the sole issue—the critical and lasting impact of stressing differences is that they commonly force the researcher to return to the original case with a set of new enquiries.

Continuing with the theoretical understanding of particular cases, George Steinmetz examines the emergence of New Social Movements in Germany after World War II. As throughout Europe, Germany during the post-war period has had a broad range of social movements which cut across class divisions. The basis of these movements reflects a series of tensions, some with the past of National Socialism, others on matters regarding post-war unification, environmental concerns, race and racism, increasing "Americanization" of Germany, moves towards re-militarization, and counter-globalization. Given that these movements straddle various segments of society and class lines, Steinmetz is cautious in working within a traditional Marxist framework, yet he thinks that certain features of post-Marxist thought might elucidate these developments. The major tool of analysis here is regulation theory based on Fordist and Post-Fordist theories as developed by Gramsci.

Fordism, as it was developed in the United States and the Soviet Union, was a semi-totalizing framework that created the New Man as factory workers from family life to assembly life. The totalizing aspects are manifest in how Ford saw the factory, as ideally devoted to re-working production in conjunction with increasing demands of high consumption, thus producing a form of hegemonic convergence in which high wages meant high production, which meant still higher consumption, and so on. In this sense the Fordist subject was ideally successful if the benefits were realized by the worker. Yet, Fordism created many of the structures and dilemmas which unleashed conflict and fueled various issues of protest. Marxist theory illuminates the internal contradictions between the system of production and the theoretical basis of the movements. An increasing sense of alienation and contradiction is partly a rejection of Fordist approaches as well as a questioning of the role of the German state. The existence of the

Nazi past blurs and obscures a positive national identity, and thus German nationalism and vitalism have become the basis of right-wing elements and political parties. The canopy of conflicting features embraced by the New Social Movements are continuously re-created, although the post-Fordist foundations may have eroded in recent times.

Raymond Grew draws forth a series of issues and concerns that are both critical to and critical of comparative history. While in quarters of the historical profession, some practitioners would contend that comparison is what one does late in intellectual life, Grew makes clear that all historians do comparative work throughout their careers. Challenges to comparison come in many forms. The essential quality of uniqueness is still a concern of many historians and one can still argue that "unique" findings can have broader implications on contextualized as well as cross-contextualized situations. If context represents one side of the equation, abstract ideal types may be its nemesis. Ideal types can be made so abstract as to diffuse their validity and power of explanation. Grew warns that hyper-abstraction of ideal types and models must always deal with contextual features which are the essence of the problem.

History, as Grew notes, has always vacillated between the particular and the general. Foucauldian history and post-modernism have had a critical impact through the over-generalizing quality of the categories they employ, and historians have been forced to critically evaluate their methods. The cultural turn has moved the discussion to texts and meanings which are intrinsically focused on difference(s). Here, of course, the issue is not only texts but the extent to which the historian's own rhetoric converges with them, and thus any interpretation must deal with a range of readings, one of which is the author's.

Yet, given the range of contemporary interests among historians, comparison must always challenge conceptual boundaries, which over time can become binding. As Grew observes, the openness of the challenge not only refutes hard categories, it also produces new directions for exploring old and new questions. Again, theory is only one facet of the comparative process.

In dealing with some of the discontents in anthropology, Aram Yengoyan also evokes some of Grew's concern but in anthropology they are more biting and more bitter. Anthropology, which at one time was seen as a theoretical endeavor, a comparative project, a generalizing form of science or humanity, a descriptive field enterprise, and the source of critical cultural portraits has barely survived deconstruction and post-modern criticism. Many of the critiques are valid, such as the questioning of objectivity in anthropology and the critique of ethnographic authority. Now, the author is part of the described milieu which also has its perils if taken to an extreme expression.

Advocating different forms of translation, Yengoyan notes a cautious warning for all translations have a heavy reliance on a meta-language. Linguistics has a sophisticated meta-language through which translations are made, yet the problem remains in that comparative work in linguistics usually verifies its meta-language. History has not been burdened with a grand meta-narrative or a meta-language and in many ways the comparative endeavor has been more fruitful. In anthropology we must also be concerned about what meta-theory or meta-languages embrace. Translations are more fruitful if we can relate texts and textual materials to the idea of a prior text. The prior text is asking what does one need to know to know something. Prior texts are local in language and culture yet they are essential to our means of knowing. The comparative question is not only one of determining the convergences of text and prior text, but also asking how far can different prior texts encounter, understand, and resonate with texts which are foreign and different. This is an empirical problem but one which will yield new insights on the extent to which texts and narratives are only historically derived. It also has the virtue of asking questions which are not apparent. Just as Foucault's portrait and narrative was on the "underbelly" (madness, asylums, sexuality, disease, punishment) of society, the move to prior texts in other contexts might direct our enquiries to other arenas of action and thought which are not voiced in particular texts and narratives.

*Comparing Globally* (section 2) moves the enquiry from the initial focus on the particular to broad comparative and global concerns. Each of these essays indicate different ways on what comparison might yield. Some approaches might have been consciously devised, others might direct the author and the reader to new and different speculations which emerge through how the work was crafted. A few of the results might be exciting, others might appear as obvious, but that is the risk of comparative scholarship.

Mary Beard's original essay dealt with the initial impact of James Frazer's *The Golden Bough* which not only dwarfed scholarship in religion, myth, and the classics for nearly thirty years, it eventually dwarfed the author. As Beard notes, Frazer's vision did not fully comprehend the lasting impact of the volumes in creating an ambitious comparative project in many directions. The work itself has its roots in Greek and Latin cultural developments which were contrasted. The remainder of the "primitive" world was a backdrop against which the classics of the Greek and Roman worlds were the pinnacle. Yet, as Beard notes these two cultural worlds were separate and contrasted, but not compared.

Classical history in its inception was two worlds (the Greeks and the Romans) which were to be understood separately through different and unique texts. This contrast is best captured in Stoppard's *The Invention of Love* (1997: 91) as follows. Young Chamberlain tells the dying classicist/ poet A. E. Housman that they have a discussion group and they discuss what they should call themselves, and "homosexuals" has been suggested. Housman responds, "Homosexuals?" to which Chamberlain lamely responds, "We aren't anything 'til there's a word for it." Housman sarcastically responds, "Homosexuals? Who is responsible for this barbarity?" and Chamberlain meekly answers, "What's wrong with it?" to which Housman retorts, "It's half Greek and half Latin!"

As Beard observes, Frazer was the great comparative departure from the classicism of the nineteenth century. As a broad comparative venture, it had its greatest impact on anthropology, although it also moved the direction of the study of the classics toward ancient history, classical philosophy, linguistics, archaeology, and philology. Within this broad shift, via the exoticism of myths and legends throughout the world, Frazer created the "other," which was as uncompromising as himself.

Comparative tensions still exist in classical studies, yet since they are now pursued through a broad range of intellectual fields, there can be no return to original foundations. Frazer's lasting impact on different and unique cultural discourses became part of the classic foundations of World's Exhibitions and Fairs from 1851 to the 1940s. *The Golden Bough* was read in the British colonies, and the colonial system created a number of responses. Portraits of other peoples and cultures in International Exhibitions (in France, the United Kingdom, the United States) gradually worked back to local contexts and created new and different practices.

Chris Gregory's approach to broader issues of colonial rule, the emergence of the informal economy, and the rise of subaltern politics is developed through the use of cowrie shells for currency in many parts of the world. In Melanesia, cowries as a medium of exchange were subject to a variety of forces such as inflation in the early colonial period. With the introduction of Western-based currencies, colonial officials attempted to end the use of cowrie shells for exchange, but the success of this venture was never totalized. As Western monetaries came into existence, and states attempted to suppress cowrie use through legislation, there was nonetheless a *rise* in local-level demand for cowries. Gregory shows that from West Africa to India to Melanesia, the cowrie became dominant in the informal economy as a means of exchange, and also as a symbol and structure of resistance to Western economic penetration. Cultural differences as responses to Western monetization policies could not be obliterated. In India, the cowrie had to compete with gold and silver and was eventually phased out. Gold and silver as cultural statements have not declined and their importance has probably increased as national currencies have fluctuated and are no longer a surety. In Melanesia in 1999, among the Tolai of Papua New Guinea, cowrie shell money was legislated as legal tender.

As Gregory shows, in Tolai the increase in shell money supply has neither debased its value or inflated shell money prices. In India, gold and silver, and earlier the cowrie, have continued to express economic status and power. We see that within the context of global economic unity and the power of the American dollar, cultures have maintained different symbols of value which create and enhance their differences.

Michael Geyer and Charles Bright tackle a broad set of issues regarding global history and the final fruition of world imperialism. A number of comparative concerns are developed by the authors for the nineteenth century which have theoretical implications for events ranging from the French Revolution to the onset of World War I. Historians have commonly accepted that the nineteenth century, the period between these two polar events, was a period of relative peace. But as Geyer and Bright note, this was a period of local and regional wars which spawned carnage in both the New World and Eurasia. Both hemispheres of the New World saw ongoing wars against indigenous peoples carried out by states as territorial units that could not be challenged.

The issues at stake were fundamentally global. Two critical changes in particular must be noted. First, Bonapartism in France established the dominance of the State over Society. This model held sway throughout the era and eventually states of mobilization became the norm in Germany, England, the United States, and France, and this brought particular problems of its own. Second, imperialism had a critical effect on the internal structure of society: agriculture as subsistence farming was gradually replaced by agriculture as regional and international commerce. Changes in tax laws enhanced this shift which internally re-peasantized the peasant as a rural proletariat.

The need to sustain control also meant that sea power became pivotal to the dominance of far-flung empires, in some regions becoming more critical than controlling land. Within this context, Germany and the United States emerged late in the imperial game by following different and yet parallel paths without having to pay the heavy costs of maintaining global empires such as that of France. As regional but not global powers, Germany and the United States became dominant areal powers.

Geyer and Bright are clear in their advocacy of traditional history, which is the foundation of their efforts, but also in their argument that a comparative task must be forged, employing new data on deaths and warfare over the time and space of the nineteenth century. By moving beyond global wars, they discovered an array of wars and massacres which would have remained obscure within the status quo of historical practice.

Appealing to hard data sets, the authors make a fine case for disciplining comparative history not simply by abandoning common analytical categories but by contextualizing those categories, and allowing data sets to provide nuanced dynamics through case-by-case analysis. By focusing on regional and semi-global contexts and on conflicts which are spatially distant but temporally connected (such as Napoleon III in Mexico and the Crimea), the pattern of interlinkages becomes more vivid and theoretically powerful. Hunches and speculations, combined with hard data sets, come to fruition.

If the essays in section 2 represent approaches which consciously seek comparative results, the articles in section 3, *Making Discoveries,* might appear to reveal curious findings with unanticipated implications. Like all "discoveries," some may have a lasting impact on future ideas, others can help us reappraise past issues, and still others create new problems.

Michael Adas examines different intersects between British science, Indian science, and the colonial system which anchored exchanges between colonizer and colonized. Scientific and technological transfers within colonial rule have normally been understood as what flows and follows from the industrial metropole to the margins of empire. Models of scientific/technological diffusion have assumed a unidirectional flow in which the colonized—either as settler or as non-settler colonies—were passive receptors.

Adas argues, by contrast, that colonial science in India was hardly passive. The excellence of Indian mathematical and statistical sciences were employed for census and cadastral surveys and for in-depth analysis of particular areas and problems, both of which were essential to the operation of the colonial system in India. However, many quarters of the colonial system still characterized the colonized "other" as a tabula rasa where no scientific knowledge or tradition existed prior to English, French, German, or American scientific penetration. In settled colonies such as Australia, the scientific savants were British who had moved to the colonies to convey their scientific activities. The settler colonies occupied by British scientists were different and apart from non-settler cases.

India did not fit into this mold. There, astronomy and mathematics were very advanced and in many ways outstripped their European counterparts. Adas asserts that India was therefore hardly a tabula rasa, but this very difference in knowledge and possible superiority nevertheless did not alter the tenets of scientific racism, which buttressed European cultural hegemony. Indian knowledge and practice in some fields, such as medicine, were highly resilient in the face of English scientific pursuits. For example, in the process of exchange, Indian medical thought successfully fought off European ideas of vaccination in preference for indigenous variolation techniques.

Throughout the early nineteenth century, nationalistic movements supported the development of a national medical theory and practice, thus enhancing an "independent" scientific framework which was neither derivative nor only applied, and which possessed its own sense of "Indianness." Moreover, over recent decades, Indian medical practice has had an immense impact on Western ideas of medicine, hence partially moving ideas towards different expressions of "wholism."

John Borneman's analysis brings us back to how issues of cultural and national identity affect categories and symbolic processes which beset the historical relations of state to nation. By analyzing the connections between horse breeds and breeding in France and the United States, Borneman points to the differences between a single performance standard for French horses and breeders, and multiple performance standards in the United States. Yet in both countries, the use of new genetic and scientific breeding techniques have resulted in another form of cultural explanation. In France, the passion for the horse in its totality has since as long ago as 1665 existed within the centralized administration of the state. State regulation of breeding policies, practices, and change is rigidly adhered to as part of an ideology for the passion of the horse. In the United States, American culture balances the language of horse commodification and profit with that of religion as a metaphor. The value of the horse is not a matter of the horse itself, but which one of its various attributes are desired and enhanced.

In theory, the passion of the horse in France is not simply a matter of the state, it is also based on the Enlightenment principle that scientific utilization creates improvement, rationalization, and enhancement of what France has to offer. Thus, the issue is one that transcends profit.

The horse as a racial category in the United States is partially cleansed as a religious phenomena, one which is within the realm of lived-in America, and thus horse beauty is semi-sacred. And better yet, in both France and the United States the object of love can be replicated without any ordinary sex act. It all comes out divine.

Beverly Heckart's essay is a critical analysis of how two European cities dealt with post-World War II urban renewal. The issues involved in the playing out of what was encountered in urban renewal and cultural impetus were highly variable against a field of competing forces and ideologies. Both Avignon in France and Worms in Germany each pursued their own re-creation, initially by re-doing the city center, the heart of the urban complex. In both cases, assessments had to be made of the past and present, intentions for the future, the impact of European views of post-World War II modernity, and the most recent expressions of modernism in urban architecture.

Avignon focused on the past, but it also had to compete in heated political battles over the extent to which economic prosperity influenced architectural stylistics. Conflicts between renovation and restoration reflected deep and contradictory currents in French society. Eventually, the city center (the Balance) became a blend of old and new, but it could not fully escape the transformative forces of time.

Worms was confronted with a destroyed inner city, and also with competing ideas of the past and the present. The inner city of Worms was the symbol of its urban identity, while cathedrals were its link to the past. Yet, the past also had to be prior to 1933, and like Avignon, the connections of Worms to Europe were in a Christian past which was basic to urban renewal. Thus, in Avignon, the future was reversed and older cultural attitudes and patterns were re-instituted. For Worms, traditionalism meant a more distant past, but the acceptance of European modernism in architecture represented a partial escape from the past.

As I have noted, anthropologists commonly relegate cultural factors to the realm of least explanatory value. Economic and structural features loom large in the construction of theoretical and/or comparative insights, while cultural features are stressed mostly in terms of particularisms. Jack Goody and Cesare Poppi's reflections on funerary practices in England

and Italy remind us to ask *just how much funeral practices can diverge.* Funeral practices imply a certain or limited variance in what are commensurable frameworks. Against a range, but not an infinite range, of possible responses, practical problems and dilemmas must be dealt with. In Italy, the dead are buried, but later the bones are exhumed, washed, and cleaned. Burial sites are moved and at times the remains occupy double burials. Flowers are used as a sign of social and personal continuity. While Italian practice involves movement of the dead, the English demand that their dead stay put. In Naples, death is a process and an ongoing connection between the living and the dead. In England the dead are at the end of a journey and the preservation of memory is linked to the permanence of death. Flowers are associated with fertility and increase in Italy, and thus for Italians living children blossom into adults, while dead children are also flowers in that their growth only lasted for a short time.

As Poppi explains in his postscript, the possible variations form a continuum which, in theory, could be utilized to encompass all possible cases. The specific cases in essence contrast what is Italian and what is English. For example, *"Ciao Lella"* on an Italian tombstone is contrasted to an English tombstone showing a cast of plastic flowers around a pint of beer for excessive drinking or a set of boxing gloves for a good boxer. The bottom line is cultural. One is Italian, one is English and they are eternally distinct, separate, and contrastive, like Greek and Latin.

## Conclusion

Institutions such as war, the state, economy, and technology are commonly utilized as comparative categories throughout the social sciences, although less so in the humanities. Current topics such as gender relations, transnational movements, globalization, and diasporas might be similarly categorized, but in reality they emerge from a single context and subsequently become the source of cross-cultural or cross-national comparisons. Either as institutions or topics of comparison, however, what is being compared must be related to the intellectual and philosophical foundations of categories. In some cases, the linkages of categories to a particular period in time and space make it difficult or virtually impossible to expand beyond initial contexts.

Comparative contextualization might sound like an oxymoron, but in reality we must always seek to learn the extent to which institutions are contextualized. At one time, we accepted the position that contexts cannot be compared, that in reality we are only comparing institutions or writing cultural portraits. This assumption is simply not warranted today. Different and even radically unique contexts are not different worlds with no interface. Although we start from the particular and the local, contextualizations do render parallel pathways of convergence and divergence; thus unique or obscure events within one context are visible in other cases.

Contextualization challenges the idea of the continuity of structures and institutions. One must ask the extent to which contexts might alter, curtail, or otherwise modify structural features, and vice-versa. This is not a new problem or a only a contemporary concern. The spread of capitalism, socialism, and communism to different nations, cultures, and contexts is a fine example of how national contexts, let alone local contexts, can change or erode the fundamental pillars of the "-isms" themselves.

Many of our findings have their start as speculations based on imagination. By this I mean that the analyst or researcher has subjective ideas and thoughts which shape the image of what the comparative task will embrace. To an extent, the image/imagination is shaped by what one knows of the evidence. Yet the question is: how far can one challenge the "facts," or go beyond the facts to what is critical and exciting?

To what extent is the past used to justify comparisons? National intellectual and political structural traditions have a critical bearing on the form of scholarship produced from one national context to another. The *Annales* in France at its inception was comparatively based on the positivistic frameworks of the nineteenth century, as seen in the works of Saint-Simon and Durkheim. Historically, comparison within the context of the writing of American history has seldom been an issue, a point noted by many writers, most visibly Raymond Grew. Yet in recent times, scholarship in the United States on slavery and on the idea of the frontier and frontier history has had a significant impact on writings about other national traditions. German interest in culture(s), not civilization, and the German tradition's unique sense of relativism have both critically influenced anthropology, though it has been somewhat less influential in the promotion of historical relativism (some quarters might argue that Marx, if not Marxists, was a historical relativist). And England, with a society dominated by rank, status, hierarchy, and a crystallized class structure based on rule, law, and social principles, has seen itself reincarnated in classical British social anthropology.

Within all of these contrasting cases, however, comparison has been a form of discovery. Comparison can destabilize what we consider natural, raising new and unforeseen implications that are as important as new findings. As a form of thought experiment, the opening of new findings and new challenges may depend on how an argument is crafted, on how it moves from narrow issues to larger openings, and vice-versa. Or it may depend on how an argument strives for in-depth analysis across the breadth of broader perceptions. In every case, as comparativists, new, unsettling findings are the grail we all seek.

NOTES

Acknowledgments: The conference "Modes of Comparison" was held at the University of Michigan, in Ann Arbor, on 4–5 May 2001. Special thanks must be expressed to the University of Michigan Office for Vice President for Research, the Rackham School of Graduate Studies, and the Department of History for assistance before, during, and after the conference. I am most grateful to all of them for seeing this venture to final fruition. Also, the efforts of Raymond Grew, Thomas Trautmann, David Akin, Ken George, and Chris Krupa have been critical at various times in assisting me in regards to particular problems and broader intellectual issues. David Akin in particular has assisted me in a variety of ways from the inception of this project. Not only were his efforts of the highest value, he also provided creative critique when I needed it. I also want to express my appreciation to Jim Reische and Kamyar Abdi for their organizational help, to David and Peg Bien for their hospitality during the conference, and finally to Daphne Grew for her gracious hosting.

    1. I highly also recommend Burguière's 1982 paper, "The Fate of the History of *Mentalités* in the *Annales*" (*CSSH* 24, 3: 424–37), which can in some ways be read as a companion piece to his new chapter here.

REFERENCES

Asad, Talal. 2003. *Formations of the Secular: Christianity, Islam, Modernity.* Stanford: Stanford University Press.

Hughes, Diane Owen. 1986. Distinguishing Signs: Ear-rings, Jews and Franciscan Rhetoric in the Italian Renaissance City. *Past and Present* 112: 3–59.

Kelly, Gail P. 1984. The Presentation of Indigenous Society in the Schools of French West Africa and Indochina, 1918 to 1938. *Comparative Studies in Society and History* 26: 523–42.

Linton, Ralph. Totemism and the A.E.F. 1924. *American Anthropologist* 24: 296–300.

Stoler, Ann. 2001. Tense and Tender Ties: The Politics of Comparison in North American History and (Post) Colonial Studies. *The Journal of American History* 88, 3: 829–97.

Stoppard, Tom. 1997. *The Invention of Love.* New York: Grove Press.

# 1. ON THINKING COMPARATIVELY

# From the History of Mentalities to Anthropological History

*André Burguière*

My point of departure here is an argument I developed in a 1982 *CSSH* piece on the fate of the history of *mentalités* in the *Annales.*[1] I want to pursue further my analysis of that then-new historiographical trend and try to explain how the study of mentalities turned into what we now call anthropological history. I will retain the distinction drawn in the previous essay between two different conceptions and lines of historiographical inheritance one identified with Marc Bloch, the other with Lucien Febvre. According to Bloch's mainly sociological approach, the *mentalités* to be observed by the historian concern preferably collective habits, repeated practices, and non-reflexive or unconscious representations imbedded in social contrasts and contradictions. According to Febvre's more psychological and at the same time more intellectual conception, the task of the history of *mentalités* is to reconstruct the unity of the mental world of a moment in the past, of a past society, as it is reflected in the unity of individual consciousness. In Febvre's conception and its line of inheritance, we can recognize the tradition of psychological history represented by Robert Mandrou, Jean Delumeau, or Alain Corbin in France, and also the extremists of *mentalités* like Philippe Aries or Michel Foucault, for whom historical reality is purely *causa mentale.* For the moment I will not add to my previous statement, although as I proceed I will encounter and again cross this line of inheritance with regard to the later use of Febvre's conception.

My focus now, however, will be the other line of development in the history of *mentalités* originating in Bloch's conception, in order to analyze the shift from the history of *mentalités* to what we now call anthropological history. Let me first consider the fact that Bloch's conception of *mentalités* was tied not only to his own problematique as an economic and social historian but also to his definition of the object of historical research. For him, as he asserts in *l'Apologie pour l'histoire,* history is not the science of time (and geography is not the science of space), these two categories being present in most scientific fields and disciplines. Rather, history is the science of change. Other disciplines among the social sciences may also take the dimension of change into account, but unlike history can ignore it if they wish to.

### Flashback on the *Annales' Enquêtes Collectives:* The History of Prices

By giving priority to collective forms and trends, to the structural aspects of historical reality, the question of change becomes crucial for those who share a secularized conception of history and do not recognize any global meaning or teleological direction in its change/evolution/development over time. What is the nature of change and how does it operate? Is it a heteronymous or an autonomous process? Is it the result of external and objective forces or produced by society itself? We can trace the transformation of the concept of change among Annalist historians by considering the development of the most successful and fruitful of the *enquêtes collectives* launched and driven by the founders of *Annales:* the cross-disciplinary research done on the history of prices, money, and economic crises. The project was presented in *Annales* in 1930 by Lucien Febvre, who emphasized the explanatory power of confronting the present with the past.[2] The key focus was the Great Depression that had just occurred. Past financial, monetary, or economic crises could help to explain this complex event, and, conversely, the Depression could also be expected to shed light on some economic crises of the past.

Marc Bloch was not officially in charge of the project, which François Simiand had been designated to manage. But he soon became more actively involved in the project than Febvre, writing articles (particularly during the late 1930s after having been elected to the chair of economic and social history at the Sorbonne), frequently reviewing new publications related to the topic . What strikes me in all of these writings is precisely his insistence on emphasizing the psychological dimension of any economic or monetary change. For instance, reviewing a work of François Simiand on the history of prices published in 1936 just after the author's death, he seeks to distance himself from Simiand's somewhat mechanical explanation of the cyclical movement of prices.[3] Simiand tends to assign a causal role to discoveries of new precious metals, such as the gold and silver imported from America in the sixteenth century as studied by Earl Hamilton,[4] which increase the volume of monetary metals and currencies and thereby boosts demand. Bloch writes that, contrary to that metalist conception, all forms of money, metal, or paper, are basically *fiduciaires* (expressions of confidence), and he wants to emphasize the psychological dimension of the market.

This non-determinist attitude toward economic questions was not restricted to Marc Bloch but it was in the mainstream of *Annales'* understanding of the Great Depression. Ernest Gutman, for instance, in his great *Annales* article of 1932 on the international role of the gold-standard,[5] considered gold to be in itself a pure regulator, a conventional means of payment but not the leading force of the economic system. And Gutman emphasized the important role of confidence in the capitalist economy. Likewise, Jean Houdaille, reviewing Georges Boris' book *The Gold Question and the World Crisis,* wrote that "gold as an inert stuff, does not expend credit; but credit, as a primarily psychological mechanism, does attract gold."[6] Economic and social change in that period was rarely portrayed in *Annales* as a modernizing process, but rather is a refraction and expression of mentalities.

### The Labrousse Moment

The study of economic fluctuations by reconstructing price movements using statistical or serial methods greatly expanded in the postwar period something under the influence of Ernest Labrousse. Promoted by the project of *Annales* on the history of prices, it followed Simiand's approach more than Bloch's for various reasons—some intellectual, others more institutional or ideological. Intellectually, Labrousse can be considered a follower of Simiand, although he considered himself to be more a disciple of the economist Aftalion, or of Jaures,[7] because of his attention to long- and short-term price and salary fluctuations, and his practice of statistical and serial analysis. His approach to the crisis of the Ancien Regime[8] appears in one sense less mechanical or less determinist than Simiand's in that he tries to show and explain divergent responses of social groups to economic difficulties (for example, a sudden increase of the price of wheat) not only according to their class interest but perhaps more importantly according to the idea they have of where their interests lie.

But Labrousse's influence on the new generation of historians in the post-war period may come more from his academic position than from his sense of the complexity of social reality. He assumed the *chaire d'histoire economique et sociale* at the Sorbonne, replacing Marc Bloch, at a time when this new field was becoming more attractive to students shaped by the spirit of the Resistance and, frequently, influenced by Marxism and the Communist Party. Marxism had little success among French intellectuals before the Second World War[9] except among a small group of militants within the socialist or communist parties and a time when it was gaining influence among German, Italian, and English intellectuals. After the Second World War, boosted by the leftist spirit of the Liberation and a sudden growth of the Communist Party, Marx made a late and spectacular entrance in France. A new generation of historians, many of them members or sympathizers of the Party, chose the field of social and economic history because of their Marxist orientation and became students of Ernest Labrousse. The historical (and partly unconscious) role of Labrousse consisted in driving them to join the *Annales* school with the illusion that in doing so they remained close to Marxism.

Among historians and social scientists more generally, the concepts of growth and development were in the air. This *Zeitgeist* had much to do with the economic voluntarism in the air during that period of reconstruction which gave the Marxists themselves a productivist tonality, and Maurice Thorez ordered his followers to 'Roll up your sleeves' (*retroussons les manches*). We must go back to the peculiar political climate of that period to understand the strange mixture of Marx and W. W. Rostow, author of *A Non-Communist Manifesto* and theoretician of takeoff[10] which inspired the disciples of Labrousse, new recruits to the *Annales* school. What interested them in Rostow's ideas was not his dogmatic quantification of the Manchesterian pattern of industrialization, but rather his problematization of economic and social change as a process of modernization that required certain *pre-conditions,* including non-economic ones, such as high literacy rates, a sense of saving, planning, and so forth. Mentalities are not only affected by economic transformation—they are part, and an active part, of that transformation. For Labrousse—as for Fernand Braudel, who was less influential among the students who at that time were reshaping the newly founded Sixth Section of the Ecole Pratique des Haules Etudes as an anti-Sorbonne—mentalities have to be taken into account by the historian; but only insofar as they are affected by and a reaction to economic or social change. Braudel speaks of *mentalités* as "jails" (prisons) of the *longue durée,* which means that they play neither a creative nor even an active role in the historical process but can merely use the force of inertia to resist change.[11] Only economic and social structures are active forces in the making of history.

Labrousse proposed a method, the statistical analysis of serial data, and an objective, the investigation on the making of modernity from the Old Regime to industrial society, starting with the most visited question of French historiography: the causes of the French Revolution. In his own work, *l'Esquisse de l'histoire des prix au XVIII siècle* and later in *La crise de l'Ancien Régime,* he wants to date the explosion of the French Revolution to a peculiar conjunction of a long trend of rising prices (in the fourteenth to eighteenth century), a hypercycle of declining prices (from 1778 onward), and a cyclical crisis (created by a cooler spring and the forecast of a bad harvest for 1789). Sudden economic difficulties for the lower classes but also for farmers amplified the climate of frustration among different social groups who thus became more receptive to discourses of political dissent. Labrousse does not pretend to explain the Revolution itself but only its causes. According to him, the Revolution did not follow from the development of economic structures but was partly an accident related to an unusual economic conjuncture. The main thread remains for him the long trend of increasing prices, of economic growth. "After the pre-revolutionary contraction, after the revolutionary cycle," Labrousse argues, "the eighteenth century starts again."[12] Economic growth continues, which is for him the main factor of historical change.

Labrousse's students were incited to extend the investigation backward to the core of the Ancien Regime and forward to nineteenth-century France's becoming an industrial power, following his method of the quantitative analysis of socio-economic serial data and, like him, ignoring the Revolution itself, as meaningless for the study of the structural transformations. Some of these students like René Baehrel, Pierre Deyon, Pierre Goubert, and Emmanuel Le Roy Ladurie went back to the seventeenth century[13] and described an Ancien Regime system in which the cyclical crisis did not progressively erode social and political stability but on the contrary completed demographic adjustment. Others, like Paul Bois, Maurice Agulhon, Pierre Barral, and George Dupeux,[14] were mobilized by Labrousse for departmental research on the social and economic history of modern France. They revealed the modernization of French society as emerging from the politicization of the countryside rather than the industrialization of the cities. Most of them had to distance themselves from Labrousse's explanation of social change through the play of economic forces and interests recognizing the specific role of cultural trends and innovations. They generally began with Marxist questions, inquiring about the structure of production, and in the end chose cultural and anthropological answers.

### Leaving the Socio-economic Paradigm: A Fruitful Heresy

With Emmanuel Le Roy Ladurie's *thèse* on the *Peasants of Languedoc* from the sixteenth to the beginning of the eighteenth century, he wanted to study the primitive accumulation of capital in land, applying a Marxist conception of the early modern period as pre-capitalist. He discovered a peasant economy without growth or savings and long-term stability in agriculture, but at another level a climate of strong cultural and political change. The diffusion of printed texts from the beginning of the sixteenth century on, and some increase in literacy, generated religious dissent and conflict. The growth of the state apparatus (French historians speak of the building of the modern state) required higher taxes which generated anti-fiscal riots among the peasantry. What we call early modernity may be characterized by this distortion between strong cultural growth and a stable economic structure.

The same shift from socio-economic questions to anthropological answers can be observed in most of the departmental studies on nineteenth-century France inspired by Ernest Labrousse. No one really discovered at this level of observation the making of a modern France uplifted and transformed by industrialization but rather a wide range of cultural developments such as a process of ideological survival in the Sarthe or the folklorization of politics in the Var, as if France were condemned to persist in its diversity. *"La France, c'est-à-dire diversité"* (France is diversity), said Lucien Febvre. Let us look at the example of Paul Bois' *Les Paysans de l'Ouest,* which explains as ideological survival the divisions between its eastern and western regions in the Sarthe. In the province of the Maine during the Ancien Regime and still present in twentieth-century Sarthe the western part of the department is dominated by the *white,* and the southeastern devoted to the *blue:* In the western part, a population of peasants in majority live as tenants in large farms with large families, go to church and vote for the conservative candidates who have a clerical and anti-republican orientation. The southeast of the department was more urbanized, and most of its peasants were either poor laborers or were engaged in the proto-industrial output system at the end of the

Ancien Regime. After the Revolution, they became micro-owners or industrial workers. These families have few children, do not go to church, and vote for the left. They voted first for the republicans and later, in the second part of the nineteenth century, for the *radicaux,* for socialists in the beginning of the twentieth century, and for the communists after 1936.

André Siegfried, who had been surprised by this regional contrast, humorously proposed a geological explanation (where the soil is from hercynian granite the people vote for the right; where the soil is sedimentary, for the left); his more serious historical explanation was that the western part of the department was conservative because of an old tradition of domination by landlords and priests, going back to the Ancien Regime.[15] Bois refuted Siegfried's interpretation, arguing that at the end of the Ancien Regime the landlords were neither more present nor the *curés* more influential in the western part of the Maine than in the southeast. Instead, Bois found that the regional difference expresses the loyalty of each to their opposing ideological choices during the great political crisis of the Revolution, when everybody was urged to choose. This was particularly evident regarding the *Civil Constitution of the Clergy,* which the Pope had urged the French clergy not to accept; the department's southeastern section welcomed the constitutional priests (the *prêtres jureurs*), while the western part preferred to protect their *prêtres réfractaires* who refused the oath and obeyed the Pope.

Their divergent political but also economic and demographic attitudes from the beginning of the nineteenth century onward can be explained as the structuration and internalization of their faithfulness to the choice they made during the Revolution, Bois' concept of *survivance idéologique.* Evidently, the foundation of this choice had been prepared by the different social features of the two regions that had appeared during the Ancien Regime. The peasants of the western part *had* lived in isolated hamlets as tenants, mistrustful of the urban world, the world of the owners and of the hated bourgeoisie of new owners who monopolized (*accaparer*) the land. To them, the Revolution had been a long series of disappointments, and they saw the new political establishment as a victory for the hated *messieurs* of the town. They decided to protect their reluctant priests, not as a testimony of deep devotion to the church but because they refused the intrusion of this urban, bourgeois power in the business of their parish. After the Revolution, they increasingly accepted the rule of religion in memory of their support for the church during the Revolution. They voted for the candidates of the castles, supporting the monarchy not as a sign of submission to the nobles but rather because these candidates declared themselves against the Republic.

In the southeastern part of the department, by contrast, the poor peasants were more integrated into the urban culture because of their economic dependence upon the urban market. They submitted to the domination of the bourgeois notables who previously had provided them with jobs and accepted their ideas and culture. They supported the revolutionary government not only as the consecration of these ideas but also because its rhetoric responded to their desire for social promotion and equality. From the nineteenth century onward their Malthusian habitus has been shaped by this desire for integration into the market economy and by their hostility to the church. The earliest evidence we have of the French Church's preoccupation with the diffusion of contraception among the popular classes is the 1834 letter written by Mgr. Bouvier, bishop of Le Mans (the principal city of the Sarthe) to the Sacred Penitentiary in Rome.[16]

By criticizing the argument of the *Tableau de la France de l'Ouest,* in the first part of his work, Bois apparently does not reject Labrousse's socioeconomic paradigm; but only Siegfried's historical determinism, which he considers historically wrong. By emphasizing the diverging interests and economic positions of the peasantry in the two parts of the Maine at the end of the Ancien Regime, Bois even seems to agree with Labrousse's explanation of the political choices made by some of the economic interests. But the most interesting aspect of his argument appears to reverse Labrousse's pattern of explanation: instead of reflecting the economic and social structure, ideological choices can change that structure by shaping a new habitus. This shift at the core of historical explanation—from the category of economic interests or their subjectivization to the structuring role of mentalities—seems to be for Bois a way to escape Labrousse's socioeconomic determinism and open the door to an anthropological history. Is Bois' argument appropriate only to the case of the Sarthe? Certainly not. Drawing on examples from the surrounding departments, he tried to show that the same pattern could be detected throughout a large part of western France. Charles Tilly, in the introduction to *The War of Vendée,*[17] writes that after having attended Bois' *soutenance de thèse* he decided to change his approach and attempt to integrate Bois' model into his own argument. Some years later I took the same path, though to a lesser degree, to explain the peculiarities and anthropological dimensions of the political partition between the white and the red of a Britton village.[18]

Another department, another question. Working on the nineteenth-century department of the Var, Maurice Agulhon became interested less by the industrialization of Toulon than by the politicization of the small peasantry in the villages. In *La Republique au village*,[19] he describes the folklorization of politics among the *provençale* peasantry after the reestablishment of universal male suffrage in 1848, not as a regressive process but on the contrary as the making of modernity in peasant society. To enter into the peasants' world, politics had to appear not only as a new right to vote that they could use but as a part of their experience, the sociability of their culture. The practice of politics took the space occupied during the Ancien Regime by religious fraternities and later by the freemasonic lodges more frequently in the small towns of Provence than in the countryside;[20] a space of masculine sociability devoted to the pleasures of speaking, drinking, being and making decisions together. The peasants, who generally did not choose their elected officials for the national or departmental *assemblées* from among the peasantry, were interested less in the formal or fictional power their vote could have on national politics than in the impact of political struggle (which sometimes turned into physical struggle) on their communities. By giving new goals to the practice of sociability, politics could ensure community cohesion, but only by accepting the ritualization and the theatre of local culture.

By becoming a formal and ritualized activity of socialization, did politics loose its ideological utility? Certainly not. Discussions of candidates' proposals and the ideas and the interests at stake in national debates were not simply a pretext for expressing and reactivating local divisions, but provided access to some sense of national identity. The culture of politics, in Provence as in other peripheral areas of French peasantry (such as Brittany), provided the population with a new link between regional and national concerns, between local interests and universal ideas. This modernization of culture by the practice of citizenship, through access to new forms of identity and without modernization of the economic structure, was the path these peasant communities chose, without the risk of splitting their local culture and social ties.

### Quantitative Methods: A Useful Purgatory

The new generation of Annalists had in mind at the beginning the need to move away from Labrousse's socio-economic paradigm, as their research led them to confront not the regional diversity of France but the complexity of historical change. What we call anthropological history is perhaps nothing more than the necessity of overcoming the reductionism of the socio-economic paradigm. This was, in a way, a return to Marc Bloch's assumption in his criticism of Simiand's approach to monetary fluctuations that historical change results not from mechanical, objective forces, but psychological ones, and must be observed through the filter of mentalities. In fact the gap between Bloch and Labrousse was not only theoretical but also epistemological. Building a pattern of explanation has for Bloch an inductive function, and for Labrousse a predictive one. In his management of Annales collective project on the history of prices, after Simiand's death, Bloch wanted to attend to the distance between, on the one hand, what can be expected from the types of data and patterns of explanation that scholars have in common in historical research, and on the other, what they observe in the specific periods and countries they study. For Bloch, a collective project has to be essentially comparative, and the virtue of the comparison lies in its ability to bring differences to light. Not only do gaps between patterns of explanation and *realia* serve as evidence of the empirical dimension of historical research but the differences are meaningful in themselves. They express the diversity and complexity of the historical process.

For Labrousse, in contrast, every monograph is expected to confirm, within its own chronological and geographical frame, the pattern he has constructed. The sophistication of his method and his accurate use of statistical analysis seem to him strong enough to reveal the basic workings of history. His project on the economic and social history of modern France's departments may be seen not only as an extensive mapping of his pattern, but as repeated confirmation of it.[21] We should be grateful to Labrousse's students for the heretical frame of mind which opened the path to anthropological history. But we have to thank Labrousse as well, for his reductionism. Although as a historian he was a bit dogmatic, as a professor and as a person Labrousse was open-minded. He gently accepted his students' later deviationism, for he himself had earlier resisted their Stalinist dogmatism. What this new generation of scholars found so unexpected and intriguing in the course of their research would have remained hidden to them without the quantitative analysis they had learned from Labrousse. The trends in historical reality brought to light by quantification gained in precision because they were designated by figures rather than texts. Indeed some of the trends and historical processes that quantitative analyses revealed never appeared in texts at all.

The fascinating power of quantitative analysis lies in its ability to expose phenomena and important changes that witnesses at the time could never have discerned. But while quantitative analysis can bring them to light, it cannot explain them, raising new questions but giving few answers. This observation regarding Labroussean scholars can be extended to the historiographical trends of the 1970s in France and elsewhere. I disagree with those who explain the development of anthropological history as a reaction of disaffection and disappointment against the low productivity of quantitative methods. On the contrary, most of the topics engaged by anthropological history emerged from questions first raised by the achievements of quantitative history; and we can consider anthropological history to be a continuation of quantitative history by other means. To address such questions about these topics it was necessary to turn from the precision of quantitative methods to seek less precise but deeper insights, meanings, and understandings.

The quantitative history of food consumption turned into the anthropological history of food and taste, demographical history became the history of the family, the quantitative history of judicial cases developed into the anthropology of violence and criminality, the quantitative history of literacy and the circulation of printed texts led into the anthropology of reading, and so on. Let me expand on one example, the making of the history of the family, the one more familiar to me. Statistical analysis of the old parish registers, the methodology for which had been developed by Louis Henry, a demographer of the Institut National d'Etudes Démograhiques in Paris,[22] was employed first by historians close to Labrousse. Scholars such as Jean Meuvret and Pierre Goubert used it to compare fluctuation in mortality to wheat prices during the period of the Ancien Regime, to see if crises of mortality (during which mortality rates could multiply five or even ten fold) were directly related to increases in wheat prices and could thus be explained as a consequence of starvation. Historians also became interested in Henry's more extended quantitative use of parish registers through his method of *family reconstruction.* He devised this method to allow him to reconstruct trends of conjugal fertility, which were also important for understanding the impact of the economic crises of the Old Regime.

The introduction of the method of family reconstruction in the practice of socio-economic history had a double effect on historians both on their problematique and on their imagination as well. Although these reconstructed families were not actual family groups but artifacts, they brought a new image of the structure of society. They were no longer constituted from abstract aggregate groups ranked by income levels or professional status but rather conceived as a huge network of households or kin-groups fulfilling both social and biological functions. Further, this method revealed trends and processes of change, such as the beginning of a decline in infantile mortality during the eighteenth century, a rise in the age at which women married from the sixteenth century onward, and the diffusion of birth control practices in Ancien Regime France in the eighteenth century—shifts that could hardly be exclusively explained by the interplay of economic forces alone. Henry's method could date with precision, at the scale of a village or town, the adoption of contraceptive practices by some proportion of couples, exposing a change of attitudes kept hidden within the secrets of conjugal space and the confessional. But how were historians to explain such a change in conjugal life? Initial evidence put the conversion to Malthusian practices in the period of the Revolution and suggested a secularization of attitudes toward life and sexuality. More recent demographical studies, however, have pushed the moment of change back to the second half of the seventeenth century, a period when the church was strengthening its control over the social body, one of great religious revival. The explanation in terms of secularization had to give way, and the change was now attributed to a civilizing process: new religious trends and the diffusion of manners from court society contributed to a reshaping of the conjugal sphere, providing couples with a new sense of responsibility and intimacy. Although the debate remains open today, its evolution can help us to understand the development of an anthropological agenda among historians as a shift away from the mechanical precision of quantitative analysis toward less certain insights into the complexity and diversity of cultural change. Considered within the long-term trend of this historiographical path, from the history of mentalities to anthropological history, the moment of quantitativism was perhaps little more than an unpleasant purgatory. Unpleasant, but also useful for the historians of my generation, who retain the impression of having been saved by this ascetic passage from the hell of a positivist erudition without ideas, and from a paradise located in a self-indulgent and linguistic subjectivization of the past.

NOTES

1. "The Fate of the History of *Mentalités* in the *Annales,*" *Comparative Studies in Society and History* 24, 3 (1982): 424–37.

2. Introducing the project in *les Annales d'histoire économique et sociale* (1930), Lucien Febvre writes, "Our project on the history of prices will try to be useful to the two categories of readers that our journal would like to attract and keep: those who are investigating the Present, and those who are exploring the Past" (*Notre enquête sur l'histoire des prix s'efforcera de servir à la fois les deux catégories de lecteurs que notre revue voudrait attirer et retenir: les enquêteurs du présent, les investigateurs du passé*).

3. "A travers l'histoire des prix et des monnaies," *Revue de Synthèse* 16 (1936): 233–37.

4. Earl J. Hamilton, "En période de révolution économique; la monnaie en Castille," *Annales d'histoire économique et sociale* 4 (1932); and, *American Treasure and the Price Revolution in Spain*. Cambridge, Mass.: Harvard University Press, 1934.

5. Ernest Gutman, "Le problème international de l'or," *Annales* 4 (1932): 359.

6. Jean Houdaille, "Les controverses relatives au rôle de l'or dans la crise mondiale," *Annales* 4 (1932).

7. Christophe Charles, "Entretien avec Ernest Labrousse," *Actes de la Recherche en Sciences Sociales* 32–33 (1979), Paris.

8. Ernest Labrousse, *Esquisse du mouvement des prix et des revenus en France au XVIII siècle*. Paris: Dalloz, 1933, 2 vols.; and, *La crise de l'économie française à la fin de l'Ancien Régime et au début de la Révolution*, t. 1. Paris: PUF, 1944.

9. Daniel Lindenberg, *Le marxisme introuvable*. Paris: Calmann-Lévy, 1975.

10. W. W. Rostow, *The Stages of Economic Growth: A Non-communist Manifesto*. Cambridge, Mass.: Harvard University Press, 1960. Rostow published "Histoire et sciences sociales; la longue durée," *Annales, ESC* 4 (1959), in which he favors that the social sciences take some distance from the determinist pattern of physics.

11. Fernand Braudel, "Histoire et sciences sociales. La longue durée," *Annales ESC* 5 (1958).

12. In, *La crise de l'économie française à la fin de l'Ancien Régime . . .* , op. cit.: xli.

13. René Baehrel, *Une croissance; la Basse-Provence rurale depuis la fin du XVI siècle jusqu'à la veille de la Révolution*. Paris: SEVPEN, 1961; Pierre Deyon, *Amiens capitale provinciale; étude sur la société urbaine au XVII siècle*. Paris: Mouton, 1967; Pierre Goubert, *Beauvais et le Beauvaisis de 1600 à 1730*. Paris: SEVPEN, 1960; Emmanuel Le Roy Ladurie, *Les Paysans de Languedoc*. Paris: SEVPEN, 1966.

14. Maurice Agulhon, *Vie sociale en Provence intérieure au lendemain de la Révolution française*. Paris: Clavreuil, 1971; and, *La République au village*. Paris: Plon, 1970 (both books are on the department of the Var); Pierre Barral, *Le département de l'Isère sous la III République*. Paris: Armand Colin, 1962; Paul Bois, *Paysans de l'Ouest. Des structures économiques et sociales aux options politiques*

*depuis la Révolution française dans la Sarthe.* Paris: Mouton, 1960; Georges Dupeux, *Aspects de l'histoire sociale et politique du Loir-et-Cher.* Paris: Mouton, 1962.

15. André Siegfried, *Tableau politique de la France de l'Ouest sous la III République.* Paris: Armand Colin, 1913.

16. Quoted by Helene Bergues, in, *La prévention des naissances dans la famille; ses origines dans les temps modernes.* Paris: PUF, Cahier de l'INED, no. 35, 1960.

17. Charles Tilly, *The Vendée: A Sociological Analysis of the Counterrevolution of 1793.* Cambridge, Mass.: Harvard University Press, 1964.

18. André Burguière, *Bretons de Plozevet.* Paris: Flammarion, 1975.

19. Maurice Agulhon, *La République au village,* op. cit.

20. Maurice Agulhon, *Pénitents et francs-maçons de l'ancienne Provence.* Paris: A. Fayard, 1968.

21. Jean-Yves Grenier and Bernard Lepetit, "L'expérience historique. A propos de C. E. Labrousse," *Annales ESC* 6 (1989).

22. Michel Fleury and Louis Henry, *Des registres paroissiaux à l'histoire de la population: Manuel de dépouillement et d'exploitation de l'état civil ancien.* Paris: PUF-Publications de l'INED, 1956.

# Regulation Theory, Post-Marxism, and the Transition from the New Social Movements to Anti-Globalization and the Far Right

*George Steinmetz*

The existence of the "new social movements" (NSMs) poses a direct challenge to Marxist theories on what should be their most secure terrain—their ability to identify the main lines of social division and conflict and to explain the broad contours of historical change in the advanced capitalist world. Many writers have seen French regulation theory as promising a reinvigorated Marxism that avoids the pitfalls of functionalism, teleology, false totalization, and class reductionism, while simultaneously offering a convincing analysis of phenomena such as the NSMs. Yet German analyses of the NSMs as responses to the contradictions and crises of the Fordist mode of regulation reveal not only the strengths but also the limits of the regulation perspective. In contrast to the abstract presentations of their perspective, historical work by regulation theorists tends to interpret social formations and historical change in terms of all- encompassing totalities. The regulation approach can remain relevant for understanding conflict and change in contemporary capitalist societies only by relinquishing such totalizing ambitions. More generally, Marxism can only remain viable as a theoretical perspective if it allows its central conceptual categories, such as commodification and social class, to coexist with a range of causal mechanisms rooted in other theoretical perspectives, that is, if it acknowledges the difference between the levels of theory (abstract) and of explanation (concrete).

My argument is presented in four parts. The first sketches the specific problems posed by the NSMs for traditional Marxist theory. The second section discusses the major attempts to analyze the NSMs in terms of

45

revised versions of traditional Marxism. The most convincing of these approaches, regulation theory, is discussed in the third part. Here I focus on the work of Joachim Hirsch and Roland Roth, especially their book *Das neue Gesicht des Kapitalismus* (1986), which presents an interpretation of the development of the NSMs in West Germany between the late 1960s and the 1980s. In section four, I sketch an alternative interpretation of the German NSMs, suggesting that they were conditioned by cultural and historical factors that cannot be subsumed under the Fordist mode of regulation or the processes of its breakdown. At the end of this section I will briefly survey some of the empirical developments in the field of German social movements since the early 1990s, when I began work on the original version of this article. The two most important changes are the development of a broad spectrum of far-right movements since the end of the 1980s, as a riposte to, among other things, the NSMs themselves, and the emergence of counter-globalization protests in Germany (and elsewhere) which synthesize the two preceding waves of critical, left-wing social movements.

## Section I

The collapse of the state-socialist regimes in eastern Europe and the Soviet Union has occasioned only the latest in a century-old series of "crises of Marxism." Against this mood, however, many Marxists have countered that the "commodification of everything" (Wallerstein 1983: 11) has only been accelerated by this collapse, making Marxism more relevant than ever (Ruccio 1992: 11–12; Jameson 1992; Hardt and Negri 2000). The crisis of Marxist theory is depicted as a fabrication of the mass media or as the triumphant battle cry of neoconservatism and victorious capitalism. Others have acknowledged the psychological costs for Marxists of the failure of the "socialist experiment," without, however, rejecting Marxism out of hand (Therborn 1992). These writers embrace what they understand as genuine Marxism, of course, rather than the official doctrine of the East European regimes, which had long been dismissed by Western Marxists.

The danger is that this discussion will forget an even more serious set of challenges to so-called Western Marxism, namely those linked to the NSMs of the past three decades. Even if Marxism were to survive as an adequate theory of capitalism as an economic and social system, the broader attacks on its claims as general social theory and guide for emancipatory political practice would remain intact. The NSMs have been crucial both as a phenomenon that apparently cannot be explained within a Marxist framework and as a source of post-Marxist and poststructuralist theoretical critiques of Marxism and other modernist theoretical perspectives. Chantal Mouffe is not alone in her view—expressed before the collapse of state socialism—that "it is unlikely that Marxism will recover from the blows it has suffered" (1981: 31).

## The New Social Movements: Class Struggle without Class Revisited

The NSMs have been paradoxical for traditional Marxism. Most importantly, Marxist categories of social class have not been able to map the frontiers of social conflict or the social composition of the movements' support groups or membership. These movements' goals have not been framed in terms of material benefits for specific social classes. Although these movements have vigorously opposed many of the same forces of power, property, and privilege as the old labor and socialist movements, the form of their opposition has differed in almost every other respect.[1] Where the socialist and communist movements were concerned with mobilizing the proletariat and allied social groups and classes to gain state power and effect a major redistribution of resources, the new movements eschew these goals. In western Europe, the NSMs have tended to spurn the "social movement entrepreneurs" central to traditional Marxist understandings of politics and to evade formal "social movement organizations" such as parties. They have not sought to gain control of parliamentary power and have had a problematic relationship even to Green parties wherever the latter have been electorally successful.[2] The NSMs often claim to abjure power altogether, as in the popular slogan of the alternative movement in West Germany during the 1970s—"*keine Macht für Niemand*" ('no power for nobody' [sic]). Instead, the new movements aim to *prevent* things from happening, such as the construction of nuclear power plants or the completion of population censuses (Nelkin and Pollak 1981; Kitschelt 1986; Taeger 1983); to secure social spaces that are autonomous from both markets and the state;[3] and to directly *perform* and *practically exemplify* an alternative version of social life.

Which conflicts fall into the category of NSMs? Strictly speaking, a coherent definition of any phenomenon, including the NSMs, can only be made from within a theoretical framework. In later sections I will argue that regulation theory permits the theoretical definition and delimitation of the NSMs by singling out their specific determinants (in terms of their relationship to so-called modes of regulation). For the moment, however, I will present a more consensual definition based on a cross-section of the literature on the new movements.[4] This definition takes the form of a cluster of characteristics, many of them specified through implicit or explicit contrast with the dominant model of social movements in the preceding historical period. According to these accounts, the NSMs:

- Focus on goals of autonomy, identity, self-realization, and qualitative life chances, rather than divisible material benefits and resources.[5]
- Are as much defensive as offensive in orientation and are often directed toward narrower demands which allow little or no negotiation.
- Are less oriented towards broad social-utopian visions or metanarratives of progress.
- Do not appeal or mobilize along class lines but cut across them. In the NSMs, socio-economic categories begin to lose their subjective salience and give way to identities that are either more flexible, fleeting, partial, and "voluntarily" chosen, or else more permanent and supposedly more natural than class.
- Refer to organizational forms that are non-hierarchical and undifferentiated with respect to roles, with unmediated direct democracy as a regulative norm if not a reality.
- Rely on temporary or part-time membership and informal or submerged networks, resulting in individual patterns of shifting but continuous involvement in various movements that are only partially differentiated from one another (Melucci 1989: 61, 78).
- Work mainly outside of the parliamentary political system, employing unconventional means such as direct action.
- Politicize aspects of everyday life formerly seen as lying outside of politics.
- Are at least partially unified through their shared opposition to a system that is itself perceived as monolithic, even if they are fragmented and diversified in terms of their demands, ideology, constituency, and organizations (Raschke 1985: 412).
- The final characteristic concerns historical periodization: the NSMs have appeared since the later 1960s or 1970s in the advanced capitalist countries (and in the wealthier sectors of the periphery and semi-periphery; see Escobar and Alvarez 1992). Thus these movements were at one moment quite literally new, in the sense of contemporary.

The new label also suggests to some readers that these movements are historically unprecedented, however; and this notion has stimulated a barrage of criticism. Tarrow (1988) points out that earlier social movements, especially in their beginning phases, shared some of the features of the NSMs. Focusing on the repertoires of collective action used by French social movements over the course of a century, Tilly (1986: 349) found little novelty in the most recent wave of protest. A small academic cottage industry grew up around the argument that the NSMs were really not so novel after all (see, for example, Kivisto 1986, and Tucker 1991). But as Dieter Rucht (1982: 278) acknowledges, the new movements "cannot be specified in their totality by their form, their varying contents . . . nor their constituency. Due to the historical parallels, every attempted definition in this direction will run into boundary problems." Although it might have been preferable to call these social movements "postmodern" rather than simply "new," the critics of the latter concept have missed its historicizing intention. The emphasis was always on the difference between the dominant patterns of social conflictuality in the postwar period (roughly 1945–75) and thereafter, and was not intended to signal that the forms of contention were unique in any world-historical sense.

Since the end of the 1980s, the NSMs have themselves been largely overshadowed in Germany and the rest of Europe by movements driven by racism and nationalism, on the one hand, and by opposition to globalization, on the other. The NSMs now constitute the prehistory of these even newer movements (which themselves, like the NSMs, formally resemble earlier movements but have emerged in a unique historical conjuncture). It might therefore seem more urgent than ever to come up with an alternative term. Yet we have grown accustomed to using terms like "modernism" and "postmodernism" to refer to historically specific periods in the arts and architecture. It might be preferable simply to accept NSMs as a term of periodization analogous to expressions like "modern," "early modern," or "ancient."[6] But as I hope will become clear below, a more historically adequate and specific alternative would be to call the NSMs "critical anti-Fordist social movements."

The definition suggested here discourages efforts to create an inventory of discrete movements that fall into the NSM category (as in, for example, Vester 1983). The new movements, given that they abstain from parliamentary politics and assume forms that look from the outside like subcultural deviance, may not even recognize themselves as social movements. Ostensibly unified social movements often contain heterogeneous conflicts and logics (Melucci 1989: 28; also 1980; 1981). A case in point is the contemporary women's movement, which is sometimes counted among the NSMs. Identity-based politics which assert difference as well as equality (Scott 1988) seem to be part of the new politics, as do consciousness-raising groups. Strands of the women's movement that focus on attaining political and market equality through electoral politics and centralized organization, however, are closer to a political paradigm that Habermas calls "bourgeois-socialist liberation movements."[7]

These examples also raise questions about the NSMs' stakes and goals. Clearly the NSMs cannot be specified simply by pointing to their novel aims, as these could also have been addressed by movements organized according to the historically preceding paradigm. Indeed, established political parties, such as the German Social Democratic Party, have often tried to appropriate themes like environmental protection from the NSMs. So the real difficulty facing any theory of the NSMs is to explain the appearance of a cluster of novel forms of political action, recruitment patterns, and distinct political stakes at a specific moment in history (the late 1960s through the 1980s), as well as the relations among these different elements.

## Section 2

Alongside the challenge from the NSMs to the Marxist belief in the primacy of social class and to the traditional Left's political strategies, the 1970s and 1980s saw the rise of popular discourses critical of traditional Marxism (see P. Berman 2005).[8] While Marxism has typically focused on relations of exploitation, that is, on relations involving transfers of (surplus) value, many of the post-Marxist social theories have moved relations of *domination* into the center. Foucault is most strongly associated with a view of power and domination as ubiquitous and not centered in capitalism or social class (cf. Foucault 1978: 94–95; 1980: 60, 89, 122). Other damaging critiques of traditional Marxism have retained a materialist sociology but have insisted on the prominence of *non-class* actors, identities, and interests in social conflict, involving race, ethnicity, nationality, gender, and religion. Class is not at the core of such antagonisms either phenomenologically or in any immediate structural way (cf. Beck 1986: 121–30; 1989). Still other theories permit social class to coexist peacefully alongside other forms of oppression or stratification, but with no claims to preeminence. These approaches range from dualistic feminist theories of class and gender (Hartmann 1981), through tripartite schemes of "race, class, and gender" (Collins 1989; Chow, Wilkinson, and Zinn 1996) or "class, status, and power" (Weber 1947; Wiley 1970), to schemes in which the bases of social differentiation are potentially infinite. Taken to its logical conclusion, for instance, Bourdieu's sociological theory allows for the construction of an infinite number of new *fields* with their specific forms of distinction, dynamics of conflict, and irreducible stakes, even if Bourdieu limits the number of metatypes of *capital* to three or four in his more abstract theoretical statements (cf. Bourdieu 1977; 1984; 1986).

Finally, there is a disparate body of culturalist or poststructuralist theories associated with the NSMs and often referred to as post-Marxist. Most influential are the elaborations of Gramsci's notion of hegemony by Ernesto Laclau and Chantal Mouffe (1985; 1987; see also Žižek 1989). Hegemony, in the broadest sense, represents a specific type of discursive and political practice in which one social actor or social class orients the perceptions and actions of another. According to Showstack-Sassoon (1982: 13–14), Gramsci uses hegemony in the sense of influence, moral leadership, and consent, rather than the alternative and opposite meaning of domination. It has to do with the way one social group influences other groups, making certain compromises with them in order to gain their consent for its leadership in society as a whole. Thus particular, sectional interests are transformed and some concept of the general interest is conjured.

Hegemonic discourse provides a weapon with which domination can be challenged, but it also limits the ways in which actors imagine themselves and their opponents. Hegemony in this view differs from other discursive logics in that it implies a relatively unified, encompassing discursive formation, and one which is actively constructed by a set of leading actors or intellectuals. In discussing the relations of hegemonizing intellectuals to the groups they attempt to shape, Gramsci makes it clear how his position differs from Leninist understandings of the role of ideological leadership in social conflict (Laclau and Mouffe 1985: 55, 65–71). The ideal-typical Leninist strategy is in this respect indistinguishable from classical Social Democracy: The party's goal in both cases was to align workers and non-proletarian groups with the putative *Weltanschauung* of the proletariat, rather than to construct some new identity and world view for leaders and led. In the radically anti-essentialist reading of Gramsci, social agents transcend their earlier identities when entering a hegemonic formation, and the hegemonizing class is also seen as leaving behind its original class identity in the process. Hegemony thus entails the discursive construction of hegemonized and hegemonizing agents alike. As one interpreter of Gramsci puts it, "the subjects of hegemonic practice at the level of their discursive constitution will not necessarily have a class character . . . to hegemonize as a class would imply a limited or unsuccessful attempt" (Rosenthal 1988). Successful hegemonizing agents must abandon their sectional interests, whether they try to align the interests of dominated groups with those of the economically dominant or to orchestrate a counter-hegemonic project which coordinates the resistance of subordinate groups.

In some post-Marxist theory, material resources and social structures do not even figure as constraint; conflict and social life become entirely intra-discursive. Laclau and Mouffe begin with Althusser's notion of "overdetermination," which underscores the role of contingency, unique constellations of events, and non-simultaneous periodicities in the genesis of historical outcomes. Yet their radical version of overdetermination breaks with the vestiges of material structuration still present in Althusser. According to Laclau and Mouffe, when actors adopt new goals or identities, they are constrained mainly by previous discursive formations or "articulations." Not only is there no "logical and necessary relation between socialist objectives and the positions of social agents in the relations of production" (Laclau and Mouffe 1985: 86), but social-structural positions are not related in any way to specific forms of consciousness or interest.[9] Indeed, it not longer makes any sense to speak of "the social" as an object realm different from "culture," "ideology," or "the political."

Hegemony in Gramscian post-Marxism thus consists of practices of discursive articulation which forge social entities by bridging structural divisions and temporarily binding the free-floating signifiers ("elements") to particular signifieds. Post-Marxism denies the existence of structural stratification outside of discourse. Hegemony is therefore an inherently conflictual process, a continual struggle among contending efforts to define reality. Such radical theories of hegemony therefore question the ability of any sociological theory, including Marxism, to provide a generalizing account of the rise of the NSMs or any other social phenomenon.[10]

## Attempts to Explain the New Social Movements in Terms of Revised Class Concepts

Rather than rejecting class analysis altogether, some researchers have tried to explain patterns of support for the new movements by using revised class concepts (often quasi-Weberian ones). The NSMs have been explained as an outgrowth of the interests of the new middle class (Brand 1982: 14; Kitschelt 1985: 278) or new class (Martin 1988)[11] the state-sector middle class (Cotgrove and Duff 1980; Mattausch 1989: 50–52, 84–85); the service class (Lash and Urry 1987: 195); the old and new petite bourgeoisie (Eder 1985); and classes located in contradictory locations between proletariat and bourgeoisie (Wright 1985; Kriesi 1989).[12] At least one author (Wilde 1990: 67) has described the NSMs as "protest movements within the working class" but without offering any evidence to support this claim. For Vester (1983), the new movements represent the reemergence of traditionally lower-class resistance among the "new plebeians," characterized as those who are highly educated but blocked in their chances for upward mobility. According to Offe (1987), at least three different groups constitute the new movements' social base: the old and new middle classes, and economically peripheralized (decommodified) strata such as the unemployed and underemployed, housewives, and students. Other characteristics of participants in the new conflicts that have been linked more or less closely to social class include high levels of education and work within the cultural sector (Kriesi 1988).

All such attempts to account for the new movements in terms of social class run into difficulties, however. First, studies indicate that the NSMs' social composition is much more diverse than any of the class-based approaches suggest; there is even evidence that non-active supporters of the new movements are drawn from the various social classes in approximately representative proportions (Roth 1989: 29). Public opinion polls on environmental issues and patterns of electoral support for Green parties indicated during the second half of the 1980s that the distribution of sympathizers was flattening out (Hülsberg 1988: 68; Brand et al. 1986: 248, 281). According to a study of the Netherlands, the "strong sympathizers for the peace movement," if not the participants, "form an almost representative cross section of the Dutch population" (Kriesi 1989: 1101). The same appears to have been true of the West German peace movement of the 1980s (Brand et al. 1986: 263).

This raises a second question about the class approaches. Even if the thesis that the "new middle class" is over-represented could be supported empirically, this might reflect its greater proclivity for protest participation, rather than its inherently stronger interest in the new grievances. Rather than being disproportionately affected by the new social problems, the new middle class may simply be better able to perceive them or more inclined to mobilize against them. As one author points out, the middle classes were also over-represented in previous waves of social movements (Bagguley 1992). Such dynamics are ignored by class-theoretical approaches, which typically posit a direct relationship between engagement in a movement and relevant structural interests.

The lack of class distinctiveness of the NSMs' base might be seen as reflecting the relative classlessness of many contemporary forms of deprivation and domination. Most of the paradigmatically new grievances (pollution, nuclear power and energy, state penetration of civil society and the life world) do not typically have a disproportionate impact on the new middle classes—or any other classes for that matter. According to an important German study originally published in 1983, "the population of those who are immediately affected (negatively by the so-called modernization process) cannot be pinned down according to clear categories of class and stratum, in contrast to other cases of social disadvantaging" (Brand et al. 1986: 33). As a result, "one should not expect to find sharply differentiated new social-structural social camps (corresponding to) the new lines of conflict, comparable to the class contradictions of class society" (ibid.: 43). Ulrich Beck's notion of a shift from class society to "risk society" (*Risikogesellschaft*) elaborates upon this idea: "the generalization of modernization risks unleashes a social dynamic that can no longer be grasped and understood in class categories" (Beck 1986: 52; cf. also Beck 1989; 1991; Lau 1991). Beck concludes that "need is hierarchical, smog is democratic" (Beck: 48).

## New Social Movements Explained as the
## Result of Structural Changes in Capitalism

Even if social class were able to map patterns of membership in the new movements, there would still be the problem of explaining the emergence of novel social problems, stakes, and forms of conflict. To address these issues, certain versions of Marxism have examined large-scale changes in the organization of capitalism, attributing to them the power to generate new social contradictions, grievances, and pershaps, social movements.

The early work of Manuel Castells (e.g., 1977; 1978) represents one such approach. Concerned specifically with urban social movements, Castells focused on capital accumulation rather than social class, analyzing urban space under capitalism primarily as the site of the reproduction of labor power. According to Katznelson's summary of this approach, as "capital concentrates the working population," it "requires collective goods that the private market is unable to provide (1981: 211). The result is an increase in the collective (that is, socialized) consumption of goods and services, such as housing, transportation, cultural and educational facilities, and welfare. The contradictions of collective consumption are especially severe (and visible) in the city and increasingly define the nodal points of urban social conflict (Castells 1983: 94; 1978: 15–36). In contrast to relations of production, the relations of collective consumption define structural positions that cut across boundaries of social class. The users of public transportation come from diverse social class positions, for example, yet their interests largely converge with respect to crises of the transportation system. The basic dynamics of social provision can nonetheless be explained in terms of the logic of capital accumulation. Urban public transportation systems, for Castells, are designed primarily to meet the needs of capital.

Castell's early work thus retained a Marxist analysis of political economy and macro-social development and analyzed certain NSMs without reducing them to expressions of social class. He did emphasize contradictions and grievances unrelated to collective consumption, including those—militarism, patriarchy, and environmental pollution—often seen as central to the NSMs. Nonetheless, it would be possible to extend Castells' logic and argue that capital accumulation remains the mainspring of advanced societies even if the sociologically defined working class is declining in relative size (Offe 1984), and that this process will continue to define the main positions in social conflict. Castells later recognized that his early work ignored the autonomous cultural determinants of urban social movements, especially the role of the defense of cultural identity (Castells 1983: xviii).[13] The more challenging problem is to account not just for the emphasis on identity in the NSMs (Cohen 1985) but for the entire set of rejections of the preceding form of politics and societalization.

## Section 3

Regulation theory presents itself as having remedied many of the short-comings of older versions of Marxism without abandoning Marxist theory altogether.[14] Regulation theory focuses on political economy rather than class and avoids teleology and functionalism. The figure of historical necessity is exchanged for an emphasis on contingency and accidents. The only historical constant in the regulationist view is the recurrence of capitalist crisis, but the outcomes of such crises are always the product of multiple forces and wills intersecting in unpredictable ways. The type of crisis outcome that attracts the most attention is the temporarily stabilized "mode of regulation," which creates orderly social arrangements that permit further economic growth and capital accumulation. But regulation theory offers no guarantee that an ordered resolution to crisis will be found. Social formations are not the correlates of specific stages of development of the productive forces, nor do they result automatically from economic crisis. Social movements, here, are interpreted in the light of interests and grievances emerging from by waning or nascent modes of regulation.

The best regulation theorists embrace a mode of explanation that is *conjunctural* and *figurational.* This epistemological inclination reflects French regulation theory's emergence out of Althusserian neo-Marxism. British regulation theory has been influenced by Roy Bhaskar's critical realism, which has similar epistemological implications. Epistemologically, French regulation theory was influenced by Althusser's redeployment of the psychoanalytic notion of overdetermination, which evolved into the concept of "aleatory materialism" in his final philosophical reflections (Althusser 1994). Bhaskar's critical realism similarly rejects the positivist search for "constant conjunctions of events" on ontological grounds, suggesting that in open systems, such as societies, causal mechanisms combine in unpredictable conjunctures to produce actual events.

Despite its willingness to acknowledge the aleatory, accidental, and contingent, the regulation approach is not totally amorphous. It operates with concepts at two different levels of abstraction. At the more empirical level are specific modes of regulation, such as Fordism. These models are realized in different ways in various national (and subnational or transnational) cases, each time with distinct emphases, subtractions, and additions. Regulation theory also proposes more abstract concepts, such as *regulation* itself. The notion of a Fordist mode of regulation is ideally suited for a presentation of regulation theory because it has been discussed most extensively and illustrates the relationship between the abstract and concrete levels of analysis. It is also seen as generating the NSMs.

## Fordism as a Mode of Regulation

Theorists associated with the theory of Fordism as a mode of economic and social regulation include Michel Aglietta (1987), Robert Boyer (1990), Boyer and Mistral (1982), and Alain Lipietz (1987) in France; Joachim Hirsch (1980; 1983; 1988) in West Germany; Bob Jessop (1983; 1989; 1990b; Jessop et al. 1991) in Britain; and David Harvey (1989) in Britain and the

United States. Much of this work draws on the original insights of Antonio Gramsci in his essay, "Fordism and Americanism" (1971 [1929–35]). Gramsci had analyzed with a mixture of admiration and abhorrence the social and economic changes in the United States during the 1920s, at a time when American industry was searching for ways to combat the falling rate of profit and to radically increase productivity through the reorganization and mechanization of the production process (Gramsci 1978: 112–13). In Aglietta's (1987) study of twentieth-century American capitalism, this involved a shift from a strategy of extensive accumulation and absolute surplus value to reliance on intensive accumulation and relative surplus value. Aglietta interprets the Fordist production process as a radicalization of the Taylorist system, the latter referring to the "sum total of those relations of production internal to the labor process that tend to accelerate the completion of the mechanical cycle of movements on the job and to fill the gaps in the working day" (1987: 114). Fordism applied the Taylorist principle of fragmenting the labor performed by the deskilled individual worker to the collective labor process.[15] The key was production on a semi-automatic assembly line, which was at first used especially for producing mass-consumer goods in long production runs and later extended upstream to the manufacture of standardized intermediate components for the production process.

The second signal feature of Fordism, the formation of a social consumption norm, resulted from the lowered costs of the means of reconstituting labor power. A historically unprecedented working-class wage level was the quid pro quo for the intensification of work; indeed, the higher living standard was necessary to "maintain and restore the strength that has been worn down by the new form of toil" (Gramsci 1971: 310). In addition, employers had to pay high wages in order to capture the workers who were "best adapted to the new forms of production and work from the psychotechnical standpoint" (1978: 113). Workers in the core mass-production industries could now purchase the commodities they produced. The generalized result, Gramsci predicted, would be "a larger internal market" and "a more rapid rhythm of capital accumulation" (1971: 291). Fordism was thus founded upon a particular combination of rising wages and productivity.

Gramsci stressed Fordism's need for a "new" man who would be psychologically and physically adapted (with heightened physical and muscular-nervous efficiency) to the new production processes. Although Fordist laborers were relatively deskilled, they needed systematic work habits: a

single unreliable worker could wreak enormous damage in the interconnected and inflexible assembly line. The new Fordist methods of work
were thus linked to efforts to rationalize sexual, emotional, personal, and
family life. Gramsci pointed to American crusades against the "exaltation
of passion," alcoholism, and the "squandering of nervous energies in the
disorderly and stimulating pursuit of occasional sexual satisfaction," and
in favor of working-class monogamy (ibid.: 304–5). He interpreted these
campaigns as tools for the creation of workers suited for the "timed movements of productive motions connected with the most perfected automa-
tism" (ibid.: 305). Creating the Fordist subject was a hegemonic project,
most successful if it was "proposed by the worker himself, and not
imposed from the outside" (ibid.: 303).

A related process only touched upon by Gramsci, but playing a central
role in later theorizations of Fordism, was the state's growing involvement
in maintaining consumer demand for mass-produced goods. A panoply of
social insurance programs supported aggregate levels of consumer
demand. This legislation originated in the nineteenth century in Europe
and during the 1930s in the United States, but social insurance benefits did
not begin to approach wage-replacement levels until after 1945. Gramsci
also discussed the political effects of Fordism on the labor movement:
Struggles between labor and capital over the wage rate became institutionalized in the form of collective bargaining (Aglietta 1987: 116). A neo-
corporatist productivist bloc between industrial workers and management
was "destined to resolve the problem of the further development of the
Italian economic apparatus" (Gramsci 1971: 291). The prescience of Gramsci's observations is underscored by the rise of neo-corporatism during the
post-1945 period and by signal events like the 1950 "Treaty of Detroit"
between General Motors and the United Auto Workers (Schmitter and
Lehmbruch 1979; Panitch 1986).

The more recent writings by regulation theorists characterize Fordism
as a specific mode of regulation articulated with a particular regime of
accumulation, the latter is defined as a set of rules determining the distribution and allocation of the social product between investment/accumula-
tion and consumption. As a regime of accumulation, Fordism is characterized by a systematic relation between mass production and mass
consumption. Regulation refers to the manner in which social relations are
reproduced despite (what is assumed to be) their conflictual and contradictory nature. A mode of regulation is a set of "rules and procedures, of
norms, institutions, procedures, and modes of calculation through which
the accumulation regime is secured. It comprises all of the institutional

forms and norms which secure the compatibility of typical modes of economic conduct" (Jessop 1989).[16] In addition to clearly economic institutions and norms such as money, the mode of regulation typically encompasses aspects of the state, culture, schools, sex and gender relations,
family forms, and so forth.

As a mode of regulation, Fordism signals a broad range of changes.
According to Jessop (1989; 1990b), Fordist regulation is characterized by
the following economic features (listed in approximately declining level of
prominence):

- The centrality of the wage as the main mechanism for securing the
  reproduction of labor power.
- Collective bargaining over wage rates and working time; and monop-
  olistic price regulation.
- The predominance of mass consumption of standardized mass-produced commodities and collective consumption of goods and services
  supplied by the state.
- The encouragement of mass consumption by a number of techniques
  such as advertising.
- The importance of credit for validating full employment levels of
  demand.

Productivism and consumerism constitute the prevailing cultural forms,
the dominant societal goals and way of life, under Fordism (Hirsch and
Roth 1986). An ideology of individualization is combined in a potentially
contradictory way with the homogenization of personal life-style orientations. Culture is institutionally centered around the mass media. Neo- corporatism and the Keynesian welfare state, finally, represent the relevant
political forms. According to Hirsch and Roth, Fordist politics are based
on social-democratic, bureaucratic societalization (*Vergesellschaftung*),
strong unions, reformist parties of mass integration, corporatist institutionalization of class contradictions, and Keynesian state interventionism.

Regulation theory does not understand modes of regulation as automatic, functionally determined responses to crisis. The only assumption
about historical change is that social arrangements for capitalist accumulation repeatedly fall apart and profit rates eventually decline, leading to a
frantic and uncoordinated search for solutions by diverse social actors.[17]
The outcome is always uncertain and differs from prior blueprints. Each
regulatory mode reflects the historical peculiarities of the nation-state (or
region) and its location in the world capitalist system and world time.

Muddling through and sub-optimal solutions are as likely as successful resolutions of crisis. Fordism itself resulted from a combination of unco-ordinated planning efforts and pure chance.[18] Once the Fordist model had been invented, it was reproduced and copied, simply because it seemed to work. But the general model of Fordism was instantiated in different ways and varied enormously in each national setting (see Jessop 1989).[19]

The more recent formulations by regulation theorists describe the rudiments of Fordism as taking shape in the United States before the 1940s, with full-blown Fordism taking root during the post-World War II years in western Europe and the United States. It is frequently argued that Fordism began to unravel during the 1970s and that the advanced capitalist world is currently in the midst of a transition to some still vaguely-defined "post-Fordist" mode of regulation (see Jessop et al. 1991; Harvey 1989; Bonefeld and Holloway 1991). Different writers disagree on the precise periodization of Fordism, and their judgments depend to some extent on their implicit reference to (or familiarity with) specific national cases.

Fordism is an abstract model describing the general, dominant features of the advanced capitalist world in a certain period. It is not a concrete description of specific countries, an essence that is instantiated identically in each case. Nationally-specific forms of Fordist regulation—what Jessop calls the "national form of growth" (1989)—depended on preexistent national conditions; thus Britain exhibited a weaker form of Fordism than West Germany, whose Fordism was in turn less pronounced than Sweden's (Jessop et al. 1991: 137–42). Even though several of the central elements of Fordism were pioneered in the United States (mass production in consumer goods based on semi-skilled labor, scientific organization of work, high wages, and mass media and advertising), Fordism was less complete in the United States than in many other countries. The welfare state and neo-corporatism were underdeveloped, and vast sectors of society were not encompassed by even the partial version of Fordism that did emerge.

Fordism does not necessarily create the institutions and social practices that it brings under its sway, nor does it fully control them. Figure 1 attempts to illustrate the congealing of Fordism as a historic *bricolage* of components from diverse social arenas that both preexist and survive it (see fig. 1). The horizontal lines in the figure represent the historical development of various social fields. The general descriptions of the fields are given in the right-hand column in bold-face type; the specific forms they assume in different periods are represented by labels interpolated into the horizontal lines. The placement of a given phenomenon, such as mass consumerism, within a time line represents the hypothetical moment at which it became prominent. (The historical placement of these phenomena is merely suggestive, of course, since the chart does not refer to a specific national or regional case.) Each of the fields develops non-synchronously and in partial autonomy from the others.

Our central concern here is with the formation represented by the box labeled Fordism. Fordism interrupts the strands containing the elements that it articulates within its specific mode of regulation. The arrows that are shown as being only partially interrupted by Fordism were more peripheral to it; their post-Fordist development should also be less strongly shaped by the Fordist era. Strands that continue uninterruptedly, such as religion and the fine arts, were less central to Fordism (even if they were influenced by the Fordist mode, which is a separate issue). The sharp vertical lines around the Fordist formation misleadingly indicate a sudden birth and an equally abrupt disappearance; it would be preferable to represent an uneven congealing on the left margin and an equally incremental dissolve on the right. Finally, figure 1 only attempts to show the approximate placement of a single regulatory mode, Fordism; other regulatory modes might be indicated both before and after, and perhaps coexisting with it.

Figure 1 suggests that Fordism is a provisional historical construction that relies on and is shaped by its own raw materials, even as it partially recasts them. This is a hypothetical example that does not represent a specific national case. Not just the form of Fordism, but the degree of Fordist development in each instance will depend on the preexisting development of each of the components.

### The New Social Movements and Fordism
### in the Writings of Hirsch and Roth

Hirsch and Roth argue that Fordism has determined the main bases of interest, grievance, and oppression in the societies where it existed, and that as a result it has structured the main social surfaces, forms, and themes of social conflict.[20] The NSMs are seen as a response to the contradictions and the crisis of Fordism but are also understood as contributing indirectly to the elaboration of a new "post-Fordist" mode of regulation (Roth 1989; Hirsch 1988: 54; Hirsch 1991). This contemporary phase is of less concern in the present context than the etiology of the NSMs during the era of Fordism and its dissolution.

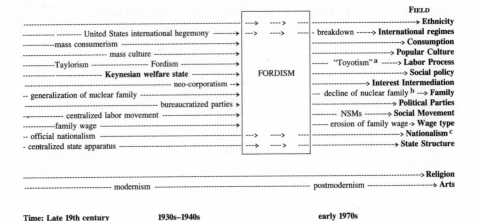

Fig. i. Hypothetical representations of the uneven history of the various strands making up the Fordist social formations. Notes: (a) Bob Jessop deserves credit for the term Toyotism. (b) See Chopra and Scheller (1992) for an overview of changes in marriage and the family in what they call "late-modern society." (c) "Official nationalism," according to Anderson (1983), arose in the late nineteenth century.

A few key aspects of Fordism should be kept in mind in order to understand its supposed contribution to social movements. Fordism was based on the centrality of the industrial laborer as producer and consumer. Male workers were relatively well-paid, and the welfare state propped up consumer demand during slack periods. The social movement sphere was monopolized by the official labor movement, centralized and bureaucratized labor unions; closely connected were social-democratic or labor parties engaged in neo-corporatist relations with employers' organizations and the state. In order to stabilize the Fordist formation, the old class actors, especially militant extraparliamentary labor, had to be either marginalized or integrated. Yet the Fordist system itself soon began to generate new areas of conflict. Just as the neo-corporatist labor movement corresponds to Fordism, so the NSMs grow out of Fordism, but they also signal (and help induce) its breakdown. Indeed, the most obvious feature shared by the NSMs is their rejection of the Fordist model of societalization. Examination of the cultural, economic, and political dimensions of Fordism can reveal the ways in which it gave rise to its own negation, partly in the form of the new conflicts.

As a regime of accumulation, Fordism involved the production of a hitherto unknown level of wealth. Due to the labor-capital accord and the welfare state, the working classes received a slightly larger amount (in absolute, not proportional terms) of this wealth than had previously been the case. The movements challenging the Fordist system were also closely tied to the social wealth produced by that very system.[21] Fordism increased levels of income, education, social security, and free time, allowing the proliferation of "postmaterialist values" (Hirsch and Roth 1986: 195; cf. Inglehart 1977; 1990). These values led in turn to a heightened consciousness of the Fordist model's shortcomings, especially its homogenization of culture and consumer goods. Sandwiched between the era of Fordist mass culture and the current postmodernist (post-Fordist) breakdown of distinctions between high and low culture was a period in which NSMs rejected both the culture industry and official elite culture.[22] Such challenges ranged from subcultural retreatism to openly oppositional milieux.

The evidence of cross-class recruitment into NSMs makes it impossible to rely uniquely on post-material values as an explanatory factor, however. The new movements also responded in part to the "leveling" class connotations of mass culture. Rejection of the culture industry was to some extent an attempted distinction strategy (Bourdieu) by *arrivé* bearers of cultural capital, themselves the product of the Fordist expansion of the educational system. Hirsch and Roth suggest that attacks on mass culture were aimed not just at its producers but also at its core proletarian and lower-middle-class audience (1986: 198). Behind student protest stood a refusal of the "degradation" of the cultural arena and university credentials. Of course, the expansion of higher education also led to struggles against a curriculum that valorized exclusionary, "classical" forms of cultural capital—struggles that were visible in the American "culture wars" of the 1990s.[23] The important point is that the Fordist expansion of mass culture and education induced both sorts of dissatisfaction.

The new movements also rejected the Fordist model of individualization and socialization. The turn to identity politics within the NSMs was a reaction to Fordism's homogenizing conformism. Traditional family and gender relations were subjected to massive criticism. The emphasis on the nuclear family as a locus of consumption and socialization in Fordism had several contradictory consequences. The women's movement(s) and social movements organized around alternative sexualities and life-styles rejected this model.[24] The nuclear family was undermined by the commodification of the family's role in the reproduction of labor power and by the sweeping entry of women into the labor force. Fordism's encouragement of a hedonistic, consumerist, narcissistic personality form (Bell 1973; Lasch 1978) created a further cultural precondition for the NSMs. Spiritual and fundamentalist movements oriented towards the recovery and solidification of identity can be interpreted partly as reactions against the lowered superego control and minimization of the self they were believed to accompany the narcissistic Fordist form of subjectivity.

The NSMs opposed not only the cultural and subjective aspects of Fordism but also its negative material externalities. The clearest example is environmentalist protest against the Fordist tenet of the unlimited exploitation of nature (Hirsch 1988: 47). The automobile was the very centerpiece of Fordist mass production and consumption (Roth 1989); Chanan and Steinmetz (2005). The collective irrationalities of reliance on individual automobiles provided the impetus for demands for cities free of automobiles, reduced speed limits, better mass transportation, and so forth. Labor and management have often been on the same side of the Fordist "productivist cartel" in opposition to movements against environmental destruction.[25]

The NSMs also respond to the specifically political aspects of Fordism. Hirsch (1980) argues that the Fordist state assumes the form of a *security state*—a term that resonates with both the "social" and the "police" connotations of security. By deepening its penetration into citizens' everyday life, the state provokes defensive reactions. Citizen opposition prevented the Netherlands from carrying out a nation-wide census starting in 1971 (Vieten 1983); in West Germany, the census originally planned for 1983 was delayed until 1987 and widely boycotted (Hubert 1983). A more extreme case involves groups like the German *Autonomen* (autonomous groups), whose attacks have been directed especially against representatives of state power (but also against private organizations and actors in civil society, from computer and genetic engineering firms to middle-class gentrifiers in the formerly alternative Kreuzberg district of Berlin).[26]

The Keynesian welfare state also had contradictory effects. On the one hand, it awakened new needs or confirmed a sense of entitlement to a certain standard of life. Writers on both the Right and Left in the 1970s claimed that they detected a system overload or immanent fiscal crisis caused in part by widespread feelings of welfare entitlement. But the decline in productivity and profits in the 1970s meant that the fiscally strapped welfare state could no longer meet such needs (Hirsch and Roth 1986: 71, 89). Moreover, the Keynesian welfare state ascertained and served peoples' needs in an authoritarian, disabling way (Lasch 1978: 154–57, 223–31; Illich 1977; Fraser 1987). Many new conflicts therefore demanded social services that would be administered democratically and locally (Handler n.d.).

The dominant neo-corporatist system of interest representation and the corresponding mass-integrative or official political parties (Poulantzas 1980: 232) provided a final impetus to the NSMs (Kitschelt 1986). As Hirsch and Roth argue, neo-corporatism systematically marginalized grievances and themes that did not fall under the purview of the peak interest organizations. This resulted in a surplus of peripheralized grievances that the political system could not address (Offe 1980). Rejecting the rigid bureaucratic form of the "mass-integrative political party," the NSMs assumed informal, non-hierarchical structures (Hirsch and Roth 1986: 68; Benton 1989). As Melucci (1984: 829–30) suggested, "the normal situation of today's 'movement' is to be a network of small groups submerged in everyday life. . . . The new organizational form . . . is a goal in itself . . . the *form* of the movement is a message, a symbolic challenge to the dominant patterns."

## Section 4

Hirsch and Roth's analysis is more solidly anchored in historical and cultural context than most writing on the NSMs.[27] They can better account for the issues, forms, and actions distinguishing the NSMs from their predecessors. Yet the regulation approach has some of the same limitations as earlier versions of neo-Marxism. It is of little help in explaining the individual motivation to join a social movement, the mobilization of resources for collective action, and the course of social conflicts.[28] Regulation theory seems best suited for understanding the patterning of grievances and the emergence and disappearance of potential collective actors. But even here the regulation approach is insufficient.

Despite their rejection of teleology and functionalism and their insistence on contingency and variation, Hirsch and Roth's ideal still seems to be the all-encompassing, totalizing form sort of analysis familiar from earlier forms of Marxism (and criticized by Althusser in his discussions of the notion of "expressive totality").[29] Hirsch and Roth do not simply present a social theory, in which it would be acceptable to mobilize only a single theoretical structure or causal mechanism; instead, they propose a history of concrete social conflicts in a specific time and place. Here they elide the distinction between theory and explanation. Nowhere in their text do they indicate that diverse theoretical systems with their particular causal mechanisms might be jointly involved in determining the concrete. Contingency is admitted to this regulationist universe, but this does not mean that diverse causal mechanisms combine in producing an empirical outcome.

Rather, contingency here only means that Marxism is unable to explain certain aspects of reality and that those aspects simply remain unexplained and untheorized. The implicit message is that aspects of the real-concrete, such as social movements, are either fully determined by the causal mechanisms central to Marxist theory or else they are underdetermined.

My aim is not to condemn the regulationists but to take the anti-reductionist tone of their programmatic statements to its logical conclusion. Although it is beyond the scope of this essay to propose a complete alternative analysis of the NSMs, this final section will make some suggestions about the sorts of additional historical and cultural factors that would need to be considered in a more complete explanatory account. I will first discuss the general importance of granting more autonomy to historical subjectivity and culture in explaining the NSMs; then I will review some of the ways in which the Nazi past shaped the German NSMs.

### Subjectivity and the New Social Movements

For Hirsch, Roth, and other regulation theorists, the Fordist regulatory mode is dialectically coupled with its own demise, producing new needs and values that lead to a rejection of its basic premises. The problematic implication of this argument, however, is that all forms of subjectivity relevant to the NSMs are part of the Fordist system, that is, that Fordism provides sufficient cultural preconditions for the NSMs. Consider Hirsch and Roth's claim that the NSMs came to focus on identity politics in reaction to the homogenization of Fordist mass culture and the penetration of the life world by the neo-corporatist security state. Fordism may have been a *necessary* condition for the new political paradigm, but it was not a *sufficient* one. The turn to identity politics in response to perceived psychological leveling depended upon prior definitions of the subject that could then be violated. In a socio-cultural setting with different preexisting constructions of individuality, autonomy, or the category of the person, Fordism might not have incited the specific reassertion of subjectivity and individualism seen in the NSMs.[30]

Differences in the NSM activities of the advanced capitalist countries cannot be attributed solely to variations in the construction of Fordism. In the United States and Great Britain, NSMs have been less prominent than in Europe; and there has been less resistance by such movements to working within the state and cooperating with authorities. The regulationist approach would tend to explain such differences by referring to the variation in the regulatory mode, pointing for instance to the differing importance of the central state as a coordinating instance in each national variant of Fordism. The fragmentation of social movements in the United States would then reflect the relatively decentered nature of American Fordism. Yet a more deeply rooted factor that cannot be assimilated to Fordism is the historical weakness of a folk concept of the state in the United States and Britain, as compared to continental Europe (d'Entrèves 1967: 33–34; Badie and Birnbaum 1983: 125–30). The example of the census boycott in West Germany during the 1980s throws an interesting light on this contrast. The regulation approach would attribute the surprising success of this boycott to the prominent role of the intrusive state in German Fordism. This begs the question of why the state was experienced as overly intrusive. The specific interpretation of the census as an issue of state intrusion was not an automatic result of Fordism but probably had to do with the salience of the folk concept of the state in Germany as all-powerful and pervasive, and with the negative coding of this concept. This image of the state could be traced to a specific construction of the collective memory of Nazism as an omnipotent dictatorship (rather than, say, a popular movement)—a construction which has little to do with Fordism.[31]

More generally, Hirsch and Roth do not carefully trace but simply assume the linkages between structural conditions and subjective responses, material grievances, and consciousness. Consider their claim that the Fordist program of universal prosperity awakens new needs, such as the expectation of a long and healthy life, but that the economic growth model itself seems to undermine the very possibility of realizing such needs (through environmental threats to health, and so forth), thus inciting opposition. Fordism cannot bear the weight of accounting for the definition of subjective expectations, perceptions of empirical reality, attributions of responsibility for grievances, notions of justice, and assessments of the value and effectiveness of opposition. Why did citizens believe the Fordist promises of the good life in the first place? Why did they understand promises as having been broken? How did people become cognizant of environmental destruction and see it as an unacceptable risk? Why did they attribute such destruction to the social system rather than, say, human nature? These are elementary questions for any investigation which takes seriously problems of ideology and the creation of hegemony, rather than deriving culture from external material conditions.

## The Presence of the Nazi Past

It is important to consider the diverse ways in which the "peculiarities of German history" (Blackbourn and Eley 1985) continue to influence many aspects of German society, including the NSMs. When contemporary historians discuss the German *Sonderweg,* they are typically referring to a period stretching backwards from 1933 to the nineteenth century or even to the Reformation (see, for example, Dahrendorf 1967; Wehler 1985). In this view, 1945 (or 1989) marks the end of (West) Germany's deviant history.[32] This model distracts attention from the continuing direct and indirect effects of Nazism on the political culture of the Federal Republic after 1945.[33] Indeed, one could argue that the German Sonderweg *began* with the unparalleled events between 1933 and 1945 and that since that time it has become impossible for Germany to be just another European country.[34] The exceptionalism thesis might make more sense if its chronology were completely reversed, projecting Germany's Sonderweg forward from 1933 rather than sequestering it in the distant past. If one ignores the peculiarities of twentieth-century German history, it is impossible to understand not just the NSMs but also the way in which Nazi ideas and slogans could have been revived and diffused so rapidly in Germany since 1990, fueling the resurgence of the current far-right movement.

The pronounced anti-authoritarianism of the German NSMs is rooted as much in the nationally specific history of Nazism as in the role of the state and centralized political parties and trade unions under Fordism.[35] The Nazi generation was fully discredited in the eyes of many of its children. The theme of rejecting the parents is especially strong in the literature of the 1968 generation (Schneider 1981).[36] Many younger Germans generalized this sentiment, turning their backs on West German society as a whole. This repudiation was facilitated by the continuing presence of former Nazis within the West German power elite after 1945.

Most importantly, the Holocaust made it impossible for many Germans to develop a positive national identity. This peculiarity of German identity politics had manifold effects on the NSMs. The hesitation to embrace a German identity has been a steady complaint of conservatives and establishment figures, culminating in the *Historikerstreit* of the late 1980s and the McCarthyite attacks on opponents of German unification in 1989–1990.[37] One result has been an overwhelmingly right-wing coding of popular German nationalism, which has had the paradoxical effect of making nationalism even more taboo for non-conservatives. The focus on identity in the

NSM milieux seems to respond to a vaguely felt subjective deficit that national feelings cannot fulfill. The NSMs often projected desires for positive identity onto non-German groups, for example, in the movement of "urban Indians" (*Stadtindianer*) during the late 1970s, the ongoing fascination with Italian social movements, the Bhagwan cult of the 1980s, alternative tourism and philo-semitism among non-Jewish Germans. With the revival of regional German folk music and dialects in the 1970s, even the internal German other became a site of counter-identification.

Another set of influences on the West German NSMs that cannot be assimilated to Fordism is related to the unusual situation of the old (postwar) German Left. Especially important here is the state's repressive orientation towards extraparliamentary opposition and the situation of the Communist Party. In contrast to most other European countries, West Germany had no viable or legal Communist Party that might have been in a position to absorb some of the new conflict issues as they arose. Many German Communists were killed by the Nazis, and West Germany then banned the KPD (Communist Party of Germany) in 1956. Even after the party was legalized in 1968 and re-founded as the DKP (German Communist Party), its close association with the GDR made it extremely unattractive to critical West Germans.[38] The FRG government's initial success in banning the KPD also created a state precedent of overreacting to supposed "threats to the constitution" from the Left, best illustrated by the Radical Law (*Radikalenerlaß*) of 1972 and the professional interdictions (*Berufsverbote*) that resulted from it.[39] West Germany's geopolitical position on the front line of the Cold War systematically reinforced its hardline approach to left-wing domestic opposition. Such official alarmism in turn intensified alienation from the state and fanned the flames of the NSMs.

The conflictory and ambivalent German relationship to the United States is yet another influence on the German NSMs that is indirectly related to the Nazi past. To some extent this highly-charged relationship to the United States was common to all countries during the Fordist era and remained a structural feature of the global order even after the demise of Fordism. When the United States assumed the role of hegemon in international relations after 1945 (Krasner 1983), it assured a period of relative free trade and held the line against insurgencies world-wide. This benefited the other Fordist national economies. America's role as world gendarme and its political/military leadership in Europe decisively influenced social movements in both the United States and Europe during the post-war period. The Vietnam War triggered startlingly simultaneous social movements around the globe (Arrighi, Hopkins, and Wallerstein 1989: 97–115; Katsiaficas 1987: 29–35). United States (and Soviet) nuclear policy again became the focus of a series of social movements across the advanced capitalist world during the early 1980s. Alongside the perceived nuclear threat, affronts to national sovereignty helped catalyze peace movements in the NATO countries in which U.S. missiles and troops were stationed. Resurgent U.S. imperialism since the late 1990s has triggered a new wave of "anti-American" social movements.

German alternative movements were shaped by the particular German relationship to the United States, a relationship that cannot be fully subsumed under the aegis of Fordism. American movies, music, fashion, and popular culture swept over West Germany during the 1950s, re-socializing a whole generation of youth (Maase 1992). While such cultural Americanization was not unique to Germany, it was coupled in the FRG with the felt humiliations of denazification (despite the limitations of the actual denazification program) and the formal Allied occupation, followed by continuing limitations on German political sovereignty until 1990 and even beyond. Denazification was not invented in Washington, of course (Bark and Gress 1989: 74ff.); but the leading American role in West German policy, the NATO alliance, and the world order tended to focus attention on the United States.[40] Most Germans readily accepted their country's junior partnership with the United States. With their informality and their use of civil disobedience tactics from the American civil rights movement, the NSMs were themselves part of an ongoing Americanization of German political culture.[41] Yet undercurrents of resentment and sweeping rejections of the United States were always evident in the German NSMs, as I discovered during my own participation as an American in the German peace movement between 1981 and 1985.[42] German peace movement supporters also paid less attention to the German and Soviet role in the arms race than to the U.S. side. Yet commentators definitely overstated the extent of anti-Americanism and nationalism in the West German peace movement during the 1980s (for example Berman 1981; Pohrt 1982: 116–17; Hollander 1992: 377–83; Herf 1991: 227).

The most direct influence of Nazism on social movements in Germany, finally, has become especially evident since the end of the 1980s, with the rapid growth of an extreme right-wing movement and other more covert expressions of far-right sentiment. The numbers of violent right-wing hate crimes have increased steadily since 1995, and twice as many were reported in 2000 as in 1992.[43] This might be construed as part of a European-wide phenomenon of neo-racism (Balibar 1991; Link 1992) and can itself be traced to the rise of a new mode of regulation (post-Fordism or flexible accumulation; see Steinmetz 1994; 1997). Several general aspects of post-Fordism could be seen as giving rise to new forms of racist mobilization: the decline of well-paid unionized jobs in the metropoles, the export of basic production jobs to the non-European countries, the opening of national borders to foreign products and workers, and the general loss of the guaranteed living conditions characteristic of the Fordist-Keynesian welfare state. Yet even if post-Fordism plays a role in these "newest" European social movements, German neo-racism is sui generis. German Nazi ideology provides a specific ideological grid connecting a variety of disparate enemies into an overarching category of the other. Thus the targets of far-right activists since 1990[44] have included not just immigrants seen as taking jobs away from Germans but also Jews, Polish tourists, homeless men, handicapped people, and participants in NSMs, such as squatters.[45] Although further research is needed to clarify the exact ways in which such ideologies are being propagated (cf. Butterwegge and Isola 1991; Schröder 1992), one condition for their particular resonance in Germany is their enhanced "realism." As Stuart Hall remarked with respect to Thatcherism, "the first thing to ask about an 'organic ideology' that, however unexpectedly, succeeds in organizing substantial sections of the masses and mobilizing them for political action, is not what is *false* about it, but what about it is *true*" (Hall 1988: 46). The partial truth lies not in the neo-Nazis' racist worldview, of course, but in the fact that an earlier German state actually put their ideas into practice. The peculiar history of Germany since 1933 continues to influence even this newest of its social movements, even if the current movement is a novel political-cultural formation that is more than a recrudescence of historical Nazism.

## From Neo-Nazism to Anti-Globalization

This said, how does the current far-right movement relate to the modes of regulation? Where the NSMs rebelled against Fordism from within, the current movement is a backward-looking one, engaged in a desperate effort to reestablish the now obsolete social conditions of what we can refer to as an imaginary Fordism. It is a rebellion of classes and groups who are losing out in the ongoing collaspse of Fordism in Germany. The neofascist movement represents a sort of nostalgia expressed as violence, intended to restore a past remembered in mediated and transfigured form. The logic of Fordism thus underpins the current movement's "immoral economy," a term I coined (building on E. P. Thompson's idea of a "moral economy") in order to draw attention to the sense of customary rights and obligations embedded in popular consciousness (Steinmetz 1994; 1997).

Like nostalgia, the Fordist immoral economy is not necessarily based on the loss or removal of an actual object, but rather on the desire for an imagined one. This is important because most of the working-class participants in the current right-wing movement have never personally experienced the full range of benefits of Fordism. During the Fordist era German workers came to view the conditions of Fordism, particularly the promise of an ever-increasing standard of living, as a kind of customary right. Other key elements of the imaginary Fordist status quo include: (1) The welfare state and its supports for working-class consumption; (2) The ideal of the nuclear family, with men the main bread-winners and women occupied primarily in the home; (3) Leisure time spent consuming homogenized cultural goods, rather than struggling for distinction in an increasingly stratified market of symbolic goods; (4) An economy defined in national terms, which is less and less the case today; and (5) foreign migrants who were mainly engaged in jobs that German workers did not want.

This model of nostalgia for Fordism is also relevant in a slightly oblique way for former citizens of the GDR or their children. The East German mode of regulation, a sort of derivative "iron Fordism" (Lipietz 1991: 88–89), promised its workers an array of economic, social, and cultural advances that bore a strong resemblance to the West German Fordist model. Starting in the 1970s, many East German citizens participated virtually in a phantasmagoric version of West German Fordism, as it was mediated by television. Achieving these benefits at their western levels was obviously only a dream for East Germans before 1989, but East German Fordism was real enough to give their aspirations a concrete basis, and to align them with West German workers' ambitions.

The current phase of social restructuring has corrosively undermined these mainstays of Fordism. Economic, political, and cultural conditions have become "flexible," and personal identities have become less secure. Groups associated with the (now no longer so new) NSMs generally welcome these changes, other sectors are experiencing them as deterioration and loss. In sum, whereas the NSMs were revolts against the Fordist mode of regulation by Fordist subjects, the mainstream of the current neofascist violence is a revolt in favor of Fordism by post-Fordist subjects. The new racist violence is a protest against the end of Fordism and the unstable, fluid, flexible world that has taken its place.[46]

The regulation-theoretical concept of Fordism allows us to make sense of a major stumbling block in the existing literature on the new right, which is the relationship between its thuggish and violent wing, which has been the most visible, and the somewhat more respectable groups with electoral aspirations, such as the German Republicans and the French National Front. Naturally, these two wings cannot be sharply separated. They have much in common ideologically and some overlap in terms of their constituencies. Since the 1980s in Germany, massive efforts have been undertaken to discover a regulatory solution for the crisis of Fordism. The ascendant socio-economic bloc under post-Fordism consists of larger employers as well as the new self-employed and highly skilled, educated workers in the new technological, information, and other postindustrial sectors. Although the dominant strand of post-Fordism is *deterritorializing* and post-national, certain groups of post-Fordist winners seek to protect their newfound advantages by embracing a form of neofascism that is *reterritorializing*. The emphases within this bloc are likely to be different from those of the backward-looking version of neofascism. Social Darwinist ideology will be directed not just against those defined as national or racial *others*, but also against the losers among what the backward-looking neofascists would regard as their national or racial *brothers*.[47] Since the halcyon days of Fordism are gone forever, the reactionary wing of the extreme right will eventually dwindle and the modernizing neofascists will present the more lasting threat. For the moment, however, the backward-looking strand is stronger and more dangerous.

Recent years have also seen the emergence in Germany and the rest of the world of the so-called anti-globalization movement. As elsewhere, the German movement is really at least two movements, but both are responses to the evolving conditions of the post-Fordist era. One tendency wants to return to a Fordist-style version of regulation centered on the nation-state, reestablishing both of its faces of security—police and welfare-statist—as well as its nationally centered mode of growth, which would imply barriers to trade. This movement represents in some respects a left-wing version of some of the themes articulated by the pro-Fordist far right (without, the latter's racism and authoritarianism).[48] The second tendency is pressing for an alternative form of globalization rather than rejecting it *tout court*. Rather than retreating into protective national and regional bunkers, this part of the movement insists that values like human rights, ecology, equality, and democracy should receive as much attention as capitalist logics within the ongoing processes of globalization/deterritorialization. This second tendency is much more "this-worldly" than the first, focused on reforming post-Fordism rather than destroying it. For example, a central demand of the organization ATTAC (Association for the Taxation of Financial Transactions for the Aid of Citizens), which has been very active in recent globalization protests in Germany and elsewhere, is the implementation of the Tobin Tax on financial transactions.[49] This suggests that ATTAC and like-minded organizations are dwelling within the post-Fordist present, in which financial markets have moved to the center of the regulatory mode (Harvey 1989).

## Regulation Theory and the Question of Comparison

In view of the topic of this volume and Raymond Grew's contributions to comparative history, I will conclude with a few remarks about the implications of regulation theory for the topic of comparison.

To clarify this problem we need to distinguish between theories and explanations and to attend to the relations between what Roy Bhaskar calls mechanisms and events.[50] Critical realism in the philosophy of science, a position that underlies much regulation theory, assumes an ontological distinction between events as they are observed and the underlying mechanisms that produce those regularities. Scientific theories, including social theories, are ultimately about causal mechanisms or structures, and are not concerned with explaining specific empirical and historical occurrences. Examples of such mechanisms include the unconscious in psychoanalysis, natural selection in evolutionary theory, and modes of production or capital accumulation in Marxist theory. Science also tries to produce explanations, which have as their object concrete outcomes or events in the world. Bob Jessop's (1990a) term, "contingent necessity," nicely expresses the relationship between theory and explanation. As he notes, "contingent" is a logical concept and concerned with *theoretical indeterminability,* "necessity" is an ontological concept and refers to *determinacy in the real world.* Thus "contingent" means "indeterminable within the terms of a single theoretical system"; it can properly be juxtaposed to the notion of "necessity," which signifies the assumption underpinning any realist scientific enquiry that "everything that happens is caused" (ibid.: 12).

Jessop's so-called method of articulation, inspired by Poulantzas' distinction between modes of production and social formation, entails a movement from the abstract to the concrete and from the simple to the complex (cf. Mahon 1991). An empirical phenomenon is explained as a conjunction of multiple chains of causation. Explaining the effects of the 1989 California earthquake, for example, might require knowledge of a variety of different mechanisms: plate tectonics, highway and building construction techniques, traffic patterns, and American conceptions of nature, culture, and civilization.[51]

The arguments advanced here clash with the standard ideal in most social science (both Marxist and non-Marxist) of attaining "parsimonious" explanations through theoretical statements that are maximally capacious.[52] Marxists have felt compelled to encompass the entirety of social reality in their accounts. "Vulgar" Marxism simply collapses across levels of abstraction, claiming to discover flesh-and-blood social classes or neatly delineated modes of production existing in reality. The more "sophisticated" variants of Marxism respected the distinction between the simple/concrete and the complex/abstract, but assumed that both levels could be understood within an entirely Marxist conceptual universe. The Althusserians in particular differentiated between the abstract level of modes of production and the more concrete level of the social formation, defining the latter as a combination of diverse modes of production. They also assimilated non-Marxist concepts, as with Poulantzas' use of mainstream political science and Macherey's employment of Russian formalism, not to mention the importance of Freud, Lacan, Bachelard, and other non-Marxists in Althusser's own thought. But the whole process took place within the homogenizing framework of Marxism. "Bourgeois" concepts were changed into Marxist ones, as in Poulantzas' discussion of state bureaucracies (1978: 331–59).[53] The social formation may have been an articulation of diverse structures for the Althusserians, but all of these structures had to be categorized as modes of production. And even if alternative levels were granted their "relative autonomy," there was an assumption that the economic level had causal primacy, that it was "determinant in the last instance."[54]

Regulation theory's approach to empirical, historical analysis breaks with the residual positivism of orthodox Marxism and with the depth-realist positivism (Steinmetz 2005b) or "theoretical realism" (Somers 1998) of the Althusserians and rational-choice theorists. Comparison here involves contrasting the effects of the same conceptual mechanism across different contexts. This approach can be differentiated from one in which the axis of comparison is organized around a certain type of empirical or concrete event. Although it might appear that regulation theory is organized around the comparison of empirical entities, this is not in fact the case. Instead it explores the ways in which abstract categories, such as capital accumulation, falling profit rates, modes of regulation, or regimes of accumulation work themselves out in differing historical and spatial conjunctures.[55] One compares the effects of underlying mechanisms or structures rather than empirical-level dependent variables. Because the effects of any mechanism are overdetermined by a variety of other ones, however, an explanation will necessarily be figurational or conjunctural.[56] This means that every empirical or historical case, national, regional, and local, is exceptional. Or better, that there are no true exceptions, because there are no empirical norms, the only "regularities" concern underlying mechanisms.

The example of contemporary neoliberal restructuring can illustrate this logic of comparison. All advanced capitalist countries may be exposed to discourses of neoliberalism, to demands for neoliberal reform from powerful international institutions, and to various economic pressures. A study of neoliberalism in the spirit of regulation theory might explore the contextually varying responses to similar pressures in different countries or regions, rather than expecting to find a consistent pattern of diffusion.[57]

## Conclusion

This article has reflected on the challenges to Marxist theory posed by the NSMs and some of the theoretical discourses associated with these movements that are grouped together under the rubric post-Marxism. Many analysts have been led to proclaim the obsolescence of Marxist theory on the basis of the NSMs' aims, form, and heterogeneous class base, together with the waning of working-class identification, the labor movement, and class differences in political behavior (Niethammer 1979; Mooser 1983; Offe 1984; but compare Weakliem 1991). I have examined regulation theory, a specific form of neo-Marxism that rejects functionalism and teleology and attempts to answer some of the other critiques without abandoning what it sees as Marxism's core: the analysis of capital accumulation, its crises, and the social arrangements that allow it to continue.[58] Given the role of the NSMs in generating the critiques of Marxism, explaining these movements within the revised Marxist approach takes on an obvious importance. Because Hirsch and Roth have presented the most extended analysis of the NSMs from a regulationist perspective, their work deserves a serious appraisal. They argue that historically stabilized social formations for regulating accumulation structure the actors, stakes, resources, and likely outcomes of social conflicts. Many of these grievances, needs, and actors cut across social class boundaries. The problem with their analysis lies in the ambition of explaining the new movements entirely in terms of regulatory modes. Arrangements for capital accumulation may not be the sole determinants of patterns of social antagonism or even necessarily the crucial ones. Marxists need to acknowledge that actors' identities, perceptions, and interests may also be shaped by discursive formations, social relations, and psychic processes whose relations to capital accumulation are only indirect or even nonexistent. Marxists need not feel compelled to explain everything in terms of the mechanisms central to its own theory.

Marxism is best understood as an abstract theory that operates with a set of simple objects and processes (such as mode of production, social class, and perhaps now mode of regulation and accumulation regime), but that is unable to claim any monopoly on explanations of the empirical and historical.[59] Marxism should respect the integrity and boundaries of theoretical systems, including its own. This self-understanding is perhaps the best definition of *post*-Marxism. Only where the theoretical core of Marxism is retained does it make sense to speak of post-*Marxist* rather than non-Marxist theory. Of course, there are varying interpretations of the term post-Marxism. For some authors, "post-Marxist" seems to be primarily an (auto)biographical description, referring to people who used to be Marxists (Wright 1987; Laclau and Mouffe 1985). In actual social analysis, however, a post-Marxist orientation seems to me to be one that continues to provisionally accept the usefulness of Marxist theory—however Marxism may be understood—while embracing a more diversified explanatory strategy that accepts a multiplicity of theoretical systems on an equal basis. It is no paradox to argue then that post-Marxism is Marxist in theory but post-Marxist in practice.

NOTES

Acknowledgements: I am grateful to Julia Adams, Julia Hell, Doug McAdam, and Moishe Postone, and members of the 1992 CSST seminar and the 2001 Raymond Grew conference at the University of Michigan. I thank an anonymous reviewer for comments on an earlier draft.

1. Without using the term "new social movements," Reinhard Mohr (1992) develops a similar contrast in political goals, styles, theories, and cultures by comparing the German "generation of 1968," which he depicts as emulating in many ways the "old social movements," and the "generation of 1978."

2. Most researchers distinguish between the Green parties and the NSMs, although the boundaries are certainly fluid. During the early years the German Green Party—with its insistence on the "rotation" of parliamentary representatives to prevent centralization, its refusal of coalition politics, and its uncompromising opposition to nuclear power, toxic chemical products, militarism, and membership in NATO—was much closer to the NSMs. See Schroeren's (1990), interview with Petra Kelly. There is still a sector of the German Green Party that adheres to these goals, but the events of the 1990s since the Gulf War and the entry of the Greens into a national governing coalition with the Social Democrats have marginalized these sectors and succeeded in tarring them with the label "fundamentalist." But for an example of the ongoing presence of these strands within the Green Party even after the bombing of the World Trade Center, see the interview with Green Party leader Antje Vollmer, "Highnoon vermeiden," *die tageszeitung* (Berlin), 22 Sep. 2001.

3. The centrality of the vision of a space "autonomous from the state" in the Berlin squatter movement since 1980 is emphasized in a documentary film, "Der Traum vom rechtsfreien Raum" (The dream of a space without laws), by Eckart Lottmann (1993).

4. This definition builds on the following articles: Offe (1987), Brand, Büsser, and Rucht (1986), Raschke (1985: 254–66, 322–36, 411–36), Cohen (1985), Roth (1989), Hirsch and Roth (1986), and Melucci (1980; 1981b; 1989).

5. It follows from this that the NSMs often look more like subcultures than movements. They can be considered movements, however, insofar as they challenge existing social structures, have some degree of organization (even if it is informal, in the sense of Melucci's "networks"), and demonstrate some congruence of grievances, aims, and identities.

6. It is necessary to define the period of the NSMs more precisely, of course, and to address problems of cross-national differences in periodization. The NSMs did not appear everywhere simultaneously in the capitalist core, and they appear to have had longer staying power in some regions than others. But such periodization difficulties can only be resolved on the basis of a model of the determinants of the NSMs. Part of the confusion stems from the different explanatory models used by adherents of the term "new social movements." Inglehart's theory (1990), for instance, virtually requires that the NSMs are historically unique, while Hirsch and Roth (1986) do not.

7. Another example of inadequacy of common-sense definitions of social movements is the peace movement of the 1980s. In many respects it assumed centralized and bureaucratic forms (Rochon 1988: 21, 210), but it also encompassed groups that emphasized localized actions, anti-statist politics, and the practical performance of new forms of social life (Hartford and Hopkins 1984; Liddington 1991: 197–286). Bagguley (1992: 31) concludes that the traditionalist tendencies in the peace and women's movements undermine arguments for the distinctiveness of

the NSMs. If one retains a distinction between abstract-theoretical and concrete-empirical levels of analysis, however, it is easy to see how a single social movement may illustrate more than one theoretical logic.

8. The relationship between theoretical discourses critical of orthodox Marxism and participation in the NSMs is illustrated by individuals such as Foucault, Touraine, E. P. Thompson, and Daniel Cohn-Bendit.

9. In a somewhat less radical critique of objectivism, Bowles and Gintis (1986: 149) argue that collective actors are created by political discourse and that "no natural boundaries to group membership" exist.

10. In the last section of their book Laclau and Mouffe actually do provide an account of the NSMs as resulting from the spread of an "egalitarian imaginary constituted around liberal-democratic discourse" and transformations of what they call "social relations," including Fordism, the welfare state, and the culture industry (1985: 165, 160–63). Although vague in many of its details, and too extreme in denying any causal role to the material, their explanation in this section is broadly compatible with the one I will propose below.

11. See also Bell (1973) and Inglehart (1990), both of whom correlate support for the NSMs with populations resembling the new class, a term used by Bell in this context (1973: 479). Inglehart also discusses the "new class" as a bearer of "postmaterial" values—his central concept—but also as one cause of the NSMs (1990: 331–32, 371–92).

12. Although he actually claims to reject "objectivist" class analysis, using Bourdieu's category of habitus to mediate between objective and subjective class position, Eder (1985) ultimately derives the putative petty-bourgeois attraction to the NSMs from their intermediate position between upper and lower classes.

13. Another problem singled out by Katznelson (1981: 211–12) is that Castells did not discuss the conditions that turn the structural possibility for social protest into its actualization. Castells' approach began to change considerably with *The City and the Grassroots* (1983).

14. Several different branches of regulation theory are discussed in Jessop (1990b). Each regulationist differs in emphasis, with some closer to traditional Marxism than others. The version discussed in this section is closest to Jessop's. I am also grateful to Bob Jessop for discussing some of the ideas in this section with me.

15. Gramsci distinguishes Fordism and Taylorism as "two methods of production and work" (1978: 112). See also Maier (1987).

16. An example of such a regulative institution, money, represents the recognition of the labor contained within an exchanged commodity and of the commodity-owner's right to an equivalent share of social labor (Scherrer 1989). Jessop proposes a third concept, "hegemonic project," which he distinguishes from modes of regulation, while Hirsch (1988: 46) equates the two.

17. Wright (1978: 111–80) also allows capitalist crises and their resolutions to

vary historically, but suggests that some sort of resolution will always be forth-coming: "In such situations [of structural accumulation crisis], typically, the forms of accumulation are themselves restructured in basic ways" (p. 165).

18. Weir and Skocpol (1985) detail the international variations and contingen-cies involved in the diffusion of Keynesianism, one of the key elements of the Fordist ensemble. Henry Ford invented many of the components of the later Fordist mode of regulation between 1913 and World War II even as he worked strenuously to prevent regulation from being carried out by the state rather than private industry (Steinmetz 2005c).

19. This process is similar to the one in which countries of the global south adopt varying versions of a standard European or "northern" model of constitu-tionalism, as detailed, for instance, by Sohrabi (1996). The analysis of varying local translations of a standard model differs from the theory of institutional isomor-phism proposed by Meyer (1980; 1999).

20. See also Hirsch (1980; 1981; 1983), Hirsch and Roth (1986; 1987), Mayer and Roth (1995), and Mayer (1991). Critiques of Hirsch and Roth are presented by Hübner (1987), Wagner and Stahn (1987), and Jessop (1988). As will become evi-dent, I am more interested in Hirsch and Roth's treatment of the connections of Fordism to the NSMs than in their discussion of Fordism per se, which is the main focus of these criticisms. The critics are probably correct in arguing that Hirsch and Roth's version of regulation theory is overly functionalist and "state-cen-tered," and that it understates the difficulties involved in constructing Fordism, especially the non-state aspects of regulation. The critics also examine various ways in which the West German case deviates from the general model of Fordism. Harvey (1989) concentrates on the relations between models of regulation and cul-tural change, and includes only a few pages on the NSMs; Epstein (1990) includes a short section on Hirsch and Roth but does not discuss *Das neue Gesicht* and their other work in German.

21. For just one example, see the comments of the director Eckart Lottmann (2001) on his work with "alternative media" in Berlin during the early 1980s and his group's reliance on money from the municipal government.

22. For instance, publicity for the 1978 TUNIX ("Do-Nothing") meeting of the "spontaneous left" in West Berlin—a manifestation of the NSM counter-scene—appealed to everyone who was sick of the "Coca-Cola-Karajan-culture" (Hoff-mann-Axthelm et al. 1978: 93).

23. This is not necessarily an argument (à la Allan Bloom) for the superiority of the traditional curriculum, but a comment on the sociological basis of struggles against it. See Delale and Ragache (1978) for the argument that the French student protests of May 1968 involved anger by "proletarianized" students about false promises of social mobility.

24. Bagguley argues correctly that feminism as an NSM can only be understood in terms of "changes in the structure and form of patriarchy," specifically the shift from private to public patriarchy, and not in terms of class structure (1992: 27,

42–45). Although gender relations certainly cannot be subsumed under regulatory modes, a more subtle analysis of changes in capitalism might also allow one to draw finer distinctions between forms of patriarchy. See Arestis and Paliginis (1995).

25. One example of this cartel can be seen in the battles over proposed anti-smog controls in Los Angeles, which were opposed by an "unlikely" coalition between labor and industry (cf. "Political Fallout from Smog Blurs Future for Los Angeles," *New York Times,* national ed., 30 Apr. 1989). Another U.S. example is labor-management opposition to tighter fuel (CAFE) standards for cars (cf. "Auto Makers see Nothing but Trouble in a Warmer World," *New York Times,* national ed., 16 Oct. 1997).

26. Lashing out against the extensions of the security state, the violence of the *Autonomen* can be seen as a Sartrian "moment of the boomerang" (Sartre 2001: 147) that symptomatically mirrors their presumed adversary (Kramer 1988; Hardt and Negri 2000: 130–32). The *Autonomen* themselves dismiss the notion of such a mirror effect, of course (cf. Lecorte 1992). In the 1990s some of the German *Autonomen* started to attack neo-Nazis and to defend foreigners against right-wing assaults. This can also be interpreted as anti-state activity insofar as the Christian Democratic government (through September 1998) tolerated anti-foreigner activities by failing to repress right-wing attacks quickly, focusing debate on restricting the right to political asylum, and paying for the return of Vietnamese guest workers and Romanian gypsies. Of course this was also the era in which Germany finally began to move politically beyond Fordism toward post-Fordism.

27. In addition to the perspectives discussed here, it would be necessary to consider the theories of late capitalism (Mandel 1978), programmed society (Touraine 1977), and Postone's (1993) thesis of a contradiction in contemporary capitalism between the ongoing structuring of society according to the labor-based form of value analyzed by Marx and the diminishing importance of labor inputs in the economy.

28. In all the theories discussed here the emphasis is on explaining very broad changes in patterns of social conflict, such as shifting ideologies, goals, forms of activity, and bases of recruitment. None of these approaches address the problem that is central to "resource mobilization theory" or RM (see Zald and McCarthy 1979), namely, accounting for differences between contending social movement organizations in recruitment success and between individuals in their proclivity to join a movement. The RM approaches, by contrast, are ill-equipped to illuminate the form and content of the new social conflicts, especially the specific nature of their grievances, as well as historic upsurges and declines in protest. The frequently expressed notion that there is a surplus of ever-present grievances that only needs to be seized on by effective organizers with sufficient resources completely ignores the relationship between evolving social problems and changing identities. How can the massive increase in peace movement activity in Europe and the United States between 1979 and 1983 (Wittner 1988: 277–86) be understood without attending to the developments in the Cold War and the nuclear arms race at that

time? The more micro-economic versions of the RM approach also must bracket the central symbolic, expressive, and moral aspects of the new movements and the non-instrumental motives which lie behind much participation. Selective incentives, a central explanatory device in the armory of RM theory, certainly could not have been operative in motivating millions of Europeans to demonstrate against nuclear missiles and other weapons and nuclear power plants during the 1980s. Most participants in the NSMs do not even belong to an organization that could provide them with so-called side benefits, and individual participants are nearly invisible at large demonstrations (see Mohr 1992: 27–31 for a vivid description of the sense of anonymity of a participant in protests against the West German Brokdorf nuclear power plant). The sheer size of these demonstrations and the lack of any single centralized organizer precluded the distribution of side benefits for most people except by their immediate group of friends. Describing such small-group reinforcements as a sort of psychological benefit not only vitiates the concept but also begs the more important question of why so many primary social groups valorized participation in precisely this sort of movement.

Of course there is another variant of RM represented by Tilly, Klandermans, and others. This variant does not focus exclusively on the choices of maximizing rational individuals but also considers political opportunity structures and the effects of a wide variety of resources, including preexisting infrastructures, on mobilization (see Perrow 1979: 199–200; Tilly 1978; Klandermans and Tarrow 1988). To the extent that Tilly (1986) also is able to account for the historical emergence of new interests through the combined processes of proletarianization and state formation, he goes beyond other RM approaches. I would argue, however, that a modified version of the regulation perspective provides a more fine-grained analysis of changes in interests and forms of social protest (Tilly's "repertoires of collective action").

29. See Althusser (1990a) for a discussion of the concept of expressive totality. As Althusser makes clear (1970: 91–119), teleology is one form of expressive totality, specifically, one in which historical change is explained in terms of a single underlying principle. Regulation theory does not engage in this particular kind of totalizing explanation.

30. The specific ideological framing work of social movement leaders and intellectuals also contributed to the negative interpretation of mass culture (Snow, Rochford, Worden, and Benford 1986; Snow and Benford 1988).

31. German anxiety around the idea of the strong intrusive state may also be related to older images of an omnipotent Prussian absolutist state. Central European absolutism, guided by Cameralist doctrine, sought to collect every possible shred of information about the territory and its inhabitants, with the avowed goal of social discipline (Maier 1980; Foucault 1989; 1991; Pasquino 1991). Regardless of the actual extent of information-gathering in the absolutist states where cameralist doctrine was taught, these states openly announced their intention to scrutinize and regulate the most minute aspects of society.

32. For an explicit statement of the "end of the Sonderweg thesis," see Kocka (1990: 495–99).

33. When the historians of German exceptionalism warned in 1989–1990 against the revival of the German Sonderweg, they were referring not to a possible revival of Nazism, but rather to the supposed dangers of retaining a second German state in the East. This shows how deep-seated the notion was that democratic West Germany had overcome Germany's peculiar legacy (see Winkler 1990: 9; Kocka 1990). Of course the same view of West Germany is equally widespread among conservative opponents of the exceptionalism thesis; see Thomas Nipperdey's exhortatively titled article, "Die Deutschen wollen und dürfen eine Nation sein," *Frankfurter Allgemeine Zeitung* 160 (13 July 1990), p. 10.

34. As Blackbourn and Eley (1985) and others have shown, pre-1914 Germany was not insufficiently bourgeois; in fact, many of its anti-democratic features reflected the power of the industrial bourgeoisie in state and society. Labor relations, economic policies, even the military were in many ways more modernized and more in conformance with capitalist interests in Imperial Germany than in neighboring countries (cf. Grebing 1986; Fischer 1987; Steinmetz 1990).

35. Radical anti-authoritarianism has been most clearly expressed in the movement-milieux of the so-called *Spontis* (spontaneous left) of the 1970s and early 1980s and the Autonomen (Brand et al. 1986: 174–76; Hoffmann-Axthelm et al. 1978). It is also striking that the earliest and largest autonomous movement arose in Italy, another country with a fascist past. The West European terrorist movements of the 1970s and 1980s, which cannot be categorized as NSMs but which originated in some of the same milieux as the latter (see Aust 1997), were also strongest in Italy and Germany.

36. The Green Party leader, Antje Vollmer (1992), even hints at a connection between the partial acceptance of Willi Brandt by the extra-parliamentary opposition and his biography as a child who never knew his father and was raised by his grandfather, allowing him to become a symbolic grandfather (rather than father) of the first NSM generation. The question of women in Nazi Germany seems to have been discussed and psychologically worked through in very different terms by the post-war generation.

37. Other appeals to this identity deficit include the Norddeutscher Rundfunk's 1991–1992 television series "Wir Deutschen," and Edgar Reitz' successful series "Heimat" (1980–1984), which proposed a nostalgic relationship to the German past and "a gratifying identification with the victims, and with oneself as victim" (Elsaesser 1989: 278).

38. While the presence of the GDR weakened conventional Left party politics in West Germany, collective war guilt toward the Soviet Union seemed to contribute to the strength of the peace movement during the 1980s.

39. The West German Radical Law of 28 January 1972 prevented anyone belonging to an extremist party or judged to be an enemy of the constitution from

holding a civil service post, which even affected teachers, professors, and mail carriers; see Komitee für Grundrechte und Demokratie (1982).

40. For a discussion of the limits on German sovereignty in West Berlin, see Tergeist (1984).

41. The late Petra Kelly, co-founder of the Green Party and the most familiar symbol of the NSMs in Germany and abroad, embodied this ambivalent relationship to the United States with her combined American and German parentage, her university education in the United States, and her insistence on the positive sides of American society despite the endemic anti-Americanism of her German cohorts.

42. See also Schmitt (1990: 249–59). I would not argue, however, that these left-wing German attitudes are equivalent to right-wing German nationalist rejections of the United States, as the latter contain unmistakable racist and anti-Semitic elements. Consider a typical statement by the extreme-right-wing German Republican party leader Franz Schönhuber:

I am struggling against a "foreignization" (*Überfremdung*) leading to a situation in which we lose our national identity; that is the decisive point for me. I am struggling against the permanent Americanization [of Germany] . . . we are on the way to becoming a Coca-Cola Republic. We are taking over slogans from the Americans . . . If you turn on the radio nowadays you have the feeling you're driving somewhere between Manhattan and Riverside [sic]" (from interview with Schönhuber in the television documentary "Mord von Rechts: Wer stoppt die Gewalt?" on the German ZDF network, 25 Nov. 1992).

43. See Bundesamt für Verfassungsschutz (1995; 2000) and Steinmetz (1997). In the year 2000, more than forty-four right-extremist hate crimes were reported daily, according to these official statistics. These numbers are of course notoriously inaccurate, but there is no reason to expect the police and citizens simply to have become more likely to report such incidents, as some commentators insist. Ongoing research by Cynthia Miller-Idriss (New York University) among technical school students in Berlin suggests that the majority of working-class youths in manual occupations identify with the far right. Political reporting supports the argument that extreme-right activism has not waned but steadily increased in Germany over the course of the last decade.

44. In 1991, skinheads in Berlin reportedly dragged a young Polish visitor into the bushes of the Tiergarten, anesthetized his tongue, and cut off the end of it with shears. Whether or not this incident is apocryphal, it illustrates in a particularly insidious form the argument about the new racism being less about biological heredity than "the insurmountability of cultural differences . . . the incompatibility of life-styles and traditions" (Balibar 1991: 21). But there are specific German elements at work here too, most precisely the long German tradition of repressing the speaking of Polish. The numerous attacks on handicapped people during 1992 were accompanied by slogans explicitly echoing the eugenic ideology (and policy) of the Nazis (Steinmetz 1994).

45. The right-wing attacks on people associated with a range of NSMs also

illustrates the way in which movements occupy a shared relational field. The far-right movement has successfully captured some of the same youthful sectors that were formerly mobilized by the NSMs. But where the NSMs rebelled against Fordism from within, the movement of right-wing hate crimes is in part a rebellion of classes and groups who are losing out in the ongoing collapse of Fordism in Germany (see below).

46. A tendency in most of the literature on German right-wing extremism since 1989 has been to argue that it is mainly coming from the eastern states, but as reports by the Verfassungsschutz (German FBI) show (e.g., Verfassungsschutz 2000: 35), the three states with the highest numbers of incidents in the 1990s were in the west. The eastern states have more active "scenes" promoting so-called national liberated zones, and four of the eastern states also had significantly higher per capita rates of right-wing hate crimes (ibid: 36). But while the state of Nordrhein-Westfalen had the fourth-lowest per capita rate, it had the largest overall number (153) of incidents. From the standpoint of the victims of such crimes, absolute numbers are more significant than per capita crime rates. The most important point is that right-wing movements grew steadily in both East and West Germany throughout the 1990s.

47. By the same token, some groups within the diverse political-ideological scene of the extreme right are staking their bets on a post-Fordist future and trying to influence its shape. This tendency surfaced in Germany during the 1990s among certain segments of the so-called Republican party as well as students, academics, and contributors to modernized right-wing journals such as *Junge Freiheit,* whose circulation in the mid-1990s was about 40,000 and could also be read on its internet site; more recently the journal has introduced on-line subscriptions, sidestepping the unwillingness of many kiosks to sell it.

48. There is sometimes a fluid boundary between the far right and anti-globalizing Fordist nostalgics. The emergence of conservative, but not right-wing extremist, framing of Fordist nostalgia can be seen in the discourse of the "Party of the Legal-State Offensive" (Partei rechtsstaatlicher Offensive), which won 19 percent of the vote in the recent elections in the city-state of Hamburg (see Jan Feddersen, "Die Rache der Verängstigten," *die tageszeitung* [Berlin], 25 Sep. 2001). On the associations between right-wing movements and anti-globalization politics, see "Right Wing Populism: Too Close for Comfort. An Interview with Chip Berlet and Matthew Lyons by Elaine Wolff," *Parallax Views* (http://www.e- venthori zon.net/democratic_ideologies/rtwing_populism.html).

49. This branch of the movement has been almost completely ignored by the *New York Times,* in contrast to the coverage in the German press. For a detailed and sympathetic discussion of ATTAC, see "'Entwaffnet die Märkte,'" *Der Spiegel* 13 Aug. 2001: 90–91.

50. See especially Bhaskar (1979; 1986; 1997); also Erik Olin Wright's discussion of these issues in Wright et al. (1989: 57–63).

51. It would be possible to combine various theoretical systems into a new

"compound" theory for every empirical analysis, thus avoiding the distinction between theory and explanation. This would provide only a temporary solution, however, as each empirical case would require the elaboration of a new compound theory. The result would be an endless proliferation of highly specialized theories with ridiculously limited ranges of applicability, thus hollowing out the very meaning of theory.

52. See Steinmetz (2005a, 2005b) on the reasons for the widespread preference for parsimonious explanations and empiricist general laws within post-war American social science.

53. An exception to this was Althusser's acceptance of the unconscious as a specific object requiring its own theory; see Althusser (1971).

54. Even if that "lonely hour" never struck. It may seem unfair to single out Marxists for criticism, since they were undoubtedly more sophisticated with respect to these issues than many others. After all, sociologists and political scientists are more frequently accused of throwing together a hodgepodge of "independent variables" in their regression equations with little attention to the theoretical systems from which the variables are derived—an approach that eliminates theory altogether, rather than just collapsing the levels of theory/mechanism and explanation/event. Althusser himself was less reductionist than many of his acolytes, and was able to inspire theorists like Laclau and Mouffe (1985); Žižek (1989); see the special issue of *Rethinking Marxism* (vol. 10, no. 3, Fall 1998), "Rereading Althusser."

55. It also may compare across slightly less abstract modes of regulation, such as Fordism or post-Fordism, but these are not considered to be empirical objects. For a more detailed discussion of critical realism and comparison, see Lawson (1998; 1999) and Steinmetz (2004).

56. The term figurational can be understood in Norbert Elias' (1978) sense as suggesting complex and dynamic process. On conjuncture, see Althusser (1990b), Matheron (1997), and Bhaskar (1979: 54; 1986: 60; 1997: 119, 165).

57. See Prasad (2000) for a closely related analysis of neoliberal restructuring. Of course one can always find evidence for repeatable diffusion if one looks hard enough, as the group around the sociologist John Meyer has shown (see note 20 above). What one is really showing in such cases, however, is not the uniformity of the diffusion process, much less the existence of a "constant conjunction of events," but rather the widespread existence of a similar set of causally effective mechanisms in each local case.

58. For an important intra-Marxist critique of the regulation approach, see Brenner and Glick (1991); cf. also Graham (1991).

59. This need not mean that Marxism is a "regional" theory in the Althusserian sense—for instance, a theory of the economy. I leave open the question of what the home terrain of Marxism really is rather than claiming that regulation theory has the correct answer.

REFERENCES

Aglietta, Michel. 1987. *A Theory of Capitalist Regulation. The U.S. Experience.* London: Verso.

Althusser, Louis. 1970. *Reading Capital.* London: NLB.

———. 1971. "Freud and Lacan." In, *Lenin and Philosophy.* New York: Monthly Review, 189– 219.

———. 1990a. "Contradiction and Overdetermination." In, *For Marx.* London: New Left Books, 87–128.

———. 1990b. "On the Materialist Dialectic." In, *For Marx.* London: New Left Books, 161–218.

———. 1994. "Philosophie et Marxisme: Entretiens avec Fernanda Navarro (1984–1987)." In, *Sur la philosophie.* Paris: Gallimard, 17–79.

Anderson, Benedict. 1983. *Imagined Communities: Reflections on the Origins and Spread of Nationalism.* London: New Left Books.

Arestis, Philip and Eleni Paliginis. 1995. "Fordism, Post-Fordism and Gender." *Economie Appliquée* 48, 1: 89–108.

Arrighi, Giovanni, Terence K. Hopkins, and Immanuel Wallerstein. 1989. *Antisystemic Movements.* London: Verso.

Aust, Stefan. 1997. *Der Baader Meinhof Komplex.* 2d ed. Hoffmann und Campe Verlag.

Badie, Bertrand and Pierre Birnbaum. 1983. *The Sociology of the State.* Chicago: University of Chicago Press.

Bagguley, Paul. 1992. "Social Change, the Middle Class and the Emergence of New Social Movements: A Critical Analysis." *The Sociological Review:* 26–48.

Balibar, Etienne. 1991. "Is There a 'Neo-Racism'?" In, Etienne Balibar and Immanuel Wallerstein, eds., *Race, Nation, Class.* London: Verso, 17–28.

Bark, Dennis L. and David R. Gress. 1989. *From Shadow to Substance 1945–1963,* vol. 1 of *A History of West Germany.* Oxford: Basil Blackwell.

Beck, Ulrich. 1986. *Risikogesellschaft. Auf dem Weg in eine andere Moderne.* Frankfurt am Main: Suhrkamp.

———. 1989. "Risikogesellschaft." *Aus Politik und Zeitgeschichte* 36 (1 Sep.): 3–13.

———, ed. 1991. *Politik in der Risikogesellschaft.* Frankfurt am Main: Suhrkamp.

Bell, Daniel. 1973. *The Coming of Post-Industrial Society.* New York: Basic Books.

Benton, Sarah. 1989. "The Party Is Over." *Marxism Today* (Mar.): 32–37.

Berman, Paul. 2005. *Power and the Idealists: Or, the Passion of Joschka Fischer, and Its Aftermath.* Brooklyn, NY: Soft Skull Press.

Berman, Russell. 1981. "Opposition to Rearmament and West German Culture." *Telos* 51: 141–58.

Bhaskar, Roy. 1979. *The Possibility of Naturalism.* New York: Humanities Press.

———. 1986. *Scientific Realism and Human Emancipation.* London: Verso.

———. 1997 [1975]. *A Realist Theory of Science.* London: Verso.

Blackbourn, David and Geoff Eley. 1985. *The Peculiarities of German History.* New York: Oxford University Press.

Bonefeld, Werner and John Holloway, eds. 1991. *Post-Fordism and Social Form.* London: Macmillan.

Bourdieu, Pierre. 1977. *Outline of a Theory of Praxis.* Cambridge, Mass.: Harvard University Press.

———. 1984. *Distinction.* Cambridge, Mass.: Harvard University Press.

———. 1986. "The Forms of Capital." In, J. C. Richardson, ed., *Handbook of Theory and Research for the Sociology of Education.* New York: Greenwood Press, 241–58.

Bowles, Samuel and Herbert Gintis. 1986. *Democracy and Capitalism.* New York: Basic Books.

Boyer, Robert. 1990. *The Regulation School: A Critical Introduction.* New York: Columbia University Press.

Boyer, Robert and J. Mistral. 1982. *Accumulation, Inflation, Crises.* Paris: Presses Universitaires de France.

Brand, Karl-Werner. 1982. *Neue soziale Bewegungen. Entstehung, Funktion und Perspektive neuer Protestpotentiale. Eine Zwischenbilanz.* Opladen: Westdeutscher Verlag.

Brand, Karl-Werner, Detlef Büsser, and Dieter Rucht. 1986. *Aufbruch in eine andere Gesellschaft. Neue Soziale Bewegungen in der Bundesrepublik.* Frankfurt am Main: Campus.

Brenner, Robert and Mark Glick. 1991. "The Regulation Approach: Theory and History." *New Left Review* 188: 45–119.

Bundesamt für Verfassungsschutz. Various years. *Verfassungsschutzbericht.* Bonn: Bundesministerium des Innern. On-line version at http://www.verfassungs schutz.de.

Butterwegge, Christoph and Horst Isola, eds. 1991. *Rechtsextremismus im vereinten Deutschland. Randerscheinung oder Gefahr für die Demokratie?* Berlin: Links.

Castells, Manuel. 1977. *The Urban Question: A Marxist Approach.* Cambridge, Mass.: MIT Press.

———. 1983. *The City and the Grassroots: A Cross-Cultural Theory of Urban Social Movements.* Berkeley: University of California Press.

———. 1978. *City, Class and Power.* London: Macmillan.

Chanan, Michael, and George Steinmetz. 2005. *Detroit: Ruin of a City.* Bristol, UK: Intellect Books.

Chopra, Ingrid and Gitta Scheller. 1992. "'Die neue Unbeständigkeit.' Ehe und Familie in der spätmodernen Gesellschaft." *Soziale Welt* 3: 48–69.

Chow, Esther Ngan-ling, Doris Wilkinson, and Maxine Baca Zinn. 1996. *Race, Class and Gender: Common Bonds, Different Voices.* Thousand Oaks, Calif.: Sage Publications.

Cohen, Jean. 1985. "Strategy or Identity: New Theoretical Paradigms and Contemporary Social Movements." *Social Research* 52: 663–717.

Collins, Patricia Hill. 1989. "Toward a New Vision: Race, Class and Gender as Categories of Analysis and Connection." Memphis, Tenn.: Research Clearinghouse and Curriculum Integration Project, Center for Research on Women.

Cotgrove, Stephen and Andrew Duff. 1980. "Environmentalism, Middle-Class Radicalism and Politics." *Sociological Review* 28, 2: 333–51.

Dahrendorf, Ralf. 1967. *Society and Democracy in Germany.* Garden City, N.Y.: Doubleday.

Delale, Alain and Gilles Ragache. 1978. *La France de 68.* Paris: Éditions du Seuil.

D'Entrèves, Alexander. 1967. *The Notion of the State.* Oxford: Oxford University Press.

Eder, Klaus. 1985. "The 'New Social Movements': Moral Crusades, Political Pressure Groups, or Social Movements?" *Social Research* 52: 869–90.

Elias, Norbert. 1978. *What is Sociology?* London: Hutchinson.

Elsaesser, Thomas. 1989. *New German Cinema: A History.* New Brunswick, N.J.: Rutgers University Press.

Epstein, Barbara. 1990. "Rethinking Social Movement Theory." *Socialist Review* 20: 35–65.

Escobar, Arturo and Sonia E. Alvarez, eds. 1992. *The Making of Social Movements in Latin America: Identity, Strategy, and Democracy.* Boulder, Colo.: Westview Press.

Fischer, Wolfram. 1987. "Wirtschafts- und sozialgeschichtliche Anmerkungen zum 'deutschen Sonderweg.'" *Tel Aviver Jahrbuch für deutsche Geschichte* 16: 96–116.

Foucault, Michel. 1978. *The History of Sexuality: An Introduction.* New York: Vintage House.

———. *Power/Knowledge.* Gordon Cohn, ed. New York: Parthenon Books.

———. 1989. "Sécurité, territoire et population." In, *Résumé des cours. 1970–1982.* Paris: Juillard, 99–106.

———. 1991. "Governmentality." In, Graham Burchell et al., eds., *The Foucault Effect. Studies in Governmentality.* Chicago: University of Chicago Press, 87–104.

Fraser, Nancy. 1987. "Women, Welfare and the Politics of Need Interpretation." *Hypatia: A Journal of Feminist Philosophy* 2: 103–21.

Graham, Julie 1991. "Fordism/Post-Fordism, Marxism/Post-Marxism: The Second Cultural Divide." *Rethinking Marxism* 4: 39–58.

Gramsci, Antonio. 1971. "Americanism and Fordism." In, *Selections from the Prison Notebooks.* New York: International Publishers, 277–320.

———. 1978. *Cahiers de prison. Cahiers 10, 11, 12, 13* (translation of *Quaderni del Carcere*). Paris: Gallimard.

Grebing, Helga. 1986. *Der 'deutsche Sonderweg' in Europa 1806–1945. Eine Kritik.* Stuttgart: W. Kohlhammer.

Hall, Stuart. 1988. "The Toad in the Garden: Thatcherism among the Theorists."

In, Cary Nelson and Lawrence Grossberg, eds., *Marxism and the Interpretation of Culture*. Urbana: University of Illinois Press, 35–73.

Handler, Joel F. n.d. "Social Protection: The Ambiguity of Decentralization, Privatization, and Empowerment." Ms., U.C.L.A. Law School.

Hardt, Michael and Antonio Negri. 2000. *Empire*. Cambridge, Mass.: Harvard University Press.

Hartford, Barbara and Sarah Hopkins. 1984. *Greenham Common: Women at the Wire*. London: The Women's Press.

Hartmann, Heide. 1981. "The Unhappy Marriage of Marxism and Feminism: Towards a More Progressive Union." In, Lydia Sargent, ed., *Women and Revolution*. Boston: South End Press, 1–42.

Harvey, David. 1989. *The Condition of Postmodernity. An Enquiry into the Origins of Cultural Change*. New York: Basil Blackwell.

Herf, Jeffrey. 1991. *War by Other Means. Soviet Power, West German Resistance, and the Battle of the Euromissles*. New York: The Free Press.

Hirsch, Joachim. 1980. *Der Sicherheitsstaat*. Frankfurt/Main: Europäische Verlagsanstalt.

———. 1981. "The New Leviathan and the Struggle for Democratic Rights." *Telos* 48: 79–89.

———. 1983. "The Fordist Security State and New Social Movements." *Kapitalistate* 10/11: 75–88.

———. 1988. "The Crisis of Fordism, Transformations of the 'Keynesian' Security State, and New Social Movements." In, Louis Kriesberg and Misztal Bronislaw, eds., *Research in Social Movements, Conflicts and Change* 10, 43–55.

———. 1991. "From the Fordist to the Post-Fordist State." In, Bob Jessop et al., eds., *The Politics of Flexibility*, 67–81.

Hirsch, Joachim and Roland Roth. 1986. *Das neue Gesicht des Kapitalismus. Vom Fordismus zum Post-Fordismus*. Hamburg: VSA-Verlag.

———. 1987. "Immer so weiter? Oder: Der Konservatismus der Linken," and "Der Kapitalismus ist enorm Anpassungsfähig" (discussion). *Sozialismus* 5 (May–June): 36–46.

Hoffmann-Axthelm, Dieter, Otto Kallscheuer, Eberhard Knödler-Bunte, and Brigitte Wartmann. n.d. [1978]. *Zwei Kulturen? TUNIX, Mescalero und die Folgen*. Berlin: Verlag Ästhetik und Kommunikation.

Hollander, Paul. 1992. *Anti-Americanism: Critiques at Home and Abroad*. New York: Oxford University Press.

Hubert, Eva. 1983. "Politiker fragen—Bürger antworten nicht! Die Boykottbewegung gegen die Volkszählung." In, Jürgen Taeger, ed., *Die Volkszählung*. Reinbek bei Hamburg: Einhorn, 254–66.

Hübner, Kurt. 1987. "Neue Gesichtszüge?" *Sozialismus* 4 (Apr.–May): 39–44.

Hülsberg, Werner. 1988. *The German Greens. A Social and Political Profile*. London: Verso.

Illich, Ivan et al., eds. 1977. *Disabling Professions.* London: Marion Boyars.

Inglehart, Ronald. 1977. *The Silent Revolution: Changing Values and Political Styles among Western Publics.* Princeton: Princeton University Press.

———. 1990. *Culture Shift in Advanced Industrial Society.* Princeton: Princeton University Press.

Jameson, Fredric. 1992. "Actually Existing Marxism." Unpublished paper, Duke University.

Jessop, Bob. 1983. "Accumulation, State, and Hegemonic Projects." *Kapitalistate* 10/11: 89–112.

———. 1988. "Post-Fordismus. Zur Rezeption der Regulationstheorie bei Joachim Hirsch." *Das Argument:* 380–90.

———. 1989. "Conservative Regimes and the Transition to Post-Fordism: The Cases of Great Britain and West Germany." In, M. Gottdiener and Nicos Komninos, eds., *Capitalist Development and Crisis Theory: Accumulation, Regulation and Spatial Restructuring.* London: Macmillan, 261–99.

———. 1990a. *State Theory. Putting States in Their Place.* University Park, Pa.: Pennsylvania State University Press.

———. 1990b. "Regulation Theories in Retrospect and Prospect." *Economy and Society* 19: 153–216.

Jessop, Bob, et al., eds. 1991. *The Politics of Flexibility. Restructuring State and Industry in Britain, Germany and Scandanavia.* Brookfield, Va.: Edward Elgar.

Katsiaficas, George. 1987. *The Imagination of the New Left. A Global Analysis of the 1960s.* Boston: South End Press.

Katznelson, Ira. 1981. *City Trenches: Urban Politics and the Patterning of Class in the United States.* Chicago: University of Chicago Press.

Kitschelt, Herbert. 1985. "New Social Movements in West Germany and the United States." In, Maurice Zeitlin, ed., *Political Power and Social Theory* 5. Greenwich, Conn.: JAI Press.

———. 1986. "Political Opportunity Structure and Political Protest: Anti-Nuclear Movements in Four Democracies." *British Journal of Political Science* 16: 57–85.

Kivisto, Peter. 1986. "What's New about the 'New Social Movements'?: Continuities and Discontinuities with the Socialist Project." *Mid-American Review of Sociology* 11: 29–43.

Klandermans, Bert and Sidney Tarrow. 1988. "Mobilization into Social Movements: Synthesizing European and American Approaches." *International Social Movement Research* 1: 1–38.

Kocka, Jürgen. 1990. "Revolution und Nation 1989. Zur historischen Einordnung der gegenwärtigen Ereignisse." *Tel Aviver Jahrbuch für deutsche Geschichte* 19: 479–99.

Komitee für Grundrechte und Demokratie. 1982. *Ohne Zweifel für den Staat: die Praxis Zehn Jahre dach dem Radikalenerlass.* Reinbek: Rowohlt.

Kramer, Jane. 1988. "Letter from Europe." *The New Yorker* (28 Nov.): 67–100.

Krasner, Stephen, ed. 1983. *International Regimes.* Ithaca, N.Y.: Cornell University Press.

Kriesi, Hanspeter. 1988. "Local Mobilization for the People's Petition of the Dutch Peace Movement." *International Social Movement Research* 1: 41–81.

————. 1989. "New Social Movements and the New Class in the Netherlands." *American Journal of Sociology* 95: (n.p.).

Laclau, Ernesto and Chantal Mouffe. 1985. *Hegemony and Socialist Strategy. Towards a Radical Democratic Politics.* London: Verso.

————. 1987. "Post-Marxism without Apologies." *New Left Review* 166: 79–106.

Lasch, Christopher. 1978. *The Culture of Narcissism: American Life in an Age of Diminishing Expectations.* New York: Norton.

Lash, Scott and John Urry. 1987. *The End of Organized Capitalism.* Madison: University of Wisconsin Press.

Lau, Christoph. 1991. "Neue Risiken und gesellschaftliche Konflikte." In, Ulrich Beck, ed., *Politik in der Risikogesellschaft.* Frankfurt am Main: Suhrkamp, 248–65.

Lawson, Tony. 1998. Economic Science without Experimentation/Abstraction. In, Margaret Archer et al., eds., *Critical Realism, Essential Readings.* London: Routledge, 144–85.

————. 1999. Feminism, Realism, and Universalism. *Feminist Economics* 5, 2: 25–59.

Lecorte, Tomas. 1992. *Wir tanzen bis zum Ende: Die Geschichte eines Autonomen.* Hamburg: Galgenberg.

Liddington, Jill. 1991. *The Road to Greenham Common. Feminism and Anti-Militarism in Britain since 1820.* Syracuse, N.Y.: Syracuse University Press.

Link, Jürgen. 1992 "Normalismus und Neorassismus." *Das Argument* 195: 714–22.

Lipietz, Alain. 1987. *Mirages and Miracles. The Crises of Global Fordism.* London: Verso.

————. 1991. "Die Beziehungen zwischen Kapital und Arbeit am Vorabend des 21. Jahrhunderts." *Leviathan* 19, 1: 78–101.

Lottmann, Eckart. 2001. "Das Endes eines Traums." *Die tageszeitung (Berlin),* 22 Sep.

Maase, Kaspar. 1992. *BRAVO Amerika: Erkundungen zur Jugendkultur der Bundesrepublik in den fünfziger Jahren.* Hamburg: Junius.

Mahon, Rianne. 1991. "From 'Bringing' to 'Putting': The State in Late Twentieth-Century Social Theory." *Canadian Journal of Sociology* 16: 119–44.

Maier, Charles S. 1987 "Society as Factory." In, *In Search of Stability. Explorations in Historical Political Economy.* Cambridge: Cambridge University Press, 19–69.

Maier, Hans. 1980. *Die ältere deutsche Staats- und Verwaltungslehre.* 2d ed. München: C. H. Beck'sche Verlagsbuchhandlung.

Mandel, Ernest. 1978. *Late Capitalism.* London: Verso.

Martin, William C. 1988. "From Class Challenge to Comfortable Collaboration? Understanding Recent Fluctuations in the Politics of the Educated Middle Class." Ph.D. Dissertation, Department of Sociology, University of Wisconsin-Madison.

Matheron, François. 1997. "Introduction." In, Louis Althusser, *The Spectre of Hegel. Early Writings.* London: Verso, 1–20.

Mattausch, John. 1989. *A Commitment to Campaign: A Sociological Study of the CND.* Manchester: Manchester University Press.

Mayer, Margit. 1991. "Politics in the Post-Fordist City." *Socialist Review* 21: 105–24.

Mayer, Margit and Roland Roth. 1995. "New Social Movements and the Transformation to Post-Fordist Society." In, Marcy Darnovsky, Barbara Epstein, and Richard Flacks, eds., *Cultural Politics and Social Movements.* Philadelphia: Temple University Press, 299–319.

Melucci, Alberto. 1980. "The New Social Movements: A Theoretical Approach." *Social Science Information* 19, 2: 201–26.

———. 1981. "Ten Hypotheses for the Analysis of New Movements." In, Diana Pinto, ed., *Contemporary Italian Sociology.* Cambridge: Cambridge University Press, 173–94.

———. 1984. "An End to Social Movements?" Introductory paper to the sessions on "New Social Movements and Change in Organizational Forms." *Social Science Information* 23: 819–35.

———. 1989. *Nomads of the Present. Social Movements and Individual Needs in Contemporary Society.* Philadelphia: Temple University Press.

Meyer, John W. 1980. "The World Polity and the Authority of the Nation-State." In, A. Bergesen, ed., *Studies of the Modern World-System.* New York: Academic Press.

———. 1999. "The Changing Cultural Context of the Nation-State: A World Society Perspective." In, George Steinmetz, ed., *State/Culture: State Formation after the Cultural Turn.* Ithaca, N.Y.: Cornell University Press, 123–43.

Mohr, Reinhard. 1992. *Zaungäste. Die Generation, die nach der Revolte kam.* Frankfurt am Main: S. Fischer.

Mooser, Joseph. 1983. "Abschied von der 'Proletarität.' Sozialstruktur und Lage der Arbeiterschaft in der Bundesrepublik in historischer Perspektive." In, Werner Conze and M. Rainer Lepsius, eds., *Sozialgeschichte der Bundesrepublik.* Stuttgart: Klett-Cotta, 143–86.

Mouffe, Chantal. 1981. "Radical Democracy: Modern or Postmodern." In, Andrew Ross, ed., *Universal Abandon? The Politics of Postmodernism.* Minneapolis: University of Minnesota Press, 31–45.

Nelkin, Dorothy and Michael Pollak. 1981. *The Atom Besieged: Extraparliamentary Dissent in France and Germany.* Cambridge, Mass.: MIT Press.

Niethammer, Lutz. 1979. "Rekonstruktion und Desintegration: Zum Verstandnis der deutschen Arbeiterbewegung zwischeu Krieg und Kaltem Krieg." *Geschichte und Gesellschaft,* Sonderheft 5, 26–43.

Offe, Claus. 1980. "Konkurrenzpartei und kollektive politische Indentität." In, Roland Roth, ed., *Parlementarisches Ritual und politische Alternativen.* Frankfurt: Campus, 26–42.

———. 1984. "Work: The Key Sociological Category?" In, *Contradictions of the Welfare State.* Cambridge, Mass.: MIT Press, 129–50.

———. 1987. "Challenging the Boundaries of Institutional Politics: Social Movements since the 1960s." In, Charles S. Maier, ed., *Changing Boundaries of the Political.* Cambridge: Cambridge University Press, 63–106.

Panitch, Leo. 1986. "Theories of Corporatism: Reflections on a Growth Industry." In, *Working Class Politics in Crisis.* London: Verso, 160–86.

Pasquino, Pasquale. 1991. "Theatrum Politicum: The Genealogy of Capital—Police and the State of Prosperity." In, Graham Burchell et al., eds., *The Foucault Effect. Studies in Governmentality.* Chicago: University of Chicago Press, 105–18.

Pohrt, Wolfgang. 1982. *Endtstation: Über die Wiedergeburt der Nation.* Berlin: Rotbuch Verlag.

Postone, Moishe. 1993. *Time, Labor and Social Domination: A Reinterpretation of Marx's Critical Theory.* Cambridge: Cambridge University Press.

Poulantzas, Nicos. 1978. *Political Power and Social Classes.* London: Verso.

———. 1980. *State, Power, Socialism.* London: Verso.

Prasad, Monica. 2000. "The Politics of Free Markets. The Rise of Neoliberal Economic Policy in Britain, France, and the United States." Ph.D. dissertation, Department of Sociology, University of Chicago.

Raschke, Joachim. 1985. *Soziale Bewegungen. Ein historisch-systematischer Grundriß.* Frankfurt and New York: Campus.

Rochon, Thomas R. 1988. *Mobilizing for Peace: The Antinuclear Movements in Western Europe.* Princeton: Princeton University Press.

Rosenthal, John. 1988. "Who Practices Hegemony? Class Division and the Subject of Politics." *Cultural Critique,* Spring: 25–52.

Roth, Roland. 1989. "Fordism and New Social Movements." Unpublished paper, Free University of Berlin, Zentralinstitut für wissenschaftliche Forschung.

Ruccio, David F. 1992. "After Communism." *Rethinking Marxism* 5, 2: 7–22.

Rucht, Dieter. 1982. "Neue soziale Bewegungen oder: Die Grenzen bürokratischer Modernisierung." *Politische Vierteljahresschrift, Sonderheft* 13: 272–92.

Sartre, Jean-Paul. 2001. "The Wretched of the Earth." In, *Colonialism and Neocolonialism.* London and New York: Routledge, 136–55.

Scherrer, Christoph. 1989. "Das Fordismus-Theorem der französischen Regulationsschule." Manuscript, Otto-Suhr-Institut, Free University of Berlin.

Schmitt, Rudiger. 1990. *Die Friedensbewegung in der Bundesrepublik Deutschland:*

*Ursachen und Bedingungen der Mobilisierung einer neuen sozialen Bewegung.* Opladen: Westdeutscher Verlag.

Schmitter, Phillipe and Gerhard Lehmbruch, eds. 1979. *Trends toward Corporatist Intermediation.* Beverly Hills, Calif.: Sage.

Schneider, Michael. 1981. "Väter und Söhne, Posthum. Das beschädigte Verhältnis zweier Generationen." In, *Den Kopf verkehrt aufgesetzt oder Die melancholische Linke. Aspekte des Kulturverfalls in den siebziger Jahren.* Darmstadt: Luchterhand, 8–64.

Schröder, Burkhard. 1992. *Rechte Kerle. Skinheads, Faschos, Hooligans.* Reinbek: Rowohlt.

Schroeren, Michael. 1990. *Die Grünen: 10 bewegte Jahre.* Wien: Ueberreuter.

Scott, Joan Wallach. 1988. "The Sears Case." In, *Gender and the Politics of History.* New York: Columbia University Press, 167–77.

Showstack-Sassoon, Anne, ed. 1982. *Approaches to Gramsci.* London: Writers and Readers.

Snow, David A., E. Burke Rochford Jr., Steven K. Worden, and Robert D. Benford. 1986. "Frame Alignment Processes, Micromobilization, and Movement Participation." *American Sociological Review* 51: 464–81.

Snow, David A. and Robert D. Benford. 1988. "Ideology, Frame Resonance, and Participant Mobilization." *International Social Movement Research* 1: 197–217.

Sohrabi, Nader. 1996. "Constitutionalism, Revolution, and State: The Young Turk Revolution of 1908 and the Iranian Constitutional Revolution of 1906 with Comparisons to the Russian Revolution of 1905." Unpublished Ph.D. dissertation, Department of Sociology, University of Chicago.

Somers, Margaret R. 1998. "'We're No Angels': Realism, Rational Choice, and Relationality in Social Science." *The American Journal of Sociology* 104: 722–84.

Steinmetz, George. 1990. "The Myth and the Reality of an Autonomous State: Industrialists, Junkers, and Social Policy in Imperial Germany." *Comparative Social Research* 12: 239–93.

———. 1994. "Die (un)moralische Ökonomie Rechtsextremer Gewalt Im Übergang Zum Postfordismus." *Das Argument* 23 (Jan./Feb.): 23–40.

———. 1997. "Social Class and the Reemergence of the Radical Right in Contemporary Germany." In, John R. Hall, ed., *Reworking Class: Cultures and Institutions of Economic Stratification and Agency.* Ithaca, N.Y.: Cornell University Press, 335–68.

———. 2004. "Odious Comparisons: Incommensurability, the Case Study, and 'Small N's.'" *Sociological Theory* 22, 1.

———. 2005a. "The Epistemological Unconscious of U.S. Sociology and the Transition to Post-fordism: The Case of Historical Sociology." In, Julia Adams, Elizabeth Clemens, and Ann Orloff, eds., *ReMaking Modernity.* Durham, N.C.: Duke University Press, 107–57.

————. 2005b. "Scientific Authority and the Transition to Post-Fordism: The Plausibility of Positivism in American Sociology since 1945." In, George Steinmetz, ed., *The Politics of Method in the Human Sciences: Positivism and Its Epistemological Others.* Durham, N.C.: Duke University Press, 275–323.

————. 2005c. "Fordism." In, John Merriman and Jay Winter, eds. *Encyclopedia of Europe: 1914–2004.* New York, Charles Scribner's Sons.

Taeger, Jürgen, ed. 1983. *Die Volkszählung.* Reinbek bei Hamburg: Einhorn.

Tarrow, Sidney. 1988. "Old Movements in New Cycles of Protest: The Career of an Italian Religious Community." *International Social Movement Research* 1: 281–304.

Tergeist, Peter. 1984. "Berlin (West): Die USA als Besatzer." *Dollars und Träume. Studien zur Politik, Ökonomie, Kultur der USA* 10: 30–41.

Therborn, Göran. 1992. "The Life and Times of Socialism." *New Left Review* 194: 17–32.

Tilly, Charles. 1978. *From Mobilization to Revolution.* Reading, Mass.: Addison-Wesley.

————. 1986. *The Contentious French.* Cambridge, Mass.: Belknap.

Touraine, Alain. 1977. *The Self-Production of Society.* Chicago: University of Chicago Press.

Tucker, Kenneth H. 1991. "How New are the New Social Movements?" *Theory, Culture and Society* 8: 75–98.

Vester, Michael. 1983. "Die 'Neuen Plebjer.' Thesen zur Klassen- und Schichtenstruktur und zu den Entwicklungsperspektiven der neuen sozialen Bewegungen." In, Hans-Hermann Hartwich, ed., *Gesellschaftliche Probleme als Anstoß und Folge von Politik.* Opladen: Westdeutscher Verlag, 215–16.

Vieten, Günter C. 1983. "Holland—ein Land läßt sich nicht zählen." In, Jürgen Taeger, ed., *Die Volkszählung.* Reinbek bei Hamburg: Einhorn, 270–82.

Wagner, Hilde and Peter Stahn. 1987. "Das neue Gesicht des Kapitalismus. Debatte des neuen Theorieentwurfs von Joachim Hirsch und Roland Roth." *Sozialismus* 4 (Apr.–May): 29–38.

Wallerstein, Immanuel. 1983. *Historical Capitalism.* London: Verso.

Weakliem, David. 1991. "The Two Lefts? Occupation and Party Choice in France, Italy, and the Netherlands." *American Journal of Sociology* 96: 1327–61.

Weber, Max. 1947 [1921–1922]. "Class, Status, Power." In, H. H. Gerth and C.-Wright Mills, eds., *From Max Weber: Essays in Sociology.* New York: Oxford, 180–95.

Wehier, Hans-Ulrich. 1985. *The German Empire 1871–1918.* Leamington Spa: Berg.

Weir, Margaret and Theda Skocpol. 1985. "State Structures and the Possibilities of 'Keynesian' Responses to the Great Depression in Sweden, Britain and the United States." In, Peter B. Evans, Dietrich Rueschmayer, and Theda Skocpol, eds., *Bringing the State Back In.* New York: Cambridge University Press, 107–63.

Wilde, Lawrence. 1990. "Class Analysis and the Politics of New Social Movements." *Capital and Class* 42: 55–78.

Wiley, Norbert. 1970. "America's Unique Class Politics." In, Edward Laumann, Paul Siegel, and Robert Hodge, eds., *The Logic of Social Hierarchies.* Markham.

Winkler, Heinrich August. 1990. "Mit Skepsis zur Einigung." *Die Zeit* 40 (28 Sep.): 8–9.

Wittner, Lawrence S. 1988. "The Transnational Movement against Nuclear Weapons, 1945–1986: A Preliminary Survey." In, Charles Chatfield and Peter van den Dungen, eds., *Peace Movements and Political Cultures.* Knoxville, Tenn.: University of Tennessee Press, 265–94.

Wright, Erik Olin. 1978. *Class, Crisis, and the State.* London: Verso.

———. 1985. *Classes.* London: Verso.

———. 1987. "Towards a Post-Marxist Radical Social Theory." *Contemporary Sociology* 16, 5: 748–53.

Wright, Erik Olin, et al. 1989. *The Debate on Classes.* London: Verso Books.

Žižek, Slavoj. 1989. *The Sublime Object of Ideology.* New York: Verso.

# The Case for Comparing Histories

*Raymond Grew*

Historical comparison has been widely praised by many of the best minds of the historical profession. Marc Bloch, whose prestige and influence have increased since his death, called for historians to work comparatively in a famous article published over fifty years ago,[1] and Lord Acton argued for historical comparison fifty years before that.[2] Indeed, the pedigree of that approach could be extended back through William Robertson and Adam Smith to Montesquieu, Vico, and Machiavelli and on to Polybius and Herodotus. Auguste Comte, that often disowned father of social science, considered comparison to be the highest form of observation and, when undertaken through "the historical method," believed it "the only basis on which the system of political logic can rest" as well as the method that would provide "philosophic character to sociology in a logical as well as a scientific sense."[3] And Marxism, perhaps even more today than in the past, is a powerful stimulus to historical comparison.

Admittedly, however, for many professional historians comparative study evokes the ambivalence of a good bourgeois toward the best wines: to appreciate them is a sign of good taste, but indulgence seems a little loose and wasteful. In part, such hesitance reflects some of the admirable if modest qualities most widely respected and fully shared within the historical profession—caution, accuracy, unpretentiousness, and respect for the integrity of documents and for the particular. In part, it reflects doubt not so much about comparison as a mode of analysis as about what it is that historians should compare. For most historians, the models that come readily to mind are troubling.

"Comparative history"—a term so compromised that, throughout the program for the Ninety-Third Annual Meeting of the American Historical

ᵗᵉʳ 1978, it was properly wrapped in quotation
ᵈ the comparison of civilizations, comparison on
manner of Spengler, Sorokin, and Toynbee. These
ᵉs part of Europe's encounter with the rest of the
o world wars, remain stimulating and provocative for
ᵉarch for the morphology of history is not intimately
ₙost practicing historians really do, very few of whom
ₜ "the most important task of the scientific study of history
ₙparative study of the development of whole civilizations."
ᵍent book Philip Bagby went on to declare, "The actual tech-
ᵉscribing cultural ideas and values is a fairly simple one. It con-
ₛting all or, at least, a number of the forms of cultural behaviour,
ₗ       ᵉch, and actions in which they are expressed, and the artifacts
which result from such behaviour."[4] And any reader knows immediately
that this student of A. L. Kroeber is not a historian.

When civilizations are compared primarily in terms of certain central
topics, the historian is on more familiar ground. Comparison, then, as in
the *grands thèmes* of international historical congresses, merely treats
familiar concerns on a broader scale. Comparative religion or the relations
of state and society are subjects of great classics of historical literature,
especially in German, and, even when segregated as philosophy of history,
such sweeping interests have animated whole schools of study. If as historians we like to call these approaches philosophy, it is because they seem,
even after more than a century of remarkable works that deny the distinction, to rest less on what historians call research than on what the very
learned already know (in short, on the state of our culture), on the wise
discernment of patterns, and on the generation of fresh hypotheses.

A third well-recognized mode of comparison treats not whole civilizations or major aspects of them but historical processes. These can range
enormously in scope, from comparative study of the "alternative modes of
production"[5] to the pace and degree of industrialization in a single industry; from the comparison of revolutions,[6] a subject of undying popularity,
to the comparison of processes still more closely defined, such as the
spread of modern educational systems.[7] This sort of historical comparison
is especially congenial to economics, sociology, and some schools of
anthropology; and, as with the now much-criticized concept of "modernization," such comparisons lead to exchanges of methods and data, interest in common problems, and a shared vocabulary that have lasting
benefits.[8] Many of the most often-cited works of recent historical compar-

ison belong in this category, although, significantly enough, most have not been written by scholars professionally trained as historians.[9]

Yet the comparison of historical processes also evokes resistance, even suspicion, among many historians. Much of that suspicion may result from methodological naiveté, intuitive nominalism, or sheer prejudice; but weightier concerns informed by an awareness of the common nineteenth-century roots of all of the social sciences also seem to be involved. Nothing is more awkwardly old-fashioned than optimism no longer felt—in this case about the nature of social knowledge, the validity of universal laws, and the meaning of history. Furthermore, our professional distaste for easy determinism deserves serious consideration on methodological grounds. Historical determinism has been one of the great spurs to comparison among Hegelians and materialists and from Buckle, Tylor, Spencer, Maine, and Morgan to the present day,[10] for determinism implies the existence of destinies and definable laws that comparison should be able to uncover. But determinism can also place an early limit on the power of comparison to uncover surprises or display variety and, thereby, to redefine traditional problems.

The nineteenth-century evolutionists tended in practice to compare stages of evolution or other analytic abstractions, and this dependence on definition is further reason for historians' discomfort. Sensitive to the differences that chronology makes, historians are bound to wonder whether a process remains the same when it lasts for decades in one instance and for centuries in another or when it occurs in different eras altogether. Are two sets of events comparable because both are called revolutions or are the crises, revolutions, and cycles assembled for analysis mere homonyms (a kind of comparison that Marc Bloch warned against), a humorless misunderstanding of a historical pun? The answer, of course, is that the validity of any comparison rests on careful definitions against which the elements compared must be systematically tested. This obvious methodological solution explains why so much of the effort in works comparing historical process is taxonomic, why so much of the actual comparison is of categories and classifications.

These problems are reduced if institutions are the unit of comparison; and much of the best work, especially in premodern history, is of this sort. But institutions that go by common names of church or party or bank may, in fact, perform quite different functions in different societies or at different times. Structural-functionalism in anthropology and sociology has helped clarify this problem and has been effectively used especially by historians of political parties and economic development.[11] Ultimately, however, social functions, like most analytic abstractions, raise for historians the taxonomic discomfort of categories that seem to lie outside the field of study (the workday historian is likely to complain of "imposing" something on the past). The emphasis on structural analysis now more in vogue lessens the abstractness, for structures are more easily tied to specific behavior. Studies of the crowd, for example, were received into the historical canon primarily as ideology[12] until Marxian concern for class differences led historians to seek a firm relationship among particular crowds, their behavior, and specific conditions. Then the comparison of crowds became especially fruitful. Yet the search for structures is vulnerable to a subtle determinism that invites merely secondary interest in *mentalités* or cultural values, and historians are wisely sensitive to modes of analysis that too readily limit or exclude. If the comparison of processes calls attention to the problems of definition, so the comparison of structures calls attention to the dangers of abstractness.

Methodological sophistication in matters of morphology and taxonomy or typology can be of great value in historical analysis, and I assume no historian so benighted as to denounce the effort in advance would have chosen to read this far. But such analytic tools require—it is their very purpose—fitting bits of history into categories already established, and conceptually that is uncongenial for most historians, even though in practice we do this all the time. It may not be more "artificial" to define a topic in terms of the available historical sources, traditional political boundaries, or conventional chronology; but historians, like everyone else, notice more readily that to which they are unaccustomed. To start with fixed categories is to admit to approaching history from the outside. To the historically sensitive, however great their gift for theory, this is not a comfortable way to work. "Events strikingly similar but occurring in a different historical milieu," wrote Karl Marx in 1877, "lead to completely different results." And, he added, "By studying each of these evolutions separately and then comparing them, it is easier to find the key to the understanding of this phenomenon; but it is never possible to arrive at this understanding by using the passe-partout of some universal historical-philosophical theory whose great virtue is to stand above history."[13] The common impression that historical comparison requires just such an approach—that it consists in comparing groups or events, institutions or ideas that in the abstract have been labeled as comparable—may in large part account for the scarcity of systematic comparison in historical writing. Significantly, the comparisons most admired and accepted tend to be of the sort that emerge in the works of Jacob Burckhardt, R. R. Palmer, or Fernand Braudel, studies whose scope was not determined by categories of comparison but that used a framework already familiar and acceptable and also large enough to include space for comparative analysis.

The willingness to compare societies rests, most attractively, on the assumption of a certain universality in the human condition, on the belief that, just as individuals and societies can learn from each other, we can learn by comparing human behavior in similar or different contexts. One of the more admirable of our own cultural traditions is thus reinforced in our times by easier communication and the methods of social science. And I believe one sees an increasing tendency among Western scholars to acknowledge, at least in their footnotes, the relevance of the African or Indian or Chinese experience to the understanding of our own behavior. Heirs of the nineteenth century, when national differences seemed fundamental, and nowadays surrounded by an intense ethnic consciousness, we have a special need for cross-national comparisons. Significantly, they remain more common in medieval than in modern history, in the study of Europe than in that of the United States. In the writing of American history it is surprising, as John Higham has commented, not that comparison "should at last have begun to flourish, but that it should have been so long delayed."[14] So great, then, is the need that "comparative history" is often taken to mean comparison between nations,[15] which has the paradoxical effect of reinforcing the tendency to consider nations the major unit of analysis. That, in turn, has discouraged comparison by those who prefer to work in primary sources; for it makes comparison seem to require an equally intimate knowledge of at least two societies, two languages, two distinct traditions of record-keeping and interpretation. Few historians are willing to abandon the benefits of a specialization that has enormously expanded historical knowledge and sophistication.[16] It is therefore important to stress that many of the benefits of comparison can result from studies in which all of the cases fall within a single nation but exemplify differences in time or space or social group or even in which the cases compared have not been investigated at equal depth. Comparative analysis, like the architect's compass, is no less useful a tool of design when the legs on which it stands are of unequal length.

Because, among professional historians, comparison is more widely admired than consciously practiced, it may be useful to set forth a fairly simple and unpretentious case for thinking about history comparatively, one that need not arouse inherited doubts and suspicions. Some of the simpler advantages of comparison are more apparent in the other social sciences. For those dealing with contemporary issues in another society, the dangers of ethnocentrism, mistranslation of culturally imbedded meanings, and false assumptions of comparability are immediate. Historians—usually analyzing a world different from the one in which they live, experienced in the culture they study, and guided by scholarly (and cultural) lore—often avoid the most blatant forms of these errors without once shuddering at the peril they missed. And when, a generation later, the historian in turn is recognized to have reflected his own times, history—the most cumulative of the social sciences in knowledge if not in method—seems hardly to have been harmed. Yet comparison, for the historian too, can help prevent the misinterpretation of other cultures.[17]

That comparison is central to any scientific method has become a truism;[18] and logicians like to point out that to declare anything unique, supposedly a penchant of historians, is by implication to compare it to a class of things to which it purportedly belongs. All historical narrative rests on some assumptions as to what constitutes normal behavior and what others have done in similar circumstances. In addition, the most consistently fruitful source of new insight into the past is probably the historian's own experience of the present. (How revealing it is that we speak of a scholar's gaining or providing a fresh perspective.) Striving for objectivity in our finished analyses, we tend to admit our grounding in the present a bit shamefacedly; but it can, like hindsight or the fact that the historian is always something of an outsider, be a welcome asset, an aid to good comparison. Similarly, the historian's preoccupation with change is a commitment to comparison. Thus, the need to compare and the habit of doing it are a large part of the practice that makes history a discipline, that enables an "experienced" historian to judge a piece of scholarship in a distant field of history. This is done by assessing the significance of the problem posed, the importance of the argument made, and the quality of the evidence presented largely by a series of comparisons both with other scholarly works and with other sets of historical problems. In short, history can be substituted for sociology in Émile Durkheim's dictum, "Comparative sociology is not a particular branch of sociology; it is sociology itself, in so far as it ceases to be purely descriptive and aspires to account for the facts."[19]

In the broadest sense, then, comparison is unavoidable. The question is not so much whether historians should make comparisons but whether the study of history benefits when those comparisons are made consciously and sometimes even systematically. Deliberately used, comparison can aid historians at four stages of their work: (1) in asking questions, (2) in identifying historical problems, (3) in designing the appropriate research, and (4) in reaching and testing significant conclusions.

In even a single piece of research, the historian may use many quite different comparisons in quite different ways. First, the initial stage of truly original historical research is the focused curiosity that comes with the asking of fresh questions. And comparison is probably their most consistent source, suggesting by examples that what looks like change may be continuity or that things seemingly unrelated may be connected. To look at other cases is to see other outcomes. By considering them, the historian wins some freedom from the tyranny of what happened and develops that awareness of alternatives—of a missing revolution, of banks that were not formed, of parliaments that did not meet, of populations that failed to increase—that underlies some of the most provocative of historical questions. We are easily blinded by the obvious. As Bloch noted of German and French ways of dividing property in the Middle Ages, either pattern studied by itself would seem natural; only comparison establishes that there is something to be explained.[20] When the historiography of one time and place develops a rich set of analytic categories, their very effectiveness tends to foreclose "inapplicable" questions—until, that is, the historical imagination is stimulated anew by the surprises that follow from applying to familiar issues some categories of questions evolved in another context. No less a thinker than Charles Darwin, one of the most effective users of comparison, expressed admiration for the brilliance of Henry Thomas Buckle (although soon adding, "I doubt that his generalizations are worth anything"),[21] and we should consider the nature of that brilliance. Confident in historical laws, Buckle was eager to seek evidence everywhere and so willing to rub one fact against another that he expanded the range of historical curiosity to touch in a few pages on climate and crime, ballads, philology, the price of wheat, the influence of the clergy, the causes of dueling, the impact of the theater, and the importance of colonies. When comparison has uncovered interrelationships usually overlooked, its effect is also to increase awareness of the differences between cases—a result often more fruitful than the initial impression of similarities. In all of these ways, comparison can lead to good historical questions. Now it may not matter how these questions are arrived at or what prejudices or misconceptions have stimulated this new awareness; but most of us need more than a falling apple. In adopting historical comparison we can make use of, for our purposes, the best thought in other fields.[22]

The purpose of posing questions is to identify historical problems that merit further research, a second stage of the historian's work. Once certain clusters of questions are identified as interrelated in ways that constitute a problem or problems for which solutions should be sought, comparison can be used with somewhat greater deliberation to determine which historical elements from an infinite variety ought to be included. Here, too, comparison is a means to breaking out of the trenches dug by received conceptions, but it should bring to bear the experience of other times and places and the work of other scholars in defining the unit of study justifying, in effect, these particular cuts across history's seamless web. Conceived comparatively, the historical problem is then more likely to determine the scope of the research—investigation that may require chronological, geographical, and social dimensions that are quite unconventional. (Acton and Bloch particularly stressed the need to use comparison to overcome the national particularism built into European historiography.) It is important to understand that the first essential of sound comparison is well-defined categories of analysis and that these, simply by being too broad or too narrow for the problem at hand, can make it difficult to uncover anything new through comparison.

In a third stage, the establishment of a research design, comparison can be used to suggest by example the applicability of evidence and methods that might otherwise be overlooked, although they have worked well elsewhere, and to search for critical variables. As most of its advocates have insisted, systematic historical comparison should often stimulate new attention to the details of individual cases and to local studies.[23] Truly original historical analysis usually strives to build its arguments from the inside out, and we should not allow the daring use of sweeping comparisons (more often ventured in our sister social sciences) to create a misimpression that comparison only moves from the abstract to the particular. To ask historians to work comparatively is not to uproot them from their sources (nor to embrace the desiccation that would be likely to follow). Whereas concern for detailed accuracy can bury significance under trivia, comparison can make the apparently trivial significant—an asset few of us can afford to ignore. As the problem is defined and a design for research established, strategies of comparison become more formal. Proper concern for the complexity of a particular context may invite comparison of its major elements with many different cases; the task is then to see wholes and compare parts[24] (for all of the majesty of his effort, Arnold Toynbee often exemplified the dangers of doing the reverse).

When research leads to the recognition of general patterns, formal hypotheses, or full-fledged theories, these can again be tested by comparison—this time in ways as methodologically systematic as possible. This fourth and most formal stage of comparison is the one most written about in works on method. But comparison can be claimed to be the historian's (or the social scientist's) form of experiment in the multiple tasks of preliminary soundings and research design as well as verification. These multiple uses of comparison form a continuum, as do the differences in scale from one instance seen comparatively to many and from comparisons within one society to those that move across countries, cultures, or time. The value of any historical comparison rests not on the importance of the cases compared or on their number or scope but on the quality of the discernment, of the research, and of the general statements that result.

This is not to say that all valuable historical work must be consciously comparative. The absolutely essential effort to determine what happened and in what sequence or to assess the validity of suspect evidence need not involve historical comparison, except in the broad sense that judgment always has some comparative elements. Nor is the scholar working on a single case so likely to use comparison when the problems posed have been fully set by historiographical tradition. Invaluable contributions have, nevertheless, been made in these ways.

The case for comparison should conclude, however, by noting that the various levels and kinds of conscious historical comparison contribute to the endless task of building a science of society, and they do so most importantly in a relatively straightforward way. The slow, concrete construction of a common vocabulary enables students of different societies working from different disciplines to speak to each other.[25] Sometimes we can even work from a shared set of questions to create the kind of dialogue that is the essence of science. We must not claim too much, for the projects devoted to interdisciplinary research during the last thirty years give reason for modesty as well as hope. Neither need we reject the vision of working to establish a common questionnaire,[26] of sharing the excitement of the hunt as well as the published reports of the kill.

In light of such broad yet gentle claims for the benefits of comparison, it is possible to say something about when historical comparison works best. For instance, it is my impression—to select two fields safely distant—that the results of comparison have been more striking and consistent in the history of art than in the history of literature. Literature, like history itself, is so easily understood as encompassing most of life that problems of focus and selectivity can be overwhelming, reinforcing a tendency we all share to let the traditions of academic monographs rather than independent analysis shape our topics. Yet there are many works of comparative literature every historian might envy. If most of us cannot assume the brilliance or adopt the erudition of Renato Poggioli or Northrop Frye,[27] we can learn from the skill with which they use the concept of established literary forms (much as historians use the idea of institutions) and mastery of rhetoric (much as sociologists use methodology). In only one respect do they enjoy an inherent advantage denied most historians: they may assume that their readers are already familiar with some of their primary sources. At more ordinary levels of scholarship, however, comparison in art history seems more often to have led to new discoveries. Perhaps because painting and sculpture, which are more removed from common discourse, are more abstractly understood, because the artistic medium itself is more expressly limiting yet universal, and because its functions and symbolic structure are more formal, the elements of comparison can be more readily defined with regard to art than to literature.

Or, closer to home, the comparisons of national character, once so fashionable, have been largely abandoned because too many different things were compared at once, leaving rules of evidence so loose that the relationship of doubtful assumption and descriptive example was circular. Demography, on the other hand, enjoys its current triumph in large part because universal elements in human biology and numerous cases permit the supreme comparability and subtle analysis of quantification, with which it is possible to distinguish significant social differences. Nevertheless, historical studies of the family have proved effective when focused on particular, well-defined problems, less so when too broadly aimed.

Similarly, the magnificent sweep of Jungian categories is only on occasion and with difficulty tied to the kind of evidence with which historians deal. Psychohistorical studies of individuals, however, are likely to leap from the absolutely particular to Freudian categories that group many cases without necessarily inviting historical comparison. When, however, psychological analysis points to social roles in specific contexts (families, generations, children, or true believers), then very fruitful historical comparisons can follow.

On the whole, historical comparison seems most effective at a kind of middle range.[28] The term is imprecise, but obviously comparison is most enlightening when the choice of what to compare is made in terms of general and significant problems, the elements compared are clearly distinguished, and attention is paid to the intricate relationships between the elements compared and the particular societies in which they are located. These criteria are most likely to be met when there are modes or theories that can be concretely applied, when the evidence is extensive and rooted in its historical context (which often means that it has been generated with just these problems in view), and when the cases are delimited. Then one seeks explanations and generalizations but not universal laws. The search is for patterns of behavior and circumscribed hypotheses, and it is as likely to result in the recognition of unexpected connections between aspects of society previously thought to be unrelated as in general theory. In practice, the importance of such findings will more often be measured by the stimulus they give to subsequent research than by formal validation.

As a faintly empirical appraisal of the sort of work currently being done in this middle range, I have attempted to analyze the last five hundred manuscripts submitted to the quarterly journal *Comparative Studies in Society and History*. Obviously, any single publication develops its own traditions and is unlikely to be very precisely representative; furthermore, although these five hundred authors come from some thirty countries, nearly two-thirds of them either are citizens of the United States or are teaching at American universities. Among these manuscripts, there is surprisingly little difference between the kinds of topics chosen by historians and those favored by sociologists, political scientists, and anthropologists. Nor is there, incidentally, any difference between the topics of that small fraction of manuscripts selected for publication and all of the rest: the printed articles tend simply to provide more carefully developed arguments (or models) and to rest on more extensive and suggestive research. Paradoxically, the ones rejected are often among the most deliberately comparative, turned down because readers felt a rather mechanical application of someone else's categories had added little either to general theory or to the understanding of particular cases.

For what it is worth, I think I see in these five hundred manuscripts support for seven general statements about the current practice of historical comparison.

1. Matters colonial constitute much the favorite subject matter, a sobering reminder of the extent to which all of the social sciences are

influenced by contemporary politics and how much the impetus to comparative study was stimulated by the West's imperial encounters with other societies (although Greece and Rome, ancient Egypt, and China have exercised a similar attraction). And a more intrinsic reason probably underlies this emphasis: the colonial experience offers a degree of analytic control not usually available to social scientists; new influences and pressures can be identified and their assimilation, distortion, or rejection can be traced. One can, perhaps with misleading ease, identify the source of social change. A similar set of advantages, I think, makes the study of ethnic or religious minorities and of migration popular; the subject may appeal to academic sensibilities, but the cases themselves, while speaking to the most universal social issues, have a closed quality that allows a distinction between internally generated and externally stimulated change and that makes more visible the confluence of old customs and ideologies with new social and political needs (the complex experience of Israel may have stimulated more good comparative study than that of any other modern nation). In historical comparison, cases that in themselves allow a kind of experimental control, that segregate certain variables from the larger social flow, offer particular advantages.

2. Articles on currently fashionable topics (such as women's history, birth control, crime, terrorism, or social services) are so frequent as to suggest something more than the latest style; comparative analysis of historical cases is especially valuable in building new sets of questions into a field of study and in connecting these questions to the established literature. Social history in general has been associated with comparative study for many reasons. It has emphasized the material circumstances that condition people's lives, and these are relatively easy to compare. It has sought to analyze social structures and, in doing so, has effectively used categories, concepts, and theories developed first by economists, sociologists, and anthropologists, making comparison at least implicit at every stage of research. Social history has welcomed quantitative methods, which facilitate comparison (and also its misuse); and relating specific phenomena to a larger society is an intrinsically comparative effort. Social historians, attentive to classes that have not left a rich, written record of their culture, are readily pushed to comparison when little encumbered by knowledge of the complexity of the lives led by anonymous people who have been seen from the first as an abstract type. Most simply, social historians have welcomed compari-

son as they saw themselves building a new subdiscipline. This may well mean that attention to comparison within social history will decline as it becomes an established field, an increasing number of whose scholars will choose to pursue in a single context questions already well developed.

3. Whenever a body of theory is already well established, it becomes easier to discern the significant elements of a particular case; empirical studies of slavery, millenarianism, land tenure, or revolution, for example, thereby gain strength. The use of theory has also become more sophisticated, and the suggestion that some general theory exists, which might be applied to real social experiences, no longer is likely in itself to seem exciting (another reason comparative study is needed). Rather, theoretical ideas are used more familiarly to illumine specific research and in somewhat scholastic logical exercises.

4. Comparative study offers a special stimulus to—and benefits by—relating categories of analysis usually left separate: peasants or workers and the larger culture, ethnic consciousness and economic structure are examples. For all of these reasons, historical comparison seems likely to flourish in the next decade or two among those analyzing the intersection of social structure and culture, the relationship of high to popular culture, and the employment of economic and political power in international relations. Important theoretical questions are at stake in each topic, and concrete comparative analysis is needed to determine where the critical connections and problems are.

5. Most of the articles submitted to *Comparative Studies in Society and History* give full attention only to a single historical case; the next largest group treats several cases across time but within a single society, and such articles are followed by those that are essentially theoretical. The minority that give equal attention to cases from several different societies are not necessarily those that most effectively use comparison to make new discoveries.

6. Although most of the authors submitting manuscripts seem to believe that social structures are more important than social attitudes, or at least are more respectable as a subject for analysis, attitudes and ideas frequently receive more space. Many explanations leap to mind, but it is possible that, whereas our vocabulary for the analysis of social structures tends to underscore the similarities between cases, it is the differences (which are more readily expressed in terms of attitudes) that are more interesting.

7. Finally, the established interests of social scientists—mobility, political behavior, law, education, religious movements, and, even more suspect, modernization or revolution—can still, through systematic comparisons, provide the occasion for fresh and exciting new understanding.

These considerations of comparative study in history—of the ways in which it is commonly understood and the somewhat different ways in which it is more often effectively practiced bring us back to questions of method. To have dealt with that more directly might have embarrassingly shortened this essay: there is no comparative method in history.[29] "The comparative method" is a phrase as redolent of the nineteenth century as "the historical method" with which it was once nearly synonymous. For historians, at least, the idea of comparison still needs to be demystified. Abstract discussion of historical comparison makes it seem so demanding in terms of knowledge and method and so taxing and complicated a procedure that only the most immodest could feel capable of attempting it and all of the rest are excused from trying. Indeed, scholars reluctant to break the framework of received opinions have an interest in adopting that view. But historical comparison is no more attached to a single method than is the discipline of history itself.

John Stuart Mill's oft-cited distinction between the Method of Agreement and the Method of Difference is a contribution to logic, but it leaves the way open to different kinds of comparisons according to whether one is exploring new questions, defining a problem, isolating a single variable, identifying general patterns, or testing a hypothesis. The criteria for selecting which elements to compare, for checking the internal logic of the analysis, or for determining the relevance of the evidence used are not fundamentally different for comparison than for social analysis of any sort. There are not even general rules, except those of logic, and they apply differently according to one's purpose, as to whether it is better to compare cases that are similar or contrasting, neighboring or distant, synchronic or diachronic.[30]

To call for comparison is to call for a kind of attitude—open, questioning, searching—and to suggest some practices that may nourish it, to ask historians to think in terms of problems and dare to define those problems independently, and to assert that even the narrowest research should be conceived in terms of the larger quests of many scholars in many fields. To call for comparison, however, says almost nothing about how to do any of this well.[31] In the United States, the excitement of comparison may be found more often in classrooms than in print and in the colleges where a few teach broadly than in the universities where many research narrowly. It may even be that this use of comparison is stimulating some of the venturesome work of younger scholars.

To admit that comparison contains no special method is not to say that methodology is unimportant. The search for problems is more than blind intuition and will benefit from the most formal methods applicable. Nor is the search for patterns mad empiricism, for it should welcome models and hypotheses that are as well developed as possible. Methods behavioral, quantitative, inductive, and even deductive, formal models, and theories of change can all be applied to comparative study and used to guide the historian in determining when comparisons support generalization and when generalization can be stretched to theory. Even the historian's concern for whether a hypothesis really fits a given context can be a disciplined test.[32]

Not only is comparison not a method, but "comparative history" is a term better avoided. In his famous call for comparison, Marc Bloch warned he would put forth no "new panacea," and it is worth noting that he spoke of *histoire comparée,* not *histoire comparative.* For historians to think comparatively, to compare histories, is to do what we already do—a little more consciously and on a somewhat broader plane. It is not to embrace some new type or genre of historical investigation. Bloch cited Fustel de Coulange's aphorism that a day of synthesis requires years of analysis, quickly adding that "analysis can be used for synthetic purposes only if it intends from the outset to contribute to such a synthesis."[33] That warning points to the essence of historical comparison—the conduct of research and the presentation of findings in the context of a larger continuing discourse about the nature of society.

There is thus no paradox in insisting that the study of a single case can be comparative.[34] The use of common terms and recognizable categories assumes comparison. The search for patterns implies comparison by seeking regularities in the behavior and issues common to a certain set—a kind of group, institution, or form of social organization—or common to a certain process.[35] In searching for patterns the historian is following François Simiand's injunction of seventy-five years ago to study classes of problems. Elegant solutions to problems carefully posed invite further comparisons, the testing of patterns and hypotheses that is most generally recognized as a form of experiment.[36] At its best, the practice of comparison can lead toward that *histoire générale* for which Lucien Febvre argued and also establish agenda for concrete, new research. At its least, comparison is an effective device for removing the inexcusable blinders of parochialism.

Articles and books need not do all of this explicitly, and, happily, it is impossible to list all possible comparisons relevant to any single case. But authors and readers who think in comparative terms enlarge the communication on which science rests. Even their tacit comparison eases the task of integrating concepts and methods from different disciplines by providing common categories of analysis and a common focus, the most effective counterweight to the penalties of specialization. Within the framework of comparison a dialogue and even a kind of teamwork can then cut across our disciplinary divisions. Arthur Wright once said that for the Chinese the discovery of comparative history and comparative sociology "was revolutionary in its effects on historical studies."[37] We would do well to work to make that revolution permanent in its historical home.

## NOTES

Acknowledgements: This paper was originally published in 1980 in *The American Historical Review* (85, 4: 763–78). I thank the editors there for permission to reprint it in this volume. An earlier version of the article was presented as a paper at the Ninety-Third Annual Meeting of the American Historical Association, held in San Francisco, December 1978. I am grateful to a number of colleagues—especially Marvin Becker, David Bien, Robin Jacoby, and Sylvia Thrupp—for stimulating criticism.

1. Bloch, "Pour une histoire comparée des sociétés européennes," paper delivered at the Sixth International Congress of Historical Sciences, held in Oslo, August 1928, printed in the *Revue de synthèse historique* 46 (1928): 15–50, and reprinted in Bloch, *Mélanges historiques* 1 (Paris, 1963): 16–40. For an English version, see Bloch, "Toward a Comparative History of European Societies," trans. Jelle C. Riemersma, in, Frederic C. Lane and Jelle C. Riemersma, eds., *Enterprise and Secular Change. Readings in Economic History* (Homewood, Ill., 1953), 494–521.

2. "The process of Civilization depends on transcending Nationality. Everything is tried by more courts, before a larger audience. Comparative methods are applied. Influences which are accidental yield to those which are rational." Note of Lord Acton, University of Michigan, Add. MSS 4908. Sylvia Thrupp used Acton's statement to begin the first issue of *Comparative Studies in Society and History: An International Journal,* in October 1958.

3. Comte, *Cours de philosophie positive,* in, Gertrud Lenzer, ed., *Auguste Comte and Positivism: The Essential Writings* (New York, 1975), 247, 249.

4. Bagby, *Culture and History: Prolegomena to the Comparative Study of Civilizations* (Berkeley and Los Angeles, 1963), 190, 192.

5. Immanuel M. Wallerstein has called for this sort of comparative study; see his "Modernization: Requiescat in Pace," in, L. Coser and O. Larson, eds., *The Uses of Controversy in Sociology* (New York, 1976), as quoted in Barbara Hockey Kaplan, ed., Introduction to *Social Change in the Capitalist World Economy* (Beverly Hills, 1978), 10–11.

6. For some recent approaches, see the articles by Perez Zagorin, Theda Skocpol, and Elbaki Hermassi, in *Comparative Studies in Society and History* 18 (1976).

7. See Michalina Vaughan and Margaret Scott Archer, *Social Conflict and Educational Change in England and France, 1789–1848* (Cambridge, 1971).

8. For some assessments of the continuing debate on modernization and its implications for comparison, see the April 1978 issue of *Comparative Studies in Society and History,* which was devoted to that question, and note the earlier articles mentioned in the Editorial Foreword, *ibid.*

9. Among others, see the works of S. N. Eisenstadt, Michel Foucault, Samuel P. Huntington, Barrington Moore, Charles Tilly, and Immanuel Wallerstein and of the Committee on Comparative Politics of the Social Science Research Council.

10. See J. W. Burrow, *Evolution and Society: A Study of Victorian Social Thought* (Cambridge, 1966); and Maurice Mandelbaum, *History, Man, & Reason: A Study in Nineteenth-Century Thought* (Baltimore, 1971).

11. S. N. Eisenstadt has seen both Claude Lévi-Strauss and Talcott Parsons, however, as providing bases for the comparison of types; Eisenstadt, *Essays on Comparative Institutions* (New York, 1965), 47. Parsons has conveyed a view of history remarkably similar to the grand histories of civilization; see his *Societies: Evolutionary and Comparative Perspectives* (Englewood Cliffs, N.J., 1966), and *The System of Modern Societies* (Englewood Cliffs, N.J., 1971).

12. Or they were received as works that could safely be ignored, as in the case of the striking *aperçus* of Elias Canetti; see his *Crowds and Power,* trans. Carol Stewart (New York, 1972).

13. Marx, Letter published in a Russian newspaper, as quoted in Edward Hallett Carr, *What Is History?* (New York, 1961), 82.

14. Higham, *Writing American History: Essays on Modern Scholarship* (Bloomington, Ind., 1970), 165. He has suggested that the vigorous effort in American studies to be interdisciplinary may have got in the way of intercultural analysis. Like so many others, historians of the United States have been transfixed by the national state. Thus, comparative analysis is central to the historiography of the colonial period but uncommon thereafter except for certain classic questions like slavery (which we would like to see as foreign anyway) and such challenges to the state as regionalism and civil war.

15. For a discussion of the development and difficulty of such ambitions, see

Stein Rokkan, "Comparative Cross-National Research: The Context of Current Efforts," in Richard L. Merritt and Stein Rokkan, eds., *Comparing Nations: The Use of Quantitative Data in Cross-National Research* (New Haven, Conn., 1966), 3–25. Terence Hopkins and Immanuel Wallerstein have distinguished three kinds of "plurinational" study, but David S. Landes and Charles Tilly have seen comparison more broadly and predicted a central place for it within the historical discipline; see Hopkins and Wallerstein, "The Comparative Study of National Societies," reprinted in Amitai Etzioni and Frederic L. Dubow, eds., *Comparative Perspectives: Theories and Methods* (Boston, 1970), 183–204; and Landes and Tilly, eds., *History as Social Science* (Englewood Cliffs, N.J., 1971).

16. The benefits of using primary materials are often misstated. In practice, greater historical understanding is threatened more by mindlessness than by error, for inaccuracies are easier to identify and correct than are misleading assumptions. The great advantage of working from primary sources is less any increased assurance that the facts are right than the increased opportunity for independent, original analysis that is at the same time sensitive to historical context.

17. Maurice Mandelbaum has made this point, significantly adding that this "need not involve an abandonment of the historian's ideographic approach"; Mandelbaum, *The Anatomy of Historical Knowledge* (Baltimore, 1977), 14. And Barrington Moore Jr., has noted that comparisons "can lead to asking very useful and sometimes new questions . . . , can serve as a rough check on accepted historical explanations," and "may lead to new historical generalizations"; Moore, *Social Origins of Dictatorship and Democracy: Lord and Peasant in the Making of the Modern World* (Boston, 1966), xiii.

18. In his admirable discussion of Claude Lévi-Strauss and Talcott Parsons, Guy E. Swanson began by noting that all research entails comparison and pungently added, "Thinking without comparison is unthinkable"; Swanson, "Frameworks for Comparative Research: Structural Anthropology and the Theory of Action," in, Ivan Vallier, ed., *Comparative Methods in Sociology* (Berkeley and Los Angeles, 1971), 141, 145.

19. Durkheim, *Rules of Sociological Method,* ed. E. F. Catlin, trans. Sarah A. Solovay and John H. Mueller (Glencoe, Ill., 1964), 139. Daniel P. Warick and Samuel Osheron have discussed the uses of comparison and noted the debate in sociology as to whether comparative sociology is a separate field. They decided it is not, citing Oscar Lewis' comment, "Comparison is a generic aspect of human thought rather than a special method." Warick and Osheron, "Comparative Analysis in the Social Sciences," in, Daniel P. Warick and Samuel Osheron, eds., *Comparative Research Methods* (Englewood Cliffs, N.J., 1973), 6–11.

20. Bloch, "Pour une histoire comparée," 39.

21. Buckle's biographer in turn attributed Darwin's skepticism to "a certain genial density"; John MacKinnon Robinson, *Buckle and His Critics* (London, 1895), 25; and Buckle, *Miscellaneous and Posthumous Works,* I (London, 1872).

22. Hugh Stretton has argued for comparison as a means of extending the investigator's experience and stimulating the imagination; but Arend Lijphart has criticized this position in favor of the conventional view that comparison serves primarily to test hypotheses; see Stretton, *The Political Sciences: General Principles of Selection in Social Science and History* (London, 1969), 69, 245–47; and Lijphart, "The Comparable Case Strategy in Comparative Research," *Comparative Political Studies* 8 (July 1975): 159–60.

23. See Bloch, of course, "Pour une histoire comparée," 40. But Lijphart has cited such sociologists as Neil J. Smelser and Juan Linz to the same effect; "Comparative Research," 67–68. And the list could easily be extended. Arthur L. Stinchcombe has provided an extended argument rejecting the idea of some tension between facts and generalization, declaring that "it is the details that theories in history have to grasp if they are to be any good" and that "social theory without attention to detail is wind"; Stinchcombe, *Theoretical Methods in Social History* (New York, 1978), 115–16, 124, 21–22.

24. Robert F. Berkhofer, Jr. has argued that in a final sense a reconciliation of the two approaches so far appears "analytically unattainable," but his standards are very high; in any case, the *effort* seems central to much of the best historical writing. See Berkhofer, "Clio and the Culture Concept: Some Impressions of a Changing Relationship in American Historiography," in, Louis Schneider and Charles M. Bonsean, eds., *Culture in the Social Sciences* (Cambridge, 1973), 99–100. Guy Swanson has cited Lévi-Strauss to the effect that the "comparative method consists precisely in integrating a particular phenomenon into a larger whole" and that research should be "so conducted that theory is at every point in touch with observations"; "Comparative Research," 146.

25. For a well-developed case for this sort of cross-disciplinary work, facilitated by the "federated" nature of American academic departments, see Bernard S. Cohn, "History and Political Science," in, Otto von Meting and Leonard Kasdan, eds., *Anthropology and the Behavioral and Health Sciences* (Pittsburgh, 1970), 89–111.

26. The term is once again Marc Bloch's, who meant by it the set of questions a Continental judge puts to a witness rather than a form to be filled out or a tool of survey research.

27. See, for example, Frye, *Anatomy of Criticism* (New York, 1967); and Poggioli, *The Theory of the Avant-Garde,* trans. Gerald Fitzgerald (Cambridge, 1968). Fitzgerald commented in his "Translator's Apology" that "it is this assembly of points into patterns that makes his [Poggioli's] book such a stimulant and a pleasure"; ibid., ix. Studies of political cartoons have offered a striking use of comparison in *Comparative Studies in Society and History.*

28. This echoes, of course, Robert K. Merton, "Theories of the Middle Range," in his *Social Theory and Social Structure* (New York, 1952). Richard H. Brown has suggested, however, that Merton merely meant testable theories; Brown, *A Poetic for Sociology* (Cambridge, 1977), 13.

29. "So the methodological problems facing 'comparativists' are the same as those facing all social-scientific investigators"; Neil J. Smelser, *Comparative Methods in the Social Sciences* (Englewood Cliffs, N.J., 1976), 3. Historians will find the discussions of method useful in Smelser's book and in Stinchcombe's *Theoretical Methods in Social History* (and especially enjoy comparing the two discussions of comparison in Tocqueville) as well as in Vallier's *Comparative Methods in Sociology* and Etzioni and Dubow's *Comparative Perspectives: Theories and Methods.*

30. Arend Lijphart's valiant effort to define a comparative methodology for political science (a discipline in which it might be expected that comparison would be more readily controlled than it is in history) does not seem to me to be convincing; see Lijphart, "Comparative Politics and the Comparative Method," *American Political Science Review,* 65 (1971): 682–93, and "Comparative Research." Also see Theodore W. Meckstroth, "'Most Different Systems' and 'Most Similar Systems,'" *Comparative Political Studies* 8 (July 1975): 132–57; and Henry Teune, "Comparative Research, Experimental Design, and the Comparative Method," ibid., 195–99. On the response to Mill by Émile Durkheim and Max Weber, see Smelser, *Comparative Methods in the Social Sciences,* 62–67, 141–43.

31. "The choice of the phenomena to be explained is the responsibility of the historian, not the comparative method"; William H. Sewell, Jr., "Marc Bloch and the Logic of Comparative History," *History and Theory* 6 (1967): 213; also see ibid., 213–18.

32. See Donald T. Campbell's article, all the more impressive for its revision of his earlier argument, "'Degrees of Freedom' and 'The Case Study,'" *Comparative Political Studies* 8 (July 1975): 178–93.

33. Bloch, "Pour une histoire comparée," 16, 38. Presumably, the analogue of the term was *grammaire comparée.*

34. William H. Flanigan and Nancy H. Zingale made this point in "The Comparative Method in Political Science," paper delivered at the annual meeting of the American Historical Association held in San Francisco, December 1978; so did E. A. Hammel in "The Comparative Method in Anthropological Perspective," a paper at the same session. An earlier version of this essay completed the panel at that meeting.

35. Alexander Gerschenkron has called the industrial history of Europe "a unified and yet graduated pattern"; Gerschenkron, *Economic Backwardness in Historical Perspective* (Cambridge, Mass., 1966), 1.

36. And these can be used to test "presumptive causal linkages"; Walter P. Metzger, "Generalizations about National Character: An Analytic Essay," in, Louis Gottschalk, ed., *Generalization in the Writing of History* (Chicago, 1963), 90.

37. Arthur F. Wright, "On the Uses of Generalization in the Study of Chinese History," in, Gottschalk, ed., *Generalization in the Writing of History,* 46.

# On Rereading an Earlier Essay

*Raymond Grew*

On rereading "The Case for Comparing Histories," I am struck by its tone: the pained assumption that most practicing historians consider comparison mildly interesting, largely irrelevant, and wholly impractical. That essay therefore opens as a kind of diplomatic *démarche* meant to persuade historians that comparison has a legitimate place in conventional historical research. No such caution is needed now, quite aside from the widespread skepticism about old-fashioned fact-garnering. Comparison has come to be accepted by historians, at least in principle, as an interesting possibility. Even narrowly focused historical monographs often proudly flag awareness of related studies that treat other societies or eras. As for works that are explicitly comparative or conceived within a comparative framework, they surely constitute a much larger proportion of historical publications now than twenty years ago.

This welcome trend owes a great deal to anthropologists, political scientists, and sociologists.[1] Less daunted by comparisons across time and space, many of them pioneered in producing important comparative historical work, and those disciplines (or important parts of them) have become more historical. The enriching effect as theories, methods, and interests move across disciplinary boundaries has encouraged comparison and facilitated it by providing a shared vocabulary. Historians now regularly attend to theory, and those who lay claim to some interdisciplinary and comparative ambition no longer risk being gently ostracized for ostentation. Before speculating on the impact of these current trends on historical research, I should concede that the future of historical study in the United States may be more affected by changes in what universities choose to support and by the economics and technology of publication than by the trends briefly considered here.

Let me also acknowledge that the historical discipline itself contains

formidable antibodies resistant to claims of methodological breakthroughs. Much admirable historical scholarship remains only marginally
affected by the trends I will comment on, a disciplinary autonomy that
merits respect. The academic trend-setters who project new directions for
the social sciences benefit from sensitive seismographs that register earth-
quakes that barely rattle the cabinets where most historians work. Historians, who know how easily the passing of time can be mistaken for
progress, remain skeptical when academics announce that they have
buried their intellectual predecessors alive and apply the prefix "post-" as
if it were a stake through the heart. Such restraint is understandable. Intellectual fashions are intellectually unattractive. They feed on proclama-
tions of newness that tend, like the manifestoes of angry artists, to exag-
gerate their own break from the past and to over-advertise their
originality. Highly partisan assessments of scholarly fields are often written in language more appropriate to an eighteenth-century military campaign: with enemy flanks being turned, lines breaking, and redoubts holding, followed (in a more contemporary gesture) by premature body counts.
Although joy in contestation can make dull thought seem lively, it is
antipathetic to many of the qualities on which serious scholarship ultimately depends. As people devoted to wringing meaning from documents,
and as students of past fallibility, historians are especially sensitive to all
this.

Perhaps the most striking trend in the social sciences and humanities is
trendiness itself, a reflection of increased self-awareness, new ideological
commitments, generational changes, and academic career pressures. By
their very nature, the trends now widely followed have contradictory
effects on the use of comparison in the human sciences. Rapidly shifting
fashions stimulate new perspectives, which in turn encourage comparison.
But trends exist only where some assumptions have come to be widely
shared, a comforting reassurance for any scholar but one not conducive to
imaginative historical comparison. Some of this cyclical engagement with
particular vocabularies and theoretical frameworks involves not so much
fresh thinking as the fairly mechanical application to one or two new cases
of an approach already well established in other contexts. Sometimes useful, such extensions of the newly familiar can also be dully predictable.
Eagerness to deploy imported vocabulary invites what Whitehead called
the fallacy of misplaced concreteness.[2] General concepts of collective
action, class conflict, modernization, or political culture have sometimes
been applied by advocates and tested by opponents with a literalness that

has undermined their significance. Seemingly exhausted, these concepts are accordingly rejected in favor of newly created frameworks and vocabularies—until, that is, the new formulations are discovered to omit some useful element of the older ones. Then calls follow to bring people, the state, culture, or history itself "back in." Doing so can of course lead to interesting uses of comparison, both methodologically and simply by widening the range of discourse. It can also result in extended exercises solving artificial puzzles. Something similar occurred a generation ago when in the name of science heuristic devices and the use of ideal types sometimes led to models so abstract that comparisons were in fact the comparison of abstractions, losing that complexity of context more likely to make comparison fruitful. Something more than mere fashion, however, seems to be opening paths to comparison through the intransigent complexity of history.

The changes in the way society is studied have been marked by a turn to history (especially in sociology and anthropology) and to language and culture (in all the human sciences).[3] Although the participants by no means all agree, they have in common many of the topics they address, the academic literature they refer to (to such an extent that it risks creating its own canon), their thoughtful attention to epistemology,[4] and the conviction that they have taken some important turn. The metaphor is significant not only for its popularity but for its implication of a growing movement and for its amiable vagueness as to who or what is changing. The belief that this constitutes a radical challenge to older ways seems to be stronger in the United States than in Europe; but there has been discussion of a methodological *crise* even in Paris, at the mother church of modern social (and comparative) history.[5] It seems to me incontestable that the study of society and culture and study of the history that encompasses both is undergoing an intellectually exciting and conceptually fundamental rethinking, that this is having lasting impact, and that the effect on academic interest in historical comparison is ambiguous.[6]

This last is my topic, and the trends affecting the use of comparison will be considered in four loosely clustered groups: those associated with the work of Michel Foucault, with poststructuralism, with the cultural turn, and with the behavioralism related to theories of rational choice. The first three are felt especially at the intersection of history, anthropology, and sociology and are best known through the work of a relatively small number of particularly able and energetic scholars. Theories of rational choice, in contrast, are most prominent in political science and economics where the interest in comparison is less often historical.

Had the original article been written even a little later than it was, it would have had to confront the ideas of Foucault, for they have inspired some of the most exciting historical studies of the last twenty years and much of that has been comparative in a variety of ways. There is no better example of how discussion of a single event, society, or period can at the same time be comparative than in Foucault's work. His writings demand a reconsideration of modernity, long a preoccupation of the social sciences, making it far more complex and problematic, while stimulating fresh attention to ideas, albeit less for what they asserted than for what they masked, implied, or left unsaid. Yet there are problems about Foucault's relationship to historical comparison. Friends and critics alike acknowledge that there is little theory of change in Foucault's analysis (or the epistemes he considers) and that the pattern of historical change he does use incorporates a very conventional chronology of European (and particularly French) history. Because France has been so central to the modern historical experience, this focus on his native land has not felt constrictive.

Foucauldian thought does encourage comparative thinking about society in several ways. Comparison between Old Regime and modernity is central to all he does; and that running comparison, by emphasizing discontinuity, calls into question any assumptions of evolution or progress and any temptation to assume that things have to be as they are. Secondly, Foucault uses the metaphor of archaeology and the idea of episteme to probe for the interconnection of every aspect of social life: ideas, structures, economic relationships, and practices at all levels. This gives him (and his followers) enormous freedom to include and exclude as they choose, while encouraging a fresh and often insightful use of historical evidence. In addition that emphasis on interconnection fits with and builds upon much other influential work in history and anthropology (including that of the Annales school and of Clifford Geertz).[7] Foucault's work also suggests a path toward the reconciliation of Marxian structuralism and his own (philosopher's) emphasis on the assumptions underlying cultural practice, a possibility his epigones have expanded on, often using the vocabulary of Antonio Gramsci.

Foucault's focus on power and on the way discourse disguises interests by excluding alternatives can be applied anywhere. This, as much as the sheer brilliance of Foucault's writing (or the delight intellectuals have in unmasking claims to objectivity or truth), explains Foucault's extraordinary influence, especially in the United States. Clearly, his invitation to expose the conservative function of established intellectual (and academic) practice met a contemporary need. His disruptive assault on the categories through which the social world is conceived opened up a myriad of questions; and among the hundreds of researchers moved to address them, many have used comparison. Most, however, have not taken it very far nor used comparison to move beyond Foucault's own ideas. The finding that a hegemonic discourse serves covert purposes in one context is so easily comparable to all other instances that the potential value of deeper comparison may go unnoticed. Moreover, because a Foucauldian sensibility deprives common analytic categories of their comforting familiarity, it calls the mechanics of comparison into question.[8] Historical comparison becomes less worthwhile (its major discoveries having already been made) and more difficult (requiring a whole new set of analyses to make comparison possible by replacing categories and techniques already dissolved).

Postmodernism, poststructuralism, or postpositivism are terms used to mean many different things. Scholars unwilling to assume the social and intellectual transformation those terms imply find it easy to dismiss them as defined merely by what they reject.[9] The fact remains that postmodernism calls into question on fundamental grounds the epistemology that produced a significant part of what social scientists thought they knew about society and many of the methods they used to discover it. It thus opens new possibilities while challenging much on which comparison rests. For postmodernism at its most skeptical, historical comparison, when not a diversion, is merely an entertainment. To those who have lost faith in progress, Marxism, modernization, or modernity, sober calls for historical comparison can seem awfully old fashioned, a gratuitous insistence on older forms, like polished silver at a picnic.

The turn to culture facilitates comparison by transgressing the boundaries between genres[10] but inhibits comparison through fear of hidden master narratives and by embedding the object of study deeply in the culture that produced it while insisting on intrinsic difference evidenced in the particularity of texts and the ambiguity of meaning.[11] Paradoxically, then, the study of culture is often thought of in comparative terms but conducted with little effective use of comparison. In practice, the complex layers of specificity unearthed by deeply burrowing into textual context risks burying what there might have been to compare. There were once historians so transfixed by historical uniqueness that they sought to eschew generalization; paradoxically, preoccupation with the subjectivity of descriptive rhetoric can have a similar effect. Hayden White's enormous impact encourages the comparison of historians' rhetoric more than of historical behaviors.[12] Called an interpretation, a statement about the past includes an implicit challenge to check its logic and supporting evidence and to look for exceptions to it and omissions within it. Called a reading, a historical assessment invites instead an evaluation of its author. The constraints—of one's own culture, of limited knowledge, and of ideological or methodological filters—invite rethinking interpretations but remain fixed signs of authenticity in readings.

In modern scholarship both the search for unseen presuppositions and the burden of reflexivity can lead to endless complications; at their disciplined best, however, cultural studies (like comparisons) prompt the fresh questions and perceptions that stimulate research leading to wider comprehension and deeper understanding.[13] As the social sciences move away from the artificial separation of culture and society, that outcome should become more common and historical comparison a more comfortable tool.[14] Postmodernist frameworks, too, can provide the basis for rational interpretation and serious comparison.[15] That requires a more traditional sort of risk taking than the admirable courage of Jacques Derrida. Using the different evidence their approaches identify while subjecting it to familiar measures of relevance and weight, postcolonial studies provide some admirable examples, and they often employ particularly refined comparisons. As postcolonial studies wrestle with the conceptual challenges of surmounting preoccupation with the Other, they displace difference to subtler levels. Historical comparison then provides essential guidance between the assimilation and reification of difference. The fresh categories that result can frame exciting, focused comparative research that moves across colonial, post-colonial, and European societies; research in which anthropologists have often taken the lead.[16]

A fourth trend in the human sciences, by far the most ambitious of all, appears comparative but uses comparison more for validation than discovery. Those who already command the universal patterns that shape social behavior, who know how societies function or how individuals, institutions, and nations make their choices may well skip exploratory historical comparison, believing sophisticated applications of their confidence more fruitful. Outstanding intellectual energy has poured into theories that aspire to universal application. For all their breadth and vitality, however, engagement with world-systems and global history, civic culture and orientalism, post-colonial and gender studies, dependency and rational choice does not automatically produce inventive comparison. Once the power of comparison is implied by a common vocabulary, its evocation facilitated by indeterminate categories, comparison is more likely to be deployed to expand the reach of a given paradigm than as a way to test or modify it. Rational choice theories carry this further, encouraging a kind of truncated comparison in which data are compared to a model rather than to other cases.[17] When they abstract beyond any particular social or cultural context—the very complexity of which so engages anthropologists and historians—comparison becomes mechanical.[18] Happily, that is not inevitable, however, and there is a growing body of work that combines the logical power of rational choice theories with an attention to context that by redefining historical problems leads to fruitful use of comparison.

In short, these current trends have in various ways, including a meritorious thrust toward the self-critical and a rethinking of methodology, enormously enriched and enlivened the human sciences. In many hands they have led away from engagement with significant historical comparison, which after all—and this must be acknowledged, too—long benefited from the hope for a science of society and the discovery of historical laws. They have also stimulated important comparative work. Historical comparison remains a conscious choice, no more the by-product of theory or method than originality.

Given these changes and possibilities, the question of when and why historical comparison may be useful takes on added interest. Ironically, some of that added interest stems from the need to contain the very virtues of self-awareness and critical analysis called for in my earlier case for comparison. Although the arguments made there still seem to me valid (and I discuss that below), the issue of focus has become more complicated. Then, the thrust was to make historians more self-aware, and historical research continues to gain when fresh questions are posed, problems are well defined, and so forth. Now, no one willing to bring pen to paper can ask all the questions implied by the ubiquitous calls to "rethink." Comparison, however, is helpful in the next step, too: identifying which problems should be investigated by which methods and in which context. Current writing on method in the human sciences, now subtler and generally more modest than twenty years ago, offers considerable guidance. Realizing that "any method, even an emphasis on comparison or non-intellectual practice, inevitably poses fundamental philosophical problems," reinforces the urge to "emphasize empirical, comparative, and theoretically informed and informing studies."[19] Challenging constructed categories (all of which, from statistics to literary criticism, carry submerged agendas) points to comparison as a kind of compass, an independent means of probing the assumptions contained in any category while at the same time using it.

Comparison offers a possible bridge between ambitions to build a science of society and to delve sensitively into the complexities and ambiguities of social context.[20] These often conflicting aims are related to a tension inherent in historical research. The tension between metahistorical explanations and the historically contingent and specific ran through nineteenth-century visions of universal history, and the tension between macro and micro analysis has been a consistent concern in the last generation.[21] These different levels of analysis constitute a formidable challenge to comparative research; yet comparison can often serve to establish relationships across them.[22] Modern interdisciplinary methods and theories and global historical interests have underscored the salience of this issue and revealed it to be something more than what historians, with their "modest qualities" of "caution, accuracy, unpretentiousness and respect for the integrity of documents and for the particular"[23] used to understand more simply as the connection between evidence and generalization.

Current discussions of methodology in the human sciences renew interest in historical comparison; and, at a simpler level, my earlier discussion of ways in which historical comparison is employed may still have some use. The assertion made then that there is no comparative method seems bland now. At the time it looked like a dangerous abandonment of claims to be a science (although to social scientists it was about what one might expect from a historian). Every method can be employed in comparative analyses, and comparison functions differently according to the problem being addressed, the evidence used, and the scale of the comparison—as the essays in this volume illustrate.[24] The question of when or why a researcher might use historical comparison thus remains. I listed four ways—to raise new questions, to identify or form a historical problem, to design a program of research, and to test conclusions.[25] In the light of recent trends, each acquires a broader utility now.

The claim that comparison is a good way to arrive at significant questions is more important than it sounds. The right questions provide the breakthrough that facilitates new understanding. Really good questions—questions that are more than an extension of previous work and partially freed of familiar assumptions—are uncommon and hard to come by. Nevertheless, that emphasis in the original article on posing questions sounded about as useful as a recommendation to think. The point is more obvious now that it has become a commonplace to declare that facts exist in terms of the question posed and now that so many discussions of methodology emphasize the importance of the questions asked.[26] How, then, are questions generated? Although imaginative genius and simple curiosity can inspire new questions, researchers most often start with questions that have worked for others, that arise from established theory, or that result from the surprise of expectations unfulfilled (those expectations may in turn come from previous experience, prejudice, or formal hypotheses). Historical comparison can point to new questions in all these ways, by drawing attention to what in a single context might go unobserved or seem simply natural—an important free benefit in itself (although workaday historians need little reminding that every situation is unique). New questions do not follow automatically from theoretical frameworks, even those conceived comparatively. For example, many historical investigations that start from a comparative perspective (as they often do nowadays in subaltern, minority, and women's studies) employ disparate cases to reach familiar conclusions without raising new questions. Paradoxically, the vibrant imperative that uncovers repression, inequality, and raw power narrows the researchers' interest in probing comparisons. Thus even when the final aim is a high level of generalization, comparison is most likely to lead to fresh questions, new discoveries, and deeper understanding when specific instances are compared in order to explore how and why general patterns vary at different times, with different groups, and in different societies.

The importance of defining a significant historical problem and the value of using comparison in doing so was another of the original article's claims for comparison. The focus on problems needed justification then because it contrasted with the historian's traditional goal of creating a balanced narrative. Now, when almost any standard used in social analysis, whether of ethics or status, is perceived to be socially constructed[27] and when the need to "problematize" is a cliché of the beginning seminar, the importance of identifying a problem is widely recognized. The argument for comparison as a means of accomplishing that, however, needs more development than the older essay gave it (and more than will be attempted here). Conceptually, posing questions and identifying problems seem barely distinct. In practice, however, they draw on different processes and apply different standards. Comparison aimed at stimulating fresh questions can be free wheeling and relatively unconcerned about how fully comparable the various instances are. Comparison intended to help identify and then define a historical problem needs to be more disciplined, assessing factors and weighing variables. This more systematic comparison attends carefully to the available evidence (and is therefore closer to previous research) and reshapes the problem in the process of making comparisons.

Identifying historical problems through comparison means accepting contingency and attending to the sequence of events (something many theorists now argue the human sciences must do), the basis of a historical epistemology, to use Margaret Somers' term. Such comparison should be ready to challenge preconceptions and foster fresh reflection on received theories, however attractive they may be. (That, after all, is only to apply to one's own work the lesson that dominant discourses promote some conceptual categories and inhibit the perception of others.) My earlier essay was surely right to emphasize the importance of the categories used and the value of comparison in shaping them. My reference to "well-defined categories of analysis," however, seems a painfully self-protective proclamation of rigor. What matters is that the categories of analysis follow from the nature of the historical problem[28] and comparison is helpful both in identifying problems and rethinking categories.

The other two ways of using historical comparison, designing one's research and testing conclusions (or hypotheses), are familiar enough and need little explication, although to the contemporary ear that borrowed language suggests neo-positivist intentions I did not have. Postmodern scholarship still generally adheres (more than is implied in its self-description or in criticisms of it) to the logic of argument, the verifiability of evidence, and the connection of both to previous historical scholarship. It is also especially attentive to the importance of theory. The greater engagement with theory that is one of the great gains in contemporary historical work implies an obligation to carefully designed research, for the challenge is not merely to apply theory but to think theoretically. The theory or theories used cannot just be pulled off some poststructuralist shelf. If they are employed as more than an article of faith, subtle and complex choices have to be made all along the way. Historical comparison can guide those decisions and weigh the hypotheses that result[29] while addressing "the core problem for all social theorists today . . . the problem of trying to comprehend and establish a general relationship between, on the one hand, subjective interpretations, understandings, intentionality, agency, and individual action, and, on the other, the macro social totality. . . ."[30] Used in this way, comparison is more fundamental than simply a device to compensate for a small number of cases, a use of comparison that arises more from the desire to validate a model than from the quest for new historical understanding.

Although I noted that they form a continuum, it was a mistake to label these ways of using comparison—asking questions, identifying problems, designing research, and testing hypotheses—as four stages. In the abstract there is a certain logic to the sequence, but each use of comparison affects the others. Along the way questions may be dropped and new ones posed, problems reconsidered, theories amended, and hypotheses, conclusions, and even cases altered or dropped.[31] Nothing is more human in the human sciences than the custom of not fully reporting one's own failures.

The original article includes a list of the kind of work in which historical comparison seemed to me especially fruitful. Primarily a reflection on my experience at *Comparative Studies in Society and History,* that list could now be read as a prediction of areas in which the next generation's research would prove most exciting. (Perhaps our disciplines have changed less over the last twenty years than we tend to think). Given the long-established practice of accepting correlations as evidence, one could even suggest that the human sciences flourish where comparison is their natural nutrient. That has certainly been the case with what were once called colonial studies. As the field moved from the comparative study of empires (with its institutional emphasis and focus on imperial policy) to the study of cultural encounters, the range of comparisons expanded exponentially to include multiple perspectives, subaltern agency, and a reassessment of European conceptions of knowledge. Moving beyond Orientalism (the recognition of Orientalism was itself an accomplishment of thinking comparatively) and across disciplinary divides, this new research has fostered theories and ways of uncovering evidence applicable to nearly every field of history.

The flourishing study of minorities and religious groups has also spurred controlled comparison; and, as expected, social history has increasingly employed comparison while refining method and expanding content. In the process social historians have indeed shifted from a focus on social structure (which was never so exclusive as current critics remember) toward the study of cultural attitudes, not only by incorporating a whole range of new evidence into social history but also by changing the conception of the field. With those changes, the framework for comparison shifted, too. That partly explains a glaring omission in the earlier list. Twenty years ago, one could see that women's history was burgeoning and even that gender studies were transforming historical consciousness,[32] but it was apparently not clear (at least to me) how this intersected with the use of historical comparison. I think my own perception was narrowed by a tendency I have often criticized in others, thinking of historical comparison as if it meant comparisons between nations. There were already notable cross-national studies of gender, but gender is so deeply embedded in the fabric of society that transnational comparison tends to become the comparison of whole nations, suggestive and interesting but diffuse in its implications. The similarities between nations with regard to gender roles and attitudes toward gender often seem quite predictable, and the telling national differences often not so clearly tied to gender. Comparison in gender studies is analytically more penetrating when centered on circumscribed topics (specific policies or comparable institutions, for example). Increasingly, scholars working in gender studies have used focused comparisons to make important findings about prominent ideologies and institutional practices and to add to a growing body of theory.

A list of topics for historical comparison would now also have to include global history,[33] for interest in thinking about history in global terms has steadily grown beyond an older conception of world history or even more recent work on world systems. The role of comparison in global history remains uncertain. Comparisons on the grand scale of civilizations tend to be useful more as an introduction to a variety of topics and societies than as a subject for research. This is primarily descriptive comparison, and it can form the basis for fascinating and valuable essays when it does more than fit borrowed information into received categories. Global history is quite different, however, in its attention to worldwide connections over time and its candid preference for working backwards from the modern experience of technology and economic development. In global history so conceived there are obvious and tempting pitfalls of teleology and technological determinism (familiar from paradigms of modernization). Paradoxically, the frequent questioning of "Western" forms of knowing, itself a product of global awareness, has not yet found a place in global history. Of course global awareness itself may prove—like the Copernican revolution or Europe's discovery of the New World—not to have had so fundamental an effect on Western consciousness as historians initially ascribed to it. Nevertheless, the best writing on the promise of global history offers the possibility of a new perspective that can reach deep into the historical past and can also identify large-scale patterns and particular historical problems overlooked before. Research into those problems may well lead global historians to shift somewhat from their foundational universalizing toward innovative uses of historical comparison. Issues of global-local interactions have some of the explosive potential, and for similar reasons, of postcolonial studies.[34]

Comparison has stimulated new work and led to the redefinition of historical problems in many well-established fields as well (one thinks of the history of education, the history of science or medicine, and legal history), encouraging and facilitated by cross-disciplinary comparisons that connect subject matter and forms of behavior traditionally studied as if distinct from each other. The areas of comparative success have in common the use of analytic categories that have themselves been shaped by comparison (between institutions and practices across time as well as regions) and that integrate new material from several disciplines. Demography, on the other hand, is no longer the model of powerful comparison that it once seemed to be, despite its lasting achievements. Ever greater refinement and precision cannot compensate for the erosion of confidence caused by awareness of how thoroughly demographic categories are necessarily the products of an era, an ideology, and an instrumental purpose.

As the gains in theoretical awareness associated with postmodernist and poststructuralist approaches appeared at last to have overcome the artificial separation between structural and cultural analysis, they deepened the methodological chasm between the social science that operates in behavioral, quantitative, and rational choice terms and the humanities that use the language of hermeneutics, deconstruction, and representation. Although dreams of a kind of unified science of society have faded, historical comparison will be especially lively where bridges across these divides seem possible and important.[35] There is, after all, much that is cumulative in modern conceptions of how societies work. Historical comparison provides a practical way of reaching toward greater coherence across fields and disciplines in a world of academic specialization. It offers a particularly trustworthy path to that "hybridization" across disciplines that has been called "the most reliable route to new knowledge."[36]

Like postmodern doubt, disciplinary complacency undermines interest in historical comparison. Comparison played a large role in the establishment of social science disciplines, as a stimulus to fresh thinking subversive of conceptual compartmentalization. Most of the founders of modern economics, sociology, anthropology, and political science wove comparison into their very definition of the new discipline. Subsequently, comparison was featured in all the social sciences when their practitioners optimistically aspired to the discovery of universal laws. As they become satisfied with the theories and problems dominant in established disciplines, they felt less need for the burden of comparing. Comparative politics, sociology, economics, and anthropology became sub-fields within their broader disciplines. Something similar may be happening now. As new movements established their own discourse (often about power or repression or injustice) and came to constitute a field with its own internal measures of achievement, they provided phrases, methods, and findings guaranteed to win praise, leaving historical comparison less appealing and riskier.

This leads to an embarrassingly unsophisticated point: Efficacious comparison still seems to me to rest on a cast of mind. More than from any particular method, theory, or topic, comparison flourishes from an imaginative openness to discovery, from an ability to recognize when assumptions need to be challenged, from a willingness to probe expectations unmet, and from the capacity to move across established conceptual boundaries. Those who share that cast of mind tend to enjoy and recognize each other's work even on seemingly unrelated subjects. But historical comparison in itself is neither a theory nor a method. The simplicity of that point is, like the original essay, a reminder that my thinking on these matters tends to sink irresistibly into the quicksand of common sense.

NOTES

1. And I have a personal debt to many of them, especially in this case to Julia Adams whose criticisms greatly improved an earlier draft of this comment, even if it still fails to meet all her concerns.

2. Craig Calhoun, "The Rise and Domestication of Historical Sociology," in Terrence J. McDonald, ed., *The Historic Turn in the Human Sciences* (Ann Arbor: University of Michigan Press, 1996), 305, makes the point about method in the course of answering his question about why, after a long record of widely admired works, historical comparison should come in the 1970s to be spoken of as if new. The emphasis on method has involved other misappropriations as well—see Ian Hacking's comment on the use of "paradigm" in the social sciences, "Five Parables," in, Richard Rorty, J. B. Schneewind, and Quentin Skinner, eds., *Philosophy in History* (Cambridge: Cambridge University Press, 1984), 115–16.

3. For an introduction to these turns and the impressive debates surrounding them: Lynn Hunt, ed., *The New Cultural History* (Berkeley: University of California Press, 1989); McDonald, *The Historic Turn;* Victoria E. Bonnell and Lynn

Hunt, eds., *Beyond the Cultural Turn* (Berkeley: University of California Press, 1999). See also Diana Crane, ed., *The Sociology of Culture: Emerging Theoretical Perspectives* (Cambridge: Harvard University Press, 1994); "Comment and Debate: Historical Sociology and Social History," *Social Science History* 11, 1 (Spring, 1987): 17–62; Joyce Appleby, Lynn Hunt, and Margaret Jacob, *Telling the Truth about History* (New York: Norton, 1994); and Jacques Revel and Lynn Hunt, eds., *Histories: French Construction of the Past* (New York: New Press, 1995). These works notably lack the univocal optimism of Philip Abrams' earlier *Historical Sociology* (Ithaca: Cornell University Press, 1984).

4. See Margaret R. Somers, "'We're No Angels': Realism, Rational Choice, and Relationality in Social Science," *American Journal of Sociology* 104, 3 (Nov., 1998): 722–84, for a particularly impressive example.

5. *Annales, Économies, Sociétés, Civilisations* 44, 4 (May–June, 1989) raised the question but presented the *"crise"* more as one of the social sciences than of history and as resulting more from the collapse of older grand paradigms than as an issue of epistemology. The responses, which were printed in 44, 6 (Nov.–Dec., 1989) in a special issue on the *"tournant critique,"* also went in many directions but differed from their American counterparts in their greater interest in forebears and a stronger sense of continuity (including an inclination to see in current tendencies the echo of concerns prominent earlier in the century). Note especially the articles by Alain Bourreau, "Propositions pour une histoire restrainte des mentalités," 1491–504, and Roger Chartier, "Le Monde Comme Représentation," 1505–20, as examples of thoughtful advocacy of new directions that is also consonant with (and even embraces) much older scholarship. These essays also contrast with American ones in seeing attention to agency prompting a return to politics, and in defending the utility of distinctive disciplines. See also the earlier book by Jacques Le Goff, Roger Chartier, and Jacques Revel, *La Nouvelle histoire* (Paris: CEPL, 1978). For a wide-ranging vision of the historical discipline: André Burguière, *Dictionnaire des Sciences de l'Histoire* (Paris: Presse Universitaire de France, 1986).

6. On different uses of comparison in anthropology and the turn from it, see the chapter by Aram A. Yengoyan in this volume. An impressive discussion of diverse trends in American historical sociology is now available in Julia Adams, Elisabeth Clemens, and Ann Shola Orloff, eds., *Remaking Modernity: Politics, Processes and History in Sociology* (Chapel Hill: Duke University Press, 2005).

7. The spread of related sensibilities and interests accounts for the much greater interest in the work of Norbert Elias in the last twenty years than in the first thirty after he first published his *Civilizing Process.*

8. Hacking warns of the danger from confusing words and things, "Five Parables," 123–24.

9. But note Juan-Hsing Chen's negative definition of his own work, as a "critical" postmodernism that draws from "the post-1968 works of Michel Foucault,

Gilles Deleuze, Felix Guattari, and Jean Baudrillard and "distances itself from a dominant 'aesthetic' criticism which privileges art works as its central site of analysis (Lyotard 1984); it departs from a philosophical criticism which locates itself within the history of philosophy (Habermas 1987); it supersedes a cultural criticism which centers on the elite sectors of cultural lives (Huyssen 1986); it diverges from a social criticism which reduces the ('postmodern') social world to a reflection of the ('late capitalist') economic mode of production (Jameson 1983; 1984); it differs from a 'moral' criticism which calls for a return to a ('post-pragmatist') ('bourgeois') social solidarity (Rorty 1984); and it also breaks away from a popular cultural criticism which focuses on the unraveling of new cultural texts," in "Postmarxism: Between/Beyond Critical Postmodernism and Cultural Studies," in David Morley and Kuan-Hsing Chen, eds., *Stuart Hall: Critical Dialogues in Cultural Studies* (London and New York: Routledge, 1996), 309. In the same volume Stuart Hall comments that "The post-marxists use Marxist concepts while constantly demonstrating their inadequacy" and is cited as noting how eurocentric the concept of the postmodern is, ibid., 25, 322. David Morley, develops the point about the multiple meanings of postmodernism in "EurAm, Modernity, Reason and Alterity or, Postmodernism, the Highest Stage of Cultural Imperialism?" ibid., 326–60.

10. Richard Biernacki, "Method and Metaphor after the New Cultural History," *Beyond the Cultural Turn,* 79–82, makes comparison central to a new cultural history.

11. The concept of a "grand narrative" was developed in François Lyotard, *The Postmodern Condition: A Report on Knowledge,* Geoff Bennington and Brian Massumi, trans. (Minneapolis: University of Minnesota Press, 1984); the still more subversive (and accusative) expression, "master narrative" is even more widely used. Lyotard's criteria of validity emphasize the local, specific context.

12. White's impact is underscored throughout the essays in Frank Ankersmit and Hans Kellner, eds., *A New Philosophy of History* (London: Reaktion Books, 1992).

13. See Stephen Bann, "History as Competence and Performance: Notes on the Ironic Museum," *New Philosophy of History,* 191–211; F. R Ankersmit, "Statements, Texts and Pictures," ibid., 212–40; and Randolph Starn, "Seeing Culture in a Room for a Renaissance Prince," in *The New Cultural History,* 205–32. The gains are especially striking when applied to scholarship itself; see S. C. Humphreys, ed., *Cultures of Scholarship* (Ann Arbor: University of Michigan Press, 1977).

14. A common theme of the essays in *Beyond the Cultural Turn* and in the work of Roger Chartier, among many others.

15. James Bohman, *New Philosophy of Social Science: Problems of Indeterminacy* (Cambridge, England: Polity Press, 1991), 112–45.

16. Without needing to resolve the tensions between ethnocentric and universalist aspirations, note Clifford Geertz's Tanner lecture, "The Uses of Diversity,"

*Michigan Quarterly Review* XXV, 1 (Winter 1986): 105–23. See Nicholas B. Dirks, "Is Vice Versa? Historical Anthropology and Anthropological Histories," *The Historical Turn,* 45–47; and the magnificent case for comparison made by Ann Laura Stoler, "Tense and Tender Ties: The Politics of Comparison in North American History and (Post) Colonial Studies, *Journal of American History* 88, 3 (Dec. 2001): 829–65.

17. ". . . Rational choice theorists generally assume that their models apply equally to all persons under study—that decisions, rules, and tastes are 'stable over time and similar among people'" although nothing in the theory requires this "homogeneity assumption," Donald P. Green and Ian Shapiro, *Pathologies of Rational Choice Theory: A Critique of Applications in Political Science* (New Haven: Yale University Press, 1994), 17. See also James Bohman, "The Limits of Rational Choice," in, James S. Coleman and Thomas J. Fararo, eds., *Rational Choice Theory: Advocacy and Critique* (Newbury Park: Sage, 1992), 207–28; and Peter Abell, ed., *Rational Choice Theory* (Aldershot: Edward Elgar Publishing, 1991).

18. The chasm between social scientists using statistical models, game theory, and rational choice theory and those in anthropology, history, and sociology using "softer" approaches may well have deepened. It is hard to imagine the paladins of cultural studies making use of the highly suggestive survey data on attitudes in Ronald Inglehart, Miguel Basañez, and Alejandro Moreno, *Human Values and Beliefs: A Cross-Cultural Sourcebook: Political, Religious, Sexual, and Economic Norms in 43 Societies* (Ann Arbor: University of Michigan Press, 1998). It is sheer prejudice, however, to reject all statistical analysis; the claims often made for it may be antipathetic to poststructuralist sensibilities, but neither its subject matter nor findings need be.

19. Victoria Bonnell and Lynn Hunt, "Introduction," *Beyond the Cultural Turn,* 13–14, 24–25.

20. Charles C. Ragin, *The Comparative Method: Moving beyond Qualitative and Quantitative Strategies* (Berkeley: University of California Press, 1987); and *Fuzzy-Set Social Science* (Chicago: University of Chicago Press, 2000), especially 35–42, on the analytical effort to keep variables separate and distinct. Consider also the work of Ian Hacking, *The Taming of Chance* (Cambridge: Cambridge University Press, 1990).

21. Allan Megill, "'Grand Narrative' and the Discipline of History," in Ankersmit and Kellner, *New Philosophy of History,* 157–58.

22. Ibid; Michael Adas, "Bringing Ideas and Agency Back In: Representation and the Comparative Approach to World History," in, Philip Pomper et al., eds., *World History: Ideologies, Structures, and Identities* (Oxford: Oxford University Press, 1998), 81–104; William B. Sewell Jr.'s, "Three Temporalities: Toward an Eventful Sociology," *The Historic Turn,* 245–80, proposes a fundamental solution. Note, too, that the works he analyzes are all works of systematic comparison. Clif-

ford Geertz and Charles Tilly offer contrasting, influential models for reaching across such differences of scale, and theories of rational choice in effect make the problem disappear through the unseen hand that operates at both the individual and the social levels.

23. Green and Shapiro, *Pathologies of Rational Choice,* 63.

24. As Calhoun comments in "Historical Sociology" (p. 309), there is "a curious tendency to try to describe historical sociology in terms of method or approach rather than substance." There is, however, a great deal to be said about methodology and the employment of comparison, on which Ragin, *The Comparative Method,* is excellent.

25. Guillermina Jasso, in "Building the Theory of Comparison Processes: Construction of Postulates and Derivation of Predictions," in, Joseph Verger and Morris Zelditch Jr., eds., *Theoretical Research Programs: Studies in the Growth of Theory* (Stanford: Stanford University Press, 1993), 213–64, has a very different sort of method and theory in mind (expecting postulates to be stated in equations); yet she divides the process of building a theory into steps—foundations (that begin with insights and early propositions), formalizations, and unsolved problems—that are not wholly dissimilar.

26. See Margaret R. Somers, "Where is Sociology after the Historic Turn? Knowledge, Cultures, Narrativity, and Historical Epistemologies," *The Historic Turn,* 91–118, for an admirably developed review of methodological issues that emphasizes the importance of the question asked, especially pp. 54–60.

27. The phrase is so freely yet somehow knowingly used that one can understand Ian Hacking's skepticism: "I have seldom found it helpful to use the phrase 'social construction' in my work. . . . It seemed to be both obscure and overused" (*The Social Construction of What?* Cambridge: Harvard University Press, 1999, vii).

28. Or rather, the nature of the problem plus the practical reality of what is feasible (what evidence is recognized by the methods employed, what of that evidence is available, its qualities, and so forth).

29. Jennifer Daryl Slack, "The Theory and Method of Articulation in Cultural Studies," discusses the use of theory as the practice of trying out and testing, in Morley and Chen, *Stuart Hall,* 113–14.

30. Christopher Lloyd, *Explanation in Social History* (Oxford: Basil Blackwell, 1986), 160–61. And see in the same volume the essays by Craig Calhoun, Antony Giddens, and Marshall Sahlins on the problems of relating action to structure, culture, and society. But contrast Jasso's three steps to theory (expressed in equations), discussed in footnote 25, with Sewell's conclusion. ". . . Rather than rejecting comparative method, we need to strip it of inappropriate scientific rhetoric and rethink it as a means of theorizing causal narratives through looping contexts of discovery," Sewell, "Three Temporalities," 274.

31. Ragin, *Fuzzy-Set Social Science,* 31–32; and note his discussion, 35–42, of

finding a middle path between complexity and generality. As Biernacki says in "Method and Metaphor" (*Beyond the Cultural Turn,* 82), "The level of analysis for cultural patterns—local network, province, civilization—is a conclusion rather than a premise of investigation."

32. Much of the material in Joan Wallach Scott's influential *Gender and the Politics of History* (New York: Columbia University Press, 1988) had appeared in her articles published earlier.

33. Note Margaret Jacob's prediction, "Sciences Studies after Social Construction: The Turn toward the Comparative and the Global," *Beyond the Cultural Turn,* 95–120, especially pp. 111–16.

34. The work of William H. McNeill reaches from Toynbeean world history to global history and, especially within his focus on material circumstance (from geography and disease to warfare), uncovers many promising possibilities for comparative research. A founding vision of global history emerges in Bruce Mazlish and Ralph Buultjens, eds., *Conceptualizing Global History* (Boulder, Colo.: Westview Press, 1993), especially in the essays by Mazlish and Wolf Schäfer (like so many others they now prefer to add the assertive adjective, "new": The New Global History). My contribution to that volume emphasizes some caveats, and I considered some of the possibilities in Raymond Grew, ed., *Food in Global History* (Boulder, Colo.: Westview Press, 1999). Schäfer presents an impressively thoughtful, systematic case in, "The New Global History: Toward a Narrative for Pangaea Two," in *Erwärgen Wissen Ethik* 13 (2002). See also Arjun Appadurai, *Modernity at Large: Cultural Dimensions of Globalizations* (Minneapolis: University of Minnesota Press, 1996); and Roland Robertson, *Globalization: Social Theory and Global Culture* (Newbury Park, Calif.: Sage, 1992).

35. Nevertheless, much of the optimism in Philip Abrams, *Historical Sociology* (Ithaca, N.Y.: Cornell University Press, 1984) about bringing history and sociology together has been fulfilled, although perhaps not in the terms the authors here had in mind.

36. The claim, as made by Mattei Dogan and Robert Pahre on the basis of their empirical study, is cited by Megill, "'Grand Narrative' and the Discipline of History," 165–70.

# Comparison and Its Discontents

*Aram A. Yengoyan*

Over the past two decades, ethnographic and theoretical writings in anthropology, and aspects of other social sciences, have moved away from problems of comparison, either as an overarching framework or as a theoretical perspective. The reasons for this come from a variety of sources, some of which will be examined in the following discussion. All the social sciences have gone through periods in which comparison has been a critical tool of explanation and interpretation. Economics and political science have had only minimal or sporadic interest in comparison, while sociology, especially historical sociology, has engaged comparative issues both prior to and after Max Weber's works. Historically, the tensions around the issue of comparison have been closely linked to how disciplines organized themselves vis-à-vis changing subject matters and changing sets of empirical evidence. If we trace these disciplinary changes over the past century, we can see how ideas about comparison have been expressed through time, a point that Raymond Grew (1980; 1986–1987; 1990) has explored insightfully throughout his broad and general works on comparison.

I do not want to restate what Grew has expressed so well in elegant exposition and elucidation. For historians, the challenges as set forth by Burckhart and Bloch remain vital. The comparative turn has always been a central intellectual anchor in history, more so than in any other social science except perhaps anthropology. The connections between history and anthropology have been long and complex, and especially the American historical school of anthropology, has had a long interest in history. Boas stressed the importance of local oral histories in his fieldwork on the native peoples of the Northwest Coast, and history was conceived of as an emergent marker of the genius/geist/essence of a people and a culture, which also demarcated one group from another. The major figure in the coupling of anthropology with history was A. L. Kroeber—the historical theme was central to his nearly six decades of research and writing. From the 1940s onward Kroeber took a more active turn toward history of historians. In his writings, Kroeber (1944; 1952; 1963a; 1963b; Coulborn and Kroeber 1956) explored broad themes such as style, civilization, feudalism, science, aesthetics, and the Oikoumene that he conveyed in historical and comparative terms. Some of his comparisons were global in scale and historically based.

More recently, writings by Bernard Cohn, Marshall Sahlins, and John and Jean Comaroff have dealt with local and national histories in a comparative historical framework, yielding great insights into issues of colonialism and post-colonial trajectories. The writings of Eric Wolf and Immanuel Wallerstein have moved anthropological and historical inquiries into the realm of regional and global capitalism as a historical process. In each of these cases, anthropologists have stressed how the local is constituted and reconfigured in terms of regional and national processes. But it also must be stressed that the local is not simply a passive marginalization within the total global process. Again, historians and anthropologists have worked on how local societies inform broader processes, and how in many cases forms of local-level resistance emerge. Both have been examined as historical process and as contemporary developments. Throughout, *Comparative Studies in Society and History* has been the central organ in conveying these perspectives and in most cases it has framed the issues which now constitute what many in history and anthropology embrace as given intellectual stances.

## Anthropology and Its Comparative Foundations

Many years ago, when I was in graduate school at the University of Chicago, we were taught two hallmarks of comparison. One was the conviction that there was a comparative method, usually voiced as "The Comparative Method." The other was that the comparative method was anthropology's equivalent to the scientific method. Both positions displayed the continuing influence of Radcliffe-Brown from when he was on the faculty in the Department of Anthropology at the University of Chicago, and both were also espoused in anthropology textbooks throughout the 1950s and 1960s.

To understand these developments, one must appreciate the intellectual framework that embraced the social sciences at that time, and to a lesser extent history, a framework which I still consider as an essential part of the humanities. From the 1920s to the 1960s, anthropology more or less defined itself as a behavioral science whose aim was to explain cultural similarities and differences in human societies. As a form of behaviorism, the conviction was that anthropology could render itself a science through which hypotheses could be formalized and empirically tested.

Two examples were critical in these developments. From the 1930s through the 1960s anthropology reached its pinnacle as a form of cross-cultural comparison and testing. Under George Peter Murdock and his colleagues at Yale, the Human Relations Area Files (HRAF) were created as a global compendium of all the world's cultures. In part, HRAF was a creation of the American involvement in World War II, but it also became an important tool to test theories and form hypotheses about human societies. Once established, it became a pivotal resource for the social sciences, especially in anthropology, psychology, and sociology. Of course, problems regarding what was being compared, the units of analysis, and the equivalency of the empirical foundations at issue (cultures), were seldom addressed. Mathematical techniques could be employed in developing comparative correlations between cultures and between cultural universals (family, kinship, household, residence rules, etc.), which became the basis for discovering co-variations, differences, and similarities. For anthropologists, Murdock's *Social Structure* (1949) is the best example of what HRAF had to offer. Again, what was being compared, why, and what the findings meant was seldom an issue. The aim was to establish co-variation through statistical means as scientific findings on the human condition.

A second example of comparison and science is evident in the writing of A. R. Radcliffe-Brown, whose early aims were to forge British social anthropology as a form of comparative sociology. Although Radcliffe-Brown's sociology is markedly influenced by Durkheim, the issue of comparison is a point of critical difference between them. For Durkheim, comparison was not involved in developing social laws. Basically Durkheim insisted that each case, well and critically analyzed, should yield a social law. Thus, to define and understand what religion is, Durkheim could not get at its foundations by studying Christianity or Judaism; such cases are too complex, expressions of historical forces that have modified or altered what religion means and how it is constituted. Accordingly, Durkheim turned to the Aranda/Arunta of central Australia to get at the essence of the idea of religion. It was a simple society (which made it privileged in his thinking) and such a case could yield the basic foundations of religion. Of course, the implication of such a method and comparison is that human societies are only quantitatively different but not qualitatively, that is, they differ only in degree, not in kind.

Radcliffe-Brown's vision of comparison was markedly different. In *A Natural Science of Society* (1957 [1937]) and in his aptly titled piece, "The Comparative Method in Social Anthropology" (1951), he makes it vividly clear that comparisons of human societies, not cultures, across types and subtypes will yield social structural laws which are found in all societies to varying degrees. Thus the alternate generations principle of symmetrical reciprocal social bonds is probably universal, while the lineage principle is only found in societies in which descent (and not alliance) is the pivotal force for social and property arrangements. Through this comparative and theoretical framework, Radcliffe-Brown had a far-reaching influence on how ethnography was conducted in Sub-Saharan Africa, Aboriginal Australia, and North America. At least one or two generations of British-trained social anthropologists wrote theoretical and comparative ethnographies under the tutelage of Radcliffe-Brown, Evans-Pritchard, and Fortes.

Yet the comparative foundations of social/cultural anthropology hearken back to nineteenth-century theories of cultural evolution promulgated both in Europe and the United States. At that time, evolutionary theory was not unique to anthropology and sociology; it had its roots in ideas of change, progress, scientific and technological advancement, and global imperialism that reached their peak in the period prior to 1914. Some writers saw progress in terms of stages, others saw evolution as a means of understanding the past, and still others conceived of it as a means in which the West situated itself within the world. Yet the comparative method was a statement that humankind is based on a uniformity that forms the basis of the psychic unity of mankind. As noted by Bock (1966), differences were cultural, thus the distinctions between the "primitive" and the "modern" were differences only of degree. Furthermore, the inspiration behind cultural evolution simply cannot be extrapolated from Darwinian thought and the biological evolution of the time. As cogently argued by Burrow (1970), most of the underpinnings of Darwinian evolutionism of the time had little impact on the idea of cultural evolution. In fact, one can read cultural evolutionary theories of the nineteenth century as moving away from Darwinian principles. In any case, the comparative method moved the argument of cultural evolution to the realm of culture, thus in part denying racial theories of their explanatory value in addressing human social variation. Of course, this matter is far from settled, since now the racial element is cast in terms of the biological, and matters of evolutionary biology.

By the 1960s, one could safely claim that there was no single comparative method, that what comparison was or could be had no connection to the idea of a scientific method (whatever that is), and that no single method or methods were essential to comparison. Some remain concerned about defining units of comparison, but as Grew has clearly argued, the unit of comparison is only an expression of the purpose of one's comparison (1986–1987: 53).

### Comparison in Its Current Context

Social anthropology is still a form of empirical/ethnographic inquiry, just as it has been from its inception. But it is hardly a positivistic endeavor or generalizing science as was claimed from the 1930s to the 1950s. Positivism as a generalizing science created descriptions that were amenable to broad and generalized ends, but this could only be accomplished if the units of analysis for each society and each case were equivalent and comparable. Again, the focus on units was based on the idea that all societies had certain categories in common. This assumption was evident in ethnographic manuals such as *Notes and Queries in Anthropology* (Royal Anthropological Institute 1951), the fieldwork Bible for British social anthropology, and its counterpart in the United States, the *Outline of Cultural Materials* produced under the auspices of HRAF.

Since the 1960s, anthropology has moved from a position of generalization to one of description (see Holy 1987). This shift, which has been manifest in different ways, has in part questioned our descriptions, our global theories such as structuralism, and also what are we describing and saying in our use of categories such as kinship, descent, and residence rules. Through the 1960s, Geertz, Needham, and Schneider, all for different reasons, severely questioned what traditional anthropological categories mean and also the extent to which they were extensions of eurocentrism.

Kinship is a good example of this change in focus from the general to the particular. From the 1960s onward, Geertz, Schneider, and Needham (who have little in common overall) implemented heavily particularistic and local understandings of kinship. They abandoned general and/or comparative categories of analysis, which they felt were only constructs from one point of view, each category being more or less meaningless in any particular case. A good example is the category of descent. From *Notes and Queries in Anthropology* to Murdock's *Social Structure,* descent was specifically defined, but the definitions were so broad and generalized that it was apparent that the particulars were lost. This meant that descent in one society might be based on land, in the next on blood, and in another on ritual affiliation. The upshot of this particularism was that kinship and what it embraced was stripped of its general comparative categories, and its theoretical formulations were rendered virtually useless. The implications of this type of analysis had the unintended consequence of making all kinship local and particularistic, and this soon became fodder to fuel sociobiological explanations (Yengoyan 1997).

This case primarily illuminates the broader trends of how anthropology turned away from comparison. Since the 1970s and more so into the 1980s, deconstructionism has been vocally debated through our journals and national meetings. While many assume that deconstruction was imported from other fields, especially those in the humanities, its roots are also found in anthropology. The writings of the early American historical school severely questioned how anthropological categories have been established and how they were utilized in fieldwork and comparative analysis. Lowie's *Primitive Society* (1920) is a clarion call for the unpacking of how categories are constituted. But the pinnacle of this trend is found almost in its entirety in the works of Paul Radin, not only in his historical and general writings, but also in *The Winnebago Tribe* (1923), which is the best example of a postmodern ethnography.

More recently, an important inspiration for deconstruction has been Claude Lévi-Strauss' *Totemism* (1962). Here again we have a fine case in which a category is unpacked as a means of drawing forth other kinds of structural connections which permitted Lévi-Strauss the means for connecting various facets of categorization as universal tendencies.

One reason behind the minimizing of comparative work in anthropology has been that the various categories and units of analysis, and potentially of comparison, have been a direct result of what we are comparing. For example, state-like structures have been described from Sub-Saharan Africa to ancient China and Bali, and one is forced to ask if these are indeed comparable states. Is the category "state" even usable? Hobart (1987), in his work on Bali, is dismissive of any attempt to characterize the state except within the terms of indigenous representations.

If the wave of deconstruction was dominant in some quarters, the impact of post-modernism in its various forms was even more critical and far-reaching. It was not only categories which went by the board—theoretical perspectives were also questioned. Many of these were dismissed as Eurocentric and others were rejected as totalizing grand theories with little or no bearing on particular cases. Furthermore, by the 1970s, the anthropological turn to agency brought forth an array of accounts, all of which were particularistic yet addressed broader issues of what motivates social action or behavior. Culture per se as a motivating factor was seen as too general, and it was usually comprehended as a static and unchanging entity with little or no bearing on how individuals work through social nuances in which they are embedded. Rational choice theories were borrowed from economics and psychology, and optimization theories from economics and in some forms of biological theory. The individual or the "abstract" individual became the unit of analysis.

Within this milieu of competing theories and frameworks, comparative work was done but no longer as a universal or generalizing or "scientific" issue. Regional comparative accounts, stemming from the seminal work of Fred Eggan (1954), attempted to understand cultural variation within particular geographic areas characterized by societies that possessed cultural similarities. The concern was to show how local histories and geographies brought forth internal variation between and within contiguous societies.

Another form of limited comparison moved away from geography as a uniting factor toward the comparison of two areas that shared interesting parallels, similarities, and differences, aligned with a category that was deemed as universal. Two good examples of this approach will suffice. *Bodies and Persons* (Lambek and Strathern 1998) is an anthology of papers comparing how cultural and symbolic representations express variations that occur in Africa and Melanesia. In each of the ethnographic papers, the concept of person is re-thought to explore the kinds of cultural constraints that shape what personhood means and how these are embedded in rituals, rites of passage, and various aspects of modernity. Tacking back and forth between African and New Guinean case studies generates an array of critical and theoretically sophisticated understandings of how far the categories of body and personhood can be pushed in different cultural milieus. A second example of such comparison is one that contrasts ideas of gender as manifest in Amazonia and Melanesia (Gregor and Tuzin 2001). Gender and gender relations are mapped against a set of different biological and cultural parameters that invoke ideas of age, marriage, systems of inequality, blood, and body.

In both of these volumes, a category (personhood, body, gender relations) becomes the over-arching basis through which comparison is understood. One can criticize these approaches by claiming that such comparisons reify the category in question. In reality, however, they work in the opposite direction by directing our attention to the variety of social, cultural, and political constraints which impact on what the category might mean. In each anthology, comparative injunctions emerge from contextualized fieldwork, but it is also apparent that the sharpness and the quality of the inquiries emerge from a wider sense of reading and thinking which can only emanate from a comparative perspective.

What is apparent from this kind of comparative perspective is that ethnography *per se,* based on fieldwork, has always stressed (consciously or unconsciously) the idea of difference. To take another perspective, one can argue that comparisons, which stress similarities, are partly a matter of distancing. Historically, it is clear that comparative frameworks have been directed toward gaining an understanding of similarities. From the nineteenth-century roots of evolutionism to more recent approaches, similarities have guided our inquiries, explicitly or implicitly, as a means of determining if these similarities actually exist and what their foundations are. To use Lévi-Strauss' *The View from Afar* (1985) as the extreme of invoking the quest for similarities, the move to universals as mental qualities can only direct us toward questions of what is common to humanity, which all societies share to varying degrees.

Among the most serious attempts to understand various forms of comparison are those found in the writings of J. D. Y. Peel, who has contributed to *Comparative Studies in Society and History* on more than one occasion. In an insightful paper, Peel discusses how culture and history are related to one another through comparisons, and sets forth what he considers as "five distinct modes" of comparison:

1. A single, universal, ideal history or "natural history of society";
2. A branching, concrete history, on the model of comparative philology;
3. Where history is denied or ignored, as comparison is used to derive sociological universals or general laws;
4. Where a degree of common history is presumed, as in regional comparative studies;
5. Where it is histories, not societies, that are compared (Peel 1987: 90).

Coming from his analyses of Sub-Saharan societies, Peel correctly stresses that the dominance of the structural-functional approach, the hallmark of British social anthropology, marginalized any interest in history and culture through almost five decades of fieldwork and theoretical

analysis. Although Radcliffe-Brown, Evans-Pritchard, Fortes, and Gluck-
man all differed in various ways in regard to comparison, the dominant
theme behind their comparative statements was an adherence to the idea
of social structure. In *African Political Systems* (Fortes and Evans-
Pritchard 1940) and ensuing volumes on kinship, marriage, and eventually
world view, the causal focus was on society and social structure which provided the unifying matrix for all comparisons.

Throughout Peel's article he stresses how history and culture were
either marginalized or treated as epiphenomena. By the 1960s, a historical
turn occurred in ethnographic accounts of societies, although history was
hardly an integrated factor—in most cases, local and regional histories
were the context or the vessel for the reproduction of social structure, and
culture was always marginalized or invoked only to explain what social
structure could not explain.

Peel (1987: 90) argues for his fifth mode of comparison, in which histories, not societies, are compared, and, he asserts, it is imperative that these
histories are informed primarily by culture, not by society. His pithy conclusion is that "What our comparison most importantly teaches is that culture is less a reflection of society, than a reflection on history" (p. 112).

The turn toward history in anthropology should not be interpreted as
simply a means of escaping from theory and comparison. For one thing,
much anthropological interpretation has played history against theory,
and in the past two decades this move has been more evident and vocal.
But more to the point, the best of our historical work has always been
informed by an acute sense of theoretical construction, an example being
the voluminous works of Marshall Sahlins on Hawaii and the Pacific.
What is evident in his writings is that history *per se* can only take us to a
certain point. The convergence of history and theory is not merely a matter of theory being imposed on history; rather, theory is embedded within
various historical profiles that emerge throughout a region or area.

## ℒ Problems and Discontents

As noted, anthropological debates regarding cultural relativism, which
have been with us for a century, are now on center stage. But relativism
comes in various forms and different degrees. In one sense we are all relativists in that we start from a relativistic position, but the issue is where we
are going and for what purposes. An acute relativism would be one which
starts and ends with a relativistic position, as found in Radin (1923), but

such a position is rare, even in more recent writings. One might cite Geertz's work as taking such a position, but his approach is better comprehended as one which tacks back and forth between readings of various European texts that illuminate what he is trying to convey.

A few examples will suffice. In *Islam Observed* (1968), Geertz utilizes the canopy of Islam to compare two different cultural profiles: Morocco and Indonesia. Although some original reviews of this work portrayed it as employing a Weberian perspective, my own reading is that it is hardly Weberian. It is essential to note that Geertz began to write cultural portraits within a broad spectrum of Islamic dogma and scriptural texts which inform each case in different ways and invoke different ideas of change. Cultural portraits are not new in anthropology, and most of them take us back to the writings of Ruth Benedict minus the psychological underpinnings. Geertz, however, develops his cultural interpretations as portraits which must be understood within themselves.

To take another example, in *Negara* (1980) Geertz's understanding of Balinese theatre and the symbology of power is developed within the writings of Kantorowicz's *The King's Two Bodies* (1957), which is largely the inspiration behind his analysis. Although Geertz's interpretive mode may be characterized by some as highly relativistic and possibly atheoretical, the idea of comparison remains central and critical to what is developed, especially in his recent work.

The most expressive form of "discontentism" emerges with postmodernism and deconstruction. Let me deal with the latter first. Extreme deconstruction, taken to its logical (or "illogical") extreme, would argue that the object of study is the problem which must be dissolved. Within anthropology, as I have noted, this emerged in various forms during the 1960s and 1970s and to a certain extent is also found in Lévi-Strauss' analyses of myths and their various expressions. External to anthropology, the move towards deconstruction is best expressed in the works of Derrida and Foucault. The range of responses have not only questioned the object of study and the theorizing of anthropology, but have collapsed the object of study.

Many quarters claim that the only way to institute subjectivism in our anthropological inquiries is to move away from what anthropology would normally accept as objects of study—be it a culture, society, institutions, the individual, or categories. Yet, subjectivism also comes in various forms. In some cases, the voice of the ethnographer/analyst looms central almost to the point that the individuals or people of the society under study vanish into the background. Again, this tradition, most of which stems from Malinowski, is still critical, although at times I (for one) weary of reading what is sometimes labeled "navel-gazing anthropology." Any comparative implications of such work are muted by what the ethnographer wants to present and how they present it.

On a more theoretical note, some of the issues that lie between comparison and subjectivism are embedded in the writings of anthropologists. Historically, our ethnographic accounts have been either in the first or third person. Movements between first and third person have reflected larger issues regarding whether anthropology is a science, a humanistic undertaking, or primarily historical. In other words, the issues have not only persevered over the last century of work, they have also markedly affected how we write. The science side of anthropology produced the third-person accounts that dominated the field for so long, but humanistic and historical developments over recent decades have pushed first-person accounts to the fore.

One of the most credible forms of humanistic understanding of cultures comes from hermeneutics, or the anthropological variant which has been labeled interpretive anthropology. It has been standard traffic to claim that the hermeneutic approach to cultures only creates separate pictures of cultures, most of which are not comparable, and which in some cases might be totally incommensurable. Issues of incommensurability have long dominated philosophical writings, which invoke ongoing debates between Hemple and Popper on one side, and Wittgenstein, Gadamer, and Lyotard on the other. The overarching issue is how comparison in any form resides within these philosophical differences.

Accounts of self-contained separate cultural worlds might be accepted as excluding any form of comparison or translation. Yet, these cultural worlds and cultural portraits are hardly infinite; they are always informed by the prior texts which all writers carry into their accounts. The unpacking of the writer/author, as Foucault (1977) has stressed, requires an understanding of how these texts and prior texts establish the parameters which are the very basis of our inquiries; what we see, feel, and think.

It is here that the writings of Gadamer become imperative. Comparison cannot be simply dealt with as either subjective or objective. On either side, different pictures of what, how, and why we are comparing create different means and ends of what is to be portrayed. Gadamer's (1975) insistence that the hermeneutic circle "is neither subjective nor objective, but describes understanding as the interplay of the movement of tradition and the movement of the interpreter," directs our interpretations as an ongoing set of evaluations which bring forth a new or even radical re-thinking of these various portraits. For Gadamer, comparison is based on the fusion of horizons which permits one to transcend an all embracing particularism.

In the past decade, one of the foremost interpreters of anthropological hermeneutics has been Michael Lambek. In an insightful and brilliant rethinking of these issues, Lambek (1991) succinctly moves the debate by philosophically arguing for various tenets of cultural hermeneutics; its openness, its pluralism, its non-subjectivism, its non-alienating properties, and its appeal to dialogue. Of critical importance for an understanding of what comparison might embrace, Lambek (1991: 47) concludes that "The fusion of horizons produces not agreement, but the clearing of common ground, the means and necessary condition for mutual intelligibility and useful argument; the difference in the discussants' positions provides its motor." It is the common ground which is essential and critical to any form of comparison, be it of cultural worlds or the imperatives of categorization.

The critique posed by deconstructionism is valid in some directions, especially in its concern to ask anthropology to rethink what we are doing, why, and for what purposes. Some might think it simply nihilistic, but in reality it has created an intellectual environment in which theoretical issues and ethnographic writing are contested from within. To a certain extent, this can be said of postmodernism in all its variants. But the total attack of postmodernism questions not only anthropology but the overall Eurocentric basis of our endeavors, from totalizing global theories, to the whole idea of theory and generalization, and the invoking of multiple voices and the margins of society which have not normally entered our accounts.

A lasting impact of Foucauldian thinking and writing on our endeavors has been his insistence that history, and to a lesser degree anthropology, has been written from the pinnacles of the past or, for ethnography, what is deemed as critical/central/diagnostic to a culture. Foucault, following Nietzsche, claims that this type of historiography or anthropology only provides one picture, and often a skewed and biased one. As a form of presentist history, Foucault questions our accounts as matters of reification and deification of the past. Thus the goal of Foucault's accounts is to convey another portrait, only one of many which might exist. Consequently, it is no accident that Foucault sees the past in terms of its "under belly," namely those features which are not discussed and those forms of thought and behavior which are minimized. The "under belly" is expressed in ideas of madness, asylums, sexuality, disease, and punishment, all reflecting the underlying dark side of the past and the present. The charges he makes against history are also valid for much of anthropology.

Within anthropology there exist other discontents stemming from post-colonial and subaltern studies writings—the creation and the use of the category "the Other." On the surface, the invocation of the Other seems valid, and one would assume that the Other has an existence apart from the West. Nonetheless, most forms of post-colonial/subaltern studies are based on an anti-essentialism which not only questions categories and comparison, but also collapses the object of study into the subject of study. The two become one for no particular purpose, and the culmination is an ongoing debate on essentialism, anti-essentialism, and anti anti-essentialism (Yengoyan 2001), debates which have no closure.

The writings in philosophy, especially in Hegel and Sartre, are vital to any anthropological understanding of what the Other means and how it is constituted. Working from Sartre, back to Hegel, Sartre's general vision is to set forth the philosophical foundations of the existence of the self and how other consciousness is experienced from one's own consciousness. Sartre's ultimate aim is to demonstrate that the Other is both a stranger and an essential part of one's consciousness. Prior to developing his own theory of the Other, Sartre examines various theories of the Other as another self or the selves of other human beings. Sartre's philosophy relies on the self as experience and as consciousness (the for-itself). Thus in order to curtail solipsistic critiques (i.e., the affirmation that it is impossible for a consciousness to prove the existence of realities outside itself) of his philosophical argument, Sartre starts his theoretical endeavors from Hegel.

Hegel's phenomenology of consciousness is the key in Sartre's argumentation and conclusion that the Other is necessary to "the very existence of my consciousness as self-consciousness" (Sartre 1956: 235). Furthermore, the Hegelian insistence that consciousness has to be perceived as a consciousness by another consciousness is central to Sartre's views. Most theories of the self are in error because they initially analyze the Other primarily on a "representational" basis, that is, they assume that the issue of the Other is tantamount only to the question of the way other consciousness is perceived. Hegel's move from a cognitive problem to one of a deeper ontological issue leads Sartre to claim: "Hegel's brilliant intuition is to make me depend on the Other in my being. I am, he said, a being for-itself which is for-itself only through another. Therefore the Other penetrates me to the heart. I cannot doubt him without doubting myself since "self-consciousness is real only in so far as it recognizes its echo (and its reflection) in another" (Hegel 1970: 20; Sartre 1956: 237).

For Sartre, the Other consciousnesses are the pivotal element in one's own constitution of one's self, thus they cannot be thought of as purely external to oneself and one's consciousness. From Sartre's view, Hegel introduces a marked turnaround in the conceptualization of the Other. Instead of taking the ego-self as the starting point for analyzing the Other's self, Hegel sets the Other's consciousness as a condition of the self-ness for one's consciousness.

Yet, the differences between Hegel and Sartre are even greater. In Sartre's view, Hegel's theory cannot fully explain the problem of the Other because it is an idealistic philosophy, namely it assumes that knowledge is the measure of being, that if we possess complete knowledge of something, we also hold that being itself as well. As clearly stated by Sartre (1956: 238), "Nevertheless, it is certain that this ontological problem remains everywhere formulated in terms of knowledge."

Consequently, Sartre refuses any idealistic approach because analyzing consciousness from cognitive perspectives reduces it to the status of mere objective phenomena. There is always an ontological gap between things and consciousness, or as Sartre states in his critique of the Hegelian Other, "We shall marshal against Hegel a twofold charge of optimism. In the first place Hegel appears to us to be guilty of an epistemological optimism" (Sartre 1956: 240). For Hegel, the optimism is in the implicit belief that the truth of self-consciousness will appear. For Sartre, there is no such entity as a true self for selves are not stable, not visible, and not describable as objective events. Only things possess a definite essence, but consciousness which is not a thing does not. In Sartre's view, the Hegelian notion of self-certainty emerging from the encounter of the Other is tantamount to reducing consciousness to an object (as opposed to a subject), because there is knowledge of things only, not of selves as selves.

Hegel's epistemological optimism relies on an ontological optimism. Such an optimism tries to fill the ontological gap between things and selves. According to Sartre, Hegel's error is thus twofold. First, he (Hegel) thinks that selves and things are commensurable, which leads him to believe that there can be a truth of the self (epistemological optimism). Secondly, assuming that selves are like things, he assumes that different selves are commensurable and that "plurality can and must be surpassed toward the totality" (Sartre l956: 240). This plurality is not an accident or a default of perception which is always directed toward a more fundamental totality. The primacy for Sartre is an irreducible condition that consciousness must always remain plural. Consequently this becomes a dilemma for rationalist thought and its conviction to reduce everything to dominant coherences and unified fields. Thus, regarding the existence of other consciousnesses, the task of ontology (as opposed to epistemology and its cognitive approach) is one of description (analysis) and not one of explanation (synthesis is impossible). "The task which an ontology can lay down to itself is to describe this scandal and to found it in the very nature of being, but ontology is powerless to overcome it" (Sartre l956: 244).[1]

No anthropologist would deny the existence of the Other, but in most writings the Other emerges as an *abstract* Other, one which may have no historical anchors, no cultural contexts, and perhaps no existence even as a self. The Other is always there, a free-floating entity/category continuously invoked.

Why and what does this mean? I submit that the abstract Other is used primarily to compare the us/West to the rest. The purpose of such comparisons, and they are comparisons, emerges as a form of critique of our own society, culture, political institutions, and forms of domination. There is very little which is inherent in the Other; it is only a means of expressing and directing critique, but now on different grounds. The Other becomes a voice which adds credibility to the critique.

Whereas earlier forms of criticism from Marx, Arnold, Simmel, Leavis, and Raymond Williams understood critique as issues of class, internal contradictions, alienation, and social ruptures, the present critiques use the abstract Other to portray a relativistic account as a means of understanding social and political ills. The comparisons are hardly comparisons and, in most circumstances, they fall far short of their intended purpose.

## Comparison and the Problem of Translation

All forms of comparison are problems of translation and all problems of translation are ultimately problems for comparison. To fully deal with this issue would require another lengthy tome, but I think I am justified in concluding this paper with a discussion of some aspects of the problems of translation.

Throughout some recent writings on translation by Becker (1995),

Hobart (1987), Overing (1987), and Yengoyan (1999; 2003), one of the constantly recurring problems is the appeal to human universals which allow us to bridge the gaps separating languages or cultures from one another. The concern is to ask if there are correspondences or equivalencies that are critical and essential in bridging differences. One position argues that there must be, since that is the only means of avoiding endless incommensurable accounts that stress differences and create particularisms. The other position would argue that invoking correspondences creates the problem of tacking back and forth from certain facets of anthropological, historical, or linguistic theory/thought which not only distorts what is conveyed, but reduces and converts the particular to an expression of what only academia can understand or even accept.

These issues have long been debated within philosophy, anthropology, and linguistics. What is critical is how meta-languages are formed in various disciplines and what their implications are. Like all inquiry, meta-languages initially come into existence through the art of labeling. Events and things exist, and this existence is initially comprehended by labeling; once this occurs the *being* of these events is established. All meta-languages are based on the idea of being, which is a crystallization of events based on some common property or properties.

We must be cautious of how meta-languages are formalized, and attentive to their impact on what we do. In most disciplines, translations from one case to another are usually glossed or parsed through meta-language(s), and this merely brings forth another level of either translation or comparison. But in many cases, the translation or the comparison only echoes the meta-language itself and, at worst, simply reconfirms what the meta-language embraces. In this scenario, particular cases—be they languages, cultures, or histories—are studied, analyzed, and created or re-created as a means of enhancing or refuting what the dominant meta-language sets forth as a totality.

Taking linguistics as a discipline, it is evident that the idea of the meta-language has been acutely developed from its inception, from Saussure to Chomsky. Indeed, the meta-language has set the dominant framework of what is asked and what the theoretical and descriptive ends are. As a science, linguistics has predominantly been a theoretical meta-language. The negative side of these theoretical developments has been a limitation in the ability to translate directly from language A to language B. All such translations must first resonate with a meta-language, which basically sets the frame from which further theoretical and empirical developments emerge.

Thus, there is no direct translation from language A to B, though such is found in the works of Carl Strehlow from Aranda/German/Aranda, or in Adoniram Judson's translation of Burmese to English to Burmese. In the context of linguistics, it is not comparison in any form, but rather a move from theory to content and back again.

If linguistics has a mixed blessing with an overabundance of meta-language which pervades all domains of inquiry, anthropology (in spite of itself) may have come off better. Theoretically, functionalism, structural-functionalism, and Lévi-Straussian structuralism have all had an important and critical bearing on the development of meta-languages. Each represents a differing version of anthropology as a scientific discipline. Earlier I discussed how structural-functionalism dominated nearly four decades of anthropological enquiry in Sub-Saharan Africa. But most of these kinds of inquiries are behind us, to varying degrees. Furthermore, as meta-languages, none of the above were ever as exacting and precise as those found in linguistics. The linguistic models pervaded phonology, morphology, and syntax, as well as what is called semantics. In anthropology, the meta-language has been porous and methodologically non-rigorous, and virtually all interest in anthropological units of analysis has ceased.

One might claim that this is an expression of the impact of postmodernism, but I do not think so. It makes more sense to argue that this form of scientific inquiry has run its course, and scientific work in anthropology is primarily now informed by biological and evolutionary perspectives. Thus, anthropological comparisons, either as cultural portraits or through the utilization of categories such as body, personhood, and gender across non-contiguous areas and regions, are a form of translation which render a more acute interpretation of the category. They thus reveal ways in which particular societies work and re-work what anthropologists might consider universal categories. Again, the translations are affected by a limited meta-language which at least establishes constraints on portraits which are internally induced.

What, then, are the meta-language(s) of history? Here I am at a loss. Comparative history might be theoretically informed, either as forms of grand theory, forms of Marxist analysis, or theories which emerge particularistically through time and space, such as theories of the state or of feudalism. But I would argue, perhaps on shaky grounds, that history has not had grand meta-narratives or meta-languages which have dominated interpretations and explanations. Thus, historical comparisons have been done in part as a matter of insight, in pursuit of the ability to generate interesting statements which can either emanate from a set of facts (the ongoing love of archives) or from limited theoretical developments primarily used to explicate parallels.

If I am partially correct in that history has not suffered through periods of dominant meta-languages/meta-narratives, we might see the ability to create and forge comparative work as an expression of this. In all of our theoretical meanderings, historians still do histories and what informs these is usually a unique combination of what the historical evidence yields and what intellectual concerns have been central to an area/region. There are reasons why American history, with the possible exception of labor history, has not taken the comparative turn that is so central to European and most other regional histories.

But again I must return to translation. Any form of comparison must always be informed by at least a minimum of theory; I think there is no escape from that. Where the danger lies is when histories and comparisons pay the price of the heavily laden meta-languages which direct and channel one's inquiries. Here I would argue that translations, or at least those which are superb, such as Alton Becker's work, have the virtue of minimizing the impact of the meta-languages within which the translator has worked. If translation is based on texts and textual analyses as they resonate from certain prior texts, it is imperative that translators be aware of these prior texts which they bring to the work. Translation, then, can be the "purest" form of comparison. In earlier days, Judson and Strehlow did not bear the burden being teased by meta-languages, which they empathically realized would distort and modify the very things they wanted to convey.

### Conclusions and a Personal Note

The insistence on a temporal perspective is critical to all forms of comparison, be they history or anthropology. History has long internalized this, but anthropology in its various theoretical expressions has in its comparative work always vacillated between the organicistic metaphor and a temporal perspective. The reasons for this have been many, but foremost has been the conviction that small-scale "primitive" societies were bereft of history. This was a basic assumption for classic British social anthropology, and in some quarters it persists, though in modified forms. The organicist focus created synchronic cases which could be compared to generate social or social structural laws. But we are now past that, and the central problem is still the ongoing debate between whether anthropology should be a science or a form of humanistic endeavor. Biological paradigms and their application to human societies, especially small-scale societies, currently tend to mute history, though that may change. Of course the problem within biological explanations is that they portray small-scale units as populations, not as cultures.

It might be warranted to re-think anthropology's paradox between science and the humanities by returning to Maitland's (1936 [1899]: 249) dictum that "by and by anthropology will have the choice of being history or being nothing." Maitland's contrast must be interpreted in terms of the intellectual debates of 1900 which embraced anthropology, sociology, and history. Nonetheless, the dictum could well be applied to social/cultural anthropology today, where we are divided between the humanities and the social sciences. The kinds of comparisons made by each side are not only different; they may have no bearing to one another. As ever, both anthropology and history face the problem of where to locate themselves.

From a more personal perspective, I think comparison(s) emerge from all fronts of what we do, from fieldwork to general and theoretical writing. I am not convinced that fieldwork must stress differences while theoretical and comparative writing stress similarities. Over the past four decades, my fieldwork has been with upland peoples in southeast Mindanao in the Philippines and with an Aboriginal Australian society in the western desert of Australia. In each case, the concept of the field situation re-emerges and is transformed as one's thought tacks between readings, and between readings and the circumstances on the ground, thus provoking imagination and curiosity and stimulating reflection on critical questions. Among the Mandaya of Mindanao, where a historical and dynamic system of orality and oral traditions is firmly developed, I seek insight from reading Irish writers, mostly Synge and Yeats. Yeats is especially insightful in his probing of how orality can be maintained within the all-embracing emergence of a written tradition, for language is always oral, and orality gradually succumbs to writing. With the Pitjantjatjara of central Australia, I have turned to some of the ethnography of native North American peoples in the Southwest, such as the Tewa and Pueblo cultures. Tewa ideas of time and space, and how they co-ordinate through history and myth, have a critical bearing on how history, time, and space are triangulated among many of the Aboriginal cultures of central Australia. But even more important for understanding Aboriginal religion and the symbolism of myth, I go back to the Old Testament, though shorn of the prophets and the prophetic tradition which are an essential component of Christianity. Prophets and personal messages are very foreign to what Aboriginal religion and myth means, but insights from early Christianity, and its impact on questions of truth, morality, and justice are always valuable and critical.

And dare I say that anthropology will have the choice of being essentially humanistic or being nothing. All of us still have our archives.

### NOTES

Acknowledgment: I would like to thank Mr. J. Plouin for his assistance in various phases of this paper.

1. One of the more perceptive readings and interpretation of Hegel's understanding of self-certainty and self-consciousness is found in *Hegel's Phenomenology of Self-Consciousness: Text and Commentary,* Leo Rauch and David Sherman, eds., Albany, New York: State University of New York Press, 1999. One should also consult the writings of Alexandre Kojeve on Hegel and Marx on ideas of the self.

### REFERENCES

Becker, A. L. 1995. *Beyond Translation: Essays toward a Modern Philology.* Ann Arbor: University of Michigan Press.

Bock, Kenneth E. 1966. The Comparative Method of Anthropology. *Comparative Studies in Society and History* 8: 269–80.

Burrow, J. W. 1970. *Evolution and Society: A Study in Victorian Social Theory.* Cambridge: Cambridge University Press.

Coulborn, Rushton and A. L. Kroeber, eds. 1956. *Feudalism in History.* Hamden, Conn.: Archon Books, Inc.

Eggan, Fred. 1954. Social Anthropology and the Method of Controlled Comparison. *American Anthropologist* 56: 743–63.

Fortes, Meyer and E. E. Evans-Pritchard, eds. 1940. *African Political Systems.* London: Oxford University Press.

Foucault, Michel. 1977. *Language, Counter-Memory, Practice.* Ithaca, N.Y.: Cornell University Press.

Gadamer, Hans-Georg. 1975 [1960]. *Truth and Method.* New York: Crossroad.

Geertz, Clifford. 1968. *Islam Observed.* New Haven, Conn.: Yale University Press.

———. 1980. *Negara.* Princeton: Princeton University Press.

Gregor, Thomas A. and Donald Tuzin, eds. 2001. *Gender in Amazonia and Melanesia: An Exploration of the Comparative Method.* Berkeley: The University of California Press.

Grew, Raymond. 1980. The Case for Comparing Histories. *The American Histori-cal Review* 85: 763–78.

———. 1986–1987. Comparison in the Social Sciences. Ann Arbor: University of Michigan, Rackham Reports.

———. 1990. On the Current State of Comparative Studies. *Marc Bloch aujour-d'hui: Histoire comparée & sciences sociales.* Paris: Éditions de l'École de Hautes Études en Sciences Sociales, 323–34.

Hegel, G. W. F. 1970. *Philosophische Propädeutik. Werke. Vol. 4. Nürnberger und Heidelberger Schriften, 1808–1817.* Frankfurt am Main: Suhrkamp.

Hobart, Mark. 1987. Summer's Days and Salad Days: The Coming of Age of Anthropology? In, Ladislav Holy, ed., *Comparative Anthropology.* Oxford: Basil Blackwell, 22–51.

Holy, Ladislav. 1987. Description, Generalization, and Comparison: Two Para-digms. In, Ladislav Holy, ed., *Comparative Anthropology.* Oxford: Basil Black-well, 1–21.

Kantorowicz, Ernst H. 1957. *The King's Two Bodies.* Princeton: Princeton Univer-sity Press.

Kroeber, A. L. 1944. *Configurations of Culture Growth.* Berkeley: University of California Press.

———. 1952. *The Nature of Culture.* Chicago: University of Chicago Press.

———. 1963a. *An Anthropologist Looks at History.* Berkeley: University of Cali-fornia Press.

———. 1963b. *Style and Civilizations.* Berkeley: University of California Press.

Lambek, Michael. 1991. Tryin' to Make it Real, But Compared to What? *Culture* 11: 43–51.

Lambek, Michael and Andrew Strathern, eds. 1998. *Bodies and Persons: Compara-tive Perspectives from Africa and Melanesia.* New York: Cambridge University Press.

Lévi-Strauss, Claude. 1962. *Totemism.* Boston: Beacon Press.

———. 1985. *The View from Afar.* New York: Basic Books, Inc.

Lowie, Robert. 1920. *Primitive Society.* New York: Liveright Publishing Corp.

Maitland, F. W. 1936 [1899]. The Body Politic. In *Selected Essays.* Cambridge: Cambridge University Press.

Murdock, George Peter. 1949. *Social Structure.* New York: Macmillan.

Overing, Joanna. 1987. Translation as a Creative Process: The Power of the Name. In, Ladislav Holy, ed., *Comparative Anthropology.* Oxford: Basil Blackwell, pp. 70–87.

Peel, J. D. Y. 1987. History, Culture and the Comparative Method: A West African Puzzle. In, Ladislav Holy, ed., *Comparative Anthropology.* Oxford: Basil Blackwell, 88–118.

Radcliffe-Brown, A. R. 1951. The Comparative Method in Social Anthropology. *Journal of the Royal Anthropological Institute* 81: 15–22.

———. 1957 [1937]. *A Natural Science of Society.* New York: Free Press.

Radin, Paul. 1923. *The Winnebago Tribe.* Washington, D.C.: Bureau of American Ethnology, Smithsonian Institution.

Royal Anthropological Institute. 1951. *Notes and Queries in Anthropology.* 6th ed. London: Routledge and Kegan Paul.

Sartre, J-P. 1956. *Being and Nothingness: An Essay on Phenomenological Ontology.* Hazel Barnes, trans. New York: Philosophical Library.

Yengoyan, Aram A. 1997. Yengoyan on Handler's *Schneider on Schneider. American Ethnologist* 24: 208–10.

———. 1999. *Racism, Cultural Diversity and the Australian Aboriginal.* Publication of the International Human Rights and Human Diversity Initiative, College of Arts and Science, University of Nebraska-Lincoln. Public lecture delivered at the University of Nebraska, 9 April 1999.

———. 2001. Essentialisms of Aborginality. Blood/Race, History, and the State in Australia. In, André Burguière and Raymond Grew, eds., *The Construction of Minorities: Cases for Comparison Across Time and Around the World.* Ann Arbor: University of Michigan Press, 269–87.

———. 2003. Lyotard and Wittgenstein and the Question of Translation. In, Paula G. Rubel and Abraham Rosman, eds., *Translating Cultures: Perspectives on Translation and Anthropology.* Oxford: Berg, 25–44.

# 2. COMPARING GLOBALLY

# Frazer, Leach, and Virgil

## The Popularity (and Unpopularity)
## of *The Golden Bough*

### *Mary Beard*

### Leach versus Frazer

In 1985 Edmund Leach, well into retirement from his chair of Anthropology in Cambridge, made his first visit to the site of the temple of Diana at Nemi, some fifteen miles southeast of Rome.[1] Leach called this visit a pilgrimage, for Nemi and the problems of its bizarre cult were the starting place for James Frazer's founding work of Social Anthropology, *The Golden Bough*. This was the spot that Frazer described in such lavish detail in his opening chapter: "the sylvan landscape [that] was the scene of a strange and recurring tragedy."[2] This was the setting for the problem that Frazer set out to solve: Why in Roman times could the priest-king of the sacred grove of Nemi (the so-called *Rex Nemorensis*) win his priestly office only by killing the previous incumbent; why would he himself lose it only through murder at the hands of his successor?[3] For those who see Frazer's work as the start of anthropological study in its modern sense, the site and the cult of Nemi must hold a particular place: this colorful, but minor, backwater of Roman religion marks the source of the discipline of Social Anthropology.

Leach used the word pilgrimage with a certain irony. Following his visit to the site, he published a short article entitled: "Reflections on a Visit to Nemi: Did Frazer Get It Wrong?[4] The aim of this essay was to show how Frazer's interpretation of the cult and priesthood of Nemi rested on a misunderstanding—or rather a willful misrepresentation—of the physical remains of the site. Even though he had visited Nemi in 1901, Frazer, in Leach's view, had seen only what fitted in with his own preconceived ideas.[5]

Leach himself was particularly struck by the prominence and size of the surviving remains of the temple and other cult buildings. These features alone suggested that the whole sanctuary had once been rather grand and imposing—quite contrary to the picture of "an unpretentious place deep in the forest" that Frazer's account conjures up. Frazer had, Leach argued, quite clearly underestimated the grandeur of the site in order to support his view that the cult was "a poverty stricken survival from 'savagery.'" "Savagery," after all, sits uneasily in grand architecture. For Leach, on the other hand, the grandeur of the remains offered an answer to the problem of the strange cult: simple economics. Why, he asked, should anyone have wanted to take on the office of priest-king at Nemi when it meant certain death at the hands of some future claimant to the title? Not, he stressed, because all these men were primitive savages, acting in a primitive and, to us, irrational way. They sought the office for the "entirely rational" reason that it gave them control of vast wealth. So exit Frazer and the whole thesis of the *Golden Bough*.[6]

This article on Nemi was only the last of a series in which Leach tried to undermine the foundations of Frazer's work in the *Golden Bough*. In one particularly vicious attack entitled "Golden Bough or Gilded Twig?"[7] Leach accused Frazer of the double crime of plagiarism and distortion. Not only, he claimed, did Frazer's anthropological writing consist of little more than a pastiche of direct quotations from earlier ethnographic accounts; but when he did choose to make his own contribution, Frazer commonly rewrote or improved his sources in order to give the impression that they backed up more strongly his own tendentious theories.[8] It might then seem surprising that Frazer should have enjoyed such an extraordinary popular reputation. But Leach found the explanation for this in the support given to Frazer by Robertson Smith,[9] and in the "propaganda" by two women: Lady Frazer, "a French widow," who was preoccupied with her husband's public renown and acted as his "public-relations officer,"[10] and Jane Harrison, historian of Greek religion and Fellow of Newnham College, Cambridge 1898–1922, whose interest in his work gave it an academic respectability.[11]

## Nemi and the Popularity of
## *The Golden Bough*—The Problem Defined

This article was originally stimulated simply by my surprise at Leach's outrage and at the vehemence of his attacks on Frazer. But this sense of surprise developed into a more pointed concern with central problems of the cultural history of late nineteenth- and early twentieth-century Britain: the interrelationship of the study of the classical past (its literature, archaeology, religious history) with the presentation, re-presentation, and negotiation of the imperial present; and the links between the imaginative exploration of the Other and the development of the disciplines of social science and anthropology. These broad issues underlie the two questions that provide the framework of my article. First, why is the site of Nemi so prominent in the structure of *The Golden Bough*? Second, why was the book so immensely popular in the late nineteenth and early twentieth centuries—not among academics and specialists (who were often, in any case, skeptical of the claims of *The Golden Bough*), but among the middle-brow reading public who bought it in staggering numbers?[12] I intend to show that these questions, separate at first sight, are directly connected, and that the prominent position of Nemi's cult in *The Golden Bough* was an integral factor in the book's extraordinary, and perhaps puzzling, success.

I do not aim to rehabilitate Frazer at the expense of Leach. It is clear that in several respects Leach did almost willfully misunderstand Frazer's methods and approach. His strident criticisms of Frazer's "plagiarism," for example, simply fail to acknowledge the nineteenth-century context of Frazer's work and the standard (to us "plagiaristic") practices of much nineteenth-century scholarship. On the other hand, a large proportion of *The Golden Bough* is inadequate, as well as irrelevant and (at least in the third edition) monstrously prolix by any reasonable standards of accuracy. I do not want to take sides but to reexamine some of the important issues about Frazer's work that Leach raised despite his vitriolic hostility. "Why was *The Golden Bough* so popular?" is a question still worth asking, whatever the intrinsic merit of the book itself.

This question necessarily touches on other issues relating to the writing and reception of *The Golden Bough*. I have chosen to concentrate on a set of material never before discussed in the context of Frazer's cultural importance: popular newspaper reports in the British and colonial press from the early decades of this century. In doing this, I have decided not to discuss in any detail Frazer's own intellectual history. This is fully treated elsewhere and does not, in my view, have much bearing on the wider popularity of his work.[13] I have also given only a little space to the question of why *The Golden Bough* remains so popular today. Part of my argument on the early popularity of the book may well help to answer that question, but additional factors, broached directly at the very end of this article, have ensured Frazer's book the status of a modern classic. My major focus is on the popular reception of *The Golden Bough* before Frazer's death in 1941.

### Nemi and Virgil's "Golden Bough"

Although every edition of *The Golden Bough* starts and finishes with the sacred grove of Nemi, the various editions have, of course, differences among them and generally tend to expand. In particular, as the whole work developed from a two-volume book in the first edition to twelve volumes in the third, and as Frazer gathered more archaeological information about the site and actually visited Nemi in 1901, the description of the grove gets markedly longer. Some of these detailed changes no doubt indicate changes in Frazer's understanding and interpretation of his subject. But none of these minor shifts of emphasis should obscure the central simple fact that in every edition of the work Nemi takes the leading position.[14]

Frazer's treatment of Nemi in the opening chapter of *The Golden Bough* is famous particularly for its evocative literary qualities and its highly crafted prose. Frazer paints a vivid picture of the priest-king of Nemi, prowling round a tree in his sacred grove, constantly on the watch—looking out for the contender who (according to the rule of the cult) would first cut a particular branch off the tree and then attack the priest himself:

> The post which he held by this precarious tenure carried with it the title of king; but surely no crowned head ever lay uneasier, or was visited by more evil dreams, than his. For year in year out, in summer and winter, in fair weather and in foul, he had to keep his lonely watch, and whenever he snatched a troubled slumber it was at the peril of his life. The least relaxation of his vigilance, the smallest abatement of his strength of limb or skill of fence, put him in jeopardy; grey hairs might seal his death-warrant. His eyes probably acquired that restless, watchful look which, among the Esquimaux of Bering Strait, is said to betray infallibly the shedder of blood; for with that people revenge is a sacred duty, and the man-slayer carries his life in his hand. To gentle and pious pilgrims at the shrine the sight of him might well seem to darken the fair landscape, as when a cloud suddenly blots the sun on a bright day. The dreamy blue of Italian skies, the dappled shade of summer woods, and the sparkle of waves in the sun, can have accorded but ill with that stem and sinister figure. Rather we picture to ourselves the scene as it may

have been witnessed by a belated wayfarer on one of those wild autumn nights when the dead leaves are falling thick, and the winds seem to sing the dirge of the dying year. It is a sombre picture, set to melancholy music—the background of forest shewing black and jagged against a lowering and stormy sky, the sighing of the wind in the branches, the rustle of the withered leaves under foot, the lapping of the cold water on the shore, and in the foreground, pacing to and fro, now in twilight and now in gloom, a dark figure with a glitter of steel at the shoulder whenever the pale moon, riding clear of the cloud-rack, peers down at him through the matted boughs.[15]

There is more in these opening passages than lavish description. By the end of the first chapter of *The Golden Bough,* Frazer has drawn two important conclusions. First, on the basis of a passage of Servius, he has identified the bough of the tree plucked by the contender for the priesthood with the Golden Bough of Virgil's *Aeneid*—the bough which Aeneas plucked, on the Sibyl's instructions, before his journey to the underworld.[16] Second, on the basis of a passage of Virgil himself, he has identified that bough as mistletoe and so the tree on which it grew in the sacred grove as an oak. These conclusions are also supported, impressionistically at least, by the visual images chosen for the book: as a frontispiece, Turner's painting entitled *The Golden Bough,* a Virgilian scene showing the Sibyl holding the famous branch beside a lake which Frazer called Lake Nemi; and on the front cover of the book, a specially commissioned design of gold embossed mistletoe.[17]

Frazer's arguments are elegantly stated and, at first sight, seducing. Closer examination, however, reveals serious inconsistencies, misinterpretations, and errors. This is not merely the judgment of hindsight. From the very moment of its first appearance, from the first reviews of the first edition, commentators have found major faults with the chain of argumentation in the opening chapter of *The Golden Bough.*

The objections are quite straightforward. It is clear, for example, that the idea of the poor priest of Nemi prowling watchfully around his tree is largely an invention of Frazer himself. The only ancient source he cites in support mentions that the priest-king of Nemi was armed with a sword but says nothing about his guarding a tree and its sacred bough.[18] It is also clear that Frazer entirely misidentified Turner's painting in his frontispiece: the distinctive landscape features make it certain that the Sibyl is standing not by Lake Nemi at all but by Lake Avernus.[19] Even more important for the structure of Frazer's argument is the lack of any firm basis for equating the branch of Nemi with Virgil's Golden Bough. The evidence offered by Frazer comes from Servius, the fourth-century commentator on Virgil. In a complicated and allusive passage, Servius appears to include the branch of Nemi as one of four possible identifications of the Virgilian Golden Bough, though the difficulties of the passage make it uncertain what Servius had in mind for the precise connection between the tree of Nemi and the Virgilian Golden Bough.[20] There is even less foundation for equating either the branch at Nemi or the Virgilian Bough with mistletoe. Frazer simply relies on the fact that Virgil compares his Golden Bough with mistletoe, which is hardly the same thing as saying that it is mistletoe. In fact, it probably implies the reverse. For, as Andrew Lang observed already in 1901, "A poet does not compare a thing to itself."[21]

Frazer was probably aware of some of these difficulties. His own copies of the various editions of *The Golden Bough,* in which he made notes, added references to new material, and tried out slight rewordings for future editions, are in the library of Trinity College, Cambridge. In his copy of the second edition, we can still see a series of attempts at rewording the crucial passage that suggested that the branch at Nemi was none other than Virgil's Golden Bough. In this edition, as in the first, the sentence as printed reads: "Tradition averred that the fateful branch [that is the branch of Nemi] was that Golden Bough which, at the Sibyl's bidding, Aeneas plucked before he essayed the perilous journey to the world of the dead." Frazer made a whole series of attempts at rewriting this in the margins of the book, finally settling on a new version for the third edition: "According to the public opinion of the ancients, the fateful branch was that Golden Bough etc." And in this last edition he also added a footnote admitting that Servius was in fact the only ancient source to corroborate what he was proposing.[22] Such changes may not seem very substantial or significant, but the repeated corrections proposed for this crucial sentence and the obvious difficulty that Frazer had in finding an appropriate wording suggest that he did recognize the problems in what he was claiming, at some level.

Frazer's own recognition of these problems is also suggested by a slight change of emphasis in the third edition. In both the first and second editions, he claimed unequivocally that the whole purpose of his book was to investigate the rules of the strange cult at Nemi: why the priest had to slay his predecessor and why first he had to pluck the Golden Bough. In the third edition, by contrast, he called the priest of Nemi only the nominal hero of the book, suggesting that its real purpose was more than merely "investigating a particular problem of ancient mythology." It is as if he was trying to push into the background some of the more inconvenient problems associated with his interpretation of the cult at Nemi.[23]

## Nemi in *The Golden Bough*—Problems of Explanation

Why then, given Frazer's own recognition of these difficulties, did he continue to lay such stress on the sacred grove of Nemi? The obvious answer would be that he saw particular importance in this type of site and its cult. Up to a point that must be true, but it cannot be the whole answer. Surprisingly, despite Frazer's elaborate description of Nemi, he offers very little analysis of the site or, in more general terms, of the nature of sacred groves in Rome or other cultures. His references, for example, to ancient discussions of groves and glades (*luci* and *nemora*) omit some of the most relevant Latin passages, which Frazer must have known well.[24] And despite an enigmatic claim at the very beginning of the book that there was "a subtle link" between the natural landscape at Nemi and the horrible rituals perpetrated there, he never explored the possible connection between the physical aspect of the site and its religious significance.[25] It is clear that the prominence of Nemi in Frazer's work has more complex roots.

J. Z. Smith reveals some of this complexity in a chapter ("When the Bough Breaks") of his famous book, *Map is Not Territory*. Smith shows that Frazer's discussion of Nemi (particularly the identification of the sacred branch of the tree at Nemi first with Virgil's Golden Bough, second with mistletoe) is central to the structure of the whole work; more than that, the bough provides the sole crucial link in Frazer's great comparative scheme. Smith's argument is simple. The main hero of the second part of *The Golden Bough* is the Norse God-King, Balder the Beautiful, who is killed, it is said, by a shaft of mistletoe plucked from a sacred oak tree. In order to show a clear and direct link between the myth of the dying king in the classical world and the myth as it appears in other European cultures, Frazer must show that the branch of Nemi was (like Balder's branch) mistletoe. There is no other direct link to keep the whole book together. Whatever the problems, Frazer was forced to lay stress on Nemi; and he was forced to make the identification with Virgil's Golden Bough because it was only through Virgil and through Virgil's comparison of that bough with mistletoe that he could make the connection with the plant that killed Balder.[26]

Recognizing that Frazer must have known that he was on shaky ground, Smith goes much further. He ends his chapter by suggesting that Frazer knew perfectly well that the interpretation he offered of Nemi, its branch, and the Golden Bough was untenable. Moreover, in offering such an absurd interpretation, Frazer was deliberately making "his central work a joke," watching in amusement as his readers failed to spot the fact that the link supposedly holding the whole thesis together was no more than an illusion. For Smith, in other words, *The Golden Bough* is a comedy of the absurd, with Frazer a self-deconstructing Derridean hero.[27]

Smith's final interpretation of the aim of *The Golden Bough* has the advantage of rescuing Frazer's intellectual standing. For Smith, Frazer remains a hero (even if in a rather odd way)—rather than a victim of his own preoccupations with god-kings, mistletoe, and oak trees. But in its most extreme form Smith's view is hard to accept. There is nothing, of course, positively to disprove the idea that the real James Frazer was constantly laughing at a world (including his wife) that took *The Golden Bough* at face value. There is, however, nothing I have seen in Frazer's writing, either in *The Golden Bough* itself or in any of the other published works or even in the letters, journals, and notebooks, to suggest any element of such wicked self-irony. If Frazer was amusing himself by using it, he kept the joke entirely to himself.

Smith's first observation on the crucial linking role of Nemi in the structure of *The Golden Bough* is surely correct. But in order to go further than that simple observation, in order to understand the importance of the site and its rituals for Frazer's project, we must consider a context wider than the author's idiosyncratic literary aims. By turning now to examine the extraordinary and immediate popularity of *The Golden Bough,* my aim is to establish not only a useful context for understanding the work as a whole but also to throw new light on the particular prominence given to Nemi and to its Virgilian associations.

## The Craze for Frazer

*The Golden Bough* has achieved classic status as one of the symbols of British middle-class culture. Perhaps not read very often now, at least not from the beginning to the end of the twelve volumes in the third edition, it still does remain constantly in print (at least in the abridged edition), bought and admired by thousands.[28] Paradoxically, its assured, apparently unproblematic place on our shelves tends to discourage analysis of the nature of the book's success. We rarely think very carefully about why we continue to buy *The Golden Bough,* and still less about the process by which the book gained its classic status in the years between its first publication and Frazer's death.

The extraordinary authority of *The Golden Bough* in popular imagination during its author's lifetime can easily be documented from contemporary press reports of Frazer and his work.[29] In the early years of this century, major newspapers as well as the local press throughout the British empire—from the *Glasgow Herald* to the *Nairobi Standard,* from the *Huddersfield Examiner* to the *Auckland Star*—carried reviews of each edition of the book and regularly referred to it, particularly when searching for an explanation for some bizarre custom. *The Golden Bough* seemed to provide a useful key to practices as diverse as the strange rituals of royal coronations, the eating of horse meat, or voodoo magic used against Hitler in 1940s America. A typical article, in the *Melbourne Age* of 27 April 1940, reported the founding of a new American women's association, one of whose aims was to find a more acceptable title for mothers-in-law. The newspaper tried to point to the wider nature of this problem, ending its article by referring the reader to *The Golden Bough* and its ample documentation (so the newspaper claimed) of the "world-wide unpopularity of the mother-in-law among primitive peoples."[30]

Equally striking is the prominence of *The Golden Bough* in the literary columns of the British and English-speaking press. Even though by the 1930s a few commentators were beginning to find Frazer's writing (and the attitudes it suggested) somewhat "Victorian,"[31] the vogue for *The Golden Bough* was unabated. In New York in 1940 it competed equally with *Mein Kampf* as the best-selling non-fiction reprint.[32] *The Golden Bough* (according to the *London Evening News)* accompanied Mrs. Neville Chamberlain on most of her travels.[33] Time and time again it found a place in the literary editors' recommendations for war-time reading. For one writer of the period, it was quite simply "one of the masterpieces of all time" and its author one of "the giants of English prose."[34]

The enthusiasm for Frazer's books, however extravagant, did not in fact equal the enthusiasm for Frazer the man. He received all kinds of formal marks of recognition: a knighthood, honorary degrees, membership of the Order of Merit. He was invited, as a celebrity, to lecture all over the country and was wheeled out (sometimes literally no doubt) to meet a strange assortment of visiting dignitaries—not just academic and literary figures, but even evangelical preachers and sportsmen. In 1936, for example, he was introduced to the Black American athlete, Jesse Owens, who was reportedly thrilled at the meeting. What Frazer himself made of the encounter, we are (perhaps fortunately) not told.[35]

Towards the end of his life the flame of Frazer's popularity was kept regularly fanned by the annual celebrations of his birthday and by a continuing stream of much heralded publications.[36] By the 1930s the birthday (which fell on the first day of January, though often celebrated a few weeks later) became the excuse for more and more extravagant festivities planned by Lady Frazer and admiringly reported in the press. Particularly notable (and particularly well publicized) were the celebrations of 1937, when he reached the age of eighty-three. A party held in London for over two hundred guests featured an enormous cake with eighty-three candles; a short operetta based on a story by Lady Frazer, entitled, appropriately enough, *The Singing Wood;* and, as a final item that particularly charmed the old man, a display of indoor fireworks.[37]

One of the most notable accounts starts to describe the party but develops into an evocative appreciation of Frazer's achievement. Under the headline, "He *discovered* why you believe what you do," it reads:

Notables from many lands made their way to the Grosvenor Hotel, Victoria yesterday afternoon to do honour to an old man with a neat white head and eyes gone blind with reading too many books.

He stood beneath the golden bough of mistletoe specially brought from Norway as a symbol of his life-work. His body rests in civilized twentieth-century London, but his spirit roams the hinterland of time and space, at home in the Polynesia of a thousand years BC or the frozen north before even the Vikings had touched its shore with dragon prow or ruthless sword.

He has been twice honoured by his Sovereign, but he is shy to the point of diffidence even in the presence of nonentities. He knows all men are fools, riddled with superstitions that, self-imposed, constrict their freedom and splinter their happiness with futile sacrifice, but he has no contempt for them.

And, though but few have read the work by which he lives, and fewer know more of him than his name, he has changed the world.

He has changed it not as Mussolini has changed it: with coloured shirts and castor oil; nor as Lenin has changed it, boldly emptying out the baby of the humanities with the filthy bath of Tsarism; nor as Hitler with the fanfarronade of physical force.

He has changed it by altering the chemical composition of the cultural air that all men breathe: as Darwin changed it, bringing to a humanity still in bondage freedom from the idol that enslaved them.

. . . This quiet sedentary student has a mind similar to the body of Sir Francis Drake, ranging distant countries and bringing back their treasures for his own kind. But Frazer left the past no poorer for his rounds—and the present infinitely richer.[38]

On other occasions, normally the publication or projected publication of some new work, profiles of the great man appeared in many British and colonial newspapers. Obviously circulated in syndicated copy through the press, they piled anecdote upon anecdote about his strange and wonderful academic habits. In 1933, for example, following the publication of *The Fear of the Dead in Primitive Religions,* an almost identical account of Frazer (based on an interview with "a close friend") was widely reported in British local newspapers:

To Sir James Frazer work is a rite. During his life as a scholar he has worked 14 to 16 hours a day, seven days a week, and the same on holidays.

The Americans once told the greatest possible lie about him. They said that he was not a man, but a syndicate. He has, in point of fact, written every line of his books himself and has read all his own proofs.

. . . He is fond of recalling an anecdote about Anatole France, who had cupboards full of magnificent inkstands that had been presented to him, but who wrote every one of his novels from a twopenny inkpot.

It is the same with Sir James. He has been presented with gold and silver fountainpens. But he is not modern. He loathes "gadgets" and has written all his books with an ordinary steel nib.

Some people think that he must have travelled in all the countries he has described, but he has not. He is fond of saying that he has never seen a savage in his life. His books are the outcome of research into original scientific works.[39]

There are a number of important themes in these characterizations, apart from the perhaps predictable, perhaps laughable, stereotype of the unworldly academic. I shall return to some of these themes below, but for the moment I simply want to emphasize the quite extraordinary degree of popular acclaim for Frazer during his lifetime demonstrated by this material and to raise the question of why Frazer and *The Golden Bough* were so popular. In what follows I shall explore several answers to this question. I hope to show particularly that Nemi and Virgil's Bough had a role in this popularity and that the supposedly classical beginning of the work served to legitimate the unfamiliar methods and claims of *The Golden Bough*. I hope also to show that the image of the Virgilian Golden Bough is central to one main theme of the book, a theme that emerges also in the popular press accounts: that is, the exploration of the Foreign, the Other.

### *The Golden Bough* and Imperialism

One obviously important aspect of *The Golden Bough* is its close links with British imperialism. The British empire largely provided the raw material for Frazer's discussion of contemporary savage customs, and the footnotes, time and time again, cite the early classics of British colonial (or missionary) ethnography: Dalton's *Descriptive Ethnology of Bengal,* Spencer and Gillen's *Native Tribes of Australia,* Biddulph's *Tribes of the Hindoo Koosh,* and so on.[40]

Some readers in the early years of this century commented on the practical usefulness of *The Golden Bough* as a compendium of native customs of empire. One of Frazer's close friends was even quoted as saying "many mistakes would have been avoided in this direction [the government of backward and primitive peoples] if more attention had been paid to the knowledge which Sir James has revealed of habits, customs and traditional beliefs."[41] But we should not understand *The Golden Bough*'s links with empire and imperialism just in practical terms. By laying out within a single framework the various customs of the different parts of the empire, Frazer provided for his readers a useful image of the British imperial enterprise: He offered a manageable way of re-presenting imperial subjects to their masters. *The Golden Bough,* in other words, acted to legitimate imperialism by turning the empire and its subject peoples into the supporting evidence in an important scholarly project. This was political domination neatly turned into academic prose.

The extraordinary popularity of *The Golden Bough* cannot depend solely, however, on the book's reassuring projection of British imperialism. First, Frazer's work was not particularly distinctive in this respect. Most late Victorian anthropological literature was concerned at some level with negotiating and justifying the role of British white imperialism. Frazer might have surpassed his contemporaries in the breadth of his geographical coverage or in the number and range of primitive customs that he managed to include. But he did not create a new or unique link between anthropology and the politics of empire.[42] Second, *The Golden Bough* covers many topics that lie quite outside the ethnography of the British colonies. The savage customs of the empire's inhabitants are certainly prominent in the book but so also (as I have already stressed) is the world of classical antiquity, as well as the folk traditions of rural Britain. No explanation of the book's success can be satisfactory if it fails to take account of the distinctive combination of themes woven together by Frazer, the combination to which I now turn.

### Frazer's Comparative Scheme and the Role of Nemi

The casual reader of *The Golden Bough* is struck immediately and forcefully by the extreme comparativism on which the book is based. The text and footnotes of almost every page present a dazzling range of material that juxtaposes the ethnography of empire with the world of classical antiquity and with British rural folklore: In *The Golden Bough* corn dollies rub shoulders with magical kangaroos, African rain-makers with Hippocratic doctors. The savages of the empire are seen here not in isolation but as part of a wider framework incorporating both the ancient world and contemporary Britain.[43]

The comparative method was not in itself new. Many of the early reviewers of *The Golden Bough*'s first edition recognized this intellectual style and saw the book as part of a recent, but nevertheless well-established, trend towards comparative study in religion and anthropology.[44] But no one before had adopted such an extreme and apparently self-confident comparative approach as this—certainly not in a work intended for a general readership.

It is helpful to contrast the books of Frazer's contemporary, Jane Harrison, the historian of Greek religion. Almost as much as Frazer's, Harrison's whole approach to her subject depended on close comparison between the classical world and modern anthropological theory and ethnography. But the final products (*Themis, Prolegomena to a Study of*

*Greek Religion*) still presented themselves as technical studies of classical religious history. It takes more than a casual glance for the reader to be aware of the wider frame of reference buried within.[45] A striking contrast may also be drawn with E. B. Tylor, whose *Primitive Culture* (1871) is probably the most direct ancestor of *The Golden Bough*. Tylor's project was essentially a comparative one, based on a conviction (shared with Frazer and others) that the fundamental unity of mankind was far more important than individual cultural differences. But he was writing for a more strictly academic readership and did not flaunt (indeed sometimes concealed) the wide range of his comparisons, particularly with respect to the domestic folk traditions of the British Isles.[46] An even more striking contrast with Frazer can be found in the material collected in ethnographic and folklore periodicals of the mid- to late nineteenth century, both in Britain and Europe. These journals certainly contained articles spanning many of the areas of Frazer's interests—from "Childbearing in Australia and New Zealand" to "The Superstitions of West Sussex." But the links between these separate pieces were rarely made clear, and it was only in very specific areas (notably physical anthropology and the anthropology of language) that contributors regularly wrote explicitly comparative articles.[47] Here was the raw material for comparison but not the comparative method itself. Even within the covers of a single journal, the different areas of research remain isolated from one another. There is no definition of an overall intellectual framework in which both the ethnography of empire and British folklore are integral parts.

Frazer's achievement was, unashamedly, to unite all these different areas as part of a single intellectual programme. Unlike Tylor, he paraded rather than concealed the full extent of the comparative approach. His comparativism was obvious and unmistakable. It defined the character of his work. The implications of this were far-reaching. Frazer was not simply meditating on the problems (or virtues) of the British empire as a phenomenon on its own. By bringing together these different areas of study, he set the subject of imperialism within the context of other central issues in the culture of late Victorian Britain: the changing face of British traditions in the face of growing industrialization; the role and importance of the classical past. Through *The Golden Bough,* questions about British imperial domination became implicated in other questions about the relations between the peoples of the empire and those of rural England, about the nature of the rural and the urban, the nature of the foreign, the domestic, and the past. The extraordinary appeal of *The Golden Bough* derived from the power of this combination: from its weaving together so many central problems of late Victorian, early twentieth-century Britain.

What then of the role of Nemi and its cult? Was it just one element of the classical side of Frazer's comparative project—an ancient Roman cult to be set against the rituals of Africa or the Scottish Highlands? Or was it just an artful frame to the whole work, the excuse for an elaborate literary exercise at the beginning and end of the book? Nemi's role is, I would argue, much more important and much more closely related to the success of Frazer's project. The problem of Nemi provided a most effective re-assurance to those readers who might reasonably have found Frazer's ambitious comparative scheme disconcerting.

The secret of *The Golden Bough* was that, within its complex web of far-flung comparisons, it offered a simple question and a surprisingly simple answer. To present an intellectual vision that embraced the foreign and savage so closely with the familiar domestic (if rural) world of England in an overtly popular book was itself a dangerous undertaking. But Frazer managed to reassure his readers while puzzling, exhilarating, even shock-ing them. For in the end (as Frazer took pains to make clear) all the dan-gerous unfamiliar learning of *The Golden Bough* was directed towards the neatly tied, elegant solution of a problem that could not have been safer—a problem drawn from classical history and scholarship. In the Victorian world in which the classics remained at the center of traditional intellectual endeavor, Frazer used the problem of Nemi to legitimate his project, to clothe it in respectability. The wild, far-reaching exploration in the main text was granted academic status and safety by the set pieces on the cult of Nemi at the beginning and end of the work.[48]

### The Theme of Exploration: *The Golden Bough* and the "Golden Bough"

The excitement engendered by *The Golden Bough* did not come only from its daring comparative framework. More than a work of comparative anthropology, it was also a tale of travel and exploration. This is not to say that Frazer offered his readers an eyewitness description of foreign coun-tries. Quite the reverse was the case. The press made a good deal of play with the fact that Frazer had never actually travelled to those countries he described. "An authority on savages. But he has never seen one" ran many headlines; and the gossip columnist of the *Sunday Chronicle* (who had naively supposed that he must have "pottered intellectually around Polynesia, New Guinea, the Great Barrier reef and a few other places where our aboriginal brothers and sisters reside") reliably reported, after a lunchtime conversation with Frazer, that the grand old man "had never been farther than Greece."[49] The Golden Bough was not a literal tale of travel. It offered the reader a metaphorical voyage into the unknown, into the wild, the Other. For a society in which travel to the Mediterranean was becoming a bourgeois reality, in which literary accounts of such travel were increasingly being replaced by direct experience, Frazer offered a view of much wilder shores.

The image of travel is partly sustained by Frazer's own language. He often writes of his book as a voyage or exploration. So, for example, at the end of the first introductory chapter, he looks forward to his wider project in these terms: "To that wider survey we must now address ourselves. It will be long and laborious, but may possess something of the charm and interest of a voyage of discovery, in which we shall visit many strange foreign lands, with strange foreign peoples, and still stranger customs. The wind is in our shrouds: we shake out our sails to it, and leave the coast of Italy behind us for a time." And at the very end of the book (in the third edition), when he returns to Nemi he returns to that image of sailing: "Our long voyage of discovery is over, and our bark has dropped her weary sails in port at last. Once more we take the road to Nemi."[50] Reviewers and commentators also picked up this metaphor of exploration. They talked of Frazer "travelling far afield in search of facts," of "following" him on his journeys around the marginal areas of the world—and even (as in the passage quoted above) compared him to such famous heroic explorers as Sir Francis Drake.[51]

The image of exploration was most strikingly developed in a novel published in 1890 and based explicitly on The Golden Bough, whose first edition had appeared some months earlier. In The Great Taboo, Grant Allen turned Frazer's metaphorical journey into a literal story of travel and adventure.[52] It is the tale of a young English couple, Felix Thurstan and Miss Muriel Ellis, washed overboard a steamer in the South Seas and cast up on an island called Boupari, where the religious customs of the natives were a composite of those described by Frazer in The Golden Bough. In the end, predictably enough, young Felix has to save his own life (and that of the delightful Muriel, with whom he has by now fallen in love) by seizing the branch of a sacred tree, killing the cannibalistic god-king and assuming the role of the deity himself. The final scene of the novel sees them back in England, rescued and just married, trying to deal with Muriel's crusty old aunt, who objects to the fact that they had spent so many months on the island together but unmarried. "Taboos," as the concluding remark of the novel goes, "are much the same in England as in Boupari."

Although this narrative is not a great novel and has no particular distinction, it does reveal, in its crude and simplified retelling of *The Golden Bough,* some of the major themes of Frazer's book, as they were perceived when it first appeared. Two particularly important aspects are apparent even from the very brief account of the novel given above. First, the final sentence of *The Great Taboo* (on the similarity of taboos in England and in Boupari) baldly states what is otherwise merely implied in much of Frazer's comparative approach: that primitive customs cannot be so clearly divided from the customs of contemporary civilization.[53] Second, the narrative of *The Great Taboo* interprets literally the metaphorical journey into the unknown that was implicit in *The Golden Bough.* The novel acts out that voyage: Two young explorers are cast ashore onto the unknown and strange island, then finally brought back to familiar civilization but now with a heightened sophistication about the taboos and constraints of their own culture. It is as if the reader's experience in traveling through *The Golden Bough* has been turned into the vivid melodrama of a voyage of discovery.

But what of Nemi in this metaphorical voyage into the Other? Nemi and its cult are doubly important in this context. First Frazer uses the classical world, with its traditional place in British culture, as the familiar firm ground in his voyage. As he made explicit in the first chapter of *The Golden Bough,* Italy (and within Italy a clear classical problem) is the starting point of the journey—and it is to Italy (to the bells of Rome itself, in fact) that the reader returns at the end of the journey. But second, and even more important, the identification of the branch of Nemi with the Virgilian Golden Bough plays a particularly crucial role because it reproduces in Frazer's text the same function it fulfilled in the narrative of the *Aeneid.* What was it that the Golden Bough allowed Aeneas to accomplish? It allowed him to enter into the underworld and to return again. By stressing (beyond what the evidence will bear) the identification of the branch at Nemi with the Virgilian Bough, by appropriating the Golden Bough as the title for his whole work, Frazer paraded the same function for his book. Like the Virgilian Bough, Frazer's *The Golden Bough* took the reader into the Other and then brought him or her safely back out again.

The importance of Frazer's title was recognized by Jane Harrison. Quite contrary to the impression given by Leach, she did not spend much time on Frazer and his work. But in a brief reference to him in her autobiography she claimed that "the happy title" of *Golden Bough* made it "arrest the attention of scholars." "Sir James," she wrote, "has a veritable genius for titles . . . at the mere sound of the magical words 'Golden Bough' we heard and understood."[54] Harrison must have seen how much was at stake in the title *Golden Bough* and in the identification of the branch at Nemi with its Virgilian counterpart. It was not just a case, as Smith would suggest, of finding a direct parallel with Balder the Beautiful. The Virgilian Golden Bough represented the function of the whole Frazerian enterprise. Much of the appeal of *The Golden Bough* lay in the fact that it was a Golden Bough for every reader.

### Postscript: *The Golden Bough* Today

*The Golden Bough* still sells in large numbers. Frazer does not today enjoy quite the heroic status that he enjoyed in the earlier years of this century. But the abridged edition has remained constantly in print, and the publishers presumably anticipated some commercial success when they decided to issue in 1990 a new reprint of the full twelve-volume edition. Why is there such unabating popularity?

It would be naïve to imagine that Frazer's theories and arguments had much to do with this popularity. Maybe (to judge from the common appearance of *The Golden Bough* in bookshops of the occult) part of the book's success comes from a link between Frazer's theories of death and rebirth and modern esoteric religion. But this can hardly be a major factor. Even the most enthusiastic followers of the occult (if they trouble to read more than a few chapters) would surely find it hard to see the relevance of much of Frazer's outdated ethnography to their own interests. The average reader, without such a particular incentive to persevere, must find *The Golden Bough* a long-winded, impenetrable text made all the more baffling for its insistent comparisons between one (now) unfamiliar world and another.

The success of *The Golden Bough* rests on the undeniable fact that it is so rarely read.[55] It is bought; is presented as a prize; takes an assured, if not honored, place on the shelves of libraries; is owned by most of those who make at least some pretence to literary culture; and is a lurking presence behind some of the greatest pieces of modern creative literature.[56] But few people would even claim to have read more than a couple of pages of *The Golden Bough.* Its importance lies no longer in what it says, but in what it is: a vast symbol of encyclopedic knowledge. Behind even the abridged edition lies the sheer bulk and authority of the twelve-volume text—a monument not so much to scholarship, but to facts; to the possibility of collecting and ordering such facts; and to the reassuring certainty that they can be explained. Paradoxically, a book which started life as a potentially dangerous voyage of exploration into the Other has grown into a symbol of the certainty of human knowledge.

NOTES

Acknowledgements: My work on Frazer started after an invitation to talk on "Fraser and Sacred Groves" at a conference on "Les bois sacres" at the Centre J. Berard, Naples in November 1989, to mark (a few months in advance!) the centenary of the publication of *The Golden Bough*'s first edition. I would like to thank the organizers of that conference, Olivier de Cazanove and John Scheid, for their invitation and for the stimulus to work further on Frazer. This article expands and develops the ideas of that earlier paper (to be published in French in the proceedings of the conference). I am also most grateful to David McKitterick and the staff of the Wren Library, Trinity College, Cambridge for their help with manuscript material relating to Frazer; to the Master and Fellows of Trinity College for permission to quote from this material; and to the editor and referees of *CSSH* for helpful comments on the final draft.

I have normally cited passages from the third edition of *The Golden Bough,* 12 vols. (London, 1911–1915) as *GB*³. Any significant differences between the various editions (*GB*¹, 2 vols. [London, 1890] and *GB*², 3 vols. [London, 1900]) are indicated. Two recent biographical studies (R. Ackerman, *J. G. Frazer, His Life and Work* [Cambridge, 1987], and R. Fraser, *The Making of The Golden Bough: The Origins and Growth of an Argument* [London, 1990]) provide the full account of the central aspects of Frazer's writing and career. They are cited (as Ackerman, *J. G. Frazer,* or Fraser, *The Making of The Golden Bough*) only in cases of disagreement or where their discussion is particularly relevant to my argument.

1. The clearest account of these remains and the complex history of their excavations is given in *Mysteries of Diana: The Antiquities from Nemi in Nottingham Museums* (Castle Museum: Nottingham, 1983). See also F. Coarelli, *I santuari del Lazio in età repubblicana* (Studi NIS Archeologia 7) (Rome, 1987), 165–85.

2. *GB*³, I, 1 (= vol. 1), l.

3. For discussion of this cult and the office of the priest-king (held in the historical period by a runaway slave), see A. E. Gordon, "The Cults of Aricia," *University of California Publications in Classical Archaeology* 2, 1 (1934): 1–20, and T. F. C. Blagg, "The Cult and Sanctuary of Diana Nemorensis," in M. Henig and A. King, eds., *Pagan Gods and Shrines of the Roman Empire,* Monograph 8

(Oxford: Oxford University Committee for Archaeology, 1986), 211–19. The practice of killing the king survived in some form into the Roman imperial period. Suetonius (*Life of Gaius,* 35) claims that the emperor, Gaius (A.D. 37–41), actually put up an opponent for a priest-king who had, he thought, held power too long—an example, for Suetonius, of the emperor's mad jealousy of even his most lowly subjects. The practice is attested also by Pausanias in the second-century A.D. (*Description of Greece* II, 27, 4).

4. *Anthropology Today* 1 (1985), 2–3.

5. Leach's particular target is the one-volume abridged version of *The Golden Bough* (London, 1922), which omits most of the archaeological information on the site included in the full-scale third edition. Leach much prefers the account given in that longer version. In fact, the inclusion of this archaeological material makes little difference to Frazer's image of the site, which remains remarkably consistent through all editions, both before and after his visit.

6. All quotations are from Leach, "Reflections on a Visit to Nemi" (see n. 4).

7. *Daedalus* 90 (1961), 371–99. See also "On the 'Founding Fathers': Frazer and Malinowski," *Encounter* 25 (1965), 24–36 (reprinted with further comments in *Current Anthropology* 7 (1966), 560–67). For a bibliography of other recent evaluations of Frazer, see Ackerman, *J. G. Frazer,* 315.

8. Leach himself ("Golden Bough or Gilded Twig," *Daedalus* 90 (1961), 375–77 analyses $GB^3$, IV, 1 (= vol. 5), 102–3 against its source (W. E. Roth, *North Queensland Ethnography* (Brisbane, 1903), par. 81–83). A similar relationship with source material can be demonstrated in earlier editions: for example, $GB^1$, I:69–72 (compare, J. Biddulph, *Tribes of the Hindoo Koosh* [Calcutta, 1880], 103–6); $GB^1$, I:85 (compare, E. T. Dalton, *Descriptive Ethnology of Bengal* [Calcutta, 1872], 261). Unfortunately, Leach's interpretation of this and other aspects of Frazer's writing is undermined by his transparent disdain, even loathing, for his subject, whom he characterizes as a self-seeking lapdog of the Establishment, devoid of intellectual originality.

9. Robertson Smith was resident in Trinity from the end of 1883 to 1885, where he became close to Frazer. As editor of the *Encyclopaedia Britannica,* he commissioned Frazer to write articles for the ninth edition, under the letters P, S, and T—from "Penates," "Pericles," and "Praefect" to (significantly) "Taboo" and "Totemism." Smith died in 1894. In Leach's view ("Golden Bough or Gilded Twig," 373), this left Frazer without intellectual inspiration and he "thereafter created virtually no fresh work throughout the whole of his long life." For a discussion of Frazer's relations with Robertson Smith, see R. Alun Jones, "Robertson Smith and James Frazer on Religion," in G. Stocking, ed., *Functionalism Historicized: Essays in British Social Anthropology* (History of Anthropology, no. 2) (Wisconsin, 1984), 31–58.

10. Leach follows the almost unanimous scholarly tradition in deriding Lilly Frazer (born Elizabeth Adelsdorfer, from Alsatian France, widow of Charles

Grove before her marriage to Frazer) as a publicity crazed harridan, who dominated her reserved husband. Even the judicious Ackerman ends his biography by quoting the jibe of the Fellows of Trinity (a group not well known for their sympathy for the female sex) to the effect that her death only a few hours after Frazer ensured that she did "not allow him even one day's peace by himself"; see also the characterization in Ackerman, *J. G. Frazer,* 124–26. This stereotype of the academic's wife (see also, for example, Lady Beazley, who is described by B. Ashmole, *Proceedings of the British Academy* (*PBA*), 56 (1970), 447–48; repr. in D. Kurtz, ed., *Beazley and Oxford* [Oxford, 1985], 60–61) would itself be worth further study!

11. Leach ("Golden Bough or Gilded Twig," 383) typically finds an unworthy secret behind Harrison's interest in Frazer: "It seems clear that part of Jane Harrison's interest in *The Golden Bough* lay in the fact that she was fascinated by the brute sadism of primitive sacrifice." For Harrison's career (which, in fact, had very little to do with Frazer's, despite their long residence in the same university), see S. J. Peacock, *Jane Ellen Harrison: The Mask and the Self* (New Haven and London, 1988), with the review by M. Beard, *Times Literary Supplement,* 27 Jan.–2 Feb. 1989, 82. It is, of course, a highly implausible suggestion that in the late nineteenth century the academic respectability of a Fellow of Trinity could have been promoted by the support of a woman—still less by the support of the eccentric Jane Harrison.

12. See below, n. 28.

13. In addition to Ackerman and Fraser, see, for example, E. Evans-Pritchard, *A History of Anthropological Thought* (London, 1981), 132–52; R. Alun Jones, "Robertson Smith and Frazer." It would be rash to deny that the higher intellectual context of Frazer's work had some bearing on his popular success; but there is little in the press reports cited below to suggest that the distinction between magic and science, the inheritance of Hume, or an intellectualist view of religion touched the public consciousness. In fact, I suspect that it has proved difficult to explain the widespread popularity of *The Golden Bough* precisely because it has always been treated from a strictly academic standpoint. This article suggests a different route toward an explanation.

14. Both Ackerman and Fraser are much concerned with the development of Frazer's thought over the three editions of *The Golden Bough* and suggest that apparently minor changes in the treatment of Nemi and its cult may relate to a more fundamental revision of Frazer's theories. See, for example, Ackerman, *J. G. Frazer,* 240–41 and Fraser, *The Making of The Golden Bough,* 160–67. Even if these revisions are as important as is suggested, they do not affect the prominence of Nemi in every edition.

15. *GB³*, I:1 (= vol. 1), 9–10.

16. Virgil, *Aeneid,* 6, 98–155, 183–211. Among the works in the vast literature on the Virgilian Bough, see R. A. Brooks, "Discolor Aura. Reflections on the Golden Bough," *American Journal of Philology* 74 (1953), 260–80; C. P. Segal, "Aeternum

per Saecula Nomen, The Golden Bough and the Tragedy of History," Pt. 1, *Arion* 4 (1965), 617–57; Pt. 2, *Arion* 5 (1966), 34–72; D. West, *The Bough and the Gate* (Exeter, 1987), repr. in S. J. Harrison, *Oxford Readings in Vergil's Aeneid* (Oxford, 1990), 224–38. Note that I use *The Golden Bough* (italics) to refer to the book and the Golden Bough (in roman type) to Virgil's branch.

17. Designed by J. H. Middleton (1846–1896), director of the Fitzwilliam Museum, Cambridge. For Frazer's detailed instructions to the publisher on the appearance of the book, see Fraser, *The Making of The Golden Bough,* 53–54, 118.

18. *GB*[3], I:1 (= vol. 1), 9, n. 1. cites (in the original Greek) Strabo's description (*Geography* 5, 3, 12): "The priest is always armed with a sword, looking around for the attacks, and ready to defend himself." In the same passage Strabo mentions the sacred grove but not a particular tree with a particular bough that must be plucked. The only ancient source to mention such a particular bough is Servius (passage cited in n. 20). Even he does not suggest that the priest-king guarded the tree, merely that combat could take place only after the assailant had plucked the branch.

19. For full details of the painting, see M. Butlin and E. Joll, *The Paintings of J. M. W. Turner* (New Haven and London, 1984), no. 355 (cat. pp. 204–5; pl. 359). Frazer himself did not know the painting at first hand. He wrongly notes on his own copy of *GB*[2] (Trinity College, Adv c 21 69): "The original is said to be in the public gallery at Dublin." In fact it had always been housed in London museums (the National Gallery and then the Tate).

20. Servius on *Aeneid,* 6, 136, trans. by J. Z. Smith, "When the Bough Breaks," ch. 10 of *Map Is Not Territory: Studies in the History of Religions* (Studies in Judaism in Late Antiquity 23) (Leiden, 1978), 215 (with full discussion, 215–21). See also West, *The Bough and the Gate,* 226–27 (page reference from reprint).

21. Virgil, *Aeneid,* 6, 201–9. The passage, translated by Cecil Day-Lewis, describes Aeneas' discovery of the Golden Bough, led by two doves:

> Then, when they [the doves] came to the mouth of foul-breathing Avernus,
> Swiftly they soared, went gliding through the soft air and settled,
> The pair of them, on a tree, the wished-for place, a tree
> Amid whose branches there gleamed a bright haze, a different colour—
> Gold. Just as in depth of winter the mistletoe blooms
> In the woods with its strange leafage, a parasite on the tree,
> Hanging its yellow-green berries about the smooth round boles:
> So looked the bough of gold leaves upon that ilex dark,
> And in a gentle breeze the gold-foil foliage rustled.

Lang was a critic of Frazer almost as vitriolic as Leach. This particular objection is from *Magic and Religion* (London, 1901, p. 215), a book which amounted to an extended review of *The Golden Bough*. For further discussion, see Smith, "When the Bough Breaks," 224; West, *The Bough and the Gate,* 227–30 (page reference from reprint); and (on the context of Lang's opposition), Ackerman, *J. G. Frazer,* 171–74.

22. *GB²*, 1, 4 (Trinity College, Cambridge Adv c 21 69), reworked into *GB³*, I:1 (= vol. 1), 11. Among the repeated amendments the order of the corrections is difficult to disentangle. He obviously considered and rejected (at least once): "Tradition, at least of the learned in the time of Servius, that is about the end of the fourth (?) century . . ."; "The general opinion of the ancients held that . . ."; "The general opinion of the ancients, as reported by the old Virgilian commentator Servius, held that . . ."; "According to the general opinion of the ancients. . . ." Earlier (on p. 4) he considered altering the first sentence of this paragraph from "I begin by setting forth the few facts and legends which have come down to us on the subject" to "facts and opinions," though he later decided to leave the sentence as it stood in the second edition. For an impression of the character of Frazer's own marginal notes (sometimes submerging the written text), see Fraser, *The Making of The Golden Bough* (Plate I, facing p. 196).

23. *GB³*, VII:1 (= vol. 10), vi (though note that the abridged edition of 1922 again claims that "the primary aim of this book is to explain the remarkable rule which regulated the succession to the priesthood of Diana at Aricia" (p. v). Smith ("When the Bough Breaks," especially 209–12) documents this change of emphasis over the successive editions very clearly, as does Ackerman, *J. G. Frazer* (especially 236–57), though, in my view, occasionally over-interpreting its significance. See also n. 14.

24. 24 *GB³*, I:1 (= vol. 1), 2, especially n. 1. Frazer's view that the Latin word *nemus* meant, in its strictest sense, a natural opening or glade, while *lucus* meant the wooded grove itself, is probably the reverse of the truth. Among relevant passages not cited by Frazer, note especially Cato, *On Agriculture,* 148. For recent discussion of sacred groves, see O. de Cazanove and J. Scheid, eds., *Les bois sacrés* (forthcoming).

25. *GB³*, I:1 (= vol. 1), 1–2. A similar claim is made in the preface to *GB³*, IV:1 (= vol. 5), v, again hardly developed. Frazer's edition of Pausanias' six-volume *Description of Greece* (London, 1898) contains a number of sometimes elegant, sometimes high-flown descriptions of landscapes; for an analysis of these scenic passages, see Ackerman, *J. G. Frazer,* 137–39, and Fraser, *The Making of The Golden Bough,* 42–43. Significantly, however, Frazer's commentary devotes almost no attention to the Greek sacred groves described in Pausanias' text.

26. See, especially, Smith, "When the Bough Breaks," 221–34. Other critics have noted the crucial importance of the similarity between Balder and the priest-king of Nemi; see Ackerman, *J. G. Frazer,* 95–110, and Fraser, *The Making of The Golden Bough,* 191. Early reviewers were struck (in different ways) by the link between the myth of Balder and that of the Golden Bough. So, for example, in the *Glasgow Herald* (4 June 1890) the anonymous reviewer suggested that Frazer "does

not succeed, unless by straining, in harmonising the act of plucking the bough with the act of striking Balder"; though reviewers in the *Pall Mall Gazette* (10 June 1890) and *The Academy* (14 June 1890, by Isaac Taylor) were convinced. Taylor even believed that that link was the strongest point in the book (*The Academy*, 14 June 1890).

27. Smith, "When the Bough Breaks," 238–39.

28. Some 36,000 copies of each volume of the complete third edition were printed between 1911 and 1922; over 33,000 copies of the abridged edition were printed between 1922 and 1933 (Ackerman, *J. G. Frazer*, 257). For figures on earlier editions, see Ackerman, *J. G. Frazer*, 96, 113, 114, 162, 177).

29. This task is made infinitely easier because of Lady Frazer's often derided preoccupation with her husband's career. It appears that from at least the mid-1920s she organized a subscription to various news clipping agencies, with the result that an extraordinary range of press reports and reviews of Frazer's work from all over the world are preserved in scrap books in the Wren Library, Trinity College (amongst other Frazer MSS 7, $22^{5-34}$, $22^{35-56}$, $22^{110-43}$, $22^{144-65}$). It is unclear how far, or in what way, Frazer's public image in this last period of his life differed from his image in the earliest years of the century or the late Victorian period, for there is no full collection of clippings within the Frazer papers before the mid-1920s. It would, of course, be possible to conduct a full survey of the British and foreign press for that earlier period in search of references to Frazer, but it seemed to me that (however interesting the question of the changes in Frazer's reputation) the results were unlikely to justify the months of time for such a survey. My material therefore concentrates on the period covered by the cuttings already assembled in the Trinity College collection.

30. See the *Daily News*, 23 May 1896 (coronations); *The Times*, 14 July 1937 (eating horsemeat); *Cavalcade*, 15 Mar. 1941 (voodoo against Hitler). Similarly, the *Melbourne Argus*, 12 June 1936 (religious associations of volcanoes); the *Manchester Evening News*, 23 Dec. 1939 (mistletoe); the *Huddersfield Examiner*, 23 Mar. 1940 (Easter customs). The comprehensive index of the third edition (stretching to almost 400 pages) no doubt partly accounts for the frequency with which *The Golden Bough is* cited. This index effectively turned the work into an easy reference encyclopedia of world customs.

31. See, for example, the *Sydney Morning Herald*, 13 Feb. 1936, reviewing *Aftermath* (London, 1936): "Sir James, a late Victorian, pities the poor savage with all his heart for being so ignorant of the blessings of civilisation. The young anthropologist of today usually envies the savage for exactly the same reason."

32. Reported in the *Saturday Review of Literature*, New York, 28 Dec. 1940.

33. 16 Apr. 1938. Apparently Mrs. Roosevelt showed similar tastes, enjoying "treatises on sociology and history," while her husband preferred "books of the sea."

34. The *Cambeltown Courier*, 22 Feb. 1941. See also (for wartime reading) the

*Baptist Times,* 28 Sep. 1939 ("I shall keep Sir James Frazer's *Golden Bough* within easy reach"); the *Auckland Star,* 24 Aug. 1940 ("Frazer's unabridged edition of *The Golden Bough* is guaranteed to keep the non-skipping reader fully occupied through another 40 years war").

35. The *Birmingham Post,* 3 Sep. 1936. The meeting with Owens was apparently arranged by Dr. Harris Kirk, an American preacher.

36. This included not only academic works (including *Creation and Evolution in Primitive Cosmogonies* [London, 1935]; *Anthologia Anthropologica,* 1–4 [London, 1938–1939]—anthologies of material relating to "native races" of different areas), but also a children's book about a dog (written with Lady Frazer), *Pasha the Pom* (London, 1937).

37. It is not entirely clear why Frazer (by this date completely blind) was so charmed by the fireworks! He is normally characterized by the press as uninterested in these gatherings, preferring the pleasure of a good day's work. See, for example, *The New York Times,* 1 Jan. 1939; *The Northern Echo,* 19 Feb. 1937.

38. Gerald Haylett, *News Chronicle,* 27 Jan. 1937, a rare signed piece.

39. Published on 15 Apr. 1936, by the *Northern Daily Mail, West Lancashire Evening Gazette, Portsmouth Evening News, Dublin Evening Mail, Oldham Evening Chronicle, Staffordshire Sentinel, Nottingham Evening Post, North Western Evening Mail, Aberdeen Evening Express, South Wales Evening Post, Cambridge Daily News* (very abbreviated), *Yorkshire Evening News;* on 16 Apr. 1936, by the *Torbay Herald;* on 18 Apr. 1936, by the *Gloucester Journal.* The account may also, of course, have been printed in other papers which did not reach the Frazers and so are not preserved in the collection at Trinity College.

40. A vast bibliography (144 pages) is included in the final volume of *GB*[3], with full details of all works cited. By the time Frazer was writing the third edition a number of the ethnographic accounts he relied upon were themselves influenced by his theories, well known from earlier editions. Frazer appears gratified by their confirmation, rather than alarmed by the circularity. The direct involvement of Frazer in Spencer and Gillen's work (effectively acting as their agent with Macmillan) is documented by Ackerman, *J. G. Frazer,* 153–57.

41. *Dublin Evening Mail,* 25 Sept. 1936—Frazer himself was reported to be pleased "that the knowledge which they [his books] contain about the customs and ways of thought of primitive peoples may be of help to those whose task it is to govern them" (quoted in fuller versions of the report cited in n. 39).

42. Aspects of the complex relation of anthropology and imperialism are explored by Gillian Beer, "Speaking for the Others: Relativism and Authority in Victorian Anthropological Literature," in R. Fraser, ed., *Sir James Frazer and the Literary Imagination* (London, 1990). See also the brief discussion with bibliography by C. R. Phillips III, "Classical Scholarship Against Its History," *American Journal of Philology,* 111 (1989), 636–57 (esp. 646–47).

43. Note, for example, *GB*[3], I:1 (= vol. 1), 148–49, where the twelve footnotes

embrace the customs of Java, North India, Mexico, the northern counties of Britain, Germany, and the Slavs, as well as references to Mrs. Gamp and the Greek scientist, Aelian. Many other openings offer a similar range.

44. See, for example, W. Warde Fowler's review in *Classical Review* 5 (1891), 48–52. See the subtitle of the first edition, "A Study in Comparative Religion," and the first advertisements for the book ("The Method of Investigation Is the Comparative One" as in *Athenaeum,* 2 Mar. 1890).

45. For Harrison's intellectual background, see R. Ackerman, "Jane Ellen Harrison: The Early Work," *Greek, Roman, and Byzantine Studies* 13 (1972), 209–30, and Ackerman's doctoral thesis, *The Cambridge Group and the Origins of Myth Criticism* (Ann Arbor, Mich.: University Microfilms, 1969).

46. The difference between Tylor's work and Frazer's partly consists in presentation and packaging (important factors in the popular reception of the work). It is striking to compare the flamboyance of Frazer's footnotes (see n. 43) with the reticence of Tylor's throughout *Primitive Culture.* Similarly Frazer's index in *GB*³ parades the range of his comparative scheme (with a column of references to the traditions of Scotland, and even eleven references to the traditions of Cambridge and Cambridgeshire), while Tylor's tends to conceal that (with fewer than five references in the whole of the index of *Primitive Culture* to subjects obviously connected with British local traditions). The wide-ranging comparative framework underlying Tylor's work is made clear in, for example, "On a Method of Investigating the Development of Institutions; Applied to Laws of Marriage and Descent," *Journal of the Anthropological Institute* 18 (1889), 245–69 (not an article for "the general reader").

47. The list of contents of various ethnographic and similar journals illustrate this clearly. Consider the range of articles in the *Journal of the Ethnological Society of London* (ns) 1 (1868–1869): from "On the Pseudo-Cromlech on Mount Alexander, Australia" and "On Some of the Mountain Tribes of the North West Frontier of India" to "Flint Instruments from Oxfordshire and the Isle of Thanet" and "On Chinese Charms." Likewise articles in the *Folk-Lore Record* 1 (1878) included: "Some West Sussex Superstitions Lingering in 1868," "The Folk-Lore of France" (by Andrew Lang), "A Folk-Tale and Various Superstitions of the Hidatsa Indians" (by Tylor himself), "Divination by the Blade Bone," and "Wart and Wen Cures." Among the European periodicals, note, for example, *Archivio per le tradizioni populari* (from 1882), *Memoires de la societé d'anthropologie de Paris* (from 1860), *Revue des traditions populaires* (from 1886).

48. Warde Fowler appreciated this point in his review of *GB*¹. In discussing the significance of Nemi for Frazer's work, he concludes that Frazer "has provided us with a thread which at once increases both our comfort and our curiosity" (p. 49).

49. *Sunday Chronicle,* 15 Aug. 1937. For headlines parading Frazer's ignorance of "savages in the flesh," see the articles cited in n. 39.

50. *GB*³, I:1 (= vol. I), 43; *GB*³, VII:2 (= vol. II), 308. This final image of sailing

was introduced only in *GB³* (compare, *GB²*, 3, 462). Frazer's own copy of this volume of *GB²* (Trinity College, Adv c 21 71) shows various attempts to elaborate these final sections. The image of travel in *The Golden Bough is* noted by S. E. Hymans, *The Tangled Bank* (New York, 1962), 264–65, though he does not investigate its significance.

51. *Manchester Examiner,* 17 May 1890; *Athenaeum,* 2 Aug. 1890; *Oxford Magazine,* 29 Oct. 1890.

52. This is discussed also by Gillian Beer, "Speaking for the Others." One of the finest moments in the novel is when a talking parrot reveals to Felix his likely fate as a god-king.

53. Wryly interpreted by the reviewer in the *National Observer,* 29 Nov. 1890: "The conclusion you reach is that it is better to be Taboo (in the degenerate sense) at home than to be Taboo (in the original sense) and a god in a cannibal island."

54. *Reminiscences of a Student's Life* (London, 1925), 82, (repr. in *Arion* 4 (1965), 312–46 (at p. 343).

55. My certainty does not derive from any statistically accurate survey. It comes from relentless questioning of friends and colleagues in humanities faculties in the Universities of Cambridge and London. If they have not read it, who has? A similar view is held by G. Steiner, who (in a recent [1990] radio broadcast) linked *The Golden Bough* with *Capital* and *The Origin of Species* as the great unread classics of non-fiction. For further discussion of the influence of unread (or rather the "not-finished") books, see G. Beer, "Ceasing to Read," in *Arguing with the Past: Essays in Narrative from Woolf to Sidney* (London, 1989), esp. 6–8.

56. For discussion of the literary influence of *The Golden Bough,* see J. B. Vickery, *The Literary Impact of the Golden Bough* (Princeton, 1973), and Fraser, ed., *Sir James Frazer and the Literary Imagination.* This literary influence of Frazer is often rated very highly; and some would argue no doubt that it is more important for the current popularity of *The Golden Bough* than the main lines of my argument might suggest. Maybe. But I sense that this literary aspect gives it a rather more tenuous hold on contemporary popular culture than many critics would like to suggest. To be sure, a diligent college student working on Eliot's *Wasteland* might feel some obligation at least to look at some passages of *The Golden Bough.* For most people the importance of Frazer for Eliot, Joyce, Yeats, and Lawrence merely gives the book a vague sense of familiarity, rather than encouraging them to pick it up and read it.

# Afterword

*Mary Beard*

Some kinds of comparative history make uncomfortable work. None more so, for the author at least, than the reflection on their own past writing and the inevitable comparison it entails between what they were once proud to write and how differently they would do it now. It is a case of two competing emotions: the hope that the work has somehow survived and that it is still worth reading, versus the aspiration to have something new and better to say, ten years on. It would, after all, be simultaneously reassuring and a terrible accusation of intellectual stagnation still to be thinking about the same problems in the same way after the interval of a decade or so.[1] I leave it to readers to judge whether, or in what sense, "Frazer, Leach, and Virgil" has stood the test of time. In this Afterword I want to raise two issues that I now feel were missed, or woefully underplayed, in the original article.

The first concerns the wider classical background to Frazer's comparative enterprise and the links between *The Golden Bough* and the institutional and intellectual history of Classics (as a university discipline) in the late nineteenth century and beyond. In "Frazer, Leach, and Virgil," I present the central classical symbol of Virgil's "Golden Bough" as a legitimating device for Frazer's radically ambitious project, and as a rhetorical model for the exploration of the Other that lay at the heart of the book. Frazer's readers, in other words, would have felt reassured that, for all the far-flung unfamiliarity of much of the book's subject matter and argument, the aim of the enterprise was rooted in a traditional puzzle of classical history (the fate of the poor priest of Nemi) and in the most canonical classical text of all, namely Virgil. They would also have recognized (as Jane Harrison certainly did) the prompt in the title itself: like its namesake, this *Golden Bough* was pledged to take you on a very dangerous journey indeed; but, journey over, (rest assured) it would bring you back home safely again.

All that remains true, but hardly sufficient. What my original argument ignored was the much more fundamental role of Classics, in its late nineteenth-century manifestation, in generating such an ambitious comparative project. Like almost every other British intellectual of his time, Frazer was before anything else a *classicist* and his work must be seen in that context. During the 1870s and 1880s when his plans for *The Golden Bough* were taking shape, Classics as a discipline was being transformed—broadening its focus, outside the narrow study of the Greek and Latin languages alone. In Cambridge, where Frazer had been a classical student from 1874, and then a fellow of Trinity College, the change was particularly striking and swift. In the mid-nineteenth century (and still the case while Frazer was an undergraduate), the examinations taken by classical students had demanded reams of translation from Latin and Greek into English and English into Latin and Greek, and very little else. By the early 1880s, after a major reform of the curriculum, which in broad terms invented the subject as it is known today, a wide range of different options became available. These included ancient history, classical philosophy, linguistics, and what its practitioners called "archaeology."

Of these, "archaeology" is the least familiar, because it extended far beyond the concerns of ancient material culture (whether marble masterpieces or fragments of bone pins) that now characterize this subject for us. In fact, one influential and dazzlingly wide definition of archaeology at the time ran as follows: "the study of the evidence for man's history not already incorporated into printed literature."[2] This could be taken to include anything from the history of carpentry to the customs of the peasantry, from ancient table manners to the comparative study of myth and ritual. Students could now be asked not only to render some elegant stanzas of John Keats into equally elegant Greek verse, but—if they chose—to write on such questions as "Compare briefly the position of women at Athens, Sparta and at Rome" ('history' for us, but 'archaeology' for them), or "Point out traces in Greek ritual of human sacrifice." This "archaeology" was a visionary new subject that derived directly from a rethinking of how Classics was to be studied; it heralded a means of access to the classical world that was no longer solely, or even principally, dependent on the literary tradition.[3]

Significantly, among the graders of one of the very first examinations in "archaeology" for classical students at Cambridge in 1883 was none other than the young J. G. Frazer. Of course, the range of subjects corralled into *The Golden Bough* is even wider than those represented by the new classical "archaeology." But there is a much greater overlap between the two than I allowed in my original article. Certainly I was wrong if I implied that the problem of Nemi might be seen as a respectable fig-leaf behind which Frazer could safely develop his wilder comparative ideas. More to the point, Frazer's insertion of classical myth and ritual into the framework of comparative mythology and folklore was one particularly flamboyant symptom of the way Classics, as a discipline, was busy redefining itself.

This reflection on the nature of Classics as a comparative discipline prompts further thoughts relevant to the theme of this volume. Far beyond *The Golden Bough,* Classical history holds a peculiarly privileged place in the historiography of comparison, for a very simple reason. In the Anglo-American tradition of classical scholarship at least (the story in continental Europe may be a little different), ancient history has always been the study of two cultures: Greece and Rome. True, the research interests of individual scholars often tend toward one more than the other; but all students start with both, and most teachers teach both. Bilateral comparison— Greece against Rome, and vice versa—is embedded in the discipline and in its traditions of pedagogy. In Classics, comparison is integral, not an optional extra ("Why was Roman slavery configured differently from Athenian?" "How far can Athenian models of political analysis be applied to Rome?" and so on). But more than that, the history of this general comparative project extends back to the ancient world itself. From the moment that Rome came into contact with the Greek world, one of the central questions posed by Greco-Roman intellectuals was always the comparison of the two cultures (which were, in some important respects, increasingly becoming one). From the historian Dionysius of Halicarnassus in the first century B.C.E., who tried to collapse comparison, by showing (comparatively, of course) that Rome *was* a Greek city, up to and beyond Plutarch in the second century C.E., whose *Parallel Lives* explicitly compared the qualities of leading historical figures from Greece on the one hand and Rome on the other, Roman imperial culture was a *comparative* culture. The genealogy of historical comparison cannot afford (as I did) to ignore this.

The second issue is more narrowly Frazerian, though it has important implications for how we understand the process of comparison, its elusiveness, uncertainties, and perilous self-reflexivities. "Frazer, Leach, and Virgil" was strikingly resistant to seeing *The Golden Bough* as a comparative *process* rather than a book. Inevitably, for us, it *is* a book—in three different editions. But those three editions were also frozen moments in an ongoing project, whose boundaries and focus changed as it went along, so that ultimately the comparative spotlight fell on the author as much as on his subjects, and the myth of Frazer and his comparativist aims were fed back into the colonial world itself. Although it remains uncertain who exactly comprised the readership of *Nairobi Standard* (more colonial administrator than native servant, one would guess), I missed a trick when I failed to emphasize that the whole "craze for Frazer" extended into the very territories from where he had drawn some of his most exotic material. And I missed another trick when I failed to emphasize the way in which popular myths repeatedly portrayed Frazer himself as if he was one of his own subjects (the man for whom work was a 'rite' and who shamanistically ranged through time and space from Polynesia to the snowy wastes of Iceland). The Frazerian comparative project, in other words, was liable to engulf its author; there turned out to be no *terra firma* from which to watch the "savages" at play.

Part of the problem was my commitment to seeing Frazer's work and the commentary on it exclusively as literary rhetoric, rather than (also) part of cultural discourse. If I had ranged more widely in the cultural practice of the late nineteenth and early twentieth centuries, I would have seen acted out many of the issues and tensions embedded in the comparativism of *The Golden Bough*. One classic example would be the great World's Fairs, particularly in the United States, around the turn of the twentieth century, which regularly offered in their ethnographic displays and tableaux of "native villages" a comparative pageant of world culture (*à la* Frazer).[4] Predictably, these also served to display many of the paradoxes generated by comparison, and to raise questions about the complicated transactions involved in watching, and comparing, other cultures: "savages" acting out their native customs right next to fresh-faced English girls with their native maypoles and thatched cottages; local lads finding friends and partners, as much as weird "specimens," among the people on display; "real" natives choosing to make a living as actors on the fair circuit, pretending to be the kind of "savages" they once, but no longer, were. For the countries of Western Europe, the price of joining in these (extremely lucrative) extravaganzas was the risk of blurring the boundary between, in their terms, "civilization" and "savagery"; and to turn *themselves* into objects of curious gaze. As I might usefully have reflected, there are close links between this and the paradoxes of the Frazerian myth, and his comparativist project in general. For ultimately, as my exploration of the popular accounts showed, Frazer was in the end "Othered" as uncompromisingly as he "Othered" his savages.

NOTES

1. Despite my anxieties, I remain extremely grateful to the organizers of the "Grew celebration" and to Ray Grew himself for having given me the opportunity to rethink my article, and for the happy occasion of the conference itself.

2. The words of Charles Newton (who was for a long time keeper of Greek and Roman Antiquities at the British Museum), first spoken in a lecture in Oxford in 1850, and later published as "On the Study of Archaeology," in *Essays on Art and Archaeology* (London, 1880), 1–38.

3. For these changes in Cambridge, see my article, "The Invention (and Re-invention) of 'Group D': An Archaeology of the Classical Tripos, 1879–1984," in, C. Stray, ed., *Classics in 19th and 20th Century Cambridge: Curriculum, Culture and Continuity* (Cambridge Phililogical Society, Sup. 24, 1999), 95–134. For the wider context, see C. Stray, *Classics Transformed: Schools, Universities, and Society in England, 1830–1960* (Oxford, 1998).

4. For details, see R. W. Rydell, *All the World's a Fair: Visions of Empire at American International Expositions, 1876–1916* (Chicago, 1984); P. Greenhalgh, *Ephemeral Vistas: The Expositions Universelles, Great Exhibitions and World's Fairs, 1851–1939* (Manchester, 1988).

# Cowries and Conquest

## Toward a Subalternate Quality Theory of Money

*Chris Gregory*

In the beginning of the world we had the forge and we forged things, we had weaving-looms and we wove our clothes, we had oracle huts where we consulted the oracle, and we had boats from which we caught fish. We had no guns. We had no cowrie-money (*akwá*). If you went to the market you took beans in order to exchange them for sweet potatoes. You exchanged something specific for something else. Then the king brought the cowrie-money. What did the king do in order to bring the cowrie-money? He caught people and broke their legs and their arms. Then he built a hut in a banana plantation, put the people in it, and fed them bananas until they became big and fat. The king killed the people and he gave orders to his servants to attach strings to their bodies and to throw them into the sea where the cowrie-shells (*akwá*) lived. When the cowrie-shells started to eat the corpses they pulled them in, collected the shells, and put the live cowries in hot water to kill them. That is how cowrie-money came to exist. This cowrie-money was white like our maize and we called it "white-corn-money" (*akwé-kún -wéé*) in order to distinguish it from other forms of money. The French came to break this country before they came to bring their metal-money (*gàn-kwé*). The other money of the French is called paper-money (*biyéé*).

—Klikpo Cece, Ayou Hannya, Benin[1]

## The Problem

If the problem of understanding the process by which a commodity acquires value is difficult enough, then the question of the process by which money acquires value is a degree of magnitude more so; and when the money in question is in the form of cowrie shells, one of the few forms of money that quite literally grows, the problem acquires yet another twist.

But what, precisely, is the problem? It is most emphatically not the hoary old definitional question of whether or not the cowries can function as money. This problem has been laid to rest by the meticulous historical work of Hogendorn and Johnson (1986) in their *The Shell Money of the Slave Trade*. Not only used by the slave traders to buy slaves, cowries were also used by the villagers of West Africa as a medium of exchange in their periodic markets. Comparative historical and ethnographic evidence from India and Papua New Guinea[2] suggests that the story that Hogendorn and Johnson tell is not restricted to the particular case of West Africa. This evidence also confirms another important observation by Hogendorn and Johnson: Cowries can also be used in bridewealth exchanges, as jewelry, as decorations for clothes, as counters in games, as gifts, and so on.

The problem to be addressed—and here credit must be given to Hogendorn and Johnson for posing it so clearly—is that of explaining the cowrie-shell bubble that occurred in the early stages of the direct colonial conquest of Africa. Put simply, the question is this: What is the relationship between the massive import of shells into Africa and the subsequent hyper-inflation and demonetization of the cowrie? This question, I will show, is a general one. The same phenomenon occurred in India and Papua New Guinea (among other places) in the early phases of colonization. Although Hogendorn and Johnson do not concern themselves with the general problem, their answer is in very general terms. Like many others who have tackled this issue, they have found the seductive explanatory power of the quantity theory of money too hard to resist. This theory, whose chief exponent these days is the Nobel-prize winning economist, Milton Friedman (1987), not only has academic authority on its side, it seems to be self-evidently true in the case of the cowrie-shell bubbles. In all three cases hyper-inflation followed a massive increase in the quantity of shells. The evidence for their case seems to be watertight, as I hope to show in the first part of this essay.

However, as the myth by Klikpo Cece above suggests, villagers in West Africa have their own story to tell. The central message of this myth is plain and clear: The elders of Ayou Hannya village, as if aware that anthropologists have a tendency to over-interpret myth and thereby to miss its simple message, made a point of telling Elwert (1989: 25) that the kings of Dahomey were not their beloved rulers and that the reason for the violence and cruelty of these rulers was their sheer quest for wealth. Elwert notes that behind the symbolic language of Cece's myth is "a very realistic interpretation of the economic history of the kingdom of

Dahomey" and a treatise on money which differs from the king's. The myth has many other meanings too, argues Elwert, because the thriftiness of mythical language means that myth can work more efficiently than handbooks and dictionaries as a means of storing information and as a means of evoking emotion.

Stories such as Cece's myth, then, are full of thought-provoking wisdom rather than truth, and contain overtones of meaning that resonate sympathetically in the ears of the initiated listener. Although they are not in the form of clearly articulated theories that can be objectively tested, these resonances are not completely esoteric either because the thoughts of an outsider can be stimulated by stories of this kind. When they are situated anthropologically, historically, and geographically, stories like this can be read as archives on the human condition that give figurative expression to unresolved antagonisms.[3] I see in the thoughts of Cece and other people like him the elements of a general criticism of the quantity theory of money. It suggests to me that money is a standard of value created by a state (be it a divine kingship as in Dahomey or an imperial nation-state like France), that it is also an instrument of the power of a king over his subjects and an instrument of the power of the imperial state. The theoretical problem that cowrie money poses, then, involves understanding the contradictions among the money-value systems of the imperial state (symbolized in Cece's myth by the metal and paper money of the French), the money-value system of the indigenous elite (symbolized by the cowrie money "caught" by the king through the sacrifice of his subjects), and the values of the subalterns for whom the things produced and exchanged by the labor of farmers and artisans is valued more highly than the inhuman mercantile dealings of a brutal king and his trading partners from over the seas. This perspective raises the question of the quality of money and throws the self-evident truths of the quantity theory of money into doubt as will be seen in the second half of this article. My starting point is the economic history of the shell money of the West African slave trade.

### The Shell Money of the Slave Trade

The trade in shell money began in the fourteenth century and was finished by the 1880s.[4] The structure and volume of trade changed greatly over this period, but its efflorescence was in the era of European mercantile imperialism. The end of the trade coincided with the emergence of capitalist imperialism and the scramble for the territories of Africa, Asia, and the

Pacific. The Maldives, a 475-mile-long stretch of nineteen atolls some 400 miles due west of Colombo in the Indian Ocean, were the basis of the whole system. Here cowrie shells (*Cypraea moneta*), in the form of small live gastropods, are prolific breeders. These shells were harvested and traded to every corner of the globe. West Africa, where the gastropods did not breed, was the ultimate destination for many of the shells, although India, and especially Bengal and Orissa, was also another major user of them.

Ecology and economy motivated the commerce in shells. The Maldivians traded shells for rice and other commodities with the Bengalis, who used the shells as currency for petty transactions and other purposes. European merchants, in turn, purchased them from Indian merchants and carried them back to Europe, where they were sold at a profit. Those purchasing the shells in Europe were slave traders who carried them to West Africa as capital to buy slaves. There, the shells were absorbed into the West African economies and used for a variety of purposes, the most important of which was as a medium of exchange for small transactions.

The eighteenth century was a prosperous one for the cowrie trade because this was when the Atlantic slave trade was at its peak. The Dutch dominated the cowrie trade until 1750. Thereafter, the proportion of shells traded by the Dutch dropped steadily, falling to zero in 1796 when the Great European War ruined Dutch commerce. The English controlled the trade until 1807, when the abolition of the legitimate slave trade rendered the system unprofitable. Statistics collated by Hogendorn and Johnson (1986: 58) reveal that during the period between 1700 and 1790, some 11,436 metric tons of shells were shipped to West Africa by the Dutch and English, the equivalent of the staggering figure of 10 billion individual shells.

The nineteenth century was one of boom and bust for the international cowrie trade; it was also one of privatization and fierce competition because the East India Company lost its monopoly in 1813. The abolition of the slave trade caused a temporary slump in the legs of the cowrie trade going between India and Europe and between Europe and Africa. Its revival was brought about by the growth of palm oil exports from West Africa. Great quantities of cowrie shells were needed to buy palm oil, which was used in Europe as a lubricant to grease the wheels of the emerging capitalist industrial enterprises and as the chief ingredient of soap to clean the grime of newly invented machines from the bodies and clothes of the working classes. The cowrie trade entered an unprecedented expansion in the 1840s. Records were repeatedly broken, and the high levels of production needed led to concerns about over-fishing. In 1840, for example, the British exported some 205 metric tons of cowries to West Africa; in 1845 an all-time high of 569 metric tons was exported.

The final phase of the shell trade was the period between 1851 and 1869, when five private German and French companies captured the trade and shipped over 35,000 tons (14 billion shells) directly to West Africa. This frenzied trade exploded the cowrie bubble, dropping the price of shells dramatically, making trade unprofitable, and stopping shipments. The beginning of this final phase saw the end of the Maldivian cowrie (*C. moneta*) and the temporary rise of the Zanzibar cowrie (*C. annulus*), a slightly larger cowrie that yielded a merchant's profit of 1,100 percent compared to a meager 100 percent for the Maldivian cowrie.

The end of the international trade in cowries also marked the virtual end of their domestic circulation in West Africa, although it took some fifty years before they disappeared from circulation completely (Ofonagoro 1979). Many shells, it seems, were buried underground in hoards, ready to be used again when their value recovered. The Nupe must have thought this day had come when their ethnographer, S. F. Nadel, arrived. He asked to be shown some cowries and was told that they were no longer in use and not available; when he said that he was prepared to pay for them, large baskets full suddenly turned up and he had to do his best not to be inundated with them (Nadel 1942: 310).

Two theoretical questions are posed from this narrative: What principles govern the emergence and explosion of shell bubbles? What are the implications of this for the theory of value in general and the theory of money and the gift in particular? Hogendorn and Johnson have a very definite point of view on both of these questions and it is worth quoting them at length for their position raises a number of general issues.

The cowrie could very well serve as an object lesson in a money and banking class today. Dramatically and convincingly, near the end of its life as a working money it suffered a hyperinflation that demonstrates nicely the wide application of both the Quantity Theory of Money and Gresham's Law. The Quantity Theory of Irving Fisher states that the stock of money (M) multiplied by the number of times that money is spent each year (velocity, V) must equal the annual value of all transactions, PQ, where Q is the number of transactions and P is the average price level. $MV = PQ$. When an economy is growing, Q rises and therefore, with V relatively constant, the stock of money M can also rise without affecting the level of prices. But should M expand much more rapidly than Q, the theory predicts the likelihood of rises in P, that is, inflation. The cowrie currency conforms to the prediction of this theory remarkably well. As long as the small shells from the atolls of the Maldives were the only ones imported to West Africa (true for half a millennium at least), the limited growth rate in M did not significantly outrun the growth of the domestic economy, so that the value of the cowrie remained relatively stable. But when the East African variety of the cowrie suddenly was poured into West Africa by European traders in the years after 1845 . . . it generated hyperinflation that ultimately destroyed the usefulness of the shell money standard (which by that time was mainly associated with palm-oil trade, and not with slaving). At the same time, Gresham's Law—"bad money drives out the good"—was in full operation. The East African shells were much cheaper than the smaller variety produced in the Maldives; wherever they proved acceptable, they were paid out by the importing merchants to the point that the shells from the atolls virtually disappeared in some areas.

> The great cowrie inflation was not the only example of a "primitive" money badly depreciated by oversupply; the copper and brass currencies of Africa were much eroded by improved manufacturing techniques in Europe, and similar advances in the fabrication of wampum beads ruined that famous American Indian currency. But the cowrie inflation is best documented, and demonstrates clearly how Fisher's rule and Gresham's Law both apply in a world far removed from the coins, paper, and bank deposits for which they were formulated (Hogendorn and Johnson 1986: 3–4).

The implications of this argument for the theory of gift exchange are spelled out in a lengthy footnote in which the West Africans are described as "intensely commercial":

> The substantivist school of anthropologists has sometimes written of the cowrie as a "special purpose money," governed by principles of reciprocity, redistribution, and ritual. It is true that very late in the life of the cowrie currency it did survive for a few more years as a means of making ritual payment. For most of its life, however, any argument that the shells were a traditional special purpose money is untenable (Hogendorn and Johnson 1986: 1, fn. 2).

The analysis of Hogendorn and Johnson is one of many studies that have used Fisher's Rule and Gresham's Law to explain the end of cowrie currencies in Africa, India, Papua New Guinea (PNG), and other places.[5] But what sets this analysis apart from all others is the fact that it is by far the best documented and most convincing treatment of the subject. Hogendorn and Johnson have introduced the skills of the professional historian into the debate and have combed the archives for data in a way that few others have done.

It is also important to note that Hogendorn and Johnson have identified an important general problem—the phenomenon of the shell bubble in early colonial history—that needs to be explained. Anthropologists have a tendency to problematize difference rather than similarity and are reluctant to accept, for example, that the economic history of PNG has anything in common with West Africa. It is true that there are a great many differences between the early colonial period of the PNG highlands (1930–1960) and the slave trade of West Africa, but these differences are defined only by the remarkable similarities between the two cases. The meticulous archival and field-work research of Hughes (1977; 1978) establishes beyond any doubt that a shell money bubble developed and exploded in PNG during the period between 1930 and 1960.

Hughes shows, for example, that cowries, both *C. moneta* and *C. annulus,* were traded up into the highlands where they were used extensively for a variety of purposes, including that of a medium of exchange. Other shells traded into the region included the dog whelk (*Nassa*), the goldlip pearl oyster (*Pinctada maxima*), the baler (*Mela aethiopicus*), the green snail (*Turbo marmoratus*), the egg cowrie (*Ovula ovum*), the Leopard cone (*Conus Leopardus*), and five others of lesser significance. In the period just prior to colonization, cowries and dog-whelk shells were the most numerous and widely spread of the eight main kinds of shells and, as a consequence, had the lowest relative value. From the archaeological evidence it is known that shells have been used in the area for at least six thousand years and possibly longer. Trade in shells in the highlands, then, is of great antiquity; but we know little about it, save that shells were bartered up to the highlands from the north and south coasts without the intervention of professional traders, merchants, or itinerant peddlers. Most of the supplies of common shells came from the north coast, reflecting, in part, the natural distribution of the species. However, there were apparently no specialist centers of the Maldivian type. Australian gold miners first visiting the area in the 1930s discovered that they could use the shells to hire workers and buy food. These transactions brought about many radical changes to the volume and structure of the indigenous exchange system, introducing a merchant capital component into the system because these miners bought shells cheap on the coast, brought them to the highlands by air freight, and sold them dear in exchange for the commodities they wanted. The miners used cowries to purchase vegetable foods, sex, and daily labor and used the more valuable shells, where they were current, to buy bigger items. Needless to say, the trade in shells boomed, and the quantity of shells available in the highlands multiplied at a geometric rate. Between the establishment of the Mount Hagen base in 1933 and 1940, up to 10 million shells were imported into the highlands. The war interrupted the flow of shells, but after the war they were flown in in even greater numbers. Complete statistics are not available, but some idea of the magnitude of the trade can be gleaned from the fact that, in the six-month period between September 1952 and February 1953, some 20 million dog-whelk shells were distributed from the Goroka base. This shell bubble, like the one in Africa, burst at different rates in different places and with differing local implications. They ceased to be used by the white colonizers after the 1960s to buy food and labor but today, like the African and Indian cowries, can still be found in some places. The evidence from India, which I shall make no attempt to summarize here, is yet a third variation on this general theme. The examples can be multiplied, and credit must be given to Hogendorn and Johnson for identifying this important general theme in the history of the use of shell money.

Another important point that Hogendorn and Johnson establish is that anthropologists are amateurs when it comes to the craft of history. By and large, the theories of the anthropologists who have tried to explain the historical relationship between metallic monies and shell monies in terms of novel anthropological theories have not performed well. These theories are logically satisfactory but historically unsatisfactory. Consider the case of Bohannan (1959), whose influential "spheres of exchange" theory has been the subject of a telling critique by the historian D. C. Dorward (1976).

Bohannan (1959: 124) notes that if "we take no more than three major money uses— payment, standard and means of exchange—we find that in many primitive societies as well as in some ancient empires, one object may serve one money use while another object serves another money use." Bohannan characterizes these economies as "multi-centric" and the "modern" European one as "uni-centric"; these economies, he argues, use "special-purpose" money and "general-purpose" money, respectively. The Tiv economy of West Africa, argues Bohannan, contained three spheres. The first sphere was associated with subsistence and was governed by the "morality of the free and uncontrolled market" (1959: 125). The second sphere was a prestige sphere in no way associated with markets: Only certain ritual objects—slaves, cattle, *tugudu* cloth, brass rods—circulated within this sphere. The third sphere was supreme and contained only one item: rights in human beings other than slaves, particularly women. Its values were expressed in terms of kinship and marriage. With the spread of the world market and the introduction of general-purpose money, argues Bohannan, the multi-centric economy of the Tiv was flattened and transformed into a uni-centric one. Another almost identical version of this theory, I was surprised to discover recently, was independently invented by Keynes (1982) in the late 1920s but not published until 1982. Keynes developed his theory from a study of the ancient Greek empire and expressed his theory in the language of multiple "standards of value" rather than multiple "spheres of exchange."

The substance of Dorward's critique of Bohannan is that he did not have access to, or was unaware of, the relevant documentation and that he relied too heavily on oral evidence. Dorward proceeds to present a wealth of new evidence that is damaging to Bohannan's case. He shows, for example, that *tugudu* cloth was a general-purpose, not special-purpose, form of money and that, because of his preoccupation with the subsistence economy, Bohannan failed to grasp the significance of the craft industry and the web of commerce in which the Tiv were caught up. Dorward's alternative explanation is a particular illustration of the general theme developed by Hogendorn and Johnson: When the colonial government began to demand payment of taxes in their own metallic currencies, Gresham's Law came into operation, and bad money (European coinage) began driving out good money (Tiv cloth currency) (Dorward 1976: 590).

The answer to the question posed above—what was the impact of European coinage on non-European economies using cowries?—seems to be obvious in light of the latest historical evidence: cowries disappeared due to the operation of Fisher's Rule (the quantity theory of money) and Gresham's Law. This conclusion would not surprise Milton Friedman, who has won a Nobel prize for his theoretical contributions to the quantity theory of money. Given the superlative academic prestige of this theory and the overwhelming weight of the supporting historical evidence, it seems ridiculous to suggest that this theory is obviously wrong. However, as I suggested in the introduction above, there is a subalternate point of view which is also obviously right. Before I can present this opposing view, a brief theoretical interlude on the question of power is necessary.

## Interlude: The Logic of Power

The thought of people such as Klipko Cece, whose version of the cowrie-shell trade in West Africa heads this essay, is a particular illustration of what Guha (1983a) calls "logic of subaltern consciousness." This is a form of *political* consciousness, a rival cognition that questions the violence and cruelty of unloved rulers. When Cece's story is read as a *political* tale of monetary conquest and as one that views this history from below, it poses the question of the political status of the quantity theory of money. Is this a theory that describes and interprets events from above, from below, or from afar? The evidence would seem to favor the latter view. The quantity theory has all the attributes of an objective scientific theory. Hogendorn and Johnson's approach, for example, is that of disinterested social scientists. They offer a compelling general explanation for the West African cowrie-shell bubble that applies to the case of India and PNG, and this explanation cannot be linked in any simple-minded way with the interests of the slave traders and the colonial state. Nevertheless, the fact that conquest involves the exercise of raw power does raise the question of the explanatory adequacy of a theory of monetary conquest that abstracts from power relations and makes no attempt to give the native point of view.[6]

Getting access to the native point of view poses special problems for the historian because such things are not the stuff of which archives are made. But Guha's method of inferring the voice of the Indian peasant from the language of the elite opens up new avenues of research for the historian and anthropologist, and his myth-as-archive thesis is an invitation for anthropologists to look anew at the content of many a myth. This is what I have tried to do with the myth by Cece, a member of the Ayizo people, who were at one time sold as slaves and who were, in another period, forced to serve without compensation in the king's slave-raiding army. This story acquires a new saliency when seen in the light of some evidence from Melanesia. Here, European conquest is a relatively recent event, and ethnographers have been able to record the memories of the people involved. These data are fragmentary and, by themselves, of limited use. However, if this evidence from PNG is seen in the comparative light of

Cece's tale and located in the context of a theory of power that identifies and inverts the central assumptions of the quantity theory, then a subalternate theory can be constructed by teasing out the generalizations that dwell in every specific instance. Such an exercise must, of necessity, be based on inference; and the conclusions, questionable. However, my aim is not to produce a theory that replaces the quantity theory but, rather, to produce an argument that can stand beside it and raise doubts about its objectivity and explanatory adequacy.

My starting point is the theory of power developed by Guha (1989: 229ff). Power, notes Guha, is a general relation of domination (D) and subordination (S). In its most brutal form, power is a relation of killer to killed, as Cece's myth illustrates. The logic of power is such that, once one side of the relation is identified, the other follows as a logical consequence. This oppositional logic is that of privation rather than axiomatic contradiction: black versus white rather than black versus non-black, to use the analogous logic of color. This logic is perfectly general, but the actual history of conquest is the outcome of an interplay between the relation of domination and subordination and its constituent elements—coercion, persuasion, collaboration, and resistance—which imply each other contingently. It follows, therefore, that the black-and-white contrast between domination and subordination defines a gray continuum, the limits of which are set by the antagonistic contradiction between coercion and resistance at one extreme and the non-antagonistic contradiction between persuasion and collaboration at the other. The history of conquest, to pursue the color metaphor further, gives this general conception of power its unique coloration. Here, the primary colors, which correspond to the political culture of the conquerors, are opposed to the secondaries, which represent the culture of the colonized. These primary colors create contrasting hues which complement and harmonize beautifully here and clash and contrast in an ugly way there. Every colonial encounter is a unique creation of these constituent elements. In colonial India, for example, British liberal political culture was expressed in an idiom defined by the terms Order, Improvement, Obedience, and Rightful Dissent corresponding to Coercion, Persuasion, Collaboration, and Resistance respectively. The Indian idiom, derived from its pre-colonial, semi-feudal culture, was expressed in the language of Danda, Dharma, Bhakti, and Dharmic Protest (Guha 1989: 270). Thus, the conquest of India must be understood not as a simple opposition of domination to subordination but in terms of a matrix of constituent elements (see Figure 2).

| Power in General | Constituent Elements of Power in General | British Paradigm of Power | Indian Paradigm of Power |
|---|---|---|---|
| Domination | Coercion | Order | Danda |
| Domination | Persuasion | Improvement | Dharma |
| Subordination | Collaboration | Obedience | Bhakti |
| Subordination | Resistance | Rightful Dissent | Dharmic Protest |

Fig. 2. Paradigmatic derivation of political idioms

Guha, the historian, uses this matrix in much the same way that the artist uses the logic of the color cube to think about his paints as he goes about mixing and applying them to the canvas.[7] Just as the logic of the color cube reveals the elementary oppositions behind the complex phenomenon of color, this matrix helps one grasp the phenomenon of the British conquest of India in all its simple complexity. But just as knowledge of the logic of the color cube does not make one an artist, knowledge of this theory of power does not make a historian. Thus, Guha's theory of power is not a model that can be mechanically applied. Rather, it serves to focus one's attention on the contradictions and paradoxes of colonialism and to pose questions that are derived from the D/S relation. To give some examples noted by Guha (1989: 272): Why was a democratic Britain happy to preside over a state without citizenship? Why was a vision of Improvement on capitalist lines implemented by means of a neo-feudal system of property? Why, on the side of the indigenous elite, was the leadership of the bourgeoisie resolute in its defense of landlordism? Why, on the side of the subaltern, was the peasant rebel's vision of God a white man who writes like a court clerk? For Guha these questions are the offspring of one central paradox, the coexistence of two paradigms as the determinants of political culture; for him "the question that calls for an answer is: why two paradigms and not just one?" (1989: 272).

## A Subalternate Quality Theory of Money

The implication of Guha's theory of power is that, whatever the merits the quantity theory of money has in explaining the impact of coins on economies using cowries, another perspective exists. As a starting point it is necessary to adopt the temporary working hypothesis that the quantity theory of money is yet another form of "bourgeois knowledge," that it is elitist in Guha's sense of the term. The legitimacy of associating the quantity theory of money with a superaltern imperial idiom can then be tested by inverting the central tenets of the theory and by grounding the resultant propositions historically and comparatively.

It follows from this that the existence of a superalternate quantity theory of money, MV equals PQ, in which money prices are held to be determined by the supply of money when velocity is constant, presupposes the existence of a subalternate quality theory of money where money prices are determined by the demand for money when velocity is constant. The basic idea here is extremely simple; the only difficulty lies in the habits of thought that govern everyday thinking about money, one of the most used and least understood symbols ever invented by *Homo sapiens.* A simple example can clarify the point I want to make. Suppose a consumer buys bread for the value of $10 from a baker and that the baker uses the same $10 note to buy flour from a miller. In this case, the quantity of money is ten dollars (M equals $10), the velocity of money is two (V equals 2) and the total value[8] of transactions is $20 (PQ equals $20). Substituting these values in the quantity equation, MV equals PQ, gives $10 times 2 equals $20. The next step is to conceive of money (M) as a commodity with its own price (quality) and quantity. In this case we have:

M equals the price of money times the quantity of money.

But what meaning can we give to a notion like "the price of money." In this example the price of money must be equal to one (1). This is because money conceived of as a commodity is $10 and the quantity of money is also $10, which means that the price of money must be one (M equals 10 equals 1 times 10). The price of money, then, is another way of talking about what is called the standard of value. For money to perform this function efficiently, the standard must be kept constant. But whose standard is to do the measuring, how is it to be kept constant, and what are the implications of all of this? An analysis of the following truncated version of Cece's myth can help us answer this question:

We had no cowrie-money. If you went to the market you took beans in order to exchange them for sweet potatoes. You exchanged something specific for something else. Then the king brought the cowrie-money [by selling slaves to overseas merchants]. . . . The French came to break this country before they came to bring their metal-money.

*We had no cowrie-money. If you went to the market you took beans in order to exchange them for sweet potatoes. You exchanged something specific for something else.* Prior to the existence of cowrie money, there was no money standard: One commodity (C), such as beans, was exchanged for another commodity (C), such as sweet potatoes, and indigenous standards of weights and measures provided the means by which the exchange-value of one commodity was measured in terms of the other. Marx (1867: ch. 1) called this exchange of one commodity for another "the relative form of value" and gave it the general symbolic form C-C. Suppose, for the sake of exposition, the standard was weight and the unit was kilograms. In this case prices would assume the form of, say, one kilogram of rice equals five kilograms of sweet potatoes. The ethnographic reality was no doubt more complicated. If my field-work experience in India is anything to go by, it probably involved mixed standards of volume such as, one tin of rice of this size equals one basket of sweet potatoes of that size, in which the sizes of the "standard" tin and the basket varied from market to market and over time. Exchange-values of the C-C form are implicit in any market and are revealed by lifting away the "veil" of money.[9] The process by which these relative values are established is the most controversial subject in the history of political economy, but, as the full version of Cece's myth suggests, labor and technology must obviously be central to any explanation: Neither the quantity of money nor its quality has a role to play in the determination of the exchange values of commodities.[10]

*Then the king brought the cowrie money.* Money, as Cece quite rightly suggests, is the creation of kings; it is their standard of value. Marx (1867: ch. 3), by contrast, assumes "for the sake of simplicity, gold as the money commodity." This counterfactual assumption has given birth to the idea that there is such a thing as a commodity-money that can exist independently of the state. The historical fact is, however, that kings created money by fixing the prices of special commodities such as gold, silver, and cowrie shells or by placing a stamp on a piece of metal or paper. This act of state power creates a new standard of money value which the agents of the state are employed to maintain. The result in Dahomey was prices in the form of, say, 1 tin of rice equals 3 *kan* (strings) of cowries, in which the *kan* was the standard required by a law of the king to contain 40 cowries on a threaded string. In Whydah, the official whose responsibility it was to ensure that this and other regulations were kept was called the Captain of the Market (Law 1991: 51). Formally, this standard has the following value form:

*Kan* equals the price of cowries times the quantity of cowries equals 1 times 40.

This standard was also the basis for higher groupings: Five *kan* made one *afo* (foot), and twenty made one *degba* (basket). Standards like this are the sign that money is an instrument of state power because they provide a fixed standard for measuring the value of all commodities and a means of levying taxes. The money veil that is thrown over commodities, then, is a form of state power that varies from place to place and time to time: Despite the positions of quantity theorists, money is *never* neutral. In this particular case the veil of cowrie money masked a brutal mercantile power that profited from the purchase and sale of human beings. The imperial monies of this time, such as the pound sterling, did much the same thing but on a much grander scale. The link between the two was established by means of such international standards as that of 16,000 cowries equal one ounce of gold equal 4 pounds sterling, which the Dahomey state struggled to maintain throughout the eighteenth century.

*The French came to break this country before they came to bring their metal-money.* Subordinate states are always subjected to the will of the dominant state; and, when the mercantile imperialism of the European states gave way to capitalist imperialism, the money standards changed as a consequence. First comes the imperialist conquest of the kingdom, which breaks the power of the king in an act of brute military force. New monetary standards follow. Prices now are required to assume the form, say, one kilogram of rice equals two French francs, and taxes are required to be paid in this new standard. The price of the French franc is now set at unity in those countries colonized by the French; and cowries are demonetized, which is another way of saying that the price of cowrie money falls to zero. But the demonetization of the cowrie does not happen over night. Rival standards of value are at stake. This is a political struggle between the citizens of the old state, who have their wealth stored in the form of cowrie money,[11] and the new rulers. The citizens who hold their wealth in the form of cowrie money have much to lose and fight it out. As the imperial state gradually assumes control, the demand for cowrie money falls because it is no longer legal tender. As this happens, sellers of commodities begin to demand payment in the new standard of value; buyers of these commodities who only have supplies of the old standard will be forced to offer increased quantities of the old standard if they are to persuade the sellers to accept it as a means of payment. This brings about a rise in prices in terms of the old standard of value (that is, cowrie money). Thus, it is this fall in the demand for cowrie money, and not an increase in their quantity, as the quantity theory of money would have it, that is responsible for the rise in the absolute level of cowrie-money prices.

This, in brief, is the political economy of the subalternate quality theory of money. Formally speaking, it means that the old quantity equation needs to be rewritten in a new qualitative form in which SMV equals PQ where S, the standard of value of the ruling state, is equal to one. The establishment of standards of significant value is the result of a struggle for prestige, and the raising of a new standard, like the raising of a new flag, is an expression of the political significance of the victor. In other words, the equation S equals 1 is a symbol of order; while the existence of multiple standards of subordinated quality represents disorder, or, to be more precise, a challenge to the order imposed by the ruling state. Since this exposition of my myth-inspired political approach to the symbolism of money is terse and somewhat unconventional, I will now restate it in the more familiar academic language of semiotics in an attempt to persuade the skeptical reader of its obviousness as against the obviousness of the quantity theory.

The expression "quality of money" refers to the value of money as a signifier, and to understand what this means, it is necessary to consider the iconic, indexical, and symbolic meaning of money. This is a vast topic, and I shall limit myself to a brief consideration of the symbolic and indexical issues which are pertinent to my discussion. "The word symbol," a high school textbook on poetry reminds us, "is related to the Greek word symbolon, which was a half-coin carried away by each of the two parties to an agreement as a pledge of their good faith. A symbol, therefore, is like half a coin—it is an object; the other half of the coin is the idea it represents. When a person understands the symbol the two parts come together and the meaning is passed on" (Boagey 1977: 40). This simple formulation of the notion of a symbol enables an equally simple question to be posed: If metallic coins are one half of a material object, then what is the other half and what is the nature of the invisible chain that binds them? The answer to the first part of the question is cowrie shells and bullion. As for the second part, the invisible chain that has bound these objects together in different times and places has been the power of various states to maintain fixed rates of exchange between these objects for long periods of time. This is because gold, silver, and cowries have historically defined the standard of value by which state-issued money is measured. In other words, the price of money has historically been defined in terms of gold, silver, and cowries. Further, the spatio-temporal dimensions of the fixed rate of exchange of metallic money is an index of the coercive power of the state. Herein lies the indexical significance of money.

Consider the facts. As Law (1991: 176) notes: "The prime cost of cowries in Europe varied considerably, but on the Slave Coast they had a fixed local or 'trade' value: . . . the grand cabess of 4,000 cowries was at first valued at 25s. 'trade,' but in the mid-1720s this valuation was lowered to £1 'trade.' The 'ounce trade,' equivalent to £4 'trade,' was therefore valued at 4 grand cabess, or 16,000 cowries." Given the fixed price of gold established by the British of approximately four pounds sterling per ounce,[12] this gives the international standard, mentioned above, of 16,000 cowries equals one ounce of gold equals four pounds sterling. Polanyi (1968), who seems to have misinterpreted the data on this rate and exaggerated the success the state had in maintaining its fixity over a long period,[13] makes the important observation that the "stability of gold in terms of cowries became the absolute requirement of Dahomey's overlordship." To extend his argument, one can note that the stability of gold in terms of the pound sterling was an absolute requirement of Britain's imperial overlordship. In other words, the fixing of the London price of gold at £3.17.10½d was an index of the imperial power of the British state. The price of gold was set at this rate by Isaac Newton when he was director of the Mint in the 1690s and continued unchanged, save for a few hiccups during the Napoleonic war period, to the First World War. Britain was the only country that maintained a fixed price of money in terms of gold for this period. This fact must be seen in the light of another: From 1934 to 1971 the price of United States money was fixed at $35 per ounce of gold; the United States was the only country in the world able to maintain a constant price of money in terms of gold for this period. This index is a measure of U.S. imperial power just as the declining value of the dollar relative to gold after 1971 is an index of the decline in U.S. imperial power.[14]

States maintain their control over money by forbidding their citizens to handle gold, the supreme standard. Thus, the U.S. government made it illegal for its citizens to hold gold for most of the period when the price of gold was fixed; likewise, in Dahomey, "gold trade was also a royal monopoly, the purchase of gold by anyone other than the king being a capital offence" (Law 1991: 308). It is possible to debate the significance of the particular dates defined above, but the general point that a constant price (or quality) of money is an index of the dominance of an imperialist state is a difficult proposition to deny. The quality of money, then, is like the mercury in a doctor's thermometer: If the reading is constant at 98.4 degrees Fahrenheit (or its equivalent in degrees Celsius), then the body is in good order; but if it starts to rise over the 100 mark, then it indicates trouble, the monetary equivalent of which is debasement of the currency, an index of declining state power. Some ultra-right-wing economists have failed to grasp the significance of this and mistakenly believe that a return to the gold standard will enable the United States to recover some of its lost power.[15] The medical equivalent of this is the doctor who believes that the temperature of a patient can be brought down by plunging the thermometer into a glass of cold water.

Monetary standards of value, then, are political standards of value: They express the values of the dominant powers. In this respect they differ from standards of weight and measure. Today, for example, the true or invariable meter is defined as "a length equal to 1,650,763.73 wavelengths of the orange light emitted by the Krypton atom of mass 86 in vacuo" (Kula 1986: 81). This definition, introduced in 1961, involved a complete break with the past in that a scientific idea was substituted for a physical object located in a carefully controlled environment. In the European Middle Ages, for example, standards were cut in stone or cast in heavy metal and displayed in public places; over time, with the need for ever greater precision in the definition of these standards, the objects were stored away in ever more artificially controlled environments until, in 1961, they disappeared altogether. Monetary standards have had a similar history: Gold has replaced silver, copper, cowries, and a host of other standards; but attempts to replace gold with a theoretical idea have been a signal failure. The result is that today gold and the U.S. dollar remain the principal standards of value for world commerce despite the best attempts of economists to emulate the physicists. The fact is, of course, that we will never succeed in eliminating material standards of money. This is because monetary standards are signifiers of political relations between people, whereas standards of weight and measure signify physical relations between objects. Thus, for as long as there is coercion, there will always be resistance; and the subordinated will never trust the motives of the elite. "The attachment to gold," as Rist (1938: 103) has noted, "is one aspect of the eternal struggle between individuals and the state, the former anxious to protect himself against the hazards of the future, the latter anxious to use money as an instrument of its power to keep for itself the monopoly thereof."

Consider, now, the explanatory adequacy of this subalternate quality theory of money. The first point is that the quality theory of money equation, SMV equals PQ, has the advantage because it combines Fisher's Rule and Gresham's Law into one new quality of money equation. In other words, it is superior to the quantity theory under the Ockham's Razor principle of explanatory parsimony. The second point is that the equation has to be modified to take account of the particular situation found in colonized countries such as West Africa, India, and Melanesia. What we had in these countries in the early colonial period was a situation of monetary and political disorder brought about by imperialist conquest or, to be more precise, a transition from one system of political order to another. For quantity theorists like Hogendorn and Johnson and others, these political factors are regarded as being of no significance. (This is rightly called Economics and not Political Economy.[16]) The quality theory, on the other hand, raises the possibility that the new order being established might be of negative significance to, say, the West Africans who were being enslaved. Could it be that the particular standard adopted by the King of Dahomey (16,000 cowries equals one ounce of gold equals four pounds sterling) signified an order that the slaves wanted to disrupt? Could it be that some of the subordinated peoples struggled to get other standards accepted?

Expressed in this way the problem is not one of explaining, say, how bad money drives out good, a theory which is concerned with quantitative changes to a standard which is qualitatively the same, but how one standard drives out another of a completely different quality. This requires a further change to the quality of money equation SMV equals PQ: The variable S must now be given a subscript according to its position on the power tetrad. Thus, $S_d$ signifies the dominant standard, and $S_s$ the subordinate standard. The latter term acquires additional superscripts according to the multiplicity of standards in existence. These matters are empirical questions, but, at a minimum, it will include two distinct subordinated standards: those of the indigenous elite and those of the subalterns.

With these modifications to the formula it is clear that the question of standards of value is a struggle for prestige, a question of politics. In other words, it is yet another variation on the general theme of resistance that Guha (1983a) has proposed. In order to illustrate this point,[17] the following lengthy quote from the autobiography of a Solomon Islander about a tax collection episode is justified:

When the tax was collected, Basiana had given four shillings to Mr. Bell instead of five. Mr. Bell had said, "No, you have to pay five shillings— that is the law!" Basiana had said "Five shillings are impossible for me. I'm a man from the bush and I haven't gone to a plantation—where could I earn a fifth shilling? I'll give you an important valuable instead of the five shillings." Mr. Bell refused: "No, You go back this afternoon and look around for a fifth shilling. Then you bring it back. You have to pay the tax tomorrow." So Basiana climbed the hill, thinking to himself. He went all the way up to the bush, to his own place, high in the mountains at Gounaile.

When he got there, he went to his men's house and got his crescent pearl shell: a sacred chest pendant inherited from his ancestors, and consecrated to them. At first he thought he might trade that *dafi* for someone's shilling. But then his mind turned another way. He was really angry. He took that *dafi,* consecrated to his ancestor, and smashed it to pieces. He took one of the pieces from the smashed pearl shell and began to grind it down. All night long, into the next day, he ground and ground and ground it down, until at dawn it was the same size and shape as a shilling piece. So he had those four shillings, four pieces of money, and his fifth was that piece of *dafi.* At dawn he went down to Gwee'abe, where Mr. Bell had had the tax house built. He went to Mr. Bell and put the four shillings and the piece of shell down on the table in front of him. "Mr. Bell, that one shilling was impossible for me. But this is my own shilling, one I ground down. You want money with the head of your king on it. But this shilling I ground for you is consecrated to my ancestor; your shilling has been passed down from my ancient ancestor. You have to accept it! You can't refuse it!"

Mr. Bell couldn't believe it. "Oh, you bastard. Don't you do that again! I want five real shillings. Not a piece of seashell like this." "This isn't just an ordinary shell. It's just the same size and shape as those of yours. But yours have your king on them, and mine has my ancestor on it. This is my fifth shilling!"

"It's all right for this time, but don't you do that again. Next time, I'll put you in jail." Basiana was very angry about that. "I've broken up that important *dafi* passed down by my ancestors, and Mr. Bell doesn't even think it's worth anything" (Fifi'i 1989: 7).

From the quantity theorist's perspective, the substitution of one standard of value for another in the colonial context appears as the workings of objective economic laws; but, from the subjective perspective of some-one like Basiana, such a theory is manifest nonsense. The other claim of the quantity theorists—that the cowrie shells were driven out because of excess supply—is also questionable from a quality of money perspective. Pax Britannica imposed its coinage in Africa, India, and Melanesia by the coercive act of demanding that taxes be paid in terms of coins of the realm instead of cowries.[18] This, not surprisingly, led to an excess supply of cowries as the result of the fall in the demand for them.

Dorward (1976: 590) noted that the colonial governments in West Africa demanded payment of tax in their own metallic money but argued that this set Gresham's Law into operation because "bad money (Euro-pean coinage) began driving out good money (Tiv cloth currency)." But Dorward has failed to understand this law because good money and bad money are relative valuations of the same standard of value, not compar-isons of different standards. Thus if a good silver coin was one in which the face value of the coin and its intrinsic metal content were in agreement, a bad silver coin was one in which the metallic content fell below the face value. For example, if one silver coin marked one pound sterling con-tained an ounce of silver and another contained only half an ounce, then the former was called good money and the latter bad money. If this law operated in West Africa, it would have to be shown, for example, that a *kan* consisting of a regulation 40 cowrie shells was ousted by a *kan* con-sisting of a number of shells less than 40. There is no evidence to show that this is what happened in West Africa (or India or PNG).

One Indian historian who has understood the politics of the demise of cowries is De, who notes that "the abnormal depreciation in the value of the cowries in the 19th century was mainly due to the fact that under the British rule the cowries were not accepted for payment of revenue; conse-quently the demand for it in the market grew less, and there was a propor-tionate fall in its price" (1952a: 10). In other words, an imperial standard was imposed by force, meaning that the subordinated standard, cowries in this case, lost its value. The British action was unique in the history of imperialist conquest of India: Previous Imperial powers had, it seems, accepted cowries as legal tender. This fact caused great hardship for all those who used cowries in India at the time. The policy was vigorously opposed by moneyed men and landlords who profited greatly from the traffic in cowries. In Orissa the Oriya Paiks, soldiers of the Raja of Khurda, rose in open rebellion against the British government in March 1817, about fourteen years after the British conquest. This rebellion was brutally suppressed by the British by October of the same year (De 1952b). This fact is sufficient to belie the claim that the cowrie is a humble currency, the coinage of the masses.[19] The cowrie can be, and has been, a standard of significant value to landlords, moneylenders, slave traders, and merchant capitalists throughout history. The fact is that cowries, dollars, gold, and so forth are mere objects; their natural properties provide no clue as to their iconic, indexical, or symbolic significance. What must be comprehended is the fact that invisible chains bind these objects together: If they are comprehended, then the symbolic meaning is revealed; if not, they remain mere objects. Many historians and economists have failed to understand the symbolism of money with the result that their theories become apolitical and objectivist.

Anthropologists, on the other hand, ever alert to the importance of the iconic and symbolic significance of money, sometimes make the most elementary mistakes and fail to realize that cowries can be money symbols. For example, in the 1940s a great debate waged in the pages of *Man* concerning the iconic significance of the cowrie. On the one side were the "horizontalists" who argued that the cowrie was "obviously" a charm against the evil eye; on the other side were the "verticalists" who maintained that the cowrie represented the human vulva and was used as a fertility charm. According to my Bengali informant (Ranajit Guha), some of the people who actually used them saw things differently: Parents put cowries around the necks of their newborn children rather than gold, so that the evil spirits would be fooled into thinking that the children had a low value. In other words, the iconic value of cowries to Bengalis was derived from their use as money symbols and not as objects which conjure up, in the anthropological imagination, likeness to various parts of the body. Thus, whereas some economists have failed to realize that money is a symbol, some anthropologists have failed to realize that cowries, as a money symbol, can have iconographic significance.[20]

The subalternate quality theory of money calls for a reassessment of Bohannan's theory of spheres of exchange and Keynes' theory of multiple standards of value. These theories, it was seen above, were found wanting by Hogendorn and Johnson and by Dorward. But the theories of Bohannan and Keynes are significant contributions to the literature and a great improvement on the quantity theory approach. Indeed, aspects of Keynes's theory of multiple standards are consistent with the quality theory approach developed here. The problem with Bohannan's and Keynes' approach is that it abstracts from power. Keynes' (1982: 259) idea that one standard is replaced by another through "the normal progress of adaera-tion" is to give objects a life of their own. There is no natural tendency for metallic standards to oust others (or for general purpose monies to oust special purpose monies), rather, there is a cultural tendency for those with power to impose their standards of value on others with different stan-dards. It is a matter of the cultural logic of power rather than of the nat-ural power of logic.

## NOTES

Acknowledgements: This essay has been a long time in the making, and I have incurred many debts over the years. An early version was first presented as a paper at an interdisciplinary conference on gift exchange organized by Natalie Davis, Rena Lederman, and Ronald Sharp at the National Humanities Research Center, North Carolina, in November 1990. I am indebted to them and to the participants of that conference for the many helpful comments I received. Particular mention must be made of Georg Elwert, who has worked on the anthropological history and oral traditions of Benin. He drew my attention to his own work on the subject (see Elwert 1973; 1989), and my essay has benefited immeasurably from this input and from our discussions. He patiently took me through a word-for-word transla-tion of the original myth by Klipko Cece which forms the prelude to this essay. The final draft was written whilst I was a fellow at the Wissenschaftskolleg zu Berlin. I am grateful to the fellows and staff of the Kolleg and especially to Hans Medick for his comments on this paper. Finally, I thank my Canberra-based colleague, Ranajit Guha, for trenchant criticisms on an early draft and for the general intel-lectual inspiration that his writings, as well as our long discussions, have provided. This is my first attempt to come to terms with some of the implications of his thought for political economy and anthropology.

　1. The quotation is translated from Ayizo by Elwert (1989), who notes that this was first published in the Ayizo language in *Gankpanvi* (1979: vol. 1), the first issue of a journal that was established as a result of the Ayou literacy movement. This translation differs slightly from the English version he published (see unnum-bered footnote.)

　2. See De (1952a; 1952b); Hughes (1978).

　3. Compare Guha (1985): "Religion is the oldest of archives" (p. 1); "once the syncretic wrapping is taken off, the content of many a myth can be identified as what it really is—that is, as a figure of some ancient and unresolved antagonism" (p. 2).

　4. The following is a much-abbreviated account of the story of the shell money of the slave trade as told by Hogendorn and Johnson (1986). I focus on this book because it provides me with a convenient rhetorical means of raising my gen-

eral comparative questions. My concern is not to develop a critique of Hogendorn and Johnson's economic history but to raise general questions about the quantity theory of money by means of the expression it gets in their book.

5. Dubbeldam (1964) and Connell (1977) are among those who have applied Fisher's Rule and Gresham's Law to the Papua New Guinea case. Perlin (1987) contains an exhaustive bibliography on cowries in India.

6. Law's (1991: 5) "scepticism about the potential value of oral tradition" for research of this kind reflects, perhaps, a more general view among historians of a non-anthropological bent. It seems to me that, when an oral tradition such as Cece's story about the cowrie-shell trade is written down, it becomes an archive like any other. One must take a skeptical approach to all archives; their relative value is not an objective property of the document but is determined by the theoretical approach of the historian as Guha's (1983b) essay on the prose of counter-insurgency suggests.

7. Guha, a sometime painter, makes extensive use of this image throughout *Elementary Aspects* (1983a) and his other writings. This, Guha informs me (1993), was not done consciously. His unconscious use of the logic of color to structure his thoughts invites comparison with Lévi-Strauss' conscious use of musical logic.

8. I omit, for ease of exposition, details of the prices (P) and quantities (Q) sold.

9. If, for example, one kilogram of rice cost $10 from this trader and five kilograms of sweet potatoes cost $10 from that trader, then the implicit exchange value of the commodities in the market is one kilogram rice equals five kilograms of sweet potatoes. Thus, the C-M-C form of money exchange reduces to the C-C of commodity exchange, which implies that barter forms of exchange are implicit in any market economy. Theories of values such as Sraffa's (1960) are premised on this fact.

10. This much should be obvious from the formula C-C. I stress this point because the relative commodity form of value (C-C) and the absolute money form (M-C) are often confused.

11. Law (1991: 67) quotes a French source which says that the rich had great treasures in cowries, beads, gold dust, women, and land.

12. The actual figure was £3.17.10½d which, if rounded up to £4, gives the standard rate of 16,000 cowries per ounce. There is some disagreement among the authorities on the interpretation of the data relating to the standard rate. Compare Polanyi (1966: 92, 159, 168); Hogendorn and Johnson (1986: 124, 132–35); Law (1991: 51–58, 176).

13. See Law (1991: 52).

14. See Gregory (1989) for a detailed exposition of this argument.

15. See the minority report to the Gold Commission (1982).

16. See Gregory (1982: 10–29) for an elaboration of this point.

17. See Vansina (1962) for another example from the Congo.

18. The situation in PNG is slightly different in that the gold-lip shell, *Pinctada maxima,* was permitted in place of legal tender until 1964 under the New Guinea Coinage and Tokens Ordinance. Its exchange rate was fixed at twelve shillings a pair. It is also interesting to note that in 1920, following the ousting of the Germans from New Guinea after the First World War, the use of German currency was prohibited; yet another illustration of the obvious fact that standards of value are the expression of political dominance. See Phillips (1972) for further elaboration of these details.

19. This term was first used by Perlin (1987) and seems to have been accepted uncritically by other economic historians of India. See, for example, Richards (1987: 5).

20. The debate was opened with a letter to *Man* by Murray (1939). One of the best contributions was made by Elwin (1942) in an article dealing with cowrie use in Bastar District India (where, incidentally, I did field work in 1983–1984). A recent monograph has been published by Safer and Gill (1982) that deals exclusively with the iconography of shells; this contains useful surveys of the literature. The iconography of coins and notes is a curiously neglected topic. Hocart (1952) contains a short but interesting essay on the topic in one of the few anthropological contributions to this topic that I have been able to find.

## REFERENCES

Boagey, E. 1977. *Poetry Workbook.* Slough: University Tutorial Press.

Bohannan, P. 1959. "The Impact of Money on an African Subsistence Economy." In, G. Dalton, ed., *Tribal and Peasant Economies: Readings in Economic Anthropology.* New York: The Natural History Press, 123–35.

Connell, J. 1977. "The Bougainville Connection: Changes in the Economic Context of Shell Money Production in Malaita." *Oceania* 48, 1: 81–101.

De, S. C. 1952a. "The Cowry Currency in India." *The Orissa Historical Research Journal* 1, 1: 1–10.

———. 1952b. "Cowry Currency in Orissa." *The Orissa Historical Research Journal* 1, 2: 10–21.

Dorward, D. C. 1976. "Precolonial Tiv Trade and Cloth Currency." *The International Journal of African Historical Studies* 9, 4: 576–91.

Dubbeldam, L. F. B. 1964. "The Devaluation of the Kapauku-Cowrie as a Factor of Social Disintegration." *American Anthropologist,* 66, 4: 293–303.

Elwert, G. 1973. *Wirtschaft und Herrschaft von Daxome (Dahomey) im 18. Jahrhundert.* Munchen: Kommissionsverlag Klaus Renner.

———. 1989. *An Intricate Oral Culture: On History, Humour and Social Control among the Ayizo (Benin),* No. 16. FU Berlin Institut Für Ethnologie.

Elwin, V. 1942. "The Use of Cowries in Bastar State, India." *Man* 72 (Nov.–Dec.): 121–24.

Fifi'i, J. 1989. *From Pig-Theft to Parliament: My Life between Two Worlds.* R. Keesing, trans. Suva: Solomon Islands College of Higher Education and University of the South Pacific.

Friedman, M. 1987. "Quantity Theory of Money." In, J. Eatwell, M. Milgate, and P. Newman, eds., *The New Palgrave: A Dictionary of Economics.* London: Macmillan.

Gold Commission. 1982. *Report of the Commission on the Role of Gold in the Domestic and International Monetary System.* Washington D.C.: United States Government.

Gregory, C. A. 1982. *Gifts and Commodities.* New York: Academic Press.

———. 1989. "How the USA Made the Third World Pay for the Vietnam War." In, P. Limqueco, ed., *Partisan Scholarship: Essays in Honour of Renato Constantino.* Manila: JCA Press.

Guha, R. 1983a. *Elementary Aspects of Peasant Insurgency in Colonial India.* Delhi: Oxford University Press.

———. 1983b. "The Prose of Counter-Insurgency." In, R. Guha, ed., *Subaltern Studies II.* Delhi: Oxford University Press.

———. 1985. "The Career of an Anti-God in Heaven and on Earth." In, A. Mitra, ed., *The Truth Unites: Essays in Tribute to Samar Sen.* Calcutta: Subarnarekha.

———. 1989. "Dominance without Hegemony and Its Historiography." In, R. Guha, ed., *Subaltern Studies VI: Writings on South Asian History and Society.* Delhi: Oxford University Press.

———. 1993. Personal communication (oral).

Hocart, A. M. 1952. *The Life-Giving Myth and Other Essays.* London: Methuen.

Hogendorn, J. and M. Johnson. 1986. *The Shell Money of the Slave Trade.* Cambridge: Cambridge University Press.

Hughes, I. 1977. *New Guinea Stone Age Trade. Terra Australis 3.* Canberra: Australian National University.

———. 1978. "Good Money and Bad: Inflation and Devaluation in the Colonial Process." *Mankind* 11, 3: 308–18.

Keynes, J. M. 1982. "Ancient Currencies." In, D. Moggridge, ed., *Collected Writings.* New York: Macmillan.

Kula, W. 1986. *Measures and Men.* Princeton: Princeton University Press.

Law, R. 1991. *The Slave Coast of West Africa 1550–1750: The Impact of the Atlantic Slave Trade on an African Society.* Oxford: Clarendon Press.

Marx, K. 1867. *A Critical Analysis of Capitalist Production,* vol. 1 of *Capital.* Moscow: Progress.

Murray, M. A. 1939. "The Meaning of the Cowrie-Shell." *Man* 165 (Oct.): 167.

Nadel, S. F. 1942 [1969]. *A Black Byzantium: The Kingdom of Nupe in Nigeria.* Oxford: Oxford University Press.

Ofonagoro, W. I. 1979. "From Traditional to British Currency in Southern Nigeria: Analysis of a Currency Revolution, 1880–1948." *The Journal of Economic History* 39, 3: 623–54.

Perlin, F. 1987. "Money-Use in Late Pre-Colonial India and the International Trade in Currency Media." In, J. F. Richards, ed., *The Imperial Monetary System of Mughal India.* Oxford: Oxford University Press.

Phillips, M. J. 1972. "Currency." In, P. Ryan, ed., *Encyclopaedia of Papua and New Guinea.* Melbourne: Melbourne University Press, 235–38.

Polanyi, K. 1966. *Dahomey and the Slave Trade: An Analysis of an Archaic Economy.* Seattle: University of Washington Press.

Richards, J. F. 1987. "Introduction." In, J. F. Richards, ed., *The Imperial Monetary System of Mughal India.* Oxford: Oxford University Press, 1–12.

Rist, C. 1938. *History of Monetary and Credit Theory.* New York: Kelley.

Safer, J. F. and F. M. Gill. 1982. *Spirals from the Sea: An Anthropological Look at Shells.* New York: American Museum of Natural History and Clarkson N. Potter, Inc.

Sraffa, P. 1960. *Production of Commodities by Means of Commodities: Prelude to a Critique of Economic Theory.* Cambridge: Cambridge University Press.

Vansina, J. 1962. "Trade and Markets among the Kuba." In, P. Bohannan and G. Dalton, eds., *Markets in Africa.* Evanston: Northwestern University Press, 190–210.

# Cowries and Conquest

Prelude to a Postscript

*Chris Gregory*

How does one rethink a paper completed over a decade ago? As my essay borders on the disciplines of political economy, economic history, and economic anthropology, three possible approaches suggest themselves. Firstly, from the perspective of political economy, there is the question of the adequacy of the theoretical formulation of my general argument; secondly, from the perspective of economic history, there is the question of revisions needed in the light of new material published (and old material overlooked) since I wrote my article and; thirdly, from the perspective of economic anthropology, there is the question of the function of shell money today. What is the current role of the cowrie? Is cowrie-money a thing of the past or is it poised to make a comeback? If so, what are the implications of this for my argument?

As economic anthropologist I am most interested in, and best qualified to handle, the third question. What is more, since I wrote my paper I have come across some interesting new evidence to suggest that, in one place at least, efforts are in place to have shells re-monetized. Since this attempt at re-monetization is going on as I write, it is too early to say anything conclusive about it. As such, this paper will be a postscript to my 1996 article and, perhaps, a prelude to a new one that may have to be written in a decade or so.

Cowries can still be found in the markets of Bastar District, central India today (where I do fieldwork) but only as commodities for sale, not as money. Diviners buy them for use in their rituals. They are the raw materials the cowrie-shell making people use to make baskets, belts, and decorated clothing; these are used by religious practitioners for various purposes and are also sold to tourists.

Cowries in Bastar were demonetized over 150 years ago and, while their former use as money is fossilised in the language of some myths, the shells show no signs of being re-monetized. The Indian rupee reigns supreme as legal tender. The lower denomination notes are tattered and torn and in very short supply, yet they face no competition from the cowrie despite growing demands for more low-denomination currency. By contrast, higher-denomination notes, sparkling clean and readily available from banks, must compete with gold and silver as a store of value. Almost a century has passed since Keynes described India as "the sink of the precious metals" and so it remains today; but the humble cowrie has lost its historical status as the small change of gold, and shows no signs of regaining it.

The current situation in West Africa, it seems, is much the same. Here too, cowries continue to be used for divination and other ritual purposes but they no longer have any monetary function. This much is clear from the recent work of Piot (1999: 36, 73–74, 84), who reports from his fieldwork among the Kabre of Togo. His book is a most important anthropological contribution to our understanding of the cowrie shells of the slave trade because, remarkably, his informants retain vivid memories of the slave-raiding times. Piot's informants challenge our orthodox assumptions because they freely admitted that kinsmen sold their children as slaves. These statements are consistent with the archival evidence and, alas, with journalistic reports of contemporary slaving practices in West Africa. Piot's work reveals the significant fact that the general practice was for the mother's brother to sell the sister's son. Much has been written about the mother's brother in West Africa, but it suffices to note here that the mother's brother, rather than the father, is the family member generally regarded as the closest and most affectionate towards a child.

Facts like this sit uncomfortably with a one-sided resistance theory of conquest. Guha (1989), who is not a one-sided resistance theorist, is careful to point out that without coercion there can be no resistance and that without the pair 'coercion/resistance' there can be no persuasion/collaboration. For him, these were the constituent elements of power in general and the historian's task was to record how these elements expressed themselves in particular historical circumstances. Piot's analysis of why West Africans sold their kin as slaves opens up new avenues for research into subaltern politics and reveals the need not only for history but also for an approach that is grounded in an anthropologically informed analysis of local-level politics. He suggests that coercion may lead to accommodation—"If some level of involvement was indeed unavoidable, then selling might have been clearly preferable to being raided" (1996: 45)—and that when this happens the culturally specific politics of the rural household comes into play. He notes, for example, that among the Kabre the mother's brother and the father have competing claims over children, claims that tip in favor of the father after initiation. The selling of children, he argues, needs to be seen in the light of this struggle between dominant male kinsmen.

The contemporary situation of shell money use in Melanesia presents an altogether different picture to that found in India and West Africa. Here indigenous currencies, some of which take the form of shells of different types, not only survive but thrive.

An important recent collection of essays, edited by Akin and Robbins (1999), reports new ethnographic research on the relationship between the state and local currencies from eight communities in Melanesia. As is usual in matters Melanesian, the picture is a complex one that varies from community to community, but, as the editors reveal, the question of social reproduction and cultural identity in an era of globalization is at the heart of the matter. The social significance of shells, they argue, becomes explicit in mortuary and marriage, and shells also play a prominent part in the formulation and display of individual and group identities.

The findings of Akin and Robbins are dramatically illustrated in further evidence from Papua New Guinea (PNG) that has come to light since their book was published. Consider the following report entitled "Shell Money to Become Legal Tender," which appeared in the *Post Courier,* PNG's national newspaper, on 26 November 1999.

> The traditional Tolai currency, shell money, or *tabu* will become legal tender in the province. This is as far as the East New Britain Provincial Executive Council [PEC] is concerned. The assembly recently endorsed a paper titled "Promotion and Mobilisation of Customs Wealth" presented by chairman of commerce, industry and tourism, Leo Dion. But before businesses and the community at large start exchanging *tabu* in their business transactions, the provincial government will sponsor a study and extensive research into the use of *tabu,* and put in place relevant legislation to regulate the use of the shell money.
>
> "The paper has been endorsed by the PEC which means *tabu* will become legal tender as a second currency to the *kina* in the province." "However, before that can happen relevant legislation will have to be adopted and put in place to regulate the use of *tabu* as a second currency." Mr Dion said shell money had been used in the province for

many generations until today, but there had never been any proper control of its use. Shell money is currently used in the villages, markets and even stores but there is wide spread misuse of it.

"There is a need to standardise and mobilise the *tabu.*" "This means there is a need to carry out extensive research into its use and recommend to the Government on ways to best standardise the shell spacing as well as the length, or fathom, of shell money," he said.

Usually, a fathom of shell money is valued at K2, but recently due to the drops in the *kina* value, the same fathom is exchangeable at K3.50. According to Mr Dion, this trend would give way to misuse and non-standardised use of the *tabu.* One of the issues which must also be regulated, before shell money gets into full use, is the spacing between shells in a fathom. Mr Dion said the normal practice was five millimetres between each shell, which means two shells will occupy a space of one centimetre. Mr Dion said the study would research the possibility of setting up a custom wealth bank which would assist to mobilise, regulate and control *tabu* currency.

"Our country's legal tender is being regulated and controlled by the Bank of Papua New Guinea whereas *tabu* is not regulated and has been manipulated by *tabu* traders who have pushed the price of a fathom up while its purchasing power is only equivalent to the *kina,*" Mr Dion said.

A K6 million estimate value of *tabu* is available.

The Tolai area, it should be noted, is Papua New Guinea's most economically developed area, and the Tolai people are the country's best educated.

What is the significance of these new findings for my argument about the quantity theory of money? They obviously raise questions that go beyond the narrowly defined problematic of my paper. I was concerned there with the general problem of understanding the de-monetization of shells in the early period of colonial conquest. The problem here has been turned upside down: how does one explain the apparent re-monetization of shells in the twilight zone of imperialism? Furthermore, why does this problem seem specific to Melanesia?

Obviously, I cannot answer these questions here, but the facts, I believe, do illustrate the general argument that I was trying to make in my paper, namely that a dramatic increase in the supply of shell money does not, of itself, debase its value and lead to inflated shell-money prices.

This argument is illustrated in the Tolai case. The shells used by the Tolai—a dog whelk (*Nassa*) rather than a cowrie (*C. moneta*)—were obtained in pre-colonial times from local shores. Coastal villagers collected them and traded them. An increasing demand meant that traders seeking shells had to start traveling to more distant shores, first on their own island of New Britain and later to other places in PNG. Today, the main source of supply is PNG's neighbor the Solomon Islands, because the shells there are of very high quality, and are the right size and color (yellowish). This international trade is monopolized by a few merchants. Statistical estimates of shell imports are non-existent but it is clear that massive amounts have been imported into the region over the past century. Furthermore, complaints about rising prices of shells in recent times are testimony that the massive increase has not led to a fall in prices. Indeed, the proposal by the Provincial Government to make them legal tender is clearly intended to bring about a reduction in their local exchange value through government regulation.

This particular case provides an intriguing contrast with the generalized case I described in my *CSSH* paper for the early colonial period. What both cases share are triangular relationships between the international merchants who supply the shells, the local communities that demand them, and the states that regulate through legislation. What is different is that here in New Britain the state is trying to achieve the same aim (a reduction in the local price of shells) through legal re-monetization rather than legal de-monetization. It remains to be seen if the provincial government of East New Britain will be able to implement this change, but given that its power does not compare favorably with that of imperial states like Britain in the nineteenth century one can only be skeptical about their strategy's ultimate success.

Another difference here is that the state is trying to establish a shell-money standard of value that the people also want. At first glance, this looks like a case where the subalterns are working *with* rather than against the state. However, a closer look at the local power relations in the East New Britain province reveals that the shell-money standard being proposed is that of the dominant Tolai community. There are three main ethnic groups in this province and three distinct shell standards. The exchange standards of the Pomic and Baining people, who use *kakal* and *mis,* respectively, would be subordinated to the proposed standards (PEC 1999). What the Pomic and the Baining people think about this new proposal is unknown, but the subalternate theory of money that I advance does suggest a number of hypotheses that need to be investigated.

If this attempt at re-monetization of shells is seen as an assertion of cultural identity and conflict in today's globalized world, then the fact that it has arisen only in Melanesia becomes comprehensible. If the U.S. dollar has replaced gold and cowries as the symbol of global economic unity today, then cultures require heterogenous symbols of value to express their difference. The various cultures of Melanesia favor the use of different types of shells for this purpose. In India, gold, silver, and cowries were used to express economic status rather than cultural identity, and gold and silver retain this function today. But when it comes to symbols of cultural identity in India, other objects, such as the cow, perform this time-honored role.

REFERENCES

Akin, D. and J. Robbins, eds. 1999. *Money and Modernity: State and Local Currencies in Melanesia.* Pittsburgh: University of Pittsburgh Press.

Guha, R. 1989. "Dominance without Hegemony and Its Historiography." *Subaltern Studies VI: Writings on South Asian History and Society.* R. Guha, ed. Delhi: Oxford University Press.

PEC. 1999. "Promotion and Mobilisation of Custom Wealth." Rabaul: Provincial Executive Council, East New Britain Provincial Government.

Piot, C. 1996. "Of Slave and the Gift: Kabre Sale of Kin During the Era of the Slave Trade." *Journal of African History* 37: 31–49.

———. 1999. *Remotely Global: Village Modernity in West Africa.* Chicago: University of Chicago Press.

# Global Violence and Nationalizing Wars in Eurasia and America

## The Geopolitics of War in the Mid-Nineteenth Century

*Michael Geyer and Charles Bright*

The histories of Germany and the United States became deeply entangled in the century of total war.[1] After (re)unification on the battlefield in the mid-nineteenth century, both countries underwent rapid transformations through national programs of industrialization based on new products and technologies and emerged as "great" powers with global pretensions at the beginning of the twentieth century. An initial, and somewhat hesitant, confrontation in World War I was followed by a period of oscillation and confusion during the 1920s and 1930s, as leading elements in the two economies sought grounds for collaboration even as the political development of the two nations diverged, one moving toward fascism, the other toward a liberal democratic renewal. This produced the deeply ideological collision of the second World War which resulted in an equally dramatic turnabout, as the Germans endured what Americans then most feared, a grim (albeit partial) communist takeover, and the United States became the staunch ally of the German west in its face-off with the east. Recently this close partnership has turned into a more perplexed and occasionally suspicious friendship, as the familiar terrain of the cold war is ploughed up.[2] This is a history of extreme reversals, tied inextricably to war and preparations for war.

It makes imminent sense to seek the origins of these parallel histories in the wars that remade Germany and the United States in the middle of the nineteenth century. The American Civil War and the wars of German unification were decisive watersheds in the history of these two nations.[3] Both were wars fought for old values and political objectives; both taught lessons, through the practice of war itself, about how to mobilize whole nations, national identities and industrial capabilities for war—knowledge that became the essential prerequisite of great power status in the international system of the next century. One might therefore expect that a comparison of these two foundational wars could offer insights into the historical trajectories that followed, or, reversing the inquiry, that the fact of the historic entanglement of Germany and the United States over the past century might highlight certain salient aspects of these formative mid-century wars.

Yet in fact, the American Civil War and the wars of German unification are extremely difficult to compare. It is easy enough to say that both conflicts pointed toward new ways of waging war which eventually resulted in the practices of "total" war. But the German wars of unification were extremely short, duel-like events that escalated from small origins in the campaigns against Denmark and Austria to a somewhat larger, but no less snappy war against France. Though certain aspects of civil war were present, these were basically interstate wars that dramatically reversed the balance of power in Europe.[4] Power, both domestic and international, was the key issue, for otherwise, war might well have been avoided; accordingly, the wars were settled by political (that is, diplomatic), rather than purely military means.[5] The American Civil War, on the other hand, was a war between member states of the union, despite some external meddling by other powers. It was a war over fundamentally different visions of rights and justice that expressed two emergent and very distinct social trajectories. Freedom in its various interpretations was the key issue, even though the abolition of slavery was not an initial goal and "emancipation" was an even more distant proposition.[6] The clash between alternative and uncompromising visions of the nation's future turned into a drawn-out war of destruction that had no ready political solution.[7] The military campaigns exhibited little of the operational mastery of the Prussian campaigns, despite flashes of gallantry and brilliance, but displayed more of the escalating and open-ended savagery of total war than the more limited and politically controlled Prussian wars. While the American Civil War started for political reasons, it found no ground for conclusion short of unequivocal military victory and unconditional defeat.

Not only are the two wars dissimilar, they were also utterly distant from each other. However much the subsequent national histories of Germany and the United States suggest that these foundational wars were or should be linked, it is their separateness that proves most striking in any effort at comparison. These wars were profoundly local affairs, indifferent to each other and conditioned by factors that were specific to utterly distinct local and regional contexts. Comparison, of course, does not require linkage, but the fact that two wars which lie at the epicenter of an arc of violence that, in the subsequent century, came to hold Europe and America together were in fact conducted with so little reference to the other, militarily or politically, is not only surprising in itself, but serves to highlight the absence of any bridging, imperial project in the middle of the nineteenth century that might have presumed, or made, such linkage. This directs analysis, not only to the specificities of separate regions, but to the conjunctural nature of these mid-nineteenth century wars, half-way between the intercontinental imperial and revolutionary wars of the eighteenth century and the intercontinental, great power wars of the twentieth century. The first step in comparing these two wars, then, becomes an exploration of the regional context of each war and of the historical particularities of the mid-nineteenth century international order which fostered distance and non-connectedness between these two watershed events.[8]

In pursuing a comparison to the specificities of time and place, however, another surprising feature of these mid-century wars emerges. There is little in the nineteenth century that prepares us for the numbing human and material losses of mass destruction in the twentieth century. In our own century, of course, the numbers—magnitude, frequency, and deadliness of violent conflagrations—explode, and the sheer destructiveness of warfare takes on overwhelming proportions.[9] But the contrasting image of the nineteenth century as a peaceful era in which wars such as those examined here, along with other, faintly remembered conflicts in the Crimea (1853–1856) or over Italian unification (1859–1871), are treated as exceptions to the tranquil norm, turns out to be patently wrong—especially for the mid-century decades. The Correlates of War Project records no less that 177 war-like confrontations in the period between 1840 and 1880.[10] Within this forty year span, moreover, the total number, duration, and deadliness of violent conflicts worldwide was markedly higher during the 1850s and 1860s than in the ten years before and after, thanks in the main to the multidimensional Taiping rebellion in China (1851–1864), the Crimean conflict, and the American Civil War (1861–1865). But together these four middle decades of the century were bracketed on either side by relatively peaceful periods, separating them from the revolutionary and Napoleonic wars, on the one side, and the second era of world war in the twentieth century, on the other. The striking feature of the period between

1840 and 1880, then, is the multiplication and intensification of violent conflicts, with the middle decades being a period of endemic violence. Rather than having two exceptional wars, fought at a distance, in conjuncture with a few other unrelated wars here and there, we face a world in turmoil.

The main analytic concern for a comparison of the American Civil War and the wars of German unification thus pertains less to the distance between them than to the location of these wars within global patterns of endemic violence. The first task is to map the actual incidence of violence in the mid-nineteenth century, using the compilations of the Correlates of War Project. This elementary task will establish that warfare in Europe and the United States was not the only, nor the most critical, conflict of the era—that, indeed, in a fully global context, the incidence of European- and American-made warfare must be radically resituated. From this perspective, the American Civil War and the wars of German unification can be seen to arise from two distinct axes of conflict—one along the Eurasian seam, the other on the Atlantic rim—both of which were formed by the on-going crisis and transformation of eighteenth-century Empires. At the same time, it will become clear that while the wars of mid-century anchored parallel national trajectories toward industrial transformation and world power, what brought Germany and the United States into collision in the twentieth century was not so much their direct competition with each other as the way this competition was mediated by British sea power. Britain's response to the new industrial challengers took the form of a wholly new and distinct kind of global imperialism which successfully framed the competing ambitions of the others and brought them into conflict. This final dimension of the argument will underscore the pivotal nature of the American Civil War and the wars of German unification—as both the last effects of eighteenth century empires in crisis and the cornerstone of the new forces of nation-based imperialism that shaped global conflict in the twentieth century.

## Wars at Mid-Century

In listing 177 war-like confrontations for the middle decades of the nineteenth century, the compilers of data for the Correlates of War Project distinguished twenty systemic wars, eighteenth extra-systemic wars, and twenty-seven civil wars. There were thus sixty-five major conflagrations according to their definitions.[11] They then listed another 112 small wars and large massacres to produce their stunning total.[12] Immediately, qualitative questions arise concerning this data—about the sheer number of conflicts, their duration and their deadliness. At first sight, the proliferation of wars and war-like incidents may appear to be a statistical artifact. We encounter not only the second Hollstein War (1864), the Austrian War (1866), and the Franco-Prussian War as three distinct wars rather than one Prussian war for German unification, we also find no less than thirteen entries for Italy, because Italian unification proceeded slowly and in stages and, furthermore, involved different kinds of violent confrontation. A more narrative history would reduce the clutter of overall numbers to some degree and a more analytical approach might streamline the multiplicity of campaigns into composite wars.[13] Still, the most striking feature of the middle of the nineteenth century is the significant number of sizeable wars and the persistent measure of low-level violence—small wars or large massacres that were organized enough to be noticed as violent conflagrations, and that were distinct from murder, mayhem, or riots which were also widely prevalent.[14]

Historians have come to assume that the most highly organized and most industrially or professionally advanced military campaigns are also generally the most deadly encounters. This throws emphasis on interstate wars, especially those within the European state system. However, the statistical data for this period suggest a quite different emphasis. First, there is no evident correlation between the degree of organization and the deadliness of wars. Of the six deadliest conflicts,[15] only two (the Crimean War and the Franco-Prussian War) were systemic wars involving several members of the European system. Another (the Russo-Turkish War) involved one European power, but was peripheral to the European state system;[16] and a fourth war in the "correlates" list of the most severe (the Triple Alliance against Paraguay) involved "minor" powers in another state system altogether, one which (like the European system) produced a number of other, smaller wars in the same period. Moreover, the two deadliest conflicts of the mid-decades were, in fact, non-European civil wars. Not only were the Taiping wars in China and the American Civil War among the costliest of the period, but several of what the Correlates Project counts as "systemic wars"—as, for example, the Franco-Mexican War (1862–1867)—were really civil wars in which external powers got involved. Indeed, it makes no sense to approach war at mid-century from the vantage point of the (European) state system, notwithstanding its extraordinary ability to project force. Systems wars were spread all over the globe, and only one of the European systems wars (the Franco-Prussian War) was a genuine "great power" (i.e., European interstate) war.[17]

Second, there is no obvious correlation between the degree of "stateness" and the deadliness of warfare. Much of the killing in this period arose from low intensity conflicts—ongoing, undecided, periodically genocidal, and with recurring edges of terrorism.[18] These may be thought of as "local wars." The local and social nature of warfare is something well understood by African historians studying violence on that continent in the nineteenth century.[19] A short while ago we might have argued that such local violence was "not yet" organized in the state—presuming that the differentiation and monopolization of violence was a matter of course in global development, dependent on the growth and expansion of the international system. Nowadays, one might prefer to say that as late as the mid-nineteenth century the overwhelming majority of deadly quarrels were local affairs in the sense that they happened apart from or underneath a forming interstate system, could not be pried out of their local power structures, and did not originate from a separate and monopolized organization of violence. But we should not then conceive of local wars as separate, somehow more authentic conflicts.[20] In the case of the Mexican war just cited, the French, seeking to recast a civil war for the Mexican nation in terms of the European state system, confronted localized violence seeping in on all sides, yet they were never able to break the fighting out of these local contexts to impose an imperial logic upon it. The imposed European emperor was thus condemned to drown in violence he could neither comprehend nor command.[21]

The nature of this pervasive local violence changes from place to place—and at best, one can try to establish regionally specific socio-cultural patterns. But its presence everywhere is an indication of the continuing strength of non-state networks of power and their ability to organize, concentrate, and project force. This is not a matter of scale or geography, for the Taiping rebellion, with its massive casualties, was in most respects local warfare, and the recurrent conflicts in Bosnia, Herzogovina, and Montenegro occurred in the face of forbidding logistics. Nor does localism imply the absence of state actors, although formal military organizations, when present, did not monopolize the violence and were often at a distinct disadvantage. Above all, local violence was not disorganized violence; rather it was the social nature of its organization, beyond the purview of the state, that made it so effective and so pervasive. What at first sight appears as a very diffuse kind of violence was, in fact, a peculiar form of "social" warfare—upheavals of ethnic groups, millenarian mobilizations, or the social and political confrontations of local strongmen, warlords, and caudillos.

Newly compiled data lend further credence to this argument. While roughly half of all "militarized disputes" between 1816 and 1976 involve major powers, the "other" half does not—and remains, quite inexplicably, unexplained.[22] This might not concern us were it not for the fact that during 1849–1870 and 1871–1890 a total of 42.4 percent and of 53.7 percent of all conflicts involved "minor" powers only (i.e., powers outside of the European state system). To be sure, the capability of "minor" powers to wage war independently of the European interstate system was punctured by the end of the nineteenth century, as the centering forces of imperial world order took hold. However, this decrease only lasted for an intermittent period which one might call the high twentieth century. Between 1890 and 1918, "minor" power violence decreased to one-third, and between 1918 and 1945 to one-fourth of all conflicts, only to change dramatically in the second half of the twentieth century. Between 1946 and 1976 the percentage of militarized disputes between "minor" powers once again increased to 65.6 percent.[23] This highlights the exceptionally centered nature of power in the world between 1890 and 1950, and it sheds light on the extremely de-centered nature of warfare in the nineteenth century. The parallels between violence in that period and our own is striking.

This is a de-centering of violence that points, not to the relative insignificance of warfare in the mid-nineteenth century—as if de-centering can be equated with unimportance—but to the truly global nature of war during this period. More warfare occurred outside Europe than within it, a fact that, given the Eurocentric nature of much historiography, may help explain why the nineteenth century has for so long been mythologized as an epoch of unusual, universal peace. The most deadly wars—five of the six most costly in the listings of the Correlates of War Project—occurred outside the European core, mostly below the level of state systems and with only limited involvement of European forces. Of the wars outside Europe, moreover, it was only in the Crimean conflict that European powers were centrally involved. Yet this was a European war only in a qualified sense, for its origins lay in the on-going confrontation between the Ottoman Empire and the Russian Empire along the Eurasian seam. This confrontation reached its peak in the Russo-Turkish War of 1877–1878, a conflict which also made the Correlates list of the six deadliest and, for the two contending parties, was far more costly than the Crimean

War.[24] The key European nation involved in the Crimean conflict was Great Britain which, however, acted more as a "global" than as a European power, concerned with the geopolitics of the India border and the security of the eastern Mediterranean (as part of its imperial interests), but rallying a supporting cast of European powers which gained regional status by joining a "global" war against the Russian "colossus."[25] It may well be argued that the Crimean War was utterly decisive for the future of Europe. But this is to say that a basically non-European confrontation between Russia, the Ottoman Empire, and Great Britain along the Eurasian seam decided what happened in the European state system and set the stage for the European confrontations to come—rather than the opposite. What gave the Crimean War its European significance was the intervening role of Louis Napoleon's France, seeking to build an alliance with Britain against the conservative powers in order to overthrow the Vienna Settlement.

The bloodiest conflict of the era, in terms of the sheer numbers of casualties, came in the imperial Chinese campaign against the so-called Taiping rebellion. This war was extremely cruel, aiming at the annihilation of the fundamentalist rebel forces in southern China, and like the overlapping wars against the minority populations of the Miao and the Nien, it is difficult to understand without reference to the European (British, French, and Russian) pressure against the borders of imperial China during the 1840s. In this sense it was a war at the periphery of an aggressively expanding (European) interstate system. But outside intervention is neither new nor unusual in the history China or any of the other land-based empires of the Eurasian rim, nor is such intervention necessary to an account of rebellion against the imperial Chinese state and its bureaucratic apparatus.[26] We might more productively interpret this war and its outcome as one episode in a complex struggle over power and its centers in the East Asian region.[27] In this context, the outcome of the struggle (in which the imperial system survived as a multi-ethnic state, under a newly forming Han-Chinese ruling tier and with a variety of competing political vanguards) may have been adequate to the immediate crisis, but left China vulnerable in the era of nationalist competition that followed—an era made more dangerous to China by the simultaneous break-out of Japan along a path of aggressive industrialization and national self-assertion. In a regional context, then, the civil wars in China were as decisive as the Meiji restoration in shaping the future of the East Asian "system." In a global context, moreover, the Taiping war, like the coeval struggle over British control of

India in the wars of the mutiny (1857–1859) and the recurrent Ottoman campaigns to defend the integrity of its borders against Russian encroachment or the coherence of its administration against provincial breakaways, was an episode in the general struggle over the future of the great land-based empires of the Eurasian seam during this period.

Of the wars included in the Correlates' list of most severe, the remaining two, outside of Europe, occurred on the American continent. They are listed under different categories, as systemic and civil wars respectively, but they were both, in fact, nationalizing wars. In this, they are not all that different from the Franco-Prussian and Piedmont-Sardianian Wars in Europe. Being a civil war, the American war between the states, like the Taiping wars in China, was about the preservation of a pre-existing sovereign entity and involved the mobilization of resources by the political center to crush rebellion. After the Taiping wars, moreover, the American Civil War was the bloodiest conflict of the period. But while the casualties were immense, they were largely off-set by the overall size and growth of the U.S. population, and like the Chinese civil war, deaths from war remained, in proportion to total population, less costly than the Franco-Prussian War was for the French, or The Pacific War between Chile, Bolivia, and Peru were for these warring populations. In this respect, the war of the triple alliance of Argentina, Brazil, and Uruguay against Paraguay appears to have been the most murderous war of all; while there is dispute among scholars about the casualty count, the proportion of killing to the populations involved was staggering, especially for the Paraguayans.[28] Moreover, the debate over numbers hides the fact that a people was brought to the brink of disaster, because war turned into a genocidal extermination of the defeated party, which was largely an Indian nation with a mestizo elite, pursuing a unique and (for the other powers in the system) a disturbingly different economic politics. The lethal nature of this ethnic extermination reminds us, moreover, of other ethnic wars in this period which, for both quantitative (the body counts) and qualitative (the racism of the victors) reasons, are not easily detected. The American wars against the Sioux nation, for example, would qualify merely as a small war or major massacre and might easily be a forgotten aspect of the violent (re)construction of the United States at mid-century.[29] Yet the Indian wars of the 1870s were the truly "destructive wars" of the North American continent and an integral part of the nationalizing outcome of the American Civil War.[30] Indeed it is worth noting, as a final comparison, that while the outcome of the civil war in China tended along a conserving trajectory toward the restoration and renewal of imperial forms (and in this resembled the aftermath of war in both the Russian and Ottoman Empires), the American Civil War produced a powerful unitary state that moved rapidly into industrial and territorial expansion. It was this nation-making, state-creating, industrially expansive outcome of war that, irrespective of causes, makes the mid-century wars of central Europe and North America similar (and comparable with the new national reformation of Japan).[31]

Looking back from the perspective of the late twentieth century, we must overcome our prevailing understanding of warfare, shaped as it is by the great power struggles for global hegemony. The defining event in this understanding is the Second World War, in which violence was globalized through campaigns that were both global and centrally coordinated, with command centers managing far-flung theaters around the world. Barely a century before, however, the majority of deadly encounters were the opposite of centrally and globally organized warfare. Violence in the period between 1840 and 1880 grew out of de-centered configurations of conflict around the world which had little to do with one another. The frequency and intensity of violent confrontations, the extremely local nature of the organization of violence, and the distance and separation of conflicts were all aspects of warfare then which resonate again in the present era. For nowadays, once again, it is the multiplicity and disaggregation of conflicts that matters most. Violence is again radically dispersed and de-centered. The mid-nineteenth century emerges in retrospect as a period of the decompression and de-centering of warfare very similar to our experience in the post-cold war epoch.[32]

What, initially, appeared as a strange separateness or distance between the American Civil War and the German wars of unification now seems to reflect a general state of affairs in the mid-nineteenth century. These two wars were episodes in a universe of endemic, world-wide violence, played out within global patterns of conflict in which warfare was dispersed, de-centered, and mostly of low-intensity, yet capable of threatening the survival of whole ethnes. There was no grand design or central nervous system that linked these conflicts. The powers of a putative core system of European states were not as apparent then as a half-century later; while the historical record tells us that a (renewed) concentration and centralization of violence was to come, this is not yet in evidence. But if there are no systemic links among these crises of power and stability around the world, they do, all of them together, constitute a global outburst of violence that thoroughly reshaped the world. Indeed, whatever the diversity of causes, this mid-nineteenth century passage of violence had distinctly unifying consequences. And it is these consequences that focus our attention on Germany and the United States.

In this first move toward a comparative history of violence in the mid-nineteenth century, we find that global patterns had two distinct axes, neither of them in Europe. First, there is a Eurasian zone of violence, with its focal points in Afghanistan, Transcaucasia, and the Caucasus and extending westward into the Near East and into southeastern Europe, where it became the flash point for major European wars. The permanence of warfare along this Eurasian seam, especially between Russia, British India, and the Ottoman Empire—but with China loosely tied into this formation and exhibiting many of the same troubles—arose from the continuing, conjunctural crises of large land-based empires in this period, and from the uses of warfare, whether civil or inter-empire, in stabilizing weakened imperial regimes. The wars of German unification arose in this context and broke clear of it. On the other side of the globe, a second concentrated belt of violence may be found in the Americas, north and south, stretching across a geographical expanse as huge as the Eurasian seam. Here we confront a wide variety of violent conflicts, ranging from internal wars of extermination against native people, civil wars among rival regions and factions, inter-state wars among regional "minor" powers, and occasionally, wars between American and European states—all stemming in one way or another from the problems associated with the consolidation of independent national states in North and South America. Indeed, if the violence along the Eurasian seam may be taken as expressive of the persistent and continuing crisis of land-based empires, the violence in the Americas stemmed largely from the aftermath and consequences of the protracted and gradual crisis of the great eighteenth-century Atlantic sea-borne empires. The American Civil War was shaped in this regional context and then transcended it. Thus the German and American wars, while distant and separate, both broke clear of regional patterns along similar trajectories and produced in the process a new crystallization and concentration of violence worldwide.

## War in Eurasia

The predominant feature of the Eurasian configuration was the tenacious consolidation and elaboration of land-based empires along the whole seam of the landmass. "Consolidation" is a more suitable term than "defense," because these empires were still dynamic, as often as not consolidating or reasserting control over territory and people which they had only recently acquired. This statement runs counter to a common assessment. In view of the eventual collapse of the Ottoman and Habsburg Empires (in 1918), it is all too easy to assume that these cumbersome, multi-ethnic empires were all bound to break apart. But this is true only inasmuch as they had no future in Europe—and, then, definitely only after their defeat in World War I. The Chinese, Indian, and Russian empires survived largely intact (albeit in a variety of guises and under various degrees of "alien" control) to enter a turbulent twentieth century of rapid modernization and, indeed, made it into the late twentieth century. It remains to be seen, if the implosion of the Russian Empire is a temporary or a permanent affair. However, none of this allows us to speak of a "natural" decline of empires. All that can be said is that the *longue durée* of empires was sorely tested in the middle of the nineteenth century.

The wars and upheavals at the margins of the Chinese Empire highlight this type of imperial conflagration quite well.[33] The campaigns of the imperial regime against the Taiping rebellion in the south, against the (Muslim) Nien uprising in the northwest, and against the ethnic uprising of the Miao in the southwest were punctuated by inter-imperial conflicts along the borders of China. While the encroachment of Great Britain, France, and Russia on Chinese territory established the principal weakness of the Empire, civil and ethnic-religious wars set the Empire ablaze and showed the incapacity of the imperial bureaucracy to guarantee domestic security, territorial integrity, or political order. These upheavals crystallized several strands of conflict. There were, first, the violent encounters with European powers who claimed special rights and access to China. Second, the upheavals of minorities like the Miao or the Nien were ethnic and religiously motivated wars of relatively compact and coherent societies fending off Chinese encroachment and trying to preserve a degree of autonomy against Chinese in-migration. The Taiping rebellion, in contrast, was a huge millenarian upheaval that sought, with a certain protonationalist appeal, to protect the integrity of China by revolutionizing it from within. There was, further, the running conflict between a (Manchu) imperial center and regional Chinese elites over the control of power and taxation which intertwined with each of these conflicts. The tension among the ruling elites was greatly exacerbated by the imperial attempt to expand or, in fact, create "central government" in order to cope effectively with these many challenges. Centralization in order to mobilize resources more efficiently and project force more effectively was the main preoccupation of the regime but, at the same time, also a major cause of continuing revolt. The empire was ultimately saved not by the old bureaucracy but by a nationalizing provincial gentry of Han-Chinese who were to become the new ruling elites of China in the twentieth century.[34] From all of this, China emerged badly shaken and, indeed, reduced in territory and sovereignty. But China remained largely intact.

The South Asian story is usefully told in the same way, even though the Correlates of War Project counts the British-Indian confrontations among the extra-systemic (as opposed to the Chinese civil) wars. Obviously, the rulers who united the Indian subcontinent were alien. British authority was firmly established by the late eighteenth century—the pivotal outcome of the first round of European world wars in the modern era.[35] Throughout the first half of the nineteenth century, the reach of this Empire into Inner Asia was contested in a long series of wars, among which the Afghan conflicts figure most prominently. But British rule, like the rule of other imperial unifiers in the Eurasian landmass, was mostly threatened from within. In 1857 a mutiny of Bengal army units, the so-called "Sepoy Revolt," spread quickly, if unevenly, to emerging centers in the Punjab and Awadh, pulling together a wide array of peasant unrest, political opposition, and armed resistance.[36] This revolt wrecked British control and revealed a profound weakness in late eighteenth-century British rule over the subcontinent, a weakness not unlike that of the Manchu in China: on the one hand there was a lack of central organization and, on the other, an inability to reach down into peasant society. The precarious order in place had been the product of a long series of alliances, state and ethnic wars, and intermittent efforts to organize government. The mid-century crisis suggested, above all, that the system of piecemeal incorporation had reached its limits. What was needed was a thorough renovation of (British) imperial rule for Empire to survive in India. The mid-century crisis ended with a re-founding of British control over a unified Indian subcontinent and the formation, within the framework of the Raj, of a nationalizing Indian elite. Britain's subsequent conflict with an all-Indian national class was not over the fact of unitary empire, but over who should rule it.[37]

On the other side of the Eurasian mountains, the advance of Russia into north, central, and south Asia was as persistent and as unflagging as Britain's consolidation of rule in India. This Russian advance dates back into the seventeenth and eighteenth centuries, but reached its apex only in the mid-nineteenth century.[38] An older tradition in diplomatic history has interpreted the dense cluster of conflicts along the Eurasian seam in a grand geopolitical manner, as the "great game" between Russia and Great Britain.[39] More appropriately, the Anglo-Russian confrontation (which, incidentally, is the most persistent rivalry in modern times) might be considered the end-game in a long-standing struggle over empire along the Eurasian seam, with China, India, Russia, and the Ottoman Empire as its main protagonists. The Crimean War was a key event in this context. At stake were no longer simply territorial adjustments in border areas, but the survival of the Ottoman Empire against the head-on military aggression of the Russians on all fronts along the Russo-Turkish border. Russia's defeat in this "global" confrontation was momentous. The check to Russian expansionism provoked a regime crisis. An overhaul of the central administration and the abolition of serfdom were required to sustain the czarist autocracy.[40] These internal renovations of the 1860s were accompanied by a renewal of Russian pressure on its southern borders,[41] leading to yet another (and as it happened, the last) Russo-Turkish War in the nineteenth century.

Centralization and nationalization (Russification) in a multi-ethnic and multi-religious context was an active, often aggressive process, fraught with the possibilities of violent conflict and war. Russia, like all the land-based empires of the Eurasian seam, was engaged in a dual process of extending control over territory and strengthening its central capacities to exploit the resources of land. That the former tended to spark conflicts that overstrained the latter and brought central regimes into crisis, was an oft-repeated dynamic of confrontation along the Eurasian rim. It is quite the wrong impression to think that the Russian empire—and one can say the same of the Ottoman or Chinese Empires[42]—as monolithic and unchanging. These imperial systems were, in fact, all in rapid motion—if acting defensively, then in innovative and adaptive ways; if giving the appearance of conserving traditional forms, yet changing every bit as dramatically, albeit in a different direction, as the emerging national states.

The Crimean War linked the struggle over Eurasian empire with the "Eastern Question," the traditional designation for the diplomatic negotiations and military confrontations over the future of the Ottoman Empire in Europe and the Near East. The historiography has retained a sense of the once formidable gravity of the "Eastern Question" for the future of Europe, both in terms of religious concerns (protection of the Holy Places; the status of Christians in the Ottoman Empire) and in terms of competitive territorial designs.[43] But the changing nature of this "question" in the middle of the nineteenth century is easily missed. The distance between the Paris Peace Conference of 1856 (which settled the Crimean War) and the Berlin Peace Conference of 1878 (which ended the Balkan crisis of 1875–1876, culminating in the Russo-Turkish War) suggests a profound transformation of international relations. Whereas the main issue of 1856 was the survival of the Ottoman empire and the future of Eurasian politics, the main subject of 1878 was Europe and the role of nation-states as (potential) successors to Empire.[44] In this sense both the focus on the Balkans and the move from Paris to Berlin as the seat of the conference was suggestive. For it was the struggle for national independence that linked the "Eastern Question" with the "German Question."[45] The Crimean War sprang both "questions" loose from their Eurasian context,[46] and established continental Europe as a congery of nation-states and as a viable alternative to land-based empires.

The salience of the "Eastern Question," then, was in its transmission of imperial conflicts along the Eurasian seam into Europe, not vice-versa, and it dramatizes the key role played by Eurasian conflict in disturbing the "concert" of powers that stabilized order and maintained peace in Europe for forty years after the defeat of Napoleon.[47] This system or balance of powers had depended upon the mediating and defensive role of the Hapsburg Empire, but had in fact been anchored by Great Britain and Russia. For both of these powers, continental Europe had been a vital, but not the only or even the main sphere of their interest. From within, the European concert system may have appeared as a self-sustaining balance, but Europe in the post-Napoleonic era was actually under the tutelary control of two grand Eurasian empires, whose conflicts with each other along the imperial seam conditioned their view of each other in Europe. Of the two, Russia was far more crucially implicated in central European affairs, shoring up monarchical rule against nationalism and social revolt throughout the region and serving as the emergency guarantor (as in the revolutions of 1848) of autocratic legitimacy. But it was the collision of the two, in the Crimean War, that "set Europe free." For the Russian defeat in that war signaled its inability to sustain global competition on the basis of territorial expansion on the Eurasian continent and blocked the strategy of continental aggrandizement that had emerged from the eighteenth-century struggles over the balance of power in Europe. Indeed the outcome of the Crimean War suggested that territorial empire would no longer, of itself, suffice as a basis of great power status. This check to Russian ambitions—indeed, to the very premise of territorially based power—allowed the British, long Russia's global rival, to be less concerned with the fate of continental Europe. The removal of the two anchors of the European concert set things in motion.

Seeing in the Eurasian rivalries of Britain and Russia a key factor in the breakdown of the European concert is also to cast light on another surprise outcome of the Crimean War. For the most likely beneficiaries of Russian defeat did not succeed in cashing in on their victory. Austria-Hungary and France were the main candidates to organize a "little Europe" in the wake of Russian and British recusal; indeed they had competed over this role since the eighteenth century. The Hapsburg Empire was, in many ways, a small, European version of the territorial empires that dominated the Eurasian landmass—a multi-ethnic amalgam centered on monarchical legitimacy, pursuing a combined policy of territorial expansion and administrative renewal in an effort to stay competitive; in the decades after the Congress of Vienna, this empire formed the bulwark of conservative hostility to revolutionary, nationalist, and democratic forces on all fronts. Its great and continuing antagonist for predominance in Europe was France, which had been ostracized in the European Concert for fostering a nationalizing Europe against monarchical rule.[48] In the 1850s, however, Napoleon III picked up this cause again, and with particular vigor. Even in its "bonapartist" guise, the French vision of a Europe of nations was a distinct one, aiming at the creation of sovereign "people's republics,"—independent, ethnic nations that shook off the imperial yoke, but remained individually too small to project force and thus fell under French tutelage and protection. Predicated upon the triumph of unitary, civil society,[49] this republican nationalism formed the key ingredient in French policies toward Poland, Serbia, Rumania, Piedmont-Sardinia, Naples, Bavaria, Wurttemberg, and other such (potential) republics. Although Austria-Hungary opposed these moves at every turn, both powers, for very different reasons, failed in fact to understand or cope with the explosive dynamics of nationalizing war or the emerging trajectories of power within Europe that were based, not upon the extent of territorial holdings nor upon "republican" civil society, but upon the ability to mobilize the resources and productive capacities of whole national systems.

Nowhere was the failure of these two powers to exert themselves in the moment of their opportunity more apparent than in the complex and multi-layered wars of Italian unification. The Austrians, in flatly opposing all nationalist manifestations, and the French, in supporting Italian nationhood, but resisting the creation of a unitary nation-state, were both outmaneuvered by Piedmont-Sardinia. The House of Savoy and its ministry in Turin could not proceed against the Austrians without French support, and they sported the hardheaded realism necessary, in the form of territorial concessions, to win that support; but at the same time, within Italy, the Piedmontese waged a refracted struggle against various forms of republican constitutionalism and more democratic aspirations, as well as against Mazzinian nationalism, with its optimistic universalism, in favor of a more limited, less liberal monarchical solution. This they imposed upon the Bourbon south, beginning with Garibaldi's expeditions and continuing in administrative efforts for the subordination in a region that, for most northern Italians, was little different from Africa. This quasi-ethnic, almost colonial conflict was paralleled by a continuing, if oblique campaign against the territorial presence of the papacy and for secular rule in Italy. The military and political fusion of these elements—systemic, extra-systemic (colonial), civil, religious, and ethnic conflict, and the effectiveness of Piedmont-Sardinian diplomacy in maneuvering between the powers, eliminated rival multi-national and republican models from the peninsula and made Italy into the first "modern" nation.[50]

We need not essay the "passive" or incomplete nature of Italian unification, nor review the halting and interrupted pace of industrial and national development thereafter to see that the Prussian solution was a much more decisive break, precisely because it grew out of direct war with both Austria-Hungary and France. A prerequisite for German unification under Prussian aegis was, first, the defeat of republican alternatives in Germany, a program accomplished in the civil war that accompanied the upheavals of 1848–1849 and clinched in the Prussian constitutional crisis of 1862. There followed a struggle against a "confederate" solution to the German question, which would have entailed a clustering of autonomous small states beneath a common umbrella, whether of monarchical conservatism under Austrian tutelage or of republican nationalism under French patronage. This provincial liberalism contained strong elements of a community and family based, small agricultural and craft-centered political system, as opposed to the nationalizing "systemic" powers of the Prussian state. This alternative was industrial, to be sure, but more on the lines of Swiss, French, or Belgian development than the powerful industrial expansion that was to come in Germany and the United States. The Prussian war against Austria was in the nature of a civil war for a Kleindeutsch solution, but it was also a bid to impose Prussian nationalism—combining centralized power, participatory politics, and comprehensive military mobilization—upon the smaller German states, many of which fiercely resisted this outcome and were able, briefly, to foster a German Confederation after the Austrian defeat. The Prussian war against France was a systemic conflict in more than one respect, for not only did it end Napoleon III's (and France's) pretensions to be the arbiter of Europe, but it redefined the nature of "great power" in Europe;[51] for the triumph of Prussia was the triumph of an integral state, whose power was based upon an ability to mobilize national populations and capacities for war. The emergent state was clearly not "neo-feudal," as is sometimes asserted;[52] rather it picked up on the centralizing, state building dimension of the French Revolution, including a bonapartist dominance of state over society. This was now the key to great power status, and France could not but follow suit.[53]

In central Europe the pursuit of ethnic nationhood succumbed to the drive for large integral nation-states that was spearheaded by Prussia and engineered by Bismarck. The Hapsburgs slipped into a subordinate relationship with Germany as the best defense of their multi-national monarchy, while the French project of republican nationalism was relegated, by default, to Eastern and Southeastern Europe. There the pursuit of integral and ethnic nationhood continued to butt up against Austrian opposition and to appeal, past the new nation-states of Europe, to more liberal (and universal) principles of self-determination. This triangle of Balkan ethnic nationalism, German and Italian national-statism, and French republicanism conditioned the diplomacy of the European state system thereafter.[54] Such a "real-political" image of Europe was the result of the transformation of that system in the aftermath of the Crimean and unification wars. It pivoted upon the Franco-German antagonism and the containment of ethnic nationalism and was predicated upon the exclusion of Russia and Great Britain, although in shaping the terrain for a new round of hegemonic wars in Europe, this new balance of power eventually (mainly after 1900) drew the two "peripheral" powers back into the European arena.[55]

## War in the Americas

It is more difficult to sketch the lineaments of development for the Americas as the second main region of endemic violence. The separateness of the "new world" throughout much of the nineteenth century was a consequence of its violent disengagement from the European-Atlantic empires between 1770 and 1820. The breakdown of these Atlantic empires at the end of the first era of European wars for global hegemony, and the tentative, even experimental nature of independence in the Americas meant that conflicts in this region during the first half of the nineteenth century were largely a matter of elaborating and working out the legacy of empire within the context of newly forming national states. In shaping a national articulation of independence, these states pioneered the paths of analogous, but later developments in Europe.[56] But the patterns of violence in the Americas were framed at every turn by the crisis of imperial systems and the aftermath of their breakdown, and in this they find much closer parallels in the violence that accompanied the protracted, but contemporaneous crises of land-based empires along the Eurasian seam. The starting point, then, for a comparison of these two regions of violence is the simple fact that the early modern European-Atlantic Empires collapsed under the weight of anti-imperial, national rebellion, whereas the Eurasian empires did not. The latter only began to fold or disaggregate in the wake of the second era of European wars for global hegemony in the twentieth century. The nineteenth-century crises of empire arose from specific conditions and proceeded according to their own, internally regulated pace with the Asian empires and the American nations moving along distinct paths into the twentieth century. But while this grand perspective may help to locate Europe in the mid-nineteenth century, as a system of states caught between the tectonic movements of two continents gravitating in different directions, it says nothing about the sources of war in the Americas—except that it was distinctly post-imperial violence and, as such, not comparable with what happened on the Eurasian continent.

The wars of the American region were of several kinds. Conflicts with European imperial powers punctuate the entire century, from the American war of 1812 with Great Britain to the Cuban war of independence with Spain. But while the "great" powers rarely hesitated to involve themselves, and the newly independent nations were moved by fears of intervention or by the recurring hope that a benevolent European tutelary might provide badly needed stability, the interventions by European powers in American affairs remained hesitant, episodic, and even when relatively massive, as in the case of the French effort to impose a European ruler in Mexico or the long Spanish campaigns in Cuba, largely unsuccessful.[57] There were, secondly, the wars that the newly independent nations waged against one another, mostly over territory and resources; sometimes these wars entailed large transfers of territory, as in the case of the conflict between the United States and Mexico over Texas,[58] but as often, these conflicts bogged down into bloody, even genocidal tussles, as in the case of the War of the Triple Alliance (Brazil, Argentina, and Uruguay) against Paraguay and The Pacific War (Chile, Bolivia, and Peru),[59] both of which made the "Correlates" list of the eight costliest wars of the era. There was, thirdly, a recurrent and general pattern of civil conflict in the region, ranging from the bloody American war between the states to the more intermittent, but often brutal caudillo wars of the Platte. And there were, finally, wars waged by newly forming nations against the indigenous peoples of the interior. These were continuing campaigns of destruction that culminated in the 1870s with the Argentine conquest of Patagonia and the U.S. campaigns against the Indian nations of the Great Plains. In one way or another, all of these conflicts erupted along the outer boundaries or at the points of rupture in nation-formation. And they were all defined, on the one hand, by the need of newly independent states to sustain independence from Europe, and, on the other, to limit the continuing internal devolution of power that the movements of national independence had set off.

Broadly speaking, a number of common themes run through the various manifestations of violence that mark the period between 1820 and 1870 in North and South America. While the four cited here do not exhaust the possibilities of comparison and parallel analysis, they will be enough to establish the central point, that there was a distinct regional band of violence in this era, stretching from the southern Pampas to the battlefields of Pennsylvania, and from the Atlantic to the Pacific Oceans, and that this violence was centrally conditioned by the consequences of independence and the struggle with the legacies of eighteenth-century European seaborne empires in decline.

Regional violence was, in the first instance, an issue of the devolution of power after independence.[60] This often took the form of breakaway movements, elaborating the colonial rebellion into a challenge to newly independent (usually coastal) centers of power. Examples include the string of anti-state insurgencies in the United States, from the Whiskey rebellion through the Jacksonian mobilization, and the procession of provincial rebellions and caudillo resistance that accompanied the consolidation of the Argentine state. It also took the form of regional and sectional tensions among provinces that had been conglomerated in colonial systems and now, with independence, felt the differences with each other overcoming the solidarities of the struggle for independence. This was most notably in the north-south tensions of the United States, but was also seen in the break up of the Gran Colombia and the continuing civil warfare in Argentina down to the liberal consolidation of the mid-century. Primarily these were disputes over the forms and powers of central or centralizing regimes. And they tended to raise a dual problem: how to consolidate a viable territorial state and how to forge social, economic, and political institutions that could command authority and assure peace. This usually involved the effort to forge and maintain constitutional structures that could balance regional differences and national cultures that could define the nation and its integral purposes. Where national institutions existed, or were invented, it was soon apparent that constitutions alone would not suffice to organize factional strife and regional competition. The possibilities of break up, or re-division, were constantly reopened. Even the vaunted flexibility of the U.S. national constitution was tested and strained to the breaking point several times after 1820 by regional differences and divergent patterns of economic development; a breakup of the northern American republic into several, rival states was never out of the question.[61]

The rickety nature of state structures and precariousness of the constitutional ligaments that bound them gave rise, secondly, to various kinds of military insurgency across the region. When administrative hierarchies and constitutional bonds faltered, power often devolved, either onto families and persons with local, frequently military standing, or onto military heroes with sectional followings. The caudillos of Argentina are usually taken as characteristic of this type.[62] Regional chieftains turned national leaders—often linked to republican cults created in war or revolution—these caudillos sometimes managed to consolidate power for extended periods. But because their power was independent of office and therefore without constitutional restraint, they tended to waver between stabilizing a legal regime and disturbing it in the interest of perpetuating personal power. Most were dictatorial figures with little sympathy for democratic forms, although occasionally, a caudillo (for example, Artigas in Uruguay and Solano Lopez in Paraguay) would align himself with popular forces, even veer along a path of agrarian radicalism, in an effort to consolidate a position of resistance to centralizing regimes. In this respect, caudillos bore parallels with the stream of military war heroes in the United States (William Harrison, Zachary Taylor, and above all Andrew Jackson) who turned martial fame into political capital. They sometimes rode populist movements of mass support, and illuminated, in their rapid rise to power, the weakness or limited legitimacy of central political institutions. And since national government with some popular participation was necessary for nations to develop civic institutions—a civil code, banking, law, a national army, etcetera—these military strong men were, not surprisingly, all engaged in conflicts over national institutions (usually in ways hostile to their consolidation). Their passage on a national stage was thus often marked by wrecking behaviors and fraught with the possibilities of civil war, even as they expressed a desire for, and attempted to realize charismatically, the dream of national unity.

Third, many conflicts in the region during this period were framed by issues of territoriality. This had two distinct aspects. One had to do with the establishment of boundaries between states, or in contests over the location of these boundaries. Thus warfare and violence sometimes accompanied the break up of states or was used by embattled nations to consolidate domestic unity against a common external enemy. Perhaps the most famous of these territorial disputes was the Mexican-American War (1846–1848), which emerged from the Texas secession but came to involve quite exorbitant territorial stakes. It was fed in part by the anxiety of some southern politicians in the United States to secure the future of slave labor, and was fought with a high level of jingoism and ethnic-cum-racial ferocity. Less well known, but far more bloody, was the so-called War of the Pacific (1879–1883), in which Chile battled its northern neighbors, Bolivia and Peru, for control of the nitrate fields of the Atacama Desert, and in winning the war consolidated a path of rapid, export-led development.[63] Similarly, Brazil's ultimatum to the conservative regime in Uruguay which opened the tripartite assault on Paraguay in 1864 was driven both by long-standing territorial claims and by Dom Pedro II's desire to deliver an "electric shock" to Brazilian nationalism and shore up the future of his throne.[64]

The other aspect of territorial warfare, until recently less well studied, had to do with the subjugation of indigenous populations in the process of extending and consolidating the nation. Wars against native populations within newly forming states, and vice versa—wars of incursion by Indian nations against colonializing settlement—were somewhat piecemeal and de-centered conflicts initially, but they became ever more systematic and comprehensive as the century wore on and national states became more consolidated. The casual violence of the famous Argentine caudillo, Juan Manuel de Rosas, may be compared with the deliberate policies of expansion and extermination pursued in the southern Pampas by the first liberal-constitutional president, Bartoleme Mitre. Similarly, the efforts of French and British imperial authorities to establish a *modus vivendi* with Indian nations along the "middle ground" may be compared with the aggressive and often murderous expansion of American settlement, and the growing role of military forces and central management in the crude removal policies of the Jacksonian presidency before, and army operations against the Plains Indians after, the Civil War.[65] These later conquests, which were carried out by newly (re)consolidated liberal democratic regimes, sometimes became genocidal. This dimension of violence may underscore a neglected feature of nationalizing wars: as new national states moved to define and fix boundaries, they also sought to subjugate ethnic autonomies and indigenous sovereignties to their particularist universal sway. Thus the less "conservative," the more "liberal," or "progressive" the politics, the greater appears the readiness (at least in the nineteenth century) to enforce territoriality to the point of unconditional surrender.

The extension of territorial holdings and the consolidation of national control over the lands of the interior opened a fourth commonality in the conflicts of the region. The violence that accompanied nation-formation was conditioned by the critical issue of how land and labor questions were addressed and resolved. Because land was abundant, but dramatically underutilized, and because the produce of the land was of crucial importance in the forging of national economies, there was a general need in the Americas to intensify the exploitation of the soil, concentrate and capitalize farming, deepen market connections for agricultural goods, and displace tenants, sharecroppers, squatters, and indigenous peoples—in short to reduce subsistence farming—in favor of more commercial forms of agriculture. How land was handled, that is, transferred to private hands and rendered productive, turned upon a number of issues: on the possible uses of land (what was produced, and what commercial openings could be developed for the sale of produce); on state policies with respect to land (how it was gotten and what procedures were established for the transfer of land to private hands); and on labor on the land (what kind of work force was available and how abundant and reproducible it was).[66] These elements, themselves complex, were mixed and mingled in a variety of situationally specific and infinitely modulated ways across the region and got mapped onto a whole series of oppositions that framed key debates and conflicts in the politics of the newly independent nations of North and South America: between city and countryside, central power and regional autonomies, merchant and farming capital, free trade and protection, slave and free labor, and autonomous and dependent paths of economic development. Issues of this kind divided regions and social groups, sparking off political crises, breakaway movements, regional conflicts, and civil war.

Yet warfare and violence, while recurrent, also tended, over time, to sort out competing possibilities and to narrow options in the region. Indeed if we conceive of the Americas as being in a state of post-imperial (re)formation, the multiplicity of possibilities that were opened up by the collapse of sea-borne empires and the experiments in independence—not to mention the potential conflicts *among* these possibilities—could not remain forever open. The struggles which rival paths of development or competitive solutions for independence engendered led, inevitably, to the elimination of some lines of possibility and the amplification, even outright triumph, of others. In moving to examine the two bloodiest wars of the era, we can notice how comparable elements combined in different ways to forge lines of battle. While any attempt to directly compare the Triple Alliance war against Paraguay (1864–1870) and the American Civil War (1861–1865) would be grasping at straws, a consideration of each should also help elaborate the role of warfare in narrowing alternatives and crystallizing trajectories of possibility in the region.

In some respects, the Paraguay war was caused by the idiosyncrasy of its autocrat, who modeled himself after Napoleon III and his army after the military forces he had seen during a visit to the Crimea.[67] As a local strongman, Francisco Solano Lopez (Jr.) was, like his father before him, not notably different from other caudillos of the Upper Platte who fought in the same period to control Argentina; for example, Justo Jose de Arquiza of the Argentine province Entre Rios (like Paraguay, populated by Guarani Indians). But Lopez, father and son, were different in several ways: they sought to transform the personal power of the caudillo into an indigenous hereditary dynasty, somewhat on the model of neighboring Brazil. Moreover, this attempt to establish dynastic rule was tied to efforts by the Paraguayan regime to foster an autonomous course of development for the country.[68] In this, they followed the lead of Paraguay's first post-independence ruler, Jose Gaspar de Francia, whose repression of the creole elite and confiscation of its lands had not only dramatically leveled Paraguayan society and restricted private ownership. It had also laid the foundations of a primitive form of state socialism, in which government-run estates dominated agricultural output and state regulations strictly controlled exchange with the outside world. Carlos Lopez Sr. had extended this program of self-sufficiency by laying the legal groundwork for the abolition of slavery and fostering a nascent technological modernization through the selective appropriation of foreign know-how in building a foundry, arsenal, shipyard, and railroad.[69] His son, Lopez Jr., rather fancied the army, and built up a comparatively huge military force of 25,000 at a time when Argentina had but a tiny national force.

These initiatives were too remote and haphazard to constitute a major threat to Paraguay's neighbors, but they did contain a certain economic and political logic. Not only did a country that was already largely self-sufficient become even more (and more self-consciously) so, but the effort to promote autonomy pointed toward a rudimentary program in import-substitution. In the context of regional conflict, this had considerable significance, since caudillos, while they had often amassed great power and could sometimes hold the interior hostage, had never been able to present a viable alternative to the market-oriented cosmopolitanism of the coastal entrepôts and merchants when it came to charting a program of national development. In a strange and slightly incoherent way, the Paraguayan experiment suggested the potential for autonomous development directed from the interior. That this demonstration was made by a largely Indian population and within a highly egalitarian social system under a Mestizo dynasty that, for all its brutality and eccentricity, seems to have been genuinely popular, made it all the more threatening to the finely-graded hierarchies of landed and administrative coastal elites, and at least potentially appealing to the dispossessed and impoverished populations subjected to these elites. And there may have been grander designs. Apparently, Lopez Jr. had the dream of forging a coalition of provinces along the Platte river system, between Argentina and Brazil, that would have reached from Uruguay through Argentine territory into Brazil's Matto Grosso province. This may explain Lopez' meddling in the political crisis of Uruguay (the immediate cause of the war).[70] Though his mixture of flamboyance and caution proved difficult to read, even then, his vision was within the realm of possibility, had military force been used more prudently.

The war against Paraguay was waged by self-declared liberals. A liberal ministry in Brazil came to the support of liberal dissidents in Uruguay (whose conservative government Lopez supported), and they drew in the liberal president of Argentina, Bartolome Mitre. Mitre had recently united the country after civil war and was committed to a constitutional consolidation that included, among other things, the suppression of interior rebels and indigenous peoples. The war ended in disaster for the autocratic project. The destruction, not only of the Lopez regime and army but of the population of Paraguay, eliminated the possibility of autonomous paths on the interior and accelerated the process by which centralizing regimes consolidated control over the hinterland. The victory of nationalizing governments was thus a blow to indigenous ethnic autonomy—another pacification campaign against the interior—and to small holder farming. It affirmed the prevailing patterns of large landownership linked to cash crop production and export markets. This in turn consolidated the maritime connections with the trans-Atlantic economy that were to orient and frame Latin American development for the next century. For Argentina, the war brought an end to a long constitutional crisis, signaled the eclipse of caudillo power, and set the country on a course of constitutionally orchestrated, export-led, agricultural growth. This course was to make it into a wealthy, if dependent, cornerstone of the emerging British-led world economy.[71] For Brazil, the war revealed the limits of a political liberalism that, as in the United States, had been forced to wink at the continuation of slavery and, thanks to a deep implication with the monarchy and its dense hierarchies of royal patronage, had eschewed alignment with more popular and republican social forces. The combination of slavery and patronage acted as a barrier to the values associated with bourgeois liberalism in the nineteenth century—a commitment to work and thrift, to the rule of law, and to representative government—and continued to reproduce the conundrums of post-independence politics in Brazil well into the 1880s.

It is here that contrasts with the United States are instructive. For nowhere in the Americas was a slave and a free labor system so tightly yoked in the same economic and constitutional system *and* so equally matched. Not only did the slave economy of the American South plough a dynamic and expansive course down to the mid-nineteenth century, but with the additional stimulus from the growth of cotton production, slave labor became the main backbone of American exports in the era of free trade development. More importantly, and in contrast with Brazil, where the monarchy, acting as a "moderating" center, was able to foster "multiple" nations, based on tiers of exclusion and heritable hierarchy,[72] the U.S. Constitution, grounded in democratic and republican forms, required the fiction of "one" nation, a people united in their equality. This forced a steady expansion of (white, male) political participation and a continual (re)negotiation of political compromises at the national center. Unlike Brazil, American politics contained the conditions for a variety of rapidly shifting alliances and combinations. It was the political coalition of farmers, including slave-owners, with the sans-culottes and urban "mechanics" of the north—the Jacksonian mobilization of the 1820s—that effectively stymied the further expansion of federal power. It was a parallel combination of cotton growers in the south and coastal merchant and manufacturing capital in the north that formed the backbone of a rival coalition favoring a more promotional state.[73] But as long as these political combinations held together, in competition with each other and across sectional lines, the union held together, at the expense of enslaved Africans.

The continued, constitutionally mandated co-existence of the two regions became increasingly difficult to sustain, however. Socially different, ideologically hostile economic systems, moving along diverging paths of development, generated a feisty competitiveness that grew more urgent with time, as the two regions became stronger, but also more entrenched and less pliable in their animosity toward one another.[74] The economic viability of slavery was never in question.[75] But southern politics was another matter. Indeed, the most striking phenomenon of U.S. politics in the period running up to the Civil War was the growing rigidity of southern political positions, the unwillingness to change and the growing popularity of a politics that aimed at preserving existing ways and institutions at all costs. Nowhere was the resistance to change so vociferous, so popular, and so powerful, and so richly developed and cleverly improvised.[76] In this uniquely popular, reactionary complex, support for slavery was the crucial litmus test, but territorial expansion was the central vision.[77] It is not difficult to see why. For southerners, westward expansion, with the incorporation of more space for slave agriculture, offered a powerful substitute to domestic urbanization and industrialization. On the one hand, there was the possibility of linking this expansion of plantation agriculture to liberal economic policies that opened domestic markets for (British) industrial imports, in exchange for the maximization of cash crop production—eventually, the Latin American path.[78] On the other, there was the hope that expansion would counter the demographic growth of the north and its increasing weight in national politics. But the stridency and rigidity of southern politics bespoke a sense of pressure, of running hard but not keeping up. There was no genteel haven where southern labor practices and social mores could be shielded from northern antagonism.

The dynamism of plantation agriculture and the rigidity of southern

politics was matched in the north by an increasingly implacable abolition-
ism and by the westward expansion of free farming. Indeed, the opening of
new agricultural regions in the Midwest and Plains states shifted the center of economic gravity in the north from a merchant-trading orientation
along the coast (the Hamiltonian vision) toward internal industrial development (the Republican program). This shift toward a "regional" combination of free farmers and new industrialists, captured in the popular campaign slogan, "vote yourself a tariff; vote yourself a farm," produced the
political revolution that elected Lincoln in 1860 and precipitated southern
secession. Yet if we reverse the usual equation of who seceded from whom,
one might just as well see the northern industrial enclave breaking clear of
the hemispheric zone of slave- and plantation-based agricultural and cash-
crop production, with its narrow power bases and hierarchical social
configurations, in order to forge a more egalitarian and self-consciously
national strategy of industrial development in North America. We need
not debate the amplifier effects of free farming upon industrial markets[79]
in order to suggest that, in the wake of the Civil War and as a result of the
productive boom it engendered, the path of national development in the
United States was grounded in a massive expansion of *both* agricultural
and industrial output. Furthermore, this dynamism was centered in the
interior, in the Midwestern agricultural and, increasingly, industrial heart-
land of the nation.[80] That the liquidity to finance these developments
remained tied to the trans-Atlantic network of banking and gold reserves,
contained, not the ligaments of dependency—for export and import were
not at the core of the new system—but the underpinnings of a distinct trajectory toward industrial transformation and world power, unique in the
Americas.

The United States was remade, in war, into an integral national state.
The unique capability of this state to project force was amply demonstrated, an ability not simply to mobilize, but to organize and focus people
and resources to distinct national ends. It was this capability, as it became
the measure of "great power" status, that enabled the United States to
assume the role.[81] In this sense, the affinity between the American Civil
War and the German wars of unification is not to be found in the causes or
any structural similarities of the wars themselves, but rather emerges in
their outcome, as a product of their consequences. In both cases, war grew
out of specific regional configurations and expressed a possible trajectory
of development within a more complicated and (at the time) obscure field
of possibilities—but a path which nevertheless proved decisive. And it was

in the practice of war itself that both nations forged the key elements of their emergent status in the world—in the organization of the nation for war, the mobilization of resources, the concentration and projection of force, and the coordination of peoples to common ends. Thus the two wars radically transformed the international environment in which they occurred, and from which they sprang. The old nexus of empire that had held the world together in the eighteenth century—the great land-based imperiums presiding over the Eurasian land mass and the equally extensive sea-based empires that colonized the Atlantic rim—was radically transcended as these powers broke with the conditions that had shaped their respective regions, and struck out along parallel paths of war-induced state-building. The point of departure of these two nations could not have been more different: the pursuit of freedom at the price of a destructive war in the United States was quite the opposite of the pursuit of power with devastation averted in Germany. Yet the contrary modes by which these two powers did the same thing was what made them at once so attractive and so distasteful to each other.

## The Axes of International Warfare

Until the mid-nineteenth century, global development rested on a series of overlapping, interacting, but basically autonomous regions, each engaged in processes of self-organization and self-reproduction, even if under alien rule. This is not to discount the quickly deepening connections and interactions in between regions, mediated increasingly, though not exclusively, by Europeans. Nor is it to gainsay the importance of their "imperial" expansion, which remapped the powerscape of the earth in the seventeenth and eighteenth centuries. But contacts among regional centers of power had more to do with keeping distance than with establishing relations. Distance, hence space, remained crucial, governing not just commerce and imaginings but also the exercise of power and the use of force. Politically, economically, intellectually, and militarily, these patterns of spatial distantiation, mediated by emissaries and interlopers, organized the world well into the nineteenth century.[82]

The kind of empires produced in this world of autonomous regions were land- and sea-based extensions of power centers which spread outward through space, establishing outposts and presences in far-flung spatial configurations. Even when bureaucratically developed, these empires remained extremely de-centered, elaborated though sub-centers and border stations, often garrisoned by locally recruited forces which supplied themselves from the land. Imperial warfare, waged against neighbor-enemies or "peripheral" border regions, was about the extension of territorial control and the subjugation of additional people at the margins of the empire. These were land wars managed and directed from regional sub-centers. Russian imperial expansion into inner Asia, like British wars on the Indian borders, proceeded, not from St Petersburg or London, but from the provinces. The backward linkages to the metropolis provided guidance, but could not manage or support war directly. Thus seventeenth- and eighteenth-century "imperial wars," as regional land wars, were fought by local armies, made up of troops recruited from the recently conquered and led by ruling castes or military satraps who defined the rationale of war and its geopolitical ends on terms negotiated with the metropolitan center. These empires and the wars that sustained them, while dominant forces in the eighteenth century, faced mounting difficulties during the nineteenth century, and it was these crises that produced the fissures and openings in which nationalizing solutions (among others) could be devised. The German wars of unification and the American Civil War emerged from these gaps and interruptions of empire and should be seen as the final act of mid-nineteenth century imperial crisis in which the crystallization of new departures turned the tables on old equations of power.

Yet while Germany and the United States transformed war, and themselves as nations fighting war, they did not thereby transform the world. And while these nationalizing wars radically narrowed the field of possibilities within the regional contexts in which they were fought, these outcomes only established a capacity for regional hegemony. Comparing these foundational wars, or the regions that produced these wars, does not explain why the nations forged in war should go to war with each other. Of course, national historians in Germany and the United States have long thought this had to do with expansionist dynamics and great power ambitions. But, for all the parallels in the modes of their achievement and the expansionist dynamics that they unleashed, there is nothing inherent in the process of establishing regional hegemony that could explain why these two nations should clash, twice, in the twentieth century. To make visible the linkages that brought Germany and the United States to war requires a different focus: on Great Britain and the role of maritime and colonial warfare, which we have thus far left to one side. This is not just to add more violence to the equation, or to make up for the neglect of Africa. Rather, it is to bring to bear an "other" history and a very different kind of warfare that also took shape at the mid-nineteenth century. It was this other dimension of war that conditioned the paths of convergence that led Germany and the United States to a head-on collision in the twentieth century.

Britain was the power most directly threatened by the formation of the new national states and their rapid industrialization, based on new products and techniques. Britain was also in possession of positions around the world, mostly in support of its commerce and its imperial project in India, which provided potential avenues of response to these new industrial challengers. In India, Britain played the role of a land-based empire, fighting imperial wars of border defense and expansion throughout the nineteenth century, while struggling to defend and consolidate its administrative hold upon the subcontinent. At the same time, it deployed networks of trade and investment throughout the world, premised upon the new principles of liberal free trade and informal control.[83] There was always the potential for Britain, like Russia, to renew its old imperial quest, based in India rather than in the Americas. But developments in the technology of naval warfare, coupled with the tremendous expansion of trading opportunities created by early industrialization, nudged Great Britain in a quite different direction, providing the capabilities for a "new" imperialism. Great Britain veered off—quite radically, if not always self-consciously—from the previous (seventeenth- and eighteenth-century) course of empire building. The latter was taken up anew by China, Russia, and British India and, not to forget, by France after the mid-century crises, emulating the new nationalizing states, Germany and the United States.

The revamping of the Raj after the mutiny went hand-in-hand with advances in communications and transportation on the sea lanes and trade linkages of the world—especially in steam shipping and telegraphy—which promoted new maritime and commercial capabilities. Again, the Crimean War proved a turning point, not so much in the manner of fighting, which remained stubbornly grounded in the principles of land-based warfare, but in the logistical revolution that made a full-scale war in this distant peninsula possible.[84] The landing forces on the Crimea were maintained entirely by sea, deployed at long distance, supplied from the metropole, and decisively, if not completely, directed from the center.[85] These were crucial indicators of change that would distinguish old-time imperial wars from a new breed of imperialist wars. And it was Great Britain that pioneered this path of development and capitalized on its possibilities. While the Great Powers negotiated in Berlin over a Balkan settlement, in 1882 Britain occupied Cyprus and Egypt after having acquired the majority of the Suez Canal stocks (1875), and thus secured a strategic cornerstone in what was to become a new imperialist game.[86] The simultaneous tightening of imperialist control over Southeast Asia and, particularly, the Malaccan Straits indicates the global nature of this process.[87] Formal control over maritime strong-points, on one hand, and the defeat of piracy on the other, gained central importance. Great Britain geared up for—in fact, quite literally invented—a global power politics which no longer depended exclusively on the occupation of territory and the surpluses that could be squeezed from the land, but aimed at controlling global lanes of communication and exchange and living off the surpluses of this circulation. If the frontline of global tensions in the eighteenth and early nineteenth centuries had been along the seams of empire, it now shifted to the sea lanes and communications lines of the world.

The advancement of communication and transportation not only allowed for a new mobility of force, but facilitated the simultaneous and coordinated deployment of force at several unconnected places, and without loosing centralized control over movements. Deployment of force was based on the metropolitan ability to concentrate resources *and* to move them at will. Power, much like money, gained an entirely new liquidity that was predicated, not on the erection of sub-imperial posts, but on "relays" (coaling depots, weather stations, naval bases, and communications knots) which converted speed into action at the will of the center. The capability to be present "globally" (and not merely at dispersed regional strong points) is perhaps the most significant aspect of this logistics revolution.[88] Empires had traditionally suffered from their limited ability to move troops over long distances; hence, the emphasis on sub-centers of power and elaborate systems of foraging and storage.[89] In contrast, new transportation and communications capabilities downplayed "stocks" and put a premium on mobilization. What mattered was no longer the force at hand, but the force that could be generated and put into place.[90]

The key issue of imperialist warfare thus became conversion—how to convert resources into military use-value as efficiently and as flexibly as possible at the right moment. Timing became everything. The imperial premium on the control of space was replaced by a premium on the control of time. Properly understood, the ability to sustain a global presence was the maritime equivalent of the newly acquired capabilities of military mobilization on land by the new national states. In both cases, military preparation and the power-potentials of mobilization became most important, and the centralized command and control of forces in-being became crucial in the deployment of power. Important differences remained, to be sure: the new nationalizing land-mobilizations moved along the inner lines of geopolitics, outward (and thus faced problems of dispersal), while the globalizing maritime-mobilizations moved along the perimeters, inward (and thus faced problems of concentration). But these merely shaped the basic strategic and operational issues of warfare in the twentieth-century world.

The comparison of the American Civil War and the wars of German unification put land warfare at the center of attention and set these two wars in the context of regional transformations. But what linked them, eventually, was a global transformation (of which they were a part) in the nature of warfare that marked the crisis of old empires and the emergence of a new imperialism. Whereas "imperial" wars among land- and sea-based empires shaped the first European struggles for global hegemony in the eighteenth century, and continued to condition violence into the middle of the nineteenth, "imperialist" wars in the new mode shaped the second round of hegemonic struggle in the twentieth century. They had already begun to affect warfare in the middle decades of the nineteenth century. As the new means, first observed in the Crimea, developed and their potential was comprehended,[91] they laid Africa open to long-distance imperialist raids in the 1880s and 1890s. Wars in southern Africa and along the Gold Coast displayed the growing capacity of Europeans to project force overseas, in several places at once, relying on metropolitan resources and naval transport to sustain far-flung, but coordinated operations. The same command of the sea and reliance on new communications technology was evident in the interventions in Southeast Asia. By the end of the nineteenth century, the spatial buffers between regional centers of power had melted away. The result was a wholesale reformation of international relations, the dissolution of autonomous power systems interacting at a distance, and the consolidation of "global" circuits of money, markets, knowledge, and force. Imperial expansion through space was left behind in favor of the imperialist control of time.

Great Britain ushered in this new age when seizing the opportunities for global power, but did so defensively, in part as an extension of its old imperial position in India and in part as a move to preempt the growing advantages of industrial power generated in Germany and the United States. Already holding many technical assets and now falling back from continental Europe and North America, its goods closed out by tariffs and stiffer competition, Britain led the way in the scramble to peg out claims for the future in the primary production and industrial potential of the rest of the world. The French followed close behind, in part seeking compensation, with German encouragement, for a diminished purview of power on the continent. Others mimicked the model as they could, and in so doing entered a new maritime space of global competition shaped by Great Britain with Africa and East Asia as its main relays. Germany and the United States entered this new age as distinctly regional powers, building on their enormous capabilities, forged in war, for industrial mobilization, but still grasping for ways to transform continental hegemony into world power. As rivals of Great Britain, they also engaged each other in the shared spaces of global competition, sharpening both their mutual admiration and enmity. The new German national state, though it eventually acquired colonies, never possessed the requisite means to succeed in the global arena. While its formidable forces could threaten every capital of Europe, including London, and thus command the interior lines of global geopolitics, it could never transcend the "landed" nature of its power. It was this that defined the predicament of German power and thus the emerging world-political dimensions of the "German Question" in twentieth century.[92] The United States, alone, managed to fuse the capacities of the national state for mobilization with the logistical capabilities of maritime power, and it did so largely through its wars with Germany in the twentieth century. In thus combining land-based and sea-borne power, it made itself the first global "superpower."[93]

NOTES

1. Paul Kennedy, *The Rise and Fall of Great Powers: Economic Change and Military Conflict from 1500 to the Present* (New York: Random House, 1987).

2. Timothy Garton Ash, *In Europe's Name: Germany and the Divided Continent* (New York: Random House, 1993).

3. One of the few studies to cover this period comprehensively is Eric Hobsbawm's *Age of Capital, 1848–1875* (New York: New American Library, 1984), but he emphasizes the role of capital rather than violence.                    ·

4. Michael Howard, *The Franco-Prussian War: The German Invasion of France, 1870–1871* (New York: Methuen, 1981).

5. The debate on this issue is about as long and involved as the concomitant debate on the origins of the Civil War. See Eberhard Kolb, ed., *Europa und die*

*Reichsgründung: Preußisch-Deutschland in der Sicht der großen europäischen Mächte, 1860–1880* (Munich: Oldenbourg, 1980).

6. Garry Wills, *Lincoln at Gettysburg: The World That Remade America* (New York: Simon & Schuster, 1992); James McPherson, *Abraham Lincoln and the Second American Revolution* (New York: Oxford University Press, 1991).

7. Charles Royster, *The Destructive War: William Tecumseh Sherman, Stonewall Jackson, and the Americans* (New York: Knopf, 1991).

8. Hedley Bull and Adam Watson, eds., *The Expansion of International Society* (London and New York: Routledge, 1992) gives an indication of the problem. The volume presumes an expansion of the European (state-)system, mapping it upon the world as a result of European expansion, and hence neglects non-European sources of violence and their impact on Europe. Our model was Andreas Hillgruber's *Bismarcks Außenpolitik* (Freiburg: Rombach, 1972), who had insisted that the Prussian wars of unification, while motivated by internal German and Prussian events, could only be understood in the light of the Crimean War (1853–1856) and the breakdown of imperial relations. We suggest that one can construct a more encompassing case for the two wars under consideration.

9. As Geoffrey Barraclough notes in his *Introduction to Contemporary History* (Basingstoke: Penguin, 1968), there was also a shift in the scale of killing in proportion to population; the period of the world wars effectively ended the era of Western population expansion.

10. Melvin Small and J. David Singer, *Resort to Arms: International and Civil Wars, 1816–1980* (Beverly Hills: Sage Publications, 1981). Compare J. David Singer and Associates, *Explaining War: Selected Papers from the Correlates of War Project* (Beverly Hills: Sage, 1979); J. David Singer and Paul F. Diehl, *Measuring the Correlates of War* (Ann Arbor: University of Michigan Press, 1990).

11. Definition of systemic, extra-systemic, civil wars are summarized in Small and Singer, Resort to Arms, p. 217. As important as these taxonomies are, they also prevent the most significant argument about this period—that this is a period of endemic violence.

12. See appendix 1.

13. This is of some import for military historians, because one might well argue that only now the "age of battle" gave way to an age of war. See Russell Weigley, *The Age of Battles: The Quest for Decisive Warfare from Breitenfeld to Waterloo* (Bloomington: Indiana University Press, 1991).

14. Small and Singer, *Resort to Arms,* 62–77.

15. See appendix 2.

16. It is commonly forgotten that the Ottoman Empire became a formal member of the European Concert with the Paris Peace Treaty (1856). Small and Singer, in *Resort to Arms,* do not count the Ottoman Empire among the system's powers.

17. The conscientious historian would note that Italy, as a source of five out of nine systemic wars, did become an official member of the European Concert in 1856. Winfried Baumgart, *The Peace of Paris 1856: Studies in War, Diplomacy and*

*Peacemaking,* Anne Pottinger, trans. (Santa Barbara: ABC-Clio; and Oxford: Clio Press, 1981).

18. Hence Latin American violence might be considered to be prototypical for the time. See the chapter "The Terror," in John Lynch, *Argentine Dictator: Juan Manuel de Rosas* (Oxford: Clarendon, 1981).

19. Michael Crowder, *West African Resistance: The Military Response to Colonial Occupation* (London: Hutchinson, 1978).

20. Compare John Keegan, *A History of Warfare* (New York: Knopf, 1993).

21. Alfred J. Hanna and Kathryn A. Hanna, *Napoleon III and Mexico: American Triumph over Monarchy* (Chapel Hill: University of North Carolina Press, 1971); Richard N. Sinkin, *The Mexican Reform 1855–1876: A Study in Nation-Building* (Austin: University of Texas Press, 1979).

22. Charles S. Gochman and Zeev Maoz, "Militarized Interstate Disputes," in, Singer and Diehl, *Measuring the Correlates of War,* 202. The positivistic blinders of much quantitative work are stunning. A great deal can be done with quantitative data. But quantitative studies of war prefer to stick to historical prejudices rather than to their data. In this particular case it is quite incomprehensible that a 1990 publication uses European events to periodize their global data (rather than using the appropriate statistical tools to see "how the data fall"), and that an overwhelming majority of disputes, involving "minor" powers, is discounted. If it is true that "for the entire 1816–1876 period, major powers have been involved in over half of all militarized disputes," this hardly warrants the conclusion that only major powers count. For it is equally true that for the entire period, 841 out of a total of 960 militarized disputes, or 87.6 percent, involved minor powers.

23. Data in ibid. Klaus Jürgen Gantzel and Torsten Schwinghammer, *Die Kriege nach dem Zweiten Weltkrieg, 1945–1992: Daten und Tendenzen* (Münster: Lit, 1992); Richard H. Sanger, *Insurgent Era: New Patterns of Political, Economic, and Social Revolution* (Washington, D.C.: Potomac Books, 1970); Martin van Creveld, *The Transformation of War* (New York: Free Press; and Toronto: Macmillan, 1991).

24. Yet the Russo-Turkish War has never attracted the same attention as the Crimean War. It might well be argued that this war broke the Ottoman Empire and was decisive in setting the stage for World War I. One of the few publications to approach this problem is Ralph Melville and Hans-Jürgen Schröder, eds., *Der Berliner Kongress von 1878. Die Politik der Großmächte und die Probleme der Modernisierung in Südosteuropa in der zweiten Hälfte des 19. Jahrhunderts* (Wiesbaden: Steiner, 1982).

25. See the discussion of British intercontinental strategic challenges in Kenneth Bourne, *Britain and the Balance of Power in North America, 1815–1908* (Berkeley: University of California Press, 1967).

26. Albert Feuerwerker, *Rebellion in Nineteenth-Century China* (Ann Arbor: Center for Chinese Studies at the University of Michigan, 1975).

27. See Key-Hiuk Kim, *The Last Phase of the East Asian World Order. Korea,*

*Japan and the Chinese Empire, 1860–1882* (Berkeley: University of California Press, 1980).

28. Vera Blinn Reber, "The Demographics of Paraguay: A Reinterpretation of the Great War, 1864–70," *The Hispanic American Historical Review* 68, 2 (1988): 289–319, questions the validity of studies like Julio J. Chiavenato, *Genocidio Americano: La Guerra del Paraguay* (Asuncion: C. Schauman Ed., 1989). Casualty figures now range from 25,000 (which is probably too low) to 310,000 (which is probably too high); this would make a casualty rate of somewhere between 9 and 18 percent. See the debate: Thomas C. Whigham and Barbara Potthast, "Some Strong Reservations: A Critique of Vera Blinn Reber's 'The Demographics of Paraguay: A Reinterpretation of the Great War, 1864–1870,'" *The Hispanic American Historical Review* 70, 4 (1990): 667–75, and Reber's response, pp. 677–78. These two critics do not recognize one of Reber's basic blunders in her analysis. She uses battle-casualty rates for modern systems wars (derived from Small and Singer, *Resort to Arms*) which were far lower than the casualty rates for early modern wars—a counterintuitive observation but quite undisputed in military history. The former are distinctly below 20 percent, while the latter are distinctly above. From what one gathers from the incidental evidence in Efraim Cardozo's *Hace cien anos: Cronica de la guerra 1864–1870 publicadas en "La Tribuna" de Asuncion en el centenario de a epopeya nacional,* (13 vols. Asuncion: Ediciones EMASA, 1967–1982), the battles in this war resemble more the deadly encounters of early modern wars. This is to be taken quite literally in that, as in early modern wars, women and children moved with (and fought with) the armed forces, and were destroyed with them. Reber's battle-related casualties appear, in any case, to be too low, although her overall assessment remains valid.

29. Robert M. Utley, *Frontier Regulars: The United States Army and the Indians 1866–1891* (New York; Macmillan, 1974); and Robert Wooster, *The Military and United States Indian Policy, 1865–1903* (New Haven: Yale University Press, 1988).

30. Compare Charles Royster, *The Destructive War.* See also James Abrahamson, *America Arms for a New Century: The Making of a Great Military Power* (New York: Free Press, 1981); and Thomas C. Leonard, *Above the Battle: War Making in America from Appomattox to Versailles* (New York: Oxford University Press, 1978).

31. This is, of course, the dominant comparison. One might also note, however, the "weak" variants of this nation-building path in Latin America and Italy which points toward more dependent forms of economic development or, indeed, to an empire-conserving strategy as in British India. See Kalevi J. Holsti, *Peace and War: Armed Conflicts and the International Order, 1648–1989* (New York: Cambridge University Press, 1991), 145–56.

32. Historians and social scientists have paid scant attention to the mid-nine-

teenth century in the past and are puzzled by the present proliferation of wars and catastrophes. They preferred a study of war that focused on the steady progression of hegemonic wars. The history of war became a history of the progression of empires asserting their hegemony over ever larger parts of the world, the Soviet-American rivalry being the latest—and some would say the ultimate—expression of this development. Accordingly, the first and second era of European wars for global domination in the late eighteenth and the first half of the twentieth century were at the center of attention. This perspective favored a whole cluster of theories about the modernization of violence. They highlighted the differentiation and monopolization of violence in the state (and in transnational alliance systems); the expansion of logistics to encompass the whole nation, and increasingly global networks of dependencies; and the intensification and concentration of violence which culminated in the threat of total annihilation. Simultaneously, these theories conjectured an increasing concentration of power first on a European and, ultimately, on a global scale in which a progression of empires would organize global conduct. George Modelski, *Long Cycles in World Politics* (Seattle: University of Washington Press, 1987); Robert Gilpin, *War and Change in World Politics* (New York: Cambridge University Press, 1981); Kennedy, *The Rise and Fall of Great Powers.*

33. Yu-wen Jen [Chien], *The Taiping Revolutionary Movement* (New Haven: Yale University Press, 1973), is the classic study. Also, Jack Gray, *Rebellions and Revolutions: China from the 1800s to the 1980s* (New York: Oxford University Press, 1990); Elisabeth Perry, ed., *Chinese Perspectives on the Nien Rebellion* (Armonk, N.J.: M. E. Sharpe, 1981); Frederic Wakeman Jr., *Strangers at the Gate: Social Disorder in South China, 1839–1861* (Berkeley: University of California Press, 1966); Wen-chang Chu, *The Moslem Rebellion in North-West China, 1862–1878: A Study of Government Minority Policy* (The Hague: Mouton, 1966).

34. Stanley Spector, *Li Hung-chang and the Huai Army: A Study in Nineteenth-century Chinese Regionalism* (Taipei: Rainbow Bridge Book Co., 1964); Philip Kuhn, *Rebellion and Its Enemies in Late Imperial China: Militarization and Social Structure, 1794–1864* (Cambridge Mass.: Harvard University Press, 1980); Mary C. Wright, *The Last Stand of Chinese Conservatism: The T'ung Chih Restoration, 1862–1874* (New York: Atheneum, 1957).

35. Stig Förster, *Die mächtigen Diener der East India Company: Ursachen und Hintergründe der britischen Expansionspolitik in Südasien, 1793–1819* (Stuttgart: Steiner, 1992).

36. Surendra N. Sen, *Eighteen Fifty-Seven* (New Delhi: Publications Division, Ministry of Information and Broadcasting, 1958); Eric T. Stokes, *The Peasant Armed: The Indian Revolt of 1857* (Oxford: Clarendon Press, 1986); Ranajit Guha, *Elementary Aspects of Peasant Insurgency in Colonial India* (Delhi: Oxford University Press, 1983); Rudrangshu Mukherjee, *Awadh in Revolt, 1857–1858: A Study of Popular Resistance* (Delhi: Oxford University Press, 1984).

37. Sarvepal Gopal, *British Policy in India, 1858–1905* (Madras: Orient Longman, 1967); Sunanda Sen, *Colonies and the Empire: India 1890–1914* (Calcutta: Orient Longman, 1992).

38. William C. Fuller, *Strategy and Power in Russia, 1600–1914* (New York: Free Press, 1992).

39. David Gillard, *The Struggle for Asia, 1828–1914: A Study in British and Russian Imperialism* (London: Methuen, 1977); Hermann Wentker, *Zerstörung der Großmacht Rußland? Die britischen Kriegsziele im Krimkrieg* (Göttingen: Vandenhoeck & Ruprecht, 1993).

40. Martin McCauley and Peter Waldron, compilers, *The Emergence of the Modern Russian State, 1855–1881* (Basingstoke: Macmillan, 1988).

41. R. K. I. Quested, *The Expansion of Russia in East Asia, 1857–1860* (Kuala Lumpur: University of Malaya Press, 1968); and "Further Light on the Expansion of Russia in East Asia, 1792–1860," *Journal of Asian Studies* 29, 2 (1970): 327–45.; W. E. D. Allen, *Caucasian Battlefields. A History of the Wars on the Turco-Caucasian Border, 1828–1921* (Cambridge: Cambridge University Press, 1953); Dietrich Geyer, *Russian Imperialism: The Interaction of Domestic and Foreign Policy, 1860–1914* (New Haven: Yale University Press, 1987).

42. Roderic Davison, *Reform in the Ottoman Empire, 1856–1876* (Princeton: Princeton University Press, 1963); Carter V. Finley, *Bureaucratic Reform in the Ottoman Empire: The Sublime Port 1789–1922* (Princeton: Princeton University Press, 1980).

43. Matthew S. Anderson, *The Eastern Question, 1774–1923: A Study in International Relations* (London: Macmillan, 1966).

44. Werner E. Mosse, *The Rise and Fall of the Crimean System, 1855–1871. The Story of a Peace Settlement* (London: Macmillan, 1964); Lothar Gall, "Die europäischen Mächte und der Balkan im 19. Jahrhundert," in Melville and Schröder, *Der Berliner Kongress von 1878*, 1–16.

45. Wolf D. Gruner, *Die deutsche Frage: Ein Problem der europäischen Geschichte seit 1800* (Munich: Beck, 1985).

46. Norman Rich, *Why the Crimean War? A Cautionary Tale* (Hanover, N.H.: University Presses of New England, 1985); David M. Goldfrank, *The Origins of the Crimean War* (London and New York: Longman, 1994).

47. Winfried Baumgart, *Vom Europäschen Konzert zum Völkerbund. Friedensschlüsse und Friedenssicherung von Wien bis Versailles* (Darmstadt: Wissenschaftliche Buchgesellschaft, 1974). F. R. Bridge and Roger Bullen, *The Great Powers and the European System, 1815–1914* (London: Longman, 1987).

48. See generally, Louis Girard, *Napoleon III* (Paris: Fayard, 1986). William H. Smith, in his *Napoleon III: The Pursuit of Prestige* (London: Juliet Gardiner Books, 1991) overestimates this particular aspect. William E. Echard, *Napoleon III and the Concert of Europe* (Baton Rouge: Louisiana State University Press, 1983);

Theodore Zeldin, *Emile Ollivier and the Liberal Empire of Napoleon III* (Oxford: Clarendon Press, 1963).

49. Rogers Brubaker, *Citizenship and Nationhood in France and Germany* (Cambridge, Mass.: Harvard University Press, 1992); and Anselm Doering-Man-teuffel, *Die deutsche Frage und das europäische Staatensystem 1815–1871* (Munich: Oldenbourg, 1993).

50. Frank J. Coppa, *The Origins of the Italian Wars of Independence* (London and New York: Longman, 1992); Franco Valsecci, *L'Italia del Risorgimento e l'Europa delle nazionalita: L'unificazione italiana nella politica europea* (Milan: Giuffre, 1978). On the battles over an Italian solution, see Raymond Grew, *A Sterner Plan for Italian Unification: The Italian National Society in the Risorgimento* (Princeton: Princeton University Press, 1963); and Clara Lovett, *The Democratic Movement in Italy, 1830–1876* (Cambridge, Mass.: Harvard University Press, 1982).

51. Eberhard Kolb, ed., *Europa vor dem Krieg von 1860: Mächtekonstellatio-nen-Konfliktfelder-Kriegsausbruch* (Munich: Oldenbourg, 1987); Idem, *Der Weg aus dem Krieg: Bismarcks Politik im Krieg und die Friedensanbahnung 1870/71* (Munich: Oldenbourg, 1989); Philippe Levillain and Rainer Riemenschneider, eds., *La guerre de 1870/71 et ses conséquences: Actes du XXe Colloque historique franco-allemand* (Bonn: Bouvier, 1990); Francois Roth, *La guerre de 1870* (Paris: Fayard, 1990).

52. Hans-Ulrich Wehler, *Das deutsche Kaiserreich, 1871–1918* (Göttingen: Van-denhoeck & Ruprecht, 1973).

53. Allan Mitchell, *Victors and Vanquished: The German Influence on Army and Church in France after 1870* (Chapel Hill: University of North Carolina Press, 1984), gives an indication of this transformation. The rise of the "mobilization state" and its problematic relation to participatory politics is discussed in the second part of this essay.

54. Generally Ludwig Dehio, *The Precarious Balance: Four Centuries of the European Power Struggle,* Charles Fullman, trans. (New York: Knopf, 1962). For Germany, see Andreas Hillgruber, *Die gescheiterte Großmacht. Eine Skizze des Deutschen Reiches, 1871–1945* (Düsseldorf: Droste, 1980).

55. Paul Kennedy, *The Rise of the Anglo-German Antagonism* (London and Boston: Allen & Unwin, 1980).

56. On the unique national trajectory of these "creole pioneers," see Benedict Anderson, *Imagined Communities: Reflections on the Origin and Spread of Nationalism* (London and New York: Verso, 1991), ch. 4.

57. Bourne, *Britain and the Balance of Power in North America;* Nancy N. Barker, *The French Experience in Mexico, 1821–1861: A History of Constant Misunderstanding* (Chapel Hill: University of North Carolina Press, 1979).

58. David Pletcher, *The Diplomacy of Annexation: Texas, Oregon, and the Mexican War* (Columbia: University of Missouri Press, 1973); Andeas Reichstein,

*The Rise of the Lone Star: The Making of Texas* (Austin: University of Texas Press, 1989).

59. Raul Rivera Serna, *La Guerra del Pacifico* (Lima: Universidad Nacional Mayor de San Marcos, 1984); Roberto Querajazu Calvo, *Guano, salitre, sangre: Historia de la Guerra del Pacifico* (La Paz: Editorial Los Amigos del Libro, 1992); and idem, *Aclaraciones historicas sobre la Guerra del Pacifico* (La Paz: Libreria Editorial Juventud, 1995); Louis Ortega, *Los empresarios, la politica y los origines de la Guerra del Pacifico* (Santiago de Chile: Facultad Latinoamericana de Ciencias Sociales, 1984); William Sater, *Chile and the War of the Pacific* (Lincoln: University of Nebraska Press, 1986).

60. Frank Safford, "Politics, Ideology, and Society in Post-Independence Spanish America," in Leslie Bethell, ed., *From Independence to ca. 1870.* Vol. 3 of The Cambridge History of Latin America (Cambridge: Cambridge University Press, 1985), 347–421.

61. Michael Holt, *The Political Crisis of the 1850s* (New York: Norton, 1978); and Richard H. Sewell, *A House Divided: Sectionalism and Civil War, 1848–1865* (Baltimore: Johns Hopkins University Press, 1988).

62. On the general phenomenon, see John Lynch, *Caudillos in Spanish America, 1800–1850* (Oxford: Clarendon Press, 1992). On the Argentine variant, see James R. Scobie, *La lucha per la consolidacion de la nacionalidad Argentina, 1852–1862* (Buenos Aires: Libreria Hachette, 1964); Carlos Chiaramonte, *Nacionalismo y liberalismo economicos en la Argentina* (Buenos Aires: Solar, 1971).

63. For an excellent comparison of copper mining in Chile and the United States, see William W. Culver and Cornel J. Reinhart, "Capitalist Dreams: Chile's Response to Nineteenth-Century World Copper Competition," *Comparative Studies in Society and History* 31, 4 (1989): 722–44.

64. David Bushnell and Neill Macaulay, *The Emergence of Latin America in the Nineteenth Century* (New York: Oxford University Press, 1994), 252.

65. Richard White, *The Middle Ground: Indians, Empires, and Republics in the Great Lakes Region, 1650–1815* (New York: Cambridge University Press, 1991).

66. For a discussion of some of these issues, see Jeremy Adelman, *Frontier Development: Land, Labour, and Capital on the Wheatlands of Argentina and Canada* (Oxford: Clarendon Press, 1994); Emília Viotti da Costa, *The Brazilian Empire: Myths and Histories* (Chicago: Dorsey Press, 1985), ch. 4; Avener Offer, *The First World War: An Agrarian Interpretation* (Oxford: Clarendon; and New York: Oxford University Press, 1989).

67. For example, Charles Kolinski, *Independence or Death: The Story of the Paraguayan War* (Gainesville: University of Florida Press, 1965). The basic, popular multi-volume history of this war is Cardoso's *Hace cien anos,* but see the competing national interpretations in Miguel Angel de Marco's *La Guerra del Paraguay* (Buenos Aires: Planeta, 1995); Jorge Thompson, *La Guerra del Paraguay* (Asuncion: RP Ediciones, 1992); Joaquim Francisco de Mattos, *A Guerra do*

*Paraguai: Historia de Francisco Solano Lopez, o exterminador da nacao paraguaia* (Brasilia: Centro Grafico do Senado Federal, 1990); Javier Alcalde Cruchaga, *La guerra increible de Francisco Solano Lopez* (Santiago de Chile: Grafico Andes, 1990). It is not quite by chance that this latest, 1990s spate of Latin American interpretations puts the blame for the war, and for the destruction which it engendered, on autocracy.

68. John Hoyt Williams, *The Rise and Fall of the Paraguayan Republic 1800–1870* (Austin: University of Texas Press, 1979).

69. Vivian Trias, *El Paraguay de Francia el Supremo a la Guerra de la Triple Alianza* (Buenos Aires: Crisis, 1975); Antonio Gutierrez Escudero, *Francisco Solano Lopez, el Napoleon de Paraguay* (Madrid: Anaya, 1988); Josefina Pla, *The British in Paraguay 1850–1870*, Brian C. MacDermot, trans. (Richmond: Richmond Publishing Co., 1976); John Hoyt Williams, "Foreign Tecnicos and the Modernization of Paraguay 1840–1870," *Journal of Interamerican Studies and World Affairs* 19 (1977): 233–57.

70. See Juan José Cresto, *La correspondencia que engendro una guerra: Nuevos estudios sobre los origenes de la guerra con Paraguay* (Buenos Aires: Ediciones Convergencia, 1974).

71. The "classic" case study is Herbert Gibson, *The History and Present State of the Sheep Breeding Industry in the Argentine Republic* (Buenos Aires [Edinburgh]: Ravenscroft and Mills, 1893); Alec George Ford, *The Gold Standard 1880–1914: Britain and Argentina* (Oxford: Clarendon Press, 1962); Eduardo José Miguez, *Las tierras de los ingleses en la Argentina, 1870–1914* (Buenos Aires: Editorial de Belgrano, 1986).

72. Da Costa, *The Brazilian Empire*, ch. 7.

73. Charles Bright, "The State in the United States during the Nineteenth Century," in, Charles Bright and Susan Harding, eds., *Statemaking and Social Movements: Essays in History and Theory* (Ann Arbor: University of Michigan Press, 1984), 121–58.

74. Bruce Levine, *Half Slave and Half Free: The Roots of the Civil War* (New York: Hill and Wang, 1992).

75. Roger L. Ransom, *Conflict and Compromise: The Political Economy of Slavery, Emancipation, and the American Civil War* (New York: Cambridge University Press, 1989).

76. Drew Gilpin Faust, *A Sacred Circle: The Dilemma of the Intellectual in the Old South, 1840–1860* (Baltimore: Johns Hopkins University Press, 1977); and idem, ed., *The Ideology of Slavery: Pro-Slavery Thought in the Antebellum South, 1830–1860* (Baton Rouge: Louisiana State University Press, 1981); and Bertram Wyatt-Brown, *Southern Honor: Ethics and Behavior in the Old South* (New York: Oxford University Press, 1982).

77. The debate on westward expansion need not be revisited here. However, the Latin and Caribbean dimension of southern visions of aggrandizement is

worth recalling: Charles H. Brown, *Agents of Manifest Destiny: The Lives and Times of the Filibusters* (Chapel Hill: University of North Carolina Press, 1980); Robert E. May, *The Southern Dream of a Caribbean Empire, 1854–1861* (Baton Rouge: Louisiana State University Press, 1973).

78. Paul Crook, *The North, the South, and the Powers 1861–1865* (New York: Wiley, 1964).

79. On the "Baldwin thesis" and the so-called "staple approaches" to development, see Adelman, *Frontier Development*, 7–8.

80. The triumph of the "interior" was politically registered in the fact that every Republican president from Grant to Hoover, with the lone exception of Theodore Roosevelt, came from Indiana, Illinois, or Ohio.

81. Herman Hattaway and Archer Jones, *How the North Won: A Military History of the Civil War* (Urbana: University of Illinois Press, 1983).

82. Charles Bright and Michael Geyer, "For a Unified History of the Twentieth-Century World," *Radical History Review* 39 (Sept. 1987): 69–91; as well as "World History in a Global Age," in *American Historical Review* 100, 4 (1995): 1034–60.

83. On the pros and cons of an "imperialism of free trade," see D. C. M. Platt, *Finance, Trade, and Politics in British Foreign Policy* (Oxford: Clarendon Press, 1968); and *Latin America and British Trade, 1806–1914* (New York: Barnes & Noble, 1973).

84. Martin van Creveld, *Technology and War from 2000 B.C. to the Present* (London: Collier Macmillan; and New York: Free Press, 1989).

85. Geoffrey Best, *War and Society in Revolutionary Europe, 1790–1870* (New York: St. Martin's Press, 1982).

86. The classic exploration of the links between British interests in the Mediterranean and the scramble for Africa is Ronald Robinson and John Gallagher, with Alice Denny, *Africa and the Victorians: The Climax of Imperialism in the Dark Continent* (New York: St. Martin's Press, 1961). The debate over this controversial study is presented in William Roger Louis, *Imperialism: The Robinson and Gallagher Controversy* (New York: New Viewpoints, 1976). See also Dwight Lee, *Great Britain and the Cyprus Convention Policy of 1878* (Cambridge, Mass.: Harvard University Press, 1934).

87. Inter alia Milton E. Osborne, *The French Presence in Cochin China and Cambodia: Rule and Response* (Ithaca: Cornell University Press, 1969); James F. Warren, *The Sulu Zone, 1768–1989: The Dynamics of External Trade, Slavery, and Ethnicity in the Transformation of a Southeast Asian Maritime State* (Singapore: Singapore University Press, 1981); Eunice Thio, *British Policy in the Malay Peninsula 1880–1910* (Singapore: University of Malaya Press, 1969).

88. This should be distinguished from the logistics debate of early-modern military history. See Martin van Creveld, *Supplying War: Logistics from Wallerstein to Patton* (New York: Cambridge University Press, 1977).

89. Harold Innis, *Empire and Communications* (rev. ed., Toronto and Buffalo: University of Toronto Press, 1972 [1950]). As an introduction, see Arthur Kroker, *Technology and the Canadian Mind: Innis, McLuhan, Grant* (New York: St. Martin's Press, 1984); Judith Stamps, *Unthinking Modernity: Innis, McLuhan, and the Frankfurt School* (Montreal: McGill-Queen's University Press, 1995).

90. Paul Virilio, *Speed and Politics: An Essay on Dromology* (New York; Columbia University Press, 1986). See also, *The Lost Dimension,* Daniel Moshenberg, trans. (New York: Semiotext(e), 1991).

91. Daniel Headrick, *The Tools of Empire: Technology and European Imperialism in the Nineteenth Century* (New York: Oxford University Press, 1981).

92. The efforts to highlight a German "middle position" in Europe misses what is important about Germany's strategic position in the nascent twentieth century. This historiography acts as if strategy and geopolitics had been frozen in the eighteenth century. Gregor Schöllgen, *Imperialismus und Gleichgewicht: Deutschland, England und die orientalische Frage 1871–1914* (Munich: Oldenborug, 1984); and his *Die Macht in der Mitte Europas: Stationen deutscher Außenpolitik von Friedrich dem großen bis zur Gegenwart* (Munich: Oldenbourg, 1992).

93. Alfred T. Mahan, *The Influence of Seapower upon History: 1660–1783* (London: Sampson, Low, Marston & Co., 1890).

# APPENDIXES

APPENDIX I: LIST OF WARS, 1840 TO 1880
[SOURCE: J. DAVID SINGER, *Resort to Arms*, 59–60, 297–340.]

A. East Asia—Pacific

Systemic Wars (0): none.
Extra-Systemic Wars (1): Holland-Anchinese (1873–78).
Civil Wars (4): China/Taiping (1851–64), China/Nien (1860–68), China/Miao (1860–72), Japan (1877).

Small Wars and Massacres (23): France-Annamese (1833–39), England-France-China Opium War (1839–42), Tibet-Dogras (1841), England-Borneo Pirates (1845), Holland-Balinese (1846–49), France-Vietnamese (1847), China-Kashagaria (1847–48), England-Burmese (1852–53), China-Triads (1854–55), England-France-China (1856–60), China-Khokand (1857), France-Annam (1857–62), Holland-Boninese (1859–60), Holland-Banjermasinese (1859–63), France-Vietnam (1861–62), China-Khojas (1862–64), Siam-Cambodia (1862–63), England-France-Holland-Japan (1863–69), France-China (1862–64), England-Maoris (1863–66), Japan (1866–68), Japan (1868–69), France-Tonkin (1873–74).

B. Eurasian Seam

Systemic Wars (3): Crimean War (1853–56), Anglo-Persian War (1856–57), Russo-Turkish War (1877–78).

Extra-Systemic Wars (10): First British-Afghan (1838–42), Second Syrian (1839–40), First British-Sikh (1845–46), Second British-Sikh (1848–49), First Turco-Montenegran (1852–53), Sepoy (1857–59), Second Turco-Montenegran (1858–59), Turkey-Montenegro (1862), Balkan (1875–77), Bosnia (1878), Second British-Afghan (1878–80).

Civil Wars (0): None.
Small Wars and Massacres (30): A.-H.-Bosnia/Hercegovina (1835–46), Turkey-Bosnians (1836–37), Afghanistan-Persia (1837–38), A.H.-Montenegro (1838), England-India-Khelat (1839), Russia-Khiva (1839–42), Tibet-Dards (1841), Turkey-Bulgaria (1841), England-India-Sind (1841), England-India-Gwalior (1841), Turkey-Maronites and Druzes (1845), Rumania(1848), Turkey-Bosnians (1849–50) Turkey-Bulgarians (1850), Russia-Turkestan (1851–75), Dards-Dogras (1852), Turkey-Montenegro (1852–59), England-

Santals (1855), Russia-Circassians (1859–64), Druses-Moslems-Christians (1860), Turkey-Hercegovina (1861–62), Turkey-Serbs (1862), Bengal (1863), Afghanistan (1864–68), England-Wahhabis (1863), England-Bhutan (1865), Russia-Bohkhara (1865–68), England-France-Greece-Turkey (Crete) (1866–69), Turkey (1876), Russia-Turkmenians (1878–81).

C. Central Europe

Systemic Wars (8): Austro-Sardinian (1848–49), First Schleswig-Holstein (1848–49), Roman Republic (1849), Italian Unification (1859), Italo-Roman (1860), Italo-Sicilian (1860–61), Second Schleswig-Holstein (1864), Prussian-Austrian (1866), Franco-Prussian (1870–71).

Extra-Systemic Wars (2):
Civil Wars (4): Hungarian (1848), Second Polish (1863–64).
Two Sicilies (1848–49), France (1848), Austria-Hungary (1848), France (1871).

Small Wars and Massacres (6): A.-H.-Poles (1846), Switzerland (1847), Baden (1848), Prussia (1848), A.-H.-Poles (1848), Austria-Hungary (1848), Modena (1848), Parma (1848), Tuscany (1848), Saxony (1849), France (1851), Modena-Parma-Tuscany (1859–60), Italy-Garibaldians (1862), France/Papal State-Garibaldians (1867), Italy-Papal State (1870–71).

D. Latin America—Iberia

Systemic Wars (7): Wars of La Plata (1851–52), Spanish-Moroccan (1859–1860), Franco-Mexican (1862–67), Ecuadorian-Columbian (1863), Paraguay (Lopez) (1864–70), Spanish-Chilean (1865–66), Pacific: Chile, Bolivia, Peru (1879–83).

Extra-Systemic Wars (2): Peruvian-Bolivian (1841), Spanish-Cuban Ten-Years War (1868–78).

Civil Wars (18): Spain (1834–40), Colombia (1840–42), Argentina (1841–51), Spain (1847–49), Chile (1851), Peru (1853–1855), Peru (1856–59), Mexico (1858–61), Venezuela (1859–63), Colombia (1860–62), Argentina (1863), Argentina (1866–67), Venezuela (1868, 1869–71), Spain (1868), Argentina (1870–71), Peru (1872–76), Colombia (1876–77), Argentina (1880).

Small Wars and Massacres (22): Central America (1831–45), Brazil (1835–46), France-Mexico (1838–39), Colombia (1839), Uruguay (1843–1851), Central America (1849–58), Argentina (1852–1853), Mexico (1853–55), Colombia (1854), Spain (1854), Haiti-Santo Domingo (1855–56), Nicaragua (1855–57), Spain (1856), Peru-Ecuador (1859), Argentina (1859–61), Central America (1863), Uruguay (1863–72), England-Jamaicans (1865), Spain (1866–68), Haiti (1867–69), Argentina (1873–74), Argentina-Patagonians (1878–83).

E. North America

Systemic Wars (0): Mexican-American (1846–48), Franco-Mexican (1862–67).
Extra-Systemic Wars (2): None.
Civil Wars (1): United States (1862–67).
Small War and Massacres (2): United States-Sioux (1862–67), United States-Sioux (1876–1977).

F. Africa

Systemic Wars (1): Spanish-Moroccan (1859–60).
Extra-Systemic Wars (2): Franco-Algerian (1839–47), England-Zulu (1879).
Civil Wars (0): None.
Small Wars and Massacres (28): Muscat-Zanzibar (1829–37), England-Hottentots (1834–35), Boers-Kaffirs (1834–35), Boers-Matabele (1836–37), Ma-Kalanga-Matabele (1837), England-Zulus (1838–40), Matabele-Mashonas (1840), France-Morocco (1843–44), France-Madagascar (1845), England-Basutos (1850–52), England-Bantu (1854), France-Fulas (1857), France-Arabs (1860), Arabs-Africans (1860–69), Ethiopia (1861), Boers-Basutos (1865–67), Ethiopia (1867), England-Ethiopia (1867–68), Egypt-Zobeir's Army (1869), France-Algerians (1871–72), England-Ashanti (1873–74), Egypt-Dafurians (1873–74), Egypt-Ethiopia (1875–76), England-Kaffirs (1877–78), Egypt-Slavers (1878–79), England-Basutos (1879–81), Uganda (1880), England-Transvaal (1880–81).

| Name of War[a] | Battle Deaths | Battle Deaths [per 1,000 population][b] |
|---|---|---|
| China Taiping | 2,000,000 | 4.3 |
| United States Civil War | 650,000 | 20.2 |
| Paraguay | 310,000 | 271.9 |
| —Paraguay | | 400.0 |
| —Brazil | | 108.7 |
| Russo-Turkish War | 285,000 | 23.1 |
| —Turkey | | 58.5 |
| Crimean War | 264,200 | 15.8 |
| Franco-Prussian | 187,500 | 23.1 |
| —Prussia | | 11.6 |
| —France | | 36.4 |
| Ten Years (Spain) | 100,000 | 61.0 |
| Pacific War | 14,000 | 215.4 |
| —Chile | | 136.4 |
| —Bolivia | | 66.7 |
| —Peru | | 357.1 |

[a] Fatalities listed by country in some instances
[b] Larger than 60 per 1,000

# Postscript

On Regional Transformation, Globalization, and War, with
some Afterthoughts on Comparative and Global History

*Charles Bright and Michael Geyer*

Initial agendas have a way of leaving traces. The project that was originally suggested to us was a comparison of the Prussian wars of German
unification and the American Civil War. The origins of total war was to be
the common theme and the aim was to show that the genesis of total war
could be located in these mid-nineteenth century wars. All this faded away
in the course of our research, however, and while the theme of total war
and its origins continued to play in the background (and has become the
topic of quite a bit of discussion recently[1]), our essay took a different turn.
The agenda that emerged and upon which we focused concerned, first, the
pattern and character of war in the middle decades of the nineteenth century and, second, the impact of these mid-century wars on the history of
globalization. Reflecting now on what we did then, the postscript for this
collection offers an opportunity to raise some issues with respect to comparative and global history.

## On the Nature of War in the Nineteenth Century

Given what happened in the twentieth century, it is perhaps only natural
to assume that there was some comparative relationship between the
American Civil War and the Prussian wars of German unification in the
1860s. The problem we encountered with this initial approach had less to
do with a comparative "method" (whatever that may be) than with the
proposed category of comparison. The project posited a parameter for
comparison, "total war," that was not only ill-defined (some scholars
argue that it does not even exist, or is only an artifact of a right-wing German ideology), but in the mid-nineteenth century could only be found, if

at all, as precursor and antecedent. Whatever the merits of a concept of total war, the de-merits of investigating a historical moment with these categorical certainties or imposing these presumptions on a different age were significant. Indeed the resistance many historians feel towards comparison has precisely to do with the nominalism of imposing abstract categories on historical subjects and the methodological formalism that arbitrarily picks two or three units or "containers" for comparison for no better reason than that they may look alike or occur at the same time.[2]

Paradoxically, the way out for us was not less, but more comparison. If "total war" proved to be a straitjacket, the practice of comparing wars across time and space was not. Hence, our first analytical move was not to particularize and nationalize (contain) wars, but to expand and globalize the sample. We tried to use comparison to establish difference and distance between the American Civil War and the Prussian wars of German unification, to tease apart these coeval events, and to seek out other wars and conflicts with which these episodes might be compared. What emerged from this exercise shatters the prevailing image of a generally peaceful nineteenth century, interrupted now and then by rare interludes of violence. The convention of the "long peace" is not only blinkered or Eurocentric; it is downright false. The predominant reality, especially in the middle decades of the nineteenth century, is one of pervasive, generalized, and often quite deadly violence, with civil and ethnic wars predominating (and we would suggest, albeit with less evidence, with non-combatants forming a significant portion of the victims). This was globally dispersed violence, running across the Americas, north, south, and central, and along the Eurasian seam, from the inner-Asian borders of China through India and the Caucasus to the Balkans and into central Europe. And while states were involved in all these wars, societal wars and civil violence predominated over state-organized or military-professional warfare. This aspect was all the more striking when we took a longer perspective, for the phase of societal warfare and violence, which was most intense between the 1840s and the 1880s, and especially so in the 1850s and 1860s, was itself bracketed by two periods of preponderantly inter-state, or rather, inter-imperial conflict, between the 1760s and 1810s and between the 1910s and 1950s. Indeed from a world-historical perspective, one might argue that in the course from the eighteenth to the twentieth centuries, warfare oscillated between the poles of state-based and societal or civil warfare. But while cyclical models of war, such as Modelski's, recognize the decompression and recompression of war over time, they have little sense for the spatial configuration and the temporal conjuncture of these oscillations.[3] In any event, the diffused, general, and societal violence of the mid-nineteenth century could not be understood in terms of the logic of the European state system, and a historical literature grounded in assumptions of the latter does not prepare us for the murderous extent or variety of violence that permeated the putatively peaceful Victorian heyday.

In developing this global picture of mid-century violence, we found ourselves depending on what, for most historians, is the most formalist kind of social scientific venture—large data sets, in this case those developed by the Correlates of War Project which tabulated and categorized wars over the last two centuries.[4] While we did not adopt the particular (and sometimes peculiar) arrangements of this catalogue, we cannot stress enough the importance of large data sets of this kind, and hence of quantification, for comparative projects. However insufficient or limited the data sets may be, they are essential in generating subjects for comparison, as soon as we step beyond the familiar European-North Atlantic world. How else to select what to compare—by what is there, by what strikes the individual historian as interesting, by what coexists in time? In order to escape the straitjacket of comparing two wars for arbitrary (i.e., "total war") reasons, we used the data sets to map warfare more generally and globally, creating a global picture or "war-scape" that gave us the basis for deciding what to compare and why, and that enabled us to discern clusters and discrete spheres of warfare and violence in time and space. To be sure, our "method" was rudimentary, but the effect of our tentative mapping proved the validity of the overall point. In the process of creating a global war-scape we "discovered" dozens of wars, conflicts, and major massacres that weren't supposed to be there—which suggests that intuition is blinkered when it comes to expanding beyond the regional horizon of experience and knowledge. The historian, in short, needs a pace- and space-maker as a means to counter his or her situated knowledge. Only by drawing a general or global war-scape can we get beyond everybody's list of ten favorite wars (and their comparison) and move toward a comparative study of warfare in full historical context.

This is not necessarily a renewed call for a "social scientific" (e.g., theory-driven) use of data, although one could imagine more theory-driven approaches. Rather, it is a plea, on the one hand, for more traditional, historiographical work such as fact-finding, and, on the other, for re-assessing the historical relevance of what is found. More of the historians' craft is needed when it comes to elaborating what happened, when and where.

In pursuing this study, we had to rely on a data set that identified wars about which we and the historical profession at large knew very little. How should social scientists who collected and codified historical data know anything about them—their causes, complexities, and consequences? As it goes, they did a reasonably good job most of the time in researching the multiplicity of wars they found, but their data are "soft." They provided a service by pointing to dozens of violent conflagrations that make up a pattern and thus disrupt the historians' favored view of things, but it then remains up to historians to do what they allegedly do best; that is, to check and counter-check as well as elaborate accounts of what happened so as to establish more reliable maps and elaborate more carefully patterns of wars and their contexts. With social scientists relying on incomplete data and historians shunning the perspectives that emerge from the empirically tentative and incomplete work of social scientists, new knowledge is forfeited and prejudice and bias are preserved.

It is fine to have a theory of war (assuming there is such a thing), but it is another thing to recognize war in all its specificity and variety when and where it occurs. Here the particularism of historians proves an advantage, for in probing the data (what is usefully defined as a war? When do the dead count as combatants, victims, or "collateral" damage?) preset or theory-driven categories, whether presentist or not, muddy the water. Not every violent conflict qualifies as war, but by the same token, not all man-made deaths can be called warfare. Famine is a form of man-made mass death.[5] Enslavement and the slave trade were often far more deadly and devastating than warfare.[6] The parameters for coding the numbers are fluid and require critical judgment. Indeed, disaggregated data ought to be made available so that they can be applied and adapted to broad historical comparisons. What we need is an electronic archive of wars, violent conflict, and man-made mass death—as we need one for trade, communication, and the movement of money. Such hard-data sets would serve to "discipline" comparative history.

The difficulties of this undertaking are immense. But none of them outweigh the advantages. Defining and mapping global "scapes" of related or interconnected processes and events is the vital first step for comparative studies in an age of globalization in which local or "situated" knowledge and the assumptions that flow from it no longer provide a reliable guide. As a startling new reality of global war presented itself, it became clear to us that there could be no recourse to self-evident, naturalized entities, no reliance on an inherited, historical sensibility of what matters and what not, no trust in seemingly self-evident pictures of the world. To throw categorical certainties—¡Kinship! ¡Total War!—after uncertain subjects—¿kinship networks? ¿Violent conflagrations?—is a waste of effort. To compare the historically self-evident—Prussia-Germany and the United States—while neglecting how they are situated globally, preserves inherited prejudice. As we approach global history and, in particular, the history of globalization, the settled subjects and relations of history are turned askew and new patterns present themselves that challenge historians to move beyond professing enthusiasm for comparative history and to get on to the hard work of elaborating the global maps of structures and events that anchor comparisons.

## On the Nature of Global History

At this point in the evolution of our study, a comparative approach to the history of war in the mid-nineteenth century might have suggested a move to treat specific kinds of warfare or violence—state-wars, civil wars, ethnic conflicts, religious massacres—comparatively.[7] If we took, for example, the instances of ethnic conflict or, more generally, of warfare directed at civilian populations (and assuming the data and coding of the Correlates of War allowed it), we could have explored the causes, dynamics, and (non)resolution of these kinds of conflicts, underscoring in the process the sad fact that genocidal wars against innocent people is not a new phenomenon, but also the more hopeful possibility that the recurrence and comparability of such violent acts make them more accessible to historical understanding. For us, however, the global picture of endemic violence that emerged in the mid-nineteenth century suggested a different challenge, one that moved us toward a global narrative rather than a comparative analysis. Following Raymond Grew's observation that "even tacit comparison eases the task of integrating concepts . . . by providing common categories of analysis and a common focus,"[8] we turned the comparative task toward assembling patterns and differences in the global warscape of the mid-nineteenth century. Our aim was to open an exploration of the global processes at work in the warfare of that epoch.

This was a move to a more explicitly global history that produced the elaboration of the two regional configurations—distinct temporal and spatial arcs of violence in the Americas and Eurasia at mid-century—that came to undergird the argument of the essay. To summarize: The dispersed, societal violence at mid-century flowed from two very different kinds of historical transformations. One was the devolution of the maritime empires of the Atlantic that began in the late eighteenth century and ran its course in the early nineteenth century. The second was the largely unrelated struggles, often surprisingly effective, of the great land-based empires of Eurasia in the first half of the nineteenth century to fend off internal crisis and renew their viability through projects of self-improvement using borrowed or appropriated techniques. Thus if it is puzzling to wonder how Napoleon III managed to get his armies into both the Crimea and Mexico in the space of ten years, it becomes even more puzzling to realize that the wars of the Crimea and of Mexico were "dots" (not especially small ones, to be sure) in wider regional configurations of violence in the Americas and along the Eurasian seam that framed quite distinct contexts for the American Civil War and the Prussian wars of German unification. Pace Napoleon's aspirations, these wars not only had little to do with one another, but arose from very different patterns of violence in regional archipelagos that were conditioned by distinct historical trajectories.

In one respect, then, the argument that emerged looked back to a previous epoch of imperial-state conflict, beyond the purview of the essay we wrote, and proposed to treat the endemic global violence of the mid-century as the consequences of a previous era and the processes of what Christopher Bayly has called "proto-globalization."[9] The early modern period is, of course, one of the current "hot spots" in the renewal of interest among historians in global history. In the work being done on networks of exchange, the movement of goods and ideas, the flows of peoples, often over great distances and in broad diasporas, and in efforts to illuminate the patterns of global interconnectivity through which localities and elites consumed a wider world via mediations and serial relays across space—as luxuries and increasingly in the drug trades of sugar, coffee, tea, chocolate, tobacco, and opium—the revival of world history in this period has benefited more from comparative analysis than from Wallersteinian "systems theory." For, in showing the degrees of global interconnection, historians are presenting less a coordinated or centered "system" than a world of regional entities and power centers that were still quite distinct and capable of producing, as it were, autonomous histories.

For us, exploring the corridors or arcs of violence that separated the American Civil War and the Prussian wars of German unification and linked them instead to quite distinct regional patterns and historical contexts produced a less systemic and, in our view, less fictional interpretation of the dynamics of warfare in the mid-nineteenth century. In this light,

German unification flowed from (and in some ways transformed) the geopolitics of empire-salvaging across the Eurasian seam, but these struggles could hardly be set aside as the peripheral jumble implied by the archaic language of "the Eastern Question." Rather they emerged as crucial coordinates for understanding the nature and timing of the Central European wars that produced a united Germany and a new geopolitics of the world. Similarly American (re)unification in the wake of civil war, seen as a break-away from prevailing patterns of post-imperial reconstruction in the American hemisphere and of its ties to the Atlantic world, came at the tail end of (and in some ways reversed), the main coordinates of regional unsettlement that had convulsed the north and south Americas for over half a century. One might sensibly see the endemic violence of the mid-nineteenth century (including these two wars) as consequences or outgrowths of imperial competition and crisis and of the resulting jockeying of local and regional centers, world wide, for survival or self-improvement within continuing cycles of commodity extraction and exchange. But the geopolitical alignments of the world were shifting dramatically in this mid-century passage and, in our view, were putting the processes of globalization into motion.

It was, therefore, upon the effects or outcomes of the global and diffuse violence of the mid-nineteenth century that our essay came to focus. For the world that produced a united Germany and a (re)United States in that period is very different from the world that was forged through and as a result of the conflict of these two powers in the twentieth century. We have moved in the last century and a half from extensions, linkages, networks and exchanges reaching across space (and because of distance, over time) through the liminal zones and border lands of deserts and pirate coves, to (or toward) a world as *an interior space* of dense, continuous, and multilateral interconnectivity carried on *in real time.* To study this transformation is to study the history of globalization, which is quite distinct from the term "global," understood as "world-wide" or extensive and far-reaching and moves beyond world history as a comparative study of civilizations (whether in contact or not) toward a world of deepening integration, in which autonomy is destroyed and separate histories grind together and become inextricably implicated in one another.

These processes of globalization that were to define the long twentieth century, we argued, crystallized out of the dispersed, societal warfare of the mid-nineteenth century—the oxymoron of dispersal and crystallization capturing precisely the unanticipated and unprecedented nature of the turn. The world-wide and diffuse violence that attended the crisis and dissolution of land-based and maritime empires did have a "resolving" effect, in that warfare tended to eliminate options and narrow possibilities, forcing new departures. These departures moved in two directions simultaneously—producing deepening processes of nationalization and of globalization at the same time.

On the one hand, the big "winners" in this warfare were newly formed, or reformed, integral nation-states. We highlighted Germany and the United States as they emerged from their respective mid-century wars along a course towards rapid, national industrial and military power. We should have paid more attention to Japan in the same passage (and in the context of a more detailed discussion of the East Asian/Pacific region, which is also missing); for not only did the Japanese ascent shift power in the Asian sphere from the Chinese interior to the "exterior" Pacific world, but in making this break-out, the Japanese pursued for a time, not only a claim of primacy in Asia, but of inclusion as equals in the circle of "great" (world) powers as well. We might also have sharpened the discussion by examining some of the "failures" in this bid for national self-assertion and improvement, such as Serbia or Egypt. And we might have elaborated the difference between nation-making and a successful mobilization of national power for a breakout into global competition by examining the case of Italy. The ability to pull free of older imperial traces and to forge a national project of mass production and military power in a bid for world power proved remarkably elusive. But where it succeeded—as in Germany and the United States—the effect was a startling and often quite dangerous ratcheting upward of national capacities to project power globally.

On the other hand, the sudden appearance of these new industrial and military challengers produced a reaction, and this response is what prompted us to introduce Great Britain late in the essay. For in falling back on and revamping the imperial estate in an effort to counteract or fend off the new mobilized power of integral nation-states, Great Britain (and to a much lesser extent, France) extended and intensified processes of globalization to counter the nationalist challenges. In extending, consolidating, and formalizing its far-flung territorial empire, Great Britain developed what one might call techniques of "transnational governance." Using the new liquidity of capital and the extended reach of maritime force and new means of communication, Great Britain developed the capacity, not only to project force into the world from core territorial bases, as the Germans and Americans did, but to be present globally in many places at once. Great Britain thus added an entirely new, transnational dimension to an inter-nation system. Notwithstanding initially quite limited capabilities, this global, transnational presence established a defining element of globalization: the capacity to draw in local self-mobilizations of people, resources, goods, and cultural artifacts and integrate or articulate them into transnational circuits of exchange and multilateral settlement. Thus emerged, towards the end of the nineteenth century, the first truly global regime of order—built by the British on the nexus of colonial empire (especially India) and the gold standard (centered on the Bank of England) which deployed the regulatory rules that organized trade and exchange among industrial powers while subordinating primary production to the disciplines of the market and the promissory tutelage of colonial administration.

It was this twin movement that we sought to capture in the title, "Globalizing Violence and Nationalizing Wars," and it is how we saw the effects of mid-century warfare as setting off processes of globalization which were, at the same time, driven by the powerful engines of nationalization. It was not some grand war between states, but the persistent and pervasive elaboration of low-level, civil-type violence that created the conditions of globality. It was this globalizing interpretation of the dynamics of mid-century violence that allowed us to see the German wars of unification as the tail end of empire-preserving (and losing) conflicts along the Eurasian seam, and the American Civil War as the outgrowth of a long process of reconstruction in the Americas around new nations groping for positions of survival in the Atlantic world. This had nothing to do with a "periphery" conditioning the "center." Rather the study of the nature and distribution of warfare in the period between the 1840s and the 1880s revealed an incipient, but world-wide transformation. It was a transformation in which the competition of early-modern empires, with their expansive outward movement and their slash-and-burn colonization gave way to—or were overlaid by—a quite different process, the dual and simultaneous consolidation of nation-states and of transnational regulatory regimes which, together, forged the history of globalization in the long twentieth century.

NOTES

1. Manfred Bömeke, Roger Chickering, and Stig Förster, eds., *Anticipating Total War: The German and American Experiences, 1871–1914.* Cambridge and

New York: Cambridge University Press, 1999. Stig Förster and Jörg Nagler, eds, *On the Road to Total War: The American Civil War and the German Wars of Unification, 1861–1871.* Cambridge and New York: Cambridge University Press, 1997. Roger Chickering and Stig Förster, eds., *Great War, Total War: Combat and Mobilization on the Western Front, 1914–1918.* Cambridge and New York: Cambridge University Press, 2000.

2. See Thomas Holt's helpful comments in "Slavery and Freedom in the Atlantic World: Reflections on the Diasporan Framework," in, Darlene Clark Hine and Jacqueline McLeod, eds., *Crossing Boundaries: Comparative History of Black People in Diaspora.* Bloomington: Indiana University Press, 2001.

3. George Modelski, *Long Cycles in World Politics.* Seattle: University of Washington Press, 1987.

4. David J. Singer. *Correlates of War Project* [cited 10 May 2001]. Available from http://www-personal.umich.edu/~dlivshiz/bib.html.

5. Mike Davis, *Late Victorian Holocausts: El Nino Famines and the Making of the Third World.* London and New York: Verso, 2001.

6. Philip Curtin's standard, *The Atlantic Slave Trade, a Census* (Madison: University of Wisconsin Press, 1969) has provoked a long debate focusing understandably more on the total magnitude of the slave trade than on its mortality. Paul Lovejoy's intervention, "The Volume of the Atlantic Slave Trade: A Synthesis," *Journal of American History* 23 (1982), suggested that some two million Africans perished in the "middle passage" alone, but this does not begin to imagine the mortality of slave hunting in Africa and slave labor in the Americas. The DuBois Institute for Afro-American Research at Harvard has been preparing a database for the transatlantic slave trade based on a comprehensive survey of ship records between 1662 and 1860 which will one day be available on CD-ROM from Cambridge University Press. (See the information web-site at: http://web-dubois.fas.harvard.edu/DuBois/Research/Research.HTML.)

7. This is done with considerable success in Wolfgang Höpken and Michael Riekenberg, eds., *Politische und ethnische Gewalt in Südosteuropa und Lateinamerika.* Cologne and Weimar: Böhlau, 2001.

8. Raymond Grew. "The Case for Comparing Histories," *American Historical Review* 85, 4 (1980): 763–78.

9. Christopher Bayly, keynote address, 2 March 2001, at the conference "Interactions: Regional Studies, Global Processes, and Historical Analysis," sponsored by the AHA and the Library of Congress.

# 3. MAKING DISCOVERIES

# Testing Paradigms with Comparative Perspectives

British India and Patterns of Scientific and Technology
Transfer in the Age of European Global Hegemony

*Michael Adas*

In what, rather remarkably, is still the fullest and most perceptive essay on the comparative method written by a historian, over seventy years ago, Marc Bloch argued that among the more promising uses of comparison one must include the framing of key issues for historical inquiry, and the posing of questions that offer new perspectives and identify issues for debate.[1] A half-century later, Raymond Grew judged that these tasks had indeed proved to be two of the most important contributions of comparative studies undertaken in the intervening decades. Drawing on his wide-ranging readings of decades of historical scholarship and his interventions as the editor of *Comparative Studies in Society and History,* which he did much to establish as the most influential periodical in the field, Grew observed that in the journal and comparative scholarship more generally, provocative questions and the identification of issues to be explored had often been raised in essays concentrating on a single case.[2] As Grew implicitly suggested, given the space constraints of the essay format that scholarly periodicals privilege, full comparisons of multiple cases were rare in *CSSH* and other journals receptive to the mode of research and thinking that Bloch sought to identify and promote.

A survey of works in comparative history over the past three or four decades provides substantial support for Grew's stress on the importance of essays that draw on patterns exhibited by individual cases to generalize about broader themes in cross-cultural and indeed global history. From millenarian movements and imperialism to protest strategies and changes in warfare, essays focusing on detailed explorations of single cases have forced rethinking of existing understandings of key historical processes.[3] Such studies have often addressed questions of comparative theory and method in more fundamental ways than have book-length studies with multiple comparative examples. Essays by Eugene Genovese and Samuel Baily, to cite two examples, contain some of the most incisive thinking we have regarding comparative techniques in their respective fields of slave systems and immigration history.[4]

In this essay, I suggest further comparative uses of the single case study. I will draw mainly on evidence relating to British colonization and rule in South Asia from the eighteenth through the early twentieth centuries to explore questions and challenges generated by a growing literature on the history of scientific and technological transfers from the industrial metropoles of western Europe and North America to colonized areas in Asia, Africa, and Latin America. I focus on cross-cultural interactions in British India involving the sciences or technology and seek to identify ways in which recent research into this vital dimension of global exchange has compelled students of colonialism, and of the history of science and technology, to adopt different perspectives, ask new questions in untraditional ways, and broadly rethink the patterns exhibited by one of the core processes of modern world history. This multifaceted testing has not only necessitated ongoing experimentation with new models to analyze these processes; it has led—in accord with the Kuhnian sequence—to a fundamental revision of the diffusionist paradigm that once held sway in research and scholarship on scientific and technology transfer.

Of all of the dependencies in Africa and Asia, India was by far the largest in area and population, and one of the earliest to be fully colonized. In fact, India can be seen as the core possession of this largest of the colonial empires. More important for the purposes of critiquing the diffusionist model of the spread of science to Europe's colonies is that India was the first non-settler colony to be caught up in this process. As recent research has shown, scientific knowledge and instrument exchanges between the Portuguese and different South Asian peoples were underway from the very first decades of European overseas expansion in the sixteenth century. Between the last decades of the eighteenth century and the early 1800s, British colonizers in the Bengal, Madras, and Bombay regions, and to a much lesser extent areas further inland, undertook the first conscious and systematic campaign to transmit to African and Asian colonial dependencies key aspects of the scientific and technological revolutions that were transforming their own societies. But India was not only the lead society in the process of the global diffusion of Western science and technology, a process that continues—vastly accelerated—in the present day. With the possible exception of Japan, it was the non-Western society to which the scientific knowledge, tools, and techniques of Europe were transmitted on the largest scale, and that into which they were the most fully integrated.

For these reasons, it is difficult to envision a better test case for the diffusionist approach to the spread of Western science in the colonial world. It is noteworthy that George Basalla, the most influential proponent of this paradigm, made little use of evidence drawn from the Indian experience. This neglect may help to explain why the diffusionist perspective has proved so problematic for scholars working on the non-settler, colonial dependencies more generally, even though there have been no extended critiques of this approach as applied to South Asia comparable to those mounted by historians of settler colonies. On the basis of the Indian historical experience, I will test the diffusionist paradigm at several levels, from questions regarding the applicability of the stage sequence of diffusion that forms the core of Basalla's model, to an inquiry into presuppositions—if often implicit and unstated ones—that underlie the diffusionist approach regarding the nature of Western or "modern" science and the inevitability of its globalization.

My emphasis on case evidence from a single colonized area, of course, raises the question of the extent to which the dynamics of British-Indian interaction can be generalized to other regions and cultures that came under Western dominance in this era. As with all comparisons that seek to address broader issues and questions primarily on the basis of single case examples, the problem of the "nth comparison" looms even larger than in book-length comparative studies that deal at length with multiple case studies. But, as even the most thorough and sophisticated of the latter demonstrate, there will invariably be comparable case examples which diverge in important ways from, or explicitly call into question, patterns or generalizations that emerge from the necessarily finite number of cases that can be explored in any depth in even the most copious tome. The nth-case objection, which is sometimes raised to dispute the validity of comparative findings, arises from a misperception of the purpose of the comparative approach. No comparison can meaningfully encompass the full range of possible cases, and very often the more case examples attempted, the thinner the evidentiary base and the more problematic the larger patterns discerned. Article or book, the main task of the comparativist is to deploy evidence from one or more cases that is suitably substantial and consciously selected to raise meaningful questions with regard to larger processes, or is sufficient to identify general patterns exhibited by critical historical processes. The aim of comparison ought not to be discerning universal laws or objectively verifiable truths, but rather to arrive at understandings about historical events and processes that are worthy of testing and refining by further study in which additional case evidence can be brought to bear.

With these concerns in mind, it is important to caution at the outset that in significant ways India was by no means typical of the colonial experience, much less of societies where the Europeans exerted hegemony informally rather than through direct rule—China, Japan, or the Ottoman Empire. For this reason, I seek to frame Indian examples with case study evidence and questions regarding scientific and technology transfer relating to other colonized areas, including those dominated informally rather than directly. Contextualized in this way, I argue that the Indian example demonstrates the difficulty of constructing models of the process of scientific transfer that do full justice to the diversity of colonial sites. It is possible to discern broad patterns and perhaps even formulate tentative generalizations about this critical global exchange. But particularly if contingency, individual agency, and epistemological negotiations are seriously taken into consideration, I have found that model building becomes a contentious and ultimately frustrating exercise. In the interest of foregrounding these dimensions of global exchange, which I have argued elsewhere have often been neglected to the detriment of well-grounded and compelling global and comparative historical narratives,[5] I begin with a biographical overview of a remarkable Indian, Jagadis Chandra Bose. His career encapsulated many of the themes, responses, and issues I wish to interrogate in the historical literature concerning the unprecedented levels of scientific and technological exchange during the age of European colonial dominance.

To a point, the scientific achievements of Bose appeared to fulfill, even excel, the most sanguine expectations of the then beleaguered British officials, who saw no upper limits to Britain's self-appointed mission to civilize India's peoples. Where devout Christian converts once exemplified the ultimate success of this enterprise, by the last decades of the nineteenth century accomplished scientists like Bose were the surest confirmation of the British confidence that India could be utterly remade in the image of the West. Bose's career provided much-needed ammunition for those, such as Henry Maine and Patrick Geddes, who struggled against the cresting tide of racist sentiment and the limits on higher education for the colonized demanded by British policy makers. The latter were persuaded that the innate deficiencies of the "quite underdeveloped minds"[6] of Indian students rendered it impossible for them to comprehend scientific instruction. Bose was able to master scientific learning and conduct original research that employed the strictest scientific procedures. Ironically, this provided a dramatic counter to widely accepted "scientific" claims of inherent differences in intelligence that rendered inferior "races" like the Indians less rational than their European masters.

Beyond his scientific accomplishments, Bose's entire career seemed to be a resounding confirmation of Britain's mission to civilize.[7] As the son of the Anglicized headmaster of the first English-language school at Mymensingh in east Bengal, Bose pursued Western learning from an early age, though his education began in a local vernacular school because his father, Bhabagan, felt that he needed to be fluent in Bengali. Bhabagan enjoyed some success as an investor in, among other things, tea plantations, and he went on to become the deputy magistrate of the Faridpur district. But his impact on his son "Jessie" went beyond financial backing and official contacts. Through his active involvement in the Brahmo Samaj, the elder Bose stimulated Jessie's lifelong commitment to the organization's goal of revitalizing (or perhaps more accurately recovering) India's religious traditions, especially Hinduism, through infusions of Western rationalism and scientific thinking. Bhabagan's involvement in the Brahmo Samaj also brought the young Bose into the intellectually charged and socially committed circles of the English-educated Bengali elite.

In 1867, Jessie began his English-language studies at the Hare school in Calcutta. There he excelled, thus assuring his admittance in 1874 to St. Xavier's College, at the age of sixteen. At St. Xavier's Bose received his first formal training in Western science, particularly under the guidance of the school's physics specialist, Father Lafont. With Lafont's enthusiastic endorsement, Bose decided to pursue a career as a scientist, and to do so at the highest level in the colonial metropolis, Great Britain. His financial support secured by his success in the all-India competition for a science fellowship, Bose majored in the sciences at Christ College, Cambridge beginning in 1881. His distinguished record at Cambridge eventually won him an appointment in 1885 in the Imperial Educational Service as a professor of physics at the Presidency College, Calcutta.

By the early 1890s, Bose had begun experiments on the transmission and effects of electrical waves. In the next decade this work would earn him an international scientific reputation and transform him into something of a celebrity in India. His experiments with wireless transmission led to a series of exchanges with Guglielmo Marconi, and the claim by some of Bose's supporters that he, not the Italian inventor, had been responsible for the discoveries that made wireless telegraphy possible. In the following decade, Bose served as the official Indian delegate to a number of international scientific congresses and delivered papers at scientific societies in London and Paris. As his research turned increasingly to electro-physiology and the growth patterns of plants, he became a scientific advisor in much demand in both Great Britain and the United States. His achievements in research and education won him an annual subsidy from the Government of India and, in 1917, a knighthood of the British empire. They also garnered him the financial backing he required to found in the same year an institute of scientific research bearing his name. There he and his colleagues and students continued his exploration of, in the words of his admiring friend Patrick Geddes, "the border region between physics and physiology," and his quest "to find the boundary lines vanishing and points of contact emerging between the reaches of the Living and Non-living."[8]

Despite Geddes' assessment that Bose was the "first Indian of modern times who has done distinguished work in science,"[9] and pursued a career trajectory that appeared to fulfill the highest aspirations of the most enthusiastic British civilizers, a subversive undercurrent in his career and scientific investigations came to dominate in the early 1900s. From the outset, Bose did not hesitate to defend vigorously his research findings when they contravened the established views of his Western peers. He refused to dissemble even in the face of dismissive, at times contemptuous, opposition on the part of his English critics. This was matched by a stubborn pride that resisted official responses explicitly designed to remind him of his inferior status as a colonized subject and member of a lesser, albeit ancient, "race." His first government appointment was won over the determined opposition of the openly racist director of public instruction, Alfred Croft, who made no secret of his conviction that "no native was fit to teach the exact sciences." Having secured his position with the backing of the Viceroy, Lord Ripon, Bose refused his salary for three years after learning that it would be only two-thirds that of his British counterparts because, whatever his credentials, he was still a "native." He accepted remuneration only after the government agreed to place him at the same level as his British colleagues who had achieved an equal level of distinction.

Beginning in the early 1900s, Bose pushed his research on the transmission of energy into realms that were increasingly transgressive in terms of establishment views of the "proper" questions to be asked and procedures to be followed in scientific research. Over the following decades, Bose's critics chafed and his supporters exulted as his experiments with the sensory responses of plants and later metals drew increasingly on indigenous epistemologies, from those relating to the natural sciences and philosophy to unabashed mysticism. Bose also became increasingly vocal in his criticisms of the overspecialization and outright arrogance of the Western scientific community. He expressed a determination to revive Indian scientific learning and methods and to forge a viable synthesis between these indigenous traditions and those of the West. Like Rabindranath Tagore, Mohandas Gandhi, and other major Indian thinkers, Bose saw the First World War as a calamity that ought to serve as a caution for non-Western peoples eager to cast off their own epistemologies and approaches and imbibe those of the West without reservations or careful scrutiny. In his inaugural address at the Banaras Hindu University in 1916, Bose observed: "In the West there has been no check or limit to the competition for personal gain and lust for power in exploiting the application of knowledge, not so often for saving as for causing destruction. And on account of the absence of this restraining force, civilization is trembling to-day in an unstable poise on the brink of ruin."[10]

The career of Jagadis Chandra Bose provides a rather remarkable example of the multifaceted ways in which scientific ideas and methodologies were transferred within the premier European imperial system of the nineteenth century. Bose's experience also encapsulates a range of more fundamental patterns that cannot be accounted for by any of the existing models that seek to explain the historical dynamics of the process of scientific and technological transfer in the age of European colonial expansion. Each of these paradigms has useful things to tell us about these exports from European metropoles to widely scattered overseas colonies. But none has been formulated with a focus on tropical dependencies, such as India or those in sub-Saharan Africa, or areas "informally" imperialized, such as China or the Ottoman Empire. As George Basalla—the first historian to attempt a model with applicability to different kinds of colonial sites distributed widely over the globe—concedes at the outset, his characterization of the receiving colonies as "nonscientific" is inappropriate for civilizations like India or China, and (though Basalla does not mention them) those of Japan, Mesoamerica, or the Islamic world.[11] This means, of course, that the experience of most of humankind falls outside of Basalla's purview. It also results in a neglect, apparent in Basalla's model and those which preceded and followed it, of virtually all of the great non-Western civilizations that constructed formal and systemic scientific epistemologies that might rival those of the West.

This lacunae is symptomatic of two other defining characteristics of available paradigms for scientific transfer in colonial situations. The first, more pronounced in some models than others, is a tendency to see this process as unidirectional, with science—in its many manifestations but always equated with Western science—flowing from European metropoles to non-Western colonies. There follows from this an almost complete absence of agency of any meaningful sort on the part of individuals or groups who are not either European or of European descent.

The earliest transfer models were quite consciously Euro- and Western-centric. These were fashioned in the early 1960s by I. B. Cohen and Donald Fleming,[12] who specialized in the history of settler colonies like Canada, Australia, and the United States. Though Fleming sought through comparison to give his findings a broader significance, both scholars focused on the nature of interactions between the scientific communities in European metropoles and emergence of what were initially satellite groups formed by European migrants or their descendants in areas of settlement. For both Cohen and Fleming, the issue of agency was critical. But their main concerns were to demonstrate if, how, and when settler scientists broke from an early position of dependence on their European colleagues and European scientific societies, publications, and standards of investigation. With strains of professional chauvinism scarcely muted at times, each sought to show how the colonials went from acting first as supplicants and exporters of exotic specimens to European classifiers and theoreticians, to then becoming scientific researchers in their own right and thinkers who began to influence the scientific debates in the European metropoli.

The perspectives and overall approach of Cohen and Fleming clearly influenced George Basalla's pioneering attempt to construct a more general model for the process of scientific transfer in the age of European colonial dominance. For nearly four decades, Basalla's diffusionist vision has informed work on the history of science and European colonialism in virtually all areas of the globe. Whether explicitly providing the contextual framework for the analysis of the spread of Western science in particular colonial societies, or serving as a background reference for more generalized discussions of what he characterizes as a diffusion process, his three-phase sequence has been widely accepted and adopted by scholars in both the West and in the formerly colonized, developing countries. The persisting influence of Basalla's paradigm is suggested by it having been a focus of discussion at a 1990s symposium in Madrid on science and European expansion. At that gathering he offered a number of additional attributes of "modern science," but he averred that his model, more or less as it was originally formulated, remained a useful way to approach the study of the processes by which Europe's scientific personnel, institutions, and learning spread to overseas dependencies.[13]

Basalla's continuing confidence in the heuristic value of his model is undoubtedly bolstered by numerous authors continuing to organize their accounts of Western science in the colonies around tests of the key attributes of each of his three stages of diffusion. References to the essay's "classic" stature and its seemingly obligatory citation by specialists in the field further lead one to infer the continuing, general utility of his framework.[14] As Patrick Petitjean has observed, Basalla's model has been both the most cited and most refuted contribution to the history of science and colonialism.[15]

Beyond the problems just discussed relating to Basalla's curiously skewed sample of colonial sites, his three-stage sequence of scientific diffusion has proved a poor fit with the findings of many of the area specialists who have attempted to apply it to specific case examples. This disjuncture is symptomatic of deeper structural and conceptual problems of the stage-sequence analysis so fundamental to Basalla's approach. To begin with, Basalla is very vague about the boundaries that demarcate the three phases of diffusion he identifies, and he has little to say about the considerable overlap between them. Thus, the defining characteristics of what he identifies as phase I of scientific diffusion remain prominent in the case of India (and those of Africa, China, and Latin America) throughout phase II, or what he terms the "colonial era." Activities such as the collection, classification, and preservation of plant and animal life, which Basalla sees as central to his first phase of transmission, persisted—and in many respects increased—in most colonial areas in phase II. The orientation of field workers and scholars in the colonies to the scientific societies, publications, and institutions of the European metropoles, a defining feature of Basalla's phase II, was, if anything, more pronounced in India, Africa, and the rest of the colonized world, including the settler colonies as they are depicted by Cohen and Fleming, in the first stage, and, moreover, continued into the period of what Basalla terms "independent science." The fact that Basalla has little to say about the causal dynamics of movement from one stage to the next[16] compounds the problems of overlap and continuity between stages.

Even if clearly bounded phases of scientific transfer could be identified for significant clusters of colonies, labeling them with reference to a particular sort of scientific activity can obscure more than it reveals. As Ian Inkster has observed with reference to Australia, scientific exchange between metropolis and colony at any point in time involved a variety of levels of interaction, reflecting everything from socioeconomic base and cultural orientation to the quality of scientific support structures.[17] Case evidence from a number of areas suggests that these are rarely in sync even within a single colony, and they are highly variable from one colonial context to the next. Thus, rather than attempting to delineate clearly bounded stages or identify a generic sequence for the spread of Western science, it has proven far more revealing to explore subtler shifts in emphasis, content, and interaction between colonizer and colonized in specific colonial areas. At best, we can work to discern broader patterns of scientific exchange within each type of colonial dependency, though even here contextual givens, such as the time of annexation and the nature of indigenous epistemologies and scientific practice, can make for contrasts so pronounced that they defy overarching typologies.[18]

A rather different set of problems arises from the diffusionist and highly Eurocentric orientation of Basalla's model. In this regard, his use of the metaphoric terminology of diffusion is highly instructive, if unsurprising, given the predominant assumptions of and lexicon employed by those working on these sorts of exchanges in the heyday of modernization theory. Though the term is not explicitly stated, Basalla's formulations are clearly informed by the dependency approach to the history of colonialism that was peaking in influence when his original essay was written. Like the structuralist framework of the dependency theorists, Basalla's model is Eurocentric in the extreme. Dynamism and agency in the process of scientific exchange belong exclusively to Europe and the Europeans, as evidenced by his vision of a one-way diffusion of "modern" (or real) science from the West. Despite Basalla's qualifications regarding the prior scientific traditions of the Indians or Chinese, European science spreads into a colonial vacuum. In the first two phases of diffusion at least, colonized peoples are scarcely mentioned. Implicitly they remain passive recipients, whose responses have little impact on the inexorable spread of Western epistemologies and practice. Resistance and reformulation, much less the persistence of indigenous traditions, are at best relegated to the status of superstitions impeding the advance of the superior learning and techniques of the West. Only in phase III do colonials—invariably the white settler variety—become active players in this process, and then only as increasingly influential practitioners of the sciences of the hegemonic West.

Even though Basalla clearly distinguishes India, China, and Japan from what he terms as "non-scientific," "uncivilized," or "primitive" societies, the latter designations suggest fundamental questions regarding Basalla's conceptualization of science and the place of the Western scientific traditions within that vision. It is not simply that the terminology that Basalla employs in characterizing areas like the Americas and Africa is no longer appropriate for scholarly discourse. His usage both privileges the Western scientific tradition, which he sees as one and indivisible, and denies scientific modes of reasoning to peoples he views as primitive and uncivilized. Although he does not explicitly say so, Basalla adopts a non-constructivist view of Western science, a view that admittedly was rarely challenged by his generation of scholars. Implicitly, and at times explicitly, Basalla equates modern science with Western science, which in his view provides a value-neutral, objective, empirically demonstrated representation of reality that transcends time and cultural givens, and is thus universally valid. Basalla's diffusionist vision is also informed by a developmental teleology premised on the assumption that the spread of Western science to the rest of the globe has been both beneficial and inevitable.[19] Much of the research of intervening generations of historians of science have, of course, stressed that Western scientific knowledge is, like other forms of knowledge, socially constructed.[20] This insight calls into question Basalla's assumptions about Western scientific and non-Western epistemologies, and thereby the very nature of the process of diffusion and the interaction between cultures that he seeks to schematize. Given the widespread acceptance, even the strident demand, for Western science in virtually all areas of the globe affected by European overseas expansion,[21] it is important to note that the ascendancy of this approach to the natural world can be attributed more to the power for extraction, production, and dominance that it offers to those who adopt it than to its objectivity or universal validity.

Basalla's Eurocentric perspectives on scientific transfer under colonialism are also apparent in the alternative framework that Lewis Pyenson has proposed for comparing this process according to the colonial power in question. Drawing on his meticulously researched studies of the pursuit of science in German, Dutch, and French colonial settings,[22] Pyenson distills the predominant purpose of scientific pursuits in each. Thus, for example, he characterizes the German as research-oriented and the Dutch and Belgian as mainly concerned with scientific investigations with a bearing on mercantile pursuits.[23] These essentialist characterizations obscure the mix of motives that prompted scientific projects and transfers in various colonial areas at different time periods—a diversity well demonstrated in Pyenson's own monographic studies. But his approach underscores the importance of differences between the Western metropoles and the purposes of each colonial power, and the impact these variations must have on the diffusion and reception of Western science and technology in different colonial sites. Colonial scientific and technological development was to a significant degree determined by the levels of research and innovation attained by the metropolitan societies to which each colony was attached. Hence, despite colonial restrictions, India benefited from Britain's early scientific and industrial leads. Spanish or Portuguese colonies, by contrast, lagged far behind India and other British dependencies, and also those of the French and Germans, in the transmission of both Western science and technology. As the British fell behind the Germans, Americans, and French in technical education in the late nineteenth century, India and other British colonies felt the repercussions.

Pyenson's framework for comparing approaches to scientific transfers within the different European colonial empires suggests that he sees more direct connections between science and imperialism than some of his critics would allow.[24] Certainly these linkages are more apparent in his most recent monograph on the place of science in France's overseas empire. In contrast to his earlier insistence that his work was concerned only with what he termed the "exact" sciences, Pyenson specifically singles out his concern to probe the "ties" between *sciences fondamentales* and *sciences appliquées*.[25] But neither his framework nor Basalla's model is conducive to a serious interrogation of factors in either the metropoles or the colonies that shape colonial scientific agendas. Neither compels a constructivist inquiry into the kinds of science privileged in colonial settings, the contextual factors that shaped the questions posed, the procedures employed, and the ways in which science was institutionalized.

The rather narrow focus of both Basalla and Pyenson on "exact" sciences, such a botany, zoology, and astronomy also results in a tendency to underestimate the importance of endeavors like geology, ethnology, and incipient anthropology, fields to which the colonial encounters gave tremendous impetus. More critically, their narrow conceptualizations of science cause them to overlook broader processes for which scientific transfer was critical. The rise of European hegemony in the India and other colonies was accompanied by ambitious campaigns to "rationalize" colonial administrations, codify laws, classify their bewildering variety of social groups, and even recast the colonizeds' senses of time and space of the colonized.[26] These projects dominated the first decades of colonial control, and each involved major transfers of Western scientific thinking, instruments, and practice. New mathematical and statistical techniques were essential for the censuses that rigidified formerly fluid social divisions. Advanced techniques of calculation and measurement and ever more sophisticated European instruments were essential to the operations of the colonial geological investigations and the massive cadastral surveying projects that became the basis for revenue collection and the determination of land ownership in colonized societies.[27]

Roy McLeod's essays on the stages of scientific interaction in the colonial era provide important correctives for many of the problems in the approaches of Basalla, Pyenson, and earlier scholars.[28] Perhaps more than any other scholar, McLeod has worked to uncover the multiple meanings of *colonial* science, and he has underscored the importance of analyzing the two phenomena—colonialism and science—in tandem. His work has been explicitly concerned with the ways in which scientific questions, communities, and procedures were constructed, and the contextual imperatives which shaped this process.[29] His stage-sequence approach to scientific exchanges is more elaborate than Basalla's, and it is explicitly devised to take into account the interplay and flow in *both directions* between metropoles and colonies.

Even though McLeod makes some effort to generalize his findings to the whole of the British empire, the stages of scientific exchange he identifies are based overwhelmingly upon and best suited to patterns exhibited by the history of settler societies. Thus, agency for the colonized invariably involves the scientific discoveries of, or influence exerted by, expatriate Europeans or the descendants of European settlers. With rare exceptions, contextual observations are made with reference to Australia, Canada, and other settler areas, not the tropical dependencies. This approach is most pronounced in the final stages of McLeod's model, which deal with the White Dominions and the decades on either side of 1900. It is clear that the "cooperative" or efficiency-minded science that

McLeod sees as defining for this period, is in effect post-colonial. Thus it was a matter for negotiation and coordination between the quasi-independent White Dominions and a vastly more responsive British metropole. Here and elsewhere in McLeod's overview of the stages of transfer, it is also apparent that even though science is constructed, it can be equated with Western science and its transmission throughout the empire is inexorable. Therefore, like the models of transfer that McLeod strives to improve upon, his formulations of the workings of colonial science cannot accommodate fundamental differences in *types* of colonies, which in turn make for distinct variations in the process of scientific transfer and exchange.

As the work of McLeod, Inkster, and others make clear, the European agents who disseminated Western science in settler societies, such as those in North America and Australia, regarded the receiving areas as *tabula rasas* as far as science was concerned; as zones where no scientific traditions had existed prior to their arrival. If they were known at all, indigenous epistemologies, curing techniques, and explanations for natural phenomena were generally disdained and pushed, along with the peoples and cultures who held to them, to the margins of expanding settler communities. Thus, as Ian Inkster has pointed out, in the settler areas "no explanation of transformation of indigenous science/culture [was] required, as the latter [was] effectively knocked out of the historical process altogether."[30] This meant that the indigenous peoples played little or no part in the transfer of European science from the metropolis to colony; that the agents of this transmission were exclusively educated European migrants and their offspring.

Because the agents of transfer were European or European in descent—many of whom had actually been educated in Europe—there was no possibility of resistance to the spread of European science rooted in indigenous, non-European epistemologies or scientific practice.[31] There were also no racial barriers to the transfer of Western science, though the arrogance of metropolitan *savants* was often a source of considerable annoyance for the colonials. As Roy McLeod has so succinctly put it: "As Europeans moved abroad, as the Empire grew, cultural dependence was an unavoidable, even necessary consequence. One could maintain a place in 'metropolitan' circles by accepting the role allotted by those circles."[32] Dependence meant that most scientists in the settler colonies keyed their investigations to the research agendas and demands of the scientific luminaries in the European metropolis. Particularly in the period that most model builders see as the first phase of scientific diffusion, European scientists in settler colonies were reduced to the status of more or less recognized collectors of samples, species, and quantitative data. Scientists based in Europe were expected to classify and draw theoretical conclusions from the information and exotic flora and fauna that their colonial collaborators sent back from the ends of the earth.[33]

Thus, a broader cultural dependence wrought subordination. But dependence and subordination had very different meanings in settlement areas than in the tropical dependencies. In addition, the different mechanisms by which settler colonies were governed and the very different routes by which they gained increasing autonomy and then independence, as compared to the dependencies, made for striking differences in the diffusion of Western science in each type of colonial setting.

As this rather abbreviated survey of the existing models for the historical analysis of scientific transfer under colonialism makes quite evident, none of them can fully account for the complexities and permutations of the career of Jagadis Chandra Bose. As his experiences and personal interventions make clear, understanding this critical process of cross-cultural transmission requires that we study not only the ideas, instruments, methodologies, and institutional frameworks involved, but also the political, socioeconomic, and cultural contexts in which the interchange was taking place. Contextualization, in turn, makes it imperative that we examine the presuppositions and motivations of the agents on all sides of the transfer process. Because the most useful models devised thus far to account for these exchanges in colonial situations are—whether intentionally or inadvertently—oriented to settler societies, even those that are attentive to the interaction between metropoles and colonies tell us little about the dynamics of the transfer process in tropical dependencies, where a large proportion of the Europeans' colonial subjects lived.

The existence of a prior, ancient, and sophisticated Indian scientific tradition, which the Europeans were forced to recognize suggests the necessity for major modifications in all of the stage-sequence models proposed thus far. Before what Basalla (after J. H. Parry) characterizes as an "age of reconnaissance" driven by European zeal for exploration and material needs, there was an era of mutual curiosity and scientific exchange. Both were prominent features of the initial encounters between the Europeans and the peoples of the Indian subcontinent. In the sixteenth and seventeenth centuries, both Portuguese and Dutch physicians made a serious study of the medicines and cures of Indian *vaidas* and *hakims,* and the Ayurvedic traditions of Indian and Ceylon more generally. Many European physicians readily conceded the superior knowledge of their Indian or Sinhalese counterparts regarding tropical diseases, and they employed local prescriptions and techniques to cure afflictions of Crown or Company employees ranging from snakebite to cholera. In Goa and elsewhere, European government officials, including at one point the Viceroy of the Indies and the Archbishop of the enclave, consulted Indian *vaidas* regarding personal ailments and measures to control epidemics. Indian physicians taught at the Jesuit College in Goa, and won posts in the Portuguese bureaucracy.[34]

Although Indian interest in European medicine was less pronounced, and Ayurvedic techniques were discouraged with mounting vehemence by European officials in the late seventeenth century, serious and sustained exchanges between European and Indian communities in medicine were paralleled by similar interaction in other fields of scientific endeavor, particularly astronomy and mathematics.[35] This pattern of mutual interest, exchange, and often genuine respect is completely at odds with the characterization of the first phase of Western scientific diffusion in all of the models offered thus far. What is true for India is also true for China, Japan, Persia, the Ottoman empire, and other centers of the Islamic world.[36]

Beginning the transfer sequence with the "age of reconnaissance" is, of course, itself a move that is premised on a Eurocentric perspective of the global process of scientific transfer. To follow this is to ignore exchanges among the civilizations of Eurasia and Africa that had been occurring for well over a millennium. The shorter-term view skews the overall process of cross-cultural interaction by excluding patterns of transmission in earlier centuries when "Europe" was mainly a receiving area, and India, China, and the Islamic world the main regions from which scientific discoveries and instruments were being transmitted.[37] Neglect of these earlier developments also distorts by omitting the critical ways in which the earlier transfers of science and technology from Asian civilizations to Europe made the age of reconnaissance itself, and thus Europe's later global hegemony, possible.

It is noteworthy that in constructing an alternative stage sequence for the history of scientific exchange in colonial contexts, Roy McLeod does not deal with the poor fit between Basalla's model (and those that preceded it) and what is actually occurring in what he and other scholars have envisioned as the initial phase of European expansion into overseas areas. Because McLeod's critique and analysis are focused on case evidence from settler colonies, the problems that prior, non-Western scientific traditions and mutual exchanges raise for Basalla's model are not as apparent as they become when Basalla's formulations are applied to areas like India, China, and the Islamic world. This suggests that, at the very least, we need to fashion different typologies of the process of scientific exchange for different types of colonies.[38] The work that has been done to date indicates at least three distinct types: settler colonies, colonial dependencies, and areas—such as China, the Ottoman empire, and the new states of Latin America—that were incorporated into the informal empires of the Western powers in the nineteenth century. In terms of the pattern of scientific exchange, it may also be important to make distinctions within each of these types. For example, we can distinguish between colonial dependencies in which the Europeans acknowledged the existence of a prior scientific tradition and those, such as areas annexed in sub-Saharan Africa or the Pacific islands in the late-nineteenth century, where indigenous epistemologies or curing techniques were dismissed as superstition or witchcraft. These variations suggest that Patrick Pettijean was right to question the possibility of a single workable framework of analysis for scientific exchanges in the highly differentiated European colonial world.[39]

In the last decade or so, something of a consensus has emerged among scholars of colonial science regarding the extractive, Europe-oriented nature of the scientific exchanges among metropoles and colonies in the early centuries of Western overseas expansion. The flow of specimens and information from the end of the seventeenth century, when Dutch administrators with naturalist inclinations had begun to show great interest in the plant and animal life of the Indian subcontinent and elsewhere, suggests that scientific investigation in the colonies in what might best be seen as the age of the collectors was overwhelmingly oriented to the needs of the European metropoles. Individuals, who were usually self-taught, amateur naturalists and who had gone out to the colonies as Crown or Company officials, missionaries or traders, avidly sought to gain esteem as the overseas correspondents of scientific societies in London, Paris, and Amsterdam or as valued collectors for the cabinets and "exotic" gardens of prominent European naturalists. By the late eighteenth century, India had become a vast storehouse for collectors and classifiers of natural phenomena. In the late eighteenth and early nineteenth centuries, thousands of specimens of Indian insects, animals, and plants—dead and alive—were shipped from India to be studied and viewed in the gardens of Kew and the laboratories and zoos of London and other European cities. These and other "exotic" creatures found in the subcontinent were described and exquisitely depicted in lavishly illustrated volumes that did much to advance the study of botany and zoology in European centers of learning.[40]

Information gathered in related scientific fields, such as astrological and meteorological readings taken from locations throughout the globe, was also funneled back to Europe. In many cases, this gathering, classification, and systematizing of information not only advanced scientific knowledge, but also bolstered the enterprise of European overseas exploration and colonization. Botanical discoveries, for example, drew attention to natural resources that might be exploited, and astronomical and meteorological data was put to good use by the naval forces that were central to European expansion in this era.[41]

Although the Europeans' needs and their agents overseas had clearly made them the driving force behind the scientific exchanges that occurred with their colonies in the late eighteenth and nineteenth centuries, the focus in the stage-sequence models of Basalla and McLeod on European activities obscures the important roles that agents in the tropical dependencies played in these enterprises. In the early centuries of European-Indian exchange, for example, the receptivity of the Indian ruling classes to European weapons, instruments, and scientific learning was critical for their introduction into the subcontinent. As we have seen, at the local level Indian *vaidas* and pundits were as essential as were the European officials and missionaries aspiring to be *savants* in facilitating scientific interaction. The work of European naturalists would have been difficult, if not impossible, without the assistance of local guides. Indian artists were extensively employed in preparing the illustrations for the great compendiums of Indian flora and fauna that were among the chief productions of colonial scientists in this era.[42] In this regard, European scientific inquiry was facilitated by longstanding Indian traditions of miniature painting, including that which flourished under the Mughal rulers in the sixteenth and seventeenth centuries, in which flowers, birds, and other forms of wildlife were depicted with exacting precision by indigenous artists.[43]

All of these developments suggest the aptness of the emphasis placed by Basalla and McLeod on the extractive or production-oriented nature of the scientific knowledge and technology that the British transmitted to India in the early phases of interaction.[44] Here there were strong parallels between the settlement colonies, where the "demon of practicality"[45] reigned in scientific endeavors, and India and other non-settler dependencies. Basalla is also correct in arguing that British interest in natural history remained high, but he fails to allow for shifts in focus within this rather large configuration of fields. As the great expansion of the operations of the Geological Survey of India illustrates, geological exploration, and related fields like hydrology, gained in importance at the expense of zoology and astronomy that had been so prominent in the early centuries of European contact with India. Because it was often closely linked with the need to improve or discover commercial and industrial plant strains, botany rose steadily in importance in the colonies. By the second half of the nineteenth century, strong institutional linkages had developed among the staffs of botanical gardens in India, Kew in London, and other parts of the empire that were aimed at enhancing the extractive potential of individual colonized regions and British dependencies as a whole.[46]

Active Indian involvement in the process of scientific and technological transfer was also evidenced by the patronage given in the first decades of the nineteenth century by Indian rulers, such as the Nawabs of Oudh and Nizams of Hyderabad, to European astronomers, and the attempts by these indigenous rulers to establish observatories equipped with Western instruments. At other social levels, members of the rising professional and mercantile elites of Calcutta frequently visited and financially supported the botanical gardens that had been established at Sibpur in 1787, and Hindu and Muslim scholars wrote treatises about the findings of famed European scientists. Indian educators and princes in a number of locales also established printing presses to publish translations of European scientific works in Indian languages. By the mid-nineteenth century, Indian financiers, princes, and professionals were funding technical schools, colleges, and professorships oriented to the sciences, and presses to disseminate both Western and Indian scientific treatises.[47]

The processes by which European scientific works were translated into the Indian vernacular languages was a pivotal enterprise that can tell us a good deal about the ways in which scientific epistemologies are transmitted across cultures. Here again, India's prior tradition of scientific learning proved critical in a number of ways. It inspired some of the most innovative colonial educators of the nineteenth century, both British and Indian, to employ Indian scientific texts to bridge the epistemological differences that their Indian students needed to negotiate in order to master European scientific theories and methodologies. On the British side, for example, Lancelot Wilkinson, a Sanskrit scholar and Assistant Resident in the princely state of Bhopal, concluded that despite recent European advances, much of value remained in Indian scientific treatises, such as the

*Siddhantas.* In the mid-nineteenth century, Wilkinson used these and other indigenous text to introduce his Indian students to scientific thinking in a number of fields, including astronomy and trigonometry.[48] Wilkinson's Indian counterparts, most notably Bal Shastri Jambhekar and Master Ramchanda, made a similar use of the Indian scientific classics, both to assist their students in their efforts to master Western epistemologies and approaches and to revitalize Indian scientific traditions in and of themselves.[49]

At other levels of the process of scientific transfer, thousands of Indian assistants were essential for the geological investigations and cadastral surveys carried out in the nineteenth century under the direction of British officials in the Geological Survey of India and the Department of Revenue and Agriculture. They were equally prominent in the cartographic and meteorological operations the British undertook in the subcontinent. These massive projects were in fact one of the major channels by which Western scientific ideas and techniques were introduced into India. Through the technical education that they received as part of the preparation for work on geological or cadastral surveys and their on-the-job training, substantial numbers of Indians became familiar with Western scientific procedures and instruments.[50]

Indian traditions of naturalistic painting and Indian aptitudes for survey operations, which were noted by numerous British officials,[51] suggest another critical oversight in all of the models of scientific transfer. None of them provide for serious consideration of the effects of the non-Western host colonial cultures into which European science was being disseminated, and the ways in which indigenous epistemologies (including in the case of India, ancient scientific traditions) and cultural predispositions shaped this process in different colonial settings. Indian skills as census takers and revenue assessors, for example, can—at the risk of essentializing—be linked in part to a longstanding Indian fascination with classification (as reflected in Hindu and Buddhist philosophical systems and treatises on subjects as diverse as Sanskrit grammar and the art of making love), and to the sophistication of the mathematical systems and techniques devised by the peoples of the subcontinent.

British awareness of these traditions and aptitudes played a major role in the policies they pursued with respect to scientific and technological transfers, and nowhere was this more apparent than in the colonizers' approach to technical training and advanced education for Indians in the sciences. As eighteenth-century officials of the East Indian Company, such as Sir William Jones, found to their delight, in astronomy, mathematics, and a number of other areas, Brahmanic India had been a fecund source of scientific knowledge and techniques of investigation for contemporary and later civilizations in Western Asia and the Mediterranean basin. Thus, rather than the *tabula rasa* that Western carriers of science saw in areas of extensive European settlement, India was clearly recognized as a receiving area with an ancient and impressive scientific tradition of its own.[52] Evidence of past achievements played a critical role in British decisions in the first half of the nineteenth century to promote both English-language education and advanced instruction in the sciences, albeit in the case of the latter for very limited numbers of Indians.[53] From the early 1800s, these policies found strong support from Indian advocates of English-language education at all levels through college. Often citing India's great scientific achievements in the past, leaders of the emerging Western-educated middle classes voiced confidence in the capacity of Indian students to master the most demanding of Western scientific disciplines. Well into the twentieth century, they celebrated the transfer of Western scientific learning as one of the chief benefits of British colonial rule.[54]

The power differential that the Industrial Revolution had created between Great Britain and India had consequences far beyond political consolidation and the expansion of markets and resource extraction. It transformed early British interest in, even admiration for, Indian scientific thinking and modes of handicraft production to scorn. With rare exceptions, British administrators, scholars, and technicians concluded that the Indians had little to offer in these areas. As a result, advanced scientific and technical education was definitely channeled and constricted, if not blatantly suppressed, by conscious colonial policy. In addition, the scientific learning of the indigenous peoples was shunted aside or contemptuously dismissed as superstition-ridden, outdated, and simply wrong. Like modernization theorists in the second half of the twentieth century, British officials and missionary educators were convinced that the sooner Indian epistemologies and technology were supplanted by superior imports from the West, the more rapidly the subcontinent could be raised up from the backward and benighted state into which it had fallen. In the guise of the credo of the civilizing mission and in accordance with the tenets of scientific racism, Western scientific and technological superiority was incorporated into nineteenth-century ideologies of European colonial hegemony. As Bose's educational experience indicates, extensive technical training and advanced education in the sciences continued to be available to small numbers of Indian students. But in the colonizers' view, only Western science mattered, and advanced training for the handful of gifted Indian students would require attendance at a British, or at least a European, university.[55]

Active Indian involvement in the processes by which Western science and technology were transmitted to the subcontinent also encompassed activities that promoted the professionalization of the scientific disciplines (as that status was understood in the West), within the subcontinent. As early as the last decades of the eighteenth century, British officials, led by the indefatigable Sir William Jones, had founded organizations devoted to the study of Indian learning, including in the sciences. Though Indians were rarely invited to participate—and never as full members—in the earliest meetings of the Asiatic Society,[56] contacts and exchanges between individual Europeans and Indian pundits were quite common. Beginning in the early 1830s, Indians began to be admitted, sometimes as full members, into the sessions of the Asiatic Society of Bengal, an early focal point for humanistic and scientific investigations. By the last decades of the nineteenth century, Indian scholars were contributing a significant proportion of the papers published by the Society and other scholarly associations, including a number devoted to the dissemination of Western scientific knowledge. Europeans and Indians also came together in support of the botanical gardens, museums, and educational institutions that were soon to be key centers for the diffusion of Western scientific thinking and invention.[57]

These manifestations of the institutionalization of Western science in India itself run counter to Basalla's contention that in phases I and II colonies lacked the scientific societies that were so critical to the dissemination of new discoveries in Europe. More broadly they call into question his assumption that even scientifically-minded Europeans in the colonies were totally dependent on the European metropolises for publications, instruments, labs, and even intellectual stimulation. Substantial Indian involvement in Western-initiated and directed scientific endeavors also underscores the fact that typologies of transfer, such as those proposed by Basalla and McLeod, do not take into account the responses of the colonized, much less their initiatives in the early phases each identifies. There is no place in their models for analysis of the effects of the process of diffusion on indigenous epistemological systems or scientific techniques—unless they prove to be tradition-bound obstacles to the introduction of Western ideas and technology.[58] The great emphasis that French *savants* and prominent British administrator-scholars themselves placed on the recovery and study of Indian scientific learning from the late eighteenth century through the nineteenth century[59] demonstrates the significance of this omission if our aim is to understand scientific interchange between metropoles and colonies. But the persistence of indigenous epistemologies and, for example, Ayurvedic medical techniques, and their incorporation by the end of the nineteenth century into broader critiques of Western civilization, on the one hand, and into genuinely innovative approaches to scientific research, on the other, suggests equally fundamental limitations of the available models of scientific transfer.

Recent research has shown that though British officials exhibited increasing disdain for Indian science as British domination in the subcontinent became more pronounced in the nineteenth century, Indian learning and practices displayed great resilience in a number of scientific pursuits. British residents in India continued to consult indigenous physicians and resort to Ayurvedic cures, which were overwhelmingly favored over Western allopathic alternatives by the vast majority of the Indian population. Until the 1830s, Indian Ayurvedic texts continued to be taught in East India Company supported schools, and through much of the rest of the nineteenth century British officials recruited indigenous physicians who employed Ayurvedic techniques to help in inoculating against smallpox and controlling epidemic diseases such as cholera.[60] Well into the nineteenth century, British administrator-scholars of the caliber of H. T. Colebrooke continued the serious study and translation of Indian scientific texts, and British travelers and technicians wrote admiringly of aspects of Indian technology and recommended Indian techniques be adapted to British manufacture in areas as vital as textiles and ceramics. A minority of British officials continued to urge support for the teaching of Indian sciences as late as the 1850s.[61]

Even after the mid-nineteenth century, when British administrators turned decisively against the advice of Indian physicians in combating epidemics and the use of Indian texts for scientific education in government-funded schools, Indian epistemologies and procedures survived, and even flourished, in many fields. Late in the nineteenth century, for example, Indians continued to prefer indigenous variolation techniques to European-style vaccination for protection against smallpox. Though heavily recruited by the British for government-sponsored vaccination campaigns, Indian *tikadars* or inoculators were reluctant to give up traditional procedures. Ayurvedic physicians borrowed Western prescriptions and practice where it proved advantageous, and even incorporated Western-style advertising and mass production techniques to increase the market for their pharmaceutical products.[62]

As David Arnold has argued, by the late nineteenth century the spread of Western science, principally in the guise of allopathic medicine, had become directly linked to government schemes to enhance the Raj's control over the subject peoples of the Indian subcontinent. Campaigns against endemic diseases, such as smallpox and malaria, and especially cholera and plague epidemics, resulted in interventions into the personal lives of the colonized peoples in both urban and rural areas that were unprecedented and considered draconian by indigenous leaders and the populace at large.[63] By the late 1800s, inoculation and anti-epidemic campaigns were often transformed by government insensitivity and overreach, and indigenous resistance, into focal points for growing nationalist opposition to British colonial rule. Nationalist leaders also championed the revival of indigenous scientific traditions and technologies, most famously in Gandhi's advocacy of *charkha* production, but also in less publicized projects such as the establishment of schools for the training of Ayurvedic physicians.[64]

However important symbolically, nationalist support for the revival of indigenous cures and handicrafts was overshadowed by mainstream sentiment in the Congress party that favored the accelerated introduction of Western science and technology into the subcontinent. From the late 1800s, when India began to move toward what Basalla terms the independent or national phase of scientific interaction with the West, prominent figures in the Congress Party lamented the slow pace of industrialization under British rule. Drawing heavily on British precedents, M. G. Ranade, G. V. Joshi, Dinshaw Wacha, and others called for the establishment of technical institutes, the upgrading of medical education, and higher levels of Indian employment in scientific and technical posts. Congress leaders blamed colonial rule for India's scientific and technical underdevelopment and argued that self-rule would bring vast improvements in these areas. In the early 1900s, industrial exhibitions were held in conjunction with the annual Congress Party sessions, aimed at popularizing the benefits of "modern" science and technology. In 1904, a special association for the Advancement of Scientific and Industrial Education of India was founded with Congress' support. Even arch-traditionalist Congress politicians, such as B. G. Tilak, argued for a blend of indigenous and Western science as the basis for Indian social and economic revitalization. After 1905, the

Swadeshi movement gave added impetus to the drive for industrialization, which was reflected in an emphasis on scientific and technical education in the independent schools set up under the auspices of the National Education movement in the years that followed.[65]

Although Indian industrialists, at times with the cooperation of the colonial authorities, established a number of advanced research institutes in the decades after World War I,[66] the Western-derived sciences in India actually become more dependent on Great Britain and Europe in the early twentieth century.[67] In fact, given the hegemonic and universalizing tendencies of Western science, it is hard to know what Basalla's notion of "national" science means. But, if the Indian experience is any gauge, the development of an *independent* scientific tradition is not one of its attributes. Despite steady growth in the size and sophistication of the Indian scientific establishment after World War I, applied scientific pursuits, very often linked to resource extraction, continued to be much more strongly supported than original research and theoretical investigation.

Despite these constrictions, India produced a number of scientists of international stature who conducted highly original and theoretical research. These individuals included both J. C. Bose and C. V. Raman, who became the first Indian scientist to win a Nobel prize in 1922. Their careers, though admittedly exceptional, suggest that colonial science was not necessarily derivative and applied, though recent research has demonstrated that these were clearly the norms.[68] As the struggles of all of the Indian pioneers in Western scientific research amply illustrate, the achievements of colonial scientists had to be won in the face of government policies that fostered racial discrimination, poor funding, and inadequate equipment. Very often their successes depended on connections to research institutions and scientific societies in the metropoles. As Bose's reliance on the support of Lord Kelvin early in his research career illustrates, winning the backing of prominent scientists in the metropole also proved critical to success, if not survival.[69] Ironically, some of the most innovative and independent scientific work done by Indians in this period, such as the vitalist experiments on metals and plants carried out by Bose, was strongly influenced by indigenous epistemologies that have no place in the models of transfer proposed to date.[70]

The critical and diverse roles played by Indians in promoting, modifying, and resisting the interchange of science and technology between metropole and colony underscores Ian Inkster's insistence that workable models of these processes must combine "local imperatives and colonial relations."[71] Again, the quality and mix of these factors at each level is likely to differ considerably between colonies, and especially between different *types* of colonies. In addition, in Basalla's formulation the spread of Western science occurs only between the European core and the undifferentiated colonized peripheries. But as Roy McLeod has observed,[72] this perspective rules out the possibility of significant exchanges *between* colonies which, as the histories of colonial agriculture and forestry/environmentalism amply demonstrate, have occurred since the earliest decades of European overseas colonization.[73]

As David Arnold has observed with regard to the history of medicine in colonial India, scientific development, according to Basalla's conceptualization, comes to be equated with the imposition of Western knowledge, institutions, and practice, rather than with a process of exchange and interaction between colonizer and colonized.[74] One is also left to assume that Western scientific and technological paths to development will inevitably triumph over the Indian alternatives that modernization theorists judged obsolescent in the 1950s and 1960s, accepting as they did the British colonizers' essentialist vision of India as spiritually rather than materially oriented, mystical, emotional, and irrational.[75]

Neglect of the agency of non-Western colonized peoples and the privileging of the Western scientific tradition render the available models of scientific transfer incapable of taking into account the fundamental critiques of Western science and the European path to development through industrialization that are a critical facet of British-Indian scientific interaction from the last decades of the nineteenth century. Indian thinkers of the stature of Vivekananda, Rabindranath Tagore, and Aurobindo Ghosh fashioned both impressive critiques of Western scientific and technological imports and precedents and spirited defenses of Indian epistemologies, values, and achievements in both the spiritual and material realms. As we have seen, both of these causes were taken up by P. C. Bose, who urged his Indian students to work for a grand synthesis between Indian and European scientific epistemologies—a task for which he believed the Indians to be culturally predisposed.[76] In the first decades of the twentieth century, Mohandas Gandhi and other Indian thinkers worked the diverse strands of these critiques into a full-fledged alternative approach to social and economic organization, inventiveness, work patterns, resource use, and social organization.[77]

In view of the clear limits in terms of resource exhaustion, environmental degradation, and social inequity of both major Western paths to development—market-capitalist and Marxist socialist command economies—the neglect of this resistance to the Western industrial juggernaut and to the alternative approaches to development it has generated may prove to be the most critical shortcoming of all of the models of scientific transfer formulated to date. It may be that the direction of the process of transfer that these assume will be reversed; that approaches to the natural world, social organization, and economic well-being pioneered by thinkers and leaders in the former colonies, such as Bose, Tagore, and Gandhi, will have much to offer the beleaguered societies of the post-industrial world.

NOTES

1. Bloch's arguments "Pour une histoire comparée des société européenes," were first presented in a paper for the Sixth International Congress of Historical Sciences in Oslo in 1928. The essay was subsequently published in a number of English translations, perhaps the most accessible being that by J. E. Anderson, in Bloch's edited volume, *Land and Work in Medieval Europe: Selected Papers by Marc Block* (New York, 1919), 44–81.

2. "The Case for Comparing Histories," *American Historical Review* 85, 4 (1980), esp. 770–72, 775.

3. See, for examples, the seminal essays in *Millennial Dreams in Action,* edited by Sylvia Thrupp (New York, 1970); the collection edited by Roger Owen and Bob Sutcliff on *Studies in the History of Imperialism* (London, 1972); and James C. Scott and Benjamin Kerkvliet's volume *Everyday Forms of Resistance in Southeast Asia* (London, 1986). On warfare in global encounters there is no better place to start than Inga Clendinnen, "'Fierce and Unnatural Cruelty': Cortés and the Conquest of Mexico," *Representations* 33, 1 (1991): 65–100; or the contributions to *War in the Tribal Zone: Expanding States and Indigenous Warfare,* R. Brian Ferguson and Neil L. Whitehead, eds. (Santa Fe, N.Mex., 1992).

4. E. Genovese, "The Treatment of Slaves in Different Countries: Problems in the Applications of the Comparative Method," in L. Foner and E. Genovese, eds., *Slavery in the Americas* (New York, 1969); S. Baily, "Cross-Cultural Comparison and the Writing of Migration History: Some Thoughts on How to Study Italians in the New World," in, Virginia Yans, ed., *Immigration Reconsidered: History, Society and Politics* (New York, 1990).

5. "Bringing Ideas and Agency Back In: Representation and the Comparative Approach to World History," in, Philip Pomper et al., eds., *World History: Ideologies, Structures, and Identities* (Oxford, 1998), 81–104.

6. I. S. Lobb, "Physical Science in the Calcutta University," *Calcutta Review* 106 (1871): 326.

7. This account of Bose's family background and career is based primarily on

S. N. Basu's *Jagadis Chandra Bose* (New Delhi, 1970); Monoranjan Gupta, *Jagadis Chandra Bose: A Biography;* and the excellent summary in David Kopf, *The Brahmo Samaj and the Shaping of the Modern Indian Mind* (Princeton, 1979).

8. Quoted in Kopf, *Brahmo Samaj,* 73.

9. Quoted in *Basu,* J. C. Bose, 13.

10. "From the Voiced to the Unvoiced," 4 Feb. 1916 (Calcutta, 1916).

11. "The Spread of Western Science," *Science* 156 (May 1967): 611.

12. Respectively, "The New World as a Source of Science for Europe," *Actes du IX Congrès International d'Histoire de Sciences* (Paris, 1960), 96–130; and "Science in Australia, Canada, and the United States: Some Comparative Remarks," *Proceedings of the 10th International Congress of the History of Science* (Ithaca, N.Y., 1962), 179–96.

13. "Science, Discovery, and the Colonial World, Madrid, 25–28 June 1991," *Isis* 83 (1992): 283–84; and a personal communication from Marcos Cueto of the Instituto Veneozolano de Investigaciones Cientifica.

14. See, for examples, Alberto Elena, "Models of European Scientific Expansion: The Ottoman Empire as a Source of Evidence," 259–67; and V. V. Krishna, "The Colonial 'Model' and the Emergence of National Science in India: 1876–1920," in, Patrick Petitjean, Catherine Jami, and Anne Marie Moulin, eds., *Science and Empires: Historical Studies about Scientific Development and European Expansion* (Dordrecht, 1992), 57–72; David Arnold, *Colonizing the Body: State Medicine and Epidemic Disease in Nineteenth-Century India* (Berkeley, 1993), esp. 15–18; and Merle Jacob, review of Petitjean et al.'s, *Science and Empire,* in *Science, Technology, and Human Values* 19 (1994): 116.

15. Patrick Petitjean, "Sciences et Empires: un thème promètteur, des enjeux cruciaux," in, Petitjean et al., *Science and Empire,* 6.

16. Ian Inkster places special emphasis on this problem in his essay on "Scientific Enterprise and the Colonial 'Model': Observations on the Australian Experience in Colonial Context," *Social Studies of Science* 15 (1985): 687–88.

17. Inkster, ibid., 688–89.

18. A conclusion shared by Roshdi Rashed on the basis of his comparative examination of two case examples of scientific transfer within Islamic areas that came under the informal imperial influence of the European powers. Cf., "Science Classique et Science Moderne," in Petitjean et al., *Science and Empire,* 21.

19. Both Roy MacLeod and Ian Inkster have stressed the many questions raised by what Inkster characterizes as the "Whiggish" cast of Basalla's formulations. See respectively, "On Visiting the 'Moving Metropolis': Reflections on the Architecture of Imperial Science," *Historical Records of Australian Science* 5 (1982): 5; and Inkster, "Scientific Enterprise and the Colonial Model," 687.

20. Over the past two or three decades a very large corpus of historical, sociological, and philosophical works exploring both specific examples and broader theoretical issues relating to the social construction of science has developed. For a superb introduction to both the larger questions and key studies in various disci-

plines, see Steven Shapin, "History of Science and Its Sociological Reconstructions," *History of Science* 20 (1982): 157–211. For thoughtful reflections on some of the central epistemological and ethical dimensions of this approach, see the contributions to Everett Mendlesohn, Peter Weingart, and Richard Whitney, eds., *The Social Production of Scientific Knowledge* (Dordrecht, Holland, 1977). "Third World" perspectives on some of the sources and uses of Western scientific knowledge can be found in J. P. S. Uberoi, *Science and Culture* (Delhi, 1978); and Ashis Nandy, ed., *Science, Hegemony & Violence.* Interestingly, Basalla's recent work on technology emphasizes historical contexts and links between inventions in advancing the evolutionary development of machines. See *The Evolution of Technology* (Cambridge, England, 1988).

21. For an extremely revealing study of the premium placed on Western scientific learning in one of the most advanced civilizations confronted by the Europeans, see D. W. Y. Kwok, *Scientism in Chinese Thought, 1900–1950* (New Haven, 1965).

22. *Cultural Imperialism and Exact Sciences: German Expansion Overseas, 1900–1930* (New York, 1985); *Empire of Reason: Exact Sciences in Indonesia, 1840–1940* (Leiden, 1989); and *Civilizing Mission: Exact Sciences and French Overseas Expansion, 1830–1940* (Baltimore, Md., 1993).

23. Cf. "Pure Learning and Political Economy: Science and European Expansion in the Age of Imperialism," in, R. P. W. Visser et al., eds., *New Trends in the History of Science* (Amsterdam, 1989), 209–78.

24. See, for example, Paolo Palladino and Michael Worboys, "Science and Imperialism," *Isis* 84 (1993): 91–102.

25. *Civilizing Mission,* xiii.

26. The colonizer's obsession with codification and classification has been extensively explored in the writings of Bernard Cohn. See, for example, the essays in his *An Anthropologist among the Historians* (Delhi, 1988). On reworking conceptions of time and space, see Michael Adas, *Machines as the Measure of Men: Science, Technology and Ideologies of Western Dominance* (Ithaca, N.Y., 1989), ch. 5.

27. On the history of these projects in the Indian Empire, see Deepak Kumar, "Economic Compulsions and the Geological Survey of India," *Indian Journal of the History of Science* 17 (1982): 289–300; B. V. Subbarayappa, "Western Science in India up to the End of the Nineteenth Century," in D. M. Bose et al., eds., *A Concise History of Science in India* (New Delhi, 1971), 507–14; and Satpal Sangwan, *Science, Technology and Colonisation: An Indian Experience 1757–1857* (Delhi, 1991), 35–39. On the complex connections between geological exploration and colonial expansion more generally, see Robert A. Stafford, *Scientist of Empire: Sir Roderick Murchison, Scientific Exploration and Victorian Imperialism* (Cambridge, England, 1989).

28. "Moving Metropolis," 1–16; and "Passages in Imperial Science: From Empire to Commonwealth," *Journal of World History* 4 (1993): 117–50.

29. These questions were already evident in McLeod's early essay on "Scientific

Advice for British India: Imperial Perceptions and Administrative Goals, 1898–1923," *Modern Asian Studies* 9 (1975), 343–84.

30. "Scientific Enterprise and the Colonial 'Model,'" 687.

31. The anthropological study of indigenous cultures in the settlement areas has revealed apparently viable alternatives to Western scientific epistemologies and practice that in recent decades have been worked into the dominant culture through channels as diverse as the writings of leading ecologists, the marketing of herbal medicines, and the popularity of films, such as "The Last Wave," and "Where the Green Ants Dream."

32. "Moving Metropolis," 4.

33. Fleming, "Science in Australia, Canada, and the United States," 182–84; and Cohen, "New World as a Source of Science," esp. 118–23.

34. See, for examples John M. Figueiredo, "Ayurvedic Medicine in Goa According to European Sources in the Sixteenth and Seventeenth Centuries," *Bulletin of the History of Medicine* 58 (1984): 225–35; and A. De Zoysa and C. D. Palitharatna, "Models of European Scientific Expansion: A Comparative Description of 'Classical' Medical Science at the Time of the Introduction of European Medical Science to Sri Lanka, and Subsequent Development to the Present," in, Pettijean et al., *Science and Empires*, 111–20.

35. Adas, *Machines as the Measure*, 100–102.

36. For useful introductions to early European scientific interaction with these other areas, see the essays by Roshdi Rashed, Ekmeleddin Ihsanoglu, Catherine Jami, and Alberto Elena, in, Petitjean et al., *Science and Empire*.

37. For the most recent overview of this process, see Toby E. Huff, *The Rise of Early Modern Science: Islam, China and the West* (Cambridge, 1993).

38. This point has been made with reference to colonial differences generally by Michael Worboys in his essay, "Science and Colonial Empire, 1895–1940," in, Depak Kumar, ed., *Science and Empire: Essays in Indian Context* (Delhi, 1991), 13.

39. Petitjean, "Sciences et Empires," 8–9.

40. Subbarayappa, "Western Science in India," 530–37; and Sangwan, *Science and Colonisation*, ch. 2.

41. S. M. Razaullah Ansari, "The Establishment of Observatories and the Socioeconomic Conditions of Scientific Work in Nineteenth-Century India," *Indian Journal of the History of Science* 13 (1976), esp. 62–65; and S. N. Sen, "The Character of the Introduction of Western Science in India during the Eighteenth and Nineteenth Centuries," *Indian Journal of the History of Science* 3 (1966), 114–15.

42. Satpal Sangwan, "Indian Response to European Science and Technology 1757–1857," *British Journal of the History of Science* 21 (1988), 214; and Mildred Archer, "India and Natural History: The Role of the East India Company, 1785–1858," *History Today* 9 (1959), 736–38, 740–41.

43. On the Mughal miniature tradition, see Percy Brown, *Indian Painting Under the Mughals* (Oxford, 1924).

44. This emphasis has been confirmed by the more recent research of a number of Indian historians of science. See, for examples, Anis Alam, "Imperialism and Science," *Social Scientist* 65 (1977), 5; Deepak Kumar, "Patterns of Colonial Science in India," *Indian Journal of the History of Science* 15 (1980): 104–13; and Sangwan, *Colonialism and Science,* 147–48.

45. Fleming, "Science in Australia, Canada, and the United States," 181–82, 189–91.

46. Though anchored in a rather problematic, structural overview of the colonial order, Lucille Brockway's *Science and Colonial Expansion: The Role of the British Royal Botanic Gardens* (New York, 1979) examines some of these connections. Much of Brockway's work has recently been superseded by Richard Grove's *Green Imperialism: Colonial Expansion, Tropical Island Edens and the Origins of Environmentalism, 1600–1860* (New York, 1995); and the contributions to John MacKenzie, ed., *Imperialism and the Natural World* (Manchester, 1990). For a recent and highly informative micro-study of these linkages, see Michael A. Osborne, *Nature, the Exotic, and the Science of French Colonialism* (Bloomington, 1994).

47. Sangwan, *Science and Colonialism,* 131–36, and "Indian Response," 229–31; Ansari, "Establishment of Observatories," 65–66; Kumar, "Culture of Science," 197–203; and Krisna, "Indian Scientific Community," 93–96. Gyan Prakash has insightfully explored the ways in which the British deployed institutions, particularly museums, and special exhibitions to project the wonders (and power) of the colonizers' science and technology to their Indian subjects. See, *Another Reason: Science and the Imagination of Modern India* (Princton, 1999), 17–48.

48. See his essay "On the Use of the Siddhantas in the Work of Native Education," *Journal of the Asiatic Society of Bengal* 34 (1834): 504–19.

49. Deepak Kumar, "The 'Culture' of Science and Colonial Culture, India 1820–1920," *British Journal of the History of Science* 29 (1996), 198–200; Adas, *Machines as the Measure,* 283–84; and, for a rather different view of Wilkinson and his project, Prakash, *Another Reason,* 64– 65.

50. Sangwan, "Indian Response," 213; and "Reordering the Earth: The Emergence of Geology as a Scientific Discipline in Colonial India," *The Indian Economic and Social History Review* 31 (1994), esp. 305–8; and Deepak Kumar, "Problems in Scientific Administration: A Study of the Scientific Surveys in British India 1757–1900," in Petitjean et al., *Science and Empires,* 274– 78.

51. Deepak Kumar, "Racial Discrimination and Science in Nineteenth-Century India," *Indian Economic and Social History Review* 19 (1983): 65–66, 69–73.

52. On the British "discovery" of the early scientific achievements of Indian civilization, see S. N. Mukherjee, *Sir William Jones* (Cambridge, England, 1968); and Adas, *Machines as the Measure,* esp. 95–108.

53. Adas, *Machines as the Measure,* 275–84.

54. See, for examples, the 1823 petition for the introduction of English education by Rammohun Roy, reprinted in J. C. Ghose, ed., *The English Works of Raja*

*Rammohun Roy* (Calcutta, 1885), vol. 1, 469–73; and K. M. Bannerjea, "The Proper Place of Oriental Literature in Indian Collegiate Education," *Proceedings of the Bethune Society,* Feb. (1868), 149, 154, 159. For a good overview of these educational efforts in the early nineteenth century, see Sangwan, *Science and Colonisation,* 122–23; and in the late 1800s and early 1900s, Shiv Visvanathan, *Organizing for Science* (Delhi, 1985), 17–23.

55. Adas, *Machines as the Measure,* 166–77, 292–318, 327–38; Kumar, "Discrimination and Science," passim; and Prakash, *Another Reason,* 64–71.

56. Sangwan, *Science and Colonialism,* 149.

57. See, for discussions of these trends, Visvanathan, *Organizing for Science,* 17–18, 26–28; and A. Rahman, "Problems and Perspectives," in, Deepak Kumar, ed., *Science and Empire: Essays in Indian Context* (Delhi, 1991), 2–3.

58. Basalla, "Spread of Western Science," 617.

59. For samples from the late eighteenth century, see Jean-Sylvain Bailly, *Traité de l'astronomie indienne et orientale* (Paris, 1787); the early volumes of the *Asiatik Researches;* and Sir William Jones, *Eleven Discourses* (Calcutta, 1783). For a mid-nineteenth century example, see "The Algebra of the Hindus," *The Calcutta Review* 4 (1845): 536–60.

60. Brahmananda Gupta, "Indigenous Medicine in Nineteenth- and Twentieth-Century Bengal, in, Charles Leslie, ed., *Asian Medical Systems: A Comparative Study* (Berkeley, 1976), 369–70; and David Arnold, "Cholera and Colonialism in British India," *Past and Present* 113 (1986): 135–37; and "Smallpox and Colonial Medicine in Nineteenth-Century India," in David Arnold, ed., *Imperial Medicine and Indigenous Societies* (Manchester, 1988), 57–59.

61. Arnold, *Colonizing the Body,* 44–54; Adas, *Machines as the Measure,* 95–108, 283–84; and Dharampal, *Indian Science and Technology in the Eighteenth Century* (Delhi, 1971).

62. Arnold, "Smallpox and Colonial Medicine," 53–62; Gupta, "Indigenous Medicine," 372–75; and Visvanathan, *Organizing for Science,* 16–17.

63. "Cholera and Colonialism," 138–47; "Touching the Body: Perspectives on the Indian Plague," in, Ranajit Guha, ed., *Subaltern Studies V* (Delhi, 1987), esp. 56–60; and the introduction to Arnold, ed., *Indigenous Medicine,* 10, 17. For similar arguments relating to colonial rule in other areas, see Megan Vaughn, *Curing Their Ills: Colonial Power and African Illness* (Cambridge, England, 1991); and Renaldo Ileto, "Cholera and the Origins of the American Sanitary Order in the Philippines," in, David Arnold, ed., *Imperial Medicine and Indigenous Societies* (Manchester, 1988), 125–48.

64. Arnold, "Smallpox and Colonial Medicine," 55; and "Touching the Body," 84–88; Gupta, "Indigenous Medicine," 375–76; and Visvanathan, *Organizing for Science,* 23–25, 34–36.

65. Jagdish N. Sinha, "Science and the Indian National Congress," in, Kumar,

ed., *Science and Empire,* 160–81; Ira Klein, "Indian Nationalism and Anti-Industrialization: The Roots of Gandhian Economics," *South Asia* 3 (1973): 93–104; V. V. Krishna, "The Colonial 'Model' and the Emergence of National Science in India: 1876–1920," in, Pettijean et al., *Science and Empires,* 62–65; and Arnold, "Touching the Body," 84–85.

66. For a detailed analysis of these efforts, see Visvanathan, *Organizing for Science,* esp. chaps. 3 and 4.

67. The tensions between metropolitan and colonial scientific institutions and communities are explored in detail in Roy M. MacLeod, "Scientific Advice for British India," 343–84.

68. In his recent study, *Science and the Raj, 1857–1905* (Delhi, 1995), Deepak Kumar argues that government policies did much to insure that the scientific work allotted to Indians and expatriate European scientists was derivative, supplemental, and applied. But Kumar allows that there were important exceptions which led to major scientific breakthroughs made by scientists working in India (see esp. 60, 71, 111, 119, 170, 176–78). For case examples on original research conducted in varying colonial contexts, see I. J. Catanach, "Plague and the Tensions of Empire: India 1896–1918," in, Arnold, ed., *Imperial Medicine,* 162–63; Arnold, *Colonizing the Body,* 22–23; and Cohen, "New World as a Source of Science," 116–20.

69. Krishna, "Emergence of National Science," 57–59, 65–69; MacLeod, "Scientific Advice for British India," 343–84; C. Ray, *Life and Experiences of a Bengali Chemist* (Calcutta, 1932), 59, 68, 131–32; and J. C. Bagal, *Pramatha Nath Bose* (New Delhi, 1955), 26–29.

70. See, Bose, *Responses in the Living and Non-Living;* V. V. Krishna, "The Emergence of the Indian Scientific Community," *Sociological Bulletin* 40 (1991): 101–3; Kumar, "Culture of Science," 203–5; and Kopf, *Brahmo Samaj,* 70–71.

71. "Scientific Enterprise and the Colonial 'Model,'" 699–70.

72. "Moving Metropolis," 5.

73. See, for examples, the contributions to David Anderson and Richard Grove, eds., *Conservation in Africa: People, Policies and Practice* (Cambridge, England, 1987); as well as Grove's *Green Imperialism.*

74. Arnold, *Colonizing the Body,* 17–18.

75. See Ronald Inden, *Imagining India* (Chicago, 1990); and Adas, *Machines as the Measure,* chaps. 3–5, and epilogue.

76. "Voiced to Unvoiced," 11.

77. Gandhi's views on Western science and technology were modified substantially over a period of decades from the mostly rejectionist position he took in Hind Swaraj, first published in 1909, to a fuller and more accommodating stance that evolved in the articles that he published in "Young India" and "Harijan" in the 1920s and 1930s. The Gandhian approach is ably summarized by A. K. Reddy in his *Technology, Development and the Environment: A Reappraisal* (Nairobi, 1979);

and "Alternative Technology: A Viewpoint from India," *Social Studies of Science* 5 (1975): 331–42. See also, Prakash, *Another Reason,* 214–16, on the place of Gandhian thinking on developmentalism in the context of the larger nationalist project. For less known, but incisive critiques and proposals contemporaneous with Gandhi's, see S. Irfan Habib, "Science, Technical Education and Industrialization: Contours of a Bhadralok Debate," in McLeod and Kumar, eds., *Technology and the Raj,* 235–49.

# Race, Ethnicity, Species, and Breed

Totemism and Horse-Breed Classification in America

*John Borneman*

Totem: the iconic representation of a specific ordering of plant and animal species. Clan: the representation of a group identity. Totemism: the relationship between totem and clan. From Emile Durkheim and his nineteenth-century antecedents to Claude Lévi-Strauss, the discussion of totemism has addressed the way in which people classify themselves with reference to the animal and plant world. This discussion began with the observation among different exotic peoples of the widespread practice of arranging certain animal and plant species into a pattern that, while differing from culture to culture in content, seemed to indicate a consistent formal relationship between totem and clan. The iconic representation of so-called nature—the totem—seemed invariably the model for the representation of intra- or inter-group identity for the clan.

This article examines the historical development of the American system of light-horse breed classification[1]—a striking instance in which the animal world is classified according to the categories used for persons, a case of "reverse totemism." The lay understanding of horse breeds is that they are particularly successful experiments in genetic engineering. Whereas voluntaristic explanations of horse-breed categories, as based on the appreciation of objective and identifiable biological differentiation, are considered quite acceptable, the same kind of explanations for people groupings, such as "race" and "ethnicity," are now generally rejected. When it comes to explaining their horse pets, most Americans—lay and scientific—will maintain that horse-breed distinctions are by and large objective issues of taste that bear little relation to concurrent developments in social structure, national identity, or state formation. In spite of the common knowledge that horse breeds differ from nation-state to nation-state, this fact of historical cultural contingency does not seem to enter into the consciousness of those who breed, own, and ride horses.

In explaining the American system of breed classification this essay will be organized around the following comparative observation: that the many light-horse breeds in the United States are organized into distinct caste-like species, with an exclusivist set of allegiances to each, whereas in continental Europe light-horse breeds are not seen as so separate and distinct. Furthermore, Europeans tend to be agreed upon a single performance standard for all such light-horse breeds, whereas Americans subscribe to a multitude of standards, some having nothing to do with, or having even an adverse relation to, performance.

The concepts of breed, species, and lineage, and the regulation of these differ markedly between America and the Continent, even though the animals involved in the classification are often of the same "stock" (consanguinity), or are put to the same use (function), or share similar morphological characteristics ("conformation"). While social scientists and historians in this century have been intensively engaged in formal structural analysis of category systems, only recently have they begun to deal with the origin, historical development, and transformation of the categories themselves (e.g., Todorov 1984; Sahlins 1981). I will examine the workings of these three primary (often-used) principles of classification in the structuring of particular breeds and their relationship to the evolution of a people, a national identity, and a state. This involves an explication of both the patterning of the underlying generative structure and the historically specific content. I will proceed via a discussion of the debate on totemism and myth within anthropology.

## What Is Totemic Classification?

> Let us be careful not to imagine that totemism has vanished like a cloud at the tap of the fairy wand—slight enough, in both senses of the word—of Malinowski.
>
> —Claude Lévi-Strauss, *The Savage Mind*

Totemism, after dominating much of the anthropological debate centered around "primitive thought" in the early part of this century, was defused as an intellectual issue by the early 1960s. Already in 1929 A. R. Radcliffe-Brown suggested a shift in the debate, away from a question about the nature of primitive thought to one about universal thought patterns: He asked, "Can we show that totemism is a special form of a phenomenon which is universal in human society and is therefore present in different forms in all cultures?" (1952: 123). In the case of Australian systems, he explained, "The only thing that these totemic systems have in common is the general tendency to characterise the segments into which society is divided by an association between each segment and some natural species or some portion of nature. This association may take any one of a number of forms" (1952: 122). In 1951 Radcliffe-Brown gave us a succinct working definition of totemism, the full import of which was not further developed until Lévi-Strauss wrote *The Savage Mind* in 1962. The Radcliffe-Brown definition reads: "The resemblances and differences of animal species are translated into terms of friendship and conflict, solidarity and opposition. In other words the world of animal life is represented in terms of social relations similar to those of human society" (1952: 116). Working with and expanding upon this general definition, Lévi-Strauss articulated precisely how particularities and generalizations about systems of difference can be fashioned out of homologies made between different levels of categories, and how metaphorical and metonymical relations constitute the socio-logic of different cultural classificatory schemes.[2] Moreover, Lévi-Strauss suggested redirecting study to "the *ritualization* of relations between man and animal" (emphasis added), which, he said, "supplies a wider and more general frame than totemism, and within which totemism must have developed" (1963: 61).

While mindful of the critical contribution of Lévi-Strauss to this debate, the simple tap of his wand—metaphorical and metonymical operations of the mind—does not complete the task of explicating totemism. The formal ordering mechanisms of cognitive categories will reveal neither the origins nor the development of the structured and structuring practices, which are, after all, the *raison d'être* of both the categories and the totems. Lévi-Strauss also acknowledged the historicity of any specific application of totemism; he concluded that in "[so-called primitive societies] there is a constantly repeated battle between synchrony and diachrony from which it seems that diachrony must emerge victorious every time" (1966: 75, 155). Yet, in his own work he ignored the implications of this statement, namely, that any account of a system of classification that focuses solely on the semiological aspects will not be able to explain the significance of the conditions of its production. Without a historical account, the most significant aspects of any system of classification—the limits of its ability to generate structures—will remain unintelligible.

We can radicalize Lévi-Strauss's contribution to *le totémisme aujourd' hui* with three further observations. First, the postulation of homologies between so-called natural and cultural distinctions is not something reserved to the "primitive" mind. While Lévi-Strauss, like Radcliffe-Brown, admitted the theoretical universality of totemic devices, he drew most of his examples from "cold societies." Nor can the use of a totemic device be reduced to "pure thought," whose contemporary manifestation is a genetic inheritance from past times. Where it exists, it does so as a motivated action with mechanisms causing its present production. Second, all totemism is initially a kind of reverse totemism. The animal and plant world does not order itself in a way that is immediately recognizable from a pan-cultural or universal-human perspective. The ordering that humans perceive to exist in the animal world is not initially an inference, it is a projection (Foucault 1973). Third, through an examination of a specific "totemic mythology" we can complete the task that Lévi-Strauss set aside, of explaining "how and why it exists" (1975: 8). Lévi-Strauss stated that the "operative value" of totemic classifications derives from their formal character: "they are codes suitable for conveying messages which can be transposed into other codes, and for expressing messages received by means of different codes in terms of their own system" (1966: 75, 76). As for mythology, he argued that it "has no obvious practical function: . . . it is not directly linked with a different kind of reality" (1975: 10). Here he is absolutely wrong. What I will argue in this essay is that the semiotic codes that make up the patterning of totemism are brought into being by ideological factors, which subsequently also determine the content of the codes. The resulting myths are never innocent, never merely a product where "the mind is left to commune with itself" (1975: 10).

### The Wide World of Horses in America: Criteria of Classification

The horse has three gaits—walk, trot, and canter—that are generic to the horse as a species. These three gaits are not in every horse manifested as "pure gaits," meaning that the gait can lose its regularity. For example, the *walk,* a four-beat gait, becomes a *pace* (an impure gait) when the horse moves the legs diagonally instead of laterally. The two-beat *trot,* a diagonal gait, becomes impure when the horse simultaneously moves a front and hind leg laterally (that is, on the same side). At that point the trot loses its moment of suspension. The three-beat *canter* becomes impure when the horse lapses into a four-beat gait. International performance horses, which compete in the three Olympic sports of dressage,[3] show jumping, and combined training, are bred according to the conformational specifications that relate to the purity of the three gaits. This single *performance* criterion is also the basic generative structuring principle of the continental European horse world. The American horse world, however, is structured upon various *breed-specific* criteria, of which the performance criterion is but one among many principles.

Most northern European horse breeding is rigidly (by American standards) regulated by the state, which tests and designates approved stallions and mares considered qualified for breeding stock. This has resulted, over the course of the last two centuries, in the production of superior warm-blood performance horses (crosses between light breeds, such as Thoroughbreds, and local carriage horses and draft horses), some of which have been imported to America, where they are now also being bred. While the international sports performance horse is the focus of European horse categories, it still constitutes but a small percentage (less than 5 percent) of American horse breeding, pleasure riding, and competition. The categorization of the other 95 percent of the light-horse breeds in the United States, which serve purely national or local purposes, is the subject of this essay.

Unlike the Europeans, Americans have more than twenty-six kinds of breed recognized nationally by the American Horse Show Association (AHSA), yet either esoteric or unknown internationally, that are deemed functional and/or meaningful for ends other than international performance sports. These ends include breed criteria of, for example, *color* (Appaloosa, Pinto, Paint, Palomino), *endurance and trail* (Morgan, Peruvian Paso Fino), *sprinting and cattle herding* (Quarter Horse), *elegant, high-stepping action* (Saddlebred, Tennessee Walking Horse). While European breeds are evaluated on a single performance criterion, American breeds are evaluated not only on multiple scales of performance, but also on arbitrary breed standards other than performance, such as temperament, conformation, and coloring (Haynes 1976: 61).

Whereas the European breeds, focused upon a single performance criterion, will readily take superior animals from other breeds into their registries in order to improve the stock, Americans place great importance on breed "purity" and invest a great amount of energy in keeping the breeds pure and separate. At times the criteria will even be redefined in order to demarcate more clearly one breed from another. While the strategies used to maintain breed distinctions are multifarious, one strategy held in common among the various breeders involves the use of polythetic classificatory devices, such as versions of unilineal or cognatic descent categories, where no single significant feature is to be found in every member of the breed, but each member is assumed to share a common ancestor. Thus mythologies are constructed around a particular prepotent foundation sire who is said to have originated the breed. Thereafter, all horses included within that breed registry, while perhaps not sharing any "substance" such as temperament, looks, or ability, are traced back to the same ancestor.

Within and across breed standards Americans have developed distinctive styles of riding, which have their correlates both in the ritually demarcated show arena and in everyday riding practices. At the most general level, Western and English styles are the major categories, but both are further subdivided in the horse-show world. For example, the "Western pleasure" (a stylized performance, aesthetically judged) and the "Western gaming" (timed competition) divisions of Western riding have their English riding counterparts in "dressage" and "hunt seat" (both aesthetically judged) and "show jumping" (timed competitions). The breed and performance standards are open to constant reformulation, depending upon changes in the state of the art for performance, and in the state of the science for breeding, and thus constitute a social field of overt struggle over classificatory schemes. Since the knowledge of the making and unmaking of the system of categories is in the public domain, it can be acquired, thus empowering individuals with various forms of ritual expertise. For example, certain performance classes for nearly all breeds are structured male/female and professional/amateur. These classes include, for example, "men's English pleasure" and "ladies English pleasure," or "Western riding, open" and "Western riding, amateurs only." Other riding domains, such as "dressage" or "combined training," require such an extensive investment in training, equipment, and time, that they become, in fact, limited to select classes of individuals. Many of these breed and performance standards conform to the major cleavages in American society and serve as indices of gender, color code, and class.

Yet, the democratic ideal in America has it that everyone has or should have equal opportunity to pursue pleasure, although this does not include a guarantee nor provide the mechanism whereby everyone will in fact have this equal opportunity. And the American myth correspondingly goes that anyone can own a horse. Anyone can also breed a horse, as there is no effective regulation of breeding by the state or by other regulatory agencies, as exists in Europe. Anyone can also show a horse. And, in fact, many people of disparate cultural groups and socioeconomic categories do own, breed, and show horses. Rather than make uniform the standards for owning, breeding, or showing horses, as in continental Europe, the American practice assumes that there is a horse to fit every pocketbook, to match every color preference, every temperament, every personal body-type, and so on and so forth. The horse in America is a democratic ideal.

To illustrate the development of specific American breeds and the distinctive strategies involved in their construction, I will offer an ethnography of four exemplary American breeds that are constituted according to the criteria of function and temperament (the Morgan), conformation (the Quarter Horse and the Arabian), and color (the Paint). These examples are intended to give the reader, on the one hand, a sense of the lack of functional necessity in breed categorization, and, on the other, a sense of the detailed elaboration of symbolic differences.

## Function and Temperament: The Morgan Horse

In the case of the first American breed, the Morgan, the origin is traced to Justin Morgan, a horse received by a Vermont schoolteacher in payment for a bad debt. Conceived in 1789 in Springfield, Massachusetts, this horse possessed excessive strength for his size and a temperament characterized as industrious, docile, kind, commonsensical, versatile, and independent (*Horse Identifier* 1980: 96).[4] A biography of this foundation sire reads, ". . . the small bay stallion entered a life of hard labor—and, at first, little recognition. Although standing only 14.0 hands and weighing scarcely 950 pounds at maturity, Figure (his original name) was put to any task which required horse power, from skidding heavy logs to racing the local talent at day's end. However the spunky little stud proved he not only had the mettle to attempt anything asked of him, but invariably left the competition eating his dust as well" (Mellin 1973: 5).

According to one widely held myth, the Morgan had been a necessity in the past: How could America have been settled without him? The founding of breed registries, of which the Morgan in 1894 was the first, is accompanied by an extensive list of rules, based on morphological criteria, to determine what the breed is and what it is not. In the words of one expert, "acknowledging that of course there are always likely to be found some variations on type within so versatile a breed, those people who are dedicated to the Morgan *per se* realize their obligation to perpetuate, in fact, his basic character and disposition" (Mellin 1973: 47). Once a breed is established, morphological criteria and a particular expression—the Morgan "look"—are used to distinguish it from other breeds: "It is a bright, proud expression, at once intelligent, mischievous, a bit defiant and—totally irresistible! It is usually coupled with a snorty attitude, a tossing mane and an abundance of nervous animation" (Mellin 1973: 47). Can it be mere coincidence that the Morgan look matches the characteristics ascribed to the archetypical Jeffersonian yeoman farmer? This Jeffersonian ideal-typical construction of The American is the sum total of perceived American virtues.

It is appropriate that the Morgan, as the first official American breed to serve as a marker of distinction, simultaneously claims to incorporate the essence of Americanism. The development of a distinctively American way of life was accompanied by what the historian John Higham, in a definitive account of this phenomenon, calls racial nativism: "intense opposition to an internal minority on the ground of its foreign (i.e., 'un-American') connections" (1967: 4). Higham points to popular movements in the 1790s and 1850s in which nativistic agitation to define The American was particularly widespread. It was assumed, in both the popular and "scientific" literature of the nineteenth century, that there were at least three distinct European and many "non-Western" races. Yet, it wasn't until the end of the nineteenth century that political and literary speculation on "racial difference" received its "scientific" legitimation from biologists, anthropologists, and genealogists (Higham 1967: 149–57). In a parallel manner, the initial political and social origin of the Morgan horse of 1789 was only later, in 1894, legitimated by "science." Not until the end of the nineteenth century did the Morgan become a separate and distinct breed, based on scientifically verifiable "natural" biological distinctions.

While the notion of breed purity is common to most American breed registry associations, European warm-blood breeders seem unconcerned with purity, often using other breeds in order to improve their own, and switching identities freely. For example, a superior horse in the Hannoverian registry may be purchased by the Westphalian registry (or vice versa) and its offspring will be registered without qualification. It is worth noting, then, what happens when Americans import these European "unprotected" breeds. To keep the imported bloodlines pure, Americans have created separate registries for each European warm-blood, reproducing the breed-exclusive registry that exists within more established American breeds. In some cases, separate registries are even kept for those bred in Europe and for those bred in America, as if the geographical locus of conception made a difference. The justification given is that the change in climatic conditions results in a loss of breed purity. The cross-breeding of imported European warmbloods with American breeds (such as Thoroughbred and Quarter Horse) has resulted in the recent creation of many half-breed registries. There have also been attempts in the past ten years in America to create single performance horse registries that would incorporate qualified "performance" horses from different breeds. But, significantly, these registries do not intend to challenge the breed-exclusive categories, for they allow and even encourage listing in both the specific breed and the performance registry. In other words, dual identities are created.

### Conformation: Arab Breeders and Quarter-Horse People

The construction of breed criteria based on morphological characteristics can be clearly illustrated by comparing two well-known and popular American breeds, the Quarter Horse and the Arabian. Although it has been an official breed only since 1940, the Quarter Horse embodies more than any other breed the American West, and its origin is often expressed in a folksy Western manner. L. N. Sikes writes, "The history of the Quarter Horse goes back a long way—back before the time when anybody kept good accounts of what stock horses in this country even looked like" (1958: 13). Of course, Sikes is not unaware of the part he plays in myth building, for he appropriates other myths of the Quarter Horse as myths, such as a virility myth told of Steel Dust, a foundation sire of the breed: "So much of a reputation did Steel Dust get that, pretty soon, he began siring colts in places he'd never been. In fact, up until recent years, lots of cowmen would refer to a Quarter-type horse as a 'steel dust'" (1958: 13). One chronicler of the Western horse, Robert Denhardt, comments that "every horse trader who has not recently joined a church will modestly admit that his horses are direct descendants of Steel Dust" (1967: 17). While the Morgan represents a particular east-coast-derived American archetype, the Quarter Horse appeals to a more general Western myth. Says Denhardt, "The Quarter Horse is a scion of the oldest and most aristocratic of American equine families, a race which can trace one side of the family to the Mayflower and the other to the Conquistadors of Spain" (1967: 178).

Arab breeders, as they are called by other horse people, are among the most eccentric horse owners in America. This is attributed to many factors: They often fear riding their own spirited horses, they usually prize beauty and sentiment over function, and they commonly display an extreme fetishization of the parts of the horse. When asked to identify what makes an Arabian an Arabian to an Arab breeder, one man replied, "They have lots of mane. Lots of head with big eyes. And they are surrounded by fog." Arab breeders have made a fetish of the head, so that regardless of how the body of the horse is put together, or of how the horse moves (how it carves its rider), a proper Arab head—bulging eyes and nostrils, dished forehead, wild and flowing mane—is the most prized and determinative characteristic of the breed. Most pictorial representations of the Arab show only the head and at times part of the neck. Sometimes it is surrounded by mist.

This contrasts with representations of the Quarter Horse, which often focus on the rear. At times the horse's head is turned so that it is staring back at the camera, though many photos in Quarter Horse advertisements show only the rear end. The history of the Quarter Horse parallels that of the territorial expansion of the United States. It originated in the southern United States, and was bred to run a sprint, a quarter of a mile. The thrusting power of a horse is to be found in a powerful rear end: a long hip with a muscular loin and well-developed gaskin muscles. The Quarter Horse was bred for this powerful rear end. Because of its special stopping and starting ability, it is particularly suited for use in cattle herding on the open range. With the western expansion and the growth of the open range, Americans, not surprisingly, found Quarter Horses to be most suited to their needs. Thus, this American sport horse was developed for purely local ends—for short-distance racing and cattle herding. Yet, a third use of the Quarter Horse arose, that of a docile and tractable show horse. The number of horses devoted to this third use presently far exceeds that in the racing and cattle-herding oriented uses for which the horse was initially bred.

Paradoxically, as the initial functions of the Quarter Horse became less important, the prime symbol of those functions—the distinctive rear end—took on increased significance. The fetish surrounding this body part has resulted in the breeding of some horses that are uncomfortable to ride, for often the rear end is out of proportion to the front, creating not a more powerful engine but an unbalanced, downhill-moving horse. This kind of horse, known as the Bull-Dog type, "hits the ground hard" when it moves, jarring the teeth of its riders and decreasing the longevity of the horse, as its legs and feet have difficulty withstanding the pounding. One admirer of the leaner type of Quarter Horse refers to the Bull Dog as a "muscle-bound weight lifter trying to be a boxer" (Davis 1962: 9).

During the 1960s the popularity of showing horses greatly increased and show classes proliferated.[5] Halter classes, where the horses are led into the ring and judged purely on conformation with no concurrent attempt to link this to a performance aspect (like a swimsuit beauty competition, where the contestants need not swim), expanded greatly in number and took on increased status and significance. This was accompanied by increased specialization within each breed, so that a racing Quarter Horse was of a type different from a Quarter Horse used for show. And the show-horse category was further subdivided into horses that could win "at halter" and those that could win "in performance." With the increased importance of the show-horse aspects to the majority of breeders, who prized (with money and status) competitive wins in the halter classes over those in performance classes, less attention was paid to those aspects that keep the horses sound, that is, physically healthy. Put simply, beauty became divorced from function. In order to accentuate the bulk (thus, the beauty) of the body, Quarter-Horse breeders during the 1960s and 1970s also selected horses with refined bones and feet, and they introduced some Thoroughbred blood—Thoroughbreds have slighter bodies and more refined limbs—into the registry. Many breeders today acknowledge that these particular conceptions of beauty, having an attenuated and even adverse relationship to function, have resulted in a physical weakening of the breed.[6]

A particularly distinctive and popular class at Arabian horse shows is the "Arabian costume class," for which owners dress their horses and themselves in what they think of as typical Arabian costumes. The horse's head is appropriately highlighted, with plumes on the top. The horse's body is covered (who wants to see the body?) by sequined silk multicolored blankets with small white or blue pompons sewed around the edges. While most of the body is cloth covered, the head and neck are further accentuated with silver-plated bridles on which are inscribed the names of the horse, names of Arabic origin that none of the participants can pronounce. After all the performers are gathered in the arena, they circle the judge, each at a pace the individual prefers. They are then asked by the judge, usually a male, to perform individually. From a line-up in the middle of the arena, the performers individually circle the judge and the other riders, displaying their costumes to best advantage. Most often this is done at a hand gallop—a very fast canter—so that the rider's long silk robe and the pompons on the horse's blanket will billow in the wind, creating the feeling of speed and light movement. In several classes that I have watched, the female performers played upon Western ideas of the sexuality of the Arab world by going braless under their light silk robes. A Wisconsin woman, who had imported an Egyptian Arabian stallion, would also, after her gallop, race up to the male judge, stopping within inches of him, and lean forward so that he could smell her perfume and see her form under her Arab silks. She was always the talk of the show, and never lost a costume class during the four years (of the 1960s) in which I knew her.

## Color: The Paint

The color breeds—for example, Paint, Appaloosa, Pinto, Albino, Palomino—while incorporating all three breed-classificatory criteria (function, conformation, and color) in both their mythology and their current registry standards, single out color as the necessary and sufficient condition of incorporation. A color breed such as the Paint, in order to constitute itself as a separate and distinct breed that is understood as a biological (that is, genetic) category, must assert that certain criteria, either singly or in combination, are uniquely Paint. In the effort to maintain and justify the distinctiveness of the color category, Paint owners and breeders engage in ceaseless semiotic and ideological maneuvering. In an article on the social uses of color codes, Marshall Sahlins provides an initial framework for explaining the semiotic aspect of the construction of the Paint breed: "Colors are in practice semiotic codes. Everywhere, both as terms and concrete properties, colors are engaged as signs in vast schemes of social relations, meaningful structures by which persons and groups, objects and occasions, are differentiated and combined in cultural orders" (1977: 166).

The Paint provides a specific example of the development of a color code, and can be used to extend Sahlins' insight. Two related questions should be kept in mind: First, can one isolate the various strategies used to produce this cultural order, and, second, what is the relationship between the ideological motivations and the semiotics of color coding?

Even though the founding of the Paint-Horse registry, with which its legitimation as a breed begins, did not occur until February 1962, much importance is placed upon its ancestry, that it has existed forever, or nearly so. Its beginnings are traced back to 20,000 B.C. in Spain, southern France, Arabia, and North Africa. There is some confusion in the early records (that is, prior to 1519, when the Paint is definitively dated as reaching America), as it is "impossible to trace the movements of each breed" because no distinction was usually made between the different kinds of spotted horses (Haynes 1976: 3).

After the fifteenth century the record supposedly becomes clearer, and we are told that, for instance, the Indians in America domesticated the Paint Horse "because they had an eye for anything bright or colorful," and that they apparently thought Paint Horses were better camouflaged than solid colored ones (Haynes 1976: 24, 25). "Paints" continue to be associated with the domesticated Other, which in this case is the American Indian. Popular forms of representation, from such diverse media as films and horse-show costume class performances, index the Paint as "colored." From the television serial "The Lone Ranger" in the 1950s, where the Ranger (white) rides a Palomino but Tonto (Indian) a Paint, to the film *Silverado* in the 1980s, where the hero rides a white horse and the buffoon a Paint, the mythical history of the breed is reconfirmed. Today the Paint Horse and the other color breeds can be found in all parts of the United States, although they tend to be more concentrated in the West.

Since 1962 the criteria of classification have changed several times because it has been difficult to decide, as one breeder put it, "How much color is a Paint Horse?" (Haynes 1976: 54). Initially, it was required that the Paint be recognizable as such from both sides, but this has been changed so that now only one side need be so recognizable. At present the other requirements for inclusion are height (fifty-six inches at age two years), gaitedness, and conformation approval (in the case of a stallion). For those that fulfill these requirements but are not offspring of registered parents, patrilateral descent, that is, paternity from a stallion in another approved registry (for example, Quarter Horse or Thoroughbred), is an added requirement. Apparently, the dam's lineage can be considered inconsequential for the purposes of breed inclusion. This American oversight—denial of the genetic importance of the mother—is not peculiar to the Paint breed; it is a quite common practice in the origin of most breeds.[7]

The requirements for participation in show classes for the Paint Horse are similar to those of the Quarter Horse, which the Paint Horse closely approximates in function and performance.[8] The one characteristic that all Paints are supposed to share—color—is also the only characteristic that is ruled out as a consideration when judging halter classes. The only class in which color is to be considered a factor is in a color class, a non-point (no cumulative year-end award) class judged solely on color. For show purposes, any Paint Horse, once accepted in the registry, has sufficient color.

What is most significant about the Paint Horse breed is that the criterion on which it bases its claim to a breed status is not and never can be genetically isolated, for "noncolor breeds" will at times produce horses that theoretically qualify as ideal Paints, and Paint Horses will often produce full-colored offspring. Many color patterns are carried by recessive genes.[9] Some horses unpredictably change color patterns several times during their lives. Nevertheless, given the social importance in America of horse breeds as a form of distinction making, each breed must necessarily be conceptualized as distinct, and invested with an ideal type. Horses not adequately measuring up to this ideal will be rejected as impure. Thus, the Quarter-Horse registry will refuse to register full-blood Quarter Horses with impeccable lineages but with too much white, or with color in the "wrong" place (that can, in other words, qualify as Paints), and will demand that the animals be withdrawn as breeding stock (by gelding the stallions and spaying the mares). The rules for inclusion as a Paint are the same as the rules for exclusion as a Quarter Horse, namely, that color markings as decided by "body contrasts" must or must not be of a particular type and in a specific location (Haynes 1976: 70).

The use of color as a "primordial classifier" illustrates the social embeddedness of semiotic codes and the consistency of ideological motivations within any particular cultural order. The resort to mythical histories, to genealogies based on shared blood or patrilateral descent, and to functional claims (conduct codes) parallels the kind of strategies most often used to constitute the kinship systems of human groups. The consistent breakdown of the category-use does not result in a denial of their naturalness, but rather in a reformulation of the color combinations that signify the breed. Color use never merely names objective differences in the visible spectrum of *signified* color patterns; it also, as Sahlins has argued, arbitrarily *signifies* and communicates culturally constituted social relationships.

### The Production of Distinction: Good Horse Flesh

As we have just seen, the practico-theoretical logics governing the life and thought of so- called primitive societies are shaped by the insistence on differentiation.

—Claude Lévi-Strauss, *The Savage Mind*

> The practice of sports . . . owes part of its "interests," just as much
> nowadays as at the beginning, to its distinguishing function, and
> more precisely, to the gains in distinction which it brings.
> —Pierre Bourdieu, "Sport and Social Class"

It should now be clear how American horse breeds, based on arbitrary distinctions of function, conformation, and color, are constantly manufactured. Furthermore, these distinctions and significations are not derived from some natural pan-cultural ordering of the animal kingdom, but are peculiarly American social distinctions that are in turn mapped onto differences found within a given species. The differences are indeed arbitrary: fetishes of parts (nostrils, eyes, and necks for the Arabian, rear ends for the Quarter Horse), priorities of color (for the Paint Horse or the Palomino), mythologies of origin and temperament (for the Morgan). By *arbitrary* I do not mean that these significations are unmotivated signs, but simply that the motivation chosen is one among other possibilities. There are, indeed, limits to the arbitrariness of a signification, but these limits are ideological constraints, not semiological ones. For the example of horse breeds, the meaning attached to function, conformation, and color is possible precisely because it is motivated by similar divisions in the social world of people.[10]

In the remainder of this essay the question to be addressed, then, is how and why this particular set of ideological constraints motivates the semiotics of horse-breed distinctions. Why do Americans set up new rules for each breed rather than, like the Europeans, agree to one set of performance rules for all breeds? A passage from Lévi-Strauss, explicating the relation of totem to caste and the "conceptual transformations marking the passage from exogamy to endogamy," suggests an answer to this question:

> But if social groups are considered not so much from the point of view
> of their reciprocal relations in social life as each on their own account,
> in relation to something other than sociological reality, then the idea of
> diversity is likely to prevail over that of unity. Each social group will
> tend to form a system no longer with other social groups but with particular differentiating properties regarded as hereditary, and these characteristics exclusive to each group will weaken the framework of their
> solidarity within the society. The more each group tries to define itself
> by the image which it draws from a natural model, the more difficult
> will it become for it to maintain its links with other social groups and,

in particular to exchange its sisters and daughters with them since it will tend to think of them as being of a particular "species" (1966: 177–78).

If Lévi-Strauss' conceptualization is correct, then the movement from exogamous to endogamous horse breeding would involve specific formative steps. How did the American horse breeds become species-like (or, one might ask, are endogamy and caste-status preconditions for constituting a breed)? This can be illustrated by examining the three processes involved in the creation of "good horse flesh": breeds are conceptualized, registries are created, and breed divisions are enforced.

While the definition of breed varies from writer to writer, certain themes are held in common. Wayne Dinsmore says a breed exists when a "substantial number of animals within a species . . . differentiat[e] them[selves] from others of the same species" (1978: 103). J. W. Evans relies on an argument of human or abstract needs to explain breeds: "Breeds were developed according to the needs of horsepeople in each locality, or they developed naturally" (1977: 101). Along with these two basic assumptions, many writers date the official origin (other than that offered in their mythologies) to the foundation of a registry. The importance placed on the official codification is often so great that, in his history of the Appaloosa (1975), for example, Jan Haddle dates the breed to the opening of its official registry in 1949, even though this is a year after the first full-Appaloosa horse show.

Haynes makes the above connections explicit: A breed is "a variety or stock of animals related by descent with certain inherited characteristics and capable of reproducing those characteristics," but has also come to mean "animals registered in some association or club" (1976: 61). This emphasis upon being recorded in the stud register or the registry of a particular breed is also regarded as the distinguishing characteristic of breed by the *Manual of Horsemanship,* which is published by the British Horse Society and The Pony Club, and is the most authoritative text on horse basics in all the Western English-speaking countries. The registry—that is, the concept consanguinity—has now taken on an institutional raison d'etre, so that superior animals fitting the breed specifications will be rejected if their progenitors are not already members of the registry.[11] This needs to be so, says Haynes, because "it takes several generations of recorded and scientific breeding to establish a family or strain" (1976: 62). Horse breeders themselves recognize the creative and constitutive nature of their endeavor. "There is no reason," says John Gorman, "why a group of horse breeders of a certain type and color cannot preserve the purity of the horses' breeding and eventually establish a breed" (1958: 229).

In order to establish "pure breeds," most breed associations at some point established extensive inspection programs through which individual animals were (or are) initially approved for a breed registry. Haynes points out that the desire to "ensure uniformity in the breed" led to "rigid stallion inspections" as one of many necessary "police actions" (1976: 52). The Quarter-Horse inspection program (no longer active because the breed registry is closed) can serve as an example of how these actions were carried out. If a horse's progenitors were not both registered, or if the progenitors were unknown, an owner could petition for inspection. After an initial inspection by an officially approved inspector, who was most often flown to the site where the petitioned animal was kept, the animal would be either rejected or accepted into the registry as an appendix-registered horse. The horse would then be required to compete and win in several different divisions (for example, racing, halter, performance) at official Quarter-Horse shows in order to accumulate the required number of points. Thereafter, animals that fulfilled these requirements were automatically admitted into the full registry, with the possibility that they could be used as breeding stock.[12]

## The State, Social Structure, Cultural Categories

Just as there are many distinct, mutually exclusive—that is, caste-like—American horse breeds, there are also many styles of riding. On the Continent[13] not only is there a single standard— performance—for breeding, but also a uniform set of presuppositions concerning how training and riding the horse should progress.[14] These continental presuppositions are formalized and systematized in the art of "dressage." I will briefly sketch how this codification progressed, concentrating on the post-Medieval period, as it allows us to bring together the interactions among cultural categories, social structures, and the nascent states of Europe.[15] This comparative discussion of the sociopolitical context in which breed categorization developed is intended to illuminate the American situation, and not to provide an exhaustive account of European state and horse-breed development.

The first written texts on the different aspects of horsemanship in the West are attributed to Xenophon in 500 B.C. For the next twenty centuries, however, there was very little written on breeding type and riding style. According to the current literature on horses and horsemanship, there were also no appreciable improvements in understanding, training, or breeding of the animals (at least in the West)[16] until the fifteenth century. After the fall of the Roman Empire, the use of infantry declined and that of cavalry increased, although this does not appear to have had any immediate effect on improving the caliber of horsemanship. Yet, between 1500 and 500 B.C. the domesticated horse, arriving from the East, became common to much of Western Europe. This "noble beast . . . was associated with a new social distinction," comments Emmanuel Le Roy Ladurie, "[and] in its way it marked the appearance of a group of aristocrats, living off contributions levied from the peasants" (1979: 80). In addition to its function in changing agricultural techniques, the horse was simultaneously appropriated as an indexical symbol, associated with the growing nobility and with knighthood.

The formalization of riding and the development of *haute école* began again during the Renaissance in the fifteenth century. It reached a fountainhead at the riding School of Naples, which served as a source for subsequent developments among the Hapsburgs (and the Spanish Riding School) in Austria, the French, and the British. A student from that school, de Pluvinel, is thought to be the originator of the French school. Antoine de Pluvinel's book, *The Instruction of the King in the Art of Riding,* printed in 1626, was written as a dialogue between the author and his pupil, Louis XIII. Following upon these beginnings, Louis XIV, from the splendor of his court, created a French riding school—the School of Versailles—in the Tuileries. In 1733 the Frenchman Robichon de La Guérnière, who conducted this school, wrote what is still considered the classic text on dressage. His teachings formed the basis for all subsequent cavalry schools, the most famous of which is the Cavalry School of Saumur, founded in 1771, a direct descendant of the School of Versailles. Advances in horse breeding and training in France subsequently emanated from contacts with the Saumur school, which to this day retains its role in licensing instructors, trainers, and judges.

What one can conclude from this account is that horse riding in France is marked by the reliance of a particular cultural standard upon the court culture and upon the development of a military elite situated in and near Paris. The growth of the performance standard in France is inextricably linked both to the process of formalization rules of etiquette among French nobility and to the utilization of the horse in the military-political centralization of France.[17] One is reminded of Alexis de Tocqueville's account of the demise of the ancien régime, his central thesis being that "in

France, more than in any other European country, the provinces had come under the thrall of the metropolis, which attracted to itself all that was most vital in the nation" (1955: 72). Despite the fact that Louis XIV "tried to check the growth of Paris" six times, administrative centralization was the marked tendency of the French territory from the beginning of the seventeenth century, where the "true owner" of the landed estates in the kingdom "was the State and the State alone" (Tocqueville 1955: 189). Tocqueville illustrates the tendency of the provinces to look toward Paris for leadership in all aspects of cultural and political life with a comment from a provincial: "We are only a provincial town; we must wait till Paris gives us a lead." He infers from this that the provinces seemed "not to dare to form an opinion until they knew what was being thought in Paris" (1955: 74). The German historian Otto Hintze is in accord that "the transition occurred only in the seventeenth and eighteenth centuries, the period of absolutism and administrative centralization; it was finally completed by Napoleon. As a unified state, moreover, France became the model of development for the entire continent" (1973: 168).[18]

Whereas the development of "France" is marked by political centralization, that of "Germany" is by bureaucratization. The most common explanation for the bureaucratic centralization of Prussia in the eighteenth century is that external, chiefly military, threats from the new states in the West forced internal developments toward increasing centralization (Cf. Hintze 1973: 168–69; Craig 1978: 1–34; Wehler 1973).[19] Thus, in the Prussian case, military needs, initially tied to cavalry effectiveness, necessitated breeding of animals that correspond somewhat to our present light-horse category.[20] This effort followed upon, and was modeled after, the successful school at Saumur in France, for monarchs and nobility commonly borrowed from each other. Since the purpose here is not to explain differences on the Continent,[21] but the differences between the American model and the continental one, it is important to emphasize that the Germans and French are much alike in holding a particular pan-national breed standard (although the manner in which and reasons for which these standards were propagated differ), whereas in America, with a weak state formed on pluralist (federalist) premises, there occurred a proliferation of breed standards.

For Americans, nation building—the creation of shared cultural-identity markers—took precedence over state building. In marked contrast to Europe, America had neither a court culture, nor large, threatening states on its borders. The classic formulation as to why political centralization never occurred to the same extent in America as in Europe was put forth by Louis Hartz, who argued that the absence of feudal social institutions, including an aristocratic cultural elite, made unnecessary the centralization of power required to dislodge it (1955: 43–46). Samuel Huntington concludes from this initial premise that, while the American state, in its subsequent development, "often helped to promote economic development, . . . it played only a minor role in changing social customs and social structure" (1973: 193). Furthermore, without "external enemies" as a backdrop against which a national identity is imagined,[22] American national identity was (and is) imagined as an internal affair. This has meant both a nativist universalism, as Higham has articulated, and a pluralist melting-pot folk ideology concerning the nature and expression of cultural difference.

In France and Germany, centralization—political in the French case and bureaucratic in the German one—played the key role in establishing a universalistic cultural standard, which for horse breeding is expressed in a single performance criterion. In the United States, diverse cultural standards and social strata were never subject to strong political or bureaucratic structures capable of or in need of bringing about a uniform performance standard. Consequently, particularistic cultural standards, as in the domain of horse breeds, were generated as "separate but equal" social-identity markers. Where state building precedes nation building on the Continent, centralized administration and hierarchical modeling leads to uniform breed standards. Where nation building precedes state building in the United States, the denial of social difference and of hierarchy leads to heterogeneous and separate but formally "equal" cultural breed standards.

### Race, Ethnicity, Species, Breed

Totemism, as Lévi-Strauss argues, is the postulation of a homology between two systems of differences. It is a way of thinking that has no intrinsic content. Lévi-Strauss makes it clear that totemism is the establishment of homologies not between the terms themselves, but only between the *differences* "which manifest themselves on the level of groups on the one hand and that of species on the other" (1966: 115). He represents this as follows:

$$\text{Nature:} \quad \text{species } 1 \neq \text{species } 2 \neq \text{species } 3 \neq \ldots \text{species } n$$
$$\mid \qquad\qquad \mid \qquad\qquad \mid$$
$$\text{Culture:} \quad \text{group } 1 \neq \text{group } 2 \neq \text{group } 3 \neq \ldots \text{group } n.$$

It is the same "pure totemic structure" that I am suggesting exists in the creation of breed categories in America. The relationships suggested are not between particular breed and particular ethnic or racial categories but between a *system of human differentiation* and a *system of breed differentiation*. It can be represented as follows:

Breeds:  Quarter Horse ≠ Morgan ≠ Paint ≠ Arabian ≠ . . . . breed *n*
         |         |        |       |
Humans: Anglo-Saxon  ≠ German ≠ Black ≠ Italian  ≠ . . . . ethnic/racial
                                                        group *n*.

The melting-pot ideology notwithstanding, American social groups increasingly tend to be in practice statistically endogamous, occupationally differentiated, and residentially separated from one another (Thurow 1980; 1975; Harrington 1984; 1980). The term *ethnicity,* which has traditionally been used to refer to forms of regional identity based upon customs and influences from outside the society in which the groups now live, is increasingly recognized as indicating relationships based upon differences used to demarcate indigenous groups from one another (Glazer and Moynihan 1975). Michael Hechter has postulated that a common form of ethnicity is a reactive group formation, where groups adopt historically established distinctions to demarcate themselves from other groups, rather than adopting these identities in an interactive, closed group (1978). Sociolinguistic work by John Gumperz (1982a; 1982b) indicating the persistence of linguistic and discourse differentiations has forced re-evaluation of the logic behind and reasons for the use of diverse discourse conventions.

There is no need to go into detail on the significance and persistence of collective descent and race as distinction-making categories in American history (Gossett 1963; on the relationship of race to ethnicity and class, see Altschuler 1982). Many writers have argued that race is *the* most significant category for Americans. A 1937 study of etiquette and race in the American South begins with the assertion that "the American people seem to exhibit a perennial interest in problems pertaining to contact and association of the many races which constitute the general population" (Doyle 1937: viii). The logic of racial differentiation is often explained in a manner similar to Hechter's reactive-group-formation thesis. L. Copeland states, "Wherever the groups and classes are set in sharp juxtaposition, the values and mores of each are juxtaposed. Out of group opposition there arises an intense opposition of values, which comes to be projected though the social order and serves to solidify social stratification" (1959: 171).

## Conclusion

That is why myth is experienced as innocent speech: not because its intentions are hidden—if they were hidden, they could not be efficacious—but because they are naturalized.

[M]ythology harmonizes with the world, not as it is, but as it wants to create itself.

         —Roland Barthes, "Myth Today"

Horse breeders and riders experience their breed classifications innocently. The myths they spin about their cultural performances, while not maliciously motivated, are also not harmless. These classifications do not arise from virginal minds. Rather, at the point of their origin and in their reproduction they serve as perpetual alibis, by naturalizing and legitimating the social order about which they speak. Unlike "the primitive," the century-old creation of anthropological study, who is said to deny nature and to reify culture, Americans seek to reify certain parts of their culture which they falsely identify as nature. Americans forget that "nature," in as far as it is experienced and becomes part of a human life-world, is also a cultural construct.

It is no accident that American notions and usage of horse breeds—where the concepts of race and ethnicity, blood and breeding, have all become reified into biological naturalisms—are first taken from human categories and then projected onto animal classifications. In the American case, Durkheim's basic insight about the relation of totem to clan can be confirmed. The concept of horse breeds is, in fact, a stolen language, stolen from our practice of social structure. This is a specific instance of a general phenomenon that can only be explained as a reverse totemism. Horse breeds are thus an example of what Sahlins has called scientific totemism (1976: 106).

The creation, in our image, of a world of differentiated animal species is also inextricably linked to the reciprocal influences of cultural categories, social-structural practices, and the formation of nation-state identities. Although in everyday speech the terms *breed* and *species,* or *race, ethnicity,* and *species* may not be confused, in practice the different horse breeds are treated as if they were separate species. Since breed, like race, is confused with and often considered a matter of genetics and biology, and not culture, and since biology is considered the ultimate arbiter of phenomenological disputes, the naturalness of this social order is never questioned. In this case, the post-Mendelian scientific discourse on genetics enters the history of horse breeding after the forms of classification and their motivations have already been culturally cast. Today, the relationship of the science of genetics to popular representations and practices, when not serving a merely legitimating role for what is already there, remains tenuous.

Though this essay focuses on the analysis of the totemic nature of horse-breed categorization in America, the theoretical implications of the argument are broader. As Roland Barthes so perspicaciously argued, and as the specific examples here illustrate, the mythical systems produced through classificatory devices, while experienced as innocent speech, are in fact constructed, first, by a plagiarism of the social world, and second, by a harmonization of that plagiarism with its dominant discourse. This kind of myth is neither simply a charter for reality nor is it an invention of pure thought. It is both a language for analogically representing and reconstituting another reality—a hierarchical system of human differentiation—and a means by which that reality can be validated.

## NOTES

Acknowledgements: I would like to thank Sally F. Moore for several critical readings of this essay. Thanks are also owed to Charles Lindholm, Chris Waters, Peter Sahlins, Daniel Goldhagen, and Carlos Forment for their suggestions.

1. When dealing with horse breed classification, one encounters several coexisting category systems. In the words of one authority, "now nearly every country has its own national, as opposed to native, breeds. . . . In each case, these breeds have been developed to meet the interest, demands and requirements of the individual country" (Skelton 1978: 10–11). The cultural differences at the linguistic level alone can be the subject of an entire book. For example, *breed* and *race* have separate, though overlapping, semantic usages in English. Yet, the words *race* in French and *Rasse* in German are used for both people and animal classifications.

There are three categories of horse generally recognized throughout the world among people who domesticate horses. The *cold-blooded* horses, which are not dealt with in this paper, are those functional draft breeds used for pulling heavy loads but generally not ridden. *Cold-blooded* can also mean phlegmatic and tractable. The term *hot-blooded* is most generally limited to horses of the Thoroughbred and Arabian breeds. Three Arabians, imported to England in 1689, 1705, and 1730, are the foundation sires of the English Thoroughbred. These two breeds are also considered *full-bloods* because they have engaged in endogamous breeding programs over a long period of time. *Full-blood* and *hot-blood* are often used, many maintain incorrectly, interchangeably. *Hot-blooded* can also mean excitable and sensitive. The third category of horse, the subject of this essay, are termed *light-horse* breeds, often a cross between the other two types and used for domestic riding and competitive performance. In the United States they are not simply animals for "ritually demarcated" use, and the theoretical distinction between ritual and everyday is not useful in explaining their categorization.

The term *warm-blood* refers to those European breeds established specifically for show purposes. They are a cross between Thoroughbreds or Arabians and local draft horses, and are the primary light-horse category in Europe. Each European country has at least several different warm-bloods, which tend to be named after their geographical origins. While draft-horse and Arab breed categories have been constant over several centuries, light-horse breeds (which also includes the English Thoroughbred) are relatively recent in origin (eighteenth and nineteenth centuries), and in the United States new ones continue to be created. The point being elaborated in this essay is that the continental European and American breeds are constituted by different generative principles. The American breeds discussed here are uniformly recognized within the American horse world (see, e.g., AHSA 1982–1983; Kays 1982; Skelton 1978; Davis 1962; Evans 1977; Gorman 1958; Haddle 1975; Haynes 1976; *Horse Identifier* 1980).

2. Lévi-Strauss has often been accused of reifying cognitive structures. Although he does not deal with the social relations out of which the ideological transformations he outlines are drawn, he recognizes their theoretical significance: "It is of course only for purposes of exposition and because they form the subject of this book that I am apparently giving a sort of priority to ideology and superstructures. I do not at all mean to suggest that ideological transformations give rise to social ones. Only the reverse is in fact true. Men's conceptions of the relations between nature and culture is a function of modifications of their own social relations. But, since my aim here is to outline a theory of superstructures, reasons of method require that they should be singled out for attention and that major phenomena which have no place in this programme should seem to be left in brackets or given second place. We are however merely studying the shadows on the wall of the Cave without forgetting that it is only the attention we give them which lends them a semblance of reality" (1966: 117).

3. *Dressage,* meaning to school or train, provides the basic principles for all hippology, but is today often narrowed to what is in the vernacular called classical riding. Classical, or "high school," riding takes many years of training and supervision, for both the horse and rider, to achieve a moderate level of accomplishment. While in most other riding sports horses can be trained to their maximum capacity in from six months (racing) to two years (show jumping), a horse gener-

ally requires seven years of methodical ballet-like training under the guidance of an expert trainer to achieve the ability to perform at the Grand Prix level of dressage.

4. Authors differ in accounting for the nature of Justin Morgan's death. Jeanne Mellin, in her idealistic biography of the horse, claims he "died of an injury" (1973: 10). Charles Trench maintains that after the death of the original owner, Justin Morgan was turned out to pasture in the harsh northeast winter, like any other horse, "where he was eaten by wolves" (1972: 28).

5. The entire "industry" of horse-breed production and showing is in fact growing rapidly. The following table listing the growth of several major breeds is taken from Dinsmore (1978).

| Registry | Year Formed | Horses in 1960 | Horses in 1977 |
|---|---|---|---|
| AQHA | 1914 | 37,000 | 1,350,000 |
| Thoroughbred | 1894 | 12,901 | 760,000 |
| Appaloosa | 1938 | 4,052 | 760,000 |
| Morgan | 1894 | 1,069 | 275,000 |
| Paint | 1962 | 2,390 | 30,000 |
| Palomino | 1936 | 657 | 9,013 |
| Half-Arab | 1955 | 2,200 | 178,400 |
| Arabian | 1908 | 1,610 | 125,000 |

6. The Arabian horse, incidentally, has always been known as an endurance horse rather than a quick stopper and starter; it has a weakly muscled rear end and often crooked hind legs (cow-hocked or sickle-hocked). Consequently, there is no fetishization of the rear. Yet, as in the case of the Quarter Horse, halter classes have increased in importance for the Arabians. Although this shift was based upon different sets of morphological criteria, in both cases less attention was paid to how the horse performed. Many Arabs, bred for heads and necks that blend gently with the rest of the body, for "smooth toplines," lack an adequate withers to hold the saddle in place. Consequently, not only the saddle, but also the rider is continually sliding forward. Such fetishization of parts and "dysfunctional developments" have not, to my knowledge, occurred in Europe, perhaps because of the close ties of function to performance in the European sport horse.

7. An old aphorism says: The mare contributes the disposition, the stallion the conformation. Then, again, there are commonly recognized stallions in each breed that are called prepotent because they pass on their characteristics to their offspring. In America, these particular stallions are said to have a lot of "type" and to be "true to their breed."

8. The exact description of the Ideal-type and conformation is given as follows: "The Paint Horse is a stock-type horse. Head relatively short and wide with small muzzle and shallow, firm mouth; nostrils full and sensitive; ears short and active, set wide apart; large eyes, set wide; well-developed jaws with width between

lower edges; neck of sufficient length, with a trim throatlatch and not too much thickness or depth joining the head at a 45-degree angle and blending into sloping shoulders which are long and relatively heavy muscled; medium-high and well-defined withers the same height as croup; deep and broad chest with wide-set forelegs and well-muscled forearm; back short, close-coupled and powerful across loin; deep girth with well-sprung ribs; broad, deep, heavy, well-muscled quarters that are full through the thigh, stifle, and gaskin; cannon bones short with broad, flat, clean, strong, low-set knees and hocks; firm ankles and medium length, sloping pasterns; tough, textured feet with wide open heel" (AHSA 1982–1983: 235).

9. For a useful discussion of the genetic component in breed reproduction, see Warwick and Legates (1979: 553–85). They conclude that although the horse appears to be a "genetically plastic species," we are still ignorant of the "genetic parameters of quantitative traits in horses" (1979: 567).

10. In an extensive discussion concerning the names given to animals, Lévi-Strauss classifies racehorses as metaphorical inhuman beings (1966: 207). He first narrows his discussion of names to racehorses, for "ordinary horses whose place approximates more or less closely to that of cattle or that of dogs according to the class and occupation of their owner . . . is made even more uncertain by the rapid technological changes of recent times" (1966: 206). Reflecting upon English names, Edmund Leach agrees with him concerning racehorses, but disagrees as to cattle and dogs (1976: 100–102). With regard to the American case, I would emphasize Lévi-Strauss's caveat concerning the historical nature of naming "ordinary horses," which, as he uses the term, are the subject of this essay. I would also extend the caveat to racehorses, dogs, and cattle. While naming always involves political power in that it never merely describes but also constitutes the object, there are serious limitations to an approach that determines the signification of animals based solely upon a study of their names as part of a semiological system. The names themselves are determined by a combination of material, symbolic, and functional aspects of the animal's relation to humans. It should be added that function, conformation, and color of horses are not merely metaphorical extensions of differences in occupation, morphology, and color of people. There is also a metonymical identification between the temperament, origins, and functions of particular horses and the corresponding would-be or aspired-to characteristics of social groups. This kind of identification has only been suggested in this essay, and deserves further study.

11. Gorman (1958: 313) elaborates the levels of categorization used in speaking about individuals who are partially or fully part of a specific breed. A purebred "is a horse whose ancestors have been recognized as a breed for several generations. They are generally registered in a breed association." "A registered horse is one that has been recorded in a registration association by name and number." "A crossbred is a horse whose sire and dam are of different purebred breeds." A *grade* usually means a horse that had one purebred parent and one of unknown or mixed

breeding. A more basic distinction is often made between hot-blood and cold-blood, which roughly corresponds to the light-horse/draft-horse division. Haynes describes a hot-blood morphologically, as having "smooth body lines, trim legs and feet, quick movement, maneuverable speed" (1976: 62).

12. For a perspective on the extensiveness of an inspection program, note the following two years of statistics for the Quarter Horse (Sikes 1958: 12):

| Years | Miles Driven by Inspectors | Horses Assigned for Inspection | Percentage Accepted | Percentage Rejected |
|---|---|---|---|---|
| 1956 | 199,011 | 5,888 | 68 | 32 |
| 1957 | 264,890 | 9,007 | 70 | 30 |

13. Although the pattern to be sketched is generally true for the Continent as a whole, I am limiting the discussion to Germany and France. Germany is today the recognized exemplary center of international horse competition, of dressage in particular, and a center of breeding for this purpose. Yet, it is in seventeenth- and eighteenth-century France that light-horse riding as we know it today became codified, and for this reason, the development of French breeding and showing served as an exemplary center for the rest of the Continent.

14. In an article on sport and social class, Bourdieu makes several related observations about the French case. He maintains that the "extension of the public beyond the circle of amateurs helps to reinforce the reign of the pure professionals," and he attributes "decisive political effects" to "the division it makes between professionals, the virtuosi of an esoteric technique, and laymen, reduced to the role of mere consumers" (1978: 829, 830). While democratization and popularization of certain sports (that is, the extension of participation from royalty in elite schools to military to mass sporting associations) in Europe may have lead to the solidification of status differences, the process in America is different. This is because, first, many sports in America were not initially confined to an elite or to a group of amateur connoisseurs (for example, racing, Western riding); rather they were initially quite democratic. Second, the movement has been toward a proliferation of breeds, sports organizations, and shows, all roughly hierarchically ranked and indexically related to the creation of class and status distinctions in the general population. The consequence has been an appropriation of particular breeds by particular social classes.

15. The account here of this history follows the similar, although more detailed, accounts in the following texts: Seunig 1956; Wynmalen 1966; Kellock 1975; Skelton 1978; Goodall 1982.

16. Xenophon's texts appear enlightened and contemporary when compared to documents published in the Middle Ages. Laurentius Rusius, in *Hippiatrica sive marescalia,* printed in Paris in 1533, notes: "The nappy horse should be kept locked in a stable for forty days, thereupon to be mounted wearing large spurs and a

strong whip; or else the rider will carry an iron bar, three or four feet long and ending in three well sharpened hooks, and if the horse refuses to go forward he will dig one of these hooks into the horse's quarters and draw him forward; alternatively an assistant may apply a heated iron bar under the horse's tail, whilst the rider drives the spurs in with all available strength" (quoted in Wynmalen 1966: 27).

17. For detailed and theoretical treatment of the history of manners in France and Germany, see Nobert Elias (1978; 1982). Elias emphasizes both the internalization of norms and the external, policing efforts toward making particular cultural standards uniform. Although, for reasons of length, I am not dealing with the social conditions that made possible the reception and adoption of a national standard, imposed from without, the social leveling processes that preceded and subsequently accelerated after the French Revolution are acknowledged as important in the creation of French nationalism.

18. Arguments concerning the effects of French political centralization on cultural development are put forth by Pierre Bourdieu and Jean-Claude Passeron (1977) on national education, and by Eugen Weber (1976) on the creation of national identity among French peasants. Pierre Birnbaum makes the strongest theoretical statement, claiming that the French state is an independent variable, setting the limits for cultural and social processes (1980; Badie and Birnbaum 1983).

19. Max Weber, commenting on the importance of bureaucratization in the development of Germany, notes that the lack of powerful status groups of notables in Germany was in part responsible for the absence of political centralization (1978: 976–77). In an extended treatment of the Prussian experience, Hans Rosenberg maintains that during the ancien régime the bureaucracy "ceased to be responsible to dynastic interest" and "recast the system of government in its own image" (1966: vii). By 1815, the "political hegemony of the bureaucracy . . . was firmly established" (1966: 227). By 1871, German political unification was complete. The interesting aspect of German breeding is that even without political centralization, each German breeding program (*Landgestüt*) bureaucratized and rationalized separately. The history of German breeding is too lengthy to deal with here; however, I might note that the Teutonic Order of Knights already owned sixty-one stallions in 1400. In 1732, Frederick William I started the Trakehner Royal stud which was later taken over by the Prussian state upon the death of his son, Frederick the Great. Yet during the nineteenth century 80 percent of breeding still lay in the hands of small breeders, and the Trakehner horses were not branded until 1888. The Oldenburg breed was constituted in the seventeenth century by Count Gunther, but not subject to licensing of stallions and breeding control until 1819. This can be compared with the early date, 1621, of the Swedish Royal Stud (Goodall 1973; 1982; Skelton 1978).

20. The infantry, not the cavalry, was the backbone of the Prussian army. Yet the Prussian cavalry enjoyed royal patronage and "in the eyes of Europe (since

Frederick the Great) was the most famous branch of the Prussian armed forces" (Shanahan 1945: 17, 19). Perhaps because of the lack of political integration, there existed great regional autonomy in breeding and training until the time of Bismarck.

21. Birnbaum maintains that "the German state was unable to differentiate itself from the aristocracy" (1980: 675), whereas in France "the institutionalization of the state was accompanied by marked differentiation from the dominant class" (1980: 676). This may explain in part some of the differences between German and French horse breeding that run contrary to what one might on the surface predict. The German standard is more uniform than the French, deriving from the close links among the German aristocracy, the military, and the bureaucracy. Yet the French, who have more centralized political administration than the Germans, also have more marked differentiation among the aristocracy, the military, and the state. Thus, the French exhibit somewhat more regional diversity in horse breeding and usage than do the Germans.

22. See Benedict Anderson's *Imagined Communities* (1985) for an extended argument on the conditions under which imagined national communities have arisen.

REFERENCES

AHSA. 1982–1983. *Rule Book, The American Horse Shows Association, Inc.* New York: American Horse Shows Association, Inc.

Altschuler, Glenn C. 1982. *Race, Ethnicity and Class in American Social Thought, 1865–1919.* Arlington Heights, Ill.: Harlan Davidson, Inc.

Anderson, Benedict. 1985. *Imagined Communities: Reflections on the Origin and Spread of Nationalism.* London: Verso.

Badie, Bertrand, and Pierre Birnbaum. 1983. *The Sociology of the State.* Chicago: University of Chicago Press.

Barthes, Roland. 1983. "Myth Today," Mythologies. In, Susan Sontag, ed., *A Barthes Reader.* New York: Hill and Wang.

Birnbaum, Pierre. 1980. "States, Ideologies and Collective Action in Western Europe." *International Social Science Journal* 4: 687–716.

Bourdieu, Pierre. 1978. "Sport and Social Class." *Social Science Information* 17, 6: 819–40.

———. 1984. *Distinction: A Social Critique of the Judgement of Taste.* Richard Nice, trans. Cambridge: Harvard University Press.

Bourdieu, Pierre, and Jean-Claude Passeron. 1977. *Reproduction in Education, Society, and Culture.* Beverly Hills: Sage.

Copeland, L. 1959. "The Negro as a Contrast Conception." In, E. Thompson, ed., *Race Relations and the Race Problem.* Durham: Duke University Press.

Craig, Gordon. 1978. *Germany, 1866–1945.* New York: Oxford University Press.

Davis, Deering. 1962. *The American Cow Pony.* Princeton: D. Van Nostrand Company, Inc.

Denhardt, Robert. 1967. *Quarter Horses: A History of Two Centuries.* Norman: University of Oklahoma Press.

Dinsmore, Wayne. 1978. *The Horses of the Americas.* Norman: University of Oklahoma Press.

Doyle, Bertram Wilbur. 1937. *The Etiquette of Race Relations in the South.* Chicago: University of Chicago Press.

Elias, Norbert. 1978. *The Civilizing Process, Vol. 1.* New York: Pantheon Books.

———. 1982. *The Civilizing Process, Vol. 2.* New York: Pantheon Books.

Evans, J. Warren. 1977. *Horses.* San Francisco: W. H. Freeman and Company.

Foucault, Michel. 1973. *The Order of Things: An Archaeology of the Human Sciences.* New York: Vintage/Random House.

Glazer, Nathan, and Daniel P. Moynihan. 1975. *Beyond the Melting Pot.* Chicago: University of Chicago Press.

Goodall, Daphne Machin. 1973. *The Flight of the East Prussian Horses.* New York: Arco Publishing Co., Inc.

———. 1982. "Breeds of Horses." *Encyclopedia Americana.* Connecticut: Grolier, Inc.

Gorman, John A. 1958. *The Western Horse.* Danville, Ill: The Interstate.

Gossett, Thomas. 1963. *Race: The History of an Idea in America.* Austin: University of Texas Press.

Gumperz, John. 1982a. *Discourse Strategies.* New York: Cambridge University Press.

———. 1982b. "Introduction: Language and the Communication of Social Identity." In, J. Gumperz, ed., *Language and Social Identity.* New York: Cambridge University Press.

Haddle, Jan. 1975. *The Complete Book of the Appaloosa.* New York: A. S. Barnes and Company.

Harrington, Michael. 1980. *Decade of Decision: The Crisis of the American System.* New York: Simon and Schuster.

———. 1984. *The New American Poverty.* New York: Holt, Rinehart and Winston.

Hartz, Louis. 1955. *Liberal Tradition in America: An Interpretation of American Political Thought since the Revolution.* New York: Harcourt Brace.

Haynes, Glynn. 1976. *The American Paint Horse.* Norman: University of Oklahoma Press.

Hechter, Michael. 1978. "Considerations on Western European Ethnoregionalism." Paper presented at the conference "Ethnicity and Economic Development," University of Michigan, Ann Arbor, Oct.

Higham, John. 1967. *Strangers in the Land: Patterns of American Nativism 1860–1925.* New York: Antheneum.

Hintze, Otto. 1973. "The State in Historical Perspective." In, Reinhard Bendix, ed., *State and Society.* Berkeley: University of California Press.

*Horse Identifier.* 1980. New York: Sterling Publishing Company.

Huntington, Samuel P. 1973. "Political Modernization: America vs. Europe." In, Reinhard Bendix, ed., *State and Society.* Berkeley: University of California Press.

Kays, John. 1982. *The Horse.* New York: Arco Publishing, Inc.

Kellock, E. M. 1975. *The Story of Riding.* New York: St. Martin's Press.

Leach, Edmund. 1976. *Claude Lévi-Strauss.* New York: Penguin Books.

Le Roy Ladurie, Emmanuel. 1979. *The Territory of the Historian.* Chicago: University of Chicago Press.

Lévi-Strauss, Claude. 1963. *Totemism.* Boston: Beacon Press.

———. 1966. *The Savage Mind.* Rodney Needham, trans. Chicago: University of Chicago Press.

———. 1975. *The Raw and the Cooked.* New York: Harper & Row.

*Manual of Horsemanship.* 1972. Kenilworth, England: The British Horse Society.

Mellin, Jeanne. 1973. *The Morgan Horse.* Battleboro, Vt.: Stephen Greene Press.

Radcliffe-Brown, A. R. 1952 [1929]. "The Sociological Theory of Totemism." In *Structure and Function in Primitive Society.* New York: The Free Press.

Rosenberg, Hans. 1966. *Bureaucracy, Aristocracy, and Autocracy: The Prussian Experience 1660–1815.* Boston: Beacon Press.

Sahlins, Marshall, 1976. *The Use and Abuse of Biology.* Ann Arbor: University of Michigan Press.

———. 1977. "Colors and Cultures." In, Janet Dolgin, David Kemnitzer, and David Schneider, eds., *Symbolic Anthropology.* New York: Columbia University Press.

———. 1981. *Historical Metaphors and Mythical Realities: Structure in the Early History of the Sandwich Islands Kingdom.* Association for Social Anthropology in Oceania Special Publications No. 1. Ann Arbor: University of Michigan Press.

Seunig, Waldemar. 1956. *Horsemanship.* New York: Doubleday & Company.

Shanahan, William O. 1945. *Prussian Military Reforms, 1786–1813.* New York: Columbia University Press.

Sikes, L. N. 1958. *Using the American Quarter Horse.* Dayton, Tex.: Saddlerock Corporation.

Skelton, Betty. 1978. *Pictorial Encyclopedia of Horses & Riding.* Chicago: Rand McNally & Co.

Thurow, Lester. 1975. *Generating Inequality: Mechanisms for Distribution in the U.S. Economy.* New York: Basic Books.

———. 1980. *The Zero-Sum Society: Distribution and the Possibilities for Economic Change.* New York: Basic Books.

Tocqueville, Alexis de. 1955. *The Old Regime and the French Revolution.* New York: Doubleday & Company.

Todorov, Tzvetan. 1984 [1982]. *The Conquest of America.* New York: Harper & Row.

Trench, Charles, et al. 1972. *The Treasury of Horses.* London: Octopus Books.

Warwick, Everett J. and James E. Legates. 1979. *Breeding and the Improvement of Farm Animals.* New York: McGraw-Hill Book Co.

Weber, Eugen. 1976. *Peasants into Frenchmen: The Modernization of Rural France 1870–1914.* London: Chatto & Windus.

Weber, Max. 1978. *Economy & Society: An Outline of Interpretive Sociology.* Guenther Roth and Claus Wittich, eds. Berkeley: University of California Press.

Wehler, H.-U. 1973. *Das deutsche Kaiserreich 1871–1918.* Göttingen: Vandenhoech u. Ruprecht.

Wynmalen, Henry. 1966. *Equitation.* London: Country Life Limited.

# Postscript

## Reflections on Totemism Tomorrow: Horse Breeds and Breeding in the United States and France

*John Borneman*

In 1984 and 1985, during my third year of graduate study, I wrote the article on Race and Breed to fulfill the requirement called the "Specials Paper" in order to advance to Ph.D. candidacy in anthropology at Harvard. Horses and horse breeds were unrelated topically to my actual Ph.D. research, which was to be on kinship and nation building in Germany, but I wanted to analyze something with which I was already familiar, experientially, unlike the mere textual knowledge I had of Germany. And I was already familiar with totemism—the relation of humans to animals and plants—for I had grown up on a dairy farm, and I had worked for eight years as an equestrian (dressage and combined training riding instructor) between the completion of my bachelor's degree and entrance into the Ph.D. program at Harvard. (Professors would come up to me and introduce themselves and say, "So I hear you write.") At the time, I was enthused about semiotics and hermeneutics, but I also wanted to understand the motivation of the sign, and the politics and perlocutionary effects of semiosis. My explicit theoretical goal was to understand the historical relation of the state to the nation—in the United States, Germany, and France—as embodied in changes in cultural categories and the symbolic work they do in everyday life. Hence, on one level, it is an article about the ideological motivation of the symbolization of breed and race in three places.

On another level the article on horse breeds is about comparison. Only through comparison could I clarify an outstanding difference that had puzzled me ever since my first trip to Europe in 1973: Americans use a multitude of standards in defining their light horse breeds whereas Europeans rely on a single performance standard. My studies in anthropology had introduced me to the debates on totemism, a mode of classification employed to relate animal and human groupings in so-called primitive societies, but had not been applied ethnographically to any particular case of the relation of animals to Western classificatory devices of race and ethnicity. I knew that breed and species classification was historical and changing, but the prevailing synchronic analyses of totemism steered me toward a fairly uncritical functionalist explanation. And, most important for me, while breeding and ethnic identification are experienced as innocuous and often naturalized, they are in fact highly political acts, "the creation, in our image, of a world of differentiated animal species." Their effect is that of a second order language, to validate systems of class, race, and ethnic differentiation. To address the question critically, I needed comparison, and comparison not of fixed national cultures that generate or reproduce themselves but of fluid and interactive units over time. I had, first, to understand how totemic classification of people and horses in Germany and France differs in the United States, and second, to trace both the historical derivation of national categories of breed and race and the ideological motivation of these categories as signs of difference.

With the benefit and clarity of hindsight, I can state this theoretically: the article compares at three levels: categories of breed and race, national societies, and state form. It compares in three places: the United States, Germany, and France. And it compares not things but relations of difference in one order to relations of difference in another. If nation and state were to be anthropological categories of analysis, I should be able to see their significance in relation to how people employ something so basic as totemic operations—establishing correspondences between people and animals—in Europe and America. If I were able to maintain the fluidity of all three units, then I might be able to understand their formation and interaction as singular yet translatable symbolic forms within world historical processes.

In the course of my research, I quickly realized that there is no simple evolutionary sequence in the development of breeds, yet as symbolic forms in any particular social formation they tend to stabilize over time. This stabilization is merely of a symbolic form, however, and not of a whole or culture. Moreover, the stabilization of form, such as in Anglo-Saxon ethnicity or in a Quarter Horse, appeared necessary for processes of differentiation at the level of state and nation. This differentiation is part of a formal operation, motivated partly by disidentifying with either some exteriorized other or an outside—what structuralism, in its Lévi-Straussian version, identified as a key determinant of human thought. I traced this differentiation process comparatively for horse breeds, people classification, nation building, and state formation, each unit or level of difference generating its own logic yet dependent on the other levels, and on comparison and translatability, for definition.[1]

I will devote the rest of this essay not to talking about "totemism *aujord'huis*" but "totemism tomorrow," and thus sustain the ethnographic and theoretical surprise about the symbolic forms of horse breeding that arrested me in the first place. For the sake of space, I will limit myself to examples from the United States and France.

### Technical Replication Replaces the Sex Act

In the nearly two decades since I wrote the article, there have been some dramatic changes in the field of breeding and training. The European "warm bloods" now being produced are far superior athletes—larger, more powerful, more balanced—to the ones I had ridden professionally. What used to take eight to ten years to train for in dressage and performance now often appears reachable within four to six. Much of this is due to advances in breeding, including contributions from new reproductive technologies—artificial insemination, in vitro fertilization, genetic planning, egg transplants, and surrogate motherhood, for example. These are also forcing changes in the language and practices of sex and breeding. But thus far, the relation between human sex and animal breeding—the totemic operation—has changed much more in the United States than in France.

Language and metaphor might index some of these changes. Consider some of the "traditional" ways of talking about procreation and reproduction for horses and people. In English, German, and French, people "make love" (*Liebe machen, faire l'amour*), they "fuck" (*ficken, baiser*), they engage in "coitus" (*Koitus, coit*)[2] or in a "sex act" (*Sexakt*) or have "sexual intercourse" (*Geschlechtsverkehr treiben, rapport sexuel*), and they "come" (*kommen, jouir*). But only in English and German do people "have sex" (*Sex machen*).

If we take up the "scientific" and supposedly neutral language of evolutionary biology, English and German terms "to mate" (*balzen*) or to engage in "mate choice" (*Balzverhalten*), referring to people or horses, also have no direct French equivalents. In French, humans "partner" (*partenaire*) and engage in "partner choice" (*choix de partenaire*), and more recently can also have a sex partner (*partenaire sexuel*)—a term borrowed from English. Animals, by contrast, engage in coupling (*accouplement*)—a term used for people only as an insult, especially about "primitives," non-whites, or "mental retards." Finally, some terms in all three languages are largely reserved for non-human animals: "breeding" (*Deckakt,* reproduction), "to breed" (*züchten, la saillie de la jument or la monte*) or "to inseminate" (*besamen*).

In sum, French terminology maintains a more radical divide between horse breeding and human sex than does German or English. Historically, all three languages developed equine terminology in the Middle Ages with respect to practices of chivalry, and later with cavalry warfare. And French, like English and German, still borrows many of the human terms of romance and applies them to horses, such as ascribing "gentleman" status to well-behaved stallions, or claiming a stud likes/loves a mare (*il l'aime bien*) or has a soft spot for some mares (*un faible*), usually gray ones. But in France, the tradition of the "noble" horse is a stronger mark of distinction, indexing both a glorious past of absolutist kings and Napoleon's victories and a bourgeois project of professionalization, including the control over highly detailed, specialized, and esoteric equine knowledge not used in everyday situations. Hence the distinction between humans and animals that is being effaced in the United States and Germany is more resistant to reworking in France, as horses stand in an indexical relationship to French nobility. They are much more than lowly pets.

With respect to language, the simple point I want to make is that the process of breeding/sex is expressed through metaphors that often try to differentiate (or to establish similarities) in language between horses and humans. But these differences have been unsettled by the introduction of new reproductive technologies used for both humans and horses, which presents the problem of putting them into language designed to maintain or bridge other differences. Especially in the United States, without a stable way of analogizing between human and animal species, the totemic operation of establishing metaphorical equivalences appears less relevant. For example, the practice of "breeding in hand," also called "natural breeding" (*natürlicher Deckakt*), where the stallion mounts the mare either freely in a field (*monte en liberté*) or on a lead rope (*monte en main*) in an environment controlled by handlers, has in many places dramatically changed or been replaced (except for the least valuable breeds), by practices associated with "artificial insemination (AI)" (*künstliche Besamung*). AI involves masturbatory ejaculation, capture of the semen, and insertion of a tube of frozen, cold, or warm semen into the mare. AI is not talked about this way; technological terms are preferred over colloquial. All of these terms in the last sentence are in fact mine. Genital sex and its imagining is no longer necessarily a part of the process of reproduction. Coitus with the opposite sex is replaced by temporally separate processes of ejaculation and insemination. The orgasm is subordinated absolutely to external conditions. A model of species replication is replacing species reproduction.

The highly erotic scenes of light horse breeding that I remember from my childhood are largely a thing of the past. I do not think these scenes are just a matter of my memory, for the fact that most breeders vehemently deny the eroticism while joking about sexual excitation (and sometimes themselves having sex after) suggests to me classic repression. The mare "in heat" will still be teased until she is in a frenzy, squealing and squirting wildly, eager to be mounted. The stallion will still be encouraged to think of his own pleasure in penetrating and dominating the mare. But now the mare's hind legs are hobbled to prevent her from kicking not the stud but the semen-handler as he enters her with his rubber-gloved arm, frozen semen tube in hand. Now the stallion's huge penis will no longer be guided by a careful stud-handler to enter a live mare but into a foam-padded wooden stockhorse dummy covered in horse hide. Gone is the speculation about whether the foal will be better if the mare and stallion are a "love match," or the mare is truly "ready to mate," or whether the stallion loses his erection because the handler touched the penis, or touched it too soon, or the mare's tail wasn't held properly to the side. Gone (I am speaking only of warm bloods here) are the stereotypes, largely projections, to which American breeders appeal for legitimation of their own practices: free range breeding as among the elegant French, disciplined and technically controlled breeding as in Germany. We still have identification with the animal as the love-object (in France they still eat horses), but it is no longer an identification with the sex act. We might call it a return to polymorphous perversity. The sex act is replaced by processes of technical replication, which are similar everywhere, in France, Germany, and the United States.

Replication, however, can be imagined for different purposes. To state the difference starkly: in France, the purpose is a strict, single performance standard arising out of a scientific and bourgeois understanding of the horse; in the United States, multiple performance standards are subordinated to fetishized differences that index class and race.

### Soring and the "Big Lick": Conformation
### and the Tennessee Walking Horse

In 1984, I identified function and temperament, conformation, and color, as three breed criteria that are symbolically elaborated in order to differentiate horses. In the interim, the criterion that has taken on the most specifically American gestalt is "conformation"—basically, how the horse looks. In photos from advertisements in trade journals back in 1983, we can see fetishization of the Arabian head is distinguished by contrast with the Quarter Horse rear-end—both index conformational qualities typical of the respective breeds. U.S. American identification with appearance and beauty may be a constant cultural theme, but since the mid-1970s there has been an explosion of interest in health and beauty and diet regimes, extending through all ages, ethnicities, races, and economic classes, manifested in activities such as weight lifting, aerobics, dieting and dietary supplements, the use of steroids and muscle enhancers, and reconstructive surgery. This remaking of the body into a more "natural beauty" has its direct counterparts in the horse world. Let me elaborate another American light horse breed that I mentioned only in passing before: the Tennessee Walking Horse.

Walking Horses claim descent from Thoroughbreds, Standardbreds, Morgans, and American Saddlebreds, with early contributions from Canadian and Narragansett Pacers. There are currently 360,000 registered Tennessee Walking Horses in the United States, and about 10 percent go to horse shows. They are primarily known for a special gliding gait, perfected for plantation owners and village doctors in early nineteenth-century Tennessee, and elsewhere in the old South. With this glide (instead of trot, walk, or gallop), one could ride for hours without fatigue, for either horse or rider. This gait is called the "running walk": the hind feet move in long flat strides while the front feet step high and the head nods in time. It is, needless to say, an impure gait, yet selective breeding has made it inheritable.

Breeders and trainers who show these horses in competitions win by exaggerating the movement of the running walk. Eighty to ninety percent of these trainers, according to most critical observers, resort to a practice called "soring." Several days before any show, trainers apply to the front legs chemical irritants, including kerosene, diesel oil, crotonaldehyde, and mustard oil (a relative of the poison gas used in World War I). The legs are left to "cook" under plastic wraps and bandages. Or, alternately, farriers over-trim the hooves or add thick pads to the shoes to raise the heels, or trainers put circular chains on the horses' ankle, the combined effect being that with every step the front feet hurt on impact with the ground.

Soring causes the horses to lower their hindquarters and snap their front feet briskly and hold them in the air longer and higher than they normally would. Known as the "Big Lick," this movement is an exaggerated parody of the breed's "natural" way of moving, but practically impossible to achieve without the use of pain. It is considered the ultimate in mainstream Walking Horse competition.

In the summer of 1999, the veterinarian Dr. Andrew Lang, who tends to the health of the ASPCA's shelter animals and heads up an Equine Advisory Committee in Tennessee, spent three days attending shows and visiting training barns. "Some horses," he wrote in his report, "appeared to be struggling just to make it around the ring. . . . When at last the horses were lined up along the rail for judgment, several appeared distressed, glistening with sweat, their eyes wide and their nostrils flaring as they caught their breath."

Dr. Lang asked a trainer if he engaged in soring. "'No,' he replied. Seconds later, he confessed. One night, years ago, he applied the caustic chemicals, wrapped his horse's front legs in plastic and bandages, and went to bed. Unable to sleep, he returned to the stable in the middle of the night, undid his handiwork and washed his horse's legs. 'Horses,' he said with tender conviction, 'are God's gift.'" To my knowledge, no German or French trainer would resort to God to justify limits on the use of torture to increase performance. To be sure, some Europeans also engage in abusive practices to increase the performance of their warm bloods, especially in the lucrative field of show jumping, but they do so clearly in the name of science or profit or national esteem. The peculiar U.S. American ideology involves the reintroduction of God, or religion, as a counterweight to the language of profit, profit earned through the production of "beauty."

Soring itself has a history, very much connected to the growth of a glamour industry in the United States. The official breed registry, later called the Tennessee Walking Horse Breeders and Exhibitors Association, was formed in 1935. Four years later, in 1939, the breed competed for the first time at New York City's Madison Square Garden, in what is called the National Walking Horse Celebration. With that national exposure, their popularity exploded, and the value of top horses rose as much as tenfold.

A recession in the 1950s reduced demand, and prices took a dive. This is when soring entered. Many say it was an accidental discovery: a horse with a sore foot lifted its foot much higher and quicker, producing a flashier running walk. Soon, trainers began treating both front feet for pain—accentuating rather than alleviating it—and voila, the result was the Big Lick! In the 1960s, the situation had deteriorated to the point where horses' feet could be seen bleeding in the show ring. In 1970, the state entered: Congress passed the Horse Protection Act, which outlawed soring. Enforcement was entrusted to the United States Department of Agriculture (USDA), but little money was allocated for this purpose. In 1976, in a wave of deregulation legislation, Congress allowed industry organizations certified by the USDA to train their own lay inspectors. Still under-funded, these inspectors attend only about 50 out of 600 shows a year. In 1999, the USDA and industry and humane groups developed a new operating plan intended to improve enforcement—clarifying procedures and increasing penalties. At the same time, the industry was given a larger role in enforcement.

Meanwhile, breeders and trainers have improved soring techniques and made them harder to detect, giving the appearance of progress. Dr. Lang writes in his report, "Painful trimming and shoeing methods that cannot be detected without removing the shoes have replaced nails hammered through hoof walls and cut off at the surface or metal objects wedged between the shoe pads and soles that are gouged to the quick. Some horses are subject to mock inspections and beaten severely if they show signs of pain. Salicylic acid is used to burn off scar tissue and dyes or tattoos hide discoloration. Topical pain-killing sprays numb the skin before inspection, but wear off while the horse is in the ring." (For documentation of these practices, and a copy of Lang's report, see http://www.aspca.org/learn/upl/AnimalWatch/sore.html.)

The framework in which I would like to interpret soring and the "Big Lick" sustains a paradox: Animals are both increasingly protected from humans (i.e., growth of societies for the protection of animals, including animal rights movements, even animal rights courses taught at major law schools) and increasingly commodified for humans in our games and competitions. We try to treat horses as forms of difference not already assimilated into our hierarchies on the basis of what they lack in human qualities, to attribute intrinsic value to them as a living species. But deprived of value based on our own explicit projections, on our anthropomorphizing, we then instead submit them to a more distanced arbiter: the market, which in turn transforms them into new commodity forms, for which we no longer feel directly accountable. Horses are both individuated family members with their own integrity and mere commodities in a big business. I will return to the economic aspects shortly, but first let me compare these changes in American breeding with the French.

### Scientific Rationality and "*La Passion du Cheval*"

Whereas in the United States the potential counterweight to commodification and the language of profit is religion; in France the potential counterweight to profit is "*passion du cheval.*" At least since the Revolution, the cultivation of horses—breeding and riding have been part of a national project of improving Frenchmen and French animals, of a general "*embourgeoisement.*" While indexing the French nation, horse breeding is also an activity connected to myths of the uniqueness and beauty of the countryside (*terroir*) and rural France. As of 1998, there were 45,000 horse breeders in France, of whom 1,023 were rated as professionals (those with at least nine mares). Today's highly subsidized farmers may still be heavily involved in breeding draft horses, but most light horse breeding (warm bloods), on which I will concentrate here, is a professional activity practiced by other social classes. The riders of warm bloods also usually come from the bourgeoisie.

The French state, through its centralized administration, has nearly total control over the regulation and direction of breeding and training. The bureaucracy charged with this task is the Haras Nationaux ('National Stud Farms'), one of France's oldest administrations. Created by Colbert in 1665 under Louis XIV, the National Studs were abolished in 1790 during the French Revolution, and then in 1806 re-established by Napoleon. Their early role was essentially military, and their royal and imperial history in defense of the French nation is integral to its attraction both in France and abroad. The National Studs represents itself as working in partnership with professional unions, local administrations, and non-profit-making associations, but unlike in the United States, it actually directs the various activities within the French horse industry, which it divides into three sectors: racing, sport, and leisure—which the Heras also ranks in this order in terms of importance for breed improvement and revenue. The category "sport," which is concerned with light horses, is further divided into dressage, jumping, and eventing.

The National Studs is entrusted with a specific mission: to promote and develop horse breeding and all horse-related activities. It lists these activities as: definition and implementation of breeding policies, breed preservation and improvement, identification and maintenance of a central file of registration, registration and surveillance of horse-dedicated premises open to the public, collection and processing of economic and financial data on markets, trades and professions concerning horses and other equines, development and promotion of products as well as promotion of sporting techniques and practices, definition and implementation of main research and design trends, as well as programs developed jointly with Ministries and other administrations or institutions. In short, this is a quintessential Enlightenment project—the use of science for improvement and continuous rationalization of activities in the service of the French people.

The National Studs is also dedicated to the sale and breeding of Selle Francais sport horses, but it also promotes other breeds, including the indigenous French Anglo-Arab (which are infrequently introduced into the Selle Francais). Napoleon himself had created the "French Anglo-Arab," importing Arabians from northern Africa and crossing them with English Thoroughbreds, with some early nineteenth-century influx of "local" mares also of Thoroughbred or Arabian descent. The Selle Francais are most similar to other European warm bloods, regional mixes of draft (Normandy cold blood) mares and English Thoroughbred stallions. Although the Haras Nationaux own only 23 percent of the stallions in the country, they sire 50 percent of French light and draft horse breeds. (Privately owned stallions sire more than 70 percent of foreign riding horses, racing horses, and ponies/donkeys.) Hence its strength rests not on having a monopoly on breeding but on its large administration that engages in research, regulates, and subsidizes local activities. Some breeds, like the Anglo-Arab, are strictly concerned with maintaining the purity of bloodlines. Others, like the Selle Francias, must balance two goals: to maintain the purity of bloodlines or to improve the quality of the breed through mixing with better stock and to maintain the purity of bloodlines.

Since 1976, most of the breeding of the Selle Francais has been done with artificial insemination, using "fresh" (warm), refrigerated, or frozen semen. (Frozen is still forbidden with thoroughbreds.) The introduction of AI and other reproductive technologies has provided the basis for further rationalization of breeding. Several French breeders use embryo transfer to prolong a top mare's competitive career, using much larger draft horse mares as surrogate mothers. All foals in a given year must be named with a word beginning with the same letter of the alphabet, making it easier to track cohorts. And, in 1976, a centralized system of identification and registration was created, with horses receiving *"papier d'identite,"* identification papers like those for people (called simply *"papiers"*). These function like a passport, containing pedigrees and health histories, which will further serve purposes of genetic planning and tracking. (For the most informative site on French breeding, see www.haras-nationaux.fr.)

Despite this devotion to science and the rationalized production of superior horses, the horse is still attached to the noble and the elegant in France, and it is still identified with a communicative rationality, or even a non-rationality, what is called *"la passion du cheval."* This side of French breeding, or the mix of the emotional and rational, is illustrated by Pierre Durand, winner of the gold medal in the 1988 Seoul Olympics in show jumping on a 1.58 meter (slightly under 15 hands) Selle Francais stallion named Jappeloup. Since the average height of show jumpers is closer to 16.2 hands, Jappeloup was absolutely tiny to go over such large jumps. Durand (whose name incidentally identifies him as prototypical Frenchman, like Joe Smith in English) has his own website, where he offers an ontology of this passion:

It was at the age of 10 that I had my first real encounter with a horse. She was called Gitane. She completely seduced me, like a bolt of lightening, which ignited a double passion that has never left me: the first for horses, and the second for the practical realm of equestrian sport. Since then, my life has been conducted and dedicated to these loves of my life—after Gitane came Bonita, Urgence, Velleda, Laudanum, Jappeloup, Narcotique and, today, once again, Gentleman. Every one gave me incomparable joy and filled my life with formidable emotions. My family did not come from equestrian traditions so it was through my first instructor that I discovered the foundations of riding that were subsequently enriched essentially by observation, reading, and discussions with other riders. In the beginning, it was three-day eventing that drew me close to the three Olympic disciplines but, following a nasty fall at the age of 12, my parents decided that I should change to showjumping, which was considered less dangerous. Very soon, I dreamed of becoming an Olympic Champion like Pierre Jonquères d'Oriola. And this childhood dream transformed into a sincere obsession in my adult years that a horse like no other gave me the opportunity to realize: he was called Jappeloup (www.annuaire-du-chre view.com).

After his gold medal victory in the Olympics, Durand became embroiled in several scandals that were perhaps related to the kind of self-promotion suggested in his description above. He appeals to both French Ur-myths, of science and of passion, but his interests clearly originate in passion. Following the seduction by the mare "Gitane" (a female gypsy and a very strong French cigarette), he engaged a succession of "lovers", many of whose names recall illicit passions: "Narcotique" drugged him, "Laudanum" (a favorite opium tincture of late nineteenth century ladies and dandies) opiated him, "Urgence" represented an irrepressible, compelling need. But not born into an equestrian family, Durand, like Rousseau's Emile, needed education: He was "enriched" through "observation, reading, and discussions," which enabled him to dream of "becoming an Olympic champion," and to transform this dream into a "sincere obsession" and to realize it with the horse "Jappeloup."

Durand's commitment to his *"passion du cheval"* was questioned in an unusual scandal concerning Jappeloup's death. After his Olympic achievement, Jappeloup became a national hero and was retired to stud. But he had problems breeding, or so it was rumored (I have been unable to find any record of foals he sired). Then one day he died in a mysterious fire. Durand, who in the interim had become not just a nouveau-riche Olympic champion but also a successful businessman and sponsor of events, with his own equestrian center and vacation and training resort, collected a large insurance premium. One high commissioner in the French Equestrian Federation said openly what many suspected: that Durand had killed Jappeloup to collect the insurance premium.[3] To make a long story short, Durand sued for libel and won. Today, he continues to advertise his *"passion du cheval"* while marketing his progeny, including most recently a foal from his mare "Narcotique," which he calls one of his *"produit"* (products, offspring).[4]

## Conclusion

Value in U.S. American light horse breeding is earned through the production of "conformation," meaning beauty, justified in the name of God; in France value is obtained through a scientific rationality that exploits the "passion for horses" with the help of the state. Let me develop this with two points by way of conclusion. First, with regard to my claim, in 1984, that all totemic classification is the result of a projection and hence inverse totemism. That was totemism yesterday. If a horse's value is intrinsic to it, as argued by many U.S. animal rights activists, arrived at without resort to analogy to humans, without resort to an identification with the animal as part of or (dis)similar to oneself, then there is no justification for a specifically human valuation of animals based on our relationship to them. How, then, to determine this intrinsic value? Without a totemic operation, where does the value of the horse come from? As I have illustrated above, herein enters the logic of profitability, value as determined by rules of market exchange, what Sahlins (1976: 211) argued made "the economic . . . the main site of symbolic production."[5] This logic holds increasingly in both France and the United States. Particularly in the horse world, initial capital and location in the economy are preconditions for participation in such an expensive activity.

While the market may be the site of symbolic production, however, it is no longer regulated by any invisible hand. Its force and motivation are discursively and publicly debated conditions for human self-definition, in which a logic of replication frequently asserts itself. Decoupling sex from breeding has enabled diverse experiments in kinship practices—sex, breeding, love, affiliation—wherein the human is radically refigured. Innovations in reproductive technologies and regimes of health and diet have been an integral factor here, contributing to a redefinition of the boundaries of life and death, and the relation of reproduction to replication. This bricolage in the kinship domain is in turn refiguring the horse as pet and commodity, as both comparable in value to humans (with its own—parallel) horoscope and lineage and diet and exercise regime and hospital and graveyard)—and as having no value outside commodity exchange—(hence valued more dead than alive as, for example, dog food or an insurance premium). There is a complicated feedback loop of desire here, in which we have a premonition of totemism tomorrow, driven by a logic of sexless identification and replication. In the United States this identification and valuation occurs partly by means of a repudiated totemism and in interaction with a highly reticent and largely ineffectual state, which, when it does enter the fray, seems largely beholden to the industry it is in charge of regulating. In France, value is still largely ascribed totemically with the state as a major player.

My second point: In both the United States and France, commodification encourages selective replication. With the possibility of replication in mind, the libidinal attachment to the animal can be divorced from any originary sex act. One's favorite horse can be replicated without sex. Both the procreative act *and* the death of the loved animal then become irrelevant when the loved object can be simply replaced through replication. Torture and death are no obstacles when replication is possible. Replication, understood as a compulsion to repeat, is in fact the opposite of eros or of love for the animal. Rather, it resembles what Freud associated with the death drive. By this he means striving to reduce tensions to null, to bring the living being back to the inorganic state. It is a drive initially directed inwards towards self-destruction but which subsequently becomes aggression directed towards the outside world. In this case, the aggression appears to be directed at the love object itself: the horse.

NOTES

Acknowledgments: My many thanks to Christophe Robert for criticisms and research assistance, especially on French breeding, about which I could not have written without his knowledge and insight.

1. In an excellent article on comparative sociology, Phil McMichael (1992: 359) sketches two methodological requirements that correspond to my approach: "first, ensuring that the units of analysis are historical, and therefore fluid, concepts; and second, employing an emergent, rather than an a priori whole, to establish historical context. . . . The diachronic form involves comparison across multiple instances of a single historical process." See Phil McMichael, "Rethinking Comparative Analysis in a Post-developmentalist Context," *International Social Science Journal* 133, 3 (1992): 351–65.

2. Hence informed French travelers find the Coit Tower in San Francisco extremely amusing.

3. Killing valuable performance horses for insurance premiums is perhaps even more widespread in the United States. A federal investigation of the killing of fifteen horses in the late 1980s and early 1990s led to several convictions, the most famous being of the George Lindemann for killing his Olympic mount, "Charisma," to collect a $250,000 insurance premium. Lindemann was convicted, along with three others, for a federal conspiracy to defraud the insurance company, using interstate telephone calls (thus the charge of "wire fraud") to electrocute Charisma on the evening of 15 December 1990 (cf. U.S. v. George Lindemann, Jr. U.S. Court of Appeals 7th Circuit, No. 96–1188, decided 4 June 1996).

4. The English language term "animal husbandry" suggests a similar relationship to animal breeding, that the human functions not as wife, uncle, aunt, or father, but as a male, married caretaker.

5. Marshall Sahlins, *Culture and Practical Reason* (Chicago: University of Chicago Press, 1976). In some other parts of the horse world, other logics, such as a logic of care or friendship, do in fact trump market logic. One salient example: For the last several decades, the U.S. Bureau of Land Management offers a Wild

Horse Adoption Program as a means to control overpopulation of wild horses in federal lands without killing them. Such horses can be domesticated, but they are rarely profitable in any sense of the word. Most frequently, they are difficult to train and, not being bred selectively for riding, they do not make particularly good mounts. Most of the adoptive parents only take them by identifying through projecting qualities onto them (such as wildness and freedom), or simply out of the joy of caring, and they in fact have to sacrifice a great deal of time, money, and even status.

# The Cities of Avignon and Worms as Expressions of European Community, 1945–1975

*Beverly Heckart*

At the end of 1978, the German art critic Walter Frentz, introducing a film and public lecture in the city of Worms, postulated that West Europeans could breathe new life into the idea of European unity by devoting greater care and attention to the shape and form of European cities. Consciously or unconsciously, Frentz, inspired by the European Heritage Year of the mid-1970s, strove to awaken a nascent European consciousness. Did such a consciousness exist?

Since Frentz spoke nearly three decades ago, scholars from various disciplines have explored the nature of European "unification." Was it merely an economic venture, innovated to bolster the economies of participating nation-states? Was it, at the time, a Cold War construct used as one weapon, among many, against the Soviet Union and the Eastern bloc? Or did, as Frentz implied, a sense of "Europeanness" already exist? Did West Europeans remember a common history and share a common vision that transcended economic and political concerns? Did Europe's treatment of its urban cores contain hints of common characteristics?[1]

A large interdisciplinary literature suggests that cities take shapes that are expressions of a total society, reflecting the spectrum of their political, economic, and cultural life. As West Europeans sought to revitalize themselves after the crisis of World War II by innovating economic unification, so cities pursued their own re-creation in order to ensure their survival. Two such cities in France and West Germany were Avignon and Worms. An investigation into how they configured their urban cores during the three decades following the war can provide insights into their images of themselves, not only as Avignonnais and Wormser, as French or German cities, but as European ones as well.[2]

366

Avignon and Worms possess striking similarities in their geographical situations and historical developments. While located on two different, major European rivers (the Rhône and the Rhine), both urban sites were settled in prehistoric times, both belonged to the Roman Empire, and both were prosperous settings for significant European events during the Middle Ages. The fortunes of each declined in the early modern period but revived in a modest fashion during the nineteenth and twentieth centuries as industrialization brought Europeans closer together both economically and culturally.

After World War II, these two old, European cities faced the task of rebuilding their city centers. In such old cities, the rearrangement of the center is a difficult task. Not only are traditional street patterns, long-established properties, and entrenched business interests difficult to dislodge, but the very role of the core for the entire urban area gives its image and configuration a strong psychological significance. The center is the original urban heart, where the sites of the original market, the original port, the original government once pulsed—and, in many cases, continue to beat. In most European cities, small and large, the center is the scene of important cultural and social activities; its high visibility makes it the symbol of urban memory and identity. How this center is changed reveals not only a city's assessment of its past and present, but its intentions about the future. Because a city's fortunes are intertwined with external developments, urban change both reflects and enriches the supra-local currents of an era.[3] In Avignon and Worms, the treatment of the urban cores was caught up in the wider European tide.

## The Rebirth of Avignon

At the end of World War II, Avignonnais hoped to recapture the prominence the city had once enjoyed as Papal residence and ecclesiastical capital of Europe. This proud past contrasted sharply with the city's immediate prospects. In 1945 Avignon was only one of many small French towns whose postwar future looked bleak. Because of restrictions on local travel during World War II, the city's function as a supply center had been assumed by outlying towns and villages. After the war, its few industries—textiles, pharmaceuticals, canning—moved away or began to decline. Although Avignon remained the administrative center of the département of Vaucluse, its leaders yearned to rebuild the city as a "regional metropolis": the economic hub of a rich agricultural area in the Provence and of a vast hinterland on the west side of the Rhône. The best hope for achieving that goal lay in the "extraordinary aptitude" of the Avignonnais to "transform themselves." Speaking to the Chamber of Commerce in 1945, the regional director of the agricultural research center, Jean Bordas, urged the assembled notables not only to modernize but to embellish the city's core.[4] Thus he created a link between economic prosperity and urban architecture.

When Bordas spoke, the heart of Avignon still lay inside its fourteenth-century walls. Practically no change had occurred to the medieval warren of winding paths and alleys; most structures predated the French Third Republic. Isolated houses verged on collapse. Avignon's faulty sewers stank during the hot Provençal summers. In contrast to scores of German and other French cities, Avignon had experienced little destruction in World War II. A transforming urbanism confronted an antiquated framework descriptive of the past and communicating different signs to various groups.[5]

These signs became important as the city pursued economic and social modernization in the postwar era. To accomplish this task, a coalition of moderate progressives persuaded Edouard Daladier in 1953 to become mayor. This former French premier and actor on the European scene was once again Vauclusien deputy to the National Assembly and a powerful member of the dominant Radical Socialist Party. Over the next five years, he secured massive government loans for a variety of projects. The damaged bridge over the Rhône was replaced; a pumping station for flood control was completed; outside the walls, numerous schools and housing complexes created extensive new quarters. Plans were made to build a larger, more modern agricultural wholesale market on the outskirts of town. Members of the construction industry—a group that strongly supported Daladier's mayoralty—benefited from these projects. In contrast, as the intramural population deserted the city's core for the new quarters on the periphery, businessmen in the center suffered economic misery.[6]

Many Avignonnais retailers commonly perceived the loss of employment due to factory closures as a major cause of the city's commercial stagnation. At least one solution to this problem was to stimulate new industrial ventures. Reduced taxes for industry were supported by the city council, and subsidies (from the national government) obtained for an industrial park, but few new enterprises opened their doors in Avignon. The extreme centralization of the French state encouraged many firms to locate in and around Paris, and Avignon, unlike the neighboring Marseilles and Lyons, offered few external economies to industries increasingly interested in efficiency. Its only advantages were the railroad's triage station, the city's proximity to a rich agricultural hinterland, and the brief history of Papal residence. Like so many cities scattered across the Midi, Avignon had long specialized in services. Conservative Avignonnais, though they desired economic revitalization, shunned the idea of an industrialized city, stressing its tradition as a center for peasants, artisans, and vacationers. Even retailers did not favor sweeping economic alterations.[7]

This ambivalent attitude toward change manifested itself in many ways. One was the growth of Poujadism. Begun by a small businessman, Pierre Poujade, as a protest against national fiscal reform, it developed into a revolt against the perceived standardization and loss of individualism that accompanied the postwar drive to modernize France. In the national elections of 1956, 20 percent of Avignon's voters supported Poujadist candidates. Locally, Poujadists elected a sizable group to the Chamber of Commerce and used their influence to counter the domination of Florentin Mouret, a modernizer who was president of the Association of Builders and an important member of the mayor's cabinet.[8] The revolt against Mouret and his influence coincided with the beginning of a sustained controversy about the renewal of the intramural city. This issue stirred up a host of civic memories that eventually resounded throughout France.

Throughout the postwar period, plans for urban renewal focused on the quarter that was both the city's worst slum and its most significant townscape. This old quarter, the Balance, lay on the western side of the Rocher des Doms—the high cliff above the Rhône that protected ancient river traders. As Europe had changed, so had the Balance. In Roman times, the area served as a depot; during the late Middle Ages, eastern access to the famous bridge traversed the quarter. The Papal Palace adjoined the cathedral on the Rocher's slope, and cardinals lived in the neighboring Balance during the Papal residence. After the Popes' departure the district remained one of the most fashionable in the city, and the Rue de la Balance was Avignon's main street. Two other routes through the district, the Rues Grande Fusterie and du Limas harbored the textile and timber industries of the old regime. Thus the entire site was associated with the city's past growth and glory. In addition, "urban renewal" in the seventeenth century had fixed its architectural image in the classical style—a genre that recalled European origins in Greece and Rome, the ascendancy of the French state in the age of Louis XIV, and the cultural consensus of the imperialist Third French Republic. For some Avignonnais the stones and red-tiled roofs of the Balance also awakened their sense of a "méridional" identity, of belonging to a region with affinities to a larger Mediterranean world.[9]

The decline of the Balance began with the French Revolution and the French state's annexation of Avignon. As the Papal Palace became first a prison and then a military barracks, the nobility and rich bourgeoisie departed; prostitutes, gypsies, and proletarians filtered in. After 1945, the French government classified most buildings in the Balance as substandard. Many reasons were advanced for its complete destruction and subsequent renewal. Not only were living conditions completely unsuitable for the twentieth century, but its narrow streets hindered traffic traveling from the modern bridge to the center of the city. Its unsightliness and inconvenience deterred both tourists and customers from visiting and shopping in downtown Avignon. Because the area's degradation diminished property values, it also reduced tax revenues. Some improvement had to occur to make access to town more convenient, to increase Avignon's attractiveness to both the casual tourist and the more frequent shopper, and to contribute more generously to Avignon's public coffers.[10]

Urban improvement can take many forms. Complete renewal involves the destruction of existing patterns and structures; renovation assumes only partial preservation of the former plan; restoration projects the complete rehabilitation of the old architectural features. In dealing with the Balance, Avignonnais first slated urban renewal. Both before and after World War II, the municipality and the appropriate national agencies anticipated razing the entire quarter. As the inheritor of this assumption, Mayor Daladier engaged a nationally known architect, M. Pouillon, who completed a small-scale model displayed at the city hall in 1956. The model foresaw the destruction of all the Balance's distinctive features. The old pattern of streets would be effaced, medieval, Renaissance, and seventeenth-century structures leveled. In their places a new, European vision, à la Corbusier, would arise.[11]

Although the modernist plans of architects and urban planners of the twentieth century now seem utopian, it is easy to forget that international movements such as the Charter of Athens and the Bauhaus, which inspired Pouillon's plans, sought not only to avert "crises" of commercial urban cores, such as Avignon experienced in the postwar period, but to change the degraded lifestyles of the urban poor who lodged in the old, airless, crowded quarters of ancient districts like the Balance. Modern buildings in the new European and International styles would obliterate the more recent memories of poverty and decline and propel the city into a more modern, orderly, and socially upgraded future. The architecture of the distant past would disappear.[12] Daladier, however was not the first to attack the old stones of Avignon. Throughout the preceding century, energetic mayors and their supporters, with similar visions of progress, had projected destruction of the medieval walls, of old mansions, and of familiar pathways. As recently as the early 1950s, determined groups had staved off a decision to alter the Balance's southern section because it portended the quarter's complete destruction. At that time, the idea of restoring the entire ensemble first arose.[13]

When Daladier's model appeared at city hall, a similar array of civic chagrin arose. The politically centrist newspaper, *Méridional,* most representative of retailers and sympathetic to the Poujadists, called for a beautification of the Balance; perhaps total destruction was unwarranted. Citizens interviewed by the Socialist newspaper, *Le Provençal,* admitted that the facades of the Balance were historically unique and architecturally beautiful, but thought restoration would be too expensive; efficient modernization pointed to destruction. Of those the paper interviewed, only a Socialist trade unionist wanted to save the quarter's image. The conservative *Gazette Provençal* supported razing and renewal. The Friends of the Papal Palace firmly rejected the "buildings" featured in city hall's model but favored renovation rather than a strict preservation of the quarter. At the beginning of 1958, the city council rejected Pouillon's plan and promised to "respect the archaeological patrimony" of the quarter, but it made no specific recommendations for the future.[14]

Long before the European preoccupation with patrimony that emerged in the 1970s, the Avignonnais began to focus on the physical memory of their European past. By the time they rejected the renewal planned for the Balance, Avignon, like other European cities, had confronted the way in which a vision of future improvement can efface the memory of a serviceable past. In France, the Revolution of 1789 had threatened to "vandalize" completely the art and architecture of the Old Regime. The Haussmannien episode in French city planning, even in Avignon, had swept away the patterns of entire urban districts. The destruction of World Wars I and II had led to the disappearance of art and architecture that anchored the memories of a communal continuum that could ease a painful transition into the future.[15] In 1958, as Avignon struggled to carve out for itself a new urban niche, it could hardly escape its national and international context. With the approaching independence of Algeria, France faced the loss of its old role as world power. It too needed a rejuvenated identity. Participation in a united Europe held out the hope of a new leadership position on the international scene. Such influence necessitated the economic modernization that caused economic and social crisis in towns like Avignon. Just as the Avignonnais chose renovation as a means of partially preserving a legacy reminiscent of the European past, so the French state aspired to remind Europe that France was the receptacle and disseminator of European cultural values.[16] With a past more European than French, Avignon could not escape its function in this larger scheme.

Even as the Avignonnais contemplated compromise in the configuration of the Balance, the French cultural elite attended to the fate of the quarter. Outsiders chastised those who favored renovation for neglecting and destroying the city's architectural legacy. Avignonnais bristled at this interference, but their objections were ambivalent. If architects and city planners, like Pouillon, projected destruction, they were dismissed, or counteracted. If nationally known critics said Avignon was callous about preserving artistic treasures, they were accused of understanding neither the city's future needs nor its financial situation. Knowledgeable Avignonnais knew that the national Service of Historic Monuments would have to approve anything done to structures inscribed on the official list, but this agency itself was equivocal. It simultaneously proclaimed the Balance to be a classified site and to possess no special architectural value. Renovation was an appropriate approach.[17] The matter rested there as the Fourth Republic ended, and the Gaullist Fifth began.

As a result of the Gaullist victory, Daladier—his usefulness to the city undermined by his strong opposition to the Fifth Republic—resigned as mayor in 1958. The less flamboyant Henri Duffaut took his place. Originally from Languedoc, he arrived in Avignon in the 1940s as an inspector of finances. Active in the local office of the social security administration, he was elected to the city council as a Socialist and had served as a member of the municipal cabinet. Quietly competent, he was elected mayor in 1958 in order to reflect a national coalition of moderate progressives and Gaullists on the local level. Locally, the reformers of the previous decade remained in place.[18]

In the years that followed, Duffaut pursued the policies of his predecessor. Industries that were new during the transitional 1950s prospered; the agricultural wholesale market was completed, an industrial zone created. In the early 1960s the city attracted a branch of the University of Provence. A theatre festival, begun just after the war by the avant-garde director

Jean Vilar in the grand courtyard of the Papal Palace, drew increasing hosts of tourists during the peak summer months. Outside the walls, the construction of new housing and schools continued. The French census of 1962 revealed that Avignon had attained the desired role of regional capital. Duffaut remained on good terms with the construction industry, as had his predecessor, but he was determined to do more for the threatened inner city.[19]

Such determination meant returning to the problem of the Balance. By the time Duffaut became mayor, renovation had replaced renewal as the official course. Both the municipality and the Service of Historic Monuments had decided to preserve certain significant historic structures, to retain the traditional street pattern, but also to construct a complex of new residences and roads to invigorate the downtown economy. In 1960, several public agencies combined to form the Société d'Équipement du Département de Vaucluse. Immediately this company began to purchase properties in the Balance. In the same year, yet another architect drafted a plan for a self-contained quarter surrounded by a peripheral road granting easy access to the city center; structures in the eastern and northern parts of the quarter would be destroyed. Even though the Service of Historic Monuments rejected this plan as too radical, it did not seriously object to destruction. It merely wanted to preserve more of the traditional image. Simultaneously, studies and projections by national experts foresaw the replacement of the area's residents with middle- and upper-income groups, as well as the elimination of most of the quarter's small, uncompetitive shops.[20] Ultimately, renovation would satisfy the psychological need of Avignon's residents for a local *lieu de mémoire* and would benefit contractors and retailers outside the Balance.

Even as renovation seemed the solution to the city's future, the idea of restoration survived. Restoration would mean the preservation of the old warren of narrow streets and the maintenance of the seventeenth-century facades with their soft, porous limestone and the traditional, red-tiled roofs. Behind the facades, modern living and working quarters would be introduced. Deemed too costly in time and money, total restoration had been rejected in all the postwar planning for the Balance. Even the Friends of the Papal Palace considered it too costly a venture. Only a small, convinced minority continued to believe in total rehabilitation.

During the Fourth Republic, a number of property owners, antique dealers, and influential townsmen had founded a Society for Safeguarding Old Residences and Sites in the Avignon Region. Originally dedicated to saving historic homes, the Society gradually concentrated on restoring the Balance as a symbol of preservationist values. In official communications, it listed its headquarters as the mansion of the Count St. Priest d'Urgel. Located on the fringes of the Balance and possibly threatened by any renewal or renovationist project, the mansion dated back to the mid-eighteenth century and retained the damask panels and painted tympana of its original style. Descended from one of the founders of Avignon's gas works—a modernizing venture of the early nineteenth century—his immediate family had acquired the mansion during the Third Republic. In 1961, St. Priest d'Urgel continued to own the gas works; and he managed the firm until it disappeared two decades hence. Though he lived and worked in Paris, he visited Avignon frequently and participated in a variety of the city's cultural organizations, including the Friends of the Papal Palace. In the preceding controversies about the Balance, he had ranged himself firmly against renewal. A self-styled poet, both his aesthetic and economic interests inclined him to preservation.[21] As plans for the renovation of the Balance seemed final, his contacts in Paris aided him in the preservationist cause.

Under pressure from groups with both economic and cultural motives, the French Minister for Cultural Affairs, André Malraux, had recently formed a committee to explore legislation for assisting localities in the restoration of traditional townscapes. One politician most interested in this activity was the Viscount Jacques de Maupeou d'Ableiger. Descended from one of Louis XV's famous reforming ministers, Viscount Maupeou was a senator from the Vendée and a leader of the Independent Republican Party, an important participant in Gaullist coalitions. He was also president of the prestigious Society for the Protection of Landscapes, to which St. Priest also belonged, and both he and St. Priest were members of the Association for the Mutual Welfare of the French Nobility. A writer like St. Priest, Maupeou's literary interests inclined him to support preservation; his political position facilitated his task. In the winter of 1962, Maupeou persuaded de Gaulle's prime minister, Michel Debré, to stop action in the Balance until the concept of restoration could be examined.[22]

Accompanying this activity was a series of articles in the national press protesting the quarter's destruction. Once again, the city bristled at the outside intervention. In April, Mayor Duffaut protested that Avignon needed renovation, not restoration; he accused the newspapers of listening to people who rarely came to Avignon. In May, a member of the mayor's cabinet explained to the Friends of the Papal Palace that restoration would cause a serious financial burden for the city. In July, the municipality threw down the gauntlet by initiating the administrative procedures necessary for condemning property and beginning renovation.[23]

Almost immediately, the national government countered with the passage by the National Assembly of the famous *loi Malraux*. This measure created the concept of safeguarded sectors and held out the promise of government aid for restoring them. Nevertheless, France was in the midst of liquidating the Algerian War, and national subsidies for local projects were scarce. The municipal government still expected to pay for any operations in the Balance. It proceeded, undeterred by the *loi Malraux,* with renovation. In response, the French government, despite its lack of funds, attempted to make good on its preservationist promise. In the fall of 1962, Malraux met with the parties most responsible for the Balance: the mayor, the prefect, representatives of the local Société d'Équipement, architects, and officials from the Ministry of Construction. He succeeded in achieving a compromise: Initially the eastern side of the Rue de la Balance would be restored; the western side would be renewed to harmonize with the older structures. Thereafter, costs and results would be compared. For the time being, the southern and extreme western ends of the Balance would remain in their existing state. Two years later, the national government declared the entire quarter a *secteur sauvegardé* under the terms of the *loi Malraux*.[24]

With the declaration of the Balance as a safeguarded district, it appeared that most of the quarter would be preserved. What was, however, the final plan for the Balance? An examination of its details revealed that the original compromise between renovation and restoration prevailed. Ultimately, only particularly valued structures and facades would be restored; contemporary architecture would be substituted in place of utterly valueless houses and blended with the old. It was merely necessary "to conserve the image of Avignon, imprinted with legendary, méridional poetry."[25]

By the end of the 1960s, Avignon had found its niche not only as regional capital but as a tourist attraction. The fledgling theatre festival of the previous decades, centered on the Papal Palace, had gained national and international renown. Francophones from all over the world inundated the city and its environs for several months during every year. Thus the city's old image had to accommodate the expectations of modern travelers. A special route through the quarter would guide visitors to the principal places of interest; hotels, restaurants, and boutiques would serve their needs. An underground garage beneath the square of the Papal Palace, easily accessible from outside the walls through a new breach in the Rocher, would provide convenient parking. The functions of the Palace itself would be expanded: In addition to serving as a tourist attraction and principal stage of the festival, part of it would be remodeled into a conference center.[26] This plan, devised in 1968, was slowly but surely achieved. In the following decade, the Balance acquired a "new personality" that matched the city's transformation.

As a renovated Balance took shape, plans were laid for preserving the "memory" of the entire intramural town. In the 1970s, as the French state provided incentives for refurbishing medium-sized cities—the *contrats villes moyennes*—a pedestrian zone was created in the major downtown shopping area; the central Place de l'Horloge was closed to traffic; and the Place Crillon, one of the major entrances to the city, was refurbished, including the facade of the eighteenth-century theatre. Avignon shared such renovation with other cities in France, and, as in Avignon, much that was restored emulated a classical European style.[27] Such construction went hand in hand with the continued erection of twentieth-century apartment blocks and tall functional buildings associated with the modernist genre.

These contradictory architectural impulses reflected deep currents in French society. Jules Gritti has demonstrated how the *Guides bleus,* in their touristic advice, use concepts borrowed from the business world. A tourist has a "duty" to "move," and to "observe"; in the process he "earns" or "increases" his field of motion or observation. Tourism must be rationally organized, and only the best sights are worth one's best effort. Worthy sites are those that are highest, oldest, and best preserved. As tourist guides, the *bleus* pretend to preserve the hierarchy of French esthetic values.[28] These values, after World War II, were also European ones. Avignon's leading citizens shared the mercantile goals of progress, rationalization, and capital accumulation as well as an admiration for artistic treasures. By the 1970s, French cities had profited from the "three glorious decades" that made France an economic equal in Europe. At the same time, economic progress had generated social tensions that divided France and its cities into contending, hostile groups. A cultural approach—reminders of a shared heritage—was one way of defusing these tensions.[29]

In Avignon, no actor disagreed that a transfigured Balance would enhance urban fortunes. Each group simply had different understandings of the relationship between past and future. These differing orientations reflected local, national, and European visions as well. On one side were those who viewed the International style of functional, streamlined structures as a projection of efficiency, hygiene, comfort, and social as well as economic progress into the future. On the other side were the proponents of the classical style, embodied in the structures of the Balance, who clung to the older symbols of themselves as urban leaders, of the quarter itself as the past home of a ruling elite, of France as a dominant state, and of the city as the center of Europe. A preoccupation with restoration is one way of escaping the future; but it can also represent a coping mechanism. Restoring the symbols of the past decelerates changes that threaten to overwhelm political, social, economic, and cultural identities. Between the two extremes is renovation. This compromise was espoused by a group that, paradoxically, represented the most locally and the most internationally focused of Avignon's elite, the *"méridionaux."*[30] While preserving the old image, both the city and the country could progress into the modern age.

It was no accident that de Gaulle's Minister of Culture, André Malraux, instigated the compact that renovated the Balance. The presidency of Charles de Gaulle was a defining event in French and European history. At least one historian has credited de Gaulle with closing the social fissures that had plagued France for more than one hundred years. As a kingly figure dedicated to the republic, de Gaulle lent to French life a stability within which old and new politics, social groups, economic organizations, and cultural orientations could be reconciled. A confirmed nationalist, he committed France to participation in European economic cooperation. For him, and for many other Frenchmen, the association with the European community would preserve France's old role of international leadership within a new framework. In this stabilizing crusade, both inside and outside France, not the least of his weapons was cultural. The treatment of Avignon's Balance was one of the first local examples of this reconciliation through cultural means.[31]

Malraux, as Gaullist Minister of Culture, effected the compromise that allowed old memories and new visions to dwell side by side. While he pursued the restoration of ancient national treasures like Rheims cathedral, he also listed nineteenth- and twentieth-century structures for the first time as historic monuments. As a friend of Jean Vilar, he no doubt relished the staging of contemporary theatre in the medieval setting of the Papal Palace. While propagating French cultural leadership throughout the world, he also innovated Maisons de Culture in provincial centers like Avignon. Regions, such as the Provence, became more equal participants in national culture, just as France began to devolve into one European region among many. The *loi Malraux* itself was a harbinger of more local initiative in determining national values.[32] Malraux's gift was to utilize the full cultural palette in remolding France for its role as a decolonialized power and an equal participant in the European community. In this drama, Avignon served as a crucial *mise en scène.*

The blend of old and new in the Balance signified a transformation of cultural symbols on the local level that reflected both national and international developments. In Avignon, old industries, crafts, and shops gave way to the new economy of a modernized France. New forms of culture, like avant-garde drama, challenged old Provençal customs. The city, as Jean Bordas foretold, had transformed itself in the brief period since World War II. France itself had recreated its old leadership role within Europe by falling back on cultural symbols. Much that was preserved in Avignon and other French cities, as a result of the *loi Malraux* and the *contrats villes moyennes,* reminded Frenchmen of their former power in the seventeenth and eighteenth centuries. Yet much of this architecture symbolized a pan-European classical style. Similarly the need to participate as an equal on the European scene and to maintain a worthy partnership with the more modern West Germany meant accepting the introduction of a more contemporary International style. Avignon, like France, like Europe as a whole, could not escape the transformative passage of time.

## The Reconstruction of Worms

An older citizen of Worms, three decades after the event, recalled bursting into tears as he viewed the almost complete destruction of Worms' inner city after the Allied bombing of March 1945. Thereafter, Worms, like Avignon, faced urban reconstruction, but in a different way. Rather than destroying the urban fabric, it needed to rebuild much of its physical environment and restore civic life. How much should it deviate from the previous urban image? What kind of architecture was desirable in the postwar political context? What kind of European city did Worms remember? What sort of city did it want to become?

Worms, like Avignon, is an ancient city. The site attracted settlement because its Rhenish marshes were relatively narrow and fringed by a steep rise of land, allowing both for fortification and activities close to the river.

Prehistoric Worms, like Avignon, became a significant node in east-west/north-south trade. In the first century A.D., the Romans conquered the settlement and made it an administrative center. Similar to Avignon, Worms had once enjoyed high urban stature. During the Middle Ages, members of the city's Salian clan became Holy Roman Emperors. There, in 1521, Martin Luther took his stand for the Reformation before the assembled German princes and clergy. As in Avignon, the city's fortunes declined in the early modern era. Contributing to Worms' precarious position was its location on the marching route of French armies from Louis XIV to Napoleon. The medieval city was almost completely destroyed by fires set by Louis XIV's soldiers in 1689. During the French Revolutionary and Napoleonic Wars, some remaining historic structures were either razed or defaced. Unlike Avignon, large parts of the *European* past could no longer be remembered in stone when the nineteenth century began. When the bishopric of Worms was absorbed into the enlarged state of Hesse in 1806, the city lost diocesan importance and local independence.[33]

During Germany's swift nineteenth-century industrialization, the town's economy revived. The discovery of the process for making patent leather, combined with supplies of hides and wood, and running streams in the environs, attracted several tanning factories to Worms. Factory workers streamed in and out of town from the outlying villages, and retail business flourished. After the completion of the Rhine bridge at the end of the nineteenth century, Worms, like Avignon, became a market and supply center for the agricultural areas on both sides of the river. The city continued to grow during the early twentieth century. In the initial stages of World War II, Worms, anticipating a victorious postwar dynamism, incorporated large amounts of neighboring territory. This expansion ceased at the end of the war. As a result of the bombing of March 1945, the chief leather factories, lying directly north and south of the city center, were severely damaged; the market square was a vast heap of rubble.[34]

Worms' urban core, like the Balance, was rich with historic memory; it contained the route of Worms' main street since Celtic times, the site of the old Roman forum, the location of the medieval market. Unlike Avignon, this core was no longer enclosed by the medieval wall but was a maze of tiny passages that had persisted into World War II. Even before the bombing, a local factory owner had invited a prominent German architect to recommend improvement for the city's physical framework. At the beginning of World War II, the municipal planner had drafted detailed designs for the postwar period when victory and wealth were assumed. Thus in

Worms, as in Avignon and numerous other French and German cities, prewar plans assuming renewal carried over into the postwar period.[35] How much would they influence the future?

To a much greater degree than in France, a conscious awareness of the symbolism of urban architecture existed in Germany. During the Weimar Republic, the Bauhaus had loudly proclaimed the new "functional," streamlined designs of the International style as the harbinger of a new society. Though they rejected the new society of the Bauhaus, the National Socialists, throughout the Third Reich, used architecture for propaganda purposes. Building styles for monuments and structures sanctioned by the party ranged from the neo-classical to the International—both forms associated with a greater Europe.[36] Yet, as postwar Worms prepared to rebuild, both its government and citizenry were conscious of rejecting the National Socialist political past. In order to provide full democratic participation in the reconstruction process, the city government held three separate exhibits of plans for reconstruction between 1945 and 1949; citizens were urged to submit their reactions. Responses supported retention of the old urban pattern. In Avignon, plans for the Balance had once envisioned total destruction. Confronted with an almost obliterated inner city, the Wormser chose preservation.[37]

As in Avignon, no one anticipated restoring the cramped urban quarters of the prewar period. Up-to-date amenities would characterize postwar housing. Streets would be widened; a main thoroughfare would extend a former dead end; squares would be enlarged. The basic pattern, however, dating back to pre-Roman times, would remain; traditional public buildings, even striking mansions, would be rebuilt, in the old style, at their former sites, and would house their prewar functions. The Wormser clung to their "places of memory" in the midst of changing times.[38]

As reconstruction began, the restoration of churches received high priority. The city's most striking visual image, the Romanesque cathedral of red sandstone occupying the site of the old Roman forum, had been little affected by bombs; its roof, windows, and bells were all quickly replaced. A Romanesque abbey housing the city's museum was quickly restored. The Magnus Church, site of the first Protestant sermon in Germany, was reconstructed to its early Gothic form. Directly opposite the cathedral, on the site of the medieval market, the Church of the Holy Trinity, originally built as a symbol of resurrection from the ruins of Louis XIV's wars, was restored in its original style. The Wormser rebuilt the synagogue, destroyed before and during the war by the National Socialists, to its medieval and early modern form. This synagogue had, during the Middle Ages, served as a scholarly center for West European Jews. This reconstruction of the city's places of worship reflected the healing qualities of religion for the Germans after World War II. Not only did Judeo-Christian ethics and their architectural incorporation symbolize a repudiation of National Socialist barbarism, the re-emphasis of the Judeo-Christian tradition was a means of reintegrating Germans into a universal European culture. In this rehabilitating process, the Wormser restored the monuments that predated the nationalistic era and symbolized Worms' past importance as a European city.[39]

The reconstruction of the churches, representing the citizens' transcendent, spiritual ideals, proceeded without conflict. In the rebuilding of secular structures, their original desire to restore their lost urban core slowly dissolved. How did this process occur?

Ever since the city's industrialization, the Heyl family, owners of the most important leather-processing firms, had dominated Worms' economic, social, and political life. This domination was due to the energy and prestige of the nineteenth-century *pater familias:* the Baron Cornelius von Heyl zu Herrnsheim. A confirmed nationalist, the "old Baron" had represented Worms in both state and national Diets and had served on the city council until the eve of World War I. His political influence won both a railway line and a Rhine bridge for Worms. As a nineteenth-century, right-wing liberal, he was the *Herr im Hause* within his own firm, and though he introduced pensions, housing, and medical care for his workers (and urged other industrialists to do the same), he rejected the welfare state and all aspirations of trade unionists and Social Democrats to greater social and political equality. This first Baron Cornelius died in the midst of the German inflation. Before his death, he divided the original leather-processing firm into two, one for each of his sons. The Heyl family continued to be important locally after 1933, but its influence declined as the National Socialist state synchronized all aspects of life to the aims of the party and Führer.[40]

When the Third Reich ended, secular life in Worms seemed to return to the normality of the Heyls' preeminence. The bomb-damaged leather factories were slowly reconstructed. In 1946, Christian Eckert, chairman of the board for Cornelius Heyl, Inc., was selected mayor by the Allied authorities. Ludwig Heyl, younger son of the old Baron and head of the firm Heyl-Liebenau, used his work force to clear away the rubble. As plans went forward for rebuilding Worms "just at it was," the dominant urban vision was the one that existed at the peak of the Heyls' influence in the city, though Worms, like Avignon, had experienced both political and socioeconomic change in the postwar era. In 1948, the Social Democrats, for the first time in the city's history, won an absolute majority on the city council. Heinrich Völker became Worms' first Social Democratic mayor, and he administered the city for the next two decades.[41]

Having moved to Worms at the age of ten, Heinrich Völker was a printer and active trade unionist. As a Social Democrat, he was imprisoned for eighteen months under the National Socialists, expelled from Worms, and drafted into the army in the middle of World War II. He reentered politics via the trade-union movement and was a member of the state Diet of Rhine-Palatinate when elected mayor. Although he lacked the flamboyant prestige of Avignon's Daladier and the analytical training of Duffaut, documents and colleagues alike testify to his integrity and authority in rebuilding Worms under extremely difficult circumstances.[42]

After the Socialists captured city hall, conflicts arose because of the struggle between old and new political forces. If the city government represented the future, the Reconstruction Society reflected the past. Initially formed with official sanction to meet the postwar housing emergency, the Reconstruction Society created a strong feeling of solidarity among all urban groups. As order and normality returned, city government assumed more responsibility for housing, and its functions became separate from that of the Reconstruction Society. As the functions diverged, so did their approaches to rebuilding the city. The Reconstruction Society, under the leadership of Ludwig Heyl Jr., the old Baron's grandson, believed that reconstruction should occur primarily under private auspices and the city should resume its prewar image. In contrast, the Social Democratic mayor and council became increasingly convinced that private capital alone was insufficient for the massive task; financially, it was impossible to restore all aspects of the old city.[43]

As approaches diverged, the Reconstruction Society increasingly collided with the municipal government. Over the years, the Society criticized the municipality's decision not to restore prominent old, inner-city buildings; it objected to the modernist designs for public housing in the urban core. Originally, the Society insisted on its right to be consulted about all urban building permits. When Mayor Völker objected that such consultation was improper, the Society tried to influence the city planner unofficially. Although no one so boldly articulated the issue at the time, it was apparent that the townscape had become the scene of a contest between the Heyls' old leadership and the new political actors from all the major parties. Throughout Völker's tenure as mayor, both Christian and Free Democrats cooperated actively with the Social Democrats in governing the city.[44] As in Avignon, a coalition of moderate groups attempted to forge a new role for Worms in the midst of changing conditions.

After the war, Worms' economic problems were similar to Avignon's. German industrial concentration hurt the city's predominantly medium-sized firms. Small manufacturing shops closed down. The loss of the East German market and increasingly stiff, foreign competition contributed to the leather industry's decline. As in Avignon, the service industries of the future only gained ground slowly. Unemployment in the early 1950s was a serious problem for the municipal government, and it tried to attract new industry by aiding fledgling firms and developing an industrial park. Due to the wartime destruction of the bridge over the Rhine, Worms was cut off from its eastern hinterland until 1952, and city shops lost much of their former business to developing towns in the east (such as Lampertheim) or to the larger cities (Mannheim, Ludwigshafen) of the south. Worms, as a county seat, remained an administrative center for two decades after the war; but it compared unfavorably with Avignon, which was capital for a much larger area and benefited from the earlier centralization of the French state. This weakened economic base engendered political and psychological insecurity. As churches, lodgings, shops, and factories were rebuilt, the highly symbolic, secular areas around the *Marktplatz* remained unreconstructed. Finally, in the mid-1950s, as the state Ministry of Finance and Reconstruction insisted on the development of the urban core, the city government made plans to erect a new city hall.[45]

Because city hall, actually and figuratively, is an expression of socio-economic and political relationships, its placement and design can affect different groups strongly. In Worms, the architecture of the old city hall was associated with the leather barons' dominance. In the postwar era, the city government decided to move the Rathaus from its peripheral site in the Hagenstrasse to a new location on the northeast side of Trinity Church. How should this new building look? The Social Democratic leadership preferred a contemporary, progressive design. To give the appearance of impartiality, it established a jury of architects and citizens to select the best form for city hall and to give advice on the arrangement of the entire urban core. When this jury urged a blend of the old urban image with modern architectural elements, both mayor and city council concurred.[46] Thus the style and placement of the new city hall combined elements of old and new.

It was easy to achieve consensus about the new city hall's placement and design because its location possessed minimal symbolic value. No group in Worms had a high psychological attachment to the space. This indifference vanished when decisions were made to reconstruct two other interrelated sites that traditionally served as icons of the urban power structure.

The first of these two locations to be considered lay on the south side of the Trinity Church. During the late Middle Ages, the architecturally elaborate old Mint, converted into city hall in 1491, had occupied this spot. City government had only come to reside in this dominant location after a long battle with bishop and emperor over the rights of the citizenry to independent action. In 1689, Louis XIV's army destroyed the old Mint, and no significant building occupied the site for two centuries thereafter. At the beginning of the twentieth century, the first Baron Cornelius erected a cultural center there and bequeathed it to the city. When finished, this neo-Romanesque structure took the name Cornelianum, for the old Baron's eldest son, Cornelius Jr.

The Cornelianum's decoration and use reflected its donor's political sentiments. The concert hall was painted with scenes from the Nibelung legend; over the entrance was a frieze depicting Siegfried's arrival in Worms; adorning one wall was a statue of Volker of Alzey. Its deed of trust dedicated the Cornelianum to the cultural improvement of the whole urban population but expressly banned all political activities. The center thus remained closed to a host of Social Democratic organizations.[47]

After the bombing of World War II, only the tower, the southern wall, and the sculptures of the Cornelianum remained. Initially, the city thought to restore it "just as it was," but the city's postwar penury meant abandoning the Cornelianum's luxurious function in favor of housing the municipal library, archive, and adult education center on the old site. The jury that judged the plans for city hall had recommended for this location a "new structural and architectural solution, corresponding to the historical significance of the site and the dignity of the surrounding cathedral district." Encouraged by the jury's advice, the city council, in 1959, voted to replace the Cornelianum with an educational center of modern design.[48]

Only after the vote did the Reconstruction Society decide to intervene. In its intervention, there was a curious intermingling of public architectural and private Heyl family concerns. Ludwig von Heyl Sr., as a member of the endowing family, had been shown the plans as a courtesy, but his suggestions were ignored, and he resented the complete change of function and style. When Ludwig von Heyl Jr., as the Reconstruction Society's chair, asked to view the designs, the city's administration demurred, saying they were not quite complete. At the end of August 1959, as the city prepared to demolish the Cornelianum's ruined remains, the Society and the Heyls furiously tried to stop the demolition. They even considered asking the state government to intervene. All these efforts were in vain. By mid-September, the site was empty, and a reconsideration of the modernistic design, brought by sympathetic independents, was defeated in the city council. As the new building neared completion three years later, there was little support for using the old name. At the structure's dedication in 1963, Mayor Völker christened it the Municipal Cultural Institutes.[49]

What did the complete change of style, function, and names at the site of the old Cornelianum signify about the Wormser's cultural memory? Why was there so little popular support for retaining the old image? The city's need to economize certainly dictated the functional change. Nevertheless many citizens clearly related the relative postwar poverty of the city to the leather industry's decline. They chose not to remember a style and a name associated with a family whose fortunes were on the wane. At the same time, evidence exists that Worms' memories of the Heyls were all too fresh and that many preferred to forget a dominance associated with undemocratic nationalism.[50]

Scholars of the postwar era have indulged in the truism that Germans preferred to forget the National Socialist past in the immediate postwar era, that they refused to probe their own contributions to the party's victory and popular appeal. In a small city like Worms, it was impossible to forget. Most people knew which neighboring families had done what, when, and where. One way of coping with the inability to forget was a refusal to restore the physical images associated with the values of a conflicted past. By failing to rebuild the Cornelianum "just as it was," Wormser, particularly the dominant Social Democrats, remembered also the era prior to National Socialism when the patriarchal Heyls had excluded them from stature and influence in local society. This conscious forgetting and remembering continued to mark the labeling process even beyond the events of the 1950s and 1960s. When, in the 1980s, the city renamed the Cultural Institutes, it chose "House at the Mint," recalling a history that signified an independent citizenry.[51]

These overtones of victorious self-government also sounded in a controversy linked to the Cornelianum: how to arrange the property of the Heylshof mansion and garden. Extending along the mansion's northern edge was the Stephansgasse, slated for enlargement by the city to accommodate increasing postwar traffic. Alterations to the street had to affect the property.[52]

Even more symbolic than the location of the old Cornelianum, the Heylshof lay adjacent to the cathedral and had been part of the bishop's residential complex. The bishop's baroque palace and garden had been destroyed during the French Revolution, and thereafter the Heyl family acquired title to all land between the cathedral and the Stephansgasse. In 1840 the leather firm's founder erected the so-called Little Palace on the eastern end of the property, and the first Baron Cornelius built the Heylshof in 1883, on its northwestern corner. Between the two mansions was a magnificent garden closed off to the Stephansgasse and to the general public by a wall and balustrade. When the old Baron died in 1923, his will created a private trust to support a museum in the Heylshof mansion. The trust document provided that the garden be left as it was at the time of his death.[53]

Plans for the expansion of the Stephansgasse foresaw an elevated walkway through the garden but did not state whether the walkway and the garden would be open to the public. Until that matter was settled, the senior Ludwig von Heyl so influenced the trust's administration that it refused to sell the land needed for the roadway to the city. He wanted the garden to remain the private preserve of family members who still lived in the Little Palace and whose terrace was fully exposed to the garden. For its part, the city government wanted the walkway open to the citizenry, thus transforming the garden into a public park.[54]

In Worms, as in Avignon, there were long-standing laments about the paucity of open green spaces, and the municipality argued that a park was desirable. Given the history of this particular spot, the conflict represented the difficult passage from the old paternalistic to the new democratic order. The dispute was already two-years old when the city government precipitously disposed of the Cornelianum's remains, and both sides paired the two issues. The Heylshof Foundation refused to give up the land; the city destroyed the Cornelianum. Until the land issue was settled, the Foundation refused to open the museum. The city could always go to court to expropriate the necessary strip for the street but it would thereby alienate vital elements of the population.[55]

Both time and effort involved the placement of the wrought-iron gate leading to the mansion and its garden. A gate is an architectural symbol. As a boundary between two places, it is a powerful image of separation, of exclusiveness, of individual control over space and people. Apart from the aesthetic worth of the gate, claimed by the Heyls and verified by the state's historic preservationist, its placement on its original site could symbolize a refusal to make the passage from one era to the next. Ludwig Heyl, Sr., upholding the old Baron's will, insisted the gate be set back from the enlarged Stephansgasse to preserve the garden's traditional entrance. The city planner claimed that such a placement would distort the architectural dimensions of the mansion; he suggested moving the gate to a less symbolic site just across the street. A political, not an architectural, principle was really at stake.[56] The gate's former location symbolized not only the Heyls' restriction of accessibility into the garden but also their domination of the city. As the leather industry declined, they could no longer restrict or dominate. As had happened so many times in the past, new urban forces were determining the disposition of sites traditionally associated with the exercise of urban power.

Early in the controversy, the junior Ludwig Heyl poignantly articulated this issue in a letter to his father. He argued that eventually people would forget both the Heyls and their contributions to Worms. The family should make its peace with the times. In such a vein, the younger Heyl achieved a compromise between the family and the city. The gate and the old wall would continue to enclose the garden but be accessible to the public by day; the municipality would assume responsibility for maintaining the garden but would close it at night. This agreement became final the year after the Cornelianum's demise.[57] The gate to the Heylshof would remain, but it, like the city's government, would be open to all.

The final passage into a new era was achieved with the reconstruction of the last symbolic site in Worms' urban core. This spot lay adjacent to the cathedral and the Little Palace and faced the Cultural Institutes across the market square. It represented several realms of memory for the people of Worms, but through most of its transformations, the style and functions of its structures had been truly commonplace. From the late Middle Ages until the twentieth century a row of small houses had stood there. The view over their gables toward the towers of the cathedral had been memorialized in a nineteenth-century print familiar to every older citizen of Worms. At the beginning of the twentieth century, Julius Goldschmidt had replaced the old houses with a modern department store, but after 1933 he was forced to sell this property to the Steffan Bank of Frankfurt.[58] During World War II, bombs totally destroyed the store and unleashed the longest city-planning controversy in postwar Worms.

Before the war, there had been a small movement to clear the property in front of the cathedral's east choir in order to reveal its full structural beauty. After the bombing, this movement experienced a rebirth. The city architect, Walter Köhler, argued that, because the plot historically contained structures, they were the correct aesthetic setting for the church. Nevertheless, in his postwar plans, he made one small concession to his opposition: A complete view of the cathedral's northeastern tower from the ground to the spire would be visible from the Hagenstrasse and market square. For fiscal reasons, the mayor and the city council decreed that the site be rebuilt; the anticipated shops on the ground floor would generate needed tax revenues.[59] Despite these decisions, the property remained vacant for more than two decades.

Empty spaces in a city, particularly in its historic core, frequently reflect conflict among various urban groups. In this particular case, the city government clearly articulated its aesthetic and practical reasons for improving the plot. It is more difficult to ascertain the motives of all advocates for an unimproved site. It is possible only to say that many, either consciously or unconsciously, shared the sentiments of Dr. Friedrich Maria Illert, the town's archivist, historian, and curator. Until his death in 1966, Illert continually fought against the idea of constructing anything on the old Goldschmidt land. This earth, he recalled, was the "great hill of the Roman forum." Here was the stage for Siegfried's entry into the Nibelung legend. Here, *he* said, was the site of Charlemagne's favorite palace. On this site, Friedrich Barbarossa had conceived his idea for a central European empire, and Martin Luther had proclaimed the Reformation.[60] For Dr. Illert and his allies, this small parcel was the symbol of a world-historical Worms set in a pre-Hitlerian German past.

Yet Illert's icons were ambiguous. On the one hand, they, like the Roman forum, recalled the commonly accepted origins of European culture; but they also, like Siegfried and Barbarossa, focused on German symbols recently tainted by National Socialist misuse. During the Third Reich, the Romanesque cathedral itself had served as an example of "German" art. In the mid-1950s, Illert had attempted to win support for a commemoration of the Battle of Lechfeld as one way of attracting tourists to Worms and reviving the city's fortunes.[61] A defeat for invading Hungarians, this battle had led to the establishment of the Holy Roman Empire under Otto I, a relative of the local Salian clan. In the postwar political climate, this nationalistic symbol was not a memory that either Wormser or Germans cared to revisit. After World War II, the city had difficulty situating itself in the continuum of time. As the leather industry declined, the city lost much of its extra-regional significance. As a small city in a defeated nation, it dared not claim to be heir to the Roman, the Carolingian, or the German empires. Nor could it reenact a defiant Lutherian reform. Thus, the empty plot before the cathedral towers harbored disguised, multi-layered, and confused memories of accomplishment and decline.

As long as Dr. Illert lived, the plot remained planted in grass. In the year of his death, however, it was bought by the Wormser People's Bank. This institution, originally a credit union serving the city's retailers and artisans, was over 100 years old. During Germany's postwar economic miracle, the bank prospered with a multitude of customers from the city's hinterland. In 1966, it desperately needed new and larger quarters. When the bank received permission to build, the plans fulfilled all the requirements for a structure situated in the cathedral's environs. The proposal projected a slightly sloping roof covering a low three-storied building shaped from materials resembling the cathedral's red sandstone. In 1974, as the last Heyl leather factory closed its gates, the new bank building was completed.[62] Only then was one struck by the fact that the new structure was hardly traditional. Architecturally, as with the other public buildings in Worms, it reflected the spirit of an internationalized, late twentieth century.

Worms' experience in the three decades after World War II was not atypical for West German cities. Even though the trauma of the immediate postwar period inspired a desire to replace the core as it used to be, they emerged as mixtures of old and new. Municipalities, both large and small, hardly questioned the restoration of cathedrals, major churches, former squares, and other images symbolic of local and national identity. The chosen symbols frequently recalled those aspects of local and national culture that integrated Germany in an older and larger European scene. Yet both citizens and government expected that improvements envisioned before the war would be incorporated into postwar urban plans. In places like Worms, a need to economize, a shift in values, and adjustment to changing elites replaced or altered former landmarks. In regional metropoli like Cologne or Stuttgart, the glorious decades of the economic miracle forced the accommodation of urban style to traffic plans, land values, and commercial expectations. By the mid-1970s, few German cities exactly mirrored their prewar images. While retaining a local flavor, they all contained resemblances to the pan-European International style.[63]

## Avignon and Worms as European Cities

How can one compare the treatment of the urban core in Avignon and Worms in the three decades after World War II? There can be no doubt that both citizens and municipal governments regarded the core as a symbol of urban identity. Each city wanted to preserve those landmarks that made it distinct and reflected the local past. These site-specific monuments, such as the Papal Palace and Worms' cathedral, were also signs of their participation in the history of Europe as a whole. In both, progressive citizens and mayors wanted modern, comfortable lodgings for the great majority. Businessmen and cultural elites alike actively sought a vital urban economy. In pursuing this goal, they chose an architecture that blended with the old but reflected the new European style.

In each city, the configuration of the urban space produced cultural contest. Like Worms' cathedral vicinity, the Balance was Avignon's original center of economic, social, and political power. Once the town decided to capitalize on the Papal Palace as a key element of urban prosperity, the Balance figured once again as a realm of social and cultural value. Count Priest d'Urgel and his restorationist allies sheltered their own distinguished pasts behind the historic facade of the Balance just as the Barons Heyl and their cultural partners fastened upon an urban image reflective of their economic, social, and political ascendancy in Worms. The new urban elites were just as determined to mold the city into a new European form. Cultural memories and values, writ large, played a role in both cities.

Pierre Nora, in seeking "places of European memory," has discovered a multitude of accumulated symbols, just as exist in each city and nation-state. Among these emblems of remembrance are urban shapes and architectural styles. In Avignon, the Rocher des Doms is a prominent geographical feature, and its slopes continue to carry the message of settlement by Greeks and Romans in the distant European past. At least one surviving Roman arch continues to remind Avignonnais that the local Roman forum once resided at the site of their central square. In Worms, Dr. Illert refused to allow his fellow citizens to forget the central location of the ancient Roman city. Both sites symbolized urban roots in a pan-European imperium. In the Middle Ages, Europe and Christendom experienced overlapping identities. Thus, the landmark of the Papal Palace was a daily reminder of the Avignon's past European significance. In Worms, the cathedral's centrality served as an icon of this old identification between the city and its European, Christian past. The structures of the

Balance and Worms' Holy Trinity Church, representing a similar historical style, recalled to both cities the aspiration to unite Europe under
French hegemony. Less ephemeral than the ever-changing definitions of
Europe, the structures of each municipality conveyed messages of a succession of European experiences, of inter-relationships among European
institutions—cities, states, universities, industries—and of a common
European culture evolving over time.[64]

If there is any prevailing definition of Europe, it is that of diversity and
flux. In the immediate postwar period, the cities and states of Europe
poised to create themselves anew. Both Avignon and Worms shared the
general European goals of democratization, of economic and social modernization, of survival as urban bodies. The architectural symbols of these
aspirations were the modernist structures associated with the Charter of
Athens and the *Bauhaus.* Their appearance in the urban fabric created new
scenes in the progressive European drama.

As expressions of the European community in the first three decades
after World War II, the compromises in Avignon and Worms over the
structure of urban space not only represented a blend of old and new on
the local level, they represented adjustments within Europe itself. If the
seventeenth-century facades of the Balance recalled the period of French
hegemony on the continent, their preservation as a result of the *loi Malraux* reflected the determination of France to maintain its leadership
through cultural means within an economically unified Europe. The modernist architecture that complemented the older image portrayed the cooperative nature of that aspiration.

Within the European community, the closest partners of the French
were West Germans. Defeated in their twentieth-century quest to dominate Europe, they adjusted to a cooperative international environment in
order to thrive. They simultaneously evoked older and younger visions of
Europe. In Worms, the icons of a more harmonious European past were
those of cathedral and synagogue. The altered sites of the Municipal Cultural Institutes and the Volksbank represented the more participatory culture of Europe after World War II.

In Avignon and Worms, the architecture of the urban cores signified
multi-layered experiences and identities: local, national, *and* European.
The Balance, as well as the well-known symbols of the Papal Palace and
the famous bridge, contained an idea of Europe. Worms' cathedral, the
Magnus Church, and the Romanesque synagogue were all signs of a
shared European heritage. Added to these older symbols was the Interna-

tional style of the "blended" buildings of the Balance and the Volksbank. In each city, political leaders, urban planners, and citizens preserved or reconstructed those structures that recalled a common European culture. Neither city, as it embarked on a new phase of European development after World War II, could escape the modernist current of Europe in the twentieth century. Old images, new structures within the urban core recalled to Avignonnais and Wormser the memory of a shared, European past and the vision of a harmonized future.

NOTES

1. Frentz's remarks were made on 12 December 1978, before the showing of the television film, "Die Kunst zu bauen-das Erbe Europas." Economic and political motives for European cooperation in Alan Milward, *The European Rescue of the Nation-State* (Berkeley, 1992); the Cold War construct in Gerard Delanty, *Inventing Europe: Idea, Identity, Reality* (New York, 1995), 115–29. For more exploration of European consciousness see *Europe sans rivage: Symposium international sur l'identité culturelle européene* (Paris, 1988); *Europäisierung Europas?*, hrsg. Peter Haungs (Baden-Baden, 1989); Michael Geyer, "Historical Fictions of Autonomy and the Europeanization of National History," *Journal of Modern History* 22 (1989), 316–42; *Das Europa der Bürger in einer Gemeinschaft ohne Binnengrenzen*, hrsg. Siegfried Magiera (Baden-Baden, 1990); *The Idea of Europe: Problems of National and Transnational Identity*, eds. Brian Nelson et al. (Providence, 1992); Stefan Immerfall, *Einführung in den Europäischen Gesellschaftsvergleich: Ansätze-Problemstellungen-Befunde* (Passau, 1994), 30–36; *Europa im Blick der Historiker*, hrsg. Rainer Hudemann, et al. (München, 1995); *Culture and Identity in Europe: Perceptions of Divergence and Unity in Past and Present*, ed. Michael Wintle (Brookfield, 1996); *Penser l'Europe—Europa Denken*, hrsg. Uwe Baumann and Reinhard Klesczewski (Tübingen, 1997); *Modern Europe: Place, Culture, Identity*, ed. Brian Graham (London, 1998); Ulf Hedetoft, "Constructions of Europe: Territoriality, Sovereignty, Identity: Disaggregations of Cultural and Political Space," in *Territoriality in the Globalizing Society: One Place or None?*, eds. Stefan Immerfall and Jürgen von Hagen (New York, 1998), 153–71. A variation on the exploration of European consciousness are some recent attempts to demonstrate Franco-German convergence in the social and economic realms after World War II: Hartmut Kaelble, *Nachbarn am Rhein: Entfremdung und Annäherung der französischen und deutschen Gesellschaft seit 1880* (München, 1991); *Nation und Emotion: Deutschland und Frankreich im Vergleich, 19. und 20. Jahrhundert*, hrsg. Etienne François et al. (Göttingen, 1995). Michel Espagne, *Les Transferts culturels franco-allemands* (Paris, 1999), argues that one cannot conceive of French culture without the German intellectual infusion, and vice versa.

2. Some examples are: D. Burtenshaw et al., *The City in West Europe* (New York, 1981), 3, 6, 8; D. Canter et al., *Environmental Interaction: Psychological Approaches to Our Physical Surroundings* (New York, 1975), 226–27; Donald Preziosi, *Architecture, Language and Meaning: The Origins of the Built World and Its Semiotic Organization* (New York, 1979), 48; Herbert Leff, *Experience, Environment and Human Potentials* (New York, 1975), 335; E. Relph, *Place and Placelessness* (London, 1976), 34, 43; Juan Pablo Bonta, *Architecture and Its Interpretation: A Study of Expressive Systems in Architecture* (New York, 1979), 30; Dieter Jürgen Mehlhorn, *Funktion und Bedeutung von Sichtbeziehungen zu baulichen Dominanten im Bild der deutschen Stadt* (Frankfurt/Main, 1979); *The City in Cultural Context,* eds. John Agnew et al. (Boston, 1984); *The City and the Sign: An Introduction to Urban Semiotics,* ed. M. Gottdiener and Alexandros Ph. Lagopoulos (New York, 1986); Wolfgang Braunfels, *Urban Design in Western Europe: Regime and Architecture, 900–1900* (Chicago, 1988); Alan Balfour, *Berlin: The Politics of Order, 1737–1989* (New York, 1990); Eduardo Lozano, *Community Design and the Culture of Cities* (New York, 1990); Spiro Kostof, *The City Shaped: Urban Patterns and Meanings through History* (London, 1991); John Tagg, "The Discontinuous City: Picturing and the Discursive Field," in *Visual Culture: Images and Interpretations,* eds. Norman Bryson et al. (Hanover, 1994); M. Christine Boyer, *The City of Collective Memory: Its Historical Imagery and Architectural Entertainments* (Cambridge, Mass.; 1994); Alex G. Papadopoulos, *Urban Regimes and Strategies: Building Europe's Central Executive District in Brussels* (Chicago, 1996); Dolores Hayden, "Urban Landscape History: The Sense of Place and the Politics of Space," in *Understanding Ordinary Landscapes,* eds. Paul Groth and Todd Bressi (New Haven, 1997), 111–33; Peter Hall, *Cities in Civilization* (New York, 1998); Stefan Immerfall, Patrick Conway, Carole Crumley, and Konrad Jarausch, "Disembeddedness and Localization: The Persistence of Territory," in *Territoriality,* 173–204; Pierre-Yves Saunier, "La Ville comme antidote? ou à la rencontre du troisième type (d'identité régionale)," in *Regional and National Identities in Europe in the XIXth and XXth Centuries,* eds. Heinz-Gerhard Haupt et al. (Boston, 1998), 125–61.

3. For the idea of core, see Dieter Prokop, "Image and Functions of the City: An Essay on Social Space," in *Urban Core and Inner City: Proceedings of the International Study Week: Amsterdam, 11–17 September 1966* (Leiden, 1967), 29–31; Herbert Lottman, *How Cities are Saved* (New York, 1976), 17; Piero Gazzola, "Back to the Agora!" in *The Conservation of Cities,* United Nations Economic, Social and Cultural Organization [hereafter, UNESCO], (New York, 1975), 57–65; Deutsche UNESCO Kommission, *Historische Städte—Städte für Morgen,* ed. Peter Breiding (Köln, 1975), 7, 16; Jean-Paul Lévy, *Centres Villes en Mutation* (Paris, 1987), 22–27, 71–73; Angret Simms, "The Early Origins and Morphological Inheritance of European Towns," and J. Vilagrasa, "Recent Change in Two Historical City Centres: An Anglo-Spanish Comparison," both in *Urban Landscapes: Interna-*

*tional Perspectives,* eds. J. W. R. Whitehand and P. J. Larkham (New York, 1992), 23–42, 266–96; Leonardo Benevolo, *The European City* (Cambridge, Mass., 1993), 211–17; Richard Rodger, "Theory, Practice and European Urban History," in *European Urban History,* ed. Richard Rodger (Leicester, 1993), 3–4, 6–13; Maurice Agulhon, "Paris: A Traversal from West to East," in *Realms of Memory,* Vol. III: *Symbols,* ed. Pierre Nora (New York, 1996), 526.

4. Jean Bordas, "Avignon, Capitale de la région du Bas-Rhône: Essai de géographie régionale," *Mémoires de l'Académie de Vaucluse,* 3. série, vol. 8 (1943–1944), 107–9; Andrée Pescayre, "Matériaux pour une Étude Urbaine de l'Avignon d'après la guerre," *Diplôme d'Études Supérieures de Géographie, Faculté des Lettres à Aix* (1958), 219; René Grosso, "Les Industries Vauclusiennes," *Méditerranée: Revue Géographique des Pays méditerranitens,* nouvelle série I (juillet–septembre 1970), 330, 335; Gaston Imbert, "L'Évolution démographique du Département de Vaucluse," *Bulletin du Chambre de Commerce d'Avignon et du Vaucluse,* vol. 58 (octobre–décembre, 1957), 29–30; also Commissariat Général du Plan d'Équipement et de la Productivité, "Agglomération d'Avignon, Mission de Reconnaissance Préalable à L'Establissement d'un Programme de Modernisation et d'Équipement," Étude réalisée par la S.C.E.T. et la S.O.F.R.E.D. (novembre 1963), 4, Archives de Vaucluse. For events during the war, see interview with Gaston Marcy, *Le Méridional* (Avignon), 9 février 1957.

5. Conseil Général de Vaucluse, Quatrième Session Extraordinaire de 1953, Rapport Spécial, *Aide à la construction de logements,* Avignon 53 (1953), 12; Nicole Annoux, "Avignon Intra-Muros: Étude Urbaine," *Études Vauclusiennes* 4 (juillet–décembre 1970), 22. Also *Le Dauphiné Libéré* (Avignon), 22 avril 1954.

6. For stench, see report on Rue des Teinturiers, *Le Méridional* (Avignon), 19 Sept. 1952. Daladier's importance and career, Aimé Autrand, *Statistique des Élections parlementaires et des Partis politiques en Vaucluse de 1848 à 1928* (Vaison-la-Romaine, 1930), 280; Francis de Taff, *The French Radical Party from Herriot to Mendès-France* (New York, 1961), 94–95. Persuasion of Daladier, *La Gazette Provençal,* 21 mars 1953, 3 avril 1953 and *Le Provençal* (Avignon) 26 mars 1953. For accomplishments in Avignon, see Pescayre, "Matériaux," 259–64; also "Enquête Le Moniteur des Travaux Publics et du Bâtiment (22 novembre 1958)," Réalisations en 1958, dossier Urbanisme, Archives Municipales Avignon.

7. For attempts to encourage business, see *Procès-Verbaux du Conseil Municipal d'Avignon,* 28 janvier 1957 and 6 mars 1957. For economic position of Avignon, see Francois Maugard, "Avignon-Esquisse de Géographie Urbaine," *Bulletin de la Société Languedocienne de Géographie,* 20 (janvier–juin 1949), 129; Françoise Carrière et Phillippe Pinchamel, *Le fait urbain en France* (Paris, 1963), 308; Journal Officiel de la République Française, *Provence-Côte d' Azur, Plan régional de développement et d'aménagement* (14 janvier 1961), 50, 80. Beginning in January, 1957, *Le Provençal* (Avignon) ran a series of articles on the plight of the city's

retailers, see 30 janvier, 7 and 25 février 1957. For attitudes toward industry, see Jean-Denis Longuet in *La Gazette Provençal,* 3 juillet 1957, and 27 septembre 1957; also Achille Ray, "Un projet du gouvernement de Gaulle menace l'avenir d'Avignon," *L'Accent,* 4 septembre 1958.

8. Dominique Borne, *Petits Bourgeois en Révolte?* *Le Mouvement Poujade* (Paris, 1977), 169, 239; Stanley Hoffmann, *Le Mouvement Poujade* (Paris, 1956), 202, 391–402. Hoffman reports that the Vaucluse returned the highest percentage of votes for the Poujadists in all of France. The vote in Avignon resembled that of the whole département. See results in *Le Méridional* (Avignon), 4 janvier 1956. For origins of Poujadism in Avignon, Alain Mistral, "Le mouvement Poujade," *L'Accent,* 15 février 1955. In 1957, the city's Poujadists reconstituted themselves as the Union des Commerçants détaillants et magasiniers d'Avignon, *Le Provençal,* 30 et 31 janvier 1957. For revolt, Procès-Verbal de la Séance du 22 janvier 1958, *Bulletin de la Chambre de Commerce d'Avignon et de Vaucluse,* 59 (janvier–avril 1958), 5–11.

9. S. Gagnière et J. Granier, *Avignon de la Préhistoire à la Papauté* (Avignon, 1970), 133; Joseph Girard, *Évocation du vieil Avignon* (Paris, 1958), 174, 225–26; André Segond, "Les Foules Révolutionnaires et les émotions populaires à Avignon de mars 1789 à octobre 1791," Diplôme d'Études Supérieures, Faculté des Lettres et Sciences Humaines à Aix en Provence (1969), 25–28; Catherine Arlaud, "L'Aménagement du Quartier de la Balance à Avignon," Mémoire pour le Diplôme d'Études Supérieures de Science Politique, Faculté de Droit et des Sciences Économiques à Montpellier (1965), 3–6. Avignon was one of the centers of the *Félibrige,* a nineteenth-century regional movement to rescue Provençal customs and language in the face of national homogenization and modernization, that made common cause with Catalans and espoused European federalism. Philippe Martel, "Le Félibrige," in *Lieux de mémoire.* Vol. III: *Les France,* pt. 2, ed. Pierre Nora (Paris, 1992), 583. Also Herman Lebovics, *Mona Lisa's Escort: André Malraux and the Reinvention of French Culture* (Ithaca, 1999), 5, 49.

10. Ibid.; Francois Loyer, "Le Quartier de la Balance à Avignon: Rénovation, Restitution, Restauration?" *L'Oeil* 158 (février 1968), 25; Annoux, "Avignon Intra-Muros," 23. For attitudes toward balance, see A. Rey, "Une Percée vers le Rhône," *L'Accent,* 31 mai 1953; Miriam Daspet, "Le Dégagement de la rue Balance," *L'Accent,* août, 1961.

11. See Arlaud, "L'Aménagement," 12, 20–23, 30–33. For prewar and postwar plans for the Balance, *L'Accent,* 11 au 18 août 1960; *Procès-Verbaux du Conseil Municipal d'Avignon,* 20 juin 1953, 702–4. The immediate postwar projections spoke of *assainissement;* it was assumed that certain architecturally valuable old structures would be preserved. Also see article by Daladier in *Le Provençal* (Avignon), 1 mars 1957.

12. Benevolo, 196–97; Edward Relph, *The Modern Urban Landscape* (Baltimore, 1987), 49–75. A detailed survey of European planners' reactions to the

"industrialized" city is found in Werner Durth and Neils Gutschow, *Träume in Trümmern: Planungen zum Wiederaufbau zerstörter Städte im Westen Deutschlands 1940–1950.* Vol. I: *Konzepte* (Wiesbaden, 1988), 220–33.

13. For previous reactions, see B. Heckart, "The Balance and the Bridge: The Origins of the *Loi Malraux* in Avignon," *Journal of Urban History* 9, 1 (1982), 57–88.

14. Reactions of 1957 in *Le Méridional* (Avignon), 9, 11, 23 février 1957; *Le Provençal,* 20 mars 1957. The newspapers were concerned about all quarters of the intramural town, and many interviewed stressed the need to attract tourists. Also *Annuaire de la Société des Amis du Palais des Papes et des Monuments d' Avignon,* 27 janvier 1958. The change in plan was motivated by the Service d'Urbanisme, itself pressured by the Service des Monuments Historiques; see Arlaud, "L'Aménagement," 12. It was reported in the finance committee that the "historic patrimony" would be conserved in its "integrality." Since plans were also laid to have private developers construct in the Balance, it is difficult to know what would be saved. See "Commission des Finances et des Travaux Publics du 15 janvier 1958," dossier Urbanisme, Archives Municipales d'Avignon.

15. André Chastel, "La notion de patrimoine," in *Lieux de mémoire.* Vol. II: *La Nation,* pt. 2, ed. Pierre Nora (Paris, 1986), 411–25, 432–33; Jean-Michel Leniaud, *L'Utopie française: essai sur le patrimoine* (Paris, 1992), 14–19.

16. Lebovics, 47, 49. Immediately after World War II, de Gaulle favored a cultural reconstruction for Germans in the French occupation zone. See Rainer Hudemann, "De Gaulle und der Wiederaufbau in der französischen Besatzungszone nach 1945," both in *De Gaulle, Deutschland und Europa,* hrsg. Wilfried Loth, Robert Picht (Opladen, 1991), 153–67. In a speech to the Council of Europe in 1946, Winston Churchill saw France as the "moral" leader of Europe; Allan M. Williams, *The European Community: The Contradictions of Integration,* 2d ed. (Cambridge, Mass., 1994), 21. Fernand Braudel sees "Paris" as the "comptroller" of European ideas; "Zivilisation und Kultur. Die Herrlichkeit Europas," in *Europa: Bausteine seiner Geschichte,* hrsg. F. Braudel (Frankfurt/Main, 1989), 172.

17. While insisting on preservation of certain facades and other architectural features, the director of the Service des Monuments Historiques seemed willing to let Pouillon's concept be realized: Aulard, "L'Aménagement," 12, 19. Pouillon was unwilling to make the alterations. See also Jean Sonnier, "Le secteur sauvegardé du quartier de la Balance à Avignon (Vaucluse)," *Les Monuments historiques de France,* juillet–septembre, 1968, 15. For press, see A. Rey, "Une nouvelle Agression de *la Provence à Paris* contre Avignon," *L'Accent,* avril–mai, 1954. Also see Yvan Christ, "Dénoncez les vandales, " *Arts,* 5 à 11 mars 1958, 13. For earlier responses to outside criticism, see Heckart, "Balance." For Boyer, 31–33, city planning is always a "struggle among discourses" such as occurred in Avignon.

18. For Duffaut, see *Who's Who in France? 1961–1962,* 5th ed., *Dictionnaire*

*biographique* (Paris, 1961), and *Le Provençal* (Avignon), 31 mars 1958. For Daladier's resignation and Duffaut's election, see *La Gazette Provençal,* 26 novembre and 6 décembre 1958; also *Procès-Verbaux du Conseil Municipal d'Avignon,* 8 décembre 1958.

19. André Demêmes, "Le Grand Avignon: Problèmes d'industrialisation et d'emploi," and G. Reyne, "Le Grand Avignon: une réalite géographique et sociologique," *Avignon-Expansion,* juillet, 1964, 29, 39. For festival, see Catherine Arlaud, "Le Festival d'Avignon, 1947–1968," Thèse presentée et publiquement soutenue devant la Faculté de Droit et des Sciences Économiques de L'Université de Montpellier (1969).

20. G. de Couyssy, "Équipment Commercial du Programme de Rénovation Urbaine du Quartier de la Balance-Avignon," *Société d'Équipement du Département du Vaucluse. Société Contrôlée pour l'Équipement du Territoire,* décembre 1961, dossier Études Préliminaires, Service de l'Équipement, Préfecture de Vaucluse. Also Arlaud, "L'Aménagement," 13–16.

21. Arlaud, "L'Aménagement," 34. For address, see *Receuil des Actes Administratifs et Bulletin d'Information des Maires,* 15 (1957), 662; René Briat, "Lumière sur les origines de l'hôtel de Saint Priest," *Plaisir de France,* novembre, 1973, 10–17; *Who's Who in France,* 1961–1962, 1967–1968; Robert Bailly, "L'Usine à Gaz d'Avignon, 1838–1982," *Comité des Oeuvres Sociales du Personnel de la Mairie d'Avignon: Revue Annuelle d'Information* 15 (1984), 62.

22. Ibid. Arlaud, "L'Aménagement," 27.

23. Ibid., 28. See Jean Escande à Directeur Général de l'Architecture, Ministère de l'Education Nationale, 4 avril 1962; Maire Duffaut à Préfet, 4 avril 1962 in dossier Correspondance Général, Service de l'Équipement, Préfecture de Vaucluse.

24. Arlaud, "L'Aménagement, 46. Annick Vignier, "Secteurs sauvegardés et restauration publique," *Les Monuments historiques de France,* novembre–décembre, 1976, 70.

25. Sonnier, "Secteur sauvegardé," 15.

26. Ibid., 15–25.

27. Incentives introduced in 1973 provided for upgrading entire inner cities, see Phillippe Leruste, *Le Contrat d'Aménagement des Villes Moyennes,* Notes et Études Documentaires nos. 4234–4235–4236 (17 novembre 1975), La Documentation française (Paris, 1975), 8–11. Also see Roger Kain, "Europe's Model and Exemplar Still: The French Approach to Urban Conservation, 1962–1981," *Town Planning Review* 53, 4 (1982), 408–11. For the effect on Avignon, see *Le Provençal* (Avignon), 29 novembre 1973; Felix Noseda, "Ville Moyenne: un dossier élargi est en cours d'élaboration, les Avignnois doivent y participer," *Avignon: Vôtre Ville,* mars, 1976, 5; Felix Noseda, "Réactualisation du dossier 'ville moyenne': démarrage des premiers travaux cet automne," *Avignon: Vôtre Ville,* juin–juillet, 1977, 7–10. The latter article announced that the city was acquiring the mansion of St.

Priest and planned to preserve it. For ongoing work in the Balance, "L'Avenir de la Balance, des hommes vivants dans leur cité," *Avignon: Vôtre Ville,* novembre, 1975. The project of the Balance was very costly and the largest (4.78 hectares) safeguarded sector created in France up to that time; see Roger Kain, "Conservation Planning in France: Policy and Practice in the Marais, Paris," *Planning for Conservation,* Roger Kain, ed. (London, 1981), 205. For modernization and preserva-́ tion experiences of other cities, Lévy, *Centres Villes* who studied Toulouse and the smaller cities of Languedoc, and Rosemary Wakeman, *Modernizing the Provincial City: Toulouse, 1945–1975* (Cambridge, Mass., 1997). Hugh Clout, "The Reconstruction of Upper Normandy: A Tale of Two Cities," *Planning Perspectives* 14 (1999), 183–207, demonstrates the different experiences of Rouen and Le Havre.

28. Jules Gritti, "Les contenus culturels de Guide bleu: monuments et sites à 'voir,'" *Communications* 10 (1967), 51–64. For French economic development, see F. Roy Willis, *The French Paradox: Understanding Contemporary France* (Stanford, 1982), 16–33.

29. Lévy, 163–64; Maurice Halbwachs, *La Mémoire Collective,* ed. Gérard Namer (Paris, 1997), 195–96; 377; Robert Archibald, *A Place to Remember: Using History to Build Community* (Walnut Creek, 1999), 17, 43; Francis Violich, *The Bridge to Dalmatia: A Search for the Meaning of Place* (Baltimore, 1998), 297–99.

30. Lévy, 44–48; Leniaud, 6–7; Chastel, 440; Boyer, 377; David Lowenthal, *Possessed by the Past: The Heritage Crusade and the Spoils of History* (New York, 1996), 6–7; G. J. Ashworth, "The Conserved European City as Cultural Symbol: The Meaning of the Text," in *Modern Europe,* 263.

31. Pierre Nora, "Gaullists and Communists," in *Realms of Memory.* Vol. I: *Conflicts and Divisions* (New York, 1996), 218–39; Anthony Hartley, *The Rise and Fall of a Political Movement* (New York, 1971), 302–4. De Gaulle's European policy embodied the ideas of many Frenchmen. See Jean Monnet to Robert Schumann and Georges Bidault, 4 May 1950, *The Origins and Development of the European Community,* eds. David Weigall and Peter Stirk (Leicester, 1992), 57–58; Gilbert Trausch, "Der Schumann-Plan zwischen Mythos und Realität: Der Stellenwert des Schuman-Planes," in *Europa im Blick der Historiker,* 115. Despite his nationalism, de Gaulle identified himself as European and could be described as seeing France as *primus inter pares,* Hans von der Groeben, *The European Community: The Formative Years: The Struggle to Establish the Common Market and the Political Union (1958–1966)* (Luxembourg, 1987); 35–36, 227; Peter Haungs, "Einleitung," in *Europäisierung Europas?,* 8. Also Gilbert Ziebura, "Nationalstaat, Nationalismus, supranationale Integration. Der Fall Frankreich," in *Nationalismus-Nationalitäten-Supranationalität,* hrsg. Heinrich August Winkler and Hartmut Kaelble (Stuttgart, 1993), 53–54; Peter Schunk, "De Gaulle und seine deutschen Nachbarn bis zur Begegnung mit Adenauer," Wilfried Loth, "De Gaulle und die europäische Einigung"; and Gerhard Kiersch, "De Gaulle und die

deutsche Identität," all in *de Gaulle, Deutschland und Europa,* 33–34, 46–47, 53, 186, 188, 191.

32. Lebovics, 4–5, 76–82, 105, 121–27; Leniaud, 23–24; Maurice Agulhon, "Le centre et la périphérie," in *Les Lieux de Mémoire.* Vol. III: *Conflits et Partages* pt. 1, 839–48. Philippe Poirrier, *L'État et la Culture en France au XXe Siècle* (Paris, 2000), 58–61, 73–115, points out that the Fourth Republic had already initiated the decentralization of culture. He emphasizes the revolutionary nature of much of Malraux's work and argues that the idea of a Ministry of Cultural Affairs was only a new form of centralization; he concludes that Malraux laid lasting foundations for the future of the Ministry. Poirrier's *La Naissance des Politiques Culturelles et les Rencontres d'Avignon, 1964–1970* (Paris, 1997), 44–52, notes that these annual discussion groups occurred in the *"malruxien"* spirit and treated, as two of their themes, the importance of cultural development at the local level and the international application of the French concept of local culture.

33. F. M. Illert, *Worms: Führer durch die Geschichte und Sehenswürdigkeiten der Stadt Worms* (Worms, 1969), 15–44; Dieter Wilhelm, *Worms: Mittelstadt am Rande des Rhein-Neckar Ballungsraumes. Eine Stadtgeographische Betrachtung seiner Entwicklung im 19. und 20. Jahrhundert,* Beiheft 24, *Der Wormsgau: Zeitschrift der Kulturinstitute der Stadt Worms und des Altertumsvereins Worms* (Worms, 1971), 4–14; Gerald Martin, *Rheinhessen und das Nahetal: Weinland und Völkerbrücke* (Essen, 1962), 95–107.

34. Leonard C. von Heyl, "Zum Geleit," *Wormser Profile: Lebensbilder zehn Wormser Persönlichkeiten,* ed. Carl Villinger (Worms, 1966), 8–10; Richard Kirn, "Kein Weg Zurück," *Frankfurter Neue Presse,* 23 August 1952; *Denkschrift der Stadt Worms zur Eingemeindung von Herrnsheim, Leiselheim, Horchheim, Weinsheim* (1941), Stadtarchiv Worms. For the effect of the bombing on different areas, see Christa Mowitz, *Der Wiederaufbau von Worms,* Diplom-Arbeit, Wirtschaftshochschule Mannheim (1958), 33–34. Illert, *Worms,* 44. Even this most enthusiastic chronicler thought Worms' position and growth in the nineteenth century was limited; see F. M. Illert, "Der Wormser Rheinübergang in seiner geschichtlichen Bedeutung," *Die Nibelungenbrücke in Worms am Rhein: Festschrift zur Einweihung und Verkehrsübergabe der neuen Strassenbrücke über den Rhein am 20 April 1953* (Worms, 1953), 28.

35. Wilhelm Kreis, "Professor Dr. Kreis über die Zukunftsentwicklung der Stadt Worms: Vortrag über die Anwendung der Grundsätze im modernen Städtebau auf die Wormser Verhältnisse," *Heimat am Rhein: Blätter zur Pflege der Wormser Geschichte und Heimatkunde: Beilage zur Wormser Zeitung,* 31 Mai 1930. Kreis was president of the German Architects' Association and was commissioned by Ludwig von Heyl Sr. For Worms' postwar expectations, see Walter Köhler, *Gedanken über das heutige Worms und seine spätere städtebauliche Entwicklung,* Pt. I: *Text* (Worms, 1941), 3. For other cities, see Durth and Gutschow, *Träume,* I, 243;

Jeffry M. Diefendorf, *In the Wake of War: The Reconstruction of German Cities after World War II* (New York, 1993), 151, 181–205. For the most part, Durth, Gutschow, and Diefendorf approach reconstruction from the planners' and the larger cities' viewpoint. Also see Rudy Koshar, *From Monuments to Traces: Artifacts of German Memory, 1870–1990* (Berkeley, 2000), 164–65.

36. Barbara Miller Lane, *Architecture and Politics in Germany, 1918–1945* (Cambridge, Mass., 1968), 3–9, 68, 141, 187, 215; Robert R. Taylor, *The Word in Stone: The Role of Architecture in the National Socialist Ideology* (Berkeley, 1974), 1–14, 99–113. For an overview of city planning during the Third Reich, see Diefendorf, 158–80.

37. Walter Köhler, *Worms am Rhein. Das Wesen der Stadt-Ihr Zustand: Erste Gedanken über den späteren Wiederaufbau* (January 1946); *Worms am Rhein. Ein Beispiel* (Oktober 1948); *Worms am Rhein. Der Wiederaufbau* (31 Dezember 1951). These three planning documents accompanied the three municipal exhibitions and can be found in the Stadtarchiv Worms. Rudy Koshar, *Germany's Transient Pasts: Preservation and National Memory in the Twentieth Century* (Chapel Hill, 1998), 292, contends that traditional tendencies dominated reconstruction until the mid-1950s.

38. Köhler, *Worms am Rhein* 1946, 1948, 1951. Klaus von Beyme, *Der Wiederaufbau: Architektur und Städtebaupolitik in beiden deutschen Staaten* (München, 1987), 173, 177 states that large-scale rehabilitation was economically impossible. Cities adopted a "harmonization" of the new construction with the remnants and the image of the old. Freudenstadt and Münster's Principalmarkt, some of the most famous "preservation" projects, were harmonizations, not rehabilitations. Also Durth and Gutschow, *Träume*, I, 247–48, 254, 258 and Diefendorf, 190, 197, 201. For reconstruction principles in Rheinland-Pfalz, Peter Heil, *"'Gemeinden sind wichtiger als Staaten.' Idee und Wirklichkeit des kommunalen Neuanfangs in Rheinland-Pfalz, 1945–1957"* (Mainz, 1997), 259–63, 277–79.

39. *Festschrift zur Wiedereinweihung der alten Synagoge zu Worms.* Ernst Roth, ed. (Frankfurt am Main, 1961), 168, 241–44. For the record of the churches' reconstruction, see Illert, *Worms: Führer.* Churches were the most frequently reconstructed German structures, von Beyme, *Wiederaufbau,* 216. For the significance of religion, Martin Kolinsky, *Continuity and Change in European Society: Germany, France, and Italy since 1970* (New York, 1974), 133. Also Koshar, *Transient Pasts,* 242.

40. An excellent biography of the "old Baron" is Günter Kriegbaum, *Die parlamentarische Tätigkeit des Freiherrn C. W. Heyl zu Herrnsheim* (Meisenheim/Glan, 1962), 18–19, 130–31, 159–60. Other information in Leonard C. Heyl zu Herrnsheim, "Cornelius Wilhelm, Freiherr von Heyl zu Herrnsheim und seine Familie," *Herrnsheim 771–1971: Landschaft, Geschichte, Politik, Kultur,* Otto Bardong, ed. (Worms, 1971). 156–66; Herbert Wust, "Wormser Geschlecht im Wandel der Zeiten im Dienst für Volk und Kirche," Teil II, *Wormser Monatsspiegel,* Oktober

1975, 32–41. For growth of firm and division, see Heyl Kasten, Stadtarchiv Worms. For position of Heyl during the Third Reich, see Aktennotiz of Ludwig von Heyl Sr., 10 Dezember 1946, in file Briefwechsel mit Herrn Geheimrat Eckert, 1939–1948, Liebenau papers, Stadtarchiv Worms.

41. For Ludwig Heyl Sr., see P. Umhauer, "Betrachtungen zur Geschäftsführung der öffentlichen Verwaltung im Stadtkreis Worms während der Zeit der ersten beiden Monate nach der Besetzung unserer Stadt—April und Mai 1945," Maschinenschrift, Kasten Denkschriften, Stadtarchiv Worms. For election of Völker, see Stadtratsprotokoll, 15 Dezember 1948, Stadtarchiv Worms. Eckert was appointed with the approval of the occupation authorities in 1946, see F. M. Illert, "Begnadete Lebenserfüllung: Zum 75. Geburtstag von Geheimrat Christian Eckert," *Allgemeine Zeitung* (Worms), 16 März 1949.

42. *Die Freiheit,* 15 Februar 1960; *Wormser Zeitung,* 25 Oktober 1971, 10 Juni 1975.

43. For a good general history of the Reconstruction Society (Aufbauverein), see Carl J. H. Villinger, *Erbe und Aufbau, 10 Jahre* (Worms, 1955); also the brochure *An unsere Mitglieder und solche die es werden sollen* (Worms, n.d.), 7–9. For positions of the city's administration and its opponents, see Stadtratsprotokoll, 28 März 1950 and Vorwort of Oberbürgermeister Völker in *Wohnungsbau: G.m.b.H. Worms* (1968). The mayor's gravest concern was the provision of adequate, low-cost lodging. For preservationist goals, see *Wormser Monatsspiegel,* August 1951, 45–49.

44. Sitzung des erweiterten Vorstandes, 24 Januar 1950, Sitzung des Gesamtvorstandes, 29 Juni 1950, file Vorstandssitzungsberichte, 1948–1951; Ludwig von Heyl Jr., an Oberbürgermeister, 12 Juli 1950, memorandum of Ludwig von Heyl Jr., 12 Juli 1950, file Allgemeine Korrespondenz, 1948–1951; report attached to Sitzung des Gesamtvorstandes des Wiederaufbauwerkes Worms, e. V., 12 Februar 1952, file Sitzungsberichte, 1952–1955; report attached to Protokoll zur Generalversammlung, 15 Mai 1956, Protokoll über die Sitzung des Gesamtvorstandes, 20 Oktober 1958, file Vorstandssitzungsberichte, 1956–1961; Abschiedsrede Ludwig von Heyl Jr., 20 September 1971, attached to Protokoll zur Generalversammlung, 22 Juli 1970, file Vorstandssitzungsberichte, 1962–1975. All in Aufbauverein papers, Stadtarchiv Worms. For a similar struggle, Klaus von Beyme, "Frankfurt am Main: Stadt mit Hohendrang," in *Neue Städte aus Ruinen: Deutscher Städtebau der Nachkriegszeit,* ed. Klaus von Beyme et al. (München, 1992), 203–7. For city planning as the scene of contest, Boyer, 33.

45. Wilhelm, *52;* Hans Münstermann, *Wirtschaftsstruktur der Räume Worms, Pirmasens, Idar-Oberstein, Ludwigshafen am Rhein and Möglichkeiten einer wirtschaftlichen Auflöckerung* (Mainz, 1956), 15–16, 20–21, 24, 26; Willi Ruppert, . . . *und Worms lebt dennoch: Ein Bericht, 1945–1955* (Worms, 1955), 112–14; *Wirtschaftsschau im Wonnegau beiderseits des Rheins: Industrie, Handel, Handwerk, Landwirtschaft Worms von 30 August–7 September 1952;* Bruno Backe et al.,

*Raumordnungsbericht,* Pt. I: *Raumordnungsplan für die Region Rheinhessen im Auftrag der Planungsgemeinschaft Rheinhessen* (Berlin, 1970); *Allgemeine Zeitung* (Worms), 2 September 1955; *Die Freiheit,* 5 August 1957; *Wormser Zeitung,* 12 Dezember 1960. For effects of the occupation, see *Allgemeine Zeitung* (Worms), 19 November 1954. For comparison between Worms and Avignon, see Paul Gerbershagen, "Worms," *Berichte zur deutschen Landeskunde* 33 (1964); Imbert, "L'Évolution démographique," 24–25; B. Barbier et al., *Zones d'Attraction Commerciale de la Région Provence, Côte d'Azur, Corse* (l'Institut de Recherches Économiques et Sociales d'Aix-Marseille, 1965), 50, 56–72; J. G. Charré et al., *Les Villes françaises, Vol. 3: Perennité et Variations de l'urbanisation française de 1806 à 1968* (Paris, 1968). For difficulties of Heyl-Liebenau with banks, see Bericht #1 an Liebenau, 30 Oktober 1951 aus New York, file Berichte, Baron Ludwig, senior, 1 Januar 1948–31 Dezember 1954; Aktennot. 12, 11 Juli 1952, file Sanierung, Umwandlung, HLL (Heyl Ludwig Liebenau); Niederschrift über die Besprechung mit dem Betriebsrat am 16 Januar 1953, file Deutscher Gewerkschaftbund, Betriebsrat, Wirtschaftsausschuss, 1946–56; Fritz Baldauf an Herrn Direktor Ludwig Kinkel, 25 November 1953, file AR Liebenau Schriftwechsel 1953; Büro-Mitteilung an Herrn Baron Gebhard von Heyl und Herrn Sattler von Ludwig von Heyl Jr., 16 Oktober 1970, file EVG (Ein-und-VerKaufsgesellschaft Liebenau/Waeldin) betr. Korrespondenzen 1968/69 Heyl und Waeldin AG (Aktiengesellschaft), Liebenau papers, Stadtarchiv Worms. For general position of the German banks, see Karl Hardach, *The Political Economy of Germany in the Twentieth Century* (Berkeley, 1980), 152–54, 157. For governmental action, Bezirksregierung für Rheinhessen an Oberbürgermeister, 9 März 1954, file Akten zum Aufbaugesetz, 1. 8. 1949, Stadtplanungsamt, Stadtarchiv Worms.

46. An old nondescript school building had previously occupied the site of the new city hall and was slated for alteration before the war, see Köhler, *Gedanken* 1941, 20–21. For Social Democratic views, see Stadtratsprotokoll, 21 September 1955. Of designs submitted, the one favored by the jury was thought by the SPD council member, Lucie Kölsch, to be "too conservative and not contemporary." The leading SPD council member said he favored a more modern design submission for its "clarity and simplicity." The drawings submitted by the finalists can be found reproduced in *Allgemeine Zeitung* (Worms), 24 August 1955. For the jury's recommendations, see *ibid.* and the document "Tagung des Preisgerichts anlässlich des Wettbewerbs zur Erlangung von Planen für den Neubau eines Rathauses und einer Polizeidirektion in Worms am 19 und 20 August 1955," Stadtarchiv Worms.

47. For deed of trust and history of the Cornelianum and its site, see *Denkschrift zur Einweihung des neuen Rathauses insbesondere des Cornelianums,* ed. George Swarzenski (Worms, 1910); also "Eine der Urkunden im Grundstein des Rathausturms eingemauert," Beilage, *Wormser Zeitung,* 29/30 November 1958. For a further description, see Georg Illert, *Worms: so wie es war,* 2d ed. (Düsseldorf, 1977), 37–39.

48. *Wormser Zeitung,* 8/9 November 1958, 16 Juli 1959; "Tagung des Preis-gerichts . . . ," and Stadtratsprotokoll, 15 Juli 1959.

49. *Wormser Zeitung,* 24 und 26 August 1959; 28 November; 4, 11, 12, 13 Dezember 1962; 25 März 1963; *Die Freiheit,* 25 März 1963. For the contretemps between Heyls and the city government, see Ludwig von Heyl Sr. an Carl Villinger, 20 Juli 1959; Ludwig von Heyl. Sr. 10 Aufbauverein, 23 Juli 1959; Protokoll über die Sitzung des Gesamtvorstandes des Aufbauvereins. 30 Juli 1959; Protokoll über die Sitzung des geschäftsführenden Vorstandes, 19 August 1959; all in file Sitzungs-berichte, 1956–61. For additional information, see records of telephone calls: Ramge an Hirschbiel, 25 August 1959; Ramge an Seifenstadt, 28 August 1959; Ramge an Arndt, 28 August 1959; Villinger an Oberbürgermeister, 28 August 1959; Ludwig von Heyl Jr. an Carl Villinger, 20 August 1959 and telegram of Ludwig von Heyl Jr. an Oberbürgermeister. 25 August 1959; all in file Rathaus, Cornelianum. Neither the Heyls nor the Reconstruction Society expected the demolition of the tower to follow quickly after the decision of the city council. Ludwig von Heyl Jr. wrote to the city's architect that he would be on vacation and wanted to talk in September. The architect replied he wanted to talk immediately. Only after the city prepared to tear down the tower in mid-August, in order to clear the area prior to the annual Fish Festival, did the Society swing into action, see Ludwig von Heyl Jr. an Stadtbaurat Listmann, 4 August 1959; Listmann an L. von Heyl Jr., 6 August 1959, file Heylshof (Stephansgasse), Aufbauverein papers. All of the above in Stadtarchiv Worms. For failure of the reconsideration motion, see Stadtratspro-tokoll, 23 September 1959.

50. Interview with Lucie Kölsch, 6 December 1978.

51. According to Jeffrey Herf, *Divided Memory: The Nazi Past in the Two Ger-manys* (Cambridge, Mass., 1997), 267–333, West German leaders, all in different ways, barely allowed their fellow citizens to forget. Also see Rudy Koshar, *Tran-sient Pasts,* 295; Alf Ludtke, "'Coming to Terms with the Past:' Illusions of Remembering Ways of Forgetting Nazism in West Germany," *Journal of Modern History* 65 (1993), 546–47, also hints at this forgetful memory when describing the reaction of young Germans to the Holocaust television series in 1979. Michael Geyer, "The Place of the Second World War in German Memory and History," *New German Critique* 71 (1997), 17, 19, suggests that Germans remembered death particularly but had difficulty "articulating" the memory.

52. Plans to enlarge the Stephensgasse dated back to immediate postwar planning, see note 31. For implementation of plan and effect on Heylshof, see Stadtratsprotokoll, 29 Mai 1957.

53. Carl Villinger, "Die alte und die neue Stephensgasse," *Wormser Monatsspiegel,* August 1964; also *Das Kunsthaus Heylshof in Worms und seine Sammlungen* (Worms, 1977), 7–8.

54. Ludwig von Heyl Sr. an Oberbürgermeister, 22 Juli 1959, file Rathaus, Cor-nelianum; Protokoll über die Sitzung des Gesamtvorstandes, 25 November 1960;

Protokoll über die Sitzung des Geschäftsführenden Vorstandes, 10 Oktober 1961, file Sitzungsberichte, 1956–61. Also Oberbürgermeister an von Heyl Jr., 10 Mai 1960; Ludwig von Heyl Jr., an Ulrich Meister, 6 Oktober 1961; Denkschrift betr. Verbreiterung der Stephansgasse, Ludwig von Heyl Jr., 2 November 1961, file Heylshof (Stephansgasse), Aufbauverein papers, Stadtarchiv Worms.

55. See previously cited correspondence between von Heyl Jr. and Listmann, n. 43; *Wormser Zeitung,* 3 Februar 1960; Stadtratsprotokoll, 16 Juli 1959. For position of Heyls and Reconstruction Society, see Protokoll über die Sitzung des Geschäftsführenden Vorstandes, 8 Oktober 1959 and 6 September 1960, file Sitzungsberichte, 1956–61. Further, Ludwig von Heyl Jr. an Baudezernent Willi Hirschbiel, 8 August 1959, file Rathaus, Cornelianum; Aufbauverein an Kulturfonds der Wormser Wirtschaft, 14 März 1961, file Heylshof (Stephansgasse), Aufbauverein papers, Stadtarchiv Worms.

56. Protokoll über die Sitzung des Gesamtvorstandes, 25 November 1960; Protokoll über die Sitzung des Geschäftsführenden Vorstandes, 10 Oktober 1961, file Sitzungsberichte, 1956–61; Protokoll über die Sitzung des Gesamtvorstandes, 11 Februar 1963, file Vorstandssitzungen Berichte, 1962–75; Denkschrift betr. Verbreiterung der Stephansgasse, Ludwig von Heyl Jr., 2 November 1961, file Heylshof (Stephansgasse), Aufbauverein papers, Stadtarchiv Worms.

57. The controversy over the gate went on and on and was not finally settled until 1964, the year after the completion of the Municipal Cultural Institutes: Ludwig von Heyl Jr. an Ludwig von Heyl Sr., 27 August 1960; Kahlert an Villinger, 20 Juli 1961, 13 Dezember 1962; von Heyl Jr. an Oberbürgermeister, 6 Juni 1963; von Heyl Jr. an Villinger, 15 September 1964, file Heylshof (Stephansgasse), Aufbauverein papers, Stadtarchiv Worms. Also *Wormser Zeitung,* 1 Juni, 7/8 Juli 1962, 16 August, 31 Oktober/1 November 1964.

58. For history, see Karl Grüber, "Der Wormser Dombezirk," *Der Wormsgau II* (1934–1943), 238–39; Carl Villinger, "Wandlungen einer Marktfront," *Wormser Zeitung,* 27 Februar 1975. For details on the Goldschmidt property, see Liegenschaftsamt Worms. Julius Goldschmidt and his wife emigrated to South America, date unknown, see information lists on former Jewish community in Stadtbibliothek, Worms.

59. For concession, see Köhler, *Worms am Rhein* 1948, 35 and *Erbe und Aufbau,* 15; also *Allgemeine Zeitung* (Worms), 31 März and 22 April 1949, 23 März 1950, *Wormser Zeitung,* 17/18 September 1960. For arguments concerning east choir, see Mowitz, 44–46; Carl Villinger, "Worms-wie ich es sehe,-wie ich es wünsche," *Wormser Monatspiegel,* August 1968; Otto Bocher, "Zum problematik der Domumbauung," *Wormser Monatsspiegel,* Dezember 1968. For decision of city council, see Stadtratsprotokoll, 7 Juli 1960 and *Allgemeine Zeitung* (Worms), 10 Juli 1950. For similar situation in Paderborn, Mehlhorn, 310–11.

60. For empty spaces, Gary McDonogh, "The Geography of Emptiness," in *The Cultural Meaning of Urban Space,* ed. Robert Rotenberg and Gary

McDonogh (Westport, Conn., 1993), 4, 7; F. M. Illert, *Im Kreuzpunkt der Welt-strassen: Eine Führung durch die Stadtmitte von Worms* (Worms, 1940); "Am Dom-portal Barbarossas; Von nun an blühe Dein Ruhm und Deine Ehre, o Worms," *Allgemeine Zeitung* (Worms), 29/30 August 1953; "Probleme im August 1955," *Wormser Monatsspiegel,* September 1960; "Die Kulissen," *Wormser Monatspeigel,* März 1966. Illert died in 1966. For his biography, see "Friedrich M. Illert zum 70. Geburtstag," *Der Wormsgau,* V (1961/62).

61. Ibid.; also Taylor, illustration #7.

62. For building requirements, see Mowitz, 44–46. For history of the People's Bank, see F. M. Illert, *100 Jahre Volksbank Worms, e.G.m.b.H.* (Worms, 1960). Also *Wormser Zeitung,* 29 Mai 1970, 22/23 January 1972, 20/21 Juni 1973. For clos-ing of Heyl firms, see *Wormser Zeitung,* 16/17 März 1974.

63. For kinds of West German reconstruction and preservationist tendencies, see John Butchard, *The Voice of the Phoenix* (Cambridge, Mass., 1966), I, 24–26; Thomas Greene, "Hannover, Kiel and Cologne: Postwar Reconstruction and Design," *Tijdschrift voor Economische en Sociale Geographie,* 52, 4 (1961), 92; Lutz Holzner, "The Role of History and Tradition in the Urban Geography of West Germany," *Annals of the Association of American Geographers,* 60, 2 (1970), 317, 319–20; Alois Giefer et al., *Planen und Bauen im neuen Deutschland* (Köln, 1960), 157. Recent works that clearly reveal the mix between old and new are: Koshar, *Transient Pasts,* 250; von Beyme, *Wiederaufbau; Neue Städte aus Ruinen;* Diefendorf, *In the Wake of War,* Durth and Gutschow, *Träume.*

64. For this and the following paragraphs, see Pierre Nora, "Les 'lieux de mémoire' dans la culture européene," and Alfonso Perez Sanchez, "Le rôle du musée et des expositions dans la formation d'une sensibilité commune," *Europe sans rivage,* 38–42, 120–23. One of the most vivid expressions of shared European values is Alan Milward, "The Lives and Teachings of the European Saints," *The European Rescue of the Nation-State,* 318–44. See also Delanty, 156; Boyer, 152, 155, 170, 174–75; Geyer, "Historical Fictions," 334–39; Michael Wintle, "Cultural Identity in Europe: Shared Experience," "Europe's Image: Visual Representations of Europe from the Earliest Times to the Twentieth Century," in *Culture and Iden-tity in Europe,* 9–16, 21–24. G. J. Ashworth, "The Conserved European City as Cul-tural Symbol: The Meaning of the Text," contends that European messages are weak; also Brian Graham, "The Past in Europe's Present: Diversity, Identity, and the Construction of Place;" both in *Modern Europe,* 29–34, 43, 45, 278. Further, Agnes Heller, "Europe: An Epilogue?" and Sven Papcke, "Who Needs European Identity and What Should It Be?" both in *The Idea of Europe,* 13–18, 23, 25, 63–69. Accumulations in Benevolo, 183, 211, 214; another view of convergence in diversity in Germano Celant, *The European Iceberg: Creativity in Germany and Italy Today* (New York, 1985), 13–21. For compromises over the urban fabric as well as the rec-iprocity between *Zeitgeist* and urban form, see "Foreward," in *Streets: Critical Perspectives on Public Space,* ed. Zeynep Celik et al. (Berkeley, 1994), 2–5. For cul-

tural interrelationships and transfers, Espagne, 6–7, 33–49. For German role, Williams, 21–24; Maurice Agulhon, "Die nationale Frage: Geschichte und Anthropologie," in *Nation und Emotion,* 64. Adjustment in Karl-Dietrich Bracher, *Turning Points in Modern Times: Essays on German and European History* (Cambridge, Mass., 1995), 269–70, 273. For sharing powers, Volker Berghahn et al., "Germany and Europe: Finding an International Role," in *After Unity: Reconfiguring German Identities,* ed. Konrad Jarausch (Providence, 1997), 180, 182, 185. Ideas of Europe in Delanty, 1–6; Hartmut Kaelble, "Europabewusstsein, Gesellschaft und Geschichte. Forschungsstand und Forschungsschancen," René Girault, "Das Europa der Historiker," and Peter Krüger, "Europabewusstsein in Deutschland in der ersten Hälfte des 20. Jahrhunderts," in *Europa im Blick der Historiker,* 3–8, 32, 47–48, 51–52, 65–68, 76–77. Just as the Avignonnais completed the structures in the Balance and Worms built the Volksbank, the European Community's Declaration of Copenhagen, 1973 articulated the idea of a shared cultural heritage for the first time, Yves-Henri Nouailhat, "Civilisations et cultures européens: Réflexions d'un historien," *Penser l'Europe,* 53– 59.

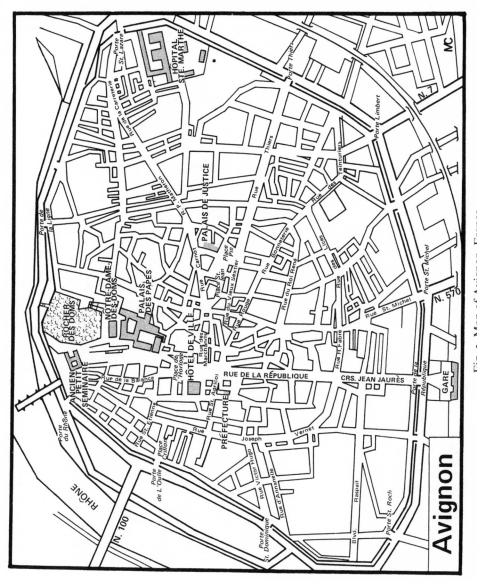

Fig. 3: Map of Avignon, France

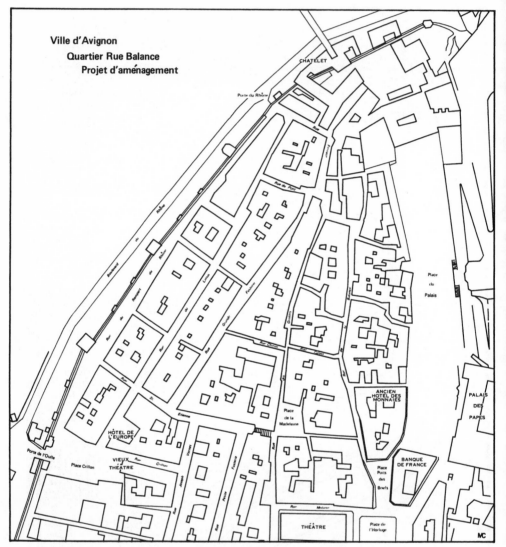

Ville d'Avignon

Quartier Rue Balance
Projet d'aménagement

CHATELET

Porte du Rhône

Place
du
Palais

Place Crillon

HÔTEL DE
L'EUROPE

VIEUX
THÉÂTRE

Porte de l'Oulle

Place
de la
Madeleine

ANCIEN
HÔTEL DES
MONNAIES

PALAIS
DES
PAPES

BANQUE
DE FRANCE

Place
Pont
des
Boeufs

THÉÂTRE

Place de
l'Horloge

Fig. 4. Map of Quartier Rue Balance, Avignon

Fig. 5. View over the Balance from tower of City Hall, pre-World War II.
(Credit: Bartesago, Collection Musée Calvet.)

Fig. 6. Aerial view of the Balance, late 1970s. (Credit: Daspet.)

Fig. 7. Entrance, Rue de la Balance, 1960s. (Credit: Robert Bailly.)

Fig. 8. Entrance, Rue de la Balance, late 1970s. (Credit: Beverly Heckart.)

Fig. 9. Corner Rue Molière and Place de l'Horloge, 1960s. (Credit: Robert Bailley.)

Fig. 10. Corner Rue Molière and Place de l'Horloge, late 1970s. (Credit: Beverly Heckart.)

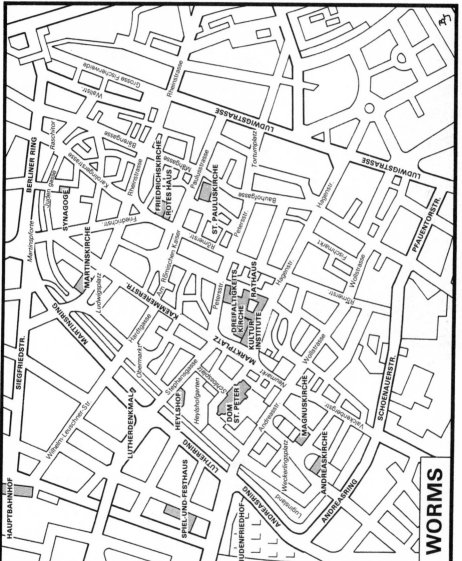

Fig. 11. Map of Worms, Germany

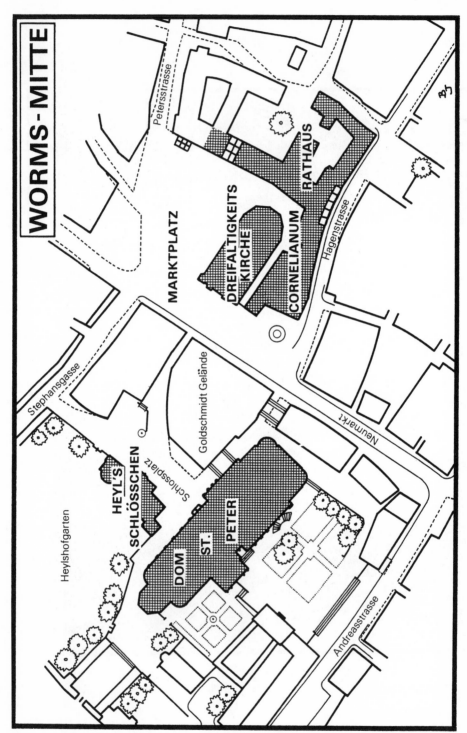

Fig. 12. Map of Worms-Mitte. Adapted: Aufbauplan der Altstadt, *Worms am Rhein: Der Weideraufbau*, 13 December 1951.

Fig. 13. Worms' new City Hall after 1958. (Credit: Stadtarchiv Worms.)

Fig. 14. Heyslof after widening of Stephensgasse. (Credit: Stadtarchiv Worms.)

Fig. 15. Cornelianum. (Credit: Stadtarchiv Worms.)

Fig. 16. Municipal Cultural Institutes. (Credit: Stadtarchiv Worms.)

Fig. 17. Houses in front of Worms' Cathedral, traditional view. (Credit Stadtarchiv Worms.)

Fig. 18. Goldschmidt's department store (on right). (Credit: Stadtarchiv Worms.)

Fig. 19. View of Worms' Cathedral, 1960s. (Credit: Stadtarchiv Worms.)

Fig. 20. Worms People's Bank, late 1970s. (Credit: Stadtarchiv Worms.)

# Flowers and Bones

## Approaches to the Dead in Anglo-American and Italian Cemeteries

*Jack Goody and Cesare Poppi*

"cui precor ut cineres sint violae sintque rosae"
(I pray that his ashes may become violets and roses)
　　　　　　　　　　　　　　—Roman Epitaph

The profusion of fresh flowers in Italian graveyards amazed nineteenth-century travelers from America, who were used to more severe practices. In England, too, flowers were sparse. Nor was their paucity unintentional. Strong sentiments were involved, for despite the increasing pomp of Victorian funerals, much ambivalence was displayed about elaborate rituals and offerings in the Anglo-American world—"a green grassy turf is all I crave," wrote Beattie in the *Minstrel.*[1] Even Loudon, the great architect of the new rural cemeteries in England, was reluctant to make a place for flowers in his plans.

Today that difference persists. The vast tracts of comparatively bare cemeteries in the United States contrast with their compact and colorful counterparts in the continent of Europe. In the States there is also a difference between the north, especially the northeast, and the south, especially the southeast. In the former, one can expect one-twentieth of the graves to be decorated with fresh flowers; in the southeast today, the figure is about one-tenth, roughly the same as England, although the flowers are usually artificial. A change was already taking place in the mid-nineteenth century, when Mrs. Stone produced her study of English cemeteries acknowledging the virtues of plain churchyards, which, however neglected, never gave the same feeling of desolation as the sight of a cemetery grave, once trim, without its "costly exotic flowers."[2] In some country churchyards people did grow sweet-smelling flowers, not those that are merely beautiful, "though it is said that these are sometimes planted by stealth, as a sort of satire, on the grave of an unpopular person." The newer cemeteries, on the other hand, gave rise to large stone-cutters' establishments which offer to decorate graves "with flowers, evergreen etc." and to carry out all other kinds of work on the tombs. Stone's own feelings are clear: "a more beautiful and luxurious garden it is impossible to conceive. . . . Such fine African and French marigolds I never saw, though I thought them in very bad taste *there*."[3] That taste relates to the teachings of the church. Ministers in the Presbyterian church, both in Scotland and the southeastern United States, still "discourage displays of ceremony or of floral tribute, focusing instead on the 'Sovereignty of God.'"[4]

Although the contrast has somewhat diminished over the past hundred years, it has by no means disappeared. The archaeologist of the gardens of Pompeii remarked, in her reconstruction of the vegetable remains of Roman culture, that Americans are surprised to find Italian cemeteries abounding in floral tributes.[5] So, too, are the British, even though they decorate their graves with fresh flowers to a greater extent than New Englanders. But in Italy the vast majority of graves are adorned with flowers, not only on special occasions but on ordinary days as well. Indeed, that difference was dramatically illustrated by the experience of an American friend whose children were playing in a cemetery near Florence. There they found an undecorated grave, so they took flowers from the others in order to cover its nakedness. In America, such a generous action would be uncalled for.

The Anglo-Americans, then, often find such display, such as the elaborate sculptures on Italian tombs or the clutter of images in a Catholic church, in bad taste, even blasphemous, when compared to their plain headstones or austere places of worship. Italians, on the other hand, often view Anglo-American practice as amounting to a neglect of the dead. As one Italian friend remarked to us: "The English dump (*scaricano*) their dead as soon as they can and then forget about them." Similar views were held by French Catholics about the practices of their Huguenot compatriots. At the time of the proposed relocation of Parisian cemeteries in 1763, a segment of the populace objected that "Parliament is treating us like Huguenots. They are sending us to the garbage dump."[6]

The contrast between the two approaches was vividly demonstrated in a recent court case in Bedford, England, where a number of Italian immigrants settled after the Second World War as laborers in the brick industry. One immigrant family wished to plant flowers to decorate the grave of a son who had died at age eighteen. This practice ran against the regulations of the local Council, which wanted to keep the cemetery clean and respectable. The family even put up fences "to stop the lawnmowers destroying the flowers we have planted and people from walking over his grave." "Our people have flowers on their graves," declared Rosanne Lombardo, "it is ridiculous that we are not allowed to honour our dead and we'll go to prison rather than agree to deface the grave."[7] The Council offered to set aside land elsewhere so that the Italians could "decorate the graves and abide by custom," but the Council's offer was not acceptable to some. The Council's refusal may well have been partly based on the higher costs required to keep up cemeteries where the lawnmowers cannot be used; that certainly seems to be the case in some American graveyards. But the issue of maintenance (and cleanliness), assumed to be a duty of the Town Council, was given pride of place over decoration, over honoring the dead as a duty of the deceased's relatives.

Nowadays this "clash of custom" is often attributed by the actors to differences in attitudes toward the dead, to bad taste, or to wasteful expenditure. Few point to the theological beliefs that encompass these practices and that undoubtedly bear upon the contrast in usage. But these beliefs do not determine these practices. For example, the activities of American Catholics in the cemetery are closer in this respect to those of their Protestant compatriots than to their Italian co-religionists. Nor is that just to be attributed to culture in any single-minded sense, though hegemony certainly plays a role. Radical changes associated not only with the advent of Protestantism but with similar movements, such as the French Revolution, have occurred over time. In this essay we want to trace some of the correlates of the difference in the use of fresh flowers in cemeteries, especially in family behavior, in the tenure of grave sites, in the practice of double interment, and in attitudes towards the bones, as well as to their theological counterparts. But in doing so we want, in this context, to break with the tradition that sees these features of Protestantism as evidence of the link with capitalism or modernization. Doubts about how to treat the dead go back much further and occur in other cultures; indeed, as we see in Stone's comments, these differences are found not only between but within societies. But first we must try to elucidate the cluster of practices linked to the constant provision of fresh flowers.[8]

## Visits to the Cemetery

The continuous supply of fresh flowers clearly means frequent visits to the cemetery, either by relatives or by employees. In Berlin many of the graves which are decorated with planted rather than cut flowers are presently maintained by outside firms or by employees of the *friedhof.* But in Italy the work is basically carried out by relatives and friends. In the dark winter of 1942–1943, one of us was living in Rome under German occupation. A regular practice of our hostess was the visit every Sunday to the Camposanto, where the remains of her dead were to be found in caskets placed in sealed recesses in walls built underground. The American Air Force's strike on the railway station caused her much greater grief by hitting the cemetery and the dead placed in caskets there than if the bombs had fallen on the living.[9] The practice of placing flowers on graves at cemeteries is very much alive today. The cemeteries of the Lake Como region are regularly filled with fresh flowers. On the banks of the Lake, at Bellagio, on an ordinary summer weekday afternoon, we observed three parties of five women in all who entered the small cemetery in the course of twenty minutes and tended seven graves, most of which were also decorated with photographs and lamps. In the case of Italian cemeteries, flowers act as the ongoing witness of the active relationship between the living and the dead. The very fact that their freshness betrays the frequency of visits compels the cult to be kept up once it has started. As a North Italian friend once commented concerning the practice of planting flowers directly on the grave, as opposed to renewing the cut variety from time to time: "It's cheating. Like inviting somebody for dinner and, on his coming, presenting him with all the ingredients for cooking and saying: 'Sorry, I cannot be with you. I must go out.' Is that good?" Relatives visiting the tomb at different times recognize the imprint of other visitors by the type of flowers they find there. The planting of flowers, as in Bedford, was very much the second-best option.

The use of cut flowers in northern Italy is taken as an outward sign of one's continuing devotion to the dead. But in both Catholic and Protestant cemeteries around Berlin, cut flowers were not the main floral tribute. Specialist firms and cemetery nurseries not only sold plants to decorate the graves but even provided the labor to tend to the plots at a fee. In Italy and in Anglo-American countries, growing plants are occasionally found but are generally looked upon with disfavor and regarded, in northern Italy, as inducing a neglect of the dead. What is remarkable about Southern France, on the other hand, is that for most of the year graves are decorated almost entirely with artificial flowers. Nowadays these are of the plastic variety, at which we have seen Parisians raise their hands in horror. Such artifice, embodied in these permanent signs of one's unfading memory, is not altogether new; for in earlier times we find crosses decorated with colored beads woven into floral designs. Visiting the dead and leaving flowers also act as ways of maintaining networks of kin. This is particularly important when the relatives in question are affines who might otherwise have little or no contact following the death of the person they had in common. If the prominence in location and the architecture of a tomb usually speak to the rank of a person in the society as a whole, floral offerings embody the continuing piety of family and close friends. In contrast with the stark tombstones of most Protestant burial places, fresh flowers represent a renewable gloss to the stone-carved garlands and other flowery allusions derived from the classical tradition. But while it is consistent with earlier Catholic practices, *la visita al cimitero* is part of the commemoration of the dead that continues to be a prominent feature of an otherwise heavily secularized society. It is as compelling for those who believe in life after death as it is for those who do not—or who so affirm. Even in Bologna, the communist-ruled capital of Emilia-Romagna, a funeral without a priest and a church ceremony is still a rare occurrence. Following the rapprochement between the Church and the Communist Party over the last twenty years, the so-called *funerali rossi* (red funerals) have declined in number.[10] As a priest who conducts funeral services in the Certosa (the main town cemetery) said: "At times it is really pitiful to see all those people coming to church for a *messa da requiem.* They just have no idea of what is going on as they never go to church. But there you are: no sooner one of their relatives dies than they all flock in." As in Protestant societies, the commemoration of the dead proves to be one of the last bastions to a complete secularization of the life cycle.

Flowers are brought to the cemetery in large quantities, both at funerals and afterwards. Outside the Certosa, about thirty fully stocked flower merchants supply a buoyant demand. As the festival of All Souls (2 November) approaches, the number of merchants increases to sixty or seventy stalls. The variety is staggering: Fashions may come and go as to which flower is appropriate to take to the gravesite, but people are profuse in their purchases. One merchant remarked: "People are going mad. I can't complain as it is all to my profit but at times I really wonder whether this isn't too much. It's got nothing to do any longer with the dead. It's just people competing with their neighbors to show that they can do better. It's all *consumismo.*"[11]

A new product in the Bologna market—silk flowers—has modified the use of fresh flowers over the last five years. Imported from Taiwan, they are considered more dignified than the plastic variety, which were regarded as disgraceful as an offering—a far worse cheating than planted flowers. "Silk on the other hand is very good," said an old lady. "It is luxurious; yes, exactly like a silk dress for the tomb, and remains bright and new for a long time." Before she discovered silk flowers, she visited only her husband's tomb. But now that silk flowers are available, she takes them to the tombs of relatives and friends in different cemeteries. "It's so handy," she continued, "as you don't have to go every week. Before I couldn't go to all the cemeteries I wanted to. If I brought flowers to my loved ones, say, once a month, next time I went I found them all dried and ugly. I just felt guilty and I would rather not go. Now I come from my village in the mountains at leisure. I go, I wash my silk flowers nice and bright, and put them back again. I think my *poveri morti* are happy, and so am I!" But the use of silk flowers is also seasonal. In the summer, before people leave for the holidays, they place silk flowers on the tombs. These will be removed at the end of the vacation and replaced with fresh ones. Other areas of Italy have not yet discovered how artificial flowers (acceptable, beautiful ones, that is) can boost the commemoration or cult of the dead[12] instead of being seen as a way to escape from one's duties. In the conservative area of Veneto and in southern Italy, silk flowers have not been taken up to the same extent as they have in Bologna. "People want the fresh, only the fresh," a salesman remonstrated, "for they say that otherwise it is like drinking watered wine and, what is worse, offering it to those you love most—your dead." The simile is particularly appropriate. Communication with the dead is sometimes thought of in terms of a *convivium* in which fresh flowers act as the metaphorical food. Even in rural cemeteries in northern Italy, like that of Bellagio, fresh flowers predominate and bear evidence of the care with which the dead are treated.

Such recurrent visits to cemeteries are not characteristic of the Anglo-American world, except for some new graves and on particular occasions, such as Memorial Day in America, major festivals in southern California, and occasional expeditions on Sunday afternoons in England. The cemeteries, especially those in New England, bleak and bare by comparison, are rarely visited. Part of the reason may be the greater internal mobility, especially in America. If kin and friends are dispersed, personal visits become more of a burden and the use of hired workers expensive. And if one is not resident in the community, social pressures to pay tribute to the dead are easily overlooked or avoided. Mobility is not an absolute barrier. Italians often travel some considerable distance to pay visits; and at Toussaints, villages in the southwest of France, a region of high emigration, are full of returning relatives coming to place fresh flowers on family graves. However, the Anglo-American world does not usually have the same continuing attachment to a particular community, or perhaps cemetery, though they may make long journeys to visit living kin at Thanksgiving and at Christmas.

Linked to the question of dispersal is the number of kin available to pay such a visit, largely the work of women, such as widows, sisters, daughters, or more distant relatives. It has often been claimed that in Italy the kinship ties (ties of *lignage* in some cases) are cast more widely than in England. Already in the sixteenth century, Francis Bacon remarked on the extended range of affective ties in Italy: "The Italians make little difference between children and nephews or near kinsfolk; but as they be of the lump, they care not though they pass not through their body."[13] The use of more distant relatives was certainly characteristic of the Italian bankers who had earlier penetrated England and northern Europe and whose activities depended upon the trust existing between kin—what Fortes called "the axiom of amity."[14] Kin groups or ranges of considerable extent and solidarity have been reported from fifteenth-century Florence, Genoa, and other cities.[15] Greater interaction among kin does not necessarily mean larger households or greater numbers of children, but it does mean that more people are available to pay regular visits to the cemetery. Where an untended grave stands out as a shameful reproach on the family, distant kin may be needed even when there is little or no movement outside the village. Under earlier demographic conditions, roughly 20 percent of families lacked immediate descendants, so that no one in the direct line was available to continue the cult of the dead. Nor could this gap be filled by the adoption of an heir, as in ancient Rome, for that practice did not form part of European law again until the last hundred years.[16] With out-migration, such ties were also brought into play. Even if the deceased had children who had left the village, calls could be made upon those kin who remained in the vicinity to tend the grave. In other words, paying regular tribute to the dead may have strengthened distant ties; and that remains true today.

These frequent visits to the cemetery are inevitably associated with different attitudes to the places where the dead are buried. Physically, the New England cemetery is a park rather than a garden. Flowers are placed there sporadically, and visitors come infrequently. The dead are largely abandoned, and the graveyard becomes the dwelling place of ghosts—the situation in much of northern Europe after the Reformation, since the cult of the dead was theologically unsound. In 1679 Pierre Muret wrote in extremely critical tones of English burial customs, claiming that although in the past the dead were honored at least once a year, their names were now not even mentioned, because that would have smacked of popery. Floral decorations, common on tombs in pre-Reformation days, had completely disappeared and in seeing tombs in English cemeteries, "one would think that they had served to bury the carcasses of a pig or an ass."[17] Although changes have occurred in more recent times, the contrast remains. In Italy and elsewhere in the south of Europe, the cemetery is the constant resort of the living, a familiar, not fearful, place for women, who are the most frequent visitors. For them it is not a place of fear, as was often the case in the folklore as well as life of more northerly climes. The deep preoccupation with people or ghosts rising from the dead, embodied in literary form in the stories of Edgar Allan Poe, was perhaps the counterpart of the abandonment of the family dead in the cemetery. Although stories of meetings with the dead in the cemeteries, always at night, do figure in Italian narratives, little of the gothic lore of northern Europe seems to have penetrated popular culture in Italy. The modern version of the encounter with the world of death, the horror movie, is far less popular in the Italian peninsula than in the British Isles; and when the products of this genre reach the Italian cinemas, they are readily identified by viewers as *film inglesi*.

## The Tenure of the Dead

A related feature of the difference between the cemeteries of the Anglo-American world and of Italy (together with much of the rest of Europe) has to do with the ownership of burial rights, whether these are vested perpetually or temporarily in the descendents. In the first case, rights are acquired by outright purchase and, in the second, by renting the land for a period of years.

By the middle of the nineteenth century, in the private cemeteries of the Anglo-American world, all graves were in theory perpetual. In Norwich, perpetual burial rights could be purchased in the Rosary Burial Ground, one of the first private cemeteries established in England in 1821 by a Presbyterian minister, whose "vision saw a general cemetery on freehold land so securely vested in trust that its use was guaranteed for all time."[18] In the municipal cemeteries that followed, perpetual freehold was an option for those prepared to pay the price.[19] Gradually, with the assistance of countless burial societies, even the poor obtained sites that were either permanent or on long lease-holds.[20]

In Italy and generally on the continent, the temporary leasing of sites is much more frequent; indeed, it is the general method of burial in many areas. The periodicity of their turnover may be quite rapid. The Napoleonic decree of 12 June 1804 (23 Prairial, Year XII), which attempted to re-establish and regularize the cult of the dead following the "scorn and insensibility" into which it had fallen during the Revolution, mandated five years.[21] Elsewhere the length of time might depend upon the rent provided, the nature of the soil, or the state of the cemetery. The length might last only for the number of years needed under specific soil conditions before the clean bones could be exhumed. That period could vary from the two years taken in Naples for the volcanic soil to mummify corpses for exhumation to the ten to fifteen years needed in Bologna. There, cemetery authorities are today under a great deal of pressure to turn over graves due to the need for space. One officer complained to us that the over-saturation of the soil necessitates an increasingly longer period of interment. This further aggravates the problem of overcrowding.

In Italy, as in France, provision is also made for family tombs on a permanent basis. The situation in Bologna has been made more difficult by the increasing demand for perpetual space, despite the fact that in the major Italian cemeteries the price of such tombs has rocketed in recent years. Moreover, unlike France, such tombs may not be places of first burial. At Bellagio, these family tombs were ranged around the outer rim of the cemetery, as envisaged in the Napoleonic decree. Of the graves in the center, none was more than fifty years old, except for a walled-off corner that included the bones of a few foreigners, some of whom had met their death in climbing accidents in the nearby Alps. Most were much more recent. It was not a particularly new cemetery, nor had the space been dug over haphazardly. Instead of freehold, *in perpetuum,* the bulk of the graveyard space was rented for terms varying between ten and fifty years.

It is this type of ownership that directly affects the matter of attendance and the use of flowers. With leasehold sites relatives do not have an open-ended commitment to decorate the graves of their dead but need only take good care of them for a limited number of years. Under the perpetual tenure of Anglo-American cemeteries, graves date from much further back, so there may be no surviving close relatives and the sites necessarily remain unattended. This phenomenon of turnover also accounts for the compact character of most Italian cemeteries in contrast to those huge straggling graveyards found in the United States, in which the space required to bury the dead expands indefinitely.

How did this difference come about? Throughout most of Europe in the later Middle Ages, especially in urban areas, it was customary to turn over any particular piece of ground in the graveyard. Except for the monumental tombs of the nobility, lay, and clerical, grave sites were reused.[22] Wooden markers would fall to pieces, and the gravedigger, like the well-known character in *Hamlet,* would disinter the bones of the former tenants in order to provide space for the new ones. Only the powerful had permanent dwelling places, either in the church or outside. Undoubtedly, one factor in the turnover of grave sites was the matter of space. The scene in *Hamlet* provides a satirical comment on that overcrowding, and it is significant that in the America of the seventeenth century, where space was not a problem, there seems to have been no question that earlier graves were ever disturbed in this way.

Space remained a problem in urban England, but other factors intervened. The extension of affluence under industrialization was followed by the establishment of the private cemeteries. The pressure for perpetual plots now came from below with the democratization of that permanent marker, the headstone. That took place early on in America and in England. But towards the middle of the nineteenth century, appalled by the chaotic and unhealthy situations existing in urban graveyards, supporters of the private rural cemetery had as one of their central aims the provision of permanent resting places for the dead. However, there were other factors related to the fate of the bones and the general attitude towards any cult or indeed prayers for the dead in certain Protestant sects.

## Moving the Bones

Not all the turnover of grave sites was done in the informal manner of Hamlet's gravedigger, nor is that how it is carried out in Italy today. In the overcrowded cemetery of Naples, the peculiar properties of the volcanic soil render it possible to exhume and shift the bodies after an interment of only eighteen months. The mummy-like, dried corpse is then wrapped in a shroud and taken to the family *loculo* in the catacombs, if one exists. Each *loculo* may contain several such corpses; and, unlike those in other parts of Italy which are walled in, its lid can be opened at will by the key holders. Relatives pay periodical visits to change the shroud and to rearrange the bones as the corpse slowly disintegrates, a process associated with a complex set of beliefs linking second burial with the progress of the soul in the afterworld.[23]

Naples represents an extreme case of cultic elaboration fostered by the early possibility of shifting the bones. Elsewhere in Italy the operation involves less complex actions. In the Certosa of Bologna these procedures for exhuming the bones take the following form. Bodies are buried in rented pits in the cemetery where row after row follow the dates of interment. After about fifteen or twenty years the bones are ready to be exhumed. Notices placed around the graves warn relatives of the dead that this will take place. These notices are displayed two months in advance, so that anyone who wishes to collect the bones can arrange to come on the date of exhumation. The casket containing the bones may be placed in the monumental family tomb, in the family *loculo,* or alternatively in a small *tombino,* a pigeon-hole where it is walled in and identified by a plaque bearing the name and eventually the picture of the deceased. If on the given date none of the relatives of the deceased shows up, the bones are collected and placed in large chambers built underground, the charnel house of old, where they are piled up anonymously. Significantly, in many old Italian graveyards such chambers were the nearest building to the church. This can be interpreted as a way of compensating for the absence of relatives (and therefore of any active attention) by placing the *ossa abbandonate* close to the center of the collective worship given in the church, so that they can benefit from some form of indirect care.

Following the Napoleonic period, cemeteries usually became detached from the church itself. Even in rural areas, they took a similar form. In Bellagio, bones are collected up when the period of lease runs out and may then be placed in one of the tall family tombs, multi-storied buildings round a miniature courtyard at the edge of the cemetery. A plaque bearing the name of the deceased is set in place, and the bones are left to rest *in perpetuum.* The use of such monumental family tombs implies a differentiation of status quite at odds with the early Puritanical stress on equality in death, the ultimate leveler, as well as with notions expounded in the eighteenth century by members of the Enlightenment and put into practice in the French Revolution.

In the Anglo-American world the notion of equality is breached by the rich, as in the Gracelands Cemetery in Chicago, where the industrial and commercial magnates have large mausoleums designed by architects; but some Protestant hackles are still raised at the sight of elaborate tombs of continental design.[24] This difference in funerary architecture is related not only to such ideological notions, as well as to theological views on the fate of the dead, but also to practical concerns about the disposition of bones.

The family tomb surrounding the cemetery is only one possibility. Another, as in Naples and Bologna, is the *loculo*. A common strategy now pursued by middle-class families is to buy a freehold concession from the municipal administration, which, as in France, is invariably in charge of cemeteries. A *loculo* is a small-sized chamber set in a wall, either in the open air or in a catacomb. It is usually of the size sufficient to hold a coffin, with some extra space at the back and the sides. Families who have moved into town with the post-war economic boom prefer to buy a *loculo* in their village of origin. Their motives of a reverential kind go hand in hand with practical reason. *Loculi* in rural villages are cheaper to buy than in the overcrowded urban cemeteries, which are always under pressure from the increasing demand for freeholds, however small. On the other hand it is said that the dead are best laid to rest with their forefathers. After the father of a Bolognese friend's mother died in the mid-1960s, when the family had attained a certain degree of economic well-being, all the siblings banded together to buy a *loculo* in his natal village and placed the dead man there.

Shortly afterwards, following a family discussion, the bones of his wife, who had died some forty years earlier, were transferred from the *ossario* (the ossuary) of the village cemetery where they had been stored after the lease on her grave site had expired, into the *loculo* next to her husband.[25] Later on, one of the couple's daughters died in town. Her husband, who lived near the town cemetery, asked her surviving siblings to be allowed to bury his wife there, as it would be easier for him to look after her grave. There is an understanding, however, that when it comes time to exhume his wife's bones, which is now approaching, these may be taken to the country cemetery to be reunited with those of her parents. The *loculo* would now be ready to receive the next child of the original couple. Meanwhile, the surviving children visit the parents' tomb, as well as that of their sister. But the main mourner at the woman's grave is her husband. His is the largest bunch of flowers, freshly renewed at least twice a week, followed in order of importance by those of her children, her siblings, and her friends.

So a *loculo* bought on a permanent, freehold basis, becomes a miniature family tomb. Bodies are first interred, later exhumed, then the bones collected together in clusters of relatives. Depending on the timing of the deaths in a given family, a fresh coffin might be immediately placed in the *loculo* as soon as the earlier one is removed and the bones arranged in the casket. This grouping of the bones of relatives in a family tomb or *loculo* is one way of disposing of them after the lease expires.

A third possibility is to employ a more impersonal treatment. The bones are taken to the *ossario* or charnel house but not placed in a separate chamber.[26] Nowadays the large majority receives a more personal treatment, as the trend is toward setting up family tombs or *loculi,* however small. In former times these bones may have been thrown anonymously on a heap of similar remains, possibly retaining some shadowy identity in a pile in the crypt.

### From Charnel House to Rural Cemetery

In Europe there are three aspects to the reverence for the bones of the dead. First, in terms of chronology, was the reverence given to the bones and other relics of the saints, the sanctified dead. The bones and dust of the early martyrs were treasured by the living, and before long church leaders "were digging up corpses and breaking them into fragments."[27] That process began by the middle of the second century A.D. The physical relics of the dead were treated with much reverence.[28] That aspect was crystallized in the festival of All Saints on 1 November. Reverence could properly be paid to these actual remains but not, at first, to representations of the dead themselves, which were often forbidden as being false and idolatrous. Second, Christian burial came to take place around the sites of churches which later occupied the centers of towns. Space was at a premium. The church sometimes had to move the bones of the dead so that they did not occupy a plot perpetually but continued to be kept *ad sanctos,* near the saints. In the Middle Ages the rearranging of bones in urban cemeteries appears to have led to the development of ossuaries and charnel houses in which to place them.[29] That aspect was later institutionalized in the celebration of All Souls on 2 November. Third, this practice developed particular features in the Baroque period, when we can speak of an elaborated cult of bones of the ordinary dead as distinct from the saints.

Although Christians, like other people, paid great attention to the burial of their relatives and circulated relics of their saintly dead from early times, there is no evidence of charnel houses before the thirteenth century.[30] Philippe Ariès sees the establishment of charnel houses and galleries as a way of coping with the pressure on graveyards.[31] That was certainly not the only reason, for later on we find ossuaries in rural areas in England and Italy, as well as in the desert of Sinai, in which the skulls of earlier monks in the Justinian monastery of Saint Catherine were piled in the crypt in order to keep them within the sacred precincts.[32] Thus, it is not so much a matter of pressure on space itself, as on holy space.

Some have seen the culture of the charnel house, the Dance of Death, the *Danse Macabre,* the worm-corrupted cadaver, the skull and crossbones, as a part of the aftermath of the Black Death.[33] Others have traced their origin to the increase in urban populations in the thirteenth or fourteenth centuries.[34] In England, when they had been disturbed in the church yard, bones were placed in subterranean chambers,[35] presumably a sign of overcrowding, as well as a way of tidying up the remains of the dead and avoiding their unseemly treatment. A concern with cleanliness lay behind the Norwich charnel which Bishop Salmon founded and to which clean bones were brought "to be decently reserved till the last day."[36] A belief in resurrection demanded bones, clean bones; the flesh was perishable, but the bones endured. In sixteenth-century Europe, and in many parts of that continent much later, the upper classes held sites in perpetuity and used them for the erection of tombs, often inside the church itself but sometimes in England in the surrounding graveyard. Meanwhile the poor were buried in a common grave and others in graves turned over with varying degrees of frequency, depending upon the nature of the soil and the pressures of space.

Although the pressure of space and tidiness were important, reverence was also at stake. The skulls of dead monks stored in Saint Catherine's monastery or the bones piled up in the church of San Giovanni in the Val di Fassa in the Dolomites had to be disposed of, but more than an utilitarian act was involved. The attention paid to them represents a more generalized conception of the cult of the bones of the dead than was involved in the earlier reverence given to the relics of saints. That cult was more than a question of the commemoration of the dead or of the *memento mori* of the Vanitas paintings of the Reformation, for the bones themselves, whether those of ancestors or of the anonymous dead, received *doulia* (reverence).[37] In many European countries this cult attained macabre heights in the Baroque age and was particularly strong in Spain, southern Italy (at the time under the Spanish rule), and in southern Germany. In these places the cult took a variety of forms. Long bones were used in making candelabra and wall decorations of various kinds.[38] In Germany bones were incorporated in the walls and ceilings of chapels, while the skulls themselves were sometimes decorated and inscribed. The tradition of southern German reliquaries carried the ornamental use of bones to a climax: Bones and skulls become beds of flowers crafted out of pearls, precious stones, gold and silver filigree, *paillettes,* and glass beads.[39] The seventeenth century saw the further elaboration of the floral style in decorating house furniture and other objects of everyday use at the level of folk art. In southern Germany, Tyrol, and the Dolomites, a distinctive manner of painting decorative flowers was developed which was also used to paint the skulls of ordinary persons well into the nineteenth century.[40] The degree of intense reverence for bones in Italy and Bavaria was unique, but it can also be seen as a special development of the practice of disinterring the bones of the dead and placing them in an ossuary, as well as of the cult of saintly relics.[41]

In England at the Reformation, both the cult of relics and the charnel house all but disappeared.[42] Bishop Salmon's charnel at Norwich was granted to the city in 1548 and then emptied of bones. The crypt, which like others was turned over to more useful purposes, became part of the Grammar School. Many of the crypts beneath English churches are emptied charnels, although a few survive with their bones[43]: Some charnel houses apparently continued to be used in London until the end of the seventeenth century. However, the vast majority disappeared for theological reasons: Most Protestants, especially radical reformers, no longer prayed to or for the dead, let alone their bones, and were more inclined to avoid the graveyard. Where space was available, as in New England, bodies were disposed of with little ceremony and then largely abandoned to the cemeteries, which were sometimes organized by the communities themselves rather than by the church. At least initially the active commemoration of the dead was kept at a minimal level.

The rejection of the Catholic cult of the dead did not solve the problem of overcrowding and the associated aspects of reverence and of health. The increase in town populations in the dense agglomerations of sixteenth-century London and Paris created difficulties for the disposing of the dead.[44] Not all was done in an orderly way. In London, too, skulls were dug up by chance and bones that had been disturbed broke through the surface of the earth. But the unsanitary aspects gave rise to concern, first among doctors and then among the general public. Provided by royal largesse, the church-yard of St. Innocents was for many centuries the only burial place in Paris. Generation after generation were buried there, with the *fosses communes* emptied once in thirty or forty years and the bones deposited in the great charnel house, which was an arched gallery created from the gifts of a variety of donors. In 1737 the Parliament of Paris asked the doctors to investigate the cemeteries and in 1763 a decree proposed to relocate and partially secularize them. However, this did not take place until the scandal at Les Innocents in 1780, when the contents of the cemetery overflowed into neighboring houses. Following a commission appointed in 1777, it was decided to transfer and display the bones (with due solemnity) in the vast quarries under the city. Although this process was interrupted by the secularizing activities of the Revolution, the use of the quarries became established in 1810. Meanwhile, the burial ground was also moved outside the city. That move happened gradually, and in 1803 the site of the future Pere-Lachaise, conceived as a sort of Elysian fields and later used as a model by many reformers, was acquired.

Even the inhabitants of urban New England were affected by the same fears, but their solution lay in a different direction. In 1831 the private cemetery of Mount Auburn in Boston was founded to take the pressure off local facilities and to create a perpetual ambiance of peace in rural surroundings.[45] By the end of the eighteenth century the situation in London had already become a cause of alarm in some quarters, of scandal in others. Not only the graves but the bones themselves were said to be recycled, and the density of deteriorating bodies led medical professionals to complain of the dangerous miasma produced by their putrefaction. In this case, the bones were not objects of cult, commemoration, or even of rearrangement, but an excrescence which needed to be covered up as soon as possible. The inevitable reform took the shape of the private rural cemetery movement of the 1840s, which developed extensive permanent plots on the edges of large towns. As in the case of Paris, the complaint was that these rural cemeteries, though sometimes placed adjacent to the new railway lines, were less easy to visit; but this difficulty was certainly of less concern to the Anglo-Americans than on the continent of Europe.

There was a further social cost to such cemeteries, namely the amount of land required to satisfy the needs of an increasing population. In America, where land is plentiful and suburbia unending, such considerations were and are of less importance. That was not so in England, where Christian fears and prohibitions connected with the resurrection of the body have not stopped the increasing trend towards the adoption of the main alternative, namely, cremation.[46]

Although the problems were similar, the Anglo-American world and the European continent moved in different directions. In the former, the new cemeteries were private, with perpetual grave sites. In France, following the pre-Revolutionary and Revolutionary moves in the same vein, the Napoleonic decree of 1804 placed all cemeteries under government control and laid down strict regulations, which promoted the turnover of those grave sites not bought in perpetuity. Even rural cemeteries were relocated and reorganized.

The disposition of cemeteries within the French Empire, which consisted of the bulk of Europe, was regulated in an Imperial Decree dated 23 Prairial, year XII, that is, 12 June 1804. The main themes were two: first, a measure of secularization and, second, the insistence on public health. As in England there was much contemporary concern with contagion by virus and with the necessity for disinfecting buildings and cemeteries.[47] Both for reasons of health and for secularization, existing graveyards were to be closed and new ones created on exposed, rising ground to the north of settlements at a distance of thirty-five to forty meters and with walls at least two meters high, with care taken to ensure the circulation of air.[48] Each burial was to be in a separate plot, with no grave being reopened for five years, so that the area should be five times that needed annually for deaths. On the other hand, when the cemetery was large enough, concessions should be made for those wanting a family plot on which to construct *caveaux, monuments,* or *tombeaux.* For this the owners would pay the commune and give money to approved charities for the poor.

It was partly through the Napoleonic empire's administration that cemeteries in France and Germany have a number of features in common with Italy, such as formal limited tenure for their graves.[49] Those similarities are related to the spread of French administration and to the general concern with matters of health and secularization. Opened already in 1801 under the administration of the Napoleonic Repubblica Cisalpina, the Certosa in Bologna remains the town's largest cemetery to this day because it maintains the large-scale turnover of graves and the retention of ossuaries for second burial (unlike France). It was founded when a fourteenth-century Carthusian monastery was purchased after the suppression of the order which gave the cemetery its name and after a long debate that began in the 1780s over the need for healthy cemeteries *extra moenia.*[50]

In Italy the adoption of such procedures for turnover meant that cemeteries could generally be kept small and central, so they could be near at hand for easy visiting. Turnover was arranged on a more formal basis than before. Instead of waiting for bones to be dug up as new graves were prepared, relatives rented space for a set number of years during which time they carefully tended the grave. After that period, the bones were shifted, either to the individual second-burial tombs or else, if not claimed by relatives, to the *ossario comune*.

The recent situation differs in other European countries, for we have found no evidence of ossuaries in France or Germany. In France they disappeared during the course of the reforms. Breton charnel houses exist but, as in England, were taken over for such municipal purposes as schools, council chambers for the commune, or as postoffices.[51] Many graves are now perpetual, that is, on ninety-nine-year leases. In urban Berlin, short-term tenure persists; but when the lease expires, the bones are simply deposited in a hole dug next to the site. Only in Mediterranean Europe, that is, Portugal, Spain, Italy, and Greece, do we find the continuation of the earlier practices that extended throughout the continent.

## The Critique and Celebration of Bones

In the nineteenth century the new cemeteries established in England and in the United States took a very different approach to the tenure of the dead than is the case in much of continental Europe. Recycling and the consequent need to shift the bones was eliminated, resulting in different attitudes towards the dead, the cemetery, and the care given to the graves. Although this difference has a theological basis, the actors tend to neglect the ideology and focus their feelings on the more proximate practice of exhumation. That practice and the subsequent reburial of the bones is seen by Anglo-Americans as tampering with mortal remains in a way that suggests disrespect for death and the dead. As an English friend commented on viewing the BBC documentary, "Mimmo Perrella non e' piu" (1985), on the reburial customs in Naples: "Why do Italians poke about with their dead? Why can't they leave them in peace?"

While the critique of the cult of bones, like the rejection of elaborate funerals, of differentiated monuments to the dead and of images themselves, was taken up by Protestants, such attitudes and practices have had a long history. Indeed the Reformers saw themselves as going back to earlier beliefs and practices, not as inventing new ones. The objections had been central to earlier moments of reform from the Waldensians onwards. The point is critical, as such changes are often viewed as intertwined with modernization, either as cause or effect. In the case of bones, such medieval writers as Geoffrey Chaucer commented satirically on the activities of the Pardonner in the *Canterbury Tales:*

> Thenne shewe I forth my longe cristal stones,
> Ycrammed ful of cloutes and of bones,
> Relikes been they
> —Chaucer 1957: Vi 347–57

Nor can the critical tone of this writing be taken as a specifically northern phenomenon. Neither the activities of the sellers of pardons and indulgences nor the criticisms that were to accompany the practice were confined to the periphery of Catholicism;[52] but it was there we find the most decisive rejection with the coming of the Reformation, when the center held and the periphery rebelled.[53] Today the Roman Catholic Church discourages the cult of bones, especially when it takes place outside the relatively enclosed and controlled environment of the monastery. So, too, did the French revolutionaries and other secular reformers. As a consequence the practice is fast disappearing, even among the laity. In 1969 the Cardinal of Naples closed many catacombs in which skulls had been kept in the open for cult purposes. In some cases the bones had to be reburied in the proper manner.

In the Val di Fassa, the change of mood occurred earlier. In 1835 a woman was tried for removing the skull of a priest from his tomb, which was set in the porch of San Giovanni, the mother church of the valley. Brought in front of a court instituted by the Austro-Hungarian administration, she explained that it was customary in the valley to remove the skull, place it in the crypt, and address it with prayers and supplication.[54] Elsewhere, in the remote village of Alba in the same valley, the *ciumitier*[55] had its skulls exposed to the prayers of the faithful until the 1930s, when it was finally demolished and the skulls buried. "It was a good thing for the people to see all their ancestors collected together," an old Ladin sexton remarked, "but the priest said the sight was not a pious one and the practice lacked respect. All the skulls were removed and the *ciumitier* brought down."

Although the cult of bones is now discouraged, that of the dead is encouraged. In the Roman Catholic Church, the main occasion for celebrating the dead is the two days of All Saints and All Souls (1 and 2 November). These dates have little meaning among Protestants, or indeed even among Catholics in the eastern United States. But in Italy, the relics of the saints are brought out of the cabinets in the sacristy and exhibited on the main altar in the church, where they are venerated by the faithful. On that same day, on the Eve of All Souls, the villagers in the Val di Fassa went to the crypt and washed the family skulls anew before *la festa*.[56] In many parts of Catholic Europe All Souls is still the time when people visit the cemetery to clean the graves and place flowers on the tomb. Even the suggestions made by the Institute for the reform of French practices included an annual ceremony for the dead.[57] Towards the end of the nineteenth century one clergyman regretted the secularization of the cemetery but took this as a reason for a renewed commitment to the cult of the dead: "Let us, therefore, decorate our graves with greater zeal than ever; let us multiply our visits as a protest against the neglect the authorities would impose."[58] In other words, the celebration of Toussaints was encouraged as a counter to the secularization promoted by reformers, as was true of other Catholic countries.

In 1985 we attended a service on All Souls Day at the convent of Nossa Senhora das Neves at Olinda, Brazil. At the end of the mass, the priest entered a courtyard, the low wall of which contained caskets with the remains of the dead, before which some had lit the remnants of candles. Candles or lamps are often placed on Catholic graves, just as they are offered to holy figures in the churches themselves; we have found these candles or lamps in Brazil (Sao Paulo); in Austria (Burg Wartenstein); and in Bologna and in Bellagio, although in the latter cases they were supplemented by little electric lights supplied by subterranean cables. Like flowers, light is an appropriate way of approaching both the saints and the dead. In Italy, as All Souls comes near, the practice of lighting candles becomes more marked. At this ritually heightened time, special candles contained in red wax paper (of the same color that burn perpetually in front of the Holy Host in churches) are placed on the steps leading to the underground *ossari*. In other words, at the approach of the Feast the *ossa abbandonate* too are addressed.

At Olinda the priest, followed by part of the congregation, walked round the courtyard, asperging the tombs with holy water, stopping here and there to say a prayer. At this time many people visited the places of the dead and decorated the tombs with flowers. Throughout South America, such visits are widespread on the Day of the Dead (All Souls). People take food and drink to the cemeteries and engage in rowdy celebrations, especially in Mexico, where the skulls, including painted pottery ones, are a major feature of the festivities.[59] The actual skulls were formerly kept in ossuaries, the notion of which was imported by the Spanish in the sixteenth century. On All Souls, the skulls, some inscribed with the name of the deceased, some becoming objects of cult, were placed on display, as was the case with the relics of saints the day before (All Saints). A heightened activity in terms of offerings and communion with the dead at All Souls appears all over the Roman Catholic areas of America and Europe. Candles are lit, food prepared, and flowers gathered.[60]

## The Theological Dimension

Our discussion so far has focused on what can loosely be called informal religion, especially the cult of the dead, which is seen by some as an alternative religion[61] and by others as the foundation of all.[62] In doing so, we have constantly encountered the influence of the more formal manifestations and, in particular, the divide between Catholic and Protestant (and more specifically non-Conformist) doctrine and practice. In the first place, the Protestants rejected the notion of purgatory, which had been consolidated between 1100 and 1300. Through the cult of the Souls of Purgatory, the *anime purganti,* the dead might be saved and translated to Heaven by means of suffrages aimed at remitting sins. But the assistance offered was reciprocal because even from purgatory the dead could intercede for the living, which is well illustrated by the standard Italian prayer, "*Sante anime del Purgaaooryo pregate per noi che preghiamo per voi*" (Holy Souls of Purgatory we beseech you to pray for us as we pray for you). That doctrine was promoted by the mendicant orders, "ardent propagandists of the new doctrine," which also received strong support from the new rituals.[63] The same orders were charged with suppressing such heretics as the Cathars, who objected to these doctrines.

The acceptance or rejection of purgatory formed part of a wider divergence of beliefs about the treatment and fate of the dead. It was associated with the objection to all payments for the remission of the sins of the dead and the living that was as intrinsic to Luther as it had been to earlier reformers. In 1529, Henry VIII passed an act forbidding payments for masses for the dead. Doctrinally there was nothing the living could do for those whose fate had already been decided. Nobody could tell who was amongst the saved and who was amongst the damned. After the denial of the doctrine of purgatory, "each generation could be indifferent to the spiritual fate of its predecessors."[64] Given this view, there was little point in going to the cemetery in order to help one's relatives. An individual could offer reverence to the dead, but even such limited attention presented problems.[65] The forefathers could be respected in other ways, so the formal occasions for visits to the graveyard disappeared. The celebration of Saints' days was much reduced in the Anglican churches or totally abandoned by non-Conformists, which was the case with All Souls, a feast closely associated with the notion of purgatory. The celebration of the saintly dead had been an early feature of the Christian Church, but that of All Souls, the day following All Saints (All Hallows), was specifically instituted by Cluny between 1024 and 1033, perhaps by Saint Odilo, its fifth Abbot.

Catholic belief asserts the possibility of mediation *in suffragium:* The fate of the dead is not completely defined in advance, so the way is open to a more collective concern, to help from others. Visiting the grave is not simply a matter of mourning an individual or revering the dead but of helping that person in the other world. As with the cult of the ancestors in many communities, there is a continuous, active relationship between the living and the dead. This is no longer true under Protestantism, although an underlying desire for it to be so may be discerned in some of its own heresies, such as in the Mormon Church or in spiritualist beliefs.[66] But the fate of the dead has already been decided, and neither they nor anyone else can intercede with God, to whom communication is direct and unmediated.

It was not only the doctrinal reasons and occasions for going to the graveyard that changed, but also attitudes towards burial places. That change was more marked among Puritans and therefore of more importance in North America, accounting for the relative uniformity of their early burial grounds. The Puritans objected to differentiating between the rites and monuments of the richer and the poorer elements in society, so these became open to attack. In 1560 Queen Elizabeth had to issue a proclamation aimed at curbing such excesses as defacing funeral monuments. In order to prevent any misinterpretation of her actions, she announced that her defense of funeral monuments was meant to preserve the historical heritage of the nation and "not to nourish any kind of superstition."[67] In the more extreme doctrines of the Puritans, memorials were in principle reduced to plain tombstones that denied all differences of status among the dead. As with the graves of soldiers, death was the great leveler.[68] Such restraint was also marked by the paucity of offerings, including flowers, placed in cemeteries. Even today, notices in American cemeteries often announce that flowers will be removed each week, a regulation explained in terms of maintenance and tidiness for which the cemetery employees are responsible.[69] In Italy one would tidy one's own plot.

The preceding discussion touches upon doctrinal elements that closely affected differences in the floral cultures of Italian and Anglo-Saxon cemeteries. Protestant reformers tended to reduce rituals of all kinds, seeking the truth in the word alone. They were often opposed to all image making of a sacred kind, whether in the cemetery or outside, as well as to the use of offerings in worship. The Christian church attempted to distinguish between the kinds of prestations made to holy figures or at the graveside, asking whether they were intrinsic to the rite (*ornamenta*) or merely for decoration. At times that distinction became blurred, especially at the level of the popular cult. Protestants saw Catholics approaching the ways of the pagans, for example in their use of flowers as *ornamenta,* intrinsic to ceremonial, rather than as decoration.[70] Protestantism revived the views of the early Church and sought to discount the value of ritual, even in the treatment of the dead, and viewed the offerings of flowers in such contexts with a critical eye.

Like Americans, English observers in the middle of the nineteenth century remarked upon the differences between their own cemeteries and those on the continent, where not only the iconography but also the offerings were more elaborate. Around that time the movement began towards the re-establishment and adaptation of earlier ritual activities and symbolism now associated with the Church of England, which was paralleled by the height of the Victorian elaboration of funeral customs.[71] That included the more extensive use of flowers inside and outside the church. English graveyards are consequently less barren than they were. Even in America, except on Jewish graves, more commemorative flowers appear, being strongly promoted by commercial interests.

Nevertheless the broad contrast remains in the eyes of both actor and observer. The actors rightly place emphasis on the religious affiliation, sometimes linking this with national characteristics. In our view there is less justification for the second interpretation, given the changes over time and the wider spread of many of these features. Historically, pre-Reformation practice regarding the use of flowers and ossuaries was undoubtedly more uniform throughout Europe, though local differences obviously occurred. The disappearance of the charnel house was first associated with the advance of Protestantism and with a different set of beliefs about the dead and about the relics of the dead, their bones, as well as about making any offerings, including floral offerings, to them. But geographically the Catholic-Protestant divide does not entirely explain the distribution of these features. German Protestants turn over the grave sites and decorate them almost as elaborately as the Italians but use plants rather than cut flowers; the cemeteries of Catholics in New England and in Quebec conform to much of the dominant Protestant practice; and the same can be said, by and large, of Catholics in England. The movement for rural or garden cemeteries promoted freehold tenure in both England and America. In Europe, administrative fiat, following the views of reformers, sanitary fears, and pressure on space, led to the regularization of procedures for turning over grave sites. Each of the features cuts across national and in some cases religious boundaries, since practice is closely linked to the dominant trends, to the hegemonic ethos, prevailing in any area regarding the tenure of the dead.

## Conclusions

We have tried to relate the differences between the uses of flowers in Anglo-American and Italian cemeteries to differences in family ties, in the tenure of grave sites and administrative practice, in the custom of double interment, and in the associated attitudes towards bones and the relics of the dead, as well as to the encompassing theological doctrines of Protestants and Catholics. In America and in England the aim for the dead became a permanent resting place, which in the nineteenth century the rural cemetery movement and its municipal followers eventually made possible. Italy and most of the continent adopted the practice of letting out sites on limited tenure, leaving the bones to be disposed of in ossuaries and elsewhere in bone pits. The Anglo-American solution was associated with ambivalence about moving bones, the continental one with the desire to preserve land, to keep cemeteries within easy reach for visiting, and to provide proper resting places for clean bones. The result was a conception of the tenure of graves that embodied short leasehold as against a freehold (or, at any rate, a long-term leasehold). Short-term allocation encourages intensive care for the dead, with frequent visits to tidy up the grave-sites, to replace the offerings of cut flowers, and to attend to the lights. This system may lead to the relocation of the bones of the dead either in a family tomb or in a charnel house and opens up the possibility of the elaborated cult of bones, especially of skulls, which was earlier found in Italy and Southern Germany but which has more recently been discouraged. And this system is in turn linked to doctrinal considerations that give a role to the living in influencing the fate of the dead (and vice versa) and that are more sympathetic to the elaboration of offerings, of images, and of ritual.

There is a tendency among Anglo-American scholars to interpret Max Weber as affirming the elective affinity among Protestantism, capitalism, and modernization which in turn led to a rationalization of religious practices and beliefs.[72] Some of the reforms that resulted in the differences we observed may have arisen out of such a developmental process, if we follow the view taken by populace and scholars alike. Elias has characterized this as civilizing, for example, interposing such intermediaries as knife and fork, handkerchief, and toilet paper between individuals and bodily functions (Elias 1978–1982). It may be that the tidying up of cemeteries and the distancing of the bones of the dead fall into this category of social act. However, many of the changes are not of this kind. Offering flowers to the dead has lately increased rather than decreased in many Protestant communities and hardly raises similar issues of hygiene or rationality, though it may raise objections on account of expense. Although the rejection of such offerings is firmly located in the practice of extreme Protestants, that feature, like others we have discussed, is not to be seen in the context of the events of the sixteenth century alone (and hence its socio-economic changes). In promoting these changes Protestants were continuing the heretical traditions of Waldensians, Cathars, Lollards, and Hussites and saw themselves as returning to the ways of early Christianity.

Central themes in the practice and beliefs of the early Church involved the rejection of offerings to the dead, advocated equality in memorials, and emphasized direct communication with God by the individual worshipper. These ideas have nothing exclusively to do with sixteenth-century Protestantism as such or with capitalism, modernity, and rationalization. They were problems of longstanding interest not only to Christians but to Muslims, Jews and, in different forms, to other written and unwritten religions. These themes concern more general problems, such as how to treat the dead (equality or the celebration of status and achievement) and what is the nature of offerings and requests made to supernatural agencies. On these topics, the ecclesia may lay down a doctrine, but that does not disperse the doubts and ambivalences of the laity and, in many cases, of the clerics too. Hence, there is differentiation within[73] and change over time, as in the case of the use of flowers, for cult purposes by some and for commemoration by others.

In this essay we have deliberately taken an observed difference which some have interpreted as indicating differing cultural attitudes to death. But, as has been observed in a critical assessment of the work of Philippe Ariès, "it is surely not enough simply to stress that there can be no strict material causation, that culture is an autonomous category."[74] In contrast with the approach of Ariès and others, we have tried to show that to deal on this level of generality brings little profit, since we need to look more closely at the interaction of specific practices, at objective constraints and their ideological counterparts, but in a wider temporal and comparative context. The same changing cultural concerns, such as a preoccupation with the improvement of decorum and respect for the dead, can accompany quite diverging practices—the perpetual grave of Anglo-American cemeteries or the secondary burial in the Italian case—and is associated with the presence of practical constraints leading to varying tenure regimes as well as with differing theological overviews. The wider temporal and geographical perspective provides a more articulate framework within which to interpret the complex dynamics we set out to investigate. Ideology is linked to practice, and theological doctrine to more immediate questions concerning the use of flowers and bones but in no single-stranded way. It is an appreciation of this cluster of specific interlinked factors, rather than any appeal to vague general concepts, such as mentalities, culture, or even attitudes, that helps to explain the dramatic contrasts in the appearance of Italian and Anglo-American cemeteries and in the meanings they have for actors and observers alike. Much of the history and anthropology of mentalities tends to look at practices in terms of overgeneralizations.

At the same time this approach is often overzealous in imposing determined developmental sequences on inappropriate data because it does not take into account a sufficiently long span of time or a sufficiently wide span of society, attributing—as in the present case in point—to sixteenth-century Protestantism a uniqueness it does not always have.

NOTES

Acknowledgements: We wish to thank Bernardo Bernardi, Carlo Ginzburg, Joanna Lanes, Italo Pardo, the members of the Art History Research Seminar at the University of East Anglia, Norwich, and anonymous readers for their useful comments and criticisms of this essay, as well as the numerous people who have accompanied us around cemeteries and provided bibliographical references. We also acknowledge the assistance of the staffs of the Archivio di Stato di Bologna, the Norwich Public Library, and the Getty Center for the History of Art and the Humanities, Santa Monica, California.

1. Quoted by Stone (1858).

2. Stone (1858: 117).

3. Stone (1858: 115).

4. Neville (1989: 163).

5. Jashemski (1979).

6. Ariès (1981: 489–90).

7. *Bedfordshire on Sundays,* 10 June 1984.

8. Our own data come mainly from the Italian cemeteries of Bellagio (Lombardy), Bologna and the Val di Fassa in the Ladin-speaking Dolomites as well as from cemeteries in East Anglia, the United States (mainly in the northeast), South and Central America, France (mainly the south), and Germany (mainly the north). Evidence has been collected both through observation and informal interviews and by direct participation in the practices under review. That includes numerical material.

9. Italian practices made a similar impact on another English prisoner in Italy during the Second World War. He recalls how he used to look from the room where he was locked away at the young Italian girls on their way to and from the *cimitero* (Newby 1983: 36–37).

10. Such funerals were found in Eastern Europe, where between the wars in Berlin a cemetery already existed to bury the socialist dead, including Rosa Luxemburg.

11. Self-criticism of funeral practice is a recurring feature of cultures of luxury at least from classical antiquity. Solon forbade elaborate funeral ceremonies and the building of monuments to the dead as unpious; there are no funeral monuments from 500 to 430 B.C. in the region of Athens (Humphreys 1983).

12. Anthropologists often distinguish between the worship and the cult of ancestors, the former implying a belief in the active participation of the object/agency addressed in human affairs. It would be misleading to speak of the worship of the dead in Near Eastern religions, as at most they can intercede with God and only he is worshipped. But the cult of the dead in parts of Catholic Europe was much more than commemoration, as Protestants recognized. Although many of these permitted some forms of commemoration, early Puritans admitted only reverence, that is, without any active rite. These distinctions we use in this essay to facilitate communication.

13. Bacon (1972: 21).

14. Fortes (1969: 219–49).

15. See for example Klapisch-Zuber (1985), and Herlihy and Klapisch-Zuber (1978).

16. Goody (1983: 101).

17. Pierre Muret 1679, *Cérémonies Funèbres de Toutes les Nations* (Paris,

quoted by Ariès, 1981: 348–49), who remarks about the use of flowers that these are *"rare* indications of a custom that may have been introduced belatedly *in imitation of antiquity"* (our italics).

18. Hamlin (n.d.), "Introduction."

19. The 1856 statues of the Norwich city cemetery prescribed a gradation in the price of freehold burial sites, according to whether there was a tomb or not. The interment fee was the same for common grave burials as for freehold burials, but it was much higher for brick and vault graves (Norwich Cemetery, *Scale of Fees and Charges,* 1856).

20. However, in more recent times there has been a tendency to turn freeholds in perpetuity into long-term leaseholds. At the Norwich City Cemetery, all concessions were turned into fifty-year leaseholds in 1971. The measure was explicitly aimed at saving space and to "lengthen the life of the cemetery." At that time, a list of 127 common graves dating from 1926 to 1945 and due for recycling was also published. The cemetery superintendent, however, specified that no grave which had a gravestone or memorial, or was still tended, was included in the list. In a further gesture to smooth the impact of a less than popular measure, he declared that, if any relatives were unable to buy the freehold rights on the graves due to be re-used and yet did not want the grave disturbed, the authorities "would not be at all bureaucratic and would agree not to use the grave again" (*Eastern Evening News,* 17 March 1991).

21. *Le Moniteur Universel,* 23 July 1804, 1357–58; see also the report of the committee of the Institute, *Le Moniteur Universel,* 1801, 796–98, 802, 806.

22. Such turnover procedures involve the recycling of tombstones of the kind we have seen in Berlin and are described by Danforth (1982), Dubisch (1989), and others for Greece.

23. In Neapolitan popular culture, the condition of dryness of the mummy signals the successful separation of the soul from the body, a further proof of a good death. It is only following such separation that a picture of the deceased can be placed at the family shrine at home and cult rendered there. On the other hand, if at exhumation the corpse is still not dry, then it is reburied for an additional period as the soul has not yet been able to leave its earthly remains. Moreover, it is only if the bones have been properly disposed of in the second burial that the soul can leave purgatory and ascend to heaven. Those who have not gone through a proper second burial are believed to remain in purgatory forever. The continuing exchange between the living and the dead takes the form of the periodic tending of the shroud and bones of the deceased, which happens when the soul manifests its desire for *refrisco* (refreshment) in dreams (Pardo 1985: 29–30; 1989).

24. Exceptions to this are the graves of gypsies and showmen in England, which tend to be highly elaborate (Pearson 1982).

25. The ossuary is also found with similar implications in modern Greece (Danforth 1982; Kenna 1991) and Portugal (De Pina-Cabral and Feijó 1983: 31),

but in Germany and France the exhumation of the bones and the turnover of graves are widely practiced, even in the absence of ossuaries. Unclaimed bones are buried in a hole near the grave site, at least since the latter part of the eighteenth century.

26. On the origin of the word *charnier,* see Ariès (1981: 53). It first carried the general meaning of cemetery, but by the later Middle Ages it came to designate a particular part, namely, the ossuary and the galleries "where bones were both stored and displayed."

27. Lane Fox (1986: 448).

28. That had earlier been the case with the bones that were collected into caskets in the middle of the first millennium B.C. in ancient Israel (Brandon 1967: 60–75; Figueras 1983; Meyers 1971).

29. Ariès (1985: 23).

30. For England, the earliest evidence of a charnel house known to us dates from 1276. A chapel dedicated to the Virgin was erected in Old St. Paul's, London. A chantry priest said commemorative masses while a warden was also employed. When the chapel was demolished in 1549, more than 1,000 cartloads of bones were reported to have been taken away. A charnel house was founded next to Norwich Cathedral by Bishop Salmon, who died in 1325. Although this charnel had a college of priests attached to it, others were maintained by church guilds. In some cases altars were set up, so that chantry masses could be sung. The statutes of the Norwich chantry explicitly mentioned that the serving priest was to say masses for the souls of the dead whose bones had been collected in the vaults and specifically for those who had left offerings to the charnel in their will (Blomefield 1805–1810, vol. IV: 55–58; Sekules 1990: 96–97). According to Stone (1858: 133), in England "charnel-houses were usual appendages to cathedral and conventual churches."

31. Ariès (1981: 54; 1985: 23).

32. Gerster (1970). There are said to be more than 30,000 skeletons of monks who were formerly placed on an iron bedstead until only the dry bones remained (Stone 1858:132–33).

33. For example, Porter 1989.

34. Ariès (1985); Morgan (1989: 95). Arms suggests that the formalized building of the charnel might have substituted for earlier places in which bones were brought when occasionally dug up. In deliberately built *charniers,* the bones could either be concealed or else displayed for visitors.

35. Litten (1991: 8).

36. Houlbrooke (1989b: 38, 211).

37. Evidence from Naples shows that anonymous skulls in ossuaries may become the focus of informally organized cults. Such skulls are given proper names and are addressed by their devotees who seek benefits in return for prayers. Such transactions are believed to be particularly successful when directed to the souls of the unburied who are said to dwell in Purgatory forever and therefore to be in con-

stant need of prayers *in suffragium*. On the other hand, the souls of near relatives will inevitably go to heaven sooner or later, thus becoming more distant and less ready to enter in a relation of mutual help with the living (Pardo 1989: 115–17).

38. Legner (1989: 140); Ariès (1985: 190).

39. The conceptual and symbolic proximity of flowers, bones, and other bodily relics is a widespread theme in Europe. The imagery of bones and ashes giving birth to flowers figures widely in Roman epitaphs (Toynbee 1971: 37). In reliquaries fragments of bone were often arranged at the center of floral creations made of precious materials (Legner 1989: Kat.–Nr. 37/38 and *passim*). In the popular culture of Europe, especially in Germany and northern Italy, the hair of a dead person (mainly those of women) was woven into wreaths of flowery patterns which were used to surround the photograph of the deceased until well into the present century (Metken 1984: 359; Raffaelli 1988: 70–71). Apart from the obvious connotations of transience, renewal, and purity, flowers become metaphors for the dead themselves: In S. Miniato, Florence, a nineteenth-century tomb portrays a young girl in the process of being transformed into a rose (Ariès 1981: 537). In contrast, fundamentalist tendencies of the puritanical kind played down the use of flowers at funerals in order to break away from the so-called paganism of the Roman tradition.

40. Examples of decorated skulls are illustrated and described in Metken (1984: 334–35). In southern Germany and amongst the Ladins of the Dolomites and Friuli (northeastern Italy), the cult continued at least until the late nineteenth century (Ghetta 1976; Nicoloso Ciceri 1982, vol. 2: 255–317). In mountainous regions, the use of the ossuary continued partly because the practical necessity of saving space by exhuming bodies was dictated not by overcrowding as such, as village communities were small, but by the desperate need for cultivable land. A cemetery *ad sanctos,* that is to say, built next to the church, such as in the villages of the highest alpine valleys, soon became full. The bones were dug up, but as at the monastery of Saint Catherine the skulls received special treatment. In the Val di Fassa, in the very heart of the Dolomites, the skull was washed in a stream and afterwards placed either in the crypt of the church (as in San Giovanni) or, alternatively, in a small building in the middle of the churchyard (as in Alba). In due course, a pyramid of skulls appeared, with each family trying to keep those of its ancestors grouped together and identifiable. In contrast to the anonymous cult of Naples, around the forehead of each skull a ribbon was tied, bearing the name of the deceased.

41. Ariès describes individual skullboxes in France as the focus of prayers for the souls in purgatory. He remarks, however, that there is no evidence of any other practices developing from this officially tolerated cult (1985: 236).

42. In France ossuaries disappeared with the relocation of the Parisian cemeteries after 1780, following the outcry against the fumes and stench from the Innocents and the subsequent secularization of death in the Revolution. They were not

restored, in the Napoleonic decree of 1804 which laid down comprehensive proce-dures for burial, nor did they return with the re-instatement of the role of the clergy in funerals at the time of the Restoration.

43. Houlbrooke (1989a: 211); Litten (1991).

44. That was the case in that other major region of Eurasia in which burial was the main means of disposing of the dead, namely China. In the nineteenth century the plant hunter, Robert Fortune, found coffins left outside the settlements and bones scattered on open ground. Proper grave sites were more usually set in hill country, where the land was of marginal use, and that is the case today (Fortune 1987 [1847]). On the other hand, the problem of space and land was avoided alto-gether in Hindu India, where corpses were disposed of by cremation, thus keeping the land for the living. However, where cremation was not customary in the Indian subcontinent, as amongst the Zoroastrian Parsis, the problem posed itself once again. The tower of silence was (and is) a tall construction used to expose bodies in the open air for disposal by vultures. Once the flesh has been consumed, the bones are thrown into a deep well at the center of the radial structure.

45. French (1975).

46. On the growth of cremation in Great Britain see Richardson (1989: 259, Figure 5).

47. "Nosologie, Topographie médicale," *Le Moniteur Universel* 294, 13 July 1804, 1323–25.

48. *Le Moniteur Universel,* 23 July 1804, 1357–58.

49. The regulations about cemetery layout and burial were published in Bologna in 1801 (Bastelli 1934), the year of the publication of the report on funeral matters of the Institute for the reform of French practices (see below). Although predating those published in the *Moniteur* by three years, they are virtually identi-cal to their French counterpart, as were the provisions for moving the cemetery outside the town walls published in Hamburg in October 1812 (Whaley 1981b: 104), a sign that a coherent policy was being pursued throughout the Empire.

50. Raule (1961: 15–16). The philosophy underlying the establishment of the Certosa is contained in a *Promemoria* circulated by the Commissione di Sanita' Dipartimentale del Reno and dated 10 Piovoso Anno IX. This was followed by a set of *Regolamenti e Discipline da Praticarsi per la Tumulazione de' Cadaveri nel Cimitero Comunale di Bologna,* drawn up along the general lines of the above French Imperial Decree and dated 9 Germile Anno IX (Archivio di Stato di Bologna, Amministrazione Centrale del Dipartimento del Reno, XI/318, 1801).

51. Stone (1858: 133).

52. The cult of relics met with some opposition from ecclesiastical leaders from its very beginning. In the second half of the fourth century, a long dispute about its theological acceptability between Vigilantius of Toulouse and St. Jerome set the scene for many more to come. Claudius, Bishop of Turin, was condemned as a

heretic by the Paris Synod of 825 for his skepticism regarding the cult of relics. He is considered a precursor of the Waldensian movement (Sox 1985: 56; Geary 1978: 18).

53. Eire (1986). The XXII Article of Religion of the Church of England states that "the Romish doctrine . . . of Reliques is rather repugnant to the Word of God" (*The Book of Common Prayer with the Additions and Deviations Proposed in 1928*).

54. Ghetta (1976).

55. In Ladin *ciumitier* denotes specifically the charnel house, whereas the cemetery at large is called *cortina*. In modem Greek, too, *kimitirio* is a church ossuary (Dubisch 1989: 191).

56. Although the practices of the Val di Fassa never reached the scale and elaboration of the Day of the Dead in Mexico, the similarities are striking (see Carmichael and Sayer 1991).

57. *Le Moniteur Universel* (1801: 798).

58. Monseigneur Gaume, *Le Cimitière au XIXe siècle* (Paris, 1874), quoted by Ariès (1981: 545–47).

59. Toor (1947: 236–44); Carmichael and Sayer (1991).

60. Numerous instances of such practices are reported. The Laymi of Bolivia hold feasts for the dead of the previous year, and wild flowers are placed on the roof of the house to welcome them (Harris 1982: 54). In southern Italy, offerings of fruit are placed on the graves (Faeta and Malabotti 1980: 58). In parts of Sardinia, the dining room is especially laid out on All Souls Eve, so that the dead can come and eat during the night. In Südtirol, a communal meal of special dishes is held at the end of the funeral service. In the monastery of Camaldoli, in Tuscany, special cakes in the shape of the trochleae of human long bones called *ex ossibus* (from the bones) are eaten on All Souls Day. Elsewhere in northern Italy little cakes in the shape of broadbeans are distributed on All Souls Eve (and at weddings). They are called *fave da morto* (broadbeans of the dead). Throughout Italy it was common practice to leave a bucket of water outside the door on the Eve of All Souls, so that the dead visiting the house could drink. In many areas the dining room was arranged so that the returning dead could sit down to dine (Pallabazzer 1992: 144–48). In the Orthodox world, such celebrations take place at other times. In Romania meals are placed and shared on the graves at Whitsuntide, during the festival of Rusalii, perhaps derived from the Roman festival of Rosalia, during which offerings of flowers were brought to the family graves (Kligman 1981).

61. Ariès (1981).

62. Tylor (1871).

63. Le Goff (1984: 280).

64. Thomas (1978: 721).

65. Beliefs and practices, such as the custom of burying grave goods with the corpse, were recorded by British folklorists well into the present century.

This way of assisting the dead has been interpreted as pointing at the persistence of views concerning the possibility that the living might influence the fate of the dead in the afterlife formalized in the doctrine of purgatory (Richardson 1989: 8).

66. The belief of the Church of the Latter Day Saints in incorporating the dead, not merely the ancestors, through posthumous baptism, has resulted in the unique collection of parish and other demographic records in Salt Lake City. On the connection between spiritualism and Protestantism, see Ariès (1981: 454ff).

67. Boase (1972: 73).

68. The earlier uniformity gave way to some differentiation, but Protestant cemeteries, especially on the east coast of the United States, are noticeably more restrained architecturally than European graveyards. For the successive waves of "display excess" and "display restraint" that followed the Reformation up to the present, see Pearson (1982), Cannon (1989), and Whaley (1981b: 82).

69. In 1991, the issue of grave decorations exploded dramatically, and all the more significantly for our present argument, in the St. Joseph's cemetery, Pittsfield, Massachusetts. The Roman Catholic priest in charge had all excessive decorations removed from the graves, including planted flowers. This provoked an uproar amongst the bereaved, who brought a $40,000 lawsuit against the priest "for breach of contract and emotional distress" (*The New York Times,* 27 August 1991).

70. Lambert (1880: 814). In the early days of Christianity, the rejection of that notion was part not only of the Judaic heritage but also of the reaction to the way in which Greeks, Romans, and other pagans treated their gods and their dead. There is little doubt that it led to a drastic diminution of people's use of flowers. However, by the fourth century some Christian leaders had already began to look anew at pagan practices. Prudentius (Spain, c.348–c.405), while praising Saint Eulalia for disparaging crowns of roses, spoke on the other hand of the use of flowers on graves as a Christian custom. He wrote in his *Hymnus circa exequias defuncti: "Nos tecta fovebimus ossa/violis et fronde frequenti,/titulumque et frigida saxa/liquidus spargemus odore"* (We shall care for the entombed bones/with violets and green leaves in plenty/and with perfumed essence sprinkle/the cold stones that bear the epitaph [Prudentius 1962, M. C. Eagan, trans.]).

71. Cannon (1989: 438–39).

72. For example, Neville (1989), but much of the literature on the history of European mentalities tends in the same direction.

73. Dubisch (1989: 191) notes two patterns in Greece, one reaffirming egalitarian values, the other asserting difference through conspicuous consumption. For emergent distinctions, see page 193. For other recent studies of death and funerals see Bloch and Parry (1982), and Huntington and Metcalf (1985).

74. Whaley (1981a, 1: 10).

REFERENCES

Ariès, P. 1981. *The Hour of Our Death.* London: Allen Lane.

————. 1985. *Images of Man and Death.* Cambridge, Mass.: Harvard University Press.

Bacon, F. 1972. "Of Parents and Children, Essay VII," In, *Essays.* London: Dent.

Bastelli, A. 1934. *Cenni Storici della Certosa di Bologna.* Bologna: N.p.

Bettenson, H., ed. 1943. *Documents of the Christian Church.* London: Oxford University Press.

Bloch, M. and J. Parry, eds. 1982. *Death and the Regeneration of Life.* Cambridge: Cambridge University Press.

Blomefield, F. 1805–1810. *An Essay Towards a Topographical History of the County of Norfolk etc. . . . ,* 11 vols. London: W. Miller.

Boase, T. S. R. 1972. *Death in the Middle Ages.* London: Thomas and Hudson.

Brandon, S. G. F. 1967. *The Judgement of the Dead.* London: Weidenfeld and Nicholson.

Cannon, A. 1989. "The Historical Dimension in Mortuary Expressions of Status and Sentiment." *Current Anthropology* 30, 4: 437–58.

Carmichael, E. and C. Sayer 1991. *The Skeleton at the Feast: The Day of the Dead in Mexico.* London: British Museum Press.

Chaucer, G. 1957. *The Canterbury Tales.* London: N.p.

Danforth, L. M. 1982. *The Death Rituals of Rural Greece.* Princeton: Princeton University Press.

De Pina-Cabral, J. and R. Feijó. 1983. "Conflicting Attitudes to Death in Modern Portugal: The Question of Cemeteries." *Journal of the Anthropological Society of Oxford* 14, 1: 17–43.

Dubisch, J. 1989. "Death and Social Change in Greece." *Anthropological Quarterly* 62: 189– 200.

Eire, C. M. 1986. *War against the Idols—The Reformation of Worship from Erasmus to Calvin.* Cambridge: Cambridge University Press.

Elias, N. 1978–1982. *The Civilizing Process,* 2 vols. Oxford: Blackwell.

Faeta, F. and M. Malabotti. 1980. *Imago Mortis: Simboli e Rituali della Morte nella Cultura Popolare dell'Italia Meridionale.* Roma: N.p.

Figueras, P. 1983. *Decorated Jewish Ossuaries.* Leiden: Brill.

Fortes, M. 1969. *Kinship and the Social Order—The Legacy of Lewis Henry Morgan.* London: Routledge and Kegan Paul.

Fortune, R. 1987 [1847]. *Three Years Wandering in the Northern Provinces of China, Including a Visit to the Tea Silk and Cotton Countries, etcetera. . . .* London: Mildmay.

French, S. 1975. "The Cemetery as Cultural Institution: The Establishment of Mount Auburn and the Rural Cemetery Movement." In, D. Stannard, ed., *Death in America.* Philadelphia: University of Pennsylvania Press.

Gaume, Monseigneur J. J. 1874. *Le Cimitiere au Dix-neuviime Siecle ou le Dernier Mot des Solidaires.* Paris: N.p.

Geary, P. J. 1978. *Furta Sacra: Thefts of Relics in the Central Middle Ages.* Princeton: Princeton University Press.

Gerster, G. 1970. *Sinai: Land der Offenberung.* Zurich: Atlantis.

Ghetta, P. F. 1976. "Il culto dei morti in Val di Fassa e il processo per la profanazione della tomba di un sacerdote." *Studi Trentini di Scienze Storiche* 1: 3–15.

Goody, J. 1983. *The Development of the Family and Marriage in Europe.* Cambridge: Cambridge University Press.

Hamlin, P. E. n.d. *Rosary Cemetery.* Norwich: N.p.

Harris, O. 1982. "The Dead and Devils among the Bolivian Laymi." In, M. Bloch and J. Parry, eds., *Death and the Regeneration of Life.* Cambridge: Cambridge University Press.

Herlihy, D. and C. Klapisch-Zuber. 1978. *Les Toscans et leur familles: une étude du catasto florentin de 1427.* Paris: Presses de la fondation nationale des sciences politiques.

Houlbrooke, R., ed. 1989a. *Death, Ritual, and Bereavement.* London: Routledge.

———. 1989b. "Death, Church and Family in England between the Late Fifteenth and the Early Eighteenth Century." In, R. Houlbrooke, ed., *Death, Ritual, and Bereavement.* London: Routledge.

Humphreys, S. C. 1983. *The Family, Women and Death—Comparative Studies.* London: Routledge and Kegan Paul.

Huntington, R. and P. Metcalf. 1985 [1979]. *Celebrazioni della Morte: Antropologia dei Rituali Funerari.* Bologna: N.p.

Jashemski, W. F. 1979. *The Gardens of Pompeii: Herculaneum and the Villas Destroyed by Vesuvius.* New Rochelle: Caratzas.

Kenna, M. E. 1991. "The Power of the Dead: Changes in the Construction and Care of Graves and Family Vaults on a Small Greek Island." *Journal of Mediterranean Studies* 1: 101–19.

Klapisch-Zuber, C. 1985. "La femme et le lignage florentin (XIVe–XVIe siècles)." In, R. C. Trexler, ed., *Persons in Groups: Social Behavior as Identity Formation.* Binghamton: N.p.

Kligman, G. 1981. *Calus: Symbolic Transformation in Rumanian Ritual.* Chicago: Chicago University Press.

Lambert, A. 1880. "The Ceremonial Use of Flowers: A Sequel." *Nineteenth Century* 7 (May): 808–27.

Lane Fox, R. 1986. *Pagans and Christians.* San Francisco: Harper and Row.

Legner, A., ed. 1989. *Reliquien: Verherung and Verklarung.* Koln: N.p.

Le Goff, J. 1984 [1981]. *The Birth of Purgatory.* London: Scholar Press.

Litten, J. 1991. *The English Way of Death.* London: Hale.

Metken, S., ed. 1984. *Die Letzte Reise. Sterben, Tod Und Trauersitten in Oberbayern.* Munchen.

Meyers, E. 1971. *Jewish Ossuaries: Reburial and Rebirth.* Rome: N.p.

*Mimmo Perrella non e' piu.* 1985. A Film written and presented by T. Harrison, produced by M. Hutchinson for BBC 2.

Morgan, J. 1989. "The Burial Question in Leeds in the Eighteenth and Nineteenth Centuries." In, R. Houlbrooke, ed., *Death, Ritual, and Bereavement.* London: Routledge.

Neville, G. K. 1989. "The Sacred and the Civic: Representations of Death in the Town Ceremonies of Border Scotland." *Anthropological Quarterly* 62: 163–73.

Newby, E. 1983. *Love and War in the Appennines.* London: Picador.

Nicoloso Ciceri, A. 1982. *Tradizioni Popolari in Friuli,* 2 vols. Reana del Royale.

Pallabazzer, V. 1992. *Paranormale e Societa' Dolomitica.* Vigo di Fassa/Vich.

Pardo, I. 1985. "Sullo studio antropologico della morte. Linee metodologiche." In, R. Huntington and P. Metcalf, eds., *Celebrazioni della Morte: Antropologia dei Rituaai Funerari.* Bologna, 5– 41.

———. 1989. "Life, Death and Ambiguity in the Social Dynamics of Inner Naples." *Man* 24, 1: 103–23.

Pearson, M. P. 1982. "Mortuary Practices, Society and Ideology: An Ethnoarchaeological Study." In, I. Hodder, ed., *Symbolic and Structural Archaeology.* Cambridge: Cambridge University Press, 99–113.

Porter, R. 1989. "Death and Doctors in Georgian England." In, R. Houlbrooke, ed., *Death, Ritual, and Bereavement.* London: Routledge.

Prudentius. 1962. *The Poems of Prudentius.* M. C. Eagan, trans. In, *Fathers of the Church.* Washington, D.C.: N.p.

Raffaelli, U. 1988. "Indagine preliminare attraverso le fonti scritte e la tradizione orale per uno studio sugh omamenti popolari trentini. Parte Prima-Trentino Orientale." *Annali di San Michele* 1: 66–87.

Raule, A. 1961. *La Certosa di Bologna.* Bologna: N.p.

Richardson, R. 1989. *Death, Dissection and the Destitute.* Harmondsworth: Penguin.

Sekules, V. 1990. The Sculpture and Liturgical Furnishing of Heckington Church and Related Monuments: Masons and Benefactors in Early Fourteenth-Century Lincolnshire. Ph.D. Thesis, University of London.

Sox, H. D. 1985. *Relics and Shrines.* London: Allen and Unwin.

Stone, E. 1858. *God's Acre: Or, Historical Notices Relating to Churchyards.* London.

Thomas, K. 1978. *Religion and the Decline of Magic.* Harmondsworth: Penguin.

Toor, F. 1947. *A Treasury of Mexican Folkways.* New York.

Toynbee, J.M.C. 1971. *Death and Burial in the Roman World.* London: Thames and Hudson.

Tylor, E. B. 1871. *Primitive Culture.* London: J. Murray.

Whaley, J. 1981a. "Introduction." In, J. Whaley, ed., *Mirrors of Mortality—Studies in the Social History of Death.* London: Europa Publications.

———. 1981b. "Symbolism for Survivors: The Disposal of the Dead in Hamburg in the Late Seventeenth and Eighteenth Centuries." In, J. Whaley, ed., *Mirrors of Mortality—Studies in the Social History of Death.* London: Europa Publications.

# Flowers and Bones

Posthumous Reflections

*Cesare Poppi*

This paper should begin with a disclaimer. Jack Goody, the co-author of the essay I am going to comment upon, could not, for various reasons, contribute his own views. What follows is entirely my own, and all the more so as various commitments and the vagaries of life have prevented us from discussing the subject further. While the usual disclaimer must therefore apply, I would feel honored if Jack—my teacher and mentor in more than one sense—could share at least some of my further thoughts upon a topic which once engaged us in a fruitful exchange.

I wish first of all to recall the general points that we were trying to raise in the original article. Here some of the evidence on which they were predicated will be reconsidered and elaborated upon. Finally, I shall expand on selected aspects of the ethnography that were left somewhat underdeveloped in the original formulation. This, I hope, will throw further light on the more general implications of our argument.

The wider area of debate engaged in "Flowers and Bones" is the relationship between belief systems and corresponding "practices." While admitting that—of course—some sort of correlation at some sort of level is to be explicitly, and more often implicitly found, we wanted to stress how the two domains are to be kept analytically separate. At the theoretical level, furthermore, they were to be articulated not in any automatic way, and even less so deterministically—whichever the direction of the *surdetermination*.

The point might seem obvious and commonsensical. The latter it might be, but the former it is not. And this must be said for in recent developments in both the historical and the social sciences—and chiefly in sociocultural anthropology—it has become almost common practice to single out "cultural" factors as *the* independent variable when explaining differences. In certain extreme cases, the notion of "culture" and its analytical specifications in terms of "attitudes," "mentalities," and the like has become *the* causal variable altogether.

This can be said, in the first place, of certain formulations stemming from the school of the *Annales*—or what the British call "continental historiography"—which prompted the critique of authors such as Geoffrey Lloyd in the 1990 book "Demystifying Mentalities." More recently—and perhaps more ominously due to wider philosophical implications—theorizing in the social sciences has made "cultural universes" some sort of self-contained wholes across which subjective interpretation is the only possible translation. This notion rests on the assumption that "culture" is a systematic, internally coherent set of correlations *causal to* the responses given to outside stimuli in a given social formation.

Locking "culture" and its practical reasons as the essential *difference* in such a cogent way militates, of course, against comparison, since the latter implies a measure of commensurability from the outset. Such commensurability is not, however, to be a priori established at the level of some (admittedly dubious) shared "universality." Rather, the possibility of comparing ranges of possible responses is set against the background of common practical problems and predicaments faced by anybody engaged in the production and reproduction of one's *lebenswelt*.

The problem that "Flowers and Bones" meant to address, instead, is one in which, precisely, "cultural" responses to "practical" problems are intertwined in a non-linear, asymmetrical, and non-systematic set of variations.

The fact we wanted to account for was the striking difference between the seemingly ornate, flower-rich Italian cemeteries and the relatively unadorned, stern, and stark burial grounds of the British Isles and North America. All too often we had heard friends and acquaintances comment about the "exuberance" of Catholic Mediterranean Italians or the "Puritanism" of the Atlantic Anglo-Saxons as the ultimate, cultural explanation for the differences in the overall attitudes towards the dead, but we were unconvinced.

We identified four areas of analysis, all relatively independent, the variety of whose possible combination and complex historical interrelations might account for differences as well as for similarities and change.

First, we saw the practice of bringing flowers to the tomb as a social sign of the continuing relationship not only between the living and the dead, but—more crucially—as a form of "presencing" that the living would signal to each other through the mediation of the dead. This, we observed with regard to Italy, was quite crucial in maintaining the relationship between affines. Increasingly, as Italian kinship ties undergo the same progressive weakening and—perhaps even more crucially—the same geographical scattering as they do elsewhere in the countries of the G7, leaving a distinctive floral offering on the grave can be the only point of contact between affines prior to the final severance of such ties at the end of what we might call "the developmental cycle" in the disposal of mortal remains. In this respect, therefore, flowers for the dead carry a contradictory message: affines are no longer in social contact with each other and yet their commitment to the common dead relation may convey the regret to see the relationship fading.

Here, as elsewhere in the paper, I would observe that the "cultural" premises and implications of the practice are at odds with their "social" counterpart: Meyer Fortes' "axiom of amity" between kin would ideally also include affines in the ideal "cultural order" of never-ending sociality. However, social reasons of a practical kind prevent this from happening well beyond the specific vagaries of each situation. Therefore, the offering to the dead can work as a sort of "social buffer" and a substitute while the relationship weakens and eventually disappears.

In this respect, there is really very little difference in the social meaning of flowers in a cemetery like that of Bologna, Italy (Fig. 21) and the cemetery of a town like Norwich (Fig. 22), in Norfolk, United Kingdom, where floral offerings to the dead *do retain*—or, perhaps, *have regained*—some aspects of pre-Reformation practice. But more of that later.

Where the difference between Italy and England becomes crucial is in what I have called—elaborating on a concept in the anthropological analysis of diachrony which Jack Goody was famously instrumental in developing—the "developmental cycle" in the disposal of mortal remains.

The consequence of the basic differences in burial patterns between Italy on the one hand and England and the United States on the other is that in Italy burial sites are periodically renewed first by digging up the bones to keep badly needed space available in burial grounds, and secondly by opening family vaults and *loculi* to accommodate the bones of the newly exhumed family members. It is easy to envisage an ideal model by which, at fairly regular intervals depending on the demography of the kin group concerned, a given burial site is renewed by the addition of a new casket of bones, while the ground is turned over to receive a new burial. It is this kind of difference, we contended, which builds up the contrast

Fig. 21. Bologna, Certosa, October 1993

Fig. 22. Norwich City Cemetery, October 1993

between the relatively dynamic, congested and ever-changing landscape of the "cities of the dead" in Italy and the tranquil, unadorned "time forever still" wildscapes of Anglo-American burial grounds. Crucially for our argument, this has important consequences for the presence of flowers on relatively old tombs in each context.

The Italian custom of double burial results in physical contact between the living and the dead being periodically renewed and kick-started again, so to speak. So does the variety of practices marking the relationship, including floral offerings. Nearing All Souls, on 2 November, most family *loculi* in the Bologna Certosa will become adorned with flowers (Fig. 23).

On this occasion, most flowers will be addressed specifically to the recently buried, be they "newly dead" or "newly added" from previous burials in the ground and—by extension—to all the family dead. This is, in the same period of heightened attention towards the dead in the Christian Calendar, in sharp contrast with the single, individual burials of Norfolk cemeteries. Here, with no periodical turnover and gathering of the bones in the family tomb being practiced, entire areas of the cemetery are deserted with burials falling into oblivion with the passing of time (Fig. 24).

These are certainly contrasting ways of dealing with the dead, but they are per se no safe indicators of contrasting "cultural" attitudes towards the dead. Paradoxically, they both stem from a strong desire to "revere" and "respect" the dead, failure to do so being the reiterated reciprocal accusation that actors of the contrasting practices throw at each other when asked to comment.

However, the contrast seen in present-day cemeteries follows developments in what were long essentially similar customs and cultural attitudes. These were the result of remarkably similar sets of intra- as well as inter-regional sets of variations in Western Europe dating from the Bronze-Age. These were possibly somehow homogenized by a variety of Roman influences and later streamlined by the Church in an uneasy tug-of-war with tenacious and amazingly resilient folk permanencies of a "structural" type (e.g., Caciola 1996; Gittings 1984; Wilson 2000: ch. 11).

So, the question is raised, where, when, and how did the contrast perceivable today actually arise? How did time-honored structural similarities rooted in the longue *durée* finally give way to divergence, change, and variations, and what brought this about?

Ironically, here we must revise the hard-to-die picture of England as the vanguard of "individualism," "secularization"—and all the rest that goes

Fig. 23. *Loculi* at the Certosa, Bologna, November 1993

Fig. 24. Norwich City Cemetery, March 1993

with "modernization" in the still dominant view of historical development. Residential patterns in the British Isles and Continental Europe (especially France and Italy) are often contrasted in terms of differing forms of tenure: rent against freehold. This contrast is strikingly consistent with what we called "the tenure of the dead." In Italy this provides rent for the period needed for the bones to become clean of bodily matter, while in the United Kingdom burial is held in freehold perpetually.

This is by no means the result of "cultural attitudes," of "mentalities" reaching back to the roots of Anglo-Saxon civilization and eventually maturing into the "modern attitude." The recent crisis in British cemeteries—on which more will be said later—has brought to the attention (and dismay) of the public opinion the fact that the law making it unlawful to disturb the remains of the dead, which virtually consigned to posterity the image of the solitary, perpetual, and romantic cemetery as quintessentially British, is as recent as 1857. This is in contrast with continental sanitary legislation regulating and often imposing the turnover of bones, since it was generally introduced by Napoleon in the first decade of the century. In the case of Britain, moreover, we are therefore dealing with an early (or belated—depending on one's perspective!) Victorian affair, and not with a Reformed, "Protestant" and "modern" attitude.

Be that as it may, in Protestant countries the ossuaries, or charnel houses, a rather late, thirteenth-century medieval institution whereby the disinterred bones were working at the same time as *memento mori* and as a focus of an ongoing dialogue of salvation between the living and the souls in Purgatory, had been dissolved with the Reformation and variously turned to "lay" use. There followed a long period during which the bones, dug up to make room for the newly dead, had been accumulated unceremoniously and piecemeal in underground chambers, very much to the delight of Catholic critics ready to accuse the Protestants of treating their dead "like dogs."

The problem, however, is that things were no different in Catholic countries. Committee reports about the appalling conditions of cemeteries in Bologna following the Napoleonic inquests of 1800 sparked a bitter exchange between the civic revolutionary administration and Church authorities. The former were eager to stem the Church's monopoly on civil matters, while the latter raised the counter-accusation that the Jacobins were trying to subtract the dead due to the influence of ecclesiastical administration, essential for salvation. Eventually a compromise was found. In Bologna and elsewhere the large sites of the Chartusian monks—the Certosas—often conveniently set just outside the city walls, were secularized. City authorities ran them for a number of years directly and exclusively, with the occasional presence of the clergy for funerals and All Souls celebrations. Slowly, however, the clergy crept back in. Today, the burial grounds in the Bologna Certosa are run by the Municipal administration, while the *Passionisti* friars inhabit the old monastic building and conduct all religious functions within the premises. Crucially for the present argument, the regulations for the tenure of the dead have remained basically unchanged since Napoleonic times. These include double-burial practices and the allocation of family vaults and *loculi in perpetuum* on a freehold basis.

This ethnohistorical excursus shows that we must revise the view that the set of differences that we are dealing has resulted from rifts happening at the time when the cultural terms of engagement with modernization were set consistently with changing religious attitudes and deeply set cultural preferences. Contemporary differences in the tenure of the dead are the work in Italy of a secular, if not altogether "atheist Jacobin" administration. In England they are the relatively late result of cultural developments well clear of the radicalism of early Protestant movements, and actually more inclined, as in High Anglicanism, to reclaim hitherto abhorred theological and cultural practices.

Perhaps most paradoxical of all is that the central contrast between double burial and perpetual burial—ultimately responsible for the different appearance of cemeteries—is the result of *the convergence between* rather than the *divergence of* cultural attitudes and expectations in the modern era. Both stem from a desire to remove the dead from the indignity of the common ossuary and provide them with a dignified, permanent "home," compatible with wider, contextual variables.

It is the latter which are responsible for the different direction taken by burial patterns in the countries in concern. Particularly important are the specific conditions under which residential areas grew, expanded, and related to both the inner space of the city and the countryside.

This fundamentally pragmatic (others would perhaps say "materialist") point must be, in turn, articulated with a further set of considerations which I wish to expound. It concerns more general and wider attitudes towards the deceased, mortal remains, and the relationship between the living and the dead. In this respect, if I were to be asked what I would change of the original article I would answer "probably nothing." I would, however, wish to elaborate further on two aspects of the problem which, as two referees for the article pointed out, remained somewhat overshadowed in the development of what was already a long and complex argument.

Such areas pertain to the intrinsic, structural relationship existing between flowers and bones and imply specific ways of understanding the relationship between the living and the dead. This in turn is underpinned by discontinuities, which I think remain crucial *cross-culturally,* between a "popular" way of approaching death rooted in agrarian social formations and urban, "bourgeois," and increasingly hegemonic attitudes towards the dead emerging in metropolitan centers with the process of modernization.

The relationship between death and renewal has been widely addressed cross culturally, and I take it for granted here (see Bloch and Parry 1982). Here I wish to expand upon Hertz's famous passage whereby "the fate of the body is the model for the fate of the soul" (Huntington and Metcalf 1979: 15).

The practice of double (or secondary) burial renders it technically possible to assess the condition of the bones in the process of decay of the flesh. This, in turn, sets the terms for the development of a semiotic system, the ideological implications of which carry important consequences for the relationship between the living and the dead, while sending signals about the final fate of the soul.

The precondition of all this is that death is conceived of as a process and a transition involving several passages, and is often articulated through contradictory, cognitively ambiguous and uncertain meanings that require management and policing.

Throughout medieval Europe the refusal of an interred body to decompose signaled that the dead person was a *revenant,* possibly possessed by a demon. Elsewhere, as in Transylvania and parts of the Hellenic peninsula, such corpses were thought to be vampires to be dealt with accordingly (Caciola 1996; Kligman 1988). But, once sanctioned by the authority of the Church or safely set in the vaults of a holy monastery, the same "unnatural" phenomenology could also send the opposite signal—that the dead in question was indeed a saintly individual whose incorruptibility was a sign of divine grace.

In the rural contexts of several Southern European regions of both Orthodox and Catholic observance, the practice of exhuming the bodies signals the final transition of the soul to the afterworld (e.g., Danforth and Tsiaras 1982). It can also mark an important change in the relationship between the living and the dead. It is at this point in the process of death, in fact, that the bones are placed in the ossuary, possibly adjoining the remains of other family members. The dead person thus becomes "an ancestor" in the full sense of the term. In a certain sense, it is at this point that the earthly identity of the deceased ceases to exist as materially attached to the bones. The dead person as an individual lodges into memory while his or her bones become altogether "other" from their previous existence. It is at this juncture that the status of the surviving relatives also changes, with the progressive lifting of mourning and the end of the various observances connected to the state of ritual pollution.

What I have outlined, *mutatis mutandis,* can apply cross-culturally to a wide section of both historical and contemporary rural social formation in the Old Continent. However, it is in the long-established urban context of Naples, demographically the most dense area in Europe, that such practices acquire a surplus of signification covering the entire spectrum of tropes enabled by the conceptualization of death as a process. In Naples, the chemical composition of the volcanic soil is such that after about twenty months bodies dry up and can be transformed into mummies. If the exhumed body is found to be still "wet," this means that the soul has not fully departed from the body and gone to heaven, and the remains are reburied for another term. Otherwise, properly cleaned and treated with naphthalene and other chemicals, the dried body is set in the family locker. This opens a new phase in the relationship between the living and the dead. Thus, for instance, periodically the dead may appear in dreams to their relatives and manifest—for instance—the desire to be wrapped in a new shroud. Such desiderata cannot be ignored. The locker is opened once again and the bones rearranged inside the new wrapping. Reward for the pious act will come again in dreams. This can take the form of forewarnings about mishaps in the family, advice on conducting a business deal, or, perhaps most common, guidance in picking *lotto* numbers. Dreams and dreamy revelations mark the ongoing relationship between the living and the dead for the time needed for the dried remains to crumble and turn to dust inside progressively smaller bundles of cloth. The time comes when the physical icon of the magnitude of the relationship will simply fade and disappear. At that point, most probably, messages from the world of the dead will be carried by the newly dead, the others gradually falling into oblivion.

While regretting not being able to expand on the hypothesis here, I would like to suggest that the all-knowing status of the dead, expressed in their divinatory capability in the *Kabbala* of *lotto,* constitutes the urban, literate and—*to an extent at least*—"modern" counterpart of the role they play in mainly rural social formations as sources of fertility and increase. The urban dead, in other words, open up access to the "chancy," "magic" money of the lottery in the same way as the rural dead preside over agricultural fertility and the increase in children and animals.

There is little doubt that the symbolic pertinence of dead and flowers is predicated upon the structural association between the dead, fertility, and increase.

One only needs to recall that, central to the initiation into the Eleusinian mysteries, was the (admittedly trivial, but that is another story) "revelation" of the death and resurrection of an ear of wheat. Both Proserpina and Artemis, goddesses of fertility, had unmistakable connections with the world of the dead, while Ephestus—Venus' husband—also had chthonic associations.

Such symbolic and ideological landscapes are structurally constituted and show great resilience and adaptability to change. Moreover, of all the possible tropes connecting the dead as ancestors with increase and fertility, the association with flowers is the most enduring. As "natural symbols" flowers lend themselves to a variety of contradictory, double-faced operations. On the one hand they are the harbingers of fruits but, as the coin is reversed, they constitute a *memento* about the fleeting nature of beauty and life. In this, they are veritable dialectical "symbols for all seasons," signifying life in death and death in life.

It is therefore not surprising to find them most closely associated with those manifestations of death where the *poiesis* fostered by the paradoxical nature of flowers can find fertile ground for expression. Whereas flowery garlands are set *in the proximity* of the bodies of adults, in the case of children up to the age of adolescence—and at any rate in the case of unmarried youths—garlands of flowers were placed *directly on the corpse,* both in the form of garlands as well as decorations of the burial dress in several European rural social formations (Metken 1984: 78, 124, 339). *Living* children "are flowers" in that they are about to "blossom" into fruitful adulthood; *dead* children "are flowers" in that their beauty and innocence only lasted a while.

By the same *pathos* the dead *turn into* flowers. Not only in the literal sense that they make the land fertile from their subterranean abodes, but because the virtues of loyalty, affection, and remembrance—the same representations said to make the bond between the living and the dead sempiternal, timeless—are themselves perceived as "flowers" adorning the moral personality of the partners.

Thus, a female lover *may be* "a flower" in life but *must be* perceived as such in death. The romantic mandatory trope of the "virginal dead lover," therefore, shapes a relic of hair of the beloved into flowers. This is specific of the condition of death: the hair of a *living* lover would never be treated in this way.

It is difficult if not impossible to pinpoint a chronology for such practices. Provided that a good number of them still characterize the lives of many people, even more thankless appears the task of defining when and why they went into decline in those parts of Europe where the Reformation's injunction of *solum verbum*—"the Word Alone"—did not clear the decks of such folk practices with a single sweep of the cognitive as well as the legal brush.

However, in those countries where the tenets of the Reformation did not attain, it was the age of the Baroque which most of all elaborated upon the proximity between flowers and mortal remains—and, namely, bones.

The arrangement of bones in patterns and the preservation of mummified bodies had been a long-standing prerogative of certain monastic orders, first and most importantly the Capuchins. Interestingly, in Italy, this branch of the Franciscan order was, and still is, responsible for perpetuating folk practices imported within the monasteries by members of the order with minimal education and a rural background, traditionally a majority within Capuchin convents. However, it was the seventeenth and eighteenth centuries in which the ancient association between flowers and bones came to the forefront of Catholic Europe *visual* culture. The exhibition *Reliquien,* held in Köln in 1989, showed a wide range of relics dating from the Baroque age in which the bones were arranged in floral patterns and motifs, imitating garlands and other decorative patterns. At the same time, in selected convents, specialist nuns were at work transforming the relics of saints into veritable "carpets of flowers" by means of beads, golden thread, *paillettes,* and so on (Legner 1989).

Truly to do justice to this type of evidence would entail a long excursus into the significance of flowers—and *artificial* flowers for that matter—in a period, the Baroque, which entertained a special relationship with everything deadly. This is beyond the scope of this paper, since in the present context I wish simply to point out how such practices developed out of two possible sources, interrelated at the structural level but historically and culturally rather distinct.

On the one hand, official Church history has fostered from the very beginning the association between moral virtues, death, sainthood, and flowers. Holy men and women died *in odore di santità*—"in odor of sanctity"—their corpses smelling of violets and roses. Similarly, the exhumation of the uncorrupted body of a candidate to sainthood letting out the smell of flowers was taken as a sure sign of heavenly connections. But also the good deeds of the saints were "flowers"—*fioretti* in St Francis' terms—offered to divinity both in a direct sense and in terms of the virtuous attitudes they prompted in others.

On the other hand, the Church fought a long battle to impose upon a culturally strong-headed peasantry that not any old bone of any old dead had miraculous powers to heal and bring fertility and riches. Thus, the author of the eighth-century treatise *Indiculus Superstitionum et Paganarium* complains how the common folk "pretend to themselves that the dead of any kind are saints" (quoted in Caciola 1996: 36). As it has been remarked, practices ranging from second-burial to the preservation and manipulation of bones are a sign of a continuing relationship between the living and the dead and are a structural feature of—at least—the European cultural area since antiquity. But so are the objections and condemnations of the selfsame practices (Davies 1999, esp. 80–81). In this and other respects, the battle over the legitimacy of relics that finally begot the extreme rejection of the Reformation is an early, structural feature in the history of death. It is rooted on the kind of inherent, implicit but not less compelling cognitive ambiguities and contradictions that almost cyclically call established practices into question in Europe and elsewhere (Goody 1997). It is not, as some theorists of modernization have claimed, a novel, hitherto unknown feature of the contrast between the Protestant, "modern" North and the Catholic, "conservative" South.

In spite of ecclesiastical efforts, the association between the bones of the dead—the ordinary dead, that is—and flowers proved persistent.

The practice of decorating exhumed skulls with flowers before placing them in the public ossuary lasted in lower Germany and other parts of the eastern Alps well into the nineteenth century (Metken 1984: 334–35). Similar care of the family skulls was recorded in the inner villages of the Dolomites in the 1920s and 1930s.

It would be wrong to think that these practices were "survivals" of increasingly obsolete systems of beliefs, fast fading under the pressure of modernizing influences. On the contrary, the most cursory look at ethnography of Southern Europe would testify that the treatment of the bones was embedded within the yearly ritual cycle of Carnival celebrations in which the dead featured prominently up to present times. There is general agreement in seeing Carnival practices as a way to connect the society of the living with the dead ancestors. More specifically, in the rural social formations of Europe, it was—and very often still is—the youths celebrating their passage to adulthood who personified the returning dead, assuring fertility and increase for the forthcoming agricultural season (Poppi 1993 and 2001).

Dancing in carnivalesque fashion inside cemeteries occurred throughout Europe up to the Modern Age and beyond, in spite of the fact that for centuries anathema had been raised against the practice. One instance must suffice. Evidence from the twelfth-century *Itinerarium Kambriae,* by Gerald of Wales, testifies that on such occasions it was the living dancers who became possessed by the spirits of the dead, lending their bodies to an inversion of the *danse macabre,* a symbolic trope spread at all levels of the popular cultures of Europe.

However, the ultimate expression of the connection between the dead increase, and calendrical events were—of course—practices connected with human sacrifice. Until the second half of the nineteenth century, *Mardi Gras* in Rome ended with the execution of a convicted criminal. If a Jew was held on death row, then this would be preferred—a grim *exemplum* of how the death and fertility symbolism of the agrarian, "pagan" cultures of all had become articulated with "urban" notions of individual salvation and damnation.

Evidence of human sacrifice, this time connected more explicitly with the agrarian cycle, appears unmistakable for large areas of Eastern Orthodox Europe up to recent times. It is reported that as late as 1840, in a village near Poniewez, in the Lithuanian province of Kaunas, a man was designated by lots from amongst the spectators of the St John's bonfire, in midsummer. He was then killed and dismembered. His limbs were scattered in the fields with the intention; "to sanctify the earth . . . and impetrate fruits from the soil" (Dowoina-Sylwestrowicz 1892: 445, quoted in Gasparini 1973: 628).

However extreme and even ethnographically doubtful such cases might appear, there seems to be a degree of continuity between such practices and more familiar forms of ongoing exchange with the deceased. In Naples, the *capuzzelle*—the skulls not reclaimed by relatives and exposed to the public in the ossuary, are singled out and "adopted" by devotees who address them in prayers. This will engender a relation of exchange with the dead. Eager to leave Purgatory, they will be ready to bestow favors onto their adopted relatives. This works at both the symbolic and cognitive levels in the relationship between the living and the dead.

In the actors' eyes as well as in terms of cogent symbolic logic, the *ossa dimenticate*—the *forgotten* bones—are all the more powerful and ready to respond to prayer as their transition to heaven has been delayed first by neglect from their relatives and secondly from having been left unburied and exposed.

By bringing the material signs of the dead once again within the reaches of memory and remembrance, a line of communication is restored, to the benefit of both parties.

In their symbolically specific way, Neapolitan practices constitute but a facet of a structural symbolic economy of memory which is set—I would like to suggest—at the very core of apparently radically dissimilar practices in Anglo-American cemeteries. Allow me to illustrate.

On 20 March 2001, Radio 4, the "cultural" programme of the BBC, raised a cry of alarm about the pitiful state of British cemeteries. It turned out that, while a great majority of them lay in a state of utter neglect, about twenty licenses are granted every year to developers to dig up the dead, summarily dispose of the bones, and turn the reclaimed land to huge profit-making. To compound the outrage, this happens in a situation wherein the authorities in charge of maintaining burial grounds are systematically denied permission to dig up old burials in overcrowded cemeteries to make space for new paying customers—so to speak. This would be the only way to earn the income needed to maintain the cemeteries in decent conditions.

The report's bottom line was that, while the Victorians invented the notion of the freehold, sempiternal burial as a measure of respect for the dead, to avoid the iniquities of the common ossuary and to foster eternal remembrance, they did not make any provisions for paying for it. By rejecting second-burial—commonly practiced until 1857—they have condemned their descendants to adopt cremation, an expensive practice increasingly criticized both for its alleged "inhumanity" as well as for its polluting implications.

What matters for the purposes of the present paper is that government agencies are reluctant to introduce a parliamentary bill allowing the recycling of burial sites for ". . . it's a sensitive issue and maybe the public is not quite ready for this yet" (BBC Online 2001: 11). Members of the public interviewed on the matter expressed disgust at the idea, with one Mr. Mackay commenting, "It is just beyond comprehension that people are put in their final resting place by people who love and respect them, . . . and then they are removed. . . . I would say it's a human right to be buried and not to be disturbed" (BBC Online 2001: 9). In fact, the Mackay family found out that their dead relatives had been removed to make room for redevelopment of the cemetery as they were trying to trace the family burials, apparently after decades of absence from the burial grounds due to their distance.

Although it would appear, *prima facie,* that "perpetual" burial entails a higher probability of the dead person being "forgotten" as it does not expose mortal remains to the kind of renewed attention shown to be the case with Italian practices, this is not the case. In British culture, the permanence of memory, the possibility, that is, of *reactivating* it irrespective of time gone by, is enabled by the certainty of the *permanence* of the tenure of the dead.

If in Italy the dead are remembered by "turn over" practices that, by moving them, force them to follow the family movements, the same result is attained in Britain by making them stay put—and forcing their descendants to travel. In both cases, "respect," "dignity," and the possibility of articulating the former with "memory and remembrance" appear to be the name of the game.

## Conclusions

I do not wish to give the impression that the final gloss to an article which tried to account for what we called "striking differences" is that *plus ça change plus c'est la même chose.* Nor is my desire to resurrect the notion of functional equivalents to describe what remain, at many levels, *moderately diverging* practical consequences of *moderately similar* symbolical and cognitive predicaments.

*Pace* Derrida's radical theory of signification, *"differences"* in comparative analysis do not result in opposing and mutually exclusive sets of meanings, for each practice must first of all be understood *within* its own system of contextual references. It is in the analysis of variations of both a historical and a synchronic nature *within* relatively homogenous contexts, in fact, that we find unexpected surprises.

Away from the urban conglomerates, where trends towards individualization and de-personification of social relations of the type described by Ariès and Elias appear to have hit less hard, things are coming back—or, perhaps more accurately, never moved far from circling a narrow radius.

Thus, in Norwich, in rural Norfolk, bereaved relatives personalize their floral homage to the newly dead in a way that many Italians would find excessive, far too literal to be respectful and altogether in poor taste (Fig. 25). Shaping flowers like boxing gloves and punching balls over the grave of a boxer; referring to excessive drinking by toasting a flowery pint of beer to the dead or addressing a dead mother with the infantile "Mum," would most probably be seen as a violation of that respectful distance close relations ought ideally to keep when addressing the dead, or—for that matter—the rest of the living too, on such occasions.

Conversely, however, evidence is there that secularization and globalizing intercultural trends in Italy are fostering a shift *away* from remembering the dead person somewhat "at a distance," in his or her new status as an ancestor finally living in a new dimension to be addressed according to the *do ut des* proper of the contract of old. The new style of photographs and inscriptions point in the direction of a close familiarity with the dead now remembered and addressed *as they were in life*—the dilemma of their new status being increasingly placed under the Wittgensteinian interdiction (Fig. 26).

In comparative analysis, differences and similarities are not the ultimate harbingers of meaning, for—in the first instance—continuities and discontinuities are to be recorded *within* apparently culturally homogeneous historical sequences. A closer look at such variations, though, would persuade that even these are consistent, *plausible* variations along a *continuum:* there is something coherently "Italian" in writing "*Ciao Lella*" on a tombstone and, by the same token, there is something coherently "English" in modelling a pint of beer from a bunch of flowers.

Across continuums, on the other hand, differences may ultimately be deemed relative and contingent, while similarities may be judged to be the result of incommensurable developments—chancy divergences and unintended convergences.

There may indeed be a mediated continuum of a cross-cultural kind between the *gnothi sauton*—"know thyself"—of the classical skeleton paraphrasing the Delphic Oracle and the cult of ancestral relics among the Kota of Gabon. But what exactly this paradigm would consist of can only be worked out by looking at the syntagmatic systems of meaning created within each signifying context, if possible through time. This is—of course—no easy task, but one that comparative analysis must keep at the core of its intellectual project.

**REFERENCES**

BBC Online. 2001. *Crisis at the Cemeteries,* 20 March.
Bloch, M. and J. Parry, eds. 1982. *Death and the Regeneration of Life.* Cambridge, Cambridge University Press.

Fig. 25. Fresh grave, Norwich City Cemetery, March 1993

Fig. 26. *Loculo* at the Certosa, Bologna, 1993

Caciola, N. 1996. "Wreaths, Revenants and Ritual in Medieval Culture." *Past and Present* 152: 3–45.

Danforth, L. M. and A. Tsiaras. 1982. *The Death Rituals of Rural Greece.* Princeton: Princeton University Press.

Davies, J. 1999. *Death, Burial and Rebirth in the Religions of Antiquity.* London: Routledge.

Dowoina-Sylwestrowicz, M. 1892. "Sobótka." *Wisa* VI.

Gasparini, E. 1973. *Il Matriarcato Slavo: Antropologia Culturale dei Protoslavi.* Firenze: Sansoni.

Gittings, C. 1984. *Death, Burial and the Individual in Early Modern England,* London: Croom Helm.

Goody, J. 1997. *Representations and Contradictions: Ambivalence towards Theatre, Relics and Sexuality,* Oxford: Blackwell.

Huntington, R. and P. Metcalf. 1979. *Celebrations of Death: The Anthropology of Mortuary Ritual.* Cambridge: Cambridge University Press.

Kligman, G. 1988. *The Wedding of the Dead: Ritual, Poetics and Popular Culture in Transylvania.* Berkeley: University of California Press.

Legner, A., ed. 1989. *Reliquien: Verherung und Verklärung.* Exhibition Catalogue. Köln: Schnütgen Museum.

Lloyd, G. 1990. *Demistifying Mentalities.* Cambridge: Cambridge University Press.

Metken, S., ed. 1984. *Die Letzte Reise: Sterben, Tod und Trauersitten in Oberbayern.* Exhibition Catalogue. München: Hugendubel.

Poppi, C. 1993. "The Other Within: Masks and Masquerades in Europe." In, J. Mack, ed., *Masks: The Art of Expression.* London: British Museum Press.

———. 2001. "*Persona, Masca, Larva:* Masks, Identity and Cognition in the Cultures of Europe." In, S. C. Malik, ed., *Rûpa-Pratirûpa: Mind Man and Mask.* New Delhi: Aryan Books International.

Wilson, S. 2000. *The Magical Universe: Everyday Ritual and Magic in Pre-Modern Europe.* London: Hambledon & London.

# Contributors

MICHAEL ADAS is the Abraham E. Voorhees Professor of History at Rutgers University at New Brunswick. He has written widely on the comparative history of colonialism and agrarian resistance movements in South and Southeast Asia. His recent work has focused on the impact of technology on colonial societies and includes *Machines as the Measure of Men: Science, Technology and Ideologies of Western Dominance,* which won the Dexter Prize in 1991. He has a book forthcoming on *Dominance by Design: Technological Imperatives and America's Civilizing Mission,* and is currently at work on *A Grave Dug in Flanders: World War I and the Crisis of the European Global Order.*

MARY BEARD is Reader in Classics at the University of Cambridge, and Fellow of Newnham College. Her books include *Religions of Rome* (with John North and Simon Price; Cambridge University Press), *The Invention of Jane Harrison* (Harvard University Press), and *The Parthenon* (Profile Books and Harvard University Press). She is currently working on the Roman ceremony of Triumph.

JOHN BORNEMAN (Harvard University Ph.D. 1989) is Professor of Anthropology at Princeton University. His current work focuses on issues of accountability and regime change, transformations in political authority, sacrifice, monetary compensation for loss, and reconciliation after violent conflict. He is the editor of *Death of the Father: An Anthropology of the End in Political Authority* (Berghahn Press, 2003).

CHARLES BRIGHT is Professor of History in the Residential College, University of Michigan, teaching in the areas of world history, Detroit urban history, and the history of prisons and punishment. His most recent book is *The Powers that Punish: Prisons and Politics in the Era of the 'Big House,' 1920–1955* (1996). His current work on the history of globalization, with Michael Geyer, includes "World History in a Global Age" in *Ameri-*

*can Historical Review* (1995); and "Where in the World Is America? The History of the United States in a Global Age" in, Thomas Bender, ed., *Rethinking American History in a Global Age* (University of California Press, 2002). They are currently completing a book on *The Global Condition in the Long Twentieth Century.*

ANDRÉ BURGUIÈRE is Directeur d'Études at the École des Hautes Études en Sciences Sociales. His publications include *A History of the Family* (with C. Klapisch-Zuber, M. Segalen, and F. Zonabend), 2 vols. (Cambridge, 1996); *Histoire de la France* (with Jacques Revel), 4 vols. (Paris, 1989–1994); and *Paysages et Paysans* (Paris, 1991).

MICHAEL GEYER is Samuel N. Harper Professor of History at the University of Chicago. He completed his Ph.D. at the Albert Ludwigs Universität in Freiburg, and began his academic career at the University of Michigan in Ann Arbor. His main areas of interest are German and European history, the history and theory of human rights and humanitarianism, and world history and globalization. Together with Charles Bright, he has published, among other work, "Where in the World is America? The History of the United States in the Global Age" in, Thomas Bender, ed., *Rethinking American History in a Global Age*" (University of California Press, 2002); and "World History in a Global Age" in *American Historical Review* (October 1995). They are currently completing a book-length study on *The Global Condition in the Long Twentieth Century.*

JACK GOODY was born in London in 1919, and educated at St. Johns College, Cambridge, and Balliol College, Oxford. After World War II, he studied English literature and social anthropology, and carried out fieldwork in Ghana, and briefly in India and China. Much of his work has focused on European historical material, and he has written on property transmission, family, kinship and marriage, the culture of food and flowers, the West African myth of the Bagre, literacy and oral societies, the East and the West, and iconoclasm and representations. He has recently published *Islam in Europe,* and *Capitalism and Modernity: The Great Debate* (both with Polity Press).

CHRIS GREGORY is a Reader in Anthropology in the School of Archaeology and Anthropology, Faculty of Arts, Australian National University. He is the author of *Gifts and Commodities* (1982), which was based on his experiences in PNG in the early 1970s. Since then he has conducted fieldwork in India and has published *Savage Money* (1997), and *Lachmi*

*Jagar: Gurumai Sukdai's Story of the Bastar Rice Goddess* (2003, with Harihar Vaishnav).

RAYMOND GREW, who edited *Comparative Studies in Society and History* for twenty-four years, also writes on global history and the history of modern France and modern Italy. He is Professor of History Emeritus at the University of Michigan, Ann Arbor.

BEVERLY HECKART is Professor of History at Central Washington University. Her primary field of interest is Modern Germany with a strong emphasis on social and economic developments. She is currently at work on a history of urban planning in the German Democratic Republic.

CESARE POPPI studies philosophy at the University of Bologna, and social anthropology at the University of Cambridge. He has conduced extensive fieldwork on the Ladins of the dolomites (northeastern Italy) and on the Gur-Grushi-speaking peoples of northwestern Ghana (West Africa). He has published on the ethnography of both ethnic groups and on theoretical issues concerning globalization and the anthropology of secrecy and knowledge. He has taught the anthropology of African art at the University of East Anglia, Norwich, and currently teaches political anthropology in the Faculty of Political Sciences at the University of Bologna.

GEORGE STEINMETZ is Professor of Sociology and German Studies at the University of Michigan. His early publications include a historical study of social policy and social discipline at the local and national levels of the German state, *Regulating the Social: The Welfare State and Local Politics in Imperial Germany* (Princeton University Press, 1993). More recently he has completed a comparative analysis of ethnographic discourse and colonial native policy in three overseas German colonies, *The Devil's Handwriting: Precolonial Ethnography and the German Colonial State in Qingdao, Samoa, and Southwest Africa* (Duke University Press, forthcoming). He also edited *State/Culture: State Formation after the Cultural Turn* (Cornell University Press, 1999) and *The Politics of Method in the Human Sciences: Positivism and Its Epistemological Others* (Duke University Press, forthcoming). Currently he is making a documentary film called "Living among Ruins: Detroit (USA) and Komsomolsk on Amur (Russia)," with Michael Chanan and Thomas Lahusen. He edits a book series called "Politics, History, and Culture" with Julia Adams for Duke University Press.

ARAM A. YENGOYAN has been involved with *Comparative Studies in Society and History* in a variety of positions from 1965 to the present. He taught at the University of Michigan from 1963 to 1990, and is currently Professor of Anthropology at the University of California, Davis. His writings cover a range of subjects from cultural theory, cultural and linguistic translation, symbolism, culture/ideology/modernity, and the history of anthropological thought with special emphasis on the writings of Georg Simmel. He has conducted fieldwork primarily on upland peoples in the southern Philippines and the Aboriginal cultures of central Australia.